Reader's Digest

Story of the
GREAT AMERICAN WEST

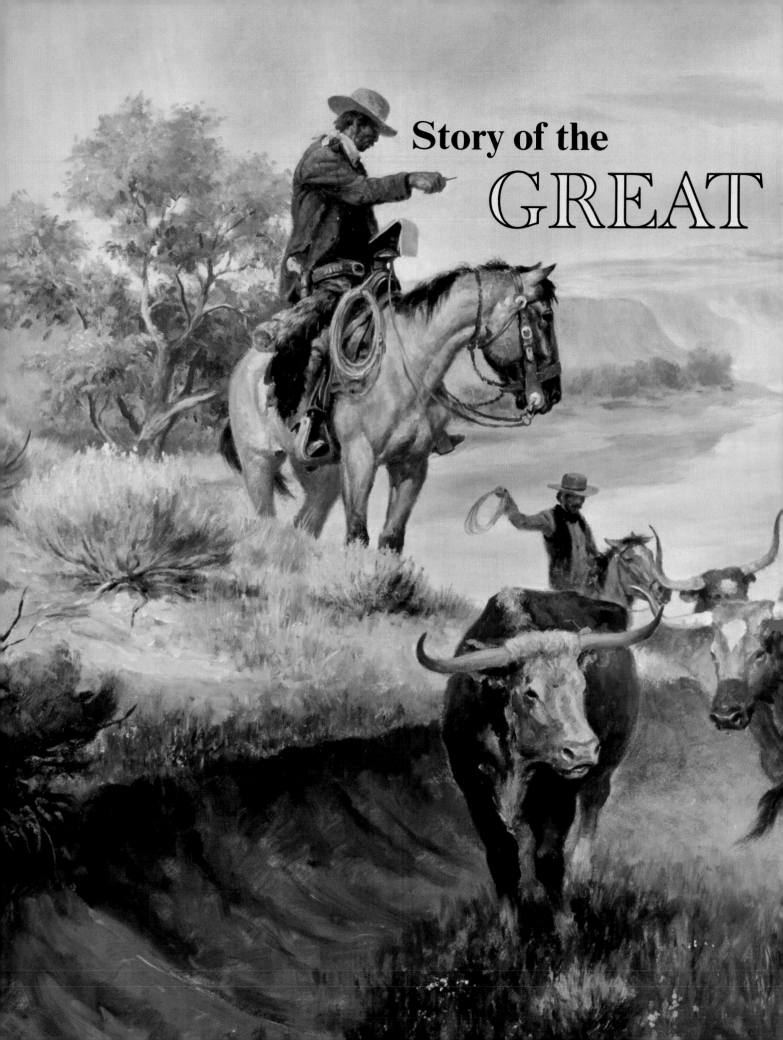

Story of the
GREAT

Reader's Digest

AMERICAN WEST

The Reader's Digest Association, Inc.

Pleasantville, New York   Montreal

Editor: Edward S. Barnard
Art Director: Gerald Ferguson
Senior Editors: Nancy F. Genet, Letitia B. Kehoe
Associate Editor: Frank B. Latham
Art Associate: Donald Spitzer
Copy Editor: Elaine Pearlmutter
Research Editors: Monica Borrowman, Susan Brackett, Helen Fisher
Research Associate: Glenda McGee
Picture Editor: Robert J. Woodward
Picture Researchers: Margaret Mathews, Richard Pasqual
Assistant Artist: Jessica L. Mitchell
Project Secretary: Helen Evans

Senior Contributing Writer: Peter M. Chaitin
Contributing Writers: Rebecca Davenport, Peter R. Limburg, Geoffrey Ward

The editors of Reader's Digest wish to express their gratitude
for the invaluable contributions of the following individuals:

Chief Consultant

Ray Allen Billington, Ph.D., *Senior Research Associate*
   Henry E. Huntington Library, Art Gallery, and Botanical Gardens

General Consultants

William Goetzmann, Ph.D., *Stiles Professor in American Studies*
   and Professor of History, The University of Texas at Austin
Bayrd Still, Ph.D., *Professor of History, New York University*

Special Consultants

Gene Ball, *Buffalo Bill Historical Center, Cody, Wyoming.* Alan L. Bates, *Author,* The Western Rivers Steamboat Cyclopoedium. Don Berkebile, *Division of Transportation, Smithsonian Institution.* Col. George M. Chinn, *Deputy Director, Kentucky Historical Society; author,* Kentucky—Settlement and Statehood. Maud Cole, *Librarian, Rare Book Division, New York Public Library.* Barry Combs, *Union Pacific Railroad.* Michael Cox, *Museum of New Mexico, Santa Fe.* Eugene D. Decker, *Archivist, Kansas State Historical Society.* Pete DeVries, *Park Superintendent, San Jose Mission State and National Historic Site.* Everett Dick, *Research Professor of American History, Union College; author,* The Sod House Frontier. Nick Eggenhofer, *Artist; author,* Wagons, Mules and Men. Robert W. Fisch, *Curator, West Point Museum, U.S. Military Academy.* Stanley A. Freed, Ph.D., *Curator, Department of Anthropology, American Museum of Natural History.* William Gannon, Ph.D., *Director, The Yakima Valley Museum and Historical Association.* Charles E. Hanson, Jr., *Director, The Museum of the Fur Trade, Chadron, Nebraska.* Don Hedgpeth, *Director, Nita Stewart Haley Memorial Library, Midland, Texas.* Leonard Huber, *Author,* Tales of the Mississippi. Ford W. Hughes, *Regional Manager and Vice President, The James Foundation, St. James, Missouri.* James Hutchins, *Dwight D. Eisenhower Institute for Historical Research, Smithsonian Institution.* Donald E. Kloster, *Division of Military History, Smithsonian Institution.*

Dean Krakel, Persimmon Hill *Magazine.* Dean Krakel II, Persimmon Hill *Magazine.* George Kraus, *Southern Pacific Transportation Company.* Douglas C. McChristian, *Supervisory Historian, Ft. Laramie National Historic Site.* Harold McCracken, *Director Emeritus, Buffalo Bill Historical Center, Cody, Wyoming.* Rodman W. Paul, Ph.D., *The Edward S. Harkness Professor of History, California Institute of Technology; author,* California Gold. Jerome E. Petsche, *National Park Service.* Byron Price, *Research Coordinator, National Endowment for the Humanities Interpretive Grant, Ranching Heritage Center, Texas Tech University.* Lois Olcott Price, *Director of Museum Planning, The Filson Club, Louisville, Kentucky.* John C. W. Riddle, *Superintendent, Lincoln Boyhood National Memorial, Lincoln City, Indiana.* John T. Schlebecker, Ph.D., *Curator, Division of Extractive Industries, Smithsonian Institution; author,* Whereby We Thrive: A History of American Farming, 1607–1972. Dan Scurlock, *Texas Historical Commission.* Tom Sitton, *Natural History Museum of Los Angeles County.* Harold K. Steen, Ph.D., *Associate Director, Forest History Society, Santa Cruz, California.* Texas Parks and Wildlife Department, *Austin, Texas.* Capt. Frederick Way, Jr., *Sewickley, Pennsylvania.* Mike Weber, *Museum of New Mexico, Santa Fe.* Roger L. Welsch, *University of Nebraska; author,* Sod Walls. C. A. Weslager, *Author,* The Log Cabin in America. George Williams, *Rodeo Division,* Persimmon Hill *Magazine.*

Printed in the United States of America
Third Printing, June 1987

The Library of Congress has cataloged this work as follows:

Story of the great American West. — Pleasantville, N.Y.: Reader's Digest Association, c1977.

   384 p.: col. ill.; 29 cm.

   At head of title: Reader's digest.
   Bibliography: p. 372–373.
   Includes index.
   SUMMARY: Recounts the settlement of the West from the first pioneers who crossed the Appalachians to the eventual disappearance of the frontier.

   1. The West—History. 2. Frontier and pioneer life—The West. [1. The West—History. 2. Frontier and pioneer life—The West]
I. Reader's digest.

F591.S857   978   76-23542
ISBN 0-89577-039-3   MARC

Contents

White-topped wagon trains, hard-riding cowboys, buckskin-clad trappers, grizzled prospectors—all are part of the image of the 19th-century Old West, an image that still stirs the hearts and imaginations of millions of Americans. But the saga of the West and of its conquest really begins hundreds of years earlier, when explorers, missionaries, and colonists from Europe moved up from Mexico and in from the eastern seaboard in search of gold, furs, souls, and land. This prologue traces the story from the arrival of the first Europeans near the end of the 15th century to the decisive confrontation of Britain and France in the New World some 260 years later.

The Coming of the Europeans

Ray Allen Billington

Aristocratically dressed Englishmen present beads and knives to American Indians clothed in skins. The 17th-century artist depicted the natives as visiting the full-sailed ships in blunt-ended dugouts of wood.

They came from Spain, from France, and from England—those first explorers and settlers who began the conquest of the Americas. Some were mere adventurers in quest of gold and glory. Others were men of the cloth, intent upon saving souls. Still others were religious dissidents, seeking a haven from persecution. All found themselves in a strange and often hostile environment, where circumstance and policy forced them to contend against each other, and against the American natives as well, for dominion.

Wherever the Europeans established their beachheads, they were met and sometimes challenged by people whom they called "Indians" because of Columbus' mistaken belief that he had happened on an outlying portion of "the Indies." Firmly established, many of these Indians lived in substantial villages and tended well-kept fields. They had created complex tribal societies and religious forms suitable to their surroundings. In defense of their homelands some of these first Americans were to prove formidable foes when white frontiersmen began their westward march across the continent.

The ancestors of most of these Indian peoples had arrived from Siberia between 10,000 and 40,000 years earlier. Wandering hunters, they had followed the migrations of bison and woolly mammoths and mastodons across the land bridge that intermittently spanned the Bering Strait as the seas rose and fell during the last ice ages. From Alaska they fanned out across North America and down into South America. At first, they continued to be hunters. Then, as their giant prey died off, they gradually adopted lifestyles suitable to the soils and climates of the lands into which they had wandered. Some in the eastern woodlands and Great Plains continued to hunt smaller game; others in the Southwest began the cultivation of corn, beans, and squash as agricultural practices spread northward from Mexico. Later, agriculturists in the center of the continent even supported sizable cities, with imposing public buildings and a highly structured society under kings and priests.

Despite the lack of the wheel, of iron, and of domesticated animals (except the dog), the Indians adapted themselves so successfully to a variety of environments that by A.D. 1400 at least 5 million of them lived in what is now the United States. By this time the differences among the tribes, both physical and cultural, far outweighed the similarities. Some Indians were light skinned, some dark. Some were squat and muscular, others tall and slender. Some were nomadic, following the game herds, others sedentary. Some lived in wigwams, others in mud huts, tepees, or apartment dwellings. Some glorified warfare, others considered fighting akin to insanity. In fact, so great were the differences among them that Indians thought of themselves not as a single people but as Choctaws or Shawnees or Sioux, just as Europeans looked upon themselves as Frenchmen or Spaniards or Englishmen. To a Mohawk, a Creek Indian was as much an outsider as a Spaniard.

When the first European explorers came to the New World, a number of small tribes were living on the Atlantic seaboard, ranging from the Abnakis and Penobscots of Maine to the Apalachees and Timucuas of Florida. The coastal tribesmen subsisted by fishing, hunting, and farming. Tribesmen in the South were especially expert husbandmen, girdling the trees to kill them and clear land. Most of these Indians were peaceful peoples who believed in living harmoniously and at first greeted the white newcomers with friendship and trust.

Inland, and covering the area that is now New York State, lay the domain of the Five Nations (later the Six Nations when they were joined by the Tuscaroras): the Mohawks, Oneidas, Onondagas, Cayugas, and Senecas. Linked in the League of the Iroquois, these Indians dominated the northern coastal and interior tribes for generations. They were expert farmers and lived in apartmentlike longhouses, which held 10 or more families.

Whether of peaceful or warlike tribes, many permanent Indian settlements were fortified. In the large southwestern pueblo above, the tiers of mud-brick homes and ceremonial buildings are protected by a front parapet and arc-shaped multistoried rear walls.

Several other sizable tribes, such as the Eries, the Miamis, and the Shawnees, occupied the Ohio Valley, basing their economies on farming, hunting, and trading. To their south was the land of the Creeks, Cherokees, Choctaws, and Chickasaws. These Indians lived in villages of 100 or more plastered dwellings grouped about a central square in which religious and social functions were regularly celebrated. They subsisted largely by farming and hunting small game.

Just beyond the Mississippi River, where the forests of the East gave way to fertile well-watered prairies, lived the Mandans, Hidatsas, Crows, Omahas, and others. These tribesmen grew corn along the Missouri and its tributaries and intermittently hunted buffalo. They lived in permanent villages of earth or bark lodges. To the northeast of them were the horticultural Cheyennes and Arapahos and the sedentary Dakotas—or Sioux—who grew corn, beans, and squash in the Minnesota lake country.

West to the Rockies stretched vast grasslands where millions of buffalo grazed in giant herds covering as many as 50 square miles. Here nomadic peoples lived by collecting seasonal vegetables and berries, hunting small game, and following the buffalo. This animal provided meat, shelter, and winter clothing, and to acquire these essentials the Indians organized buffalo drives in which they stampeded herds over bluffs or into gullies. Large family groups traveled by foot (they had no horses), hauled their few belongings with them on poles strapped to their dogs, and made camp along protected streams and in valleys. Possibly the ancestors of the Blackfeet, Arapahos, and Shoshones, these nomads were widely separated in 1400, and intertribal warfare was rare.

Among the first villages visited by white settlers in Virginia was Pomeioc, drawn here by John White in 1585. Palisades enclosed the Indians' barrel-roofed longhouses, which were covered with bark sewn in layers like shingles. Each communal dwelling housed members of one family, who slept on raised platforms.

Diverse Tribes of the Far West

Across the Rockies there were the tribes of the Great Basin—the Bannocks, Utes, Paiutes, Goshutes, and Washoes. Food gatherers rather than hunters, they lived by foraging in small bands and shunned warfare. The several hundred thousand red men along the California coast were similarly compelled to wander about constantly seeking food, with little time left for fighting. Their poverty and the roving quality of their life contrasted sharply with the prosperity and sedentary ways of the salmon-fishing Indians of the Pacific Northwest and the agricultural pueblo dwellers of the Southwest who wanted nothing more than to be left alone.

Although the Indians varied in cultural traits, they generally displayed a gracious and trusting hospitality toward the first Europeans to arrive. "I assure you," wrote an Englishman who had lived among them, "that . . . they are hospitable, friendly, and civil to an immense degree; in good breeding I think they infinitely surpass the French or any other people that I ever saw, if you will allow good breeding to consist in the desire to do everything that pleases you, and in strict carefulness not to do anything that may offend you." Here was a sound judgment. Unfortunately, white racism reinforced by land hunger made most European settlers see the red man as simply an obstacle to be overcome.

Bias aside, the confrontation between red man and white was bound to explode into warfare. At issue were two mutually exclusive philosophies of life. To the European, the land, the forests, the rivers, and the streams of the New World were all resources to be

At mealtime a Virginia Indian man sat on one side of a mat, his wife on the other. They ate corn, venison, and fish. Whites soon became dependent on such native food crops as corn, beans, squash, and pumpkin. From the Indians they also learned to grow tobacco and tap sugar maples.

Equipped with armor and horses—animals then unknown to this continent—Spanish soldiers of fortune conquered much of North America. Their horses had a tremendous impact on Indian economy and society; many sedentary tribesmen stole them and became not only superb horsemen but also aggressive nomads.

Juan Ponce de León, a Spanish nobleman, may have been on Columbus' second trip to Hispaniola. Later he found gold in Puerto Rico, then led the first European expedition to what his men called Florida (*"full of flowers"*), *because of its foliage or because they discovered it on Easter feast day* (Pascua Florida).

exploited, divided into parcels, and apportioned among individuals for their own profit. Such concepts of property and ownership were utterly foreign to the American Indian, who believed that land and its resources should be shared by the entire community and passed on virtually unchanged to succeeding generations.

Tribes might clash over hunting grounds, but the notion that an individual could own a portion of nature was so alien to the Indian that he rarely understood the threat that the settlers' land hunger posed to his domains and way of life until it was too late. Many of the Indian tribes, notably those in the woodlands, believed that a vast spiritual force was inherent in every living thing, a force the Iroquois called *orenda*. Their belief in the oneness of man and his environment endowed the earth with an importance that whites rarely felt.

In the struggle to possess the land, the white men availed themselves of many weapons. Their advanced technology enabled the settlers to overwhelm superior numbers of hostile Indians time and again. Diplomatic skill made it possible for the whites to divide and conquer. But most important of all, at least in the early days, was a weapon that the newcomers were probably unaware of, at first: disease. Through the centuries Europeans had contracted and developed a partial immunity or a sturdy resistance to a variety of ills unknown to the Indians, who thus had neither immunity nor resistance. Traveling inland with the very first explorers to probe the New World were the agents of measles, malaria, typhus, influenza, the bubonic plague, and smallpox. All took their toll of the Indians, but particularly virulent was smallpox, which wiped out whole villages. In fact, hundreds of thousands of eastern Indians who had never laid eyes on a European died, victims of the bacteria and viruses that were Europe's first gifts to the New World.

Three Disappointed Conquistadors

The European invasion began in the early 16th century. Spaniards, capitalizing on Columbus' landfall, were the first on the scene. They overran the Caribbean islands, which during those years served as a training ground for a brand of adventurers known as conquistadors—minor noblemen who had lived by their swords during the recently ended wars that had driven the Moors from Spain. These devout, hard-fighting men were to blaze a path of conquest westward as they planted the flag of their king and the cross of their church between Florida and the deserts of the Southwest.

Juan Ponce de León was the first. In 1513 he led an expedition northwest from Puerto Rico to quest for a mythical land in which gold was plentiful and a magical spring restored youth to all who drank from it. He discovered Florida but found neither wealth nor restorative waters and was mortally wounded by Indians in 1521.

Two other conquistadors were similarly disappointed in their search for treasure: Hernando de Soto and Francisco Vásquez de Coronado. De Soto, a wealthy nobleman, landed with some 600 followers in western Florida in 1540 only to endure three years of fruitless wandering and continual clashes with Indians. He died in 1542 and was buried in the river he had discovered: the Mississippi. In February 1539 Coronado started northward from Mexico with an expedition of 2,000 cavaliers, soldiers, Negro slaves, and Indians. He sought the legendary Seven Cities of Cíbola, whose streets were said to be paved with gold, but he found only the mud-walled pueblos of the Zuni Indians. The brave Spaniard wandered on as far as the area that is now Kansas before turning back. Finally he returned to Mexico in 1542, a defeated man.

The conquistadors and the Spanish colonizers who followed triggered a social revolution. They introduced the horse into America, and that animal eventually changed the whole way of life of the Indians throughout the plains and much of the Southwest. Able to run with the buffalo and kill them from horseback, once sedentary tribesmen became migrants, following the herds for months at a time. With their food supplies so vastly increased, populations began to grow, and intertribal warfare soared. What the buffalo and extensive trading did not provide, the buffalo hunters got by raiding neighboring peoples. Tribe preyed upon tribe, and the weaker were forced to migrate to new areas.

Thus the Spaniards unintentionally brought a new kind of wealth to the western Indians, yet they themselves returned from their expeditions emptyhanded, convinced that the new northern lands held nothing to compare with the golden hoards of Mexico and Peru. By the early 1500's, however, explorers from France and England were probing the Northeast, readying themselves to challenge Spain for a share of the New World's wealth.

8

Later in the 16th century, France and England intruded directly, if briefly, on Spain's domain. Starting in 1562 Admiral Gaspard de Coligny sent three expeditions of French Huguenots to plant colonies in Florida, but the Spanish quickly drove them out. In 1578 and 1579 an Englishman, Francis Drake, sailed his ship, the *Golden Hind*, through the Strait of Magellan, looted Spanish shipping in the Pacific, and claimed California for his queen but left no colony.

The Advancing Mission Frontier

Spain's response to the meddling of France and England was initiated mainly by her men of religion who established missions among the Indians. Dressed in simple robes, devout friars learned the native tongues and spread the Word of God, opening the way for the power of Spain. Franciscan missionaries, impelled by a zealous quest for souls, first arrived in Florida in the year 1593. They founded a succession of stations where natives were gathered together to be taught not only Christianity but the agricultural and mechanical arts. By 1650 a chain of missions, ministering to some 26,000 Indians, stretched from southern Florida northward to the Savannah River and westward far into the interior. In 1598 in what is now New Mexico, missionaries joined soldier-colonizers in founding the village of San Juan in the Rio Grande Valley, setting a pattern to be followed in Texas, Arizona, and eventually California. The advance of the mission frontier gave Spain a foothold in southern and southwestern North America that rival colonizing powers would later challenge.

At first, however, France posed no threat to Spain. Frenchmen set their sights on the dense forests of the St. Lawrence River Valley even before Spaniards began to seek yellow gold and red men's souls in the Southwest. Jacques Cartier, the skilled navigator who first explored the Gulf of St. Lawrence in 1534, led the way, but the true builders of New France were unsung fishermen who over the next years regularly visited the Newfoundland banks for the cod and halibut demanded by their countrymen. One of these fishermen, landing on the coast of Newfoundland to salt and dry his catch, noted the covetous glance of an Indian as his gleaming knife slit open a fat cod. The equally envious fisherman managed to signal that he would trade the knife for the fine cloak of beaver skins worn by the Indian, and thus was born the fur trade on which the economy of New France would rest.

In the Canadian wilds a coureur de bois ("woods runner") greets an Indian. French authorities demanded fees for, and limited, fur-trading licenses; in the 1680's they even ordered unlicensed hunters executed. So, impoverished young Canadiens disappeared into the forests as outlaw coureurs, exploring new regions, living and trading with the Indians—and badly depopulating French settlements.

In the beginning the trade was haphazard, carried on by the fishing vessels' crews, who bartered beads, mirrors, and gimcracks for pelts. But as news of the enormous profits spread, royally licensed companies entered the field. The most important of these, chartered in 1603, was blessed with the services of Samuel de Champlain, a 36-year-old visionary who was happy only when questing for unseen lands. Founding the village of Quebec in 1608 as a center for his explorations, Champlain and the young men he trained ranged far over the Great Lakes country. They cemented Indian alliances that sent canoes paddled by Hurons and Montagnais along the waterways leading to Quebec—canoes deep-laden with furs to exchange for guns and blankets and brandy.

Traders pressed westward in an attempt to reach unsophisticated inland tribes who had not yet learned the true value of their furs. Such was the momentum of expansion that by 1673 Father Jacques Marquette and Louis Jolliet had reached the Mississippi River from the Great Lakes and brought back word of an all-water route between the lakes and the Gulf of Mexico. This news inspired Robert Cavelier, Sieur de La Salle, to launch a giant enterprise in 1675. He planned to dot the entire interior with trading posts that could ship furs down either the Mississippi or the St. Lawrence and thence to Europe. La Salle lost his life while trying to plant a colony at the mouth of the Mississippi, but dozens of trappers and traders, operating out of a base at Michillimackinac at the head of Lake Michigan, were roaming the West by the 1680's. Enduring incredible hardships, they paddled their canoes day after day, their legs cramped against bales of fur, pausing only now and then to gulp down cornmeal mush flavored with salt pork. Their wearisome toil built a network of Indian alliances that gave New France supremacy in the Mississippi Valley and challenged the Spanish in Texas and New Mexico.

The gold and furs that won empires for Spain and France also doomed those empires to destruction, for both colonizing powers were so bent on skimming surface wealth from the New World that they left unoccupied the central coastlands of North America. This proved a fatal error, for the region between Canada and Florida possessed more enduring attractions: the temperate climate and tillable soils necessary to sustain a large agricultural population, which is vital to any permanent colonial enterprise.

It was England's good fortune that when she was ready to enter the race for empire, this potentially fruitful land remained available. During interminable wars with Spain, the English were content mainly to reap the results of Spain's labors in the New World by raiding her treasure-rich galleons. But by the early 17th century, England was anxious to compete for New World riches. In 1606, after earlier expeditions backed by Sir Walter Raleigh had failed, two groups of merchants petitioned James I for the right to risk their fortunes in founding new colonies. One of these, the London Company, acting under its authority to "deduce a colony of sundry of our people" into the lands north of the 34th parallel, succeeded. Three ships made their way to the James River of Virginia in 1607. The men and women they brought built the village of Jamestown on a low-lying peninsula. For a time the colonists starved amidst plenty, for the English settlers of that day were too undernourished to endure the backbreaking labor of frontiering, too untrained in wilderness ways to capitalize on nature's riches, and too busy looking for gold to plant crops. Gradually, however, they became seasoned, acquiring work habits and rudimentary frontier skills suited to the environment. The "Starving Time" was ended, but the colony still could not prosper until it developed a crop suitable for export to England.

The Westward March Begins

Virginians found their key to prosperity when one of their number, John Rolfe, began experimenting with Indian tobacco. By 1613 he had developed a plant "strong, sweet, and pleasant as any under the sun." Good bottomland would produce 500 pounds of tobacco to the acre, salable in England at five shillings a pound. Here was a source of wealth to rival that of New Spain! For a time even the streets of Jamestown were plowed up for planting, but only expansion of the colony would provide tobacco in the quantities needed to satisfy Britain's demands.

Expansion meant incursion on Indian lands and the inevitable reaction. The Massacre of 1622 cost the lives of 357 Englishmen, but sparked such savage retaliation that the red men were virtually wiped from the coastal lowlands. So the westward march began again, joined in 1634 by settlers from another colony, Maryland, which had been established just to the north. This migration inland followed what was to become a set pattern, with colonists moving westward up the rivers to the first waterfalls that stopped navigation from the sea, then spreading out over the interior. By the 1670's the tidewater in both Virginia and Maryland was comfortably settled.

Indeed it was so well settled that the population spilled southward into the Carolinas. This region was granted to eight commercially minded proprietors in 1663, but their principal settlement at Charles Town grew slowly, partly because tobacco proved unsuitable to the semitropical climate, partly because newcomers hesitated to risk living on the fringes of Spanish Florida. Casting about for an enterprise appropriate to the situation, the Carolinians hit on the fur trade; this would provide needed capital and would also undermine Spain's hold on the Indians, already wavering in their allegiance. By the 1690's great caravans of packhorses regularly left the frontier post of Savannah Town to journey far into the interior in quest of "deare skins, furrs, and younge Indian slaves." The traders were a rowdy crew who brought joy to the tavern keepers when they returned from their months-long expeditions and brought prosperity to merchants, who yearly shipped some 54,000 deerskins to London markets. The southern frontier was not only well established, it was ready for the day when Spanish control of the Floridas would be challenged.

The fur trade was also the principal capital-raising device of the first occupants of New England. These were the Pilgrims, a group led by religious separatists who dissented against the formalism of the Church of England. In 1620 the Pilgrims set out aboard the *Mayflower* for Virginia, only to be blown northward by an Atlantic storm. When the 102 colonists finally began building their homes at Plymouth, they had to find an economic enterprise suitable to a region unable to produce crops salable in Britain. Thus they too

NOVA BRITANNIA.

OFFERING MOST

Excellent fruites by Planting in VIRGINIA.

Exciting all such as be well affected to further the same.

LONDON
Printed for SAMVEL MACHAM, and are to besold at his Shop in Pauls Church-yard, at the Signe of the Bul-head.
1 6 0 9.

In a travel folder of 1609, on whose title page appears the type of ship that carried the Jamestown settlers, English colonial speculators recruited colonists for Virginia, advertising it as an "earthly paradise," whose climate was "most sweet and wholesome, much warmer than England," and whose tribes were "very loving and gentle." Actually, in the marshy Jamestown area the pioneers faced famine, malaria, dysentery, and arrows of antagonized Indians.

settled on the fur trade. Small expeditions that bartered for peltry along the Maine coast provided them with the money needed to pay off their London backers, while corn and cattle assured them self-sufficiency. Gradually the Plymouth Colony spread over the coastal lowlands of southern Massachusetts. It was soon overshadowed by another colony, just to the north, which was the haven of a larger dissenting group, the Puritans. In 1630 the Puritans from England founded Salem and Boston. Over the next years religious turmoil in England sparked a great migration that brought 25,000 Puritans to Massachusetts. Most of them tarried only briefly in Boston; overcrowding, inadequate pasturage, religious conflicts, and "a strong bent of their spirits for change" (as one group of petitioners put it) sent great numbers of them into the interior. There they spread over the Connecticut River Valley, where Hartford was founded in 1636. They also settled around the shores of Narragansett Bay, where the colony of Rhode Island took shape, and moved into southern New Hampshire.

As in Virginia, expansion toward tribal lands drove the Indians to rebellion. In 1637, just 17 years after the Plymouth Rock landing, the Pequots of Connecticut rose in a desperate bid to retain their hunting grounds. Puritan retaliation was awesome. William Bradford, governor of Plymouth Colony, wrote of one episode, the burning of a Pequot village: "It was a fearful sight to see them . . . frying in the fire . . . and horrible was the stink and scent thereof." In the end the Pequots were either slaughtered or sold into slavery. For the next 38 years expansion could go on uninterrupted.

Fur traders led the way, as they did on most frontiers, building their "trucking houses" at Springfield, Northampton, and even more distant points. In the 1640's and 1650's they began intruding in areas claimed by New Netherland, the Hudson River Valley colony settled by the Dutch in 1624. The Dutch had already been challenged in 1638 when the Swedes planted a colony in the nearby Delaware River Valley. The Dutch ousted the Swedes in 1655, but when they sought to protect their trade with the Mohawk Valley Iroquois from intruding New Englanders, England retaliated by seizing New Amsterdam, the capital of New Netherland, in 1664. Renamed New York, the entire colony, including the city, became part of the expanding English empire.

In New England farmers followed close on the heels of the fur traders. As they moved, they devised a frontier system vastly different from that of their countrymen in Virginia. Knowing profits comparable to those of the tobacco planters were denied them by the short growing season and rocky soils, New Englanders were content to move in groups under the guidance of their leaders rather than as individuals scattering widely to find the richest land. Areas adjacent to already settled communities were granted by the Massachusetts Bay Colony Legislature to groups of petitioners. These men then laid out building lots, fields for farming, and a village green, around which were clustered a church, a parish house, and usually a school. Thus the New England frontier advanced in orderly tiers of adjacent communities, assuring the settlers "safety, Christian communion, schools, civility, and other good ends." This system also encouraged community enterprise; fields were cleared by joint labor, village herdsmen watched over the cattle, and common effort aided in marketing the small agricultural surpluses.

Conquest of the Appalachian Country

So expansion went on, at first following the river valleys, then spreading over upland Connecticut, New Hampshire, and what is now Maine. By 1675 there were some 60,000 settlers in this northern frontier, pushing the Indians from their ancestral homelands and threatening their way of life. In desperation a brave Wampanoag chief, King Philip, rallied his tribesmen for a last futile stand. He might as well have tried to halt the wind. During the next year and a half Philip's warriors, allied with those of the Narragansett tribe, killed some 600 New Englanders (one-sixth of the total male population) before they themselves were slaughtered or sold as slaves. As in all such wars, the ultimate result was to cow the red men so completely that for a time the colonists could move westward again without meeting resistance. And so the frontier advanced beyond the coastal lowlands into the hills that merged with the Appalachian Mountains.

The conquest of the Appalachian country proceeded most rapidly in the South, where the spread of settlement whetted the appetite of speculators for lands that could be converted into real estate bonanzas through subdivision and sale to immigrants. As early as

In 1620 this wicker cradle, brought to Plymouth, Massachusetts, on the Mayflower, *rocked the first child born to the Pilgrims.*

Made by a skilled artisan, Shem Drowne, this weathervane—its Indian motif taken from the Massachusetts coat of arms—adorned the governor's mansion in Boston, around 1720.

A New Amsterdam house of 1626 displays the characteristic steplike gable and narrow, steep wooden-shuttered stone or brick construction of the Dutch. Famed as bricklayers, they started brick kilns along the Hudson River.

A plain Bible title page and a pewter bowl (above), belonging to Scottish settlers, contrast with the ornate Bible leaf and the ceramic plate, with its practical motto (below), of the Pennsylvania Germans. Each group brought distinctive arts and crafts to America.

1650, just 43 years after the first permanent English settlement at Jamestown, Virginia, Capt. Abraham Wood, a profit-minded fur trader whose ventures roused interest in the interior, led an expedition along the Piedmont's Roanoke River Valley in search of choice land parcels for future resale.

One who was fascinated by the possibility of wealth from the West was Sir William Berkeley, governor of Virginia. His interests included land speculation and an expanded fur trade, both of which required the discovery of passes through the mountains. This was the purpose of three expeditions launched by Berkeley under the command of John Lederer, a German physician, in 1669 and 1670. None of these three expeditions found a passage, but another one in 1671 was more successful. Led by Thomas Batts and Robert Fallam, this party followed the Staunton River through a gap in the Blue Ridge Mountains and emerged in a broad valley, where the westward-flowing New River promised an easy route to the heart of the continent—or even beyond. For a slight ebb and flow of the water led the explorers to think that they had discovered tidal movements from the west and were but a short distance from the Pacific.

The tales of these explorers and of others who followed described hilly lands, where the soil was deep and good, and mountain passes that led to a broad valley blessed with limestone soils of unbelievable fertility. This was the Great Appalachian Valley, which runs from south of the Carolinas to northern New York. "The best, richest, and most healthy part of our Country," one explorer labeled it, and those who listened had no reason to doubt his description.

The population tide was in full flow by the early 1700's, as cattlemen and, later, farmers migrated into the hilly Piedmont and then pushed beyond the Blue Ridge. Meanwhile, another group of settlers were descending into the Great Appalachian Valley from the north. Most of the settlers of this second group had come originally from certain troubled parts of Europe, notably Germany and Ireland. The Rhenish Palatinate, a usually fruitful area in Germany, had been laid waste by war and plundering princes. Some of the peasants displaced from this unhappy land had made their way to the upper Hudson River Valley, but many more moved to Pennsylvania, having heard that all newcomers were welcome there. Unable to afford high-priced farms in the East, they sought their haven in the interior. "The farmers or husbandmen live better than lords," one of them wrote. "If a workman here will only work four or five days a week, he can live grandly."

The Sturdy Germans and Scotch-Irish

Enticed by such good reports, more displaced Germans came, crowding the trails that led westward. The rolling hills and fertile soils of the Susquehanna River Valley reminded them of their homeland, and so they settled by the thousands, and their descendants, misnamed the "Pennsylvania Dutch," remain there to this day. As the Susquehanna Valley filled, latecomers moved on into the Potomac River Valley in Virginia, where the town of Winchester was laid out by merchants to meet their needs. The Yadkin River Valley in North Carolina was occupied during the 1750's. By that time a band of German settlements fringed the colonial backcountry from New York to the Carolinas.

Another group of immigrants to the western frontier was made up largely of the Scotch-Irish, a sturdy peasant people of Scottish ancestry who had lived in northern Ireland for several generations. Dislodged from their tenant farms by English threats to their economy and religion, great numbers of these fearless people, who had cleared the forests in their homeland and fought Catholic clans in the name of the righteous God of their Presbyterian faith, came to the New World. Some went to frontier New England, others to the Mohawk Valley of New York, but most to inland Pennsylvania. Because the best lands were already occupied by Germans, the Scotch-Irish moved farther west and south, settling down first in the Juniata River Valley of western Pennsylvania, then in western North Carolina. The population of North Carolina doubled between 1732 and 1754, largely due to the influx of Germans and Scotch-Irish. Within a few years the Scotch-Irish immigrants were venturing westward along the streams that formed the headwaters of the Tennessee River. A people of grit and determination, they honed their backwoods skills to become America's first true westerners—democratic in spirit, fierce in battle, and ever eager to move beyond the next range, across the next river, to conquer whatever challenges the unknown might pose.

The Scotch-Irish, and to a lesser degree the Germans and English who mingled with them on the fringes of the colonies, brought frontiering to maturity. Generations of experience had taught them how to live from the wilderness while conquering it. Skilled in the use of the ax and rifle—the two essential tools of the woodland frontiers—these pioneers could live handsomely from game and fish as they carved their farms from the forest. There was little in their appearance to distinguish them from the Indians. "The clothes of the people," wrote a visitor, "consist of deer skins, their food of Johnny cakes, deer and bear meat. A kind of white people are found here, who live like savages." Such were the hardy souls who, a few years later, were to push beyond the Appalachian Mountains and occupy the Mississippi River Valley. They had learned much of westering since the first pioneers had starved to death amidst nature's plenty at Jamestown.

Such bold spirits were needed if England's advance westward was to continue, for beyond the Appalachians there were not only hostile Indians to be displaced but equally hostile Europeans. By the time British pioneers were ready to move into the Ohio Valley in the mid-18th century, French officials and trappers had staked their country's claim to half the continent, and French trading posts dotted the countryside from the Great Lakes, down the Ohio and Mississippi Rivers, to the Gulf of Mexico, supported by loyal Indian allies who were eager to repel all invaders.

Conflict on the Frontier

The inevitable clash between the French and the advancing English frontier erupted in 1689 into a conflict between France and England known as King William's War. That struggle, which ended indecisively in 1697, bred two more wars: Queen Anne's War (1702-13), which cost France Nova Scotia, Newfoundland, and the Hudson Bay area; and King George's War (1744-48), another indecisive struggle. Between these wilderness conflicts, both sides maneuvered for position. The French tightened their grip on the interior by occupying the mouth of the Mississippi in 1699 and by building palisaded posts in the Illinois country. The British cemented a hold on the region about Hudson Bay and founded the colony of Georgia in 1732 as a center for traders who would undermine Spanish-Indian alliances that had been made in East and West Florida. Both powers felt confident when the last great war for empire, the French and Indian War, or Seven Years' War, broke out in 1754.

The tensions that underlay that final conflict originated during King George's War, when Britain's superior navy so disrupted French commerce that goods needed to sustain the fur trade in America could not be imported. Sensing the dissatisfaction of the Indians, who were by this time dependent on the guns, bullets, and blankets of the white men, well-supplied British traders from backcountry Pennsylvania began invading the Ohio Valley. They were welcomed with such enthusiasm that a leading trader, George Croghan, ordered a post to be built at the Miami village of Pickawillany. That was a threat to the very heart of the French Empire in North America. Unless the British could be expelled, the trade routes between the Great Lakes and the Gulf of Mexico would be severed and the whole interior lost.

France struck back as soon as "peace" allowed the flow of trading goods to resume. A band of French traders and Ottawa Indians attacked Pickawillany so suddenly in 1752 that the post was destroyed, its defenders killed, and a Miami chief who had sided with the Pennsylvania traders slaughtered, boiled, and eaten by the Ottawas. With the prestige of New France again high, Governor Duquesne decided on a bold stroke. He would build a chain of forts along the portage route that connected Lake Erie with the Ohio River, thus sealing off the Ohio Valley from the troublesome Pennsylvanians. Four forts would do the job: Fort Presqu'isle on Lake Erie; Fort Le Boeuf on French Creek; Fort Venango, where French Creek emptied into the Allegheny River; and Fort Duquesne at the Forks of the Ohio. Work began early in 1753 and before the summer was out the first three forts were occupied. Fort Duquesne was completed in 1754.

This chain of fortifications posed a challenge that Britain had to face or else lose the Ohio Valley—and with it the whole interior. To meet the French challenge meant war, but war was necessary not only to preserve Britain's national honor but to keep the West open to her demanding traders. The confrontation on the frontier could only be resolved by a clash of arms with the fate of North America at stake.

Far-ranging French-Canadian trappers, like this snowshoed woodsman, penetrated the Ohio Valley and upper Great Lakes, coming into conflict with the British. Other Frenchmen, the voyageurs, paddled pelt seekers even farther west, working first for the French, later for the British in Canada.

The borderers who thronged across the [mountains], the restless hunters, the hard, dogged, frontier farmers . . . were led by no one commander . . . they were not carrying out the plans of any far-sighted leader. In obedience to the instincts working half blindly within their breasts . . . they made in the wilderness homes for their children.

— *Theodore Roosevelt,* The Winning of the West

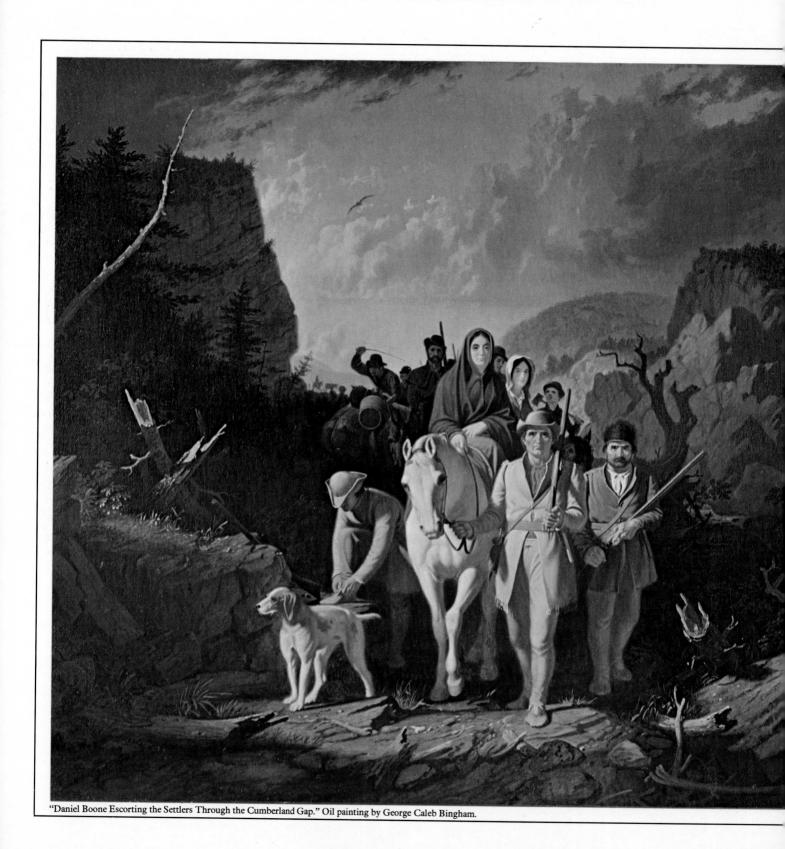

"Daniel Boone Escorting the Settlers Through the Cumberland Gap." Oil painting by George Caleb Bingham.

Chapter 1

The West Beckons

The first pioneers who pushed beyond the Appalachian range were unknowingly entering a contest that would ultimately give their descendants control of almost half a continent. From the breaching of the Appalachians to the War of 1812, the story of America is one of continuous expansion west—expansion made possible by countless battles that dispossessed the French and Indians, two successful wars against Britain, and negotiations with the European countries that claimed the land. But most of all it is the story of the people whose blood and sweat won the trans-Appalachian West: heroes and heroines, leaders and followers—rugged, independent souls all.

In the middle of the 18th century most of the non-Indian population of North America (about 1.2 million) lived in Britain's colonies on a relatively narrow strip of land along the Atlantic seaboard. To the south and southwest lay the thinly defended outposts of Spain's empire in the New World; France possessed land to the west and the north. Unsettled border zones, claimed by both France and Britain, were the scenes of frequent, often bitter, skirmishes. Victory in the French and Indian War (1754–63) would place most of the eastern third of the American continent in Britain's hands.

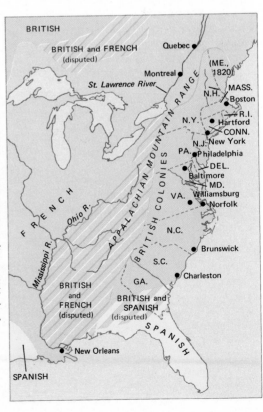

A Clash of Empires

The word was "War!" It echoed across the Atlantic from England and France to the coast of North America. For the fourth time in less than 70 years the two European powers were preparing to contend for the future of America. As the year 1754 approached, a thin stream of English colonials was wending its way west through the recently discovered Cumberland Gap in the Appalachian mountain wall. They were mostly traders, determined to challenge the French monopoly of the North American fur business. But others were farmers who hoped to find in the western wilderness free land on which to build prosperous lives. All were trespassing on territory that France called its own, and the servants of Louis XV were determined to preserve their sovereign's New World wilderness domain.

Young George Washington

As early as 1752 the British colonial trading post of Pickawillany in the back country of Pennsylvania—claimed by Virginia—was overrun and its defenders slaughtered by the French and by the Indians with whom the French had cemented alliances. Eighteen months later Virginia's governor, Robert Dinwiddie, who had strong personal interests in both wilderness fur trading and land speculation, dispatched the young George Washington into the Ohio Valley to warn the French away. The French told Washington, he later reported, "that it was their Absolute Design to take Possession of the *Ohio*, and by G— they would do it." Undeterred, Dinwiddie once again sent Washington westward, this time in command of 150 militiamen, to show the flag and, if necessary, oust the French by force. Instead, the well-prepared French repulsed Washington's troops.

Washington's humiliation was repeated in 1755 on a far grander scale, but this time the fault lay with Britain's Gen. Edward Braddock. As overconfident as he was shortsighted, Braddock ignored the warnings of Washington and other Colonial officers and marched 1,200 men directly into a French and Indian trap in a Pennsylvania forest clearing near Fort Duquesne, the main French base located where Pittsburgh now stands. Washington, Braddock's aide, almost lost his life. "I luckily escaped without a wound," the future president wrote, "though I had four bullets through my coat and two horses shot under me." The rout taught the British a costly lesson: Never again would they venture into the wilderness as if on review.

Three years later a new British commander, Gen. John Forbes, cautiously led a force of 1,700 Regulars and 5,000 Colonials against Fort Duquesne. As Forbes inched forward, with Washington at his side, hacking out what became known as the Forbes Road, his advance guard was chopped up by the French, but the main army repelled a French and Indian assault on October 12, 1758. Realizing he was heavily outnumbered,

and further weakened by the desertion of his Indian allies, the French commander abandoned Fort Duquesne, and the British occupied it on November 25, renaming this vital bastion Fort Pitt.

Meanwhile, in western New York's Mohawk Valley, an Anglo-Irish immigrant, Sir William Johnson, was busy forging an alliance between Britain and the League of the Iroquois. Controlling the primary routes to the south and west, the Iroquois were able to block French efforts to protect their inland posts. Armed with British weapons, they

George Washington, at the age of 23, was General Braddock's aide on the disastrous 1755 expedition against the French. (This portrait of him was painted in the year 1772.)

The grandly uniformed British Regulars and Colonial militia under General Braddock marched in ordered ranks toward Fort Duquesne along a 12-foot-wide road cut in the thick forest. Surprised by a smaller force of French and Indians, the British were trapped in a clearing. The Colonials fought from cover, but the Redcoats, maintaining formation and firing blindly into the forest, were mowed down by their concealed foes. Two-thirds of the bewildered British were casualties. Braddock died from his wounds.

In an 18th-century engraving (left) Sir William Johnson presents a friendly Indian with a silver medal like the one shown above, which depicts King George III on the obverse and an idyllic scene of friendship between Indian and white on the reverse. A former fur trader—and one of the few colonials who genuinely liked Indians—Johnson was made superintendent of Indian affairs north of the Ohio River in 1756.

proved more than a match for the Algonquin tribes, allied with the French.

Besides the Iroquois, Britain had another weapon against the French—a hard-drinking young frontiersman and alleged counterfeiter named Robert Rogers. Whatever Rogers' character deficiencies, and they were legion, he was a superb military leader whose ability to operate in the wilderness at least matched that of the Indians themselves.

England Victorious

Commanding a force of irregulars, Rogers struck terror into the hearts of Frenchmen and their Indian allies. Often operating deep behind enemy lines, he pushed his men to the limits of their endurance but made them experts in forced marches, traveling light, and living off the land. Swift, punishing raids were Rogers' stock-in-trade, and the ambush was his most successful tactic.

Though the French and Indian War was fought largely in the wilderness, its climax came on the Plains of Abraham beside France's proud New World capital, the city of Quebec. There, on September 13, 1759, a British force under Gen. James Wolfe overwhelmed the French defenders in a bitter engagement during which both Wolfe and the French commander, Louis Joseph de Montcalm, were mortally wounded. With Quebec's fall French ambitions in America withered; they ended in 1760 when Montreal was taken. Though peace did not come officially for more than two years, the trans-Appalachian West was already British in fact if not in name. But whether the future of this vast land was to be shaped by Englishmen in London or English colonists in America remained to be decided.

Maj. Robert Rogers of Rogers' Rangers

Frontiersman, Indian fighter, and author of a play about Chief Pontiac, Maj. Robert Rogers (1731–95) became something of a hero by following his natural bent for forest warfare. A man of prodigious strength, Rogers grew up on the New Hampshire border, where he roamed the forests and gained a thorough knowledge of the terrain. During the French and Indian War he led a force of volunteers, Rogers' Rangers, who won fame for their daring raids on French forts and the towns of hostile Indians. In their most famous exploit, the Rangers wiped out the village of the St. Francis Indians near the St. Lawrence River in 1759. The removal of this source of bloody Indian raids brought joy throughout New England. During the Revolution Rogers was on the side of the British.

Sir William Johnson Addressing the Indians of the Six Nations (1753)

I can not leave disswading you from going to Canada, the French are a delusive people, always endeavouring to divide you as much as they can, nor will they let slip any opportunity of making advantage of it. 'Tis formidable news we hear that the French & some Indians are making a descent upon Ohio; Is it with your consent or leave that they proceed in this extraordinary manner, endeavouring by force of arms to dispossess your own native allies as well as your brethern the English, and establishing themselves? . . .

I take this opportunity to return you the three Belts of Wampum sent by you to the Governor with a request to hinder the Rum from coming among You. He was very glad to gratifie you in it, and that you had seen the ill consequences of that bewitching liquor, and hopes you will continue in that resolution always. The proclamation forbidding Rum to be sent or sold anywhere among you (except at Oswego) is already published. I have now to recommend what I have said in your Brother the Governor's name to your serious consideration, and . . . I should be glad to hear [your answer]."

The Indian Menace

With the victory of Britain and her colonies over the French in America, the Indians of the trans-Appalachian country had reason to be fearful about the future. They foresaw that swarms of settlers would soon invade their domains, killing the game, felling the forests, tilling the soil, and destroying the basis of tribal life—if not the tribes themselves. Indeed, though the Indians had no way of knowing it, Gen. Jeffery Amherst, British commander in the New World, had actually recommended that smallpox germs somehow be spread among the tribesmen to destroy them. Against this threat of white domination and eventual annihilation, the Indians' only hope lay in sudden, explosive action against the still lightly defended forts of the West. Their passions were inflamed by the sudden appearance of an Abnaki "prophet" who ranged through the trans-Appalachian region claiming that the Great Spirit had charged him to rouse the Indians against the British. With considerable prescience he declared, "I give you warning, that if you suffer the Englishmen to dwell in your midst, their diseases and their poisons shall destroy you . . . and you shall die."

Pontiac, chief of the Ottawas, took such words to heart. He roused his tribe to action in the spring of 1763 and, in a swift and sudden blow, struck the British outpost at Detroit. News of Pontiac's attack set the frontier aflame, and within a month most of the tribes of the region followed his example.

The Proclamation Line

Some Indians joined Pontiac at the siege of Detroit, others surrounded Fort Pitt, still others laid waste to smaller fortifications, leaving a trail of death and pillage in their wake and sending British and colonial fur traders and settlers scurrying back east for shelter. Britain's reaction was swift, and a few months later the rebellion was quelled. Yet while

The Proclamation of 1763 banned expansion west of the Appalachians (left). Yet settlers defied it, coming into Kentucky by the river route (red, above), the Wagon (black) or Wilderness (green) Roads, trespassing on the Indians' hunting grounds.

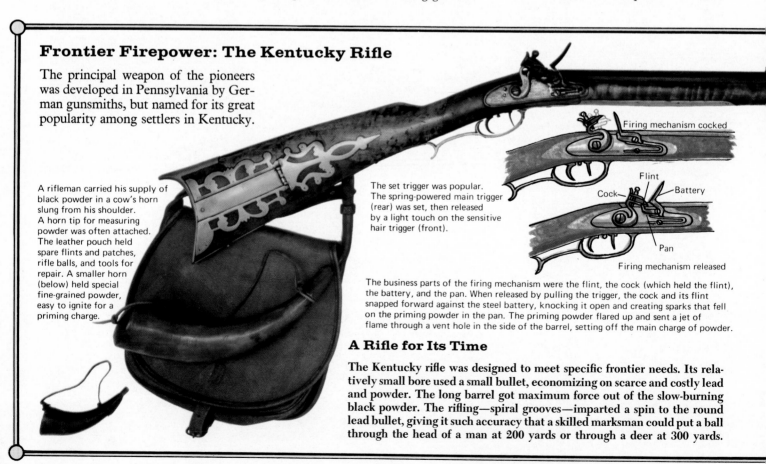

Frontier Firepower: The Kentucky Rifle

The principal weapon of the pioneers was developed in Pennsylvania by German gunsmiths, but named for its great popularity among settlers in Kentucky.

A rifleman carried his supply of black powder in a cow's horn slung from his shoulder. A horn tip for measuring powder was often attached. The leather pouch held spare flints and patches, rifle balls, and tools for repair. A smaller horn (below) held special fine-grained powder, easy to ignite for a priming charge.

The set trigger was popular. The spring-powered main trigger (rear) was set, then released by a light touch on the sensitive hair trigger (front).

Firing mechanism cocked

Flint
Cock
Battery
Pan

Firing mechanism released

The business parts of the firing mechanism were the flint, the cock (which held the flint), the battery, and the pan. When released by pulling the trigger, the cock and its flint snapped forward against the steel battery, knocking it open and creating sparks that fell on the priming powder in the pan. The priming powder flared up and sent a jet of flame through a vent hole in the side of the barrel, setting off the main charge of powder.

A Rifle for Its Time

The Kentucky rifle was designed to meet specific frontier needs. Its relatively small bore used a small bullet, economizing on scarce and costly lead and powder. The long barrel got maximum force out of the slow-burning black powder. The rifling—spiral grooves—imparted a spin to the round lead bullet, giving it such accuracy that a skilled marksman could put a ball through the head of a man at 200 yards or through a deer at 300 yards.

Pontiac lost power when he failed to win a quick victory against the English. An Indian, perhaps bribed by whites, killed him.

revolt was raging, Britain recognized that the Indians remained a power in the West whose interests could not be totally ignored—at least not yet.

To protect the Indians from further encroachment by the colonists and to reinforce royal control of the potentially rich trans-Appalachian fur trade, the British government on October 7, 1763, issued a proclamation limiting white settlement to the region east of the Appalachian crest. News of this proclama-

tion line stunned the Colonies. With a comparatively easy passage through the mountains via the Cumberland Gap and the removal of the French threat as a result of the French and Indian War, thousands of settlers were expected to swarm into the Ohio country. Many of them were militia veterans to whom land beyond the mountains had been promised by colonial assemblies. Hundreds of men—prominent easterners, including George Washington and Benjamin Franklin—were deeply involved in western land speculation and stood to lose immense fortunes if the royal decree remained in effect. In fact, vast chunks of wilderness territory had already been carved up by these speculators, and maps of the period showed as accomplished facts the dreams of the would-be real estate magnates.

But after the first shock of the proclamation had passed, it became apparent that Britain had no way of enforcing her edict. Pioneers filtered through the Cumberland Gap into Kentucky and Tennessee and pushed through the Alleghenies, establishing settlements of squatters around Pittsburgh. Speculators came to regard the line as a temporary imposition, and Washington, for one, observed that: "Any person . . . who neglects the present opportunity of hunting out good

lands and . . . marking . . . them for his own . . . will never regain it." Nor was Britain completely deaf to the arguments of settlers and speculators. Adjusting herself to reality, she steadily pushed the proclamation line westward. Perhaps she hoped in this way to solve one colonial issue while the growing disputes over taxation, the Navigation Acts, and the like were pushing the Colonies toward revolution.

Peace With Pontiac

Pondiac is a shrewd sensible Indian of few words, & commands more respect amongst those Nations, than any Indian I ever saw could do amongst his own Tribe. He and all his principal men of those Nations seem at present to be convinced that the French had a view of interest in stirring up the late differance between his Majesties Subjects & them. . . . It will require . . . a very even Conduct in those that are to reside in their Country, before we can expect to rival the French in their affection.

—Report Made to Sir
William Johnson, 1764

The Kentucky rifle's heavy octagonal barrel averaged four feet in length. Stocks were made of maple or walnut, often patterned.

The shooter cast his own lead balls in a metal mold (left) matching the caliber of his rifle. Some molds cast as many as a dozen balls at a time. Rifle calibers of this period ranged from about 0.45 to 0.60 inch; later the caliber became even smaller.

The ball, slightly smaller in diameter than the bore of the rifle, was wrapped in a greased cloth patch (left) that gave a snug fit yet allowed the ball to be pushed down the barrel easily. The ball was first trimmed to make it smooth and regular.

How To Load a Kentucky Rifle

Loading followed a strict step-by-step sequence. First, the shooter poured a measured charge of powder down the muzzle. (A rough-and-ready way of measuring was to place the ball in the palm of one's hand and pour enough powder over it to cover it.) Next, he placed a greased patch over the muzzle and carefully centered the ball in it. He then pushed the ball and patch down with a long stroke of his hickory ramrod, taking care not to pound the ball and knock it out of shape. He pulled back the cock, which latched automatically into place, opened the pan cover, and poured in a small amount of priming powder. When the cover was closed, the rifle was ready to fire.

Measuring powder   Pouring powder into muzzle   Seating patched bullet   Ramming bullet home   Priming

Daniel Boone, Bold Tamer of the Frontier

He became a legend in his own lifetime, famed for his exploits as hunter, wilderness explorer, and Indian fighter. His other roles included surveyor, negotiator, strategist, state legislator, magistrate, and land speculator. Folk tradition and hero-worshiping biographers have attributed countless mythical feats to the man, but the solid facts are remarkable enough.

Daniel Boone was born on November 2, 1734, to Quaker parents on a frontier farm near the present city of Reading, Pennsylvania. His schooling was scant; although he liked to read and learned to write a neat, legible hand, Daniel never mastered grammar or spelling. In the woods, however, he was an apt pupil. Friendly Indians taught him the art of spotting and tracking game as well as other ways of living in the wilderness. From these early contacts Boone probably also gained his deep understanding and appreciation of Indians.

Clearer of the Wilderness Road

Not a tall man—he stood about five feet nine—Boone had unusual strength, agility, and presence of mind. Once, cornered by Indians at the edge of a cliff, he leaped onto the top of a tree growing at the foot of the cliff and made his way to safety. Years later, trapped in his tobacco loft by Shawnee raiders, he threw an armful of dry, dusty tobacco leaves down on the astonished red men, escaping while they were temporarily blinded.

Boone was not the first white man to reach Kentucky, but he was the foremost of its explorers. On one expedition (1769–71), alone for much of the time, he explored most of central and eastern Kentucky. He helped a North Carolina land speculator, Judge Richard Henderson, negotiate the purchase of a huge tract of Kentucky land from the Cherokees in 1775; then, with a company of 30 axmen, he cleared the Wilderness Road through the Cumberland Gap to the Kentucky River, and founded Boonesborough at the terminus. Boone was rewarded with a large grant of land from Henderson's Transylvania Company, only to lose it a few years later when the company foundered.

This portrait of Boone at 85, the only likeness from life, was painted in Missouri by Chester Harding, a traveling artist.

At the outbreak of the American Revolution, Boone was instrumental in organizing the defense of Kentucky's scattered settlements. In 1778, captured by a band of Shawnees while leading an expedition to obtain salt at Blue Lick, he persuaded the Indians to hold him and his men as hostages and postpone their planned raid on Boonesborough, where the women and children were virtually defenseless. Taken to the Shawnee homeland north of the Ohio River and adopted into the tribe, he pretended enthusiasm for Indian life; but he squirreled away a gun, ammunition, and a store of dried meat. Then, waiting until the Shawnees were preoccupied with a turkey hunt, he slipped away into the woods, arriving at

In 1776 Indians captured Daniel Boone's daughter, Jemima, and two of her companions while they were boating on the Kentucky River. Boone and a small party, following a trail of broken twigs

and cloth scraps the girls had left behind, rescued them. Seventy-six years after this happened, French artist Jean-François Millet painted these extremely romanticized versions of the incidents.

The Pioneer's Garb

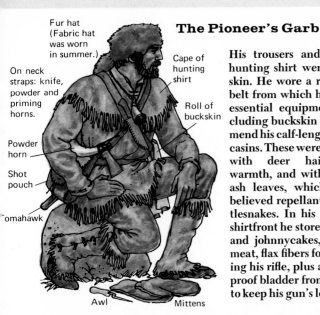

Fur hat (Fabric hat was worn in summer.)

Cape of hunting shirt

On neck straps: knife, powder and priming horns.

Roll of buckskin

Powder horn

Shot pouch

omahawk

Awl

Mittens

His trousers and caped hunting shirt were deerskin. He wore a rawhide belt from which he hung essential equipment, including buckskin used to mend his calf-length moccasins. These were stuffed with deer hair, for warmth, and with white ash leaves, which were believed repellant to rattlesnakes. In his pouchy shirtfront he stored bread and johnnycakes, jerked meat, flax fibers for cleaning his rifle, plus a waterproof bladder from a deer to keep his gun's lock dry.

Boonesborough in time to help defend it against a large Indian force sent by the British. Although Boone's delaying tactics had undeniably saved the Boonesborough settlement from immediate annihilation, rivals later accused him of treasonable dealings with the Indians and the British. He was forced to stand trial and was exonerated, but the resentment felt by some settlers lingered.

Land, however, was Boone's real downfall. By the end of the Revolution he claimed title to well over 10,000 acres. But much of it was forfeited because of improper registration, and most of the rest went to satisfy the claims of creditors, for the unexcelled woodsman was a very poor businessman. On top of this, he had sold much land to which his title was later declared invalid. The disappointed purchasers blamed Boone rather than the crafty speculators who had wangled the claims themselves. Impoverished and embittered, Boone left Kentucky in 1788 for a sojourn in what is now West Virginia, then in 1799 moved to a new frontier in Spanish-controlled Missouri, where he was greeted by the Spanish with full military honors and appointed a district magistrate. Once more he was rewarded with a huge grant of land—and once more he lost most of it when the government changed with the Louisiana Purchase in 1803. Despite this blow, Boone remained active and hardy, hunting and trapping well into his eighties. Near the end of his life he returned to Kentucky to pay off the last of his creditors. He died in Missouri in 1820, and 25 years later his body was brought back to Kentucky, the state that had rejected him, to be buried with full honors.

Boone's Trip to Kentucky in 1769

I was happy in the midst of dangers and inconveniences. In such diversity it was impossible I should be disposed to melancholy. No populous city, with all the varieties of commerce and stately structures, could afford so much pleasure to my mind, as the beauties of nature I found here. . . . I returned home to my family with a determination to bring them as soon as possible to live in Kentucke, which I esteemed a second paradise, at the risk of my life and fortune.

James Harrod, Also of Kentucky

Two years before Daniel Boone trod the bluegrass of central Kentucky, a 25-year-old Pennsylvanian with dark eyes, spade beard, and long black hair explored the forests edging the Kentucky River. His tread as quiet as an Indian's, the six-footer followed wide buffalo traces and found a lake-sized spring and creek. The year was 1767, the man James Harrod, the site his choice for what became Kentucky's first town. Seven years later he returned by canoe with 32 men, paddling down the Monongahela and Ohio Rivers and up the Kentucky River. They cleared a wide path along the creek, called it Water Street, lined it with half-acre allotments (which had 10-acre outlots), and built 5 small cabins along it and 27 more within 10 miles. The group dubbed the development Harrodsburg, drew lots for land ownership, and staked claims to all the good springs within 20 square miles (Harrod himself ultimately was to own 2,818 acres and a farmhouse big enough to entertain 65 guests).

Scarcely had the settlement been laid out than a threat of Indian war swept the backcountry, and Boone came to Harrodsburg to give warning. Harrod and most of his men left to take part in putting down a Shawnee uprising, but returned the following year. Soon their families and some slaves joined them, and they raised a fort for defense. This was essential, for in 1777—"The Year of the Bloody Sevens"—renewed Shawnee raids reached a peak. So many settlers were scalped that those who survived left their crops and stations (below) and crammed into the fort, often hungry and short of gunpowder and lead for making bullets. At a crucial stage Harrod saved them all by sneaking past Indian forces with 30 men to retrieve 5 large buried caches of gunpowder.

A Woodsman Who Came to a Mysterious End

During peaceful intervals Harrod loved to disappear on long, lone treks, hunting, surveying, and spying on Indian camps. He would even sneak into Indian villages at night to discover plans for attack. Superbly skilled in woodcraft, he repeatedly outwitted the Indians. Once, while crouching to shoot a deer, he sensed himself surrounded by three hidden Shawnees. He put his wolfskin cap on his rifle tip and slowly raised it, drawing the Indians' fire so that he could locate and kill them. Like most of his colleagues, he was a rugged individualist, and fond of drink and gambling as well. But unlike some of them, he was literate. He entertained itinerant preachers at his farm and founded the Harrod Latin School. Harrod was elected to the Virginia Legislature in 1779 and 1784. In 1791 he left home, presumably to search for a silver mine, but never returned. His wife and daughter believed he was murdered by a settler who bore him a grudge over a land claims suit.

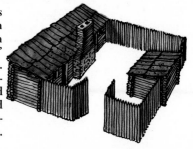

More than 30 families farmed several miles from Harrodsburg, living in twin-house log "stations" surrounded by stockades. Harrod solicitously visited each, helping find horses when they strayed or bringing a hungry settler a bear or a buffalo.

The Revolution in the West

The American Revolution was largely fought and won in a series of coastal engagements, from the battle on Lexington Green in 1775 to the siege of Yorktown six years later. At the same time, however, lesser known but often savage encounters rocked the West, where patriot victories helped win a vast hinterland for the new Union.

Of the 2.4 million colonists in 1775, only a small percentage of those in the North had abandoned the safety of the coast for the inland valleys beyond the Alleghenies, and in the South even fewer had gone through the Cumberland Gap into Kentucky and Tennessee. To the Colonies' Continental Congress, the fate of the West was of small import at first, and in any case the loyalties of the frontiersmen were often in doubt.

Settlers in the West had ample reason to distrust both patriots and loyalists. The cry of "No taxation without representation" rang hollow in the ears of the pioneers, who had long complained that colonial assemblies disregarded their interests in favor of those of the eastern merchant-planter elite. But the British were even more suspect. For years they had, however ineptly, discouraged settlement; then, faced with rebellion, they began sealing alliances with the Indians. Consequently, most pioneers were forced to the side of rebellion. In the warfare that soon erupted, neither Indians nor settlers gave or asked any quarter; its ferocity appalled a great number of British and Continental Army officers alike.

One Britisher who was particularly dismayed by the viciousness of frontier warfare, even when its victims were rebels, was Britain's superintendent of Indian affairs in the South, John Stuart. Unable to hold the Cherokees in check, he committed an act of humanitarian treason in 1776 by having a warning of impending raids given to settlers in Tennessee. Thus, when the Cherokees approached Eaton's Station on July 20, they were met by withering fire from the frontiersmen in the settlement's stockade. Thrown back from the hamlet, the Cherokees moved on to Fort Watauga, only to be routed again. To avenge this double humiliation, the Indians of the region struck at isolated farms and settlements in western Virginia, the Carolinas, and eastern Tennessee, until a strong force of militia, which had swept through the backlands, temporarily broke their power in October.

In Kentucky the situation was much the same. Shawnee and Delaware attacks drove farmers to fortified strongpoints such as Harrodsburg and Boonesborough until militiamen from Virginia cleared the areas around the major settlements. Even then the Indians continued their devastating forays.

The Indians in the North

Indians also disrupted the peace of farming settlements in New York's Mohawk Valley and Pennsylvania's Wyoming Valley. In the prewar years many German farmers had settled and prospered in these regions, and their harvests were vital to General Washington's hard-pressed army. By 1778 their fields were ablaze, and those farmers who still clung to their lands lived in fear of being murdered by the Iroquois and the bloodthirsty Butler's Rangers, a band of loyalists led by John Butler and his son, Walter.

The Iroquois leader was a remarkable Mohawk chief named Thayendanegea, better known to whites as Joseph Brant. Butler's Rangers and Brant's Iroquois stormed through the Mohawk Valley

This superbly confident letter, plus adroit bluffing, tricked British commander Henry Hamilton into giving up the strategic fort at Vincennes to Colonel Clark's small force.

George Rogers Clark led his ragged, half-starved troops 180 miles through freezing floodwaters to capture Fort Sackville, at Vincennes. Here General Hamilton surrenders the fort to Clark.

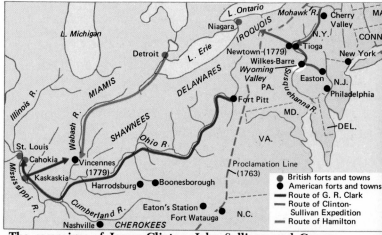

The campaigns of James Clinton, John Sullivan, and George Rogers Clark were major patriot victories in the war in the West.

and southward into the Wyoming Valley. By late 1778 it appeared that every American settlement along the Pennsylvania and New York frontiers might be wiped out.

Early in 1779 General Washington felt he could spare troops to answer the frontier farmers' desperate plea for aid, and he resolved to accomplish "the total destruction and devastation of [Iroquois] settlements." His plan called for Gen. John Sullivan to bring an army of 2,500 inland from eastern Pennsylvania and make camp at Tioga Point on the New York–Pennsylvania border. There he would await a second force of 1,500 under Gen. James Clinton, which would move from the Mohawk Valley southwest along the Susquehanna River. Once the two had joined, they would drive deep into Iroquois country.

General Sullivan's Mistake

After many delays the combined American force began moving west along the Chemung River. It had gone only 12 miles when it was challenged by an entrenched Tory-Indian force near Newtown, New York, on August 29, 1779. The American artillery blasted the enemy defenses, and an infantry charge then scattered the Tories and Indians. The rest of the campaign proved to be an exercise in pillage rather than combat. Forty Iroquois towns were destroyed, as well as 160,000 bushels of corn, standing crops of vegetables, and acres of apple, peach, and pear orchards. Although the expedition left the Iroquois country a smoking ruin, Sullivan made a serious error. Assuming that he had broken the Iroquois' power, he failed to push on and destroy the British supply base at Niagara on Lake Ontario. Stripped of their possessions and homes but not of their will to fight, the Indians provisioned and armed themselves at Niagara. For the next two years they joined the Tories in rampaging through the Mohawk Valley until John Butler's son was killed in the last major raid in October 1781.

Meanwhile, another huge chunk of western wilderness had fallen to patriot arms. Between mid-1778 and early 1779 a tiny force of Kentucky sharpshooters, led by Virginia's Col. George Rogers Clark, trekked through the Illinois country. They defeated the British at the key fort of Vincennes, immeasurably strengthening American claims to the region stretching northward from the Ohio River to the Canadian border and westward to the Mississippi.

George Rogers Clark, Hero of the Northwest

Tall, lean, and redheaded, George Rogers Clark (1752–1818) was a boy prodigy of the war in the West. The son of a Virginia planter, he explored part of the Ohio River in a canoe at the age of 19, then moved to Kentucky early in 1776. At the outbreak of the Revolution the 23-year-old Clark was sent as a delegate to the Virginia Legislature. With the help of Gov. Patrick Henry, he obtained 500 pounds of gunpowder for the defense of the imperiled Kentucky settlements. Clark and seven companions ran a 400-mile gauntlet of ambushes to get this gunpowder into the hands of Kentuckians. After fending off Indians in 1777, Clark went back to Virginia and persuaded officials to mount a counterthrust against the British in the Illinois country. He and 175 Virginia volunteers, whom he had partially equipped himself, boated down the Ohio in late June 1778, then made a swift march to take Kaskaskia by surprise on July 4. By mid-August they also held Cahokia and Vincennes and had won the alle-

For reasons known only to the artist, this portrait shows General Clark wearing a uniform of the U.S. Navy.

giance of the French inhabitants of the region. When lightly garrisoned Vincennes was retaken by the British, Clark made yet another remarkable march in 1779 to recapture it. In 1780–82, he won climactic victories over the Shawnees in Ohio. After the Revolution Clark was impoverished, as Virginia failed for years to repay money he had spent on his troops.

Women played an active part in defending the isolated, fortresslike frontier villages against sudden raids by Indians siding with the British. This 20th-century painting shows them molding bullets (far left), giving water (left center), and bandaging the wounded (center). One woman (right foreground) measures a charge of gunpowder in her hand.

Fort Harrod, a Haven in the Wilderness

To many a settler headed west, the sturdy stockade below was a welcome oasis on the Wilderness Road, a refuge from still-persistent Indian attacks. It was a self-sufficient community whose population of about 200 included 37 outlying farm families. Its strategic site on high ground was chosen by James Harrod in 1775 as more defensible than lower lying Harrodsburg. His group, all experienced frontiersmen, erected a 264-foot-square fort on the rise, clearing trees 300 feet beyond it—the extreme range of their rifles. Then, within ramparts that never fell to an enemy, they developed the first permanent settlement in Kentucky. Laboriously creating fields from forest, they pastured the cows, planted the seeds they had brought from the East, and ate the game and wild fruit of the new West. From the beginning, the pioneers included a carpenter, schoolteacher, hatter, stonemason, and a preacher who arrived "with Bible in one hand and ax in the other." In the artist's reconstruction on these pages, the residents are shown engaging in their varied activities on a peaceful autumn afternoon in 1780.

A Settlement Hewn From the Forests

The fort's seven cabins, three blockhouses, and schoolhouse are of foot-thick logs that are squared top and bottom to fit snugly when chinked with clay and straw. The logs of the 10-foot-high stockade are embedded in a trench and are pointed to make notches in which riflemen on the firewalk can rest gun barrels and fire without being seen from outside.

Multipurpose Blockhouses

Blockhouses are not only military centers but leaders' dwellings. Their ample size—25 by 44 feet—also shelters farm families in times of danger. The two-foot overhang of the second story allows defenders to pour lye onto Indians from trapdoors and enables men stationed at the portholes to shoot anyone climbing the stockade. Ground-floor windows are too high for Indian bullets to hit the inhabitants, but the latter can stand on benches to shoot out.

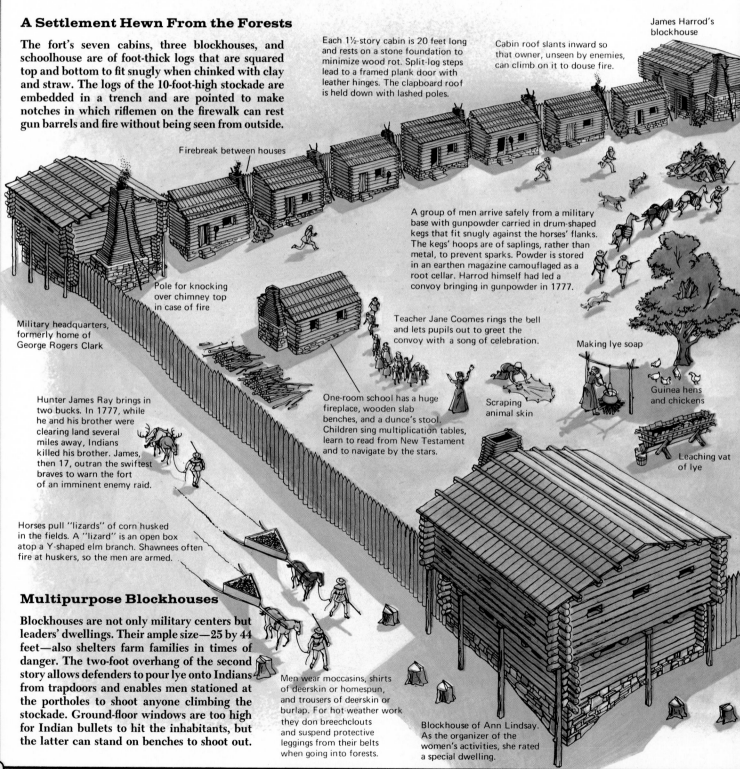

James Harrod's blockhouse

Each 1½-story cabin is 20 feet long and rests on a stone foundation to minimize wood rot. Split-log steps lead to a framed plank door with leather hinges. The clapboard roof is held down with lashed poles.

Cabin roof slants inward so that owner, unseen by enemies, can climb on it to douse fire.

Firebreak between houses

A group of men arrive safely from a military base with gunpowder carried in drum-shaped kegs that fit snugly against the horses' flanks. The kegs' hoops are of saplings, rather than metal, to prevent sparks. Powder is stored in an earthen magazine camouflaged as a root cellar. Harrod himself had led a convoy bringing in gunpowder in 1777.

Pole for knocking over chimney top in case of fire

Military headquarters, formerly home of George Rogers Clark

Teacher Jane Coomes rings the bell and lets pupils out to greet the convoy with a song of celebration.

Making lye soap

Hunter James Ray brings in two bucks. In 1777, while he and his brother were clearing land several miles away, Indians killed his brother. James, then 17, outran the swiftest braves to warn the fort of an imminent enemy raid.

One-room school has a huge fireplace, wooden slab benches, and a dunce's stool. Children sing multiplication tables, learn to read from New Testament and to navigate by the stars.

Scraping animal skin

Guinea hens and chickens

Leaching vat of lye

Horses pull "lizards" of corn husked in the fields. A "lizard" is an open box atop a Y-shaped elm branch. Shawnees often fire at huskers, so the men are armed.

Men wear moccasins, shirts of deerskin or homespun, and trousers of deerskin or burlap. For hot-weather work they don breechclouts and suspend protective leggings from their belts when going into forests.

Blockhouse of Ann Lindsay. As the organizer of the women's activities, she rated a special dwelling.

Technique for making clapboards and shingles

Froe

Maul

"Jaw"

Working on a hot day, the carpenter wears a breechclout.

Drawknife

Piggins

Noggin

Powder keg

Alphabet paddle

Broadax

Adz

The Carpenter's Woodworking Skills

To make clapboards and barrel staves, he splits them from a half log by hitting the froe with the maul. To finish staves, he sits at his shaving horse, clamps the stave with the "jaw" by pressing a foot lever, and shaves the wood with his drawknife. He also fashions plow handles, powder kegs, furniture, washboards, piggins, noggins, and paddles used to teach the alphabet to children.

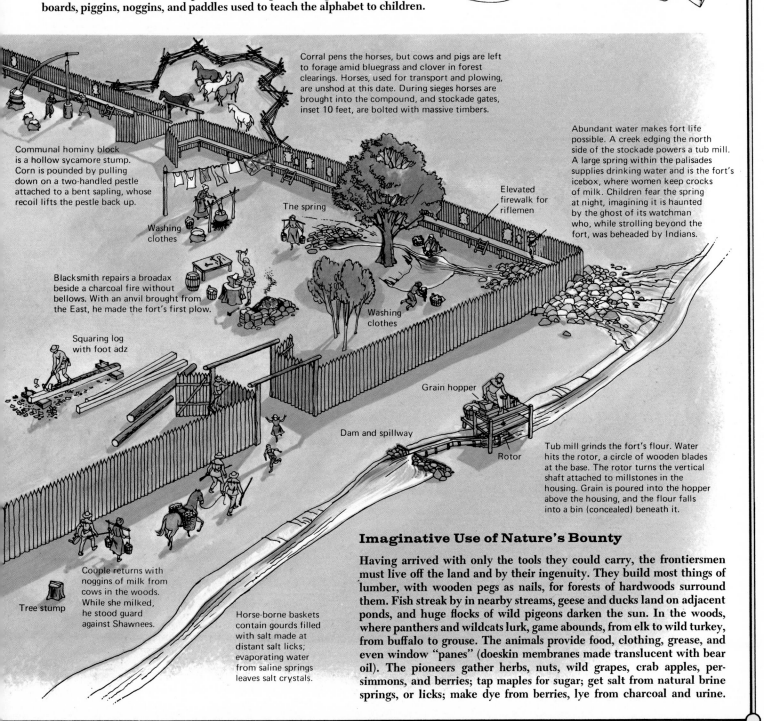

Corral pens the horses, but cows and pigs are left to forage amid bluegrass and clover in forest clearings. Horses, used for transport and plowing, are unshod at this date. During sieges horses are brought into the compound, and stockade gates, inset 10 feet, are bolted with massive timbers.

Communal hominy block is a hollow sycamore stump. Corn is pounded by pulling down on a two-handled pestle attached to a bent sapling, whose recoil lifts the pestle back up.

Washing clothes

The spring

Elevated firewalk for riflemen

Abundant water makes fort life possible. A creek edging the north side of the stockade powers a tub mill. A large spring within the palisades supplies drinking water and is the fort's icebox, where women keep crocks of milk. Children fear the spring at night, imagining it is haunted by the ghost of its watchman who, while strolling beyond the fort, was beheaded by Indians.

Blacksmith repairs a broadax beside a charcoal fire without bellows. With an anvil brought from the East, he made the fort's first plow.

Washing clothes

Squaring log with foot adz

Grain hopper

Dam and spillway

Rotor

Tub mill grinds the fort's flour. Water hits the rotor, a circle of wooden blades at the base. The rotor turns the vertical shaft attached to millstones in the housing. Grain is poured into the hopper above the housing, and the flour falls into a bin (concealed) beneath it.

Tree stump

Couple returns with noggins of milk from cows in the woods. While she milked, he stood guard against Shawnees.

Horse-borne baskets contain gourds filled with salt made at distant salt licks; evaporating water from saline springs leaves salt crystals.

Imaginative Use of Nature's Bounty

Having arrived with only the tools they could carry, the frontiersmen must live off the land and by their ingenuity. They build most things of lumber, with wooden pegs as nails, for forests of hardwoods surround them. Fish streak by in nearby streams, geese and ducks land on adjacent ponds, and huge flocks of wild pigeons darken the sun. In the woods, where panthers and wildcats lurk, game abounds, from elk to wild turkey, from buffalo to grouse. The animals provide food, clothing, grease, and even window "panes" (doeskin membranes made translucent with bear oil). The pioneers gather herbs, nuts, wild grapes, crab apples, persimmons, and berries; tap maples for sugar; get salt from natural brine springs, or licks; make dye from berries, lye from charcoal and urine.

At Home With Ann Lindsay, Leader of Women

Life at Fort Harrod was extremely difficult for the women especially, because most were used to comforts back east. But they were adventurous and spunky. One of them could not speak: her tongue had been slit by Indians. Another saw her lame husband, who couldn't run, tomahawked beyond the stockade. All dreaded the return of a riderless horse with its saddle bloody—Whose husband this time? Among the bravest was the indomitable Ann Lindsay, a self-reliant "home economics" innovator, who was eventually widowed three times. When she first rode into Kentucky, Ann carried her

spinning wheel on her horse and soon used it to spin buffalo wool. During the year that the fort was founded, while trees were being felled for the planting of flax and corn, she discovered that the fiber of nettles made an acceptable substitute for linen thread for weaving. She and the other women also knit wool stockings, fashioned doeskin underwear and buckskin winter moccasins (in summer the settlers went barefoot), and created pottery from nearby clay. They made cheese, prepared tea, using the buds of spicebushes, and poured candles of buffalo fat or bear grease, spinning milkweed wicks.

Dried apples, pears, peppers, and ginseng roots

Pressing iron

Pewter plates and tankard from back home

Gourd of salt

Sausage mill

Waffle iron

Three-tined wooden fork

Trencher (wooden platter)

Piggin

Milkweed candlewicks

Life Centers Around the Fireplace

Extending along most of one wall, Ann's fireplace is an earthen pit sunk below the plank floor. Ann tries never to let the fire die, but, if it does, she can start it up again with her rifle's flint and a tinderbox. The chimney has a base of stone seven feet high and is of stick and mud above. If it should catch fire, fort rules decree that Ann rush out and push over the upper part with a long pole. The mantel is for some of Ann's most precious possessions—from long-handled cooking utensils to pressing irons, which will be heated in the coals. Two other essentials stand nearby—a small

barrel containing a year's supply of salt and a large barrel filled with the winter's supply of cornmeal. From the hearth comes all of Ann's heat and much of her light, and most indoor household chores take place near it. Here she is making candles. In the base of each mold is a small hole; she has threaded wicks down the centers and through the holes and tied knots at the tail ends. Fastening the wick tops to a stick for taughtness, she fills the tapered molds with melted fat. Meanwhile, in the ashes, eggs roast and potatoes bake in front of a pot of beans and a tin oven in

One corner of the house's downstairs room is lighted by a doeskin-membrane window and a lamp that contains a milkweed or moss wick floating in bear grease. The protective plank shutters can be bolted on the inside. A ladder leads to the attic bedroom for older children and guests; the trundle bed is for a small child. Ann's bed is attached to the corner walls, has small branches for posts and crossed thongs for support. Her doeskin mattress is filled with cornhusks in summer, partridge down in winter. Ann made the quilt, obtaining dyes from nuts, roots, berries, and bark. She gets jet-black dye by boiling oak bark, but for rusty-black color she squeezes juice from walnut hulls in a wooden press (right). She extracts yellow-brown dye from the inner bark of white walnut trees. Blue comes from the bark of the blue ash because indigo, used in the East, seldom reaches Kentucky. Dyes must be good, for, in laundering, the clothes are smeared with homemade soap, thrown twice into a cauldron of boiling water softened with ashes, and pounded with a paddle between boilings. Ann saves dyed remnants of cloth to braid small rugs for her puncheon (timber-slab) floor and makes mats from cornhusks for her doorstep, sweeping them with a broom.

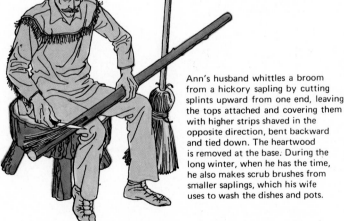

Ann's husband whittles a broom from a hickory sapling by cutting splints upward from one end, leaving the tops attached and covering them with higher strips shaved in the opposite direction, bent backward and tied down. The heartwood is removed at the base. During the long winter, when he has the time, he also makes scrub brushes from smaller saplings, which his wife uses to wash the dishes and pots.

which huckleberry-and-maize bread is baking. Above the andirons hangs a pot of hominy; in front of them, on a stone slab, are johnny-cakes of scalded cornmeal, their name possibly derived from "journey," for the men carry them on their travels. Other favorites are corn pone with fresh butter and buttermilk, venison, wildfowl, buffalo hump with turnips, sweet potatoes, peppers, and string beans. For dessert, Ann serves maple-tree treacle, paw-paws (a native "banana"), and tarts of crab apples, strawberries, wild cherries, and the hips of the sweetbrier roses that grow beside her doorstep.

From Flax to Cloth

Around June the long, blue-flowered flax stems are pulled up, soaked, and spread on the grass to rot. This softens their hard outer sheaths and tough inner cores, loosening the soft fibers sandwiched between them. When dry, the stalks are crushed by the interlocking teeth of the wooden flax brake (see below).

"Jaws" of the hinged flax brake are slammed together to "chew" the stems. They then will be draped atop a "swingling" post (right) and slashed with a wooden blade to knock off the woody parts.

Next, the fibers are pulled some six times through the spines of a hatchel until coarser bits are combed out and long fibers separated from short ones. The finer lint is then ready to be spun into thread on a spinning wheel.

Distaff

Spindle

Ann feeds fibers from the distaff to the rotating spindle, which twists them into thread. Thread passes to a bobbin, which by rotating pulls it taut and winds it. Separate cords lead from the spindle and bobbin to two grooves in the wheel, turned by a treadle. The coarsest thread becomes sacking, the next grade, men's scratchy work clothes. The finest grade goes into women's and youngsters' garments, including loose "slips" that children wear indoors.

At a homemade loom Ann presses pedals to raise and lower alternate threads of the vertical warp while passing the woof (the thread on a shuttle) horizontally under and over them. Her left hand jams a comblike reed against each new woof to pack it into a tight, strong fabric. If it is of fine grade, the tan-gray linen will be bleached white in the sun, then sewn into scarves and sunbonnets. Often strands of buffalo or sheep wool are combined with linen to produce warmer linsey-woolsey. Women's dresses—wool, linen, or a mixture—have long, full skirts and are protected by gay aprons. Buttons are of wood or the halves of walnut shells, which are pierced in the center.

Carving Up a Continent

The British defeat at Yorktown in 1781 virtually assured the independence of the United States. But although fighting soon sputtered to a halt along the East Coast, frontier warfare between pioneers and Indians continued unabated. And there were others besides the Indians who challenged American claims to the vast interior. To be sure, the Continental Army had secured western New York, and Colonel Clark's epochal trek through the Illinois country had given the Continental Congress at least a tenuous and temporary grip on the Old Northwest. Nevertheless, Spain held the great trans-Mississippi country, and Britain still occupied Detroit and other forts in the Northwest—strong bargaining cards in the coming peace talks.

The Articles of Peace

France, although America's ally, wished her protege to remain a convenient satellite, not to become a truly sovereign nation that one day might span the continent. Yorktown had hardly passed into history when the French Foreign Minister, the Comte de Vergennes, remarked, "We have no interest . . . to see America . . . a power."

France had her own view of postwar arrangements. Spain would be granted sovereignty over Florida and the Gulf Coast all the way to the Mississippi. Most of western Kentucky, Tennessee, and Georgia would become a Spanish-American protectorate to be reserved for the Indians (the white settlers would be expelled), and the Old Northwest would be retained by England or at best divided with the United States.

On learning of the French plans, the American peace commissioners defied their instructions and immediately asked for separate talks with Britain. Only too happy to drive a wedge between the allies, Britain complied and soon demonstrated her willingness to concede most of the American demands, at least on paper.

To the astonishment of France and the gratification of the United States, Britain yielded territory in exchange for goodwill. Not only was America's sovereignty over Kentucky and Tennessee assured, but also her far less secure claim to the wilderness empire north of the Ohio. Britain vowed to evacuate her forts in the area—though this was a promise she long delayed in keeping—and in later negotiations with France and Spain she yielded Florida and its Gulf Coast strip (East and West Florida) to Spain. The land to the north, the so-called Yazoo Strip, became the object of conflicting American and Spanish interests. On January 14, 1784, the Continental Congress ratified the Treaty of Paris, which had been signed by negotiators on September 3, 1783, and the United States officially became a sovereign nation at peace with the world.

The mill at Wolf Creek in the Ohio Valley served one of the growing number of settlements that sprang up after the Revolution.

Even before the treaty was ratified Congress was wrestling with the problems that peace would impose, not the least of which was control of the West. By 1780 Kentucky had some 45,000 settlers, Tennessee about 10,000; more were streaming in daily to push the line of settlement toward the Mississippi. Neither region was slated for statehood, as the Kentucky country was part of Virginia, and Tennessee was a part of North Carolina. But many along the frontier bitterly resented rule from the

As early as the beginning of the Revolutionary War, seven states pressed conflicting claims to the lands between the Appalachians and the Mississippi. The problem was solved only when the states ceded their claims to the central government. New York led off in 1780; the rest followed slowly, one at a time, ending with Georgia in the year 1802.

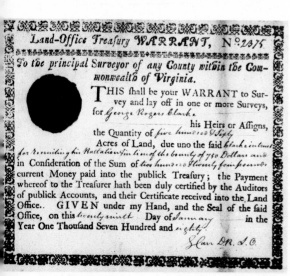

Several states granted lands in the West as enlistment bounties to soldiers—a far more solid attraction than the states' shaky currency. This Virginia land warrant, issued to George Rogers Clark in 1780 (note that the name has been misspelled), was ordered by Thomas Jefferson, then governor of Virginia, to spur recruiting for Clark's western campaigns. To meet the expected flood of veterans' claims, the states established large "military reserves" to which they retained title after they had ceded their western lands.

Yazoo Strip disputed between U.S. and Spain (ceded by Spain, 1795) (ceded by GA., 1802)

East. They felt that the eastern elite was far less interested in protecting the settlements from Indian raids than in securing vast wilderness land grants from the state legislatures, which would then be subdivided and sold to future settlers. For their part, Virginia and North Carolina complained that most of the frontier people were not much more than paupers who contributed little to tax revenues and demanded much in return. Virginia, especially, was awash with speculators looking for the main chance, for that state claimed not only Kentucky but the entire Northwest as well, thanks to vaguely worded colonial charters and George Rogers Clark's Revolutionary War forays into the region.

In fact, several states had western land claims. States that did not, fearing the potential power of those whose territorial pretensions spread far into the West, refused to ratify the Articles of Confederation until all claims were ceded to the Continental Congress.

The Cession of Western Lands

Early in 1780 New York took the lead, ceding to the central government claims she could in no way enforce. Virginia followed suit later in 1780, offering her territories north of the Ohio, but only if Congress agreed not to recognize purchases from the Indians by private land companies—a provision that kept Congress from accepting the gift until 1783. Though a few states were to retain their claims for several years, Virginia's land cession, even with strings attached, led Maryland to approve the Articles of Confederation in February 1781. (She was the last claimless state to refuse to ratify until the nagging land question was settled.) And on March 1 the Continental Congress declared this act of union to be in effect.

In those states that put off the cession of their western lands, a wild flurry of speculation developed, as their legislatures expected to reap a bonanza in revenues from the sale of wilderness lands. North Carolina, for example, put the vast but largely unsettled Tennessee region on the block in 1783 at about five cents an acre. By the end of the summer eager speculators had snapped up 4 million acres. Having thus secured a nest egg for the future, North Carolina—which had grown weary of settlers' demands for military protection and internal improvements—grandly ceded her Tennessee province to the Continental Congress in June 1784.

Detroit in 1794, as sketched by a British officer. Not until 1796, 13 years after the peace treaty, did Britain give it up and a chain of other Great Lakes trading posts on U.S. soil.

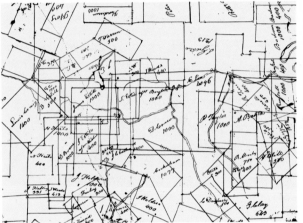

An early Kentucky land map shows a welter of overlapping land claims from the Transylvania Company, Virginia military grants, and lands awarded to surveyors for their services. Lax surveyors' descriptions, using trees as boundary markers, added to the confusion. Such "shingled" claims were bitterly contested. The map shown at the left was used in one of a series of lawsuits that lasted for some 30 years.

Surveyors—Forerunners of Orderly Settlement

The surveyor of the late 1700's relied principally on his compass and chain (right). The compass, mounted on a tripod, gave the direction of survey lines; the 66-foot chain, with links of standardized length, measured distances. A plumb bob hung from the tripod marked the starting point for measurement. In the field, the surveyor sighted on some prominent landmark, or his sighting pole, while his chainman measured the distance.

George Washington, looking suspiciously neat in the wilderness, runs a survey in 1749 with the same type of equipment used half a century later in Kentucky. The chainman anchors one end of the chain before laying it out; the sighting pole is against a tree. A well-trained surveyor could get accurate results even with his simple instruments; however, errors often occurred, giving rise to disagreements and lawsuits among later landholders.

Rumblings of Discontent

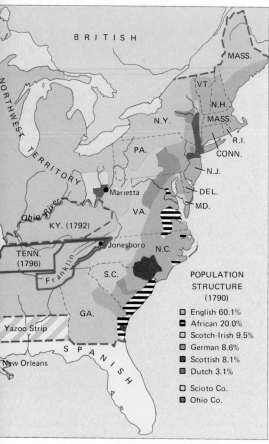

Settlers of diverse ethnic groups, led by the restless Scotch-Irish, streamed into the newly opened West from the crowded East.

POPULATION
STRUCTURE
(1790)

- English 60.1%
- African 20.0%
- Scotch-Irish 9.5%
- German 8.6%
- Scottish 8.1%
- Dutch 3.1%

- Scioto Co.
- Ohio Co.

Among the frontiersmen of Tennessee, North Carolina's gift of her western province to the central government aroused scant enthusiasm. Although few wished continued rule by the mother state, neither did they want a waiting period as a territory—and presumably more land grabs—under the Continental Congress. In 1784 settlers' representatives met at the town of Jonesboro and voted to seek immediate admission to the Union as the state of Franklin—so named in hopes of enticing Benjamin Franklin's aid for their cause. The borders they proposed extended far south and west of the area already settled and northward into Kentucky, then a part of Virginia.

Meanwhile, North Carolina had come to regret her offer to Congress and was soon to withdraw it. By then frontier unity had broken down, and two contending factions emerged, the North Carolina loyalists led by John Tipton and the advocates of statehood under John Sevier, a local land speculator. A constitution was drawn up for the proposed state, but the appeals to Congress by Sevier and his followers fell on deaf ears. North Carolina merely passed some placating laws, which won over most Franklinites—but not Sevier. After the Carolina forces under Tipton put the secessionists to rout in a somewhat farcical battle near Jonesboro in 1788, Sevier repented of his rebellion and found shelter in the North Carolina Legislature as a representative of the Tennessee country. Finally, in early 1790, North Carolina, having enriched itself anew from Tennessee land sales, again ceded the region. After six years as a U.S. territory the released lands joined the Union as the state of Tennessee, with the irrepressible Sevier as governor. Kentucky, which had endured similar upheavals, had been yielded by Virginia, entering the Union in 1792.

The admission of Kentucky and Tennessee as states equal in all respects to the original 13 (plus Vermont) was the fruit of long debates in the Continental Congress. During the early 1780's some Congressmen believed that the West would forever remain a financial burden on the East—too poor and underpopulated ever to take an equal place among the states. Even so devoted a partisan of western expansion as Thomas Jeffer-

Marietta, Ohio, as it looked in 1791, three years after its founding. It was the first planned community of the West, with a church, a school, and some industrial sites.

son had grave doubts that the interests of the staid East and the raucous West could be reconciled. "God bless them both," he remarked, "and keep them in union, if it be for their good, but separate them, if it be better." Yet others saw the West as America's future, the wellspring of a mighty nation, and even the less visionary among them viewed the region as a rich source of revenues from land sales and a buffer separating the East from Spain's trans-Mississippi holdings.

Military hero, frontier aristocrat, and land jobber, John Sevier failed to establish the new state of Franklin but became six-term governor of the new state of Tennessee.

The result of congressional debates on western policy was a series of ordinances, ending with the Northwest Ordinance of 1787, one of the last acts of the Continental Congress before the new U.S. Constitution went into effect. Under the terms of the ordinance, the region north of the Ohio, the Old Northwest, was to be divided into no more than five districts and ruled at first by administrators and judges appointed by Congress. When each district attained a free male population of 5,000, an appointed governor and a locally elected legislature would rule.

Colonies Become Partners

On reaching a population of 60,000, a territory could write a constitution and petition Congress for statehood. All such constitutions were to guarantee a great measure of civil liberties and provide for a degree of public education. And slavery was to be prohibited in the constitutions of all the states organized in the Old Northwest.

Behind the legalistic language of the ordinance lay a revolutionary concept. For the first time in human history, regions that were, in effect, colonies were given the means to join the mother country as equal partners in determining the national destiny. While the Northwest Ordinance specifically applied only to the region north of the Ohio and east of the Mississippi, it established the basic principles governing the admission of new states—though not all of them would be required to outlaw slavery.

To America's early legislators, pursued by the specter of national bankruptcy, the problem of raising revenues from land sales in the new western territories loomed at least as large as the question of the area's future political status. Moreover, there was the problem of convincing settlers to work there and the difficult question of how to dispose equitably of vast expanses of public land. Scandals surrounding the get-rich-quick schemes of speculators had made the central government somewhat wary of their flowery promises.

By the mid-1780's Congress had de-vised a plan to raise the much-needed funds and, at the same time, permit bona fide settlers to acquire land. The public domain was to be sold in large parcels at auction. Though the minimum bid was set at $1 per acre, no bid would be accepted for less than a whole parcel—640 acres. Thus, the plan proved a speculator's delight after all, for few authentic pioneers had ever seen as much as $640, and 640 acres were far too extensive for a single farmer to clear and cultivate.

Instead of settlers, land companies (often controlled by unscrupulous promoters) were the major bidders. With their considerable means and political influence, they were sometimes able to win preferential legislation allowing them to purchase large tracts with small down payments. Having secured the land, the trick was now to sell it to would-be pioneers in small plots at high prices. Typically, the promoter out for a quick killing published a pamphlet filled with praise for acreage he had probably never seen but might nonetheless describe as "the most salubrious, the most agreeable . . . the most fertile."

Among the pitiful victims of such tactics were hundreds of French citizens who had bought land from the speculators of the Scioto Company. Although the hapless victims eventually found shelter, the Scioto scandal raised new doubts about America's competence to manage western settlement.

The Scioto Scandal

The 1787–90 venture of the Scioto Company was a devious scheme by which a group of speculators attempted to gain title to a huge chunk of public land in the West when existing policy was against the purchase of large tracts by speculators. The leading conspirators were William Duer, the official who handled government land sales; Gen. Arthur St. Clair, president of the Continental Congress; and Rev. Manasseh Cutler, who represented the Ohio Company, a group of New Englanders. In a complex web of shady transactions, the Ohio Company was to buy 6.5 million acres in Ohio, then secretly turn over 5 million acres to Duer, St. Clair, and their associates known as the Scioto Company. To finance the scheme, an office was opened in Paris, where seductive prospectuses promising well-developed land persuaded some 600 prosperous city dwellers to buy lots in the Scioto territory.

French burghers throng the Paris sales office of the Scioto Company, manned by a naive poet from Connecticut, Joel Barlow, and a corrupt English promoter, William Playfair.

Rev. Manasseh Cutler: To get orderly government for those who bought his land, he helped frame the Ordinance of 1787.

From a Scioto Prospectus

A climate wholesome and delightful, frost, even in winter, almost entirely unknown, and a river called, by way of eminence, the *beautiful,* and a-bounding in excellent fish, of a vast size. Noble forests, consisting of trees that spontaneously produce sugar . . . and a plant that yields ready made candles. . . . Venison in plenty, the pursuit of which is uninterrupted by wolves, foxes, lions, or tygers. A couple of swine will multiply themselves a hundred fold in two or three years. . . . No taxes to pay, no military services to be performed.

A Visitor's Reaction

These munificent promisers forgot to say, that these forests must be cut down before corn could be raised . . . that hunting and fishing are agreeable amusements, when pursued for . . . amusement, but are widely different when followed for the sake of subsistence: and they quite forgot to mention, that though there be no bears or tygers in the neighbourhood, there are wild beasts infinitely more cunning and ferocious, in the shape of men, who were at that time at open and cruel war with the whites. . . . The picture was defective.

Plots, Foreign and Domestic

From her outposts in Louisiana and the Floridas, Spain viewed America's western ambitions with a baleful eye and determined to obstruct settlement in Kentucky and Tennessee. Madrid's strongest weapon was New Orleans, near the mouth of the Mississippi, which had been ceded to her by France in 1762. By closing that port, she could threaten western farmers with ruin, for New Orleans was their only outlet to European and American markets.

On June 26, 1784, Spain took this long-feared step. Then she opened talks with John Jay, the U.S. secretary of foreign affairs. In an effort to divide American sentiment she offered tempting trading privileges to eastern merchants, who were not about to give up potential profit for the sake of a few rowdy frontiersmen. In return, Spain's minister demanded that America agree to the closing of New Orleans for 25 years and accept postponement of the Yazoo Strip boundary dispute. When the tentative agreement was placed before Congress, seven northern states voted to accept it. Although the proposal failed to receive the required vote of nine states, the demonstrated willingness of the

Northeast to sacrifice western rights sent a wave of fury across the frontier. To make matters worse, Spain was busily arming the Creek, Chickasaw, and Choctaw tribes against American settlers in the South. Caught between their rage at the East and their fear of the aroused Indians, many frontiersmen began to question the wisdom of remaining loyal to the United States.

A Republic of the West

One who sensed an opportunity for power and profit in these events was an eastern-bred Kentuckian named James Wilkinson. Already a man of wealth and influence, Wilkinson imagined himself as the president of a new Republic of the West, a nation he believed Spain would be delighted to sponsor as a buffer against the United States. After rousing fellow Kentuckians against Congress, Wilkinson in 1787 headed for New Orleans, where he met with the Spanish governor, Esteban Miró. In exchange for Wilkinson's oath of allegiance to Spain—a loyalty he would shed soon enough—Miró granted him trading privileges at the port and urged him to sow dissent among frontiersmen.

That Wilkinson's hopes came to nothing was due, at least in part, to a sudden shift in Spanish policy. In 1789 Madrid abruptly reopened New Orleans, allowing American traders entry on payment of a 15 percent duty on their goods. Although farmers protested this stiff fee, at least they regained access to world markets. Still, the allegiance of the West seemed so tenuous that George Washington, who became president in 1789,

The Miami chief Little Turtle, a fierce opponent of the Americans, advocated peace by the time of the Battle of Fallen Timbers.

preferred to purchase the loyalty of the area's chief troublemakers rather than risk their continued plotting. Wilkinson, for one, suddenly found himself a lieutenant colonel in the U.S. Army. He soon became a general, and from these martial heights he continued to sell his loyalties.

While Spain plotted to block American expansion in the lower Mississippi Valley, Britain sought the same end in the Old Northwest. Violating her treaty obligations, Britain clung to her forts. She also encouraged the Iroquois chief Joseph Brant to forge a new coalition of tribes pledged to cede no more land to the United States and, instead, to insist on an Indian buffer state in the territory. Kentuckians stymied U.S. efforts to negotiate a settlement with Brant by making forays against Indian villages in

Military and diplomatic victories in the 1790's brought new territories in the Northwest and the Southwest under U.S. control.

James Wilkinson to Governor Miró of Louisiana (1787)

Be it known to your Honors that the Notables of Kentucky, the place of my residence, chafing under the inconveniences and privations they suffer through the restrictions placed on its commerce, suggested and pleaded that I make this voyage in order to penetrate, if this were possible, the attitude of Spain toward their country and to discover, if this were practicable, whether it would be agreeable to open a negotiation, *to admit us under its protection as vassals,* with certain privileges in matters

of religion and politics in accordance with the temper, and necessary to the welfare of the present generation. . . . I will . . . employ all my abilities to this end . . . . If in the reply which I may receive . . . my propositions are admitted, I shall on my return to Kentucky proceed with careful deliberation, take advantage of my personal consideration and political influence . . . to familiarize the people with whom I live with and make popular . . . the aims that constitute the purpose of my present voyage.

The Battle of Fallen Timbers

In the spring of 1794 Gen. Anthony Wayne led 3,000 disciplined troops slowly north from his winter base at Fort Greenville in the Northwest Territory. His object was to attack an Indian force of some 2,000 warriors from half a dozen tribes who were armed and supplied by the British at recently built Fort Miami on the Maumee River in northwestern Ohio. Leading the Indians was Blue Jacket, a powerful Shawnee orator noted for his bravery in combat. (He was thought to be a white man who had been kidnapped by the Shawnees.) After beating off one major Indian attack late in June, Wayne pushed north toward the Indians, who made their stand in a thick tangle of fallen trees along the banks of the Maumee River. Wayne, knowing that the Indians fasted before a battle, held off his attack for three days. When many of the warriors grew impatient and wandered off to get a meal at Fort Miami on August 20, Wayne launched his attack. Under cover of fire by sharpshooters and a charge by saber-swinging dragoons, the well-drilled American infantry made a bayonet charge into the fallen timbers. The Indians, dismayed by such disciplined ferocity, broke and fled for safety to Fort Miami, only to find the gates closed in their faces, as the commander did not wish to openly violate British neutrality. This rejection by their British protectors broke the morale of the Indians, and by the following year the tribes were ready to make peace with their conquerors.

A prosperous tanner in 1775, Anthony Wayne found his true profession in war. During the Revolution his dashing behavior won him the nickname "Mad Anthony," and in 1792 President Washington called him out of retirement to take command of the American army in the Northwest. Belying his nickname, Wayne did not act impetuously. He took advantage of delays brought on by renewed negotiations with the Indians and patiently drilled his men in marksmanship and tactics.

the Ohio country. In retaliation, the braves struck at isolated Ohio settlements. Two U.S. punitive expeditions against the Indians in 1790 and 1791 ended disastrously. The red men easily evaded Gen. Josiah Harmar's main force while trapping his militia and killing 183 men. Then Gen. Arthur St. Clair, first governor of the Northwest Territory, led the American army into an ambush on November 4, 1791, and suffered more than 900 casualties.

Military and Diplomatic Triumphs

In 1794 the U.S. reverses were erased by Gen. Anthony Wayne, who revitalized the hangdog army and won the decisive Battle of Fallen Timbers. In the Treaty of Greenville that followed, the Indians ceded most of what is now Ohio and a slice of Indiana.

The fate of the British forts remained to be settled, and Britain, now embroiled in European wars, was inclined to negotiate. In Jay's Treaty of 1794, she agreed to evacuate her forts in exchange for recognition of prewar debts owed British merchants. Britain retained trading rights among the Indians of the Old Northwest, a provision that was cursed by westerners. But this treaty and the Treaty of Greenville helped open the Old Northwest to settlers.

Then, with the British threat eased, it was time to settle accounts with Spain. By 1794 Madrid was becoming increasingly weary of her entanglements with Indian allies who rarely fought and American plotters who failed to rouse the West to rebellion. With war a constant reality in Europe, it seemed prudent to reach accommodation with the United States. On October 27, 1795, in the Treaty of San Lorenzo, Spain yielded the Yazoo Strip to the United States, opened the Mississippi to Americans, and permitted them to deposit goods in New Orleans and ship them without paying customs duties. Then, in late 1800, Spain signed a treaty ceding the entire Louisiana Territory to France. Suddenly the United States found herself with a far more powerful potential adversary on her western border. But the situation was less threatening than it appeared at the time, for this transfer of territory would soon lead to one of the most far-reaching real estate transactions in history: the Louisiana Purchase.

In August 1795, after weeks of negotiating with General Wayne, Little Turtle and other leaders representing tribes of the Northwest signed the Treaty of Greenville. This agreement opened vast new lands in the West to American settlers. (The symbol of Little Turtle is next to the bottom.)

Jefferson Buys an Empire

On October 18, 1802, Spain—still administering the city of New Orleans until France should find it convenient to take over again—once more closed down the port to free American trade, thus threatening frontier farmers with bankruptcy. President Thomas Jefferson, determined to solve the problem once and for all, responded with both guile and foresight. While ordering the U.S. minister to France to negotiate for the purchase of New Orleans, he encouraged rumors that the United States was considering a military alliance with Britain in order to clear the Americas of both French and Spanish influence. Napoleon, his vision beclouded by dreams of a vast New World empire, took little heed of this threat and scorned all efforts to negotiate the sale of New Orleans. Only in early 1803, after French attempts to suppress a slave revolt on the island of Santo Domingo had ended in disaster and a new war loomed with Britain, did the French emperor shift his stance. On Easter Monday Napoleon announced his decision to sell to the young American republic not only New Orleans but the entire Louisiana Territory of more than 800,000 square miles, an area slightly larger than the entire United States at that time. The agreed-upon price was about $15 million (3 cents an acre). Only the most short-sighted and ardent Jefferson haters could deny that the United States had fallen into what was surely one of the greatest land bargains in history.

The American Bargain Hunters

Thomas Jefferson's negotiating team for the purchase of New Orleans consisted of Robert R. Livingston and James Monroe. Livingston, an aristocratic New Yorker, was minister to France. Slightly deaf and speaking poor French, he could hardly believe he heard correctly when the French offered to sell all of Louisiana. Monroe, a Virginia politician and personal friend of Jefferson's, was the president's special emissary. He arrived the day after the French made their proposal, but he did take part in the lengthy bargaining talks.

Jefferson

Livingston

Monroe

The French Wheeler-Dealers

Negotiating for Napoleon were his foreign minister, Talleyrand, and his treasury minister, François Barbé-Marbois. Napoleon, dictator of France but not yet emperor, wanted quick cash and a good price for the Louisiana real estate. It was the wily Talleyrand, an ex-bishop, who proposed to Livingston that the United States buy Louisiana. Barbé-Marbois, an elder statesman known for his integrity, handled the details of the bargaining with such finesse that he gained $6 million more than Napoleon would have settled for.

Napoleon

Talleyrand

Barbé-Marbois

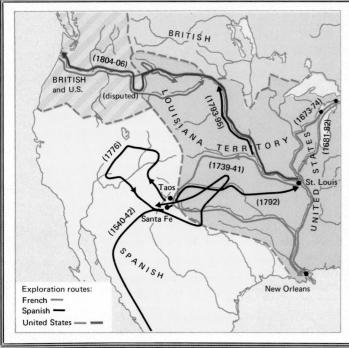

Exploration routes:
French ——
Spanish ——
United States — —

Louisiana: The Great Unknown

When the United States bought Louisiana, just what was included was a complete mystery. France refused to specify the southern and western boundaries, implying that the Americans should use force to extract the best possible terms from Spain. Said Talleyrand: "You have made a noble bargain for yourselves, and I suppose you will make the most of it." However, what was known of the resources, terrain, and climate of the new acquisition was as vague as its boundaries. The few Europeans to penetrate the region—mostly Spaniards seeking gold and Indian alliances, and Frenchmen seeking furs and illicit trade with New Mexico—had explored only narrow, if long, ribbons of land, chiefly along major rivers. To remedy this lack of knowledge, President Jefferson decided to send out the Lewis and Clark expedition, which he had commissioned months before the actual purchase. In addition to exploring Louisiana, he hoped to strengthen U.S. claims to the fur-rich Oregon Country and possibly to find a water route to the Pacific. A Britisher, Alexander Mackenzie of the North West Company, had crossed Canada in 1793, increasing Jefferson's anxiety. With the acquisition of Louisiana, its exploration became more urgent than ever before.

A French Conference

Napoleon discusses the progress of the negotiations with his bargainers. One stumbling block was that the Americans lacked the required money. The solution was to let them borrow it from Britain. The British, informed of the dealings by spies and anxious to see Louisiana occupied by a weak United States rather than Napoleon's powerful army, gladly offered the large sum at 6 percent interest.

Double Transfer of Sovereignty

Poor communications from New Orleans and an ice-choked Mississippi River delayed the transfer of northern Louisiana until March 9, 1804. Then, the Spanish flag came down at St. Louis and a U.S. officer took possession in the name of France. Toasts were drunk, and the French flag went up. Immediately afterward, American troops marched into the fort and the same officer then ceremoniously signed the territory over to the United States.

Southern Louisiana Passes to the United States

Amid happy crowds and salutes of musketry and cannon, the French flag is lowered and the Stars and Stripes raised at New Orleans on December 20, 1803. The artist took some liberties with facts; contemporary accounts say only the small group of Americans present cheered. The majority of the people, the French, were unenthusiastic.

Jefferson's Opposition

I believe [the annexation of Louisiana] will be the greatest curse that could at present befall us. . . . The inducements [for settlement] will be so strong that it will be impossible to restrain our citizens from crossing the river. . . . Thus our citizens will be removed two or three thousand miles from the capital of the Union. . . . They will gradually begin to view us as strangers; they will form other commercial connexions, and our interests will become distinct.

—Samuel White
Senator from Delaware

The principles of these people [the inhabitants of Louisiana] are probably as hostile to our Government . . . as they can be, and the relative strength which this admission gives to a Southern and Western interest, is contradictory to the principles of our original Union. . . . The words of the Constitution are completely satisfied, by a construction which shall include only the admission of domestic States, who were all parties to the Revolutionary war, and to the compact.

—Uriah Tracy
Senator from Connecticut

Beyond the Wide Missouri

On their 28-month journey in search of a water route across the uncharted vastness of the American West, Captains Meriwether Lewis and William Clark endured months of cold, weeks of hunger and fatigue, days of backbreaking labor under the prairies' sweltering summer sun, and occasional harassment from Indians. Despite such trials, they maintained nearly perfect discipline among their roughhewn subordinates; of their permanent party, which included 26 soldiers and one civilian, only one was lost—a sergeant who died of natural causes, probably appendicitis.

After spending months training their Corps of Discovery for the rigors of wilderness life, Lewis and Clark began their arduous journey on May 14, 1804. Clark left from Camp Dubois, near St. Louis, and Lewis joined him soon afterward at St. Charles. Inching up the Missouri in a 55-foot-long keelboat and two pirogues, they left all signs of civilization behind them within a few days, and the river began to reveal all its treacherous power—shifting sandbars, crumbling banks, underwater obstacles, crazily changing currents, and whirling eddies, all combining to make the upriver passage a nightmare. Against such perversities of nature the expedition struggled northwestward. Clark generally supervised the navigation while

Lewis ranged along the riverbanks, making notes for his reports and joining hunting parties in their search for game. By late July the explorers had passed the mouth of the Platte. Above it, at the site of Council Bluffs, they held their first parley with Indians: Otos, Omahas, and Missouris. As they would do many times in the months to come, they urged the red men to live in peace, gave them medals bearing President Jefferson's likeness, and told them that the Great Father now lived in Washington.

Confrontation With the Tetons

These Indians were relatively tractable, unlike the Teton Sioux whom they were to meet farther upriver. Fierce warriors, expert hunters and horsemen, the Tetons were the brigands of the Great Plains, terrorizing weaker tribes and demanding tribute in exchange for safe passage from the few French and Spanish fur traders who came their way. After a council with three chiefs who had been invited aboard the keelboat, Clark accompanied the Indians to the riverbank, where he was suddenly surrounded by warriors with drawn bows. Enraged, the captain drew his sword while men on the boats aimed their rifles into the Indians' ranks. For a moment that must have seemed an eternity, white men and red faced each other in stony

silence. Then, seeing their disadvantage, the Indians withdrew. News of the humiliation of the mighty Tetons spread quickly among the Plains tribes, earning Lewis and Clark a high respect that would greatly ease their passage.

When the plains winter with its chilling blasts closed in, the little party made haste to erect cold-weather quarters in what is now central North Dakota, among the Mandan Indians. For five months they were frozen in, but life was made relatively pleasant by the hospitable Indians. Here the explorers met a French fur trader, Toussaint Charbonneau, and his Indian wife, Sacajawea. A Shoshone from the Far West, Sacajawea had been taken captive in 1800 and sent eastward. Now she and Charbonneau offered to join the expedition as guides and interpreters. The lazy, complaining Frenchman was to prove more troublesome than useful, but Sacajawea would be of inestimable value.

On April 7, 1805, the party broke camp. The keelboat, together with some extra soldiers and rivermen, was dispatched downstream with reports and natural specimens for President Jefferson. The rest of the group, whom Lewis described as "zealously attached to the enterprise," boarded the two pirogues and six dugout canoes and struck out to the west. Although the Missouri con-

In an artist's idealized conception, Sacajawea stands at the Three Forks of the Missouri River, pointing the way to her homeland, where Lewis and Clark hoped to acquire horses for their journey. Sacajawea proved an invaluable interpreter at a crucial point of the expedition.

tinued to show its fiercest face, progress was steady, except for a short detour in early June up a tributary that Lewis named Marias River, in honor of a lady love. Ever gallant, he noted in his journal that its muddy waters "but illy comport with the pure celestial virtues . . . of that lovely fair one."

Into the Mountains

By mid-June the party reached the Great Falls of the Missouri, beyond which lay 18 miles of raging white-water rapids. To bypass this obstacle, the men were forced on a 25-day portage over difficult trails, often in gale winds or under the burning summer sun. By the time they were waterborne again they had reached the foothills of the Rockies, and the Missouri had become a swift mountain stream requiring fearful exertions to make headway against the current. Sacajawea now came into her own. She was near home country and could point out landmarks and act as guide. Lewis, heading an advance party, struck out overland, following an Indian trail through the Beaverhead Range, and then crossed the Continental Divide at the Lemhi Pass to make initial contact with a Shoshone hunting band. The braves were at first edgy and ready to scatter, but after the main party of explorers approached and Sacajawea appeared, suspicious grumbles suddenly turned to shouts of joy. Incredibly, the Shoshone leader was Sacajawea's brother, and by this most fortunate circumstance the Indians were won over.

Delighted by the whites and anxious

Explorers of the Unknown West

Lewis

Meriwether Lewis (1774-1809), a Virginia neighbor of Thomas Jefferson's, shared the president's interest in science and exploration. An experienced woodsman and soldier, Lewis became Jefferson's private secretary in 1801 and helped him plan the details of a western expedition. When the project was authorized by Congress in 1803, Jefferson named Lewis as its leader, sending him to Philadelphia for a crash course in science and medicine. For his second in command, Lewis chose an army friend, William Clark. After the expedition Lewis was appointed the first governor of the Louisiana Territory.

Clark

William Clark (1770-1838), younger brother of George Rogers Clark, was the perfect complement to Lewis. The Virginia-born Kentuckian was an even better woodsman, and as outgoing as the intellectual Lewis was withdrawn. A born diplomat, Clark so skillfully handled most of the negotiations with the Indians—who called him "The Red-Headed Chief"—that the expedition had only one violent encounter. (He was later appointed superintendent of Indian affairs for the Louisiana Territory.) Clark made the maps and drawings the men brought back with them and edited his and Lewis' diaries for publication.

for their support (and their firearms) in a continuing struggle with the neighboring Blackfeet, the Shoshones described the mountains ahead as impassable. But Lewis and Clark could not be dissuaded from pushing on, even when they learned that the broad river they had hoped to find, which would send them floating swiftly downstream to the Pacific, was nowhere nearby. Instead, the trip westward promised excruciating mountain travel before navigable waters could be reached.

York, Black Explorer

An unexpectedly valuable member of the expedition was York, Clark's Negro slave, shown here in a detail from a Charles Russell painting. Not only did York do his share of the camp chores, he was also extremely helpful in dealing with the western Indians, who had never seen a black man before. Clark's journal recounts several instances when the Indians gathered around to see the strange black man with short curly hair. The tall, powerful York obliged audiences with feats of strength and agility. After returning home, Clark freed York, who later died of cholera in Tennessee.

The Air Gun, a Toy That Proved Its Worth

One of the most surprising items carried by the expedition was Lewis' air gun. Why Lewis chose to take it is a mystery. Perhaps, as a friend of the gadget-minded Jefferson, he was intrigued by mechanical novelties and planned to test the air gun's capabilities under field conditions. He may have thought it would conserve the expedition's supply of gunpowder. At any rate, he carried the air gun with him throughout the journey. It proved of little use in bagging game—its .28-caliber bullet lacked punch—but it could wound or kill a human being at 50 yards. (In fact, it nearly did kill a bystander when discharged accidentally.) But the gun gave notable service in one department: it impressed the Indians, who were certain that any gun that could fire repeatedly without gunpowder must be magical. Lewis encouraged them in this belief.

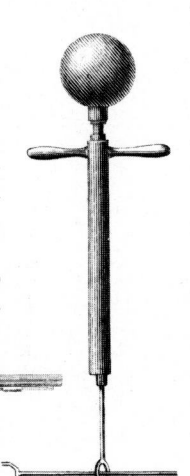

Compressed air for Lewis' gun was stored in a removable, globular metal chamber. When fully charged—by over 300 strokes of a hand pump—it held enough air for 15 to 16 shots.

Through the Rockies to the Sea

On August 30, 1805, Lewis and Clark struck northwestward once more, using packhorses obtained from the Shoshones. Their course took them through narrow, rocky defiles, where horses and men had to struggle constantly to keep their footing. Inching along 7,500-foot-high ridges, the party was assailed by snow, hail, sleet, rain, and hunger as well, all game having disappeared. After 10 days of misery, they emerged into a gentle valley, the home of the Flathead tribe. The Indians proved friendly and helped guide the explorers to a westward-flowing river, the Clearwater, which was difficult but navigable.

After pausing to build dugouts, the party took to the water on October 7. For three days they ran dangerous rapids, then debouched into the Snake River and still more rapids. It took all their painfully acquired skill as rivermen to avoid the boulders toward which the rushing white water propelled their canoes. It was madness, but the alternative was portage and delay, and the perils of the river seemed preferable to the prospect of winter in the mountains.

Down the Columbia

On October 16 the Snake took them into the Columbia, the legendary River of the West, one of the major objects of their journey. But the explorers were so exhausted that they barely noted the event. In his journal, Clark merely states: "After getting Safely over the rapid and haveing taken Diner Set out and proceeded on Seven miles to the junction of this river and the Columbia." Ahead lay more days of running rapids, a final portage around the upper and lower Cascades of the Columbia, and then bouts of seasickness as the river broadened near its mouth and choppy wavelets buffeted the canoes.

On November 7, 1805, Clark recorded in his journal: "Great joy in camp we are in *view* of the *Ocian*, this great Pacific Octean which we been so long anxious to See." The explorer was deceived, for they were still deep within the river's broad estuary. But a week later the explorers did arrive on the Pacific coast, their journey of discovery completed. On what is now the border between Washington and Oregon they built Fort Clatsop, where they spent a soggy, uncomfortable winter. The next spring they hurried homeward along much the same route they had blazed, until on July 3, 1806, the expedition split into two parties. Clark, as leader of one

From the Journals of Lewis and Clark

- **May 21, 1804 (CLARK, after Lewis has joined the party):** "Set out at half passed three o'Clock under three cheers from the gentlemen on the bank."
- **AUGUST 1, 1804 (CLARK):** "The Prarie . . . is . . . rich covered with Grass from 5 to 8 feet high interspersed with copse of Hazel, Plumbs, Currents . . . Rasberries & Grapes of Dift. Kinds."
- **SEPTEMBER 26, 1804 (CLARK):** "Those Men began to Sing, & Beet on the Tamboren, the Women came foward highly Deckerated in their Way, with the Scalps and Tropies of War . . . & proceeded to Dance the War Dance."
- **FEBRUARY 11, 1805 (LEWIS):** "Sacajawea gave birth to a boy with the help of a rattlesnake's rattle; two rings of it [were administered] to the woman broken in small pieces . . . she had not taken it more

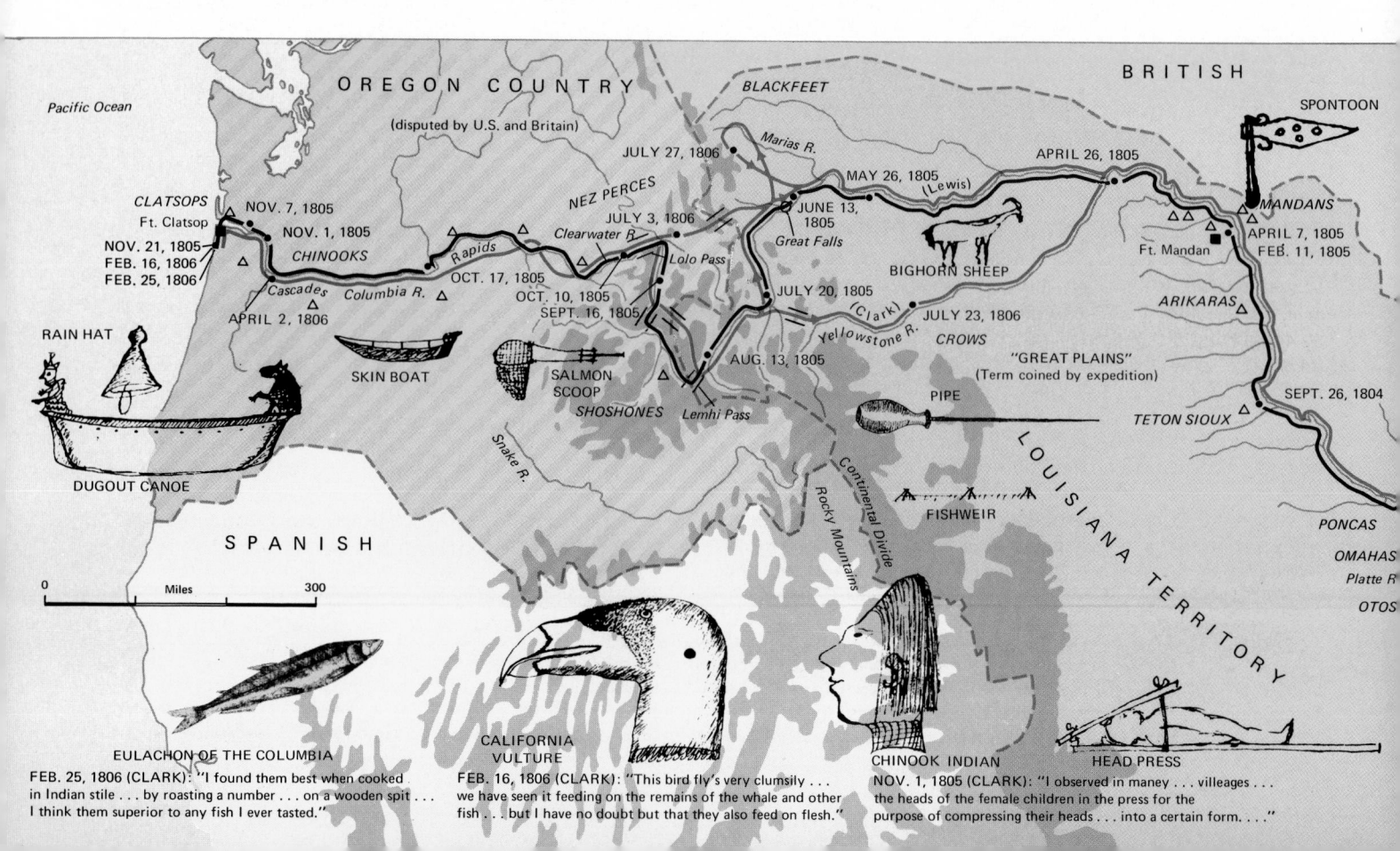

FEB. 25, 1806 (CLARK): "I found them best when cooked in Indian stile . . . by roasting a number . . . on a wooden spit . . . I think them superior to any fish I ever tasted."

EULACHON OF THE COLUMBIA

FEB. 16, 1806 (CLARK): "This bird fly's very clumsily . . . we have seen it feeding on the remains of the whale and other fish . . . but I have no doubt but that they also feed on flesh."

CALIFORNIA VULTURE

NOV. 1, 1805 (CLARK): "I observed in maney . . . villeages . . . the heads of the female children in the press for the purpose of compressing their heads . . . into a certain form. . . ."

CHINOOK INDIAN   HEAD PRESS

group, explored the Yellowstone River and followed it to its meeting with the Missouri, passing through territory that would soon be exploited by scores of American trappers. Lewis explored the Marias River and was involved in a melee with a band of Blackfeet in which two Indians were killed.

Near the joining of the Yellowstone and the Missouri, the two parties were reunited for the last leg of the journey; they arrived in triumph in St. Louis on September 23, 1806. Although they had found no easy route west, Lewis and Clark had proved the continent could be conquered and had brought back titillating and valuable information about the unknown country west of the Mississippi. Not far from the Mandan villages on the Missouri River they had met the first of the hardy mountain men heading west, their footsteps leading toward the setting sun.

In this painting by Charles Russell, Sacajawea converses in sign language with a canoeful of Chinook Indians near the mouth of the Columbia River. Lewis, his gun at the ready, is standing beside her, while Clark, wearing a cocked hat, sits behind his slave York.

than ten minutes before she brought forth."
- APRIL 7, 1805 (LEWIS): "We were now about to penetrate a country at least two thousand miles in width, on which the foot of civilized man had never trodden; the good or evil it had in store for us was for experiment yet to determine."
- APRIL 26, 1805 (LEWIS): "We ordered

a dram to be issued to each person; this soon produced the fiddle, and they spent the evening . . . singing & dancing."
- MAY 26, 1805 (LEWIS): "From this point I beheld the Rocky Mountains for the first time. . . . I felt a secret pleasure in finding myself so near the head of the heretofore conceived boundless Missouri."
- JUNE 13, 1805 (LEWIS): "From the reflection of the sun on the sprey . . . which arrises from these falls there is a beautifull rainbow produced which adds not a little to the beauty of this . . . grand senery."
- JULY 20, 1805 (LEWIS): "About 10 A.M. we saw the smoke arrise as if the country had been set on fire up the valley . . . by the natives as a signall among themselves on discovering us, as is their custom."
- AUGUST 13, 1805 (LEWIS): "[The Shoshonis] embraced me very affectionately . . . and we wer all carressed and besmeared with their grease and paint till I was heartily tired of the national hug. I now had the pipe lit and gave them smoke."
- SEPTEMBER 16, 1805 (CLARK): "I have been wet and as cold in every part as I ever was in my life, indeed I was at one time fearfull my feet would freeze in the thin Mockirsons which I wore."
- OCTOBER 10, 1805 (CLARK): "Our diet . . . bad haveing nothing but roots and dried fish to eate, all the Party have greatly the advantage of me, . . . as they all relish the flesh of the dogs."
- OCTOBER 17, 1805 (CLARK): "The number of dead Salmon on the Shores & floating in the river is incrediable to say— and at this Season they have only to collect the fish Split them open and dry them on their Scaffolds."

- NOVEMBER 21, 1805 (CLARK): "An old woman & Wife to a Cheif of the *Chunnooks* came and . . . brought with her 6 young Squars (*her daughter & nieces*) I believe for the purpose of Gratifying the passions of the men of our party."
- JULY 3, 1806 (LEWIS): "I took leave of my worthy friend and companion Capt. Clark and the party that accompanyed him. I could not avoid feeling much concern on this occasion although I hoped this seperation was only momentary. I proceeded down Clark's river seven miles."
- JULY 23, 1806 (CLARK): "Sgt. pryor found an Indian Mockerson and a Small piece of a roab, the mockerson worn out on the bottom & yet wet, and have every appearance of haveing been worn but a fiew hours before. those Indian Signs is conclusive with me that they have taken the 24 horses which we lost on the night of the 20th instant, and that those who were about last night were in serch of the ballance of our horses."
- JULY 27, 1806 (LEWIS): "I called to them [Indians] as I had done several times before that I would shoot them if they did not give me my horse and raised my gun, one of them jumped behind a rock and spoke to the other who turned arround and stoped at the distance of 30 steps from me and I shot him through the belly."
- SEPTEMBER 23, 1806 (CLARK): "Took an early breckfast . . . and Set out, decended to the Mississippi and down that river to St. Louis at which place we arived about 12 oClock. we Suffered the party to fire off their pieces as a Salute to the Town. we were met by all the village and received a harty welcom from it's inhabitants."

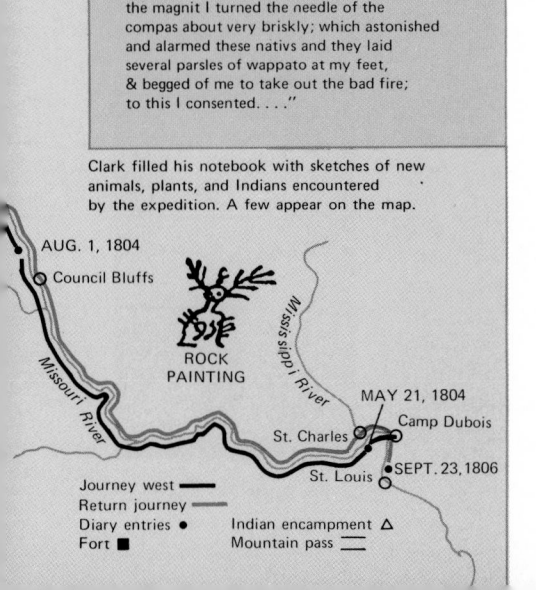

APRIL 2, 1806 (CLARK): "I entered one of the rooms of this house and offered several articles to the nativs in exchange for wappato. they were sulkey and they positively refused to sell any. I had a small pece of port fire match in my pocket, off of which I cut a pece · one inch in length & put it into the fire and took out my pocket compas and set myself down on a mat on one side of the fire, and [also showed] a magnet which was in the top of my ink stand the port fire cought and burned vehemently, which changed the colour of the fire; with the magnit I turned the needle of the compas about very briskly; which astonished and alarmed these nativs and they laid several parsles of wappato at my feet, & begged of me to take out the bad fire; to this I consented. . . ."

Clark filled his notebook with sketches of new animals, plants, and Indians encountered by the expedition. A few appear on the map.

AUG. 1, 1804
Council Bluffs

ROCK PAINTING

Missouri River

Mississippi River

MAY 21, 1804
Camp Dubois

St. Charles

St. Louis

SEPT. 23, 1806

Journey west ———
Return journey ———
Diary entries ●   Indian encampment △
Fort ■   Mountain pass ———

Treason in the Air

Zebulon Pike's two expeditions added to the geographical knowledge of Louisiana and helped to strengthen the U.S. position along its vague boundaries in the West.

As Lewis and Clark neared St. Louis on their homeward trek, fur traders along the Missouri informed them of happenings back east. Thus they learned the stunning news that Aaron Burr, vice president of the United States, had killed the Federalist leader Alexander Hamilton in a duel. Of course, they had no inkling that Burr, indicted for murder but never brought to trial, would seek to recoup his fortunes in the West. In the devious Gen. James Wilkinson, governor of the Louisiana Territory, Burr found a willing ally in murky schemes that bordered on treason.

Burr and the West

Exactly what Burr had in mind remains unknown. Rather than settling on a single plot, he seemed content to conduct vague negotiations with foreign powers to discover which one might offer the most tempting price for his services. Among his intimates he described his plans as everything from a simple land speculation scheme to the creation of a new Mexican empire on lands seized from the Spanish. In April 1805, shortly after he left the vice presidency, Burr began a tour of the frontier, the one region where his popularity had probably soared because of his duel with the archconservative Hamilton. Everywhere, he spoke darkly, if vaguely, of his plans, and vowed that those who fol-

lowed him would become rich. Often he conferred with Wilkinson, whose nervousness was growing in direct proportion to Burr's increasingly bombastic oratory. One whom Burr impressed, however, was an Ohio man named Harman Blennerhassett, who placed what was left of a declining fortune at the adventurer's disposal and offered his private island on the Ohio River to serve as a rendezvous for Burr's followers.

Even as Burr departed from Blennerhassett Island in the fall of 1806—with a small flotilla of flatboats and a motley group of followers, headed no one will ever know quite where—his jerry-built schemes began to come unstuck. Wilkinson had opted out, and to save his own skin he had written President Jefferson to accuse his erstwhile friend of treason. Though he viewed Burr's plots as "the most extraordinary since the days of Don Quixote" and just about as realistic, Jefferson ordered Burr arrested. Although Burr was later acquitted of treason, his political career was finished, and

he went into voluntary exile in Europe for four years. The grand jury that indicted Burr came within one vote of indicting Wilkinson for his part in the affair, but as usual he got off scot-free.

Pike's Explorations

Curiously, the United States derived some benefit from Burr's activities in the form of new explorations generated by his plots. In the summer of 1805 Wilkinson ordered Lt. Zebulon Montgomery Pike, a young officer under his command, to lead an expedition up the Mississippi, ostensibly to locate the source of the great river, inform the Indians of American sovereignty, and warn Canadian fur men off U.S. soil. Pike may also have been asked to report on lead-mining activities around the French settlement near present-day Dubuque—lead being necessary for making bullets, useful in any rebellion. But it is reasonably certain that Pike knew nothing of any plots and undertook his job with no thought of treason.

Aaron Burr, Adroit Intriguer

Aaron Burr (1756-1836) was graduated from the College of New Jersey (now Princeton) at 16. He served in the Army during the Revolution and in the U.S. Senate. Later he made New York City's Tammany Society into a political machine. In 1800 he tied in electoral votes for the presidency with Thomas Jefferson; the decision reverted to the House of Representatives, which, on the 36th ballot, named Jefferson president and Burr vice president. In 1804 Alexander Hamilton published insulting remarks about him when Burr was seeking to become governor of New York. Their fateful duel followed. Then Burr began to plot with Wilkinson.

James Wilkinson, Master of Deceit

The handsome, smooth-talking son of a Maryland planter, James Wilkinson (1757-1825) maneuvered his way to the top with the aid of his persuasive pen, a genius for deceit, and a passion for intrigue. After a scandal-ridden army career, including a scheme to oust Washington, he surfaced as a politician in Kentucky. There he undermined George Rogers Clark through a campaign of innuendo and began his machinations with Spain. Serving under Anthony Wayne in the Northwest, he plotted against his chief, succeeding to the command on Wayne's death. The Burr trial did not end Wilkinson's army career, but his ineptness during the War of 1812 finally did.

Zebulon Pike, a bold and resourceful explorer, reached the rank of brigadier general before being killed in the War of 1812.

Fearing that his former partner Wilkinson would kidnap him, Burr tried to escape to Spanish Florida, but he was recognized and arrested within a few miles of the border.

On August 9, 1805, with 20 soldiers, he began his ascent of the Mississippi. By September the lead mines had been inspected and the party was in what is now Minnesota, where Pike parleyed with the Sioux. Though the chill nights already presaged winter, Pike pushed his men north, until at the site of Little Falls, Minnesota, they built winter quarters. In December, however, Pike set out on foot with a small party to find the Mississippi's headwaters. They were saved from freezing to death by being given shelter in a string of Canadian trading posts along the upper Mississippi, but Pike—never forgetting his mission—ordered his hosts to pay American duties or evacuate the region. When one commander refused to lower the British flag, Pike ordered his troops to shoot it down. After this episode Pike reached Leech Lake and mistakenly assumed it to be the river's source.

Into Spanish Territory

By the time Pike returned to St. Louis on April 30, 1806, Wilkinson was ready to dispatch him into the Southwest. Although his official orders were to avoid Spanish territory, the young officer may have received secret instructions to range far into Spain's domains. On July 15, 1806, he and 23 men moved up the Osage River on two barges. Then after trading their boats for horses, they followed the Arkansas River, Pike keeping careful notes on the terrain. Significantly, his view of the plains as a treeless wasteland would help establish the myth of the Great American Desert, inhibiting settlement for decades. By mid-November, Pike's company was dangerously close to Spanish territory, and the men were beginning to suffer from cold weather, which they had not expected in the Southwest. After the party sighted the southern reaches of the Rockies, Pike and three companions made an unsuccessful attempt to climb one of the higher peaks, a mountain that would later bear Pike's name.

Winter was closing in with a rush, and deep within Spanish territory the men, who suffered horribly in their summer uniforms, built crude shelters. Meanwhile, local authorities (who had been informed of Pike's presence) sent out parties to locate and arrest him. Captured by the Spanish, the Americans were taken to Santa Fe—which, ironically, may have been Pike's objective from the start. The few private American traders who had reached the city earlier had all been forbidden to leave. Pike, being an officer of a technically friendly power, could not be treated quite so cavalierly. He and his company were dispatched under guard to Chihuahua, Mexico, and escorted back to U.S. territory via Texas. His maps and papers had been confiscated, but on his return in the summer of 1807 Pike remembered enough to write a report that greatly expanded his countrymen's knowledge of the Southwest.

From Pike's Report on Mexico (1808)

[Spain's] Mexican dominions . . . might be termed a conquered kingdom. . . . The approximation of the United States . . . began to rouse up their dormant qualities, and to call into action the powers of their minds, on the subject of their political situation. . . . Twenty thousand auxiliaries from the United States, under good officers, joined to the *independents* of the country, are at any time sufficient to create and effect the revolution. . . . The details requisite for the equipment . . . could be easily formed, but would be impertinent here.

This sail-equipped keelboat took Pike and his men on the first leg of their journey up the Mississippi; they finished it on foot.

The Drift Toward War

William Henry Harrison retreated after the Battle of Tippecanoe but managed to inflate the encounter into a major victory.

Although the machinations of Burr and Wilkinson came to nothing, other problems were arising in the West. In 1803 Ohio had entered the Union as the first state to be carved from the Northwest Territory, and its representatives in Congress plus those of Kentucky and Tennessee formed a highly vocal frontier bloc. With Kentucky's young congressman Henry Clay in the vanguard, the West began to voice its demands for internal improvements at federal expense, protection from the Indians, and territorial expansion. Moreover, as the first decade of the 19th century drew to a close, there was talk of war everywhere in the West. And if some feared its cost in blood and treasure, others could see only profit and glory.

To those along the West's southern tier—Tennessee and the Mississippi and Alabama country—the enemy of choice was Spain, for the sight of Madrid's ensign fluttering over both East and West Florida was an ever-present goad to action. In more practical terms, Spain's hold on the Gulf Coast was a threat to the prosperity of inland farmers, whose direct access to the sea might be closed at any time.

In September 1810 American adventurers struck. In swift succession they overran the Spanish fort at Baton Rouge, captured the governor, formed their own government, and then appealed for U.S. annexation. President James Madison complied, annexing the western portion of West Florida on the dubious grounds that the region was included in the Louisiana Purchase. Still, much of the Gulf Coast and all of East Florida remained in Madrid's hands, but with war between the United States and Britain in the offing by this time, and with Spain a British ally, many frontiersmen were confident that soon these choice morsels would be theirs.

Troubles With Britain

If Spain was a minor roadblock to frontier ambitions, Britain—"Perfidious Albion"—was widely perceived as a dire threat to both the nation in general and the West in particular. Embroiled in her wars with Napoleon, Britain had enshrouded Europe in a tight blockade, closing off a major western market for cotton, tobacco, salt pork, and grain. Due in part to this policy—and to limited routes for shipping, as well as sheer overproduction—the agricultural West was in a severe economic depres-

The Prophet, Tecumseh's one-eyed brother, wielded enormous spiritual power until his magic was tested at Tippecanoe and failed.

sion. To add to the frontier's woes at this time, rumors persisted that British officials in Canada were once again arming the Indians of the Northwest Territory and encouraging them to stop land cessions and to attack the settlers so that Britain might retain a hold on the fur trade of the Great Lakes region.

By 1806 the Shawnee chief Tecumseh was ranging the wilderness from the Great Lakes to the Gulf of Mexico and urging the tribes to form a great coalition to resist U.S. territorial demands and forge a sovereign Indian state in the yet unsettled upper Mississippi Valley. These goals he hoped to gain by negotiation, but he was willing to fight for them if necessary.

Tecumseh's hopes suffered a setback on November 7, 1811, when, at the Battle of Tippecanoe, an army under William Henry Harrison (then governor of the Indiana Territory) defeated the chief's warriors and put the torch to his headquarters at Prophetstown, founded by Tecumseh and his brother, a religious leader. Harrison's victory—although casualties had been high—proved to be that politician's first big step toward the presidency. More significant, however, was the governor's charge that the Indians were armed with British weapons. In the tense atmosphere along the frontier, that accusation heightened already pervasive anti-British feelings. And in Washington, where the issue of British impressment of American seamen and British violations of American rights on the high seas burned with fierce intensity, the surge toward war grew stronger.

At Tippecanoe, the Indians attacked Harrison's invading army at dawn. With Tecumseh away, they were beaten off, and about 40 were killed. American dead numbered 61.

Tecumseh: Great Indian Statesman and Warrior

More than any other Indian leader, Tecumseh (1768–1813) saw the necessity of uniting his people to resist white encroachment on the land. And he came closer than any other to persuading the perpetually warring tribes to abandon their narrow interests and traditional hostilities in order to achieve his dream of pan-Indian unity.

The son of a Shawnee war chief named Puckeshinwa and a woman named Methoataske, probably a Creek, Tecumseh was born near the present site of Dayton, Ohio. When he was six years old, the murder of his father by white hunters trespassing on the tribal lands left him with a deep, lifelong detestation of white men.

The young Tecumseh was adopted by the noted Shawnee chief Blackfish, the man who later adopted Daniel Boone. Tecumseh accompanied war parties as an observer and did not take part in actual combat until he was about 15, but then he quickly gained a reputation as a skillful and fearless warrior. At the same time, he developed an unusual quality of humaneness in dealing with white prisoners.

By his early twenties, Tecumseh was the leader of his own band of devoted warriors, drawn to him by his growing reputation. By 1792 he was the acknowledged leader of the Shawnees all along the southern border of the United States. Fighting doggedly against the Americans, he steadfastly opposed each Indian cession of land, maintaining that no individual and no tribe had the right to sell any part of the common heritage. "Sell a country?" he exclaimed to his old antagonist General Harrison, "Why not sell the air, the clouds, and the great sea, as well as the earth?"

When Tecumseh was about 30 he fell in love with the daughter of a white settler, Rebecca Galloway, under whose guidance he studied the Bible, Shakespeare, and classical history. He proposed marriage, but the romance ended when the girl insisted that he live as a white man.

An Indian Confederation

In 1805 Tecumseh's brother Laulewasika, an alcoholic, experienced a religious conversion. He changed his name to Tenskwatawa ("The Open Door")—white men called him "The Prophet"—and began preaching that Indians should return to their traditional ways, cease making war on one another, and avoid contacts with the whites. These doctrines fitted in with Tecumseh's plan of forming an Indian confederation and gave great impetus to the movement. In 1806 the brothers led their followers away from the strife-ridden frontier to found a new town deep in Indian territory.

From his headquarters at Tippecanoe, or Prophetstown, Tecumseh traveled throughout the Northwest Territory, recruiting tribes to his confederation. Later he went as far afield as Florida and Arkansas. When the War of 1812 broke out, he led his warriors into action on the British side. The Indians scored notable victories at Detroit and Raisin River, but Tecumseh was killed in the Battle of Thames River, a U.S. victory. With him died the hope of an Indian union.

In 1810, calling upon Harrison, governor of the Indiana Territory, Tecumseh denounced the latest Indian land cessions. Harrison drew his sword, but fortunately violence was averted.

In this dramatic scene, Tecumseh intervenes to prevent the torture of white captives. His great charity won him the respect of many settlers.

This painting is thought to portray Tecumseh. Despite his rejection of white culture, the Shawnee leader was much influenced by it.

In 1812 Tecumseh joined the British Army as a brigadier general. The daughter of a British officer stationed at Fort Malden, near Detroit, painted him in a feathered headdress and military trousers.

This beaded ceremonial belt was presented by the British to Shawnee leaders in the 1760's. It is believed to be the same belt that Tecumseh brought to a meeting with British officials in 1810 in a dramatic bid for their support against U.S. advances.

Blood Along the Frontier

The fever for combat was running high in early 1812, and few challenged Congressman Henry Clay's grandiloquent assertion that "the militia of Kentucky are alone competent to place Montreal and Upper Canada at your feet." But when Congress finally declared war on June 18, belligerent pronouncements could not mask the fact that America was challenging the awesome might of Britain with a 6,700-man Army and a 16-ship Navy. True, state militia units were counted on to bolster the nation's armed forces, but the New England states, openly opposed to "Mr. Madison's War," as they dubbed it, called only a fraction of their militia into service, vowing to let the West and the South bear the brunt of the fighting.

Prescription for Disaster

To command the U.S. thrust into Canada, the War Department picked the 59-year-old William Hull, governor of the Michigan Territory, whose primary qualification for the task was his utter lack of enthusiasm. Hull was to move

Oliver Hazard Perry, standing erect under a hail of British fire at the Battle of Lake Erie in 1813, transfers from his disabled flagship *Lawrence* to the undamaged brig *Niagara*. Within half an hour, Perry's audacious tactics crippled the two main enemy ships; the remaining four surrendered, giving his forces control of the vital lake route.

At the Battle of the Thames, in Ontario, the Americans under Harrison annihilated the primary British force in western Canada.

across the Detroit River on to the Ontario peninsula with a mixed force of Regulars and militiamen. After reducing Britain's Fort Malden, he was to advance along the rim of Lake Erie and link up with New York militia units moving west. Hull took his army into Canada on July 12, 1812, but instead of attacking Fort Malden, which was weakly defended, he sat down to await reinforcements that never arrived and a planned diversionary action in the east that did not take place. Learning that British forces had taken Fort Michilimackinac far to the north and Browns-

town on his supply line from the south, he hastily fell back to Detroit.

Meanwhile, the British under the energetic Isaac Brock and their Indian allies under Tecumseh went on the offensive. On August 15, 1812, Detroit awoke to find the Anglo-Indian force at its gates, demanding immediate surrender. To Brock's astonishment, Hull tamely complied on August 16 and some 2,000 U.S. troops laid down their arms. Hull became a British captive, and America had suffered one of its most ignominious defeats.

Far from celebrating a triumphal march through Canada, the West now faced grim battles on its own soil. Gen. William Henry Harrison's army of Regulars and Kentucky militiamen was so busy fending off Indian and British attacks on Fort Wayne, Fort Harrison, and other outposts that there had been no time to mount an offensive.

The Road Back

When Harrison's army finally started its march toward Canada in October 1812, it was slowed to a crawl by the bottomless mud of the Black Swamp in northwestern Ohio. The final blow to Harrison's plans came when one wing of his army under the incompetent Gen. James Winchester was surprised by British and Indians at Frenchtown, near Fort Malden, on January 22, 1813, and decimated. "General Winter" then took over and Harrison's army was frozen in until spring. In May and July the emboldened enemy struck again, attacking first Fort Meigs and then Fort Stephenson, both in northern Ohio, but Harrison's troops repulsed them and sent them reeling back to Fort Malden on August 1, 1813.

On September 10 Harrison's long delayed offensive was given a needed boost when Master Commandant Oliver Hazard Perry's ships—most of them

built by Perry and his men—routed a British flotilla on Lake Erie. The victory cut the British supply line to the West, and Harrison's army hastened north to reap rich rewards. He took Fort Malden and Detroit, then pushed along the Thames River in Ontario to rout an Anglo-Indian force in the Battle of the Thames on October 5, 1813. This victory secured the Northwest Territory from invasion.

Southern Campaigns

In the South, U.S. hopes of taking East and West Florida rested on the belief that Spain would join Britain in the war. But, frustratingly, Spain refused. To goad Madrid into action, a hotheaded Tennessee lawyer-politician named Andrew Jackson was ordered to march 1,500 militiamen (more than 2,000 volunteered for duty) to New Orleans and to combine that force with the city's garrison, commanded by none other than James Wilkinson. President Madison asked Congress for authority to take over both Floridas on the premise that Britain or France would take them if the United States did not act.

When New Englanders joined other northern foes of southern expansionists to defeat this proposal on February 2, 1813, Jackson's army was disbanded. Before long, however, Congress did authorize the occupation of Mobile and most of West Florida by Wilkinson's force. Spain fumed but did not fight.

Back in Tennessee, Jackson was soon raising troops once more, this time to use against the Creek Indians, who had gone on the warpath. On March 27, 1814, after months of raids and minor clashes, he and 3,000 men fought a showdown battle with the Creeks at Horseshoe Bend in the Mississippi Territory. Artillery blasted the Creek barricades, and infantry overwhelmed the defenders, killing more than 700

A Western Hero Stands Against the Redcoats at New Orleans

The Battle of New Orleans, fought on the plains of Chalmette, was one of the few American victories on land in the War of 1812. It pitted Andrew Jackson's badly organized assortment of fighting men against British veterans of the Duke of Wellington's European campaigns against Napoleon. With more than 2,000 Redcoat casualties versus only 21 for the United States, it gave Americans a badly needed psychological victory and created a new national hero in Jackson. Popular opinion, immortalized in the song at right, held that the battle was won by keen-eyed Kentucky riflemen. In fact, most of the damage was done by the artillery and a Tennessee contingent. Two-thirds of the Kentuckians had arrived in New Orleans unarmed and were equipped with old smoothbores from the armory. Most were held in reserve by General Jackson, who was a Tennessean.

The Hunters of Kentucky

But Jackson he was wide awake,
And was'nt scar'd at trifles;
For well he knew what aim we take,
With our Kentucky rifles.
So he led us down to Cyprus swamp,
The ground was low and mucky,
There stood John Bull in martial pomp,
And here was old Kentucky.
Oh, Kentucky, the hunters of Kentucky.

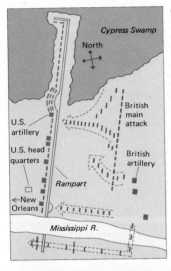

On the morning of January 8, 1815, the main British column was to hit the American left. A second column was to attack along the river; a third was to join whichever of these was more successful. Part of a fourth column, hampered by lack of boats, crossed the river and routed a Kentucky detachment before being ordered to retreat.

Andrew Jackson, sword in hand, directs artillerymen and top-hatted Tennessee volunteers as the British advance. In the center, a small British party scales the ramparts—the only ones who got that far before dying.

Based on a field sketch by a U.S. officer, this panorama shows an early stage of the Battle of New Orleans. British troops approach the mud-and-log ramparts with scaling ladders and bundles of sugarcane to fill a ditch; American artillery forces mow down the attackers.

Indians and ending Creek power forever.

The defeat of the Indians in the Northwest and South accomplished one goal of the war. But by early 1814 war weariness was sweeping the United States, and American emissaries pressed peace negotiations with the British. After first attempting to drive a hard bargain that would have carved an Indian buffer state out of the Northwest, the British relented when they suffered reverses at Fort McHenry in Baltimore harbor and at Plattsburg on Lake Champlain, and the Treaty of Ghent was signed on December 24, 1814. It was more a mutual admission of stalemate than a confirmation of victory for either side. Before news of the pact reached America, however, there was one final burst of fury. On January 8, 1815, Jackson's forces at New Orleans overwhelmingly repelled a British assault. New Englanders grumpily insisted that the war had accomplished nothing, but most Americans agreed with Albert Gallatin, who helped negotiate the peace treaty, that the war "had renewed and reinstated the national feelings. . . . The people . . . are more American; they feel and act more like a nation." Westerners, rejoicing in the ending of the Indian menace, hailed a new national figure, Andrew Jackson. In the wake of his rapidly ascending star the West would soon exercise a new power as an arbiter of the young nation's destiny.

It is a wandering people whom rivers and lakes cannot hold back, before whom forests fall and prairies are covered in shade.

—*Alexis de Tocqueville,* Journey to America

To the Mississippi and

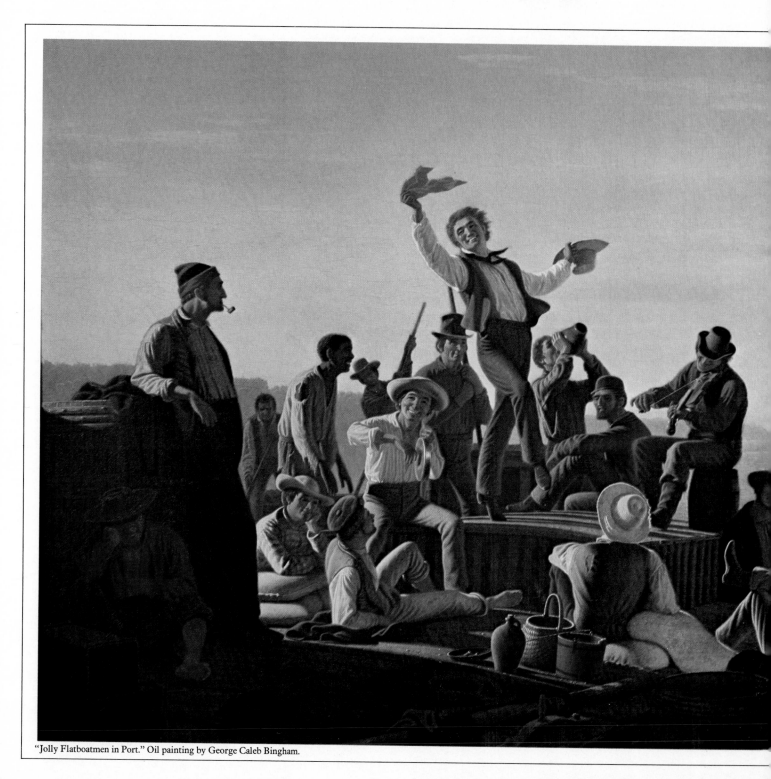

"Jolly Flatboatmen in Port." Oil painting by George Caleb Bingham.

Chapter 2

Beyond

With the peace that followed the War of 1812, the tide of migration moved the frontier steadily westward. The "movers" came by foot, on horseback, in wagons, and since roads were wretched, countless numbers used the rivers as their highways. To many a chore-burdened farm boy, the carefree life of the far-roaming boatman seemed the ultimate in freedom and glamour. But it was land, not adventure, that lured most migrants to the Great River and beyond. Canals and railroads sped the pace, and within a generation industrial cities were thriving—Cincinnati, Detroit, Milwaukee, Chicago— where not too long before Indians had hunted and fished.

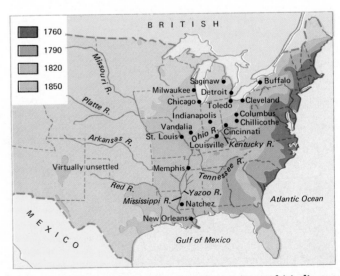

The shifting of the frontier (shown at 30-year intervals) indicates the rapid westward movement. The map's patchwork appearance is due to the fact that settlement leapfrogged areas where Indian resistance was tenacious or farming conditions poor. Despite such obstacles, the eastern half of the nation was populated by 1850.

The Great Migration Begins

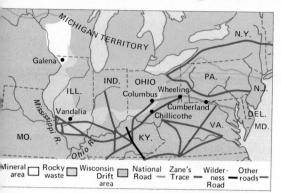

Mineral area ☐ Rocky waste ☐ Wisconsin Drift area ☐ National Road — Zane's Trace — Wilderness Road — Other roads —

An ice sheet called the Wisconsin Drift created vast areas of rich, fairly level soil. Early settlers flocked to these lands, avoiding the rocky waste—stony, uneven moraine regions left by earlier glaciers. In the unglaciated mineral area the discovery of rich deposits of lead caused a mining rush.

In 1818 Morris Birkbeck, an Englishman living in the Illinois wilderness, wrote a letter to friends in Britain, urging his countrymen "to transplant, into these boundless regions of freedom, the millions grovelling in ignorance and want." During the next decades Birkbeck's advice would be echoed thousands of times, generating an enthusiasm for the American West that sent scores of thousands across the Appalachians to turn wild forests and empty prairies into well-tended farms, bustling villages, and even great cities.

But for the Indians this westward surge was a signal of doom. The War of 1812 had destroyed their capacity to defend themselves, and now, as the whites moved in, the Indians had no choice but to make way. Neither treaty obligations nor Indian attempts to adapt to the white man's ways could stay the course of American expansion. Piecemeal land cessions might briefly appease the whites, appeals to the courts might temporarily stay their hand, calls to arms might yield a few white scalps—but nothing could long delay the Indians' disappearance from their land.

The Idea of Removal

As early as the beginning of the 19th century the notion of moving the Indians to the west of the Mississippi began to take root in the minds of America's leaders. Even as vaunted a humanitarian as Thomas Jefferson believed that the tribes should be transported beyond the pale of white settlement. As president, Jefferson ordered his representatives in the Old Northwest to conclude treaties with tribal spokesmen—usually Indians handpicked by the whites for their cupidity—for the westward removal of their peoples. His successors continued on this course, forcing tribe after tribe to exchange its holdings in the East for new lands beyond the Mississippi. That these new lands were sometimes more fertile and richer in game than the old was scant recompense for the forced upheaval from former tribal domains. Yet from the government's point of view, resettlement was the most humane of all practical alternatives. The spread of the white man's diseases and his alcohol among the Indians, the refusal of the courts to hear their side of controversies, and the killing that was done by both sides made it impossible for the two races to live side by side. Any serious effort to protect the red man's domains at the expense of the white man's ambitions would have been swept aside by an outraged American public. The harsh fact was that the nation's politicians answered to the wishes of their con-

Artist Joshua Shaw, who went west in 1819, sketched his fellow travelers. Some packed their belongings on mules, but many used crude homemade three-wheeled carts, or "horse barrows," with heavy, solid wheels sliced from tree trunks.

Inns were few and far between in the sparsely populated Old Northwest. Emigrants—as westward movers were called—often bivouacked in the open along the road, a pleasant change from a stuffy farmhouse as long as the weather was favorable.

A coach lurches slowly and dangerously along a muddy, potholed, stump-studded western road. Behind it a corduroy section, made of rough logs laid crosswise, spans a swampy stretch. Coach travel, except on parts of the National Road, was a bruising, bone-tiring experience.

stituents, who were white men, not red.

As the Indians left the Old Northwest, whites quickly replaced them. Some bought wilderness properties from the government at the going minimum rate, at first $2 an acre, later $1.25. Others bought up land warrants issued to veterans as payment for their services. Still others darted ahead of government survey teams to become squatters on land not yet surveyed and put up for sale, hoping that their physical presence would strengthen their claim when survey teams at last overtook them.

An Unstoppable Surge

To many in the East with an economic stake in the status quo—the owners of New England's new textile factories, the shippers and merchants in towns up and down the coast—the westward exodus was alarming. Fearing a wholesale loss of cheap labor in their own regions, they bent their efforts to inhibit emigration. They financed pamphlets describing in grimly exaggerated detail the hardships of frontier life; they lobbied in Congress against cheap public land; in editorial columns and from the pulpit, they warned that to go west was to find oneself among the kind of "people [who] . . . have got away from all restraint . . . and conscience."

Such efforts were bound to fail, for in the West lay the stuff of dreams: pelts to be taken; timber to be felled; pastures to be grazed; metals, such as the lead deposits at Galena, Illinois, to be mined; towns to be established; and best of all, inexpensive and abundant land to be farmed. As usual, it was the southerners who led the way. In Kentucky a second generation of pioneers was growing to maturity. Footloose and eager for adventure, hundreds sold their holdings

Many emigrants went west in flatboats roomy enough to hold farm and household equipment and even livestock. Long steering oars gave them the name "broadhorns."

The National Road, America's First Superhighway

On a turnpike feeding into the National Road, bustling traffic converges outside an inn where stagecoaches changed horses, and passengers and wagoners could find food and shelter. The National Road, built with federal funds and a vital link between the East and the Ohio Valley, was begun in 1811, the original section snaking its way across the mountains from Cumberland, Maryland, to Wheeling on the Ohio River. Extensions reached as far as Illinois by the 1850's. The eastern section was noted for its careful engineering and fine construction. A 20-foot central strip paved with crushed stone and crowned to shed water made it one of the country's few all-weather roads. A well-traveled thoroughfare, it accommodated not only emigrant wagons but also a wide variety of traffic: gaily painted coaches of competing lines, often racing dangerously; huge freight wagons carrying manufactured goods to the West and farm produce to the East; and droves of cattle on their trip to market in towns and cities along the way.

and headed for the virgin wildernesses of southern Indiana, southern Illinois, and even Missouri. Some crossed the Ohio River and picked their way northward along Indian trails until they found likely spots on which to build their cabins. Others moved west along the Ohio and other tributaries of the Mississippi, floating downstream on crude barges toward the land of their hopes.

Hard on the heels of the Kentuckians came pioneers from the seaboard states. Thousands traveled the National Road westward from Cumberland, Maryland, the poorer families on foot. The luckier ones traveled by wagon, "so light that you might almost carry it, yet strong enough to bear a good load of bedding, utensils and provisions."

At Wheeling those with a bit of money to spare boarded flatboats to float westward along the Ohio. The river promised more comfort than the overland route, but it was at least as risky. Sandbars, shifting currents, snags, and sudden storms claimed scores of craft, and many pioneers left all they owned on the Ohio's muddy bottom. Yet despite the perils of the trails and the waters, most eventually reached a homesite in the West, there to begin the arduous but rewarding task of bending the wilderness to civilization's design.

On the National Road

By far the greatest portion of travellers one meets with, not to mention the ordinary stagecoach passengers, consists of teamsters and the emigrants. . . . It would astonish you to witness how [the emigrants] get along. A covered one-horse wagon generally contains the whole worldly substance of a family consisting not unfrequently of a dozen members. . . . The strength of the poor animal is of course half the time unequal to the demand upon it, and you will, therefore, unless it be raining very hard, rarely see any one in the wagon, except perhaps some child overtaken by sickness, or a mother nursing a young infant. The head of the family walks by the horse, cheering and encouraging him on his way. The good woman, when not engaged as hinted above, either trudges along with her husband, or, leading some weary little traveller by the hand behind, endeavours to keep the rest of her charge from loitering by the wayside. The old house-dog . . . brings up the rear.

—Charles F. Hoffman, *A Winter in the West by a New Yorker,* 1835

Shelter for a Frontier Family

The log cabin was introduced into America by Swedish and Finnish colonists on the Delaware in the 1630's and spread later by the Germans and Scotch-Irish. Predominantly a feature of the backcountry, it really came into its own with the great migrations across the Appalachians after the Revolution. The advantage of the log cabin was that it could be built quickly, needed few tools—in a pinch, an ax alone would do—and the building material grew on the site. Never intended as a permanent dwelling, it provided a durable shelter until a family could afford a larger, more comfortable house of framed lumber, brick, or stone. The old log cabin was often built thriftily into the new house or turned into a shed. The one shown below in the process of construction is based on the description of an actual cabin built in Illinois in 1820 for a well-to-do family. The log cabin became a sentimental symbol of pioneer days during the presidential campaign of 1840, when William Henry Harrison's supporters claimed that he would be happy in a log cabin, like a man of the people.

Building Styles

The basic log cabin is a one-room structure with a maximum size of about 30 by 20 feet (straight, smooth logs of greater length are hard to come by). When time permits, the pioneer may add a porch in front and a back shed. "Catted" chimneys are common but apt to catch fire.

Catted chimney of logs daubed and chinked with clay

Although notched-corner construction gains space, it prevents lengthening the walls of a cabin. Scotch-Irish settlers hit on a scheme of building a second cabin and connecting it to the original with a common roof. One serves as a bedroom, the other as a kitchen-family room. Such "dogtrot" cabins are common in the South and Midwest, where the breezeway makes a cool place to go in summer. The chimneys in the cabin shown here are made of stone and are fireproof.

Central chimney is a German feature.

When well-to-do, an ambitious settler may build a substantial two-story log house with several rooms. Later he may give it a covering of weatherboards.

Roofing

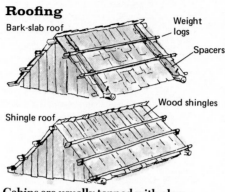

Bark-slab roof
Weight logs
Spacers
Shingle roof
Wood shingles

Cabins are usually topped with clapboards, wood shingles, or bark. The roofing is kept in place by weight logs held by wooden spacers or tied to the roof beams beneath them. Only the most prosperous of frontier families can afford to use nails for building.

Common Corner Notches

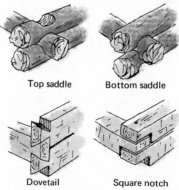

Top saddle
Bottom saddle
Dovetail
Square notch

Corner notches key the logs together and hold them in place. Four of the most common types are shown above, a fifth—the V notch—at right. Top and bottom saddles, the simplest to cut, are almost always used with round logs. Dovetails, which require considerable skill, make the firmest joint. Square notches are neat, but they must be held together by pegs.

A catted chimney, coated inside with clay to reduce danger of fire, goes up on a base of stone. Quickly built, catted chimneys are usually only temporary makeshifts and are replaced as soon as possible with stone or brick.

Shingles are rived (split) by hand from a short log of straight-grained wood with a wooden mallet and a heavy-bladed cleaving knife called a froe. They are then shaved thin at one end with a drawknife.

Notches in ends of upper logs hold horizontal roof beams in place. In less carefully built cabins, beams may simply be pegged on. In nailless roofs, bottom edges of shingles or clapboards rest against lowest beam, which keeps them from sliding off. Top row of shingles on one side projects.

Raising a Cabin: A Community Effort

A man could build a log cabin by himself, but if he had neighbors, custom obliged them to help. The building of the cabin followed an orderly sequence of steps. If there were enough neighbors they split up into parties for each task, speeding the work. Here, work parties fell trees (A), cut logs to length (not shown), and haul them to the cabin site with oxen (B). Others notch logs (not shown) and raise them into position (C). As the walls rise, the upper logs are rolled up on skids. Two men pull with ropes while two push from below (D). When the walls and roof are up, crude augers and saws (E) are used to cut openings for the door, windows, and fireplace (F). Young boys help with light tasks, while the women and girls prepare meals for the workers.

Children sleep in the open loft, reached by a ladder or by pegs driven into the wall; parents sleep in the main room. Privacy is unknown. The loft is also used for storing ears of corn, strings of dried apples, and other foodstuffs.

Ridgepole

Roof beam

The roof is the only part of the cabin where nails are used. Made by hand, nails are too expensive for general construction work, even in long-settled areas. However, they do make a sturdier, more windproof roof.

Door and window openings are made after walls are up and roof completed. (To show details of roof construction, the normal order is reversed here.) A starting hole is first bored with an auger, then a pointed saw is used to cut out openings. Boards are pegged to ends of logs to hold them securely in place and form a serviceable frame.

Rafter

Latchstring of rawhide

Latch is made of hard, tough wood.

A stout wooden latch fastened on by pegs secures the door. Latch can be opened from outside by a string passing through door. Latchstring left out during day signals "visitors are welcome." For security's sake, latchstring is pulled in at night.

Cracks between logs are chinked with mud or clay, often mixed with sticks or small stones for solidity.

Cabin is built of square-hewn logs. Hewn logs take much more work to prepare than round logs, but they fit more snugly. V-notching makes a simple, sturdy joint. As in this cabin, logs are often sawed off flush with corners to produce a neater appearance.

Door will pivot in sockets in doorsill and at top of frame.

Scoring a log for barn

Sleepers to support floor

A large, flat stone serves as doorstep.

Stone footings hold bottom logs off ground to protect them from rotting. But slovenly builders lay logs right on soil.

When squaring logs, the axman lays out a chalkline as a guide, then scores (notches) the log to this line. Notched sections are easily split off and the surface smoothed. The broadax, with its massive, chisellike head, is used for hewing. Offset handle keeps ax-man's fingers away from log.

Hewing log square with broadax

A Farm Amid a Sea of Trees

At the dawn of the 1800's western settlers labored under the delusion that the most fertile soil lay in forests. If woodland leaf mold nourished gigantic oaks 24 feet in circumference, then, they reasoned, it must be incredibly rich. In fact, the prairies beyond were far richer, but, ignorant of this, the farmer moving west stopped at Kentucky, Indiana, Illinois, and Missouri—in what one witness described as "woods, woods, woods, as far as the world extends"—and doggedly undertook the herculean task of clearing land. If he did not find a natural oak clearing, he faced a dark sea of huge hardwoods and underbrush so thick that he struggled for years with scythe and brush hook to remove briars, shrubs, and towering grape vines. He cut small trees with an ax; for the "big 'uns" he borrowed the Indian method of girdling (bottom left). The first year he planted corn and flax amid the stumps of a few felled or burned giants. Meanwhile, his wife gathered wild fruits, nuts, and lettuce. By the second year the girdled trees would die, and he could begin removing stumps, gradually making room for outbuildings and fields such as those shown in the scene below on an Indiana farm in 1820.

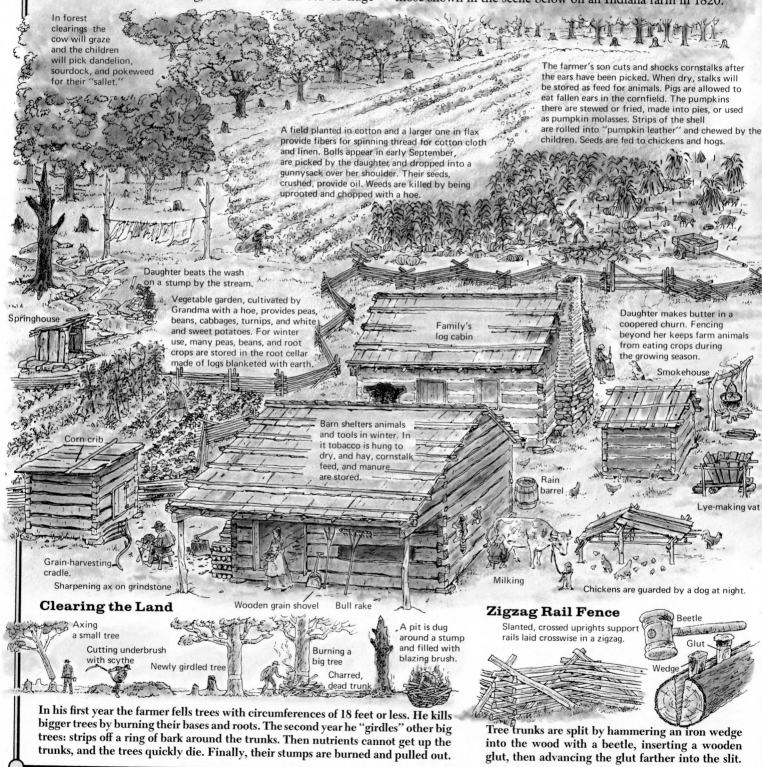

In forest clearings the cow will graze and the children will pick dandelion, sourdock, and pokeweed for their "sallet."

The farmer's son cuts and shocks cornstalks after the ears have been picked. When dry, stalks will be stored as feed for animals. Pigs are allowed to eat fallen ears in the cornfield. The pumpkins there are stewed or fried, made into pies, or used as pumpkin molasses. Strips of the shell are rolled into "pumpkin leather" and chewed by the children. Seeds are fed to chickens and hogs.

A field planted in cotton and a larger one in flax provide fibers for spinning thread for cotton cloth and linen. Bolls appear in early September, are picked by the daughter, and dropped into a gunnysack over her shoulder. Their seeds, crushed, provide oil. Weeds are killed by being uprooted and chopped with a hoe.

Daughter beats the wash on a stump by the stream.

Springhouse

Vegetable garden, cultivated by Grandma with a hoe, provides peas, beans, cabbages, turnips, and white and sweet potatoes. For winter use, many peas, beans, and root crops are stored in the root cellar made of logs blanketed with earth.

Family's log cabin

Daughter makes butter in a coopered churn. Fencing beyond her keeps farm animals from eating crops during the growing season.

Smokehouse

Corn crib

Barn shelters animals and tools in winter. In it tobacco is hung to dry, and hay, cornstalk feed, and manure are stored.

Rain barrel

Lye-making vat

Grain-harvesting cradle.

Sharpening ax on grindstone

Milking

Chickens are guarded by a dog at night.

Clearing the Land

Wooden grain shovel   Bull rake

Axing a small tree

Cutting underbrush with scythe

Newly girdled tree

Burning a big tree

Charred, dead trunk

A pit is dug around a stump and filled with blazing brush.

In his first year the farmer fells trees with circumferences of 18 feet or less. He kills bigger trees by burning their bases and roots. The second year he "girdles" other big trees: strips off a ring of bark around the trunks. Then nutrients cannot get up the trunks, and the trees quickly die. Finally, their stumps are burned and pulled out.

Zigzag Rail Fence

Slanted, crossed uprights support rails laid crosswise in a zigzag.

Beetle

Glut

Wedge

Tree trunks are split by hammering an iron wedge into the wood with a beetle, inserting a wooden glut, then advancing the glut farther into the slit.

The farmer plows for winter wheat, used to make bread. In the spring he will harvest it with a "cradle" —a scythe with four long fingers. Although of a soft variety, this wheat is harder to grind than corn and has a lower yield per acre; threshing it is also more tedious than husking corn. So the largest acreage is devoted to corn. Corn seeds are planted at intersections of furrows plowed at right angles to each other, two feet apart. In the spring the farmer makes a hole with a hoe, drops in a few seeds, and covers them with his heel. The roots of the growing cornstalks help break up the soil, making next year's plowing easier. By early autumn small ears develop. The stalks are almost nine feet tall, and pole beans climb up them. Gourds grow among the corn, as well as pumpkins weighing up to 60 pounds.

Grazing sheep are somewhat protected from predators by a fence and dog.

Harrow for breaking up soil after plowing

Outhouse

In the orchard of yellow apples children pick fruit to eat, bake in pies, and make into apple butter and cider. Nearby are pear and peach trees.

Root cellar

A sow nursing piglets is prized, for pork is the family's staple meat, along with wild game. Hams, shoulders, and sides of pigs are cured in brine, then hung in the smokehouse for two days.

Evolving Plow Types of Pre-1835 Woodland Farmers

A. Shovel Plow

It was cheap, light.

Hardwood

Iron tip caused little erosion; its furrow was shallow.

B. Wooden Moldboard Plow

Moldboard

Sharp iron share

C. Metal-Sheathed Moldboard Plow

Metal strips cover wood.

Iron share

D. Cast-Iron Plow

All-metal moldboard and share

Colter

Type A plow needed only one mule, but B and C required four oxen and two men. The advantages of B and C: each had an iron share to cut a deeper furrow, a moldboard to turn the furrow's soil, and often a knifelike colter to cut the turf. Drawbacks of B and C: they caused erosion, and B broke easily. Although D needed only one man and two oxen, it was at first cast in one piece; if one section broke, the whole plow was useless. Later, type D was made of separate, replaceable parts.

The Peripatetic Lincolns

The new westerners were a restless lot, moving from cabin to cabin. Typical was Thomas Lincoln, Abe's illiterate father, a small landowner. After marrying Nancy Hanks in 1806 he lived first in Elizabethtown, Kentucky, where his daughter Sarah was born and where he worked as farmer, carpenter, house-joiner, and cooper. Then he moved to Nolin Creek, Kentucky, arriving in midwinter of 1809 in time for Abe's birth. There he built a one-room log cabin with a dirt floor, a stick-and-clay chimney, and one window. He lost it over a title dispute and in 1811 pushed on to Knob Creek, Kentucky. Upset by the increase of slavery in the state, and for a second time driven from his land by a title suit, he decided to buy government land in Indiana and crossed the Ohio River by ferry in December 1816. He followed a wagon road, at the end of which he and Abe had to hack through dense underbrush to reach Little Pigeon Creek, a community of hard-drinking and practical-joking backwoodsmen. In freezing weather Thomas put up a three-sided log shelter, roofed with branches and warmed only by a fire on the open side. He fed his family on bartered corn and wild game. Seven-year-old Abe even shot a wild turkey. Come spring, he and Abe, with neighbors' help, built a one-room cabin with no windows and only an uncovered opening for a door. Wall pegs led to a loft where the children slept. As they cleared land that summer, chiggers, ticks, and mosquitoes plagued them, and rattlers and copperheads were a constant danger. Abe saw wolves and bears, and chilled in his bed to the night screams of a panther.

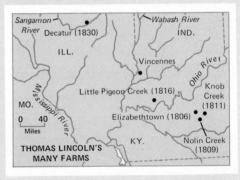

THOMAS LINCOLN'S MANY FARMS

The following year, Mrs. Lincoln died of the dreaded "milk sickness"—poisoning from the milk of cows that had eaten snakeroot. After one forlorn year Thomas married Sarah Bush Johnston, an energetic widow with three children, who arrived in a four-horse wagon loaded with pots, pans, blankets, and what seemed to the Lincolns wondrous luxuries: a feather bed and a bureau. She got Thomas to mend the leaky clapboard roof, cut a puncheon floor (halved logs with the smooth side up), hang a door, whitewash the interior, and build furniture. For a decade the family farmed more than 40 acres of corn, wheat, and oats, had a garden, and kept sheep, hogs, and cattle. Then Thomas heard from Decatur relatives about the fertility of the Illinois prairies. So, piling belongings into wagons for the last time, he led his family again, in 1830, to find new land.

Trails to Oblivion

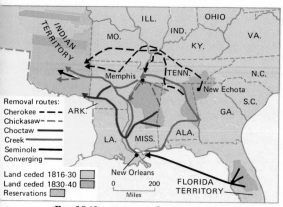

Removal routes:
Cherokee – – –
Chickasaw – · – ·
Choctaw ———
Creek ———
Seminole ———
Converging

Land ceded 1816-30
Land ceded 1830-40
Reservations

0   200
Miles

By 1840 most southeastern Indians had been removed by different routes to the same general area. The Seminoles, however, were not driven from Florida until 1842.

The march of settlers into the Old Northwest was undisturbed for the most part, save for an incident that history has recorded as the Black Hawk War, although in reality it was no more than a series of skirmishes.

In keeping with treaty obligations forced upon them as far back as 1804, the Sac and Fox Indians vacated their Illinois holdings in 1829 as hordes of whites moved into the Fever River district around Galena. Most of them were hard-bitten Kentuckians, to whom Indian fighting was a way of life, and they regularly harassed the Sac and Foxes. Tension built up on both sides until, in 1831, a group of whites attacked the main Sac and Fox village of Saukenuk. Finding it empty, they burned it. The Indians, realizing that to remain in Illinois was to court disaster, had already moved across the Mississippi into the

Iowa country. Many hoped that somehow they might return to their ancient homeland, and in 1832 about 1,000 Sac and Foxes, including more than 600 women and children, recrossed the river to reclaim their lands. Their leader was the warrior Black Hawk, who naively believed that the whites would see the justice of the Indians' cause and vacate their homes to make way for the returnees. The arrival of his pitiful band had precisely the opposite effect, generating a panic among the white settlers, who rushed to join the militia to throw out the "invaders."

Even as optimistic a soul as Black Hawk was quick to realize the hopelessness of his cause. He hastened to surrender and ask for safe conduct back to the Iowa country, but the settlers promptly fired on his emissaries. Unable to retreat and too weak for an all-out battle, Black Hawk took to the forests and formed his fewer than 400 warriors into raiding parties. In less than three months of hit-and-run warfare, he killed some 200 whites but lost an equal number of his own men. Finally, on August 3, 1832, a large militia unit caught up with Black Hawk's decimated band, killing all but about 150 of them.

Indian Land Cessions

News of the carnage traveled to the remaining tribes of the Old Northwest, and they hastened to meet the demands of the government lest they too be slaughtered. In the next five years nearly 200 million acres of Indian land were ceded to the whites, and in exchange the tribes received some cash, annuities, and new lands in the still unwanted Far

West. By 1845 hardly a red man remained in the Old Northwest.

In the South and the Old Southwest the process of Indian removal was no less brutal. In Florida, Mississippi, Tennessee, Alabama, Georgia, and the western parts of the Carolinas lay the lands of the Cherokees, Chickasaws, Creeks, Choctaws, and Seminoles—known collectively as the Five Civilized Tribes because of their ready adaptability to white men's ways. Visitors to their domains often marveled at their prosperity, built upon agriculture, animal husbandry, and cottage industry. Most admired were the Cherokees, whose villages boasted schools and churches, sawmills and gristmills. Some of these tribesmen even owned slaves and grew cotton on large plantations.

If ever there were Indians capable of blending peacefully with white society, it was these southern tribes. But, like their neighbors to the north, they held lands coveted by whites, and in the minds of local and federal officials this was reason enough for their removal.

The War of 1812 had hardly ended when the federal government began efforts to shift the Five Civilized Tribes onto reservations in the so-called Indian Territory in present-day Oklahoma. By the late 1820's this process of removal was well under way, with most of the Creek tribes of Georgia and Alabama already relocated. The Cherokees, however, refused to budge and appealed to the courts. They formed themselves into a republic and charged that the whites' efforts to remove them violated lawful treaty obligations between the Cherokee Nation and the United States. Though

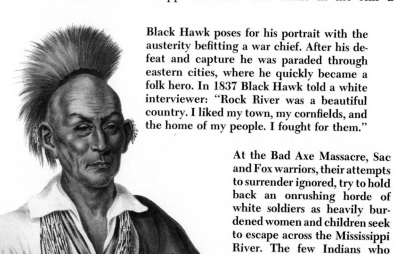

Black Hawk poses for his portrait with the austerity befitting a war chief. After his defeat and capture he was paraded through eastern cities, where he quickly became a folk hero. In 1837 Black Hawk told a white interviewer: "Rock River was a beautiful country. I liked my town, my cornfields, and the home of my people. I fought for them."

At the Bad Axe Massacre, Sac and Fox warriors, their attempts to surrender ignored, try to hold back an onrushing horde of white soldiers as heavily burdened women and children seek to escape across the Mississippi River. The few Indians who reached Iowa were killed or imprisoned by Sioux Indians.

Sequoyah, the Cherokee Genius

Sequoyah (1773–1843), inventor of the Cherokee alphabet, was the son of a white trader and a Cherokee mother. His alphabet—86 symbols, one for each syllable in the Cherokee language—was based on English characters and on signs of his own. During the 12 years Sequoyah spent developing his system of writing, he was ostracized by most of his tribe for meddling with the white man's secrets. But in 1824 his work won the approval of the tribal council. Within months hundreds of Cherokees were learning to read and write.

A Cherokee newspaper page.

Rather than sign a land-cession treaty, the fiery Seminole chieftain Osceola plunges his dagger through it. Soon afterward he led his tribe into a bloody war of resistance that lasted for nine years. In the end all but a few of the surviving Seminoles moved west.

Herded along by U.S. troops, these Cherokees plod west from Georgia along the Trail of Tears to Indian Territory. There the survivors of the journey built a proud society despite the loss of lands after the Civil War. Finally, the Cherokees accepted U.S. citizenship and joined whites in organizing the state of Oklahoma, which entered the Union in 1907.

many whites, particularly in the North, supported the Cherokee cause, the state of Georgia, where most of the tribesmen lived, demanded their immediate departure. On December 6, 1830, President Andrew Jackson threw the power of his administration behind the removal policy, which he termed a "benevolent" effort to open to a "dense and civilized population" a region inhabited by only "a few savage hunters."

The fate of the Cherokees was sealed a few months later when the Supreme Court held that the Indians' claim to sovereignty within their territories was specious. The Cherokees, said the High Court, were not a foreign nation whose rights were secure but a "domestic dependent nation." The following year, although the Court decreed that the state of Georgia must not harass them, Jackson and the Congress made it clear that the Cherokees could not look to the federal government for protection.

Though continued legal maneuvers helped delay the forced removal of the Cherokees, the end finally came in December 1835 when the federal government pressured a minor chief into signing away all the tribe's land titles. Soon soldiers were swooping down on Cherokee towns, routing families at bayonet point and setting them, under armed guard, out on the long road west. Throughout the late 1830's convoys of helpless red men were herded into Indian Territory along a route the Cherokees called the Trail of Tears, for fully a quarter of their number died from mistreatment and neglect on the trek.

By 1840 just the Seminoles remained in their ancient homeland, there to wage a magnificent but bitter guerrilla war against the power of the United States. Only after uncounted Seminoles and some 1,500 soldiers had died did these Indians agree to removal, and even then a few bands remained active in the Florida Everglades, where their descendants live today. But such resistance was as fruitless in the South as it had been in the Old Northwest. The red man's day was ended; the time of the white man had begun.

The Lure of the Old Southwest

Behind the expulsion of the Indians from their lands in the South and the Old Southwest lay a simple mechanical device called the cotton gin. Cotton had yet to dominate the economy of the South in the early 1790's, but hundreds of planters were already aware of its vast potential. They knew that Britain's booming textile industry would buy all the fiber the South could produce if just one technological problem were overcome. The short-staple cotton plant, suitable to the soil and climate of much of the South, was filled with tightly clinging seeds, each of which had to be removed by hand. Such an expensive, time-consuming operation was enough to make growing the plant unprofitable despite the great demand for it. But all this changed in 1792, when Eli Whitney, a Yankee teacher living in the South, came up with a machine that quickly separated the seeds from the fiber.

Rarely has an invention so dominated and defined a society as the cotton gin did the South. It touched off a tidal wave of emigration from the coast to the rich, loamy regions of the trans–Appalachian South—western Georgia and Alabama, Mississippi, Tennessee, and even Arkansas—and it gave birth to the legendary South of columned mansions.

The World King Cotton Made

Most important of all, however, the cotton gin made slavery a primary element in the prosperity of the planters, providing them with the armies of laborers needed to harvest the crop. At the same time, cotton relegated free labor to a marginal status. The subsistence agriculture of free men on cheap land that would help make the Old Northwest a land of opportunity for all emigrants was of secondary importance in the Old Southwest. There, with remarkable speed, the finest land was snapped up by perhaps 50,000 major planters supporting regiments of slaves. Small planters, who had 1 to 20 slaves, came next in southern class structure. Although they lacked the capital to join the ranks of the rich, most members of the middle class lived with the illusion that someday they would do so.

Far more benighted were the mass of whites, perhaps 75 percent of the free population in the South and the Old Southwest, whose condition ranged from poor to destitute. These were farmers eking out meager livings on

This painting depicts dominant features of Louisiana life around 1800: the Mississippi River busy with barge and boat traffic and an opulent mansion of one of the early planters.

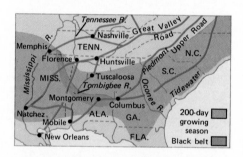

Having exhausted the tidewater's fertility, southern planters moved west over poorly maintained roads and by riverboat into a region where the cotton-growing season lasted some 200 days. North of this area mountains impinged; south of it a 10-inch autumn rainfall ruined harvests. The best zone in the Cotton Kingdom was known as the Black Belt for the color of its rich soil.

hardscrabble hill lands, hunters, trappers, herders, woodcutters, and at the very bottom the ne'er-do-wells who even in the early 19th century were dismissed as "crackers." Yet they, too, generally supported the status quo, believing that their white skins at least made them members of a racial elite.

Cotton's unfortunate influence on the society of the South and Old Southwest extended to its effects on the land itself. The soils of the Piedmont, already weakened by successive plantings of tobacco, were drained of their nutrients by the cotton crop; the once-lush region became a land of "desolation that baffles description," according to one observer. The desperate need for virgin land drove both farmer and planter ever westward. The hunter, the trapper, and the small farmer formed the cutting edge of settlement. Only when they had tested an area and found it livable and fertile did the planter follow, leading his family and his slaves through wilderness trails to the new cotton lands that lay in the Old Southwest.

Cotton's Rival, Sugar

Newspaper editors called this migration the Alabama Fever, and between 1816 and 1820 the population of Alabama and Mississippi rose from 75,000 to 200,000, while cotton production soared from 37,000 to 161,000 bales annually. A decade later almost half a million bales of cotton would be exported through the port of New Orleans.

As a cash crop, cotton had but one rival: sugar. Grown and processed on vast estates in Louisiana's rich Mississippi Delta country, the crop brought higher profits than cotton but required initial investments that only a handful could afford. As a popular saying of the day had it, only a rich cotton planter had the funds to become a poor sugar planter. By 1850, however, Louisiana

The sawtooth cotton gin was a sturdier version of Whitney's original machine. Easily copied by local craftsmen, gins were soon commonplace.

Gangs of slaves worked the plantations of the Old Southwest. While most southern whites were small farmers, who owned no slaves, the big plantations dominated the economy. Cotton was the major cash crop, but corn occupied about the same acreage.

boasted some 1,500 plantations, on which about 100,000 slaves labored to produce a quarter of the world's sugar exports. Successful sugar planters vied with one another in contests of opulent display. And none was more successful than John Burnside, whose 22,500 acres of prime delta land were valued at more than a million dollars. His mansion, Houmas House, offered such amenities as portable tubs, which slaves filled with ice-cooled water for the pleasurable immersion of guests seeking relief from the delta's awesome heat.

Despite the ostentation of the sugar and cotton planters, the Old Southwest did retain, at least in small ways, a smattering of frontier democracy. Poor whites, locked into their poverty within an ossified social and economic system, were nonetheless loath to bend the knee to persons of power and wealth. Three French aristocrats traveling on a Mississippi keelboat learned as much, to their displeasure. When the vessel became stranded on a sandbar, its captain, heedless of his passengers' rank, rudely shouted: "You kings down there! Show yourselves and do a man's work, and help us . . . pull off this bar."

All this—the conspicuous consumption of the sugar planters and the leisure and refinement of the cotton "snobs" —was made possible by the labor of blacks. In 1790, before the explosion of cotton cultivation and the westward expansion of the plantation system, there were only 750,000 slaves in the nation. By 1830 their number had grown to 2.3 million, and by 1860 to 4.5 million—almost all of them in the South and a majority in the new trans-Appalachian lands. To the planter the slave represented a capital investment from whom a maximum amount of work was expected. Undoubtedly, some slave owners and their overseers believed that only the constant threat of punishment could drive the blacks to efficient labor, but many successfully used a carrot-and-stick approach. Mississippi planter Bennet Barrow, for example, fed, housed, and clothed his slaves more than adequately and offered cash prizes for those who picked the most cotton.

The Southern Commitment

Yet even Barrow was not above administering harsh beatings for infractions of his rule. Concerning one runaway, he recorded this statement in his diary: "Ran and trailed [him] about a mile, treed him, made the dogs pull him out. . . . Bit him very badly, think he will stay home awhile." Had anyone suggested to Barrow that such punishment—indeed that slavery itself—was inhuman, the planter would have responded with incredulity. For by the 1850's the Old Southwest was almost totally committed to a society based on slavery and cotton. Its lifestyle made the region, together with the coastal South, a nation apart and, for all its glamour, a mere economic colony of the industrializing North and of Britain.

Equipped with masts and auxiliary sails, Nicholas Roosevelt's *New Orleans* (1811) was the first steamer on a western river.

Daniel French's *Enterprise* (1814), with riverman Henry Miller Shreve in command, took part in the Battle of New Orleans.

The *Paragon* (1819) exhibits traditional riverboat features—enclosed paddlewheels and an elevated deck for the passengers.

Steamboats Open Up the Old Southwest

The steamboat was the key to the rapid growth of the Old Southwest, moving cotton crops cheaply and rapidly to distant markets and transporting passengers in the nearly roadless new land. Nicholas Roosevelt, an associate of Robert Fulton, brought the steamboat west. On its maiden voyage down the Ohio and Mississippi his Pittsburgh-built *New Orleans* survived an earthquake and an attack by a canoeload of enraged Indians. A few Fulton-type boats were soon shuttling between New Orleans and Natchez, and in 1815 Daniel French's *Enterprise*, captained by Henry Shreve, bucked the current upstream as far as Louisville. Learning from this experience, Shreve pioneered in designing a new kind of steamboat for the swift and shallow rivers that flowed through the West. He used a lightweight, powerful high-pressure engine located up on deck.

Boom and Bust in the Old West

Many easterners of wealth and position regarded their countrymen beyond the Appalachians as a curious breed, but their condescension was mixed with foreboding. They mocked the westerners' crude manners and lack of education, while feeling genuine alarm at the egalitarianism of the frontier —especially its opposition to a limited suffrage based on wealth and property. The first trans-Appalachian states to enter the Union—Kentucky, Tennessee, Louisiana, and Ohio—had mandated universal white male suffrage within their borders. One New York newspaper stated in alarm: "By throwing open the polls to every man that walks, we have placed the power in the hands of those who have neither property, talents, nor influence . . . and who require in their public officers no higher qualifications than they possess themselves."

The Land Issue

Nowhere was eastern consternation over western democracy more apparent than in the debate on how best to dispose of the immense public domain beyond the Appalachians. The "best people" of the East—those who elected congressmen and controlled the selection of senators—thought of this virtually limitless acreage as a public trust that should be sold off by the federal government at relatively high prices. Such a policy, it was supposed, would limit westward emigration and bring enormous amounts of money into the federal treasury through land sales to wealthy speculators. (The speculators were often the same men who decried the westward

In 1817 a St. Louis bank issued this private note, a common practice in the cash-short West. Notes such as these could be made payable either to a specific person or to any bearer. Both kinds circulated freely, although the first type needed an endorsement.

movement, but they were not adverse to profiting from it.) Westerners, for their part, generally took exactly the opposite position on the land question, favoring the sale of the public domain at prices so cheap that everyone could afford a piece of Eden; some even maintained that the land should be distributed free to bona fide settlers.

The Land Act of 1800, which with one change remained in effect for two decades, was a compromise between the eastern and western viewpoints. It stipulated that land in the public domain could be purchased only after it had been surveyed. The minimum size of a plot was reduced from 640 to 320 acres (further reduced in 1804 to 160 acres), and the land was sold at a minimum price of $2 an acre. But many pioneers could not afford an expenditure of $640, or even $320. Time payments were permitted, but they too eventually

worked against the small farmer, who often found himself burdened with a debt he could never repay.

For a time after 1815 such practical considerations seemed relatively unimportant to the pioneer. The nation was enjoying an unprecedented boom as Europe, emerging from decades of war, clamored to obtain American grain. Throughout the harvest season barges loaded with foodstuffs plied the Ohio and Mississippi Rivers, their cargoes bound first for New Orleans and then for Europe. Adding impetus to the boom were the scores of loosely regulated local financial institutions. In the absence of quantities of specie (gold and silver coins), these banks embarked on an orgy of note printing, even though backing for this paper currency was virtually nonexistent. In this wildly inflationary atmosphere even the most ragtag of pioneers could get a loan for the purchase of land, as long as he was willing to pledge his holding as collateral.

The Panic of 1819

Then, in 1818 the bubble was about to burst. Europe was completing her recovery; the demand for American produce suddenly slackened and prices fell sharply. At about the same time the powerful, semiofficial Second Bank of the United States, which had done little to discourage reckless loans by the state-chartered banks, adopted a hard money policy, demanding payment in nonexistent specie for its outstanding loans. State and local banks, themselves heavily in debt to the Bank of the United States, followed suit. No one, from farmer to merchant to banker, could pay his debts. Boom had turned to bust.

Eastern Condescension Toward Westerners

WESTERN EMIGRATION.

JOURNAL
OF
DOCTOR JEREMIAH SIMPLETON'S
TOUR TO OHIO.

CONTAINING
An account of the numerous difficulties, Hair-breadth Escapes, Mortifications and Privations, which the Doctor and his family experienced on their Journey from Maine, to the Land of Promise, and during a residence of three years in that highly extolled country.

BY H. TRUMBULL.

Nulli Fides Frontis.

BOSTON—PRINTED BY S. SEWALL.

[In the West] if you wish to converse in any human language out of your family, you must go twenty or thirty miles to your next door neighbor, with your axe instead of staff—for you must cut your way thither, for want of roads—and perhaps, after all, find him almost as hoggish as the "swines in your pens" or the more numerous class of the inhabitants of Ohio, the wild-cat, panther, etc. who frequently associate with our tame animals to their sorrow, and sometimes with young children, to *our* mourning;—and, fags, I'd rather be a hog-reeve in good New-England, than hold any office in this back woods country, where the inhabitants walk on all fours, with the exception of a few double headed fools.

—Henry Trumbull, *Western Emigration*, 1819

The question of whether newly organized western states should be slave or free agitated the young United States. For years Congress kept the number of slave and free states in balance. But heavy migration of nonslaveholders and their families into the West eventually tipped the congressional power balance in favor of the free states.

A flatboat drifts downstream past an upward-bound keelboat. When steamboats replaced man-propelled keelboats in western waters, flatboats continued to be used for nonperishable cargoes. Unable to travel upstream, they were sold as lumber at their destination.

The economic crisis of 1819 hit the frontier with all the fury of a prairie thunderstorm, washing out the hopes of thousands of families who now saw their land devalued, their savings wiped out, and their holdings at the mercy of creditors, most of whom were themselves victims of the panic. James Flint, a Scotsman traveling in Indiana in 1820, observed the plight of workers in the debt-ridden infant industries of the Old Northwest. "The poor laborer," he wrote, "is almost certain of being paid in depreciated money, perhaps from 30 to 50 percent under par. I have seen several men turned out of boardinghouses where their money would not be taken. They had no other resource left but to lodge in the woods, without any covering except their clothes."

But it was the farmers, whose produce had become a glut on the market, who may have been worst off. Unable to pay their debts, they were now faced with the threat of eviction. The primary holder of their mortgages was, of course, the U.S. government, which had the right to foreclose. But political considerations usually stayed the government's hand, for the West was no longer America's stepchild. Thanks to the great migration of the boom years, almost a quarter of the nation's population now lived beyond the Appalachians. By 1820 Illinois, Indiana, Alabama, and Mississippi had been added to the roll of states, and Missouri would join the Union the next year, adding a trans-Mississippi bridgehead to the growing nation. Thus, in the aftermath of the Panic of 1819, the government hesitated to enrage so formidable a region as the West by massive foreclosures. Instead, men of the East and West, including Kentucky's Representative Henry Clay, began to consider together the problem of how the conflicting interests of the two regions might be resolved.

Henry Clay, Westerner

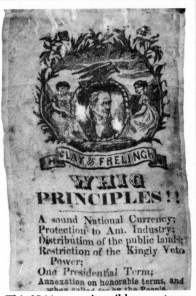

This 1844 campaign ribbon portrays Clay, perennial seeker of the presidency, and outlines his platform.

Virginia-born Henry Clay moved to Kentucky as a young man and made his mark in politics as a champion of the West. No mere sectional politician, Clay dreamed of a national unity based on what he called the American System, by which food would come mainly from the Old Northwest, cotton from the South, and manufactured goods from the Northeast. A vast network of federally financed roads and canals would tie the country together and get goods to market, while a protective tariff would nurture infant industries. His program appealed to businessmen and bankers.

When John James Audubon painted this Natchez scene in 1822, Mississippi had become a state, and commerce on the river had made Natchez a leading city of the Old Southwest.

The Erie Canal: Gateway to the West

An engineering marvel in its day, the Erie Canal stretched 363 miles from Albany on the Hudson River to Buffalo on Lake Erie. Built at a cost of $7 million and more than eight years of backbreaking labor, it became one of the most important arteries of transportation in the United States, linking the Great Lakes with the Atlantic Ocean by a safe, cheap, and reliable passage. Its slow-moving barges carried goods from the East to eager customers in the West, while western farm produce moved east, forging a strong economic bond between Northwest and Northeast. Exports from the Old Northwest that had formerly floated down the Mississippi to New Orleans now went via the canal to New York. In addition, the canal made it easy for movers from the Northeast and immigrants from Europe who had landed in the New World in New York to reach the Old Northwest. Heavily trafficked from the day it opened, at times the Erie had so many barges waiting to pass through a lock that a man could walk a mile down the canal, from boat to boat, without getting his feet wet. The brawling "canawlers" with their mule-drawn barges became a colorful part of American life.

DeWitt Clinton, the Man Behind the Canal

On November 4, 1825, DeWitt Clinton ceremoniously poured a keg of Lake Erie water into New York Harbor (right). The "wedding of the waters" symbolized the completion of the Erie Canal—a personal triumph for Clinton. That ambitious politician (10 years mayor of New York City and in 1825 serving his third term as governor of the state) had tied his career to the canal, which he saw as the key to the Northwest trade. Named to the New York State Canal Commission in 1810, Clinton had battled to get the project approved and funded by the state legislature, then kept it going for eight years of construction.

The Route West to the Great Lakes

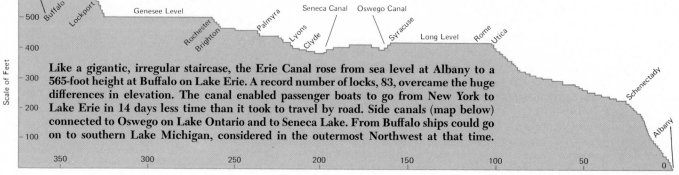

Like a gigantic, irregular staircase, the Erie Canal rose from sea level at Albany to a 565-foot height at Buffalo on Lake Erie. A record number of locks, 83, overcame the huge differences in elevation. The canal enabled passenger boats to go from New York to Lake Erie in 14 days less time than it took to travel by road. Side canals (map below) connected to Oswego on Lake Ontario and to Seneca Lake. From Buffalo ships could go on to southern Lake Michigan, considered in the outermost Northwest at that time.

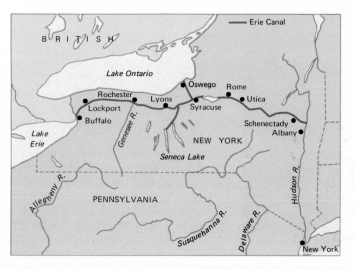

The construction of the Erie Canal was a task of tremendous magnitude. Over 360 miles in length, 40 feet wide at the surface, 28 feet wide at the bottom, and 4 feet deep—the sheer volume of earth and rock to be moved was staggering. And it had to be moved by the raw musclepower of men and animals with the aid of blasting powder. Moreover, this gigantic task was planned, designed, and carried out by amateurs. The chief engineer was a country lawyer with a bit of surveying experience. Learning as the job progressed, the men quickly developed into outstanding engineers. Work was speeded by devices invented on the spot: a horse-drawn scraper to loosen and move earth; a giant horse-powered windlass on 16-foot wheels to uproot stumps left by clearing crews; an endless-screw machine with which a single man could tear down an entire tree with its roots. After the canal was completed, graduates from the "Erie School of Engineering" took the lead in building canals and railroads in many other states.

Derricks and Aqueducts

Above, ingenious derricks powered by a horse on a treadmill, devised by Erie's self-taught engineers, hoist rubble from a deep cut through a rocky ridge at Lockport, New York, near the western end of the canal. Below, a massive 802-foot stone aqueduct carries the canal across the Genesee River at Rochester. Aqueducts were often the simplest way of getting the canal across valleys, avoiding the time-consuming construction of locks. In all, the Erie Canal had 18 aqueducts, most of them of wood atop stone piers.

Freighters, Mainstay of the Canal

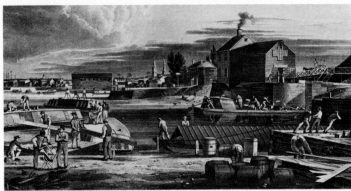

Freight barges throng the basin at West Troy, New York. Compared to the cost of hauling goods by wagon, shipping rates from Buffalo to New York City dropped from $100 to $15 a ton. Time was cut from 20 to 8 days. The canal was so popular that in its first year of operation it collected $750,000 in tolls—more than 10 percent of construction costs. Passengers camped on the decks of slow horse- or mule-drawn line boats or traveled on fancy packets that traversed the canal in six days, running day and night at the legal limit of four miles per hour.

Song of the Muleteers: "The Erie Canal"

I've got a mule an' her name is "Sal,"
      Fifteen miles on the Erie Canal.
She's a good ol' worker an' a good ol' pal,
      Fifteen miles on the Erie Canal.
We've hauled some barges in our day
      Filled with lumber, coal, an' hay.
And we know ev'ry inch of the way from Albany to Buffalo.

The Lockport "Fives," an Engineering Marvel

Travelers came from as far away as Europe to see the famous set of five double locks that took the Old Erie down a precipitous 76-foot drop in level at Lockport, northeast of Buffalo. They are shown here in an 1832 watercolor. Double locks, one set eastbound and one westbound, were necessary in order to avoid a bottleneck.

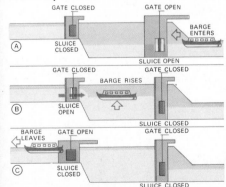

(A) To rise to a higher level of a canal a barge enters the open lock gates at the lower level. (B) The lower gates are shut, and a sluice in the upper gates admits water, gently raising the barge. (C) When the lock is filled, the upper gates are opened, and the barge goes on its way.

New Waterways West

In good weather canalboat passengers gathered on the roof, escaping for a time from the cramped confines of their stuffy cabins and shelflike bunks. However, the packet barges offered more comfort than the dusty, bone-rattling, even more cramped stagecoaches.

By the late 1820's a veritable tide of settlement was once again flowing westward to the Mississippi and beyond. To the debt-ridden settlers of the Old West the Panic of 1819 had seemed a catastrophe comparable to the Flood of Biblical times. Yet such was the nation's resilience that the effects of economic depression had proved transitory. Using the Erie Canal, pioneers now surged into such previously neglected regions as the Great Lakes plains, while some particularly hardy settlers even pushed into the wilds of Wisconsin and scouted Iowa on the far side of the Mississippi.

By 1826 about 100 steamboats were plying the rivers of the frontier and the Great Lakes, bringing down freight costs and passenger fares to just a fraction of what they had been. In 1810, for example, it had cost $5 to ship a hundred pounds of goods from New Orleans to Louisville. Three decades later the steamboat had lowered the rate to only 25 cents.

Thus the Old Northwest and Old Southwest were being brought into a closer economic relationship than ever before. But an even stronger bond of commerce was being forged between the northeast coastal states and the prairie lands via the Erie Canal and the Great Lakes. Nothing could impede the flow of trade between these two sections. Before the completion of the Soo Canals in 1855, ships too large to negotiate the rapids at Sault Ste. Marie were dragged on rollers across the spit of land between Lakes Huron and Superior.

With each new resource tapped, each new town laid out, and each new area surveyed came a rush of settlers from New England, New York, and western Europe. Although these immigrants came from various social classes and economic backgrounds, most opposed slavery and favored cheap land, and the New Englanders, in particular, were dedicated to the founding of industries, schools, and towns. Where Kentuckians had dominated the Old Northwest at first, the New England influence became predominant in the 1830's, a development that would have far-reaching consequences for the nation as the debate over slavery brought the Union ever closer to civil war.

Canal Fever

The vital element in this Northwest-Northeast alliance was the Erie Canal. Along the major trade routes that the canal opened, hamlets blossomed almost overnight into major cities. Buffalo and Cleveland were transformed from slumbering villages into busy ports and industrial centers. In 1833 Massachusetts' famous Daniel Webster remarked upon Cleveland's astonishing growth: "Eight years ago, I enjoyed a brief visit to this place. There was then but one steamboat on Lake Erie; it made its passage once in every ten or fifteen days . . . there are now eighteen steamboats plying the lake, all finding full employment." Of Detroit, an English visitor, Harriet Martineau, wrote in 1836: "Thousands of settlers are pouring in every year . . . many are Irish, German, or Dutch, working their way into the backcountry, and glad to be employed for a while." Most of America, and particularly the Old Northwest, was in the grip of canal fever.

The success of the Erie Canal sparked

A family of movers watches as a flatboatman dances to the tune of a homemade fiddle. Fiddlers, important members of the crew, were exempted from a good deal of menial labor, except when a snag, sandbar, or eddy sent all to the oars.

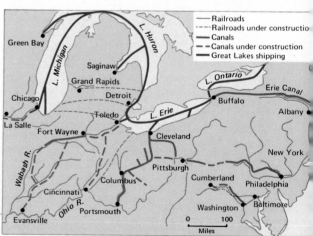

By the mid-1840's farmers had settled in forest clearings around and between Lakes Erie and Michigan, arriving by road, ship, canal, and rail.

The Versatile Keelboat

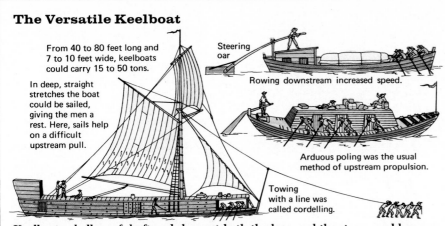

From 40 to 80 feet long and 7 to 10 feet wide, keelboats could carry 15 to 50 tons.

In deep, straight stretches the boat could be sailed, giving the men a rest. Here, sails help on a difficult upstream pull.

Steering oar

Rowing downstream increased speed.

Arduous poling was the usual method of upstream propulsion.

Towing with a line was called cordelling.

Keelboats, shallow of draft and sharp at both the bow and the stern, could go upstream as well as down. To do so, 5 to 12 brawny men braced long poles against the river bottom and propelled the boat ahead with their feet as they walked from the bow to the stern. As a last resort they towed the boat from the shore with a heavy line.

Mike Fink, Keelboater

Mike Fink bolsters his reputation as a marksman by shooting a cup filled with whisky off a close friend's head.

similar ventures throughout the West. Government officials, land speculators, promoters, and ordinary settlers—from Ohio and Indiana westward into the Wisconsin wilderness—dreamed of the prosperity that would be theirs if only a canal were dug to link their particular backwater with the Mississippi or with Lakes Michigan or Erie. In Indiana, as early as 1826, the governor waxed eloquent in the manner of a patent-medicine salesman when he claimed that a major canal linking the state to eastern markets would "increase the value of the soil, lead to culture and refinement . . . broaden the horizon of the people, and prevent feuds and political brawls." There were few so churlish as to dampen the governor's enthusiasm by asking whether it was feasible to build expensive arteries that in many cases would serve only a tiny population. Instead, there was general agreement that the building of canals would trans-

form one-horse towns into metropolises and generate so much business that the construction costs would soon be forgotten. By 1840 such thinking had plunged Ohio, Illinois, and Indiana tens of millions of dollars into debt, for few of the new manmade waterways ever paid their way. But, financially successful or not, they were a testament to the Old Northwest's confidence in the future, and generally this confidence was well founded.

An Emigrant Song

*My eastern friends who wish to
  find
A country that will suit your
  mind,
Where comforts all are near
  at hand,
Had better come to Michigan.*

"I'm a Salt River roarer, half horse and half alligator, suckled by a wildcat and a playmate of the snapping turtle!" boasted Mike Fink, semilegendary hero of the keelboatmen. The man behind the legend was a brawling, boastful, champion bully of western rivers, who, tall-tale tellers claim, never lost one of the eye-gouging, nose-biting fights that were the keelboaters' chief sport. Mike Fink, born about 1770 in Pittsburgh, appeared as a hand on a keelboat that worked the Ohio-Mississippi run two decades later. Strong, shrewd, and aggressive, he was soon captain of his own boat. By 1822 steamboats had cut deep into the keelboat trade, and Mike joined a fur trappers' expedition to the Rocky Mountains. He is thought to have been shot in winter camp by a friend of a young man he had killed in a shooting contest.

Steamboat service was in operation on the Great Lakes even before the Erie Canal opened. This 1820 painting shows the Buffalo-built *Walk-in-the-Water* as it approached Detroit.

Primarily a fur-trading center a mere generation earlier, Detroit had become a major port by 1836—the date of this picture—thanks to the thriving Lake Erie traffic serving settlers who poured into Michigan.

Steamboats—Queens of the Western Rivers

In 1850 steamboats dominated transportation in the West. Their classic design had become standardized: a long, narrow hull for speed, boilers and engines on the main deck, and passenger accommodations above. Drafts were shallow, enabling many boats to travel far up the rivers that tied the West together. More than mere transportation for travelers and freight, steamboats served as meetingplaces for politicians and businessmen, as floating hotels and gambling parlors. But they could become deathtraps when passengers succeeded in persuading the captain to tie down the safety valve for a race with another steamer. Ornately and gaudily decorated, the boats seemed the pinnacle of elegance and glamour to westerners. Residents of river towns learned to recognize each vessel's bell or whistle and flocked to greet boats as they arrived.

Side-wheeler or Stern-wheeler?

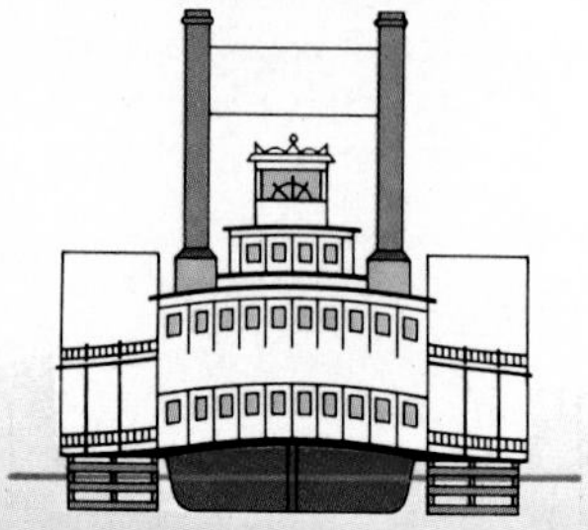

Side-wheelers are faster and more stable than stern-wheelers; they are also more maneuverable. Stern-wheelers, long used mainly as towboats, are easier to manage in shallow water and in narrow channels.

Jack staff

A Small World

Passengers of every class travel by steamboat. There is, to be sure, no contact between impoverished deck passengers and travelers in cabin class. But many ordinary folk can afford the inexpensive cabins and so mingle with wealthy merchants, planters, land speculators, preachers, and gamblers. Deck passengers include immigrants, farmers, and flatboatmen returning home from downriver ports.

The tall jack staff serves the steamboat pilot as a guide to steer by.

At this time steamboats are not only the most comfortable and fastest but also the cheapest means of transportation in the West. Cabin fares average 1 to 1½ cents a mile.

Spars and derricks are used to "grasshopper" boats over sandbars.

BONNIE GIBSON

Main deck

Docks are few; boats nose up to the bank and make fast to large trees or stumps.

Freight Produces Profits

The aristocrats of the river are the sleek packets, which carry both passengers and freight and run on a regular schedule. But even the most elegant of packets depend on freight to maintain their profits.

The Men in Command

A steamboat's captain holds supreme command. However, few captains have the nerve to interfere with a pilot's navigation. A skilled pilot's encyclopedic knowledge of the river can make the difference between calamity and a successful journey over muddy, snag-studded waters. He is often the highest paid officer on the boat.

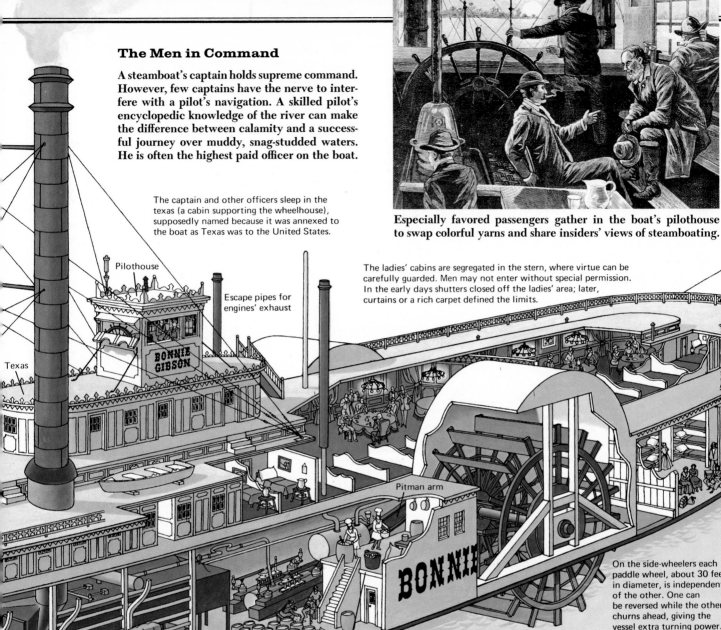

The captain and other officers sleep in the texas (a cabin supporting the wheelhouse), supposedly named because it was annexed to the boat as Texas was to the United States.

Pilothouse

Escape pipes for engines' exhaust

Texas

BONNIE GIBSON

Especially favored passengers gather in the boat's pilothouse to swap colorful yarns and share insiders' views of steamboating.

The ladies' cabins are segregated in the stern, where virtue can be carefully guarded. Men may not enter without special permission. In the early days shutters closed off the ladies' area; later, curtains or a rich carpet defined the limits.

Pitman arm

BONNIE

On the side-wheelers each paddle wheel, about 30 feet in diameter, is independent of the other. One can be reversed while the other churns ahead, giving the vessel extra turning power.

The twin engines, with cylinders 24 to 30 inches in diameter, are connected to the paddle wheels by long wooden pitman arms. They run at pressures of 150 pounds per square inch or higher.

In his tiny galley the cook produces elaborate meals of many courses. Quantity and variety are the main goals.

The magnificent saloon, sometimes over 200 feet long, is the combined dining room and social hall, the showpiece of the boat. It is lighted by bright crystal chandeliers and stained-glass skylights.

The wood-burning boilers devour huge quantities of fuel; boats stop twice a day to "wood up." Poorly built and badly maintained, the boilers frequently explode.

Steamboats draw from two to six feet of water when loaded. To reduce drafts and cut construction costs, they are lightly built to the point of flimsiness. The average life for a western steamboat is four years. These mid-19th-century vessels range in length from the lordly 350-foot *Eclipse* to mere washtubs barely able to contain a boiler. The length-width ratios of hulls vary from about 8:1 to 6:1—the slimmer the hull, the faster the boat. Smokestacks tower as high as 95 feet. The tall stacks are hinged to tilt down so that they can pass under bridges.

Cabins, Plain and Fancy

Most steamboat staterooms are spartan, with built-in bunks, a washstand, a few hooks for clothes, and possibly a mirror— but no running water or heat. (Even so, they are far more comfortable than cramped stagecoaches and squalid wayside inns.) Real luxury is sometimes provided in the South aboard the great packets that cruise between the major river cities.

Sojourners in Exotic Lands

Lesueur sketched his house at New Harmony (right) and part of the community hall (left). The rustic buildings were a far cry from the city Owen had once planned.

It was late fall in 1825 when a large, lumbering keelboat, aptly named the *Philanthropist,* pushed off from a Pittsburgh landing and nosed down the Ohio River toward its destination in Indiana. Aboard was one of the most impressive collections of intellectuals ever to brave a wilderness. Many were foreigners drawn to the American West for idealistic and scholarly reasons. Among them was the British industrialist-reformer Robert Owen, who planned to raise on American soil "an entire new state of society, to change it from an ignorant, selfish system to an enlightened social system which shall gradually unite all interests into one, and remove all causes for contests between individuals." One of Owen's companions on the drafty vessel was a French naturalist and artist, Charles Alexandre Lesueur, who saw the West as a rich virgin territory for scientific exploration.

The Lure of the West

Although within a few years Owen's dreams of an equitable cooperative society were shattered by the harsh realities of frontier life and human imperfections, Lesueur was to remain in the West for a decade to tramp the backwoods trails and riverbanks. Endowed with a draftsman's skill and an artist's insight, Lesueur sketched scores of charming scenes—several of which appear on these pages. They capture the vitality of the frontier in all its variegated lifestyles.

For decades the moving frontier had exerted an almost magnetic pull on a host of European scholars, adventurers, aristocrats, and writers. These men journeyed deep into the American interior to study exotic flora and fauna, hunt down the animals of the forest and plain,

observe American democracy at work —and cheer or jeer at what they saw. Among the very first of the breed was Lesueur's countryman, François-André Michaux, who visited the Ohio Valley in 1802. Like many who followed in his footsteps, Michaux came away with mixed feelings, exhilarated by the freedom of the frontiersman's life but appalled at his treatment of the Indians and repelled by the pioneers' "miserable log huts, with no windows, and so small that two beds fill most of the room."

It was a very different Ohio that Swiss traveler Philippe Suchard visited a mere 22 years later, an area that was already on the edge of prosperity. Suchard admired just about everything, from the politeness of the children to the political wisdom of backwoods farmers and the hospitality of their wives. Once, after tramping several days in the Ohio back-

country, Suchard chanced upon a cabin in a clearing. The lady of the house immediately bade him stop for refreshment. "This good lady enquired whether I should prefer tea or coffee for supper, and what sort of poultry I should like." In his reminiscences, Suchard then cataloged a Lucullan feast set out for him on the "whitest linen." It began with pie, then moved on to ham, chicken, salad, stewed plums, and hot cakes. Such fare, Suchard reported, "is what people usually have for supper in the West."

Not every foreign visitor delighted in western ways. In 1842 novelist Charles Dickens grumbled across America by riverboat, stagecoach, and railroad, a journey that, in the author's view, was punctuated by bad food, slovenly accommodations, rude officials, and dreary conversations. Even the great Mississippi River failed to impress him. Per-

Robert Owen's *Philanthropist* prepares to leave its landing at Pittsburgh, carrying its famed "Boatload of Knowledge" on the long river journey to New Harmony, Indiana.

Women and children peer from the cabin door of the *Philanthropist* (note Lesueur's misspelling) for a final look at Cincinnati, where the New Harmony colonists spent several days during their trip. Though still essentially a frontier village at this date, Cincinnati was on the way to becoming one of the educational and artistic hubs of the Ohio Valley.

At dinnertime the *Philanthropist's* passengers sat at a long table that ran the length of the cabin. Bunks with trunks stowed below them lined the walls. Quarters were cramped and menus monotonous on board a keelboat, and with frequent delays and stopovers the voyage to New Harmony took all of two months. Lesueur passed the long days fishing and making sketches.

A slaughtered hog—on the tree at the left —is ready for a New Harmony barbecue.

Early in 1826, while his boat was delayed by floating ice on the Ohio River, French artist-naturalist Charles Lesueur sketched this lonely cabin with its cleared fields.

haps what really drew Dickens' ire was the indifference to rank and position. Frances Trollope, Dickens' compatriot and contemporary, caught some of the West's spirit when she disapprovingly sniffed: "And . . . it may be observed that the theory of equality may be very daintily discussed by English gentlemen in a London dining-room, when the servant . . . respectfully shuts the door, and leaves them to their . . . wisdom; but it will be found less palatable when it presents itself in the shape of a hard, greasy paw, and is claimed in accents that breathe less of freedom than of onions and whiskey. Strong, indeed, must be the love of equality in an English breast if it can survive a tour through the Union."

A Visitor From the East

Saturday September 8, 1832. Wabash enters peacefully into the peaceful riv—water clear, greenish blue —Ohio yellow. Men on sand bar with a seine sack. Aground near natives house—show boat on the Illinois shore with flag—groups assembled there—rifle shooting—horse race along shore—negro laugh—sunset—party breaks up—some in boat across glassy river singing ballad— others on horseback through the woods—some on foot—some loiter on the shore—beautiful, clear ev sky. . . . Gross plenty that prevails . . . in hotels, steam boats, &c. —meats, poultry, vegetables, excellent bread, pies, puddings—food seems to be wasted—as if of no value.
—*The Western Journals of Washington Irving*

Henry Lewis, Panorama Artist of the Mississippi

"The Artist's Encampment" is the title of this engraving. The scene is an island in the Mississippi River near Nauvoo, Illinois. Behind the fallen tree is the prow of Lewis' homemade catamaran, the *Mene-ha-hah*, on which he floated down the great river. He used the roof of the 8- by 11-foot cabin, mounted on two 50-foot canoes, as his sketching post.

A picturesque river barge sails toward Hannibal, in Missouri, which the artist described as a "considerable trade center." His accompanying notes, however, reveal that Lewis was more interested in the legend of the Lovers' Leap jutting up at the left—one of half a dozen along the Mississippi River.

Henry Lewis, born in England in 1819, came to the United States as a boy. He was working as a stage carpenter in a St. Louis theater when, inspired by the previous theatrical successes of panoramas of the lower Mississippi, he got the idea of painting a mobile panorama of the river's upper part. In preparation Lewis spent three summers exploring the Mississippi above St. Louis, making detailed sketches and taking copious notes. His panorama was completed in 1849, after the self-taught Lewis and four experienced landscape painters had worked on it daily for nine months. It occupied a roll of canvas 12 feet high and 825 yards long. As an assistant unwound scene after scene across the stage, Indian war dances, buffalo hunts, battles, steamboats, and picturesque scenery passed before the audience, accompanied by brief commentaries. A later panorama of the lower Mississippi was 500 yards long. After a successful tour of the States, Lewis exhibited his work in Europe, where he remained. He also published an illustrated guide to the Mississippi Valley, from which the scenes above are taken.

Entertainment in the Backwoods

Wherever cabins were close enough for one backwoodsman to reach another by foot or horse, families would relieve their monotonous isolation with "frolics." When a farmer needed another building, or help in beating his flax, or new bedcovers, his wife would cook hams, bear, venison, vegetables, and fruit pies, and he'd invite his neighbors to a frolic—a house-raising, a swingling or quilting bee. When his new-spun wool needed fulling, he'd saturate the cloth with hot soapsuds and plop it on his puncheon floor; then his guests would sit around it on stools and, while singing and swapping yarns, stomp on the cloth with bare feet. At sugaring time his friends—partying with home-made wine and whisky—would help cook the maple sap, make the sugar, and pour lollipops for the children. Thus tedious chores were done quickly and gaily. Afterward, while the women sewed, smoked pipes, told tales about witches, and gossiped, the men wrestled, raced horses, and competed in marksmanship, logrolling, and the lifting of heavy flour barrels. Best of all was a wedding, usually at home because churches in the backcountry were rare. After feasting and square dancing to music from a squeaky fiddle, the groom, with his bride behind him on a pillion, would ride off to their new cabin—built, of course, at *his* house-raising.

During a swingling bee, neighbors playfully bop one another after beating off the woody parts from flax stems. Bringing their own swingling posts and paddles, they go from farm to farm, helping each in turn. They end with a big supper, singing, and a hoedown. This is a Pennsylvania scene, but the tradition moved on westward.

A family hosts a quilting bee in a meetinghouse for more room. A courting couple holds hands and men visit. Friends help the hostess sew together the quilt's three layers, stretched out on a frame: the top of patches stitched together in a traditional pattern; the middle of cotton batting; the bottom a homespun sheet.

Marksmen compete for the prize of a steer. Artist George Caleb Bingham, who grew up on the Missouri frontier in the early 1800's, took part in backwoods social activities and riverboat life. He painted portraits for $20 apiece but is more famous today for his genre scenes.

Dressed in their best, young people husk a neighbor's corn. He who finds a red ear can kiss the girl sitting next to him. Later the group will sup on pork 'n' beans, pumpkin pie, and cider; a caller will lead square dances.

As roads penetrated northwest, more affluent settlers heading for the new towns stopped at inns like this, where four travelers stretch their legs. Frontier dances were based chiefly on the Virginia reel and Irish jig.

This 1850's doll journeyed to Missouri and later to Oregon. Adults in the wagon train made the doll clothes, the tin cradle, and its miniature patchwork quilt.

An Economic Roller Coaster

The transportation revolution wrought by steamboats and canals played an important role in the rapid economic recovery of the Old West after the Panic of 1819, as did new federal policies aimed at making land purchases reasonably easy for pioneers. In a series of measures Congress pursued an ever more openhanded land policy. It culminated in the Homestead Act of 1862, an act that would transfer millions of acres to settlers virtually free of charge. The process began in 1820, with the reduction of the base price of public land from $2 to $1.25 an acre and the lowering of the minimum purchase from 160 to as few as 80 acres.

The next step in meeting the demands of settlers was to recognize the squatters' claims to the land they inhabited. In the 1830's Congress enacted a series of temporary measures to grant a degree of legitimacy to these claims, and in 1841 it passed the Pre-Emption Act, which made these temporary measures permanent. Under its terms, those who had occupied portions of the public domain in advance of government surveys were permitted to buy their land at $1.25 an acre, rather than being forced to bid on their holdings at public auction. Or, if they chose, squatters could sell their preemption rights to the highest bidder, who in turn could purchase the land at the minimum rate.

Squatters were a mixed lot. Many were genuine farmers who had moved

The hopes of Hamburg, Illinois, in 1836 were dashed by the depression of 1837.

west ahead of government survey teams. Some hoped to take over choice acres without having to bid for them. Other men with little capital sought to acquire land that would pay for itself. While waiting for the surveyors—usually four or five years—they would farm the property and then purchase it with what they had saved in that time. By contrast, there were the free spirits who had rushed farther west to escape the humdrum existence imposed by society. When settlement finally overtook them,

they were eager to move on; they preferred to clear a new patch of wilderness, hunker down in a rough shelter, and spend their hours in the happy pursuit of game, farming as little as possible.

A Land-Office Business

Always on the move, these peripatetic souls kept one step ahead of conventional folk and their rules, their churches, their schools, and their ambitions, and for them the land acts of the 1830's and the Pre-Emption Act of 1841 were boons. These rulings allowed the frontiersmen to sell their improvement rights and secure a grubstake for future ventures. The typical process by which land changed hands between frontiersman and settler was described by a Mrs. Rebecca Burlend, a British immigrant to Illinois in the 1830's. "An improved eighty acres was the first land we purchased," she reported. "A person named Mr. Oakes having heard that a family about to settle was sojourning at Mr. B's came to invite my husband to buy some venison. . . . My husband . . . in conversation found he was disposed to sell his improvement right. . . . For this right he wanted sixty dollars. . . . As we liked the . . . land very much . . . the agreement was completed that evening, and the money paid and possession obtained the following day. The reader is aware that the sixty dollars . . . were only for his . . . improvement right. . . . One hundred more we paid at the land

---

An 1832 cartoon shows President Jackson destroying the Bank of the United States, depicted as a many-headed monster. Walking stick, spectacles, and high-crowned hat were Jackson trademarks.

Jackson and the National Bank

Andrew Jackson's battle against the Second Bank of the United States, chartered in 1816, won him great popularity. This was particularly true in the West, where people distrusted the Philadelphia capitalists who controlled the institution. The first blow fell in 1832, when Jackson, labeling the bank a monopoly, indicated that he would refuse to renew its charter when it expired in 1836. Then in 1833 he withdrew all government deposits from the bank and placed them in chosen state banks. The result was financial chaos. The Bank of the United States had kept a tight rein on the issue of currency by state-chartered banks. Now with this stiff control removed these banks began printing unlimited amounts of paper money. Businessmen, land speculators, and others who wanted to borrow cheap money were delighted. But the result was runaway inflation, escalated in 1836 by another government decision: to hand over most of the $36 million surplus in the national treasury to the states. This largesse loosed a deluge of ambitious western state projects for building canals and railroads. Excessive business expansion and land speculation followed, as banks loaned every scrap of their shaky currency.

George Caleb Bingham painted this family of squatters on the western frontier, complete with the ever-present hunting dog.

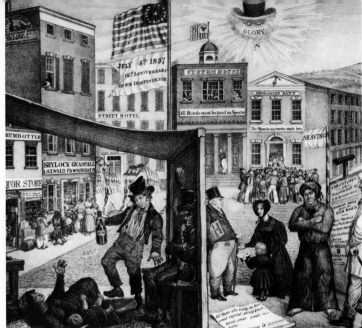

In a biting political cartoon, Andrew Jackson's familiar spectacles and hat beam down on scenes of poverty and misery in the 1837 panic.

office [for the] . . . title deeds." The Burlends were just one family among thousands. Between 1834 and 1836, for example, sales of the public domain more than quadrupled, rising from 4.6 million to 20 million acres. Government agents literally did a land-office business, and the national treasury swelled with the paper bills issued by state-chartered banks. Once again, as in the years following the War of 1812, the West wallowed in an orgy of speculation fueled by the printing presses of the hundreds of state-chartered banks that once more operated virtually without supervision. Huge parcels of land were changing hands like so many sacks of potatoes; hawkers of townsites were gulling naive easterners into buying lots in wholly imaginary western cities; and normally levelheaded settlers began pledging their homesteads as collateral for loans of paper money with which to speculate in land.

Phantom Cities

The plight of one Major Wilkey, a fictional Yankee farmer appearing in an 1839 volume, *Western Emigration*, illustrates the fate of thousands of real people. Upon arriving at a rundown inn on an Illinois prairie void, the major inquired of the landlady the exact location of the metropolis of Edensburgh:

Landlady—"Wha! . . . This here city is Edensburgh—so named but a-three months ago by Squire Soaper . . . who bought the land!" Major—"But where . . . woman, are its public and private edifices, its

increased population, its . . . State House, and other squares?"
More disappointment awaited the major when he discovered that Edensburgh was a phantom city, its entire population consisting of the landlady and her husband, the other six residents having "died with the *Fever* and *Ague*."

The boom that turned dour Yankees into high-stakes gamblers overnight was bound to bust. But few imagined that its nemesis would be the West's own darling, President Andrew Jackson. Jackson's fiscal policies—including a campaign against the national bank in favor of the state banks—had in large measure generated the speculative fever. But this did not prevent the stern old man from applying the brakes when inflation began to get out of hand. In July 1836, at the height of the boom, Jackson suddenly issued his Specie Circular, demanding that henceforth all public land purchases be paid for in silver or gold. The effect of Jackson's order was startling and disastrous. If the government would not accept paper, neither would the merchants, nor the banks that had printed the notes in the first place. Soon all credit disappeared. Loans were canceled and collateral snapped up by frightened creditors. It was 1819 all over again, a period of "hard times, hard customers, hard creditors, suits, failures . . . and epidemic woe." Some thought the West was dead but, as in 1819, they were too pessimistic. For the West's real wealth lay in the fertility of its soil and the grit of its people. A currency crisis could delay growth—but not for long.

The Independent Squatter

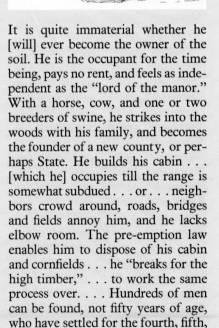

With haughty indifference a woodsman of Indiana posed for a British traveler in 1827. The oversized plug hat was popular at the time; the long rifle was vital to the squatter's way of life.

It is quite immaterial whether he [will] ever become the owner of the soil. He is the occupant for the time being, pays no rent, and feels as independent as the "lord of the manor." With a horse, cow, and one or two breeders of swine, he strikes into the woods with his family, and becomes the founder of a new county, or perhaps State. He builds his cabin . . . [which he] occupies till the range is somewhat subdued . . . or . . . neighbors crowd around, roads, bridges and fields annoy him, and he lacks elbow room. The pre-emption law enables him to dispose of his cabin and cornfields . . . he "breaks for the high timber," . . . to work the same process over. . . . Hundreds of men can be found, not fifty years of age, who have settled for the fourth, fifth, or sixth time on a new spot.

—John Mason Peck
Guide for Emigrants, 1831

Andrew Jackson: First Western President

"I could throw him three times out of four," said a boyhood friend of Andrew Jackson, "but he would never *stay* throwed." This fierce will to win would fuel Jackson's climb from obscurity on the frontier to fame as the foremost soldier-statesman of his time.

The third son of Scotch-Irish immigrant parents, Jackson was born March 15, 1767, in the Waxhaws, a frontier tract claimed by both North and South Carolina. There he received a country school education and helped out on his uncle's farm, where he lived with his two brothers and widowed mother. Then came the Revolution and personal tragedy. His mother and one brother died of disease and the other brother fell in battle. Jackson himself was badly wounded—slashed by his British captor's sword while a prisoner of war. In 1781 the 14-year-old boy was left to make his way alone.

Young Andrew toiled through a brief apprenticeship to a saddler in the Waxhaws, then returned even more briefly to school. Hot-tempered, incautious, and self-assertive, he got into numerous scrapes. Then a sizable inheritance that came from a grandfather in Ireland gave him the chance to live the life of a young man of fashion in Charleston. When the

Every inch a general, Jackson posed for this portrait in 1820, the year his friends first urged him to run for his country's presidency to "put things right in the White House."

When Jackson died in 1845, at the age of 78, he was mourned throughout the nation as the first champion of the people. This photograph was taken a short time before his death.

Enraged when his 14-year-old prisoner refused to clean his boots, a British officer took his saber to Jackson in 1781 and created lifelong scars on the young boy's head and left hand.

During the Creek campaign in 1813 Jackson cowed a company of mutinous militiamen with a leveled musket and a warning that he would gun down the first one who shirked his duty.

money was gone, the headstrong Andrew returned home for a stint of schoolteaching. At age 17 he left the Waxhaws for wider horizons. A lucky encounter at a Salisbury, North Carolina, inn led to his reading law with a local attorney and launched the shrewd, combative young man on a career in which he was to excel.

Admitted to the bar in 1787, Jackson soon decided to seek his fortune in Nashville, the "Wild West" of its day. Prospering as an attorney and public prosecutor, he married a dark-eyed divorcee named Rachel Donelson Robards, who belonged to a family of influential local gentry. Two years later the devoted couple discovered that their union was illegal; only then was Rachel's first husband granted a divorce—she assumed he had gotten it two years before—on grounds of her adultery with Jackson. Stunned, Jackson and Rachel remarried, but the scandal was to haunt them for life. Defending his wife's good name, Jackson met one Charles Dickinson on the field of honor in 1806. Dickinson was a renowned marksman, Jackson only an average shot. Coolly, Jackson allowed Dickinson to fire first, taking a bullet within an inch of his heart. Then, aiming carefully, he wounded his antagonist mortally. He later told his seconds, "I should have hit him if he had shot me through the brain."

Political and Military Battles

Jackson brought the same grim determination to politics, where he vaulted to prominence at an early age. At 30 he had twice been to Washington, as congressman and senator. At 31 he was elected judge of the Superior Court of Tennessee. In another four years he had been given command of the Tennessee militia as major general—high rank for a man whose military credentials were limited to youthful skirmishes against the British. Yet he had an instinctive genius for leading men.

In the War of 1812 Jackson soon won acclaim as the one general who could win victories while others suffered defeat after defeat. He crushed the Creeks at Horseshoe Bend, drove

When he made liberal use of the spoils system, Jackson's critics painted him as a demon who traded appointive offices for political power.

the British from Pensacola, and cut a crack British force to ribbons at New Orleans. At war's end he was lionized as Old Hickory, hero of the nation.

By then 48, Jackson retired to his Nashville estate to resume the life of a country gentleman. But in 1817 he was recalled to duty along the Alabama-Georgia border, against the Seminoles, and caused an uproar when he pursued them into Spanish-held Florida. In 1823 his admirers persuaded him to run for the Senate, and the following year they nominated him for president. Austere and aloof, the old general all but ignored his own campaign. Even so, he polled more electoral votes than his three rivals—but not the required majority. The election was thrown to the House, which chose John Quincy Adams. Jackson shrugged—until rumors (that have since been proven false) reached him of a corrupt bargain between Clay and Adams, whereby Clay supported Adams in return for a Cabinet post. Outraged, Old Hickory declared

political war, and four years later he easily trounced Adams.

King Andrew, as his critics called President Jackson, was denounced for his gargantuan spoils system, his frequent use of the veto, his imperious nature, and the "mob rule" of Jacksonian Democracy. But to the masses who put him in office, Andrew Jackson could do no wrong. Antagonistic to what he saw as vested interests, he toppled the Second Bank of the United States. Himself a self-made aristocrat, he appointed men of humble origin to high office. While the critics ranted, the masses roared their approval as Jackson held the line on federal spending and erased the national debt, and squelched an attempt by South Carolina to nullify a federal law.

Though his health was failing, the iron-willed old general served a second term as president, welcoming Arkansas and Michigan to the Union and preparing the way for the annexation of Texas. Then the man who had climbed from the Waxhaws to the White House went home.

From a cluster of cabins, Andrew Jackson's Hermitage grew to rival Washington's Mount Vernon and Jefferson's Monticello as a place of beauty. It was here, near Nashville, that Jackson lived the life of a gentleman farmer, planting cotton and tobacco, racing his stable of thoroughbreds, and indulging his wife and their adopted son. It was to the gentle banks of the Cumberland that Jackson retired from his wars, though he remained a power in the Democratic Party, which he had helped to found. He was buried at his beloved Hermitage, in the shade of the towering hickory trees that have always symbolized his indomitable strength.

Building New Jerusalems

For the isolated frontier family, prey to illness, loneliness, and fear of the unknown, one of the few comforts that could be depended on was religion, usually of the evangelical variety. In response to the call of circuit-riding preachers, many of them self-ordained, the families of farmers and woodsmen loaded their wagons with provisions and traveled long miles to join camp meetings at some designated spot in a forest clearing. Even confirmed sinners and skeptics often came, particularly when a preacher famous for his skill in breathing fire into the Word of God was scheduled to sermonize.

There were other reasons for the repentant and unrepentant alike to rally to an evangelist's call. Such a gathering afforded a rare opportunity to meet with distant neighbors, gossip, arrange trades of livestock, and perhaps even find a husband or wife, or at least enjoy some distinctly secular pleasures. William Jennings Bryan (perennial Democratic presidential candidate and no mean evangelist himself) was reputed to have said many decades later that more souls were made than saved at these meetings.

But the main business of a camp meeting took place at an outdoor log pulpit where preachers would spell one another for several days, rousing their congregants to a fever pitch of religious zeal. Recalling the galvanic style of Peter Cartwright, a renowned backwoods preacher, a frontiersman wrote that on hearing Cartwright's "glowing metaphors describing the beauties of heaven and terrors of hell, waves of excitement swept over the vast audience. There were tears and shouts and screams. Some . . . fell to the ground helpless; pandemonium reigned for hours."

The Christian Utopians

Although most westerners took their religion in large if infrequent doses, there were some for whom the Word of the Lord was a constant companion. Among these were the Christian Utopians—Amanists in Iowa, Shakers in Ohio and Indiana, and Jansonists in Illinois, to name just a few. Despite differences in doctrine and customs, all shared a common goal: to raise upon the prairie a New Zion of righteousness, of shared joy and labor. Because most of these groups held highly unconventional religious and social views and believed in the common ownership of property, they were often unwelcome in more settled regions of the country. But for a time the Old Northwest offered the space, isolation, and inexpensive land that enabled them to carry out their religious and social experiments with little interference from outsiders. Few of the colonies established by the Christian Utopians survived into the 20th century. Some of them failed because of the death of a charismatic leader, others because a policy of celibacy doomed their experiment to an early demise, and still others because the ready availability of cheap land made private enterprise a temptation too strong for most of their members to resist.

A circuit-riding preacher braves a downpour to keep his commitment to one of his many scattered backwoods congregations.

A fervent sermon makes Methodists gesticulate, shout, and faint in an ecstasy of repentance at a camp meeting in the South. A team of preachers keeps the exhortation flowing.

Building a bridge at Bishop Hill, women operate a hand-powered piledriver.

Disciplined teamwork was the keynote at Bishop Hill. Here a team of three sowers plants grain, plowing teams break new ground ahead of them, and a woman marks the rows with a staff.

Among the earliest and most successful of the Christian communitarian societies was New Harmony, established in Indiana in 1814 by the messianic German preacher George Rapp and later bought by Robert Owen. From the first, New Harmony was a success. More than 500 members labored cooperatively on 24,734 prime Indiana acres, tilling the fields and establishing small industries. Rapp, a man fervently convinced of the imminent Second Coming of Christ, bent his every effort toward the perfection of his followers so that they would be fit to receive the Messiah. All were required to surrender their personal property to the commonwealth and labor for the common good. Rapp also imposed celibacy upon his Harmonists, believing that God had originally created man as a self-reproducing creature whose appetites had been born only with the "fall from grace." Through celibacy, Rapp thought, man would be restored to his original state. Under Rapp's strict but innovative rule New Harmony prospered. Its fields along the banks of the Wabash became a veritable Garden of Eden; its cottage industries turned out a variety of goods—wagons and woolens, rope and leather goods, even beer and whisky. Then in 1825 Rapp decided to sell New Harmony and establish an industrial society in Pennsylvania. The Rappites continued to prosper in their new home, but were disappointed in the Messiah's apparent reluctance to reappear. It was the doctrine of celibacy, however, that spelled their doom. George Rapp's beliefs notwithstanding, none of his followers achieved the hoped-for capacity to reproduce without a mate, and by 1905 only two communicants remained alive

Formerly a raw prairie, Bishop Hill within a few years boasted sturdy buildings of brick made by members of the colony, one of whom, Olof Krans, painted these three scenes.

to dispose of the vast wealth their movement had created.

No less fantastic and eccentric, although short-lived, were the Jansonists of Bishop Hill, Illinois. Founded in 1846 by Eric Janson, a Swedish nonconformist who had been driven from his homeland for his unorthodox views, Bishop Hill eventually attracted about 1,500 members, almost all of them Swedes. The first years of the experiment were hard beyond all reckoning; the faithful lived in dugouts and almost starved or froze to death before the crops could be brought in.

The Faithful Begin to Doubt

Under Janson's leadership, privation turned to prosperity, and Bishop Hill expanded to 12,000 acres, complete with neat houses, a large communal kitchen and dining room, and an immense meeting hall. With the community's success, however, Janson grew increasingly capricious and dictatorial. Each morning and evening and thrice on Sundays, his followers gathered to hear his two-hour sermons, in which he claimed that "since the time of the

Apostles there has been found no true preacher before me." At times he was said to have even threatened God Himself, warning that "if You . . . do not give good weather . . . I shall depose You from Your seat of omnipotence."

That the colonists could put up with such pretensions says much for Janson's persuasiveness, but even some of the faithful began to doubt him when the preacher claimed the right to bed any female in the community who caught his eye. Before incipient rebellion could blossom, Janson fell victim to an assassin, the husband of the preacher's cousin. For three days Janson's most fervent followers prayed at his bier, certain of his resurrection from the dead. Finally, all hope gone, they buried their leader and chose a new one. Bishop Hill survived its founder by a decade, but the spark had gone out of the community. An effort to enforce celibacy among the members led to the mass apostasy of the young, and finally even common ownership of property was abandoned as the last members of Bishop Hill carved up the colony into private holdings and blended into the society around them.

The Pioneer Ironworks of Maramec

One day in 1825 Thomas James, the bank president in Chillicothe, the capital of the Northwest Territory, was entertaining some Shawnee Indians when he noticed that their faces were painted with red powder. To his trained eye—he came from an ironmaking family and had built furnaces in Ohio—it looked like hematite, an iron ore. When he asked the Indians if they would reveal its source, they agreed. So he assigned his assistant to ride with them to the distant Ozark foothills. They reached a huge natural spring flanked by forests—and slopes that were rich in hematite. Sensing the possibilities, James bought the 10,000-acre tract from the government, showing the same enterprise as he had in his youth when he left his Maryland home, trekked over the Zane Trail, loaded iron kettles onto a flatboat, floated down the Mississippi to trade with settlers, and later prospered as a banker. Then he gambled $40,000 to construct a blast furnace by that spring in the Missouri wilderness. Called Maramec (below), during 1830–70 it became the most successful of all trans-Mississippi ironworks. To follow Maramec's operations, see the opposite page and read clockwise from the upper left.

Maramec Village, an Iron Plantation

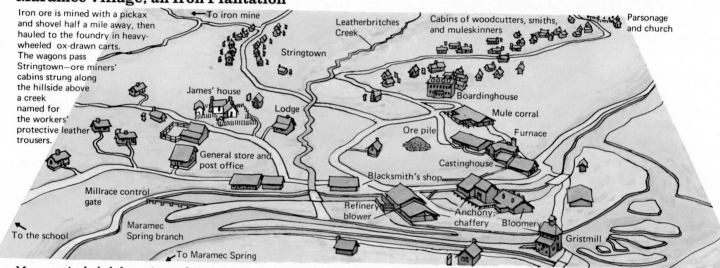

Iron ore is mined with a pickax and shovel half a mile away, then hauled to the foundry in heavy-wheeled ox-drawn carts. The wagons pass Stringtown—ore miners' cabins strung along the hillside above a creek named for the workers' protective leather trousers.

← To iron mine

Leatherbritches Creek

Stringtown

Cabins of woodcutters, smiths, and muleskinners

Parsonage and church

James' house

Lodge

Boardinghouse

Mule corral

Ore pile

Furnace

General store and post office

Castinghouse

Blacksmith's shop

Millrace control gate

Refinery blower

Anchony; chaffery

Bloomery

Maramec Spring branch

To the school

Gristmill

← To Maramec Spring

Maramec included the spring and river, mines, ironworks buildings, and a village run as an early company town. James and his descendants forbade liquor, owned all property and equipment, and rented two-room cabins to married workmen and rooms in a boardinghouse to bachelors. At the company store in the 1830's shoes cost $1.25 a pair, potatoes 82 cents a bushel, and, per pound, 62 cents for bacon, 8⅓ cents for butter, and 25 cents for coffee. By the 1850's Maramec could boast some 500 inhabitants. Malaria killed many, and fire was a constant danger, the shingled foundry roofs blazing up periodically until covered over with metal.

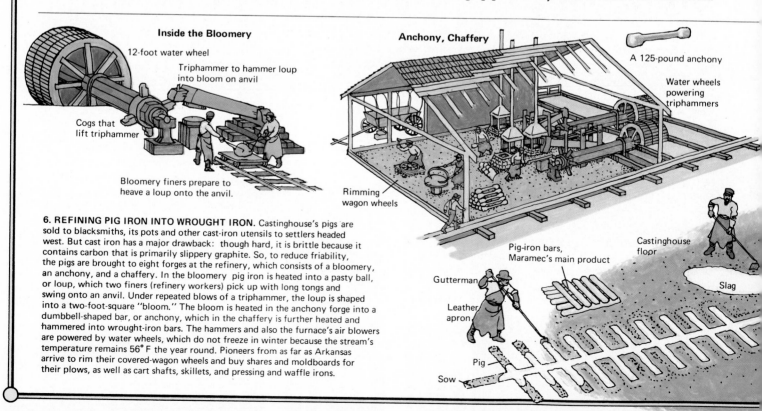

Inside the Bloomery

12-foot water wheel

Triphammer to hammer loup into bloom on anvil

Cogs that lift triphammer

Bloomery finers prepare to heave a loup onto the anvil.

Anchony, Chaffery

A 125-pound anchony

Water wheels powering triphammers

Rimming wagon wheels

Pig-iron bars, Maramec's main product

Castinghouse floor

Slag

Gutterman

Leather apron

Pig

Sow

6. REFINING PIG IRON INTO WROUGHT IRON. Castinghouse's pigs are sold to blacksmiths, its pots and other cast-iron utensils to settlers headed west. But cast iron has a major drawback: though hard, it is brittle because it contains carbon that is primarily slippery graphite. So, to reduce friability, the pigs are brought to eight forges at the refinery, which consists of a bloomery, an anchony, and a chaffery. In the bloomery pig iron is heated into a pasty ball, or loup, which two finers (refinery workers) pick up with long tongs and swing onto an anvil. Under repeated blows of a triphammer, the loup is shaped into a two-foot-square "bloom." The bloom is heated in the anchony forge into a dumbbell-shaped bar, or anchony, which in the chaffery is further heated and hammered into wrought-iron bars. The hammers and also the furnace's air blowers are powered by water wheels, which do not freeze in winter because the stream's temperature remains 56° F the year round. Pioneers from as far as Arkansas arrive to rim their covered-wagon wheels and buy shares and moldboards for their plows, as well as cart shafts, skillets, and pressing and waffle irons.

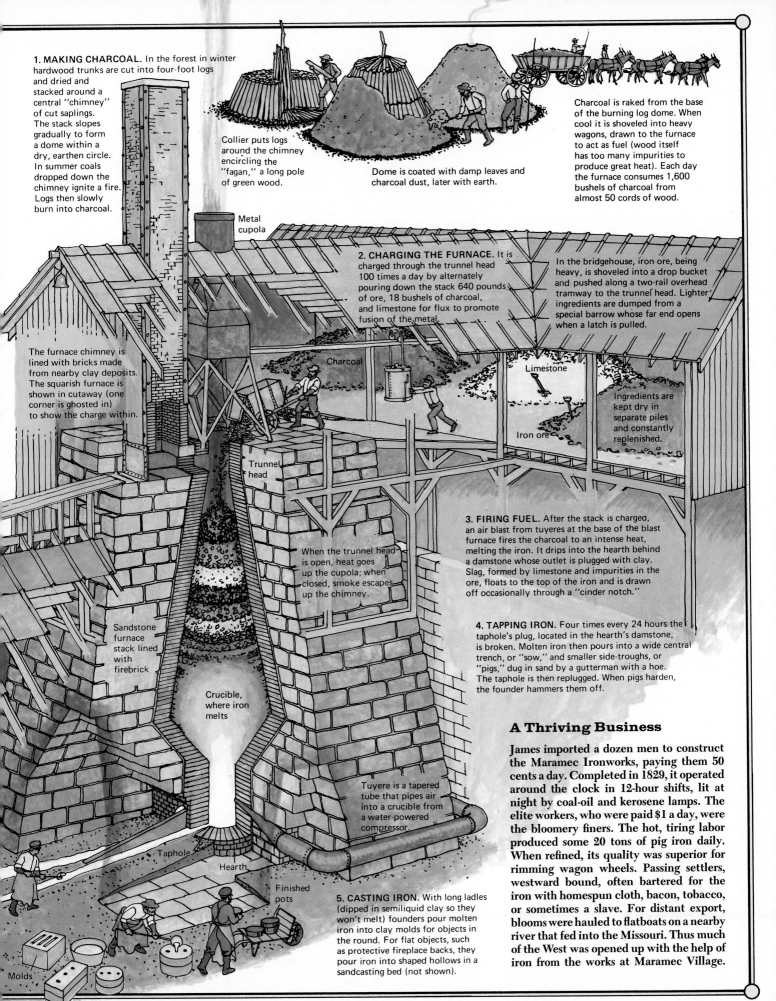

1. MAKING CHARCOAL. In the forest in winter hardwood trunks are cut into four-foot logs and dried and stacked around a central "chimney" of cut saplings. The stack slopes gradually to form a dome within a dry, earthen circle. In summer coals dropped down the chimney ignite a fire. Logs then slowly burn into charcoal.

Collier puts logs around the chimney encircling the "fagan," a long pole of green wood.

Dome is coated with damp leaves and charcoal dust, later with earth.

Charcoal is raked from the base of the burning log dome. When cool it is shoveled into heavy wagons, drawn to the furnace to act as fuel (wood itself has too many impurities to produce great heat). Each day the furnace consumes 1,600 bushels of charcoal from almost 50 cords of wood.

Metal cupola

The furnace chimney is lined with bricks made from nearby clay deposits. The squarish furnace is shown in cutaway (one corner is ghosted in) to show the charge within.

2. CHARGING THE FURNACE. It is charged through the trunnel head 100 times a day by alternately pouring down the stack 640 pounds of ore, 18 bushels of charcoal, and limestone for flux to promote fusion of the metal.

In the bridgehouse, iron ore, being heavy, is shoveled into a drop bucket and pushed along a two-rail overhead tramway to the trunnel head. Lighter ingredients are dumped from a special barrow whose far end opens when a latch is pulled.

Charcoal

Limestone

Iron ore

Ingredients are kept dry in separate piles and constantly replenished.

Trunnel head

When the trunnel head is open, heat goes up the cupola; when closed, smoke escapes up the chimney.

3. FIRING FUEL. After the stack is charged, an air blast from tuyeres at the base of the blast furnace fires the charcoal to an intense heat, melting the iron. It drips into the hearth behind a damstone whose outlet is plugged with clay. Slag, formed by limestone and impurities in the ore, floats to the top of the iron and is drawn off occasionally through a "cinder notch."

Sandstone furnace stack lined with firebrick

Crucible, where iron melts

4. TAPPING IRON. Four times every 24 hours the taphole's plug, located in the hearth's damstone, is broken. Molten iron then pours into a wide central trench, or "sow," and smaller side-troughs, or "pigs," dug in sand by a gutterman with a hoe. The taphole is then replugged. When pigs harden, the founder hammers them off.

Tuyere is a tapered tube that pipes air into a crucible from a water-powered compressor.

Taphole

Hearth

Finished pots

Molds

5. CASTING IRON. With long ladles (dipped in semiliquid clay so they won't melt) founders pour molten iron into clay molds for objects in the round. For flat objects, such as protective fireplace backs, they pour iron into shaped hollows in a sandcasting bed (not shown).

A Thriving Business

James imported a dozen men to construct the Maramec Ironworks, paying them 50 cents a day. Completed in 1829, it operated around the clock in 12-hour shifts, lit at night by coal-oil and kerosene lamps. The elite workers, who were paid $1 a day, were the bloomery finers. The hot, tiring labor produced some 20 tons of pig iron daily. When refined, its quality was superior for rimming wagon wheels. Passing settlers, westward bound, often bartered for the iron with homespun cloth, bacon, tobacco, or sometimes a slave. For distant export, blooms were hauled to flatboats on a nearby river that fed into the Missouri. Thus much of the West was opened up with the help of iron from the works at Maramec Village.

The New Technology

For a few days in 1837, while speculators in the canal-building boom were reeling under the impact of financial panic, farmers and strollers along the banks of the Erie Canal could have seen a strange and majestic sight on the waterway. Inching its way up the canal was a huge barge, bearing but a single item of freight: a large iron object surmounted by what looked like a smokestack. Those who recognized it as a locomotive must have wondered what possible use such a machine could ever have in the West.

Revolution on Rails

Only eight years before, in 1829, America's first locomotive—a British-made engine—sputtered and clanked its way along a three-mile stretch of track in Pennsylvania, and only seven years had gone by since the first U.S.-built "iron horse"—the famous *Tom Thumb*—took part in a highly publicized race with a horse-drawn coach. But already the coastal states were on a railroad-building spree that seemed certain to spread to regions beyond the Appalachians. In fact, the barge-borne locomotive on the Erie Canal was bound for a railroad that had been in operation for about a year, a single-track 33-mile line on which horse-drawn cars moved produce from Adrian, Michigan, to the Lake Erie port of Toledo, Ohio. Now the tiny Erie & Kalamazoo Railroad was ready to switch to steam, and with the arrival of the locomotive a new era would open both for the Old Northwest and for the nation as a whole.

The Old Northwest took to railroads as an empress takes to diamonds. At first the newfangled means of transportation was considered a mere supplement to the

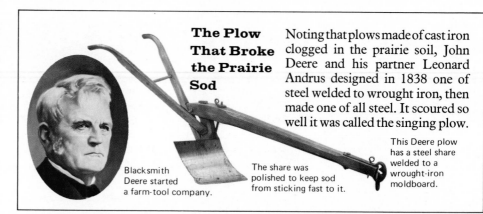

The Plow That Broke the Prairie Sod

Blacksmith Deere started a farm-tool company.

The share was polished to keep sod from sticking fast to it.

Noting that plows made of cast iron clogged in the prairie soil, John Deere and his partner Leonard Andrus designed in 1838 one of steel welded to wrought iron, then made one of all steel. It scoured so well it was called the singing plow.

This Deere plow has a steel share welded to a wrought-iron moldboard.

waterways, a means of bringing back-country produce and minerals to the ports of the rivers, canals, and Great Lakes. By the 1840's, however, men of vision believed that railroads would eventually become the nation's most important form of transportation. And although the West lacked the money to finance their construction, there appeared to be no lack of rich backers in New York, Boston, Philadelphia, and Baltimore, particularly after the government began to sweeten the pot in the 1850's by authorizing vast land grants to rail lines pushing westward. By 1860, Ohio alone boasted nearly 3,000 miles of track, making it America's premier railroading state. That same year, Chicago, with nearly a dozen lines converging on the city, had become the nation's unchallenged rail hub.

Rails Create New Export Centers

Wherever the railroads went, small towns grew into prosperous cities; wherever the railroads failed to go, prosperous cities lapsed into somnolence and decay. Newport, Wisconsin, for example, had once been a thriving lumber center, but after it was bypassed by the railroad, it declined into little more than a ghost town. Stacey Corners, Illinois, virtually committed suicide when the railroad bypassed it: its citizens departed en masse, moving not just their furniture but also their houses to Wheaton, which was near Chicago and on the rail line.

If the exact routes of the long-distance railroads were items of intense local concern, their general routes were matters of great national importance. To the South's undying chagrin, its entrepreneurs were slower than those in the North to grasp the potential of the rail-

roads and for years neglected to finance lines linking the upper Northwest with such coastal cities as Mobile, New Orleans, Savannah, and Charleston.

Thus, the trend established with the building of the Erie Canal, which helped divert the trade of the Old Northwest to New England and the Middle Atlantic states, waxed ever stronger. Just a few figures tell the story: in 1840 the Old Northwest still shipped 53 percent of its flour exports and 98 percent of its corn to the South; 13 years later these percentages were down to 28 percent and 37 percent respectively. Similarly, in 1840 New Orleans was the nation's leading port, but just 10 years later both New York and Philadelphia surpassed the lovely Louisiana city as export centers. With railroads stretching westward from New York, Baltimore, and Philadelphia to Cincinnati, Cleveland, Indianapolis, and Chicago, the Northeast

An artist's conception of the Erie & Kalamazoo Railroad shows only one passenger car—a small train even for the backwoods.

At a 76-foot shot tower in St. Louis, molten lead was poured through perforated plates at the top. It solidified into shot as it fell.

The McCormick reaper could cut up to 12 acres of wheat a day, while a strong man could cut only 2 acres by hand at best. Later models automatically bundled and tied the grain.

The mechanical thresher, developed in the 1830's, did away with one of the most laborious jobs on the farm. Horses on a treadmill power this Case thresher; later, portable steam engines replaced the horse.

and Old Northwest had become literally bound together with bands of steel.

The men who financed the railroads were neither ideologists seeking to isolate the South nor visionaries investing millions of dollars against some distant day when their lines might make profits. They were hardheaded businessmen who recognized a solid investment when they saw one. For it was a fact that a revolution was in progress on the farms of the Old Northwest in the 1840's and 1850's, particularly on the broad prairies along its northern rim.

A Spurt of Farm Production

Unprecedented farm surpluses, which were desperately needed in the industrialized New England states and in western Europe, were being produced. By 1850, when the average American consumed 25 bushels of corn per year, the farms of the Old Northwest were growing nearly 44.2 bushels for each resident of the region. Just the cost of hauling this grain virtually guaranteed a profit to the railroads with terminuses located at major eastern ports. What made this gigantic spurt in agricultural production possible was a series of technological innovations that brought the broad prairies under cultivation and extended the practical limits of the family farm from a relatively small forest clearing to scores of acres.

This agricultural revolution was born with the invention of a new plow devised by a Vermont-born farm boy named John Deere. In 1838, after moving to Grand Detour, Illinois, he perfected a self-polishing, steel-bladed plow capable of turning the loamy but root-matted prairie soil, and that same year he established a small workshop in which to manufacture it. Two decades later, demand for Deere's plow had grown so great that his thriving factory in Moline, Illinois, was turning out 10,000 a year.

(It was this plow that helped build the American steel industry, which was hard put to keep up with Deere's orders.)

While John Deere was still servicing a local clientele in the 1840's, another innovator, Cyrus McCormick of Virginia, was perfecting his mechanical reaper. This rotating, multibladed contraption on wheels, pulled by a team of horses, was capable of cutting an acre of wheat faster than a score of men armed with scythes. To produce his laborsaving device, McCormick established factories in Cincinnati and later in Chicago, from which thousands of these machines would pour forth. These inventions and others—the mechanical mower, the horse-powered thresher, and the grain binder—combined to make the great agricultural surpluses of the Old Northwest possible. At the same time, their manufacture brought booming industry and astounding economic

and population growth to the cities of the region.

But it was not just agricultural implements and railroading that created the cities of the Old Northwest. The discovery of mineral ores and their conversion into useful metals also brought great prosperity to Cleveland. Midway between the coalfields of western Virginia and the iron deposits of Michigan and strategically located on the shores of Lake Erie, it grew into a major steel-producing city before the Civil War. Detroit, which had a large community of European craftsmen, became a city of ironworkers and carriagemakers whose skilled labor prepared the way for the fabulous rise of the automotive industry. By the time the Civil War began, the ax, the hoe, and the rifle were joined by the locomotive, the reaper, and the factory smokestack as symbols of the Old Northwest.

By 1860 rails outranked canals. The Midwest had the most trackage and trunklines to the Northeast. Thus the main western trade was with the East and no longer with the South.

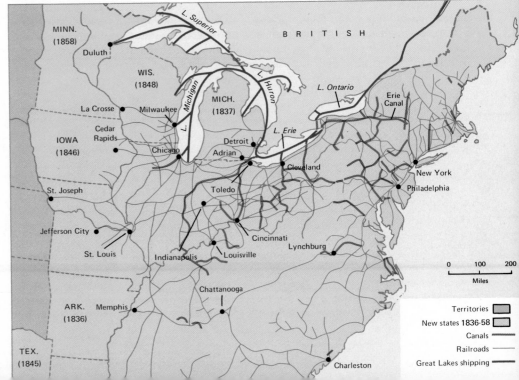

Life in Western Cities

The imposing St. Louis courthouse, built in 1847, served both as a rallying point for mass meetings and as a temple of justice.

Mrs. Frances Trollope, whose book *Domestic Manners of the Americans* set a standard for acerbic wit that few writers could match, considered the cities of the American West in general, and Cincinnati in particular, to be among the Almighty's lesser creations. An Englishwoman of studied refinement, she bemoaned the fate that had decreed her sojourn in the late 1820's in the Ohio community that many residents proudly called the Queen City. But even Mrs. Trollope could not fail to be impressed by the energy of its citizens, at least in their pursuit of wealth. "During nearly two years that I resided in Cincinnati,"

she wrote, ". . . I neither saw a beggar, nor a man of sufficient fortune to permit his ceasing his efforts to increase it; thus every bee in the hive is actively employed in search of that honey . . . vulgarly called money; neither art, science, learning, nor pleasure, can seduce them from its pursuit."

A Time of Soaring Growth

Even allowing for Mrs. Trollope's penchant for venomous exaggeration, the redoubtable lady had hit upon the primary allure of the cities of the West —the almost limitless opportunity to make money. For communities like Cincinnati, Cleveland, Chicago, Milwaukee, St. Louis, and Detroit, opportunity and growth were practically synonymous, and civic leaders in each of these towns vied fiercely with their opposite numbers in other communities to attract immigrants and the trade and the industries they would spawn. No strategy was too raw, no plot too low, in the effort to build one's own community and hinder the growth of rivals. During the 1840's the tiny town of Milwaukee, for example, actually sent out onto Lake Michigan touts whose aim was to divert to its shores shiploads of Chicago-bound immigrants by telling hair-raising tales of epidemics, vice, and crime in the Illinois city.

Since nearly all of the new cities engaged in dirty tricks of one sort or another to swell their populations, it is likely that the net effect of such efforts was minimal. But more important, of course, was the geographic location of a city. If it adjoined a primary artery of trade, as did Buffalo at the terminus of the Erie Canal, or if it lay between two of the Great Lakes, as did Detroit, growth

and prosperity were assured. If, in addition, geographical advantages were combined with shrewd promotional campaigns and legislative muscle to attract railroads, as was preeminently the case with Chicago, there was practically no limit to what might be achieved.

In 1845 the editor of the Milwaukee *Daily Sentinel* summed up popular feeling when he wrote: "The tide of emigration to the West seems to increase daily. . . . What an enterprising spirit characterizes the American people. . . . In no other country have towns and villages sprung up so suddenly as in this. Everything seems to go ahead with railroad velocity. . . . Cities grow up here to more importance in ten years than they do in Europe in a century." For proof the editor needed only to point to his own city. In 1840 Milwaukee had a mere 1,712 residents, but within a decade it would boast more than 20,000. In the same period Cleveland grew from 6,071 to 17,034, Detroit from 9,012 to 21,019, and Chicago from 4,470 to 29,963—and that was only the beginning. By 1870 Chicago's population stood at nearly 300,000, and it was well on its way to becoming the nation's second largest city and its leading transportation and meatpacking center.

Civic Affairs

Although the "railroad velocity" growth of western cities meant prosperity, it also brought previously undreamed-of burdens for which local governments were not prepared. In spirit most of the cities of mid-America remained frontier communities long after the frontier had moved far to the west. Self-help and self-protection were much-prized virtues, while large-scale

In 1820 Milwaukee consisted of a fur trader's log cabin surrounded by Indian tepees. Thirty-three years later it had grown into a prosperous port with broad avenues, diversified industries, and a short railroad. There were also musical societies and a public library.

"Queen City" of the West

Cincinnati in the 1850's possessed not only industries, including pork packing (more than 25 percent of the U.S. production), but had also become a center of commerce, finance, the arts, and education, with colleges, a law and a medical school.

The city's fire engines send competing jets of water skyward to honor the grand opening of the Ohio and Mississippi Railroad.

Steamboats throng the busy waterfront of Cincinnati. From its earliest days it was one of the leading ports for Ohio River traffic.

Droves of pigs on their way to slaughter clogged—and scavenged—the streets of Cincinnati, which was called Porkopolis.

government with its rules and regulations and its bureaucracy was scorned. In keeping with democratic tradition, mayors were often figureheads while unwieldy city councils—in some cases elected every year—brawled over budgets, expenditures, and construction contracts. Funds for municipal projects often depended more on subscriptions from wealthy merchants anxious to attract new business than upon the tax rolls, and in some cities roads were built and maintained by annual drafts of all able-bodied male citizens. All in all, there was a charming air of amateurism about the governing of western cities. But the charm could pall quickly when a citizen was set upon by thugs because of the lack of a professional police force, or when his building burned to the ground while rival volunteer fire companies came to blows over the honor of putting out the blaze, or when he died of cholera because of the absence of even a primitive sanitation code.

By the mid-1850's health and safety conditions in most cities had become so bad that the need for the professionalization of city services was generally acknowledged. Cincinnati, perhaps the most sophisticated of the western cities, led the way. Its volunteer fire department had become infested with political and individual corruption. One outraged observer wrote: "The engine houses became places of resort of evenings . . . not only of a large share of the members, but of their acquaintances, and every species of immorality was the consequences." In 1853 the city dissolved the volunteer companies, replacing them with the West's first professional fire department, much to the benefit of the city's residents.

Cincinnati's initiative seemed to break the logjam of resistance to professional services in other communities. In a few years paid fire departments were common, and professional police replaced the volunteer watchmen who had sometimes acted as little more than vigilante committees. Slowly, in the cities of the West, the rawest qualities of frontier life were being sanded down and covered with a veneer of calm, culture, and eminent respectability.

Land Boom in Chicago

'Tis very droll to hear the comic stories of the rising values here, which, ludicrous though they seem, are justified by facts presently. Mr. Corwin's story of land offered for $50,000, and an hour given to consider it. The buyer made up his mind to take it, but he could not have it; it was five minutes past the hour, and it was now worth $60,000. After dinner, he resolved to give the price, but he had over-stayed the time again, and it was already $70,000; and it became $80,000, before night—when he bought it. I believe it was Mr. Corwin's joke, but the solemn citizens who stood by, heard it approvingly, and said, "Yes, that is about the fair growth of Chicago *per hour*." However, a quite parallel case to this, I am told, actually occurred in the sale of the "American House" lot, which rose in a day from perhaps $40,000 to 50, 60, 70, 80, or 90,000.

—Ralph Waldo Emerson
Journals, 1857

Education and the Arts Come to the West

During the early years of settlement in the trans-Appalachian West education was a sometime thing. Most frontier children were more than happy to make do with occasional lessons from itinerant teachers. "Schools in this part of the country," wrote Zerah Hawley, a New Englander visiting Ohio in 1821, "are necessarily very indifferent. Young men and women, in many cases, can read and write, but very badly." This dolorous situation would soon change, particularly in the northern parts of the region, where migrating New Englanders, with their long tradition of scholarship, were settling in large numbers. In his letters to his fellow New Englanders, Zerah Hawley appealed to their Puritan consciences. "Missionaries," he wrote, "are . . . almost as much needed here as in the Islands of the Seas. . . . [It is] an *urgent necessity*, to send . . . well-instructed teachers." Hawley's call, and the pleas of others like him, found a ready response among New England's Congregational and Presbyterian elite, for whom the most worthy expression of the Word of God was man's pursuit of knowledge. By the late 1820's New England's missionary-educators were tramping through the West, and if they found only a few converts to their high-minded principles among camp-meeting audi-

In this 1839 engraving the chapel bell tower dominates the campus of Oberlin, the college that pioneered in higher education for women and Negroes. Caroline Rudd (right) was one of the first women to get a degree in the United States (1841). The first black woman, Mary Jane Patterson (far right), graduated in 1862. At first females were not allowed to study Latin or Greek, which were considered far too difficult for them.

ences, they did build as monuments to their zeal a host of colleges that would bring light into the darkness.

One of these was Oberlin Collegiate Institute (now Oberlin College), which opened its doors in Ohio in 1833. The nation's first college to admit women and the first to accept Negroes, Oberlin reflected the righteous attitudes of its New England Congregational founders in every way. Students—denied tobacco,

liquor, and most of the lesser pleasures —were expected to divide their time between scholarship and labor in the fields. Upon graduation they were urged to go out into the wilderness and build new schools while preaching God's message to the Indians, the Baptists, the Methodists, and others whose immortal souls they considered in peril. Countless grammar and secondary schools were started throughout the West by early graduates of Oberlin. Some of the colleges they helped found were Ripon in Wisconsin, Carleton in Minnesota, and Hillsdale in Michigan—a network of institutions that helped reinforce the New England atmosphere of the Great Lakes district.

An Emerging Middle West

From the lecterns of Oberlin and its sister schools came ringing denunciations of slavery, and by the 1850's graduates, students, and teachers alike had become very active participants in the Underground Railroad, shepherding scores of fugitive slaves to freedom. When the Civil War finally came, an Oberlin clergyman characteristically urged that the Southern Confederacy be destroyed by massing thousands of the righteous along the Mason-Dixon Line to pray for Dixie's salvation.

The New England conscience and New England morality were not welcome everywhere on the frontier. In the Gulf states, of course, antislavery sentiments were considered close to treason, while in slaveholding Missouri, and

McGuffey's Readers, Schoolmasters to the Nation

These down-to-earth little books were a true product of the pioneer Midwest. The author, Pennsylvania-born William Holmes McGuffey (1800–73), grew up on an Ohio farm. A leading educator, he was a college professor at 25, a college president at 36, and played a major part in establishing public schools in Ohio. McGuffey, who was a licensed Presbyterian preacher as well, liked to claim later in life that he had preached 3,000 sermons, all without notes.

McGuffey's Readers, which first appeared in 1836, combined reading instruction with varied facts, poems, stories, and drawings. They also taught such basic virtues as honesty, thrift, kindness, and industry. An instant success, the series eventually sold more than 120 million copies and was used in 37 states. In 1857 a high school Reader was also published. The influence of the books was greatest in the Midwest, whose values they molded—and mirrored as well.

A page from a McGuffey primer. There were six editions of the books.

even in the southern reaches of Illinois, Indiana, and Ohio, many of the stern preachments of transplanted New Englanders were anathema. As for the cities, where commerce was king, the Oberlin view of life was merely irrelevant. There were just too many other things to concentrate on to leave much time for theological speculation. By the 1840's and 1850's merchant princes were taking the time to enjoy their fortunes with displays of conspicuous consumption.

A New American Elite

Every city had its millionaires' row of sturdy mansions, some of which even boasted such newfangled luxuries as central heating. One such was the Amasa Stone residence on Cleveland's Euclid Street, which an admiring reporter in *The Cleveland Leader* described in 1858: "The ceilings of the parlor and library are of recess, panel, and cornice work, and have a most handsome effect. The staircase . . . is finished in mahogony . . . parlor, reception room, and library are finished with rose wood."

Such were the homes of a new American elite. Here these men and their wives planned for the transformation of their raw cities into major cultural centers, with concert halls, opera houses, theaters, and restaurants that would adequately reflect their wealth and social standing. By the time Jenny Lind, the world-renowned Swedish Nightingale, made her American tour in the early 1850's, the cities of the West were ready to receive her. Overflow audiences packed into auditoriums where, in the weeks before, opera troupes, symphony orchestras, and touring theatrical companies had played.

The simple fact was that the trans-Appalachian frontier was rapidly coming of age. Writing in 1853, newspaperman Jesup W. Scott reflected: "The West is no longer the West. . . . It is the great center. It is the body of the American eagle, whose wings are on the two oceans." However, if the old frontier was closing down, new ones were opening. For farther to the west lay half a continent, much of it already in the first stages of exploitation.

Edwin Booth and other famous actors graced Wood's Theater in Cincinnati. Programs ranged from classic drama to farce.

Ceramic figures of Jenny Lind sold by the thousands, mute testimony to the Swedish Nightingale's popularity. Jenny Lind captured American hearts by her modesty, sweet nature, and generosity—she gave innumerable benefit concerts for local charities without a fee. Capitalizing on her popularity, her astute promoter, P. T. Barnum, created a veritable Jenny Lind craze. Local merchants happily cashed in by selling to her admirers "Jenny Lind" hats, gloves, gowns, and a wild profusion of knickknacks including decorated plates and dolls.

Ladies of Leisure in Chicago

Fashionable matrons exchange gossip and local social notes over coffee.

I have gained twelve pounds in six weeks, and my weight is now 116 pounds, *just think of it!* . . . I am almost to the end of my plain sewing. I have my cloak to make and then I shall go at my quilt, and that is all I expect to do this winter. I mean to go out and enjoy myself, study French, etc. I have a great many plans laid out for the winter. I have just got an extract book to try to improve myself in writing and I shall practice on my guitar all I can. The piano is sold.

—Letter to a friend from Mrs. Walter Burley Chicago, 1845

Luxurious emporiums like Nathaniel Phillips' Piano, Music, and Military Goods Store in St. Louis catered to wealthy, discriminating men and women in their search for culture.

This was the way to live, free and easy, with time all a man's own and none to say no to him. A body got so's he felt everything was kin to him, the earth and sky and buffalo and beaver and the yellow moon at night. It was better than being walled in by a house, better than breathing in spoiled air and feeling caged like a varmint.

—A. B. Guthrie, Jr., The Big Sky

Of Mountain Men and

"Breakfast at Sunrise." Watercolor by Alfred Jacob Miller.

Chapter 3

Indians

Long before the lands of the Louisiana Purchase were settled, the lure of the lucrative fur trade drew trappers to the wild Rockies and beyond. Loving the wilderness and shunning the life of town or farm, these hardy hunters were known as mountain men. On the trek across the Great Plains to reach the beaver streams, they met a new kind of Indian: fiercely proud mounted nomads with a culture based on buffalo hunting and devoted to warfare. To survive, the mountain men learned Indian ways, often equaling the red men in skill and toughness. Though their days of glory lasted little more than two decades, these ruggedly individualistic trappers left a permanent mark on the history and legendry of the West.

By 1812 British trading posts dotted western Canada, and the two titans of the fur trade—the North West Company and the Hudson's Bay Company—were battling for control of the fur-rich Oregon Country to the south. An American interloper, John Jacob Astor, helped establish a future American claim to the region through the activities of his Pacific Fur Company.

The Race for Furs

This melodramatic 19th-century print shows Astor's trading ship *Tonquin* crossing the bar into the mouth of the Columbia River; a longboat full of crewmen founders.

As the forests of the Old Northwest yielded to the pioneer's ax, a few men restlessly cast their eyes far beyond the edge of settlement to the Rocky Mountains and the Pacific Coast. Neither gold nor land whetted their appetites. Instead, the focus of their dreams was a small furry animal noted for its dam-building propensities. This was, of course, the beaver, and there was a time when the rivers of the continent swarmed with them. Unfortunately for this engaging creature, its smooth fur was prized by fashion-conscious gentlemen both in Europe and in America. To obtain beaver pelts—"hairy bank notes," as they would soon be called—Frenchmen, Spaniards, Englishmen, Scotsmen, Indians, and finally Americans participated in an epic animal slaughter. A fierce no-holds-barred competition sprang up among rival companies, Indian tribes, and freelance trappers for control of the beaver country.

The first to exploit North America for its wealth of peltry were the French of 17th- and 18th-century Canada. However, Britain's victory over France in 1763 gave the British a monopoly of the American fur trade, and during the next decades the Hudson's Bay Company and independent traders extended the trade across the continent into the Rockies' northern ranges. By 1787 the independents, organized as the North West Company, were challenging Hudson's Bay's supremacy, leapfrogging over the latter's domains to establish posts in what is now west-central Canada and eventually on the Pacific Coast.

Traders of the new group explored virgin territories and cemented their own ties with Indian tribes. Inevitably, the two British concerns clashed. Avarice for monopoly led each to engage in bribery, thievery, arson, and murder, as Indian tribe was set against Indian tribe for the benefit of the rival companies. At length the stench of death and scandal reached all the way to London, and in 1821 the British government forced the two competitors to merge into a single, enlarged Hudson's Bay Company.

Enter John Jacob Astor

By then Britain had a new rival to cope with in the fur trade. Westering Americans had begun to penetrate the Rockies in their search for pelts. An augury of intense American competition in regions the British considered their own had come in 1810. The New York merchant John Jacob Astor, whose American Fur Company was already dominant in the Great Lakes region, organized a subsidiary, the Pacific Fur Company, to challenge the North West Company on its home grounds. Astor's plan was to build a large trading post, Astoria, near the mouth of the Columbia River in the Oregon Country. There furs would be collected from subsidiary posts in the interior and loaded on company ships for direct delivery to China, which had become a rich market for American sea otter pelts.

Astor moved quickly. In September 1810 he dispatched the ship *Tonquin*, under a crusty New England captain named Jonathan Thorn, around Cape Horn. Aboard were four Astor partners and 29 employees, charged with building Astoria and opening the fur trade to the company. Meanwhile, a second party was gathering at St. Louis to journey overland to Astoria. Unfortunately, Astor's scheme began to unravel almost from the start.

Dissension on the Tonquin

The *Tonquin* was hardly out of port before dissension between the captain and the partners began—Thorn was an overstrict disciplinarian, and one of the partners muttered threats on the captain's life. Upon arriving at the mouth of the Columbia in March 1811, Thorn was so eager to rid himself of his passengers that he dispatched a longboat in stormy seas to sound out a channel. The small craft foundered and sank, drowning all aboard. Only with the greatest difficulty did the *Tonquin* reach safe harbor two days later. On April 12, 1811, Astor's small party began the task of building Astoria.

While the remaining party completed the fort, the *Tonquin*, their chief link

German-born John Jacob Astor migrated to England at the age of 17, then to America, where he grew so wealthy that he was able to lend money to the federal government.

Fort Astoria, on the Columbia, was the hub of Astor's ill-starred Pacific fur empire.

with the outside world, engaged in brisk trading with the coastal tribes of the Northwest. At first all went well. But one day Thorn, quick-tempered as ever, slapped a chief across the face.

Overland to Astoria

The Indians' revenge for this insult was swift. They swarmed all over the ship, belaboring their hosts with clubs and dispatching them with knives. Only five whites survived the massacre by barricading themselves in a cabin, and four of these were later captured and tortured to death when they made for shore under cover of darkness. The fifth, who remained aboard ship, escaped detection. The following day, when the Indians returned to the ship for a round of looting, the sailor fired the ship's powder supply, blasting himself and the marauders to kingdom come.

The loss of the *Tonquin* proved a portent of more trouble ahead. The overland party of Astorians, under wilderness neophyte Wilson Price Hunt, had left St. Louis in early 1811 to follow the Lewis and Clark route west. But, fearing attack by the Blackfoot Indians, they took long detours and, when they reached the Snake River, then made the mistake of giving up their horses and taking to the river in canoes. After two days the Snake grew unnavigable, and four men drowned. The party separated into small groups to travel on foot. All came close to starvation, and one man went mad. Finally, in the winter of 1812, the survivors staggered into Astoria, but by June of that year war with Britain had broken out. Anticipating a British naval attack, the Astorians had little choice but to accept an offer for their holdings in 1813 (at only a fraction of their worth) from the North West Company. Thus the first American effort to outflank the British in the Pacific Northwest was a failure in all but one sense: the establishment of Astoria strengthened U.S. claims to the Oregon Country—claims that would be successfully pressed in years to come.

Fur and Mr. Astor

[En route from London to Baltimore in 1783-84] Mr. Astor became acquainted with a countryman of his, a furrier by trade . . . . He made many inquiries of his new acquaintance on the subject [of fur], who cheerfully gave him all the information in his power as to the quality and value of different furs, and the mode of carrying on the traffic. He subsequently accompanied him to New York, and, by his advice, Mr. Astor was induced to invest the proceeds of his merchandise [purchased in London with his small life savings] in furs. With these he sailed from New York to London in 1784, disposed of them advantageously, made himself . . . acquainted with the . . . trade, and returned the same year to New York . . . [to devote] himself to the branch of commerce with which he had thus casually been made acquainted.

—Washington Irving, *Astoria*, 1836

The Big-Toothed Prize That Helped Open Up America

The treasure that lured eastern adventurers northwest in the early 1800's was a thickset, placid, industrious rodent, *Castor canadensis*, whose glossy tan-to-dark-brown underfur has a natural tendency to mat, or "felt." This oily coat is waterproof, for the beaver lives along streams and lakes, eating water plants and willows, aspen and alders. When alarmed, it slaps the water with its flat tail. With oversize lungs and fleshy valves that keep water out of its ears and nostrils, it can swim underwater for 10 minutes. Its tail acts as a rudder, and its webbed hind feet propel it at two miles per hour. A sociable, mostly monogamous mammal, it constructs a dome-shaped, mud-covered aquatic lodge of interlaced branches that provides a nest for its family. This unique home has two or three underwater basement exits. They open below the ice in winter, the beaver's breeding season, allowing *Castor* to gnaw on a food supply of timber stored outside its door. To maintain an even water level for the lodge, the rodent dams its lake with stones, mud, and trees that it fells and then tows along canals it has dug from the pond to outlying groves. Its long incisors can topple a five-inch-thick tree in three minutes.

John J. Audubon depicted the beaver's scaly tail, dexterous forepaws, sharp yellow teeth, and tiny eyes that see well underwater. An adult beaver may weigh more than 60 pounds.

Lady's jockey helmet | Quaker hat | Paris beau | Stovepipe | Bicorn | Tricorn

From tricorn to topper, the stylish beaver felt hats shown above were in such demand that hatters bought 100,000 pelts each year. Discarding the long, coarse guard hairs, the hatter shaved the soft underfur from the skin, then twanged the string of a huge bow through it. The vibration of the string made the hairs hook together. The matted pile was flattened, covered with wet linen, and kneaded into a conical hood that was shrunk and thickened by being boiled, treated with acid, and beaten. While hot, the felt was molded into the desired shape over a wooden block, then dried and ironed; its nap was raised with a wire paddle.

Rocky Mountain Beginnings

Even before Mr. Astor's ill-fated venture into the Pacific Northwest, other Americans had been trapping in the Rocky Mountain region. The first were encountered in August 1806 as the Lewis and Clark expedition made its way eastward toward what would be a triumphant homecoming. The explorers were near the mouth of the Yellowstone River, some 1,500 miles from St. Louis, when they were astonished to come upon two shabby fellow Americans who had been trapping beavers. The trappers made camp with the soldiers and suggested that perhaps one of the explorers might like to join them in their hunt. Pvt. John Colter of Virginia requested his commanders' permission to do so.

That fall Colter and his new associates worked along the Yellowstone River. In the winter they took shelter in a Rocky Mountain valley, but by spring Colter's two companions had endured all they could of wilderness life and made haste back to civilization. Colter, however, stayed on to trap, hunt, and hone his woodsman's skills.

Manuel Lisa, Entrepreneur

In June of 1807 Colter was on his way to St. Louis to sell his catch when he met a swarthy entrepreneur named Manuel Lisa. A St. Louis businessman and promoter of grandiose schemes, Lisa was the kind of man who aroused strong feelings. One employee described him this way: "Rascality sat on every feature of his dark-complexioned, Mexican face." Meriwether Lewis, whose expedition Lisa and a partner named Benoit had helped outfit, was driven to write in exasperation: "Damn Manuel and triply damn Mr. B. . . . They give me more vexation . . . than their lives are worth."

Yet some saw in Lisa a kind of genius, and one contemporary referred to him as "a man of bold and daring character, with an energy and spirit of enterprise like that of Cortez or Pizarro." Friend and foe alike agreed on one point—that Manuel Lisa could sniff out the possibility of profit from a distance of a thousand miles. It was profit that had led him in 1807 to load a party of some 50 frontiersmen onto two keelboats and move up the Missouri toward the Far West.

Exactly what arguments Lisa used to turn John Colter around are not known, but the Virginian agreed to join Lisa's outfit as a guide. On Colter's advice, the party halted at the confluence of the Yellowstone and Bighorn Rivers to build a fort, and from there Lisa sent out his men to trap beavers and entice the Indians into trading arrangements. Colter was sent out to find new trapping coun-

Conflict With the Hudson's Bay Company

As American trappers and traders ventured into the Rockies, they ran into stiff opposition from far-ranging agents of the Hudson's Bay Company. Since it was chartered by the British Crown in 1670, the "Honourable Company," as the giant organization was often called, had gradually built a tightly organized fur-trade network across most of Canada. By absorbing its bitter rival, the North West Company, it acquired additional territory in the far Northwest in 1821.

The governor of the merged fur companies, George Simpson, was a pompous, penny-pinching martinet, but also an exceptionally able, if ruthless, administrator—and a determined opponent of American expansion. To discourage American entry into Hudson's Bay trapping grounds, Simpson instructed his agents to range as far west and south as possible and to trap the beavers to extinction. In this way he planned to create a buffer zone that would be worthless to American fur seekers.

The men of his Snake River brigades, under the leadership of Peter Skene Ogden, pushed into what is now Montana, Utah, Nevada, Idaho, Washington, and Oregon, and even reached California. They competed with Americans for furs and Indian friendship and incidentally contributed greatly to the knowledge of the geography of the West. But when the beavers were trapped out of the Rockies and the Oregon Country, the company lost interest in the region (whose ownership was unsettled) and left it open to American settlers.

Governor Simpson liked to travel by birchbark canoe on his tours of inspection. He wore a top hat and frock coat as a sign of rank and took along a Scottish bagpiper to announce his arrival at a post.

A snowshoed Hudson's Bay Company agent has finished bargaining for furs with an Indian. The sturdy dogs will pull his laden sledge.

The Honourable Company's crest (left) includes moose and a fox and commemorates the beaver that made it prosper. High-quality goods, such as warm striped blankets, tools, metal cooking utensils, cloth, and sparkling jewelry, helped trade relations with the Indian trappers.

Hancock-Dickson route (1806)
Lisa's route (1807)
Colter's route (1807)

BRITISH

BLACKFEET

Henry's Fort
Yellowstone R.
MANDANS
ARIKARAS
CROWS
Ft. Manuel
Bighorn R.
Colter's Hell
Union Pass
N. Platte R.
Missouri R.
Continental Divide
Rocky Mountains
Great Salt Lake
SPANISH

UNITED STATES

0   300
Miles

From Fort Manuel, Lisa's men secured the loyalty of the regional Indian tribes, except the Blackfeet, and opened the upper Missouri. Between the Bighorn and Yellowstone Rivers, Colter discovered odorous tarpits and thermal springs—Colter's Hell. Hancock and Dickson were two mountain men encountered by Meriwether Lewis.

try and to reach agreements with distant tribes, especially the Blackfeet, against the day when Lisa would spread out into new territories.

In the winter of 1807–08 Colter began his solitary odyssey on foot. His route took him through much of present-day Wyoming, Montana, and Idaho. He crossed the Continental Divide at Union Pass and became one of the first whites to gaze upon the wonders of what is now Yellowstone National Park.

Escape From the Blackfeet

While in the Wyoming country, Colter came upon steaming geysers and bubbling caldrons of mud. His tales of these marvels would later mark him as a madman; his stories were dismissed as figments of a deranged imagination and his discovery mocked as "Colter's Hell."

Without knowing it, and certainly with no intention of establishing a way of life, John Colter had become the prototypical mountain man. His ability to survive alone in the wilderness, to slay his own game, to trap his own beavers, to make his own clothes, to endure months

Manuel Lisa, Pioneer Fur Trader of the West

Mounted on an Indian pony, Manuel Lisa watches his men construct a log fort at a strategic point on the Yellowstone River, near the edge of the beaver-rich Rockies.

Manuel Lisa's great hunger for profit helped open up the fur-rich region of the upper Missouri watershed. From the chain of forts and trading posts he built along the Missouri and its tributaries his men fanned out to collect information on fur sources, to map the country, and to establish trade connections with the Indians. Lisa also had his own trappers working on contract. Ruthless, unprincipled, and violent, he was hated by his competitors and by his own men, on whom it was said he dared not turn his back. Yet he skillfully managed the Indians by showing a willingness to fight or to proffer gifts in return for friendship. In the War of 1812 he served as U.S. agent for the upper Missouri tribes and kept them on the American side.

of extreme heat or cold, and to match the Indians in stealth, prowess, and bravery became legendary and encouraged many others to follow in his footsteps.

At least twice, Colter's escapes from death were almost miraculous. In the fall of 1808 he was captured by the ever-hostile Blackfeet, stripped of his clothes, and told to run for his life while a score

of braves pursued him. Normally swift, he now ran with a speed born of desperation, ignoring the burrs and stones that tore at his naked feet as he dashed for a river some six miles distant. At one point a brave overtook him, but by wheeling suddenly Colter threw his pursuer off balance and swiftly killed the Indian with his own spear. Finally he reached the river, dove in, and hid for hours under some flotsam. After dark he made his way back to Lisa's fort.

A year and a half later, Colter again escaped death from Blackfeet warriors, though five of his companions did not. At last he had had enough and vowed: "If God will only . . . let me off I will leave the country day after tomorrow—and be damned if I ever come into it again." As good as his word, he returned immediately to St. Louis, where he died impoverished in 1813.

Meriwether Lewis Meets Two Mountain Men

August 12, 1806. At 8 a.m. the bowsman informed me that there was a canoe and a camp he beleived of whitemen on the N.E. shore. I . . . found it to be the camp of two hunters from the Illinois by name Joseph Dickson and Forest Hancock. these men informed me that . . . they had left the Illinois in the summer [of] 1804 since which time they had been ascended the Missouri, hunting and traping beaver. . . . I gave them a short discription of the Missouri . . . and pointed out to them the places where the beaver most abounded. I also gave them a file and a couple of pounds of powder and some lead.

—Expedition Diaries of Lewis and Clark

The Heyday of the Mountain Men

Even without John Colter to guide him, Manuel Lisa did well with his Missouri Fur Company, and when he died in 1820—of natural causes, to everyone's surprise—he was accounted a man of respectability and wealth. Yet Lisa's success would prove modest compared with that of two fellow St. Louisans, William Henry Ashley and Andrew Henry, a former partner of Lisa's.

The Rocky Mountain Trade

Ashley and Henry began operations conventionally enough, advertising in 1822 in local newspapers for "enterprising young men" willing to ascend the Missouri River to its source. Among the recruits there were many whose names would become synonymous with western exploration and feats of daring or villainy—men like Jim Bridger, James Clyman, William and Milton Sublette, Edward Rose, Hugh Glass, Thomas Fitzpatrick, Jim Beckwourth, and the most famous of all, Jedediah Strong Smith. Some, like Smith and Fitzpatrick, were reasonably well educated; others, like Bridger, were illiterate, and the half-black, half-Cherokee Rose had been a Mississippi River pirate. But whatever their backgrounds, all were Jacksonian Americans incarnate, true believers in the power of the individual to alter his condition, to rise from poverty to wealth by his own exertions. Many among them would prove out this faith and end their lives as bankers, merchants, Indian agents, or great wilderness guides.

In 1822 Ashley's and Henry's men moved up the Missouri by boat to build

Arrows show the first trails mountain men blazed into beaver country. The years indicate when each rendezvous site was used.

a fort and trading post. The next year, however, several of Ashley's men were attacked while on shore by Arikara Indians, and Ashley, who had decided that the river route west was too dangerous, hit upon a new method of tapping the beaver country. He would send his men overland in small groups, staking them to a year's provisions in exchange for a portion of their catch, which he would collect at a yearly rendezvous in the wild. Once in the mountains, the men, instead of trading with the Indians, would trap on their own, living off the land, seeking out fresh beaver country, and dealing with the natives as best they could. Henry retired in 1824, but Ashley continued to rendezvous with the trappers at some predesignated spot for several more summers. There he collected the pelts and reprovisioned the men, exchanging the necessities of life and the trinkets of civilization for the year's catch. Thus was born the freelance white

Jim Bridger: Trapper, Trader, Explorer, Scout

Jim Bridger (1804–81) was the epitome of the hardy mountain man. As a child he went from Virginia to the frontier metropolis of St. Louis with his family and at 13 was apprenticed to a blacksmith. At 19 he became a member of William Henry Ashley's first expedition to the Rockies. A quick learner, the tall, keen-eyed youth soon became expert in wilderness craft and Indian ways. Although he later gained renown as an Indian fighter, Bridger always tried to get along with Indians. He had three Indian wives, each from a different tribe and each died young.

"Old Gabe," as Bridger's friends called him, was notorious for his tall tales, but many of his wild yarns described real exploits. Once he floated down the rapids-filled Bear River in a skin boat to settle a bet on the river's direction of flow; he ended in Great Salt Lake—probably the first white man to see it. The saltiness of the water is said to have convinced him that he had reached the Pacific. The maps Bridger drew, based on his own observations, were among the most accurate of the period. Although illiterate, he spoke French, Spanish, and several Indian tongues.

Bridger roamed the Rockies as a trapper, trader, and eventually as part owner of a fur company. In 1843 he built a fort on the Oregon Trail, where he sold supplies, did repair work, and gave advice to the trail-weary immigrants. The business flourished for 10 years until a raid by some Mormon vigilantes destroyed the fort. The old mountain man moved his half-Indian family to the safety of a Missouri farm and returned to the West as a guide. He served as a scout for the U.S. Army in the "Mormon War," guided mapping expeditions throughout the West, and in 1866 marked the 967-mile Bozeman Trail from Nebraska to the gold mines of Montana. Disabled by arthritis and failing eyesight, he retired in 1867. By then, the coming of railroads heralded the end of the West he so dearly loved.

Many a restless young man succumbed to Ashley's promises of adventure and more money than could be made as a farmhand.

Alfred Jacob Miller, who spent about six months among the mountain men, made this painting of a group of them shooting elks for their food.

Miller caught two youthful trappers in a rare moment of rest between the chores of trapping and preparing beaver furs.

trapper who gloried in the name of "mountain man." And the rendezvous became an eagerly anticipated wilderness fair where businessmen traded goods for pelts against a riotous background of drunkenness, high-stakes gambling, contests of strength, and a general atmosphere of mayhem.

Life in the Wilds

For Ashley this system worked so well that after the 1826 rendezvous he was able to retire, selling out to Jed Smith and two other commercially minded mountain men. Four years later Smith and his associates followed suit. Tom Fitzpatrick, Jim Bridger, Milton Sublette, and two additional partners then became the proprietors of the trading corporation, which they dubbed the Rocky Mountain Fur Company.

The men from whom the company bought beaver pelts were a hardy, self-sufficient lot. They had to be to live through the winter's subzero cold, to wade day in and day out during the spring and fall in icy mountain streams, to outwit and often outshoot hostile Indians, and even to survive the manic conviviality of the annual rendezvous.

Most of the year the typical mountain man lived either alone, in a small group, or among friendly Indians. Many a trapper, his skin tanned and hardened by wind and sun, appeared to be at least a close cousin to the red man. Dressed in elaborately decorated buckskins, he was

Ashley's Farewell

Mountaineers and friends! When I first came to the mountains, I came a poor man. You, by your indefatigable exertions, toils, and privations, have procured me an independent fortune. . . . For this, my friends, I feel myself under great obligations to you. . . . I shall always be proud to testify to the fidelity with which you have stood by me through all danger. . . . I now wash my hands of the toils of the Rocky Mountains. Farewell.
—James P. Beckwourth
The Life and Adventures of James P. Beckwourth, 1856

a figure of romance at a distance, but close up or downwind he radiated an overpowering stench.

Life in the mountains was too uncertain to encourage intense loyalties. Though small groups cooperated in searching out new beaver country and setting traps, the ultimate code of the trapper was each man for himself. He lived in an environment that imposed harsh decisions upon him. Thus two frightened trappers could leave apparently dying Hugh Glass alone on an isolated mountain trail, abandoning him without so much as a rifle for protection from animals or marauding Indians. At

rendezvous, besotted trappers fought deadly duels over trifling gambling disputes, the favors of a willing squaw, or even a harsh word.

Yet, at bottom, the average trapper was probably not too different from the typical American of his day—only his environment was different. In the lonely country of the high grass and arching mountains, where danger lurked on every side, the tendency toward extremes was understandable.

Even in his attitude toward food the mountain man was excessive. Buffalo provided him with the dishes he loved most; given his preference, he would rarely dine on anything else. A wilderness banquet might begin with a soup made from buffalo blood and bone marrow, followed by a main course of broiled buffalo ribs and raw buffalo liver. "If a man could always live on such 'didins' [fare]," rhapsodized one trapper, "he would *never* die."

To an easterner reading in the popular press of the trappers' feats, their lives must have seemed a fairytale of romance, adventure, and freedom. A more realistic appraisal was offered by writer Thomas J. Farnham, who lived among the mountain men for a time. "Habitual watchfulness," Farnham wrote, "destroys every frivolity of mind and action. . . . They ride and walk like men whose breasts have so long been exposed to the bullet and the arrow, that fear finds within them no resting place."

The Two Toughest Trailblazers

The only portrait of Jed Smith, the great pathfinder, shows him in unlikely garb.

Jed Smith and his men crossing the Mojave Desert in 1826. They were puzzled by their Bible-toting leader, and one of them decided: "Jed is half grizzly and half preacher."

Jedediah Strong Smith and Joseph Reddeford Walker, born less than a month apart, were brave men with the same mission in life—but there the likeness ends. Smith was a devout Yankee, who liked to sing Methodist hymns as he rode wilderness trails, and a clean-shaven stranger to all the "manly vices," up to and including willing women. Walker was a bearded bear of a man who wenched with abandon and turned hellion come rendezvous time. Smith spent nine years in a compulsive, single-minded probing of unknown lands—the greatest pathfinder of the West. During his far-ranging treks Smith lost at least two score of his men to overwhelming Indian assaults. But his powers of command, foresight, and knowledge of wilderness travel were such that he never lost a single man to starvation or thirst. The mountain men knew that Jed Smith rode a hard, dangerous trail, but they were always ready to follow him. Walker, in his 47-year career, was a trapper, trader, trailblazer, guide for J. C. Frémont's third

expedition (1845–46), adviser to wagon trains to California, cattle seller, and leader of gold prospecting parties. Even in death the two went their separate ways: Smith at 32, ambushed on the Santa Fe Trail; Walker at 78, abed in California. But if Jed Smith and Joe Walker stood poles apart as men, they stood as brothers in history, for it was their iron will that opened trails to the golden West.

Jedediah Strong Smith (1799–1831)

With a butcher's knife in his belt and a Bible in his bedroll, 23-year-old Jedediah Smith entered the Rocky Mountain fur trade in 1822 with the avowed intent "of becoming a first-rate hunter . . . of making myself thoroughly acquainted with the Indians . . . of tracing out the sources of the Columbia River . . . and of making the whole profitable to me." Wild dreams for a greenhorn, but as time would show, this pious son of New Hampshire Methodist stock was born to be a mountain man. At 25 he had survived an Arikara massacre, had been mauled by a grizzly but was back on the trail in 10 days, and had led a command exploring the Wind River and traveling through the South Pass, thus opening this mountain portal to later settlers bound for California and Oregon. At 26 he was the proud holder of what is possibly the single-season record for a beaver catch (668 pelts). And at 27 he was in partnership with trappers David Jackson and William Sublette. But the year was 1826, a time when the mountains swarmed with trappers and competition over the known beaver country stiffened. So the three made a fateful decision: Jackson and Sublette would trap the Snake River country to the north, and Smith would push south to find the fabled Buenaventura River, said to flow westward through mountains rich in beavers and to provide a water route to the coast.

For three more years Smith rummaged the wilderness—and though he found no Buenaventura, his epic treks (see

From their great villages—this one had 600 tepees—the Comanches roamed the Southwest. One band killed Jed Smith.

map) gave him a list of firsts unmatched by any western explorer: he was the first white man to travel overland from the Rocky Mountains to California; the first to cross the Great Salt Lake Desert; the first to cross the Sierra Nevada from west to east; the first to travel overland from southern California to the Pacific Northwest, thus arousing the interest of the U.S. government in California and the Oregon Country.

With these deeds behind him, Smith retired to St. Louis in 1830. But city life soon palled for this restless searcher; in 1831 he saddled up for Santa Fe—and rode to his death. "Yet was he modest," wrote an unknown eulogist, "a man whom none could approach without respect, or know without esteem. And though he fell under the spears of the savages, and his body has glutted the prairie wolf, and none can tell where his bones are bleaching, he must not be forgotten."

Joseph Reddeford Walker (1798–1876)

With his good looks and plumed slouch hat, Joe Walker was the romantic embodiment of the mountain man. And if his escapades with the ladies were legend, so was his knowledge of the West. For about 12 years he operated as a trader and trapper out of Independence, Missouri, and for a time rode herd on the lawless as sheriff of Jackson County. As field commander for U.S. Army Capt. Benjamin Bonneville, Walker came to the 1833 rendezvous to recruit men for an expedition to California. Walker's promises of waters rich in beaver, of wine, women, and song for all on the slopes of the Pacific brought him a rush of recruits, including Zenas Leonard, a clerk from St. Louis. Leonard noted in his journal: "Mr. Walker was a man well calculated to undertake a business of this kind. He was well hardened to the hardships of the wilderness—understood the character of the Indian very well—was kind and affable to his men, but at the same time at liberty to command without giving offense—and to explore unknown regions was his chief delight."

Walker's 1833 trail took him from Salt Lake down the Humboldt River and over the towering Sierras near Yosem-

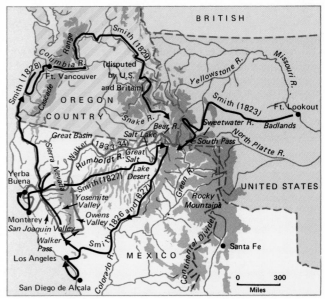

While seeking fresh beaver grounds, both Jed Smith and Joe Walker blazed new trails to California. Smith's routes in 1826 and 1827 (black) crossed perilous stretches of desert. Walker's safer trail in 1833–34 (red) followed the Humboldt River.

ite, where he saw some trees of the redwood species "incredibly large." Reaching the coast, Walker's men spent the winter carousing in Monterey, then turned homeward early in 1834 by way of the San Joaquin Valley, what came to be called Walker Pass, the Owens Valley, and back again to the Humboldt and Salt Lake. Walker's expedition found no rich beaver country, but it established his reputation as a pathfinder. Walker Pass provided an easy wagon-train trail around the south end of the Sierra Nevada; in 1869 the transcontinental railroad would follow his Humboldt River route.

When he arrived at the rendezvous of 1837, Joseph Walker brought his Indian bride along with him, and Alfred Jacob Miller was there to record the scene.

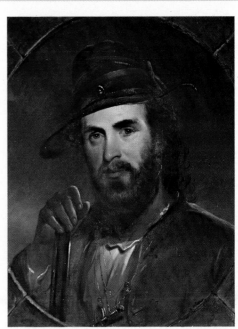

Joe Walker stood more than six feet tall and was a bit of a dandy for a mountain man.

The Trapper Takes a Wife

So rigorous was the mountain man's life that he often bought an Indian wife to help him, paying as much as two horses for her, or six pounds of beads, or, if she was a chief's daughter, perhaps $2,000 worth of furs. Such expense was borne best by the "free trapper," who owned his equipment and sold pelts wherever he chose, rather than by the "hired hand" trapper, who was given horses and traps by a company and paid fixed prices for his skins. The bride found such a match prestigious—from then on she rose high in her tribe's esteem. She also received gifts of jewelry, bangles, cloth, ribbon, and, equally important, "modern" utensils such as metal cooking pots. In exchange she made her man's clothes and tepee, cooked for him, gathered firewood, and cheered him during months of rugged isolation between the yearly rendezvous.

At dusk the suntanned trapper leads his packed mule home for dinner. Up since dawn, he has collected all beavers trapped overnight, skinned them, and cut off their tails for food and their castoreum glands for bait attractant. Then, having waded upstream for half a mile so the beavers will not smell him, he has reset six or eight of his $14 five-pound traps (below) underwater in the animals' runways. After a snack of jerky and nuts kept in his food sack, he has hunted game. Now he returns to his squaw, famished—he can eat eight pounds of buffalo a day and at times suffers intestinally from too much fatty meat, fried strips of buffalo fat being a favorite delicacy.

The mule carries a deer carcass, beaver pelts, tails, and glands, a sack for traps, and a "possible sack" that contains ammunition, tobacco, long-lasting pemmican, and deerskin for mending moccasins. The mule transports the trapper and his camping and trapping gear and acts as a sentinel, for it distinguishes the odor of strangers, such as Indians, and will bray in warning at their approach.

Its bridle removed and put in a sack so the mule can graze and drink, the animal is led by a horsehair rope braided by the mountain man's squaw.

A pipe stuck into his beaded hatband, the trapper wears a buckskin hunting shirt, leggings, and moccasins, all ornamented with beads and porcupine quills. Fringes help shed rain. From a shoulder thong hang his bullet pouch, powder horn, and wooden castoreum bottle. At his belt are a pistol; a beaded pouch for fruits, pemmican, and jerky; and a sheathed knife, which he wipes on his clothes to add to the grease used for their waterproofing. His Hawken rifle has a shorter barrel and larger bore than a Kentucky rifle. The power of its heavier ball can kill a grizzly or buffalo at up to 200 yards. A percussion rifle, it is ignited by a copper cap—better in rain than the flintlock of a Kentucky rifle.

His arms, legs, and feet are sopping wet and chilled from repeated immersion in icy streams, and he aches from the trappers' main complaint, rheumatism.

The squaw pounds wild cherries, pits and all, for pemmican. Behind her a stew of buffalo hump cooks in a prized present from her husband: a brass pot. It has replaced her Indian "pot"—a buffalo stomach held up, pouchlike, on four poles. The stomach pot was filled with water, which boiled when hot stones were dropped into it. After three days the pot would get too soggy for use and was eaten. The new brass container can hang directly over a fire of wood or of buffalo chips (dried dung).

From Trap to Bale

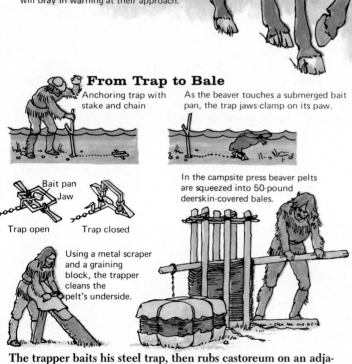

Anchoring trap with stake and chain

As the beaver touches a submerged bait pan, the trap jaws clamp on its paw.

Bait pan
Jaw

Trap open   Trap closed

Using a metal scraper and a graining block, the trapper cleans the pelt's underside.

In the campsite press beaver pelts are squeezed into 50-pound deerskin-covered bales.

The trapper baits his steel trap, then rubs castoreum on an adjacent twig so that the musky odor will attract a beaver to its death. After processing and pressing skins, he will bring, on the average, 300 to 400 1½-pound pelts to rendezvous to sell for $3 to $6 each.

A Home for All Seasons

Gravely handicapped by winter's deep snows, the mountain man traps from the spring thaw to midsummer, when the beavers molt, and again in autumn until the waters freeze. He camps in sheltered groves close to the animals' haunts and moves his home almost weekly to new beaver runs. His tepee is a cover of buffalo hides stitched with sinews and wrapped around a conical frame of poles, slightly tilted for more rear headroom. The cover is pegged down and closed with lodge pins except for an entrance hole with a door flap. With smoke flaps for ventilation, the tepee is cool in summer and, facing away from gales, is windproof in winter. In November the fire is moved inside, and buffalo robes and Hudson's Bay blankets keep the trapper and his wife as cozy as beavers in their lodges.

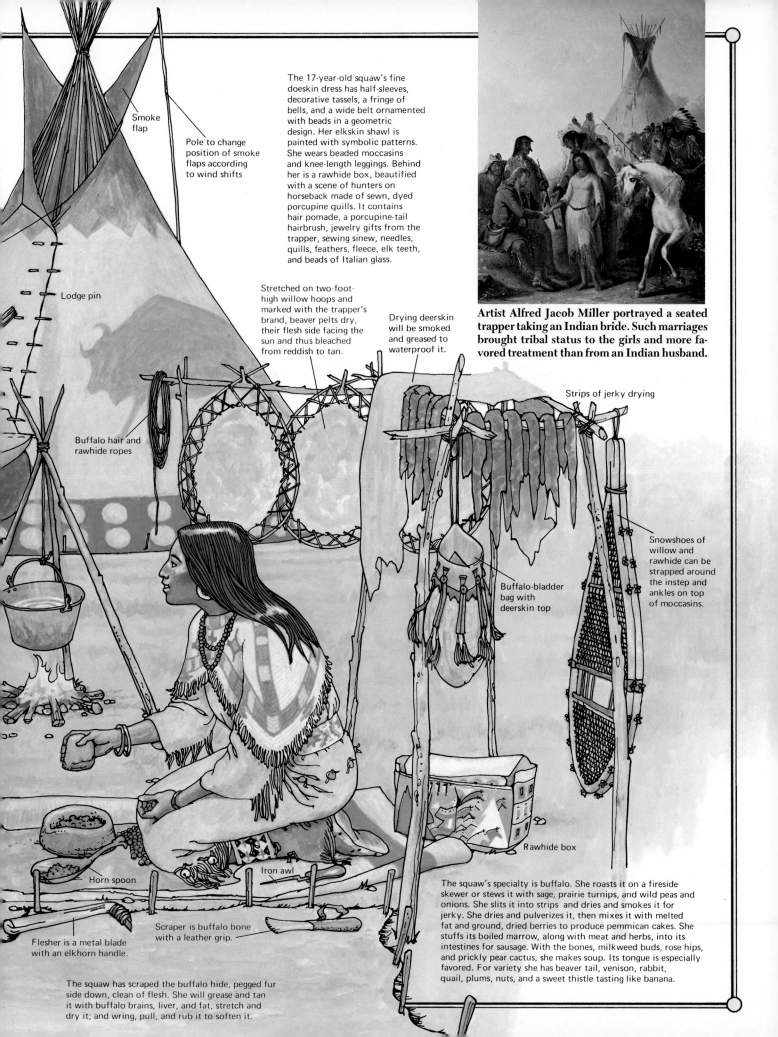

Smoke flap

Pole to change position of smoke flaps according to wind shifts

Lodge pin

Buffalo hair and rawhide ropes

The 17-year-old squaw's fine doeskin dress has half-sleeves, decorative tassels, a fringe of bells, and a wide belt ornamented with beads in a geometric design. Her elkskin shawl is painted with symbolic patterns. She wears beaded moccasins and knee-length leggings. Behind her is a rawhide box, beautified with a scene of hunters on horseback made of sewn, dyed porcupine quills. It contains hair pomade, a porcupine-tail hairbrush, jewelry gifts from the trapper, sewing sinew, needles, quills, feathers, fleece, elk teeth, and beads of Italian glass.

Stretched on two-foot-high willow hoops and marked with the trapper's brand, beaver pelts dry, their flesh side facing the sun and thus bleached from reddish to tan.

Drying deerskin will be smoked and greased to waterproof it.

Artist Alfred Jacob Miller portrayed a seated trapper taking an Indian bride. Such marriages brought tribal status to the girls and more favored treatment than from an Indian husband.

Strips of jerky drying

Snowshoes of willow and rawhide can be strapped around the instep and ankles on top of moccasins.

Buffalo-bladder bag with deerskin top

Rawhide box

Horn spoon

Iron awl

Scraper is buffalo bone with a leather grip.

Flesher is a metal blade with an elkhorn handle.

The squaw has scraped the buffalo hide, pegged fur side down, clean of flesh. She will grease and tan it with buffalo brains, liver, and fat; stretch and dry it; and wring, pull, and rub it to soften it.

The squaw's specialty is buffalo. She roasts it on a fireside skewer or stews it with sage, prairie turnips, and wild peas and onions. She slits it into strips and dries and smokes it for jerky. She dries and pulverizes it, then mixes it with melted fat and ground, dried berries to produce pemmican cakes. She stuffs its boiled marrow, along with meat and herbs, into its intestines for sausage. With the bones, milkweed buds, rose hips, and prickly pear cactus, she makes soup. Its tongue is especially favored. For variety she has beaver tail, venison, rabbit, quail, plums, nuts, and a sweet thistle tasting like banana.

Indians of the Eastern Plains

A Mandan medicine man—his name, Old Bear—waves a pair of eagle-feather pipes. His body is painted with mystical signs.

When Ashley's and Henry's trappers moved up the Missouri in 1822, they entered the world of the Plains Indians, a world utterly different from that of the forest tribes back east. Hard by the silt-laden Missouri and its tributaries lay the villages of the Iowa, Omaha, Arikara, Mandan, Oto, and Hidatsa tribes. These semisedentary people led a fairly settled life, tending corn and other crops, weaving, and making pottery for a good part of the year; in the summer they took to their horses for far-ranging expeditions to track down the buffalo. Those that they did not get through their own efforts they obtained through trade with nomadic tribes farther west, with whom they came in frequent contact.

Both the fully nomadic and the semisedentary tribes admired physical courage, and this is reflected in some of their ceremonies. In the sun dance of the Hidatsas, warriors reenacted their victories in battle. Among the Mandans, the most sacred religious ritual was the *Okipa*, a dramatization of the creation of the earth and the history of the tribe.

Enacted to mollify the spirits and thus ensure the welfare of the Mandan tribe, the ceremony was also a test of courage and endurance for young braves.

An Ecstasy of Pain

In the summer of 1832 artist George Catlin, sojourning among the Mandans in what is now North Dakota, described the four-day-long *Okipa*.

After reporting on the preliminaries, which included fasting and ceremonial dances, Catlin wrote that the initiates crawled, one by one, to the medicine men "and submitted to the knife, which was passed under and through the integuments and flesh . . . on each arm, above and below the elbow . . . and on each leg, above and below the knee . . . and also on each breast and each shoulder." Through these wounds, the medicine men passed splints; then "a cord of raw hide was lowered down through the top of the wigwam, and fastened to the splints on the breasts or shoulders, by which [each] young man was . . . raised up and suspended . . . [from] the top of

George Catlin, Painter With a Mission

This man, whose lifetime (1796–1872) spanned the conquest of the Great Plains, was one of America's most noted painters of Indians. Trained as a lawyer, young Catlin soon switched to full-time painting and became a successful portraitist; among his clients were DeWitt Clinton and William Clark. However, his real interest lay in painting Indians, particularly those tribes as yet unchanged by white influence. Fascinated by their primitive cultures and foreseeing that they would soon be destroyed by white expansion, Catlin determined to record for posterity every possible detail of Indian life and culture. The products of his self-imposed mission, his painstakingly accurate paintings, sketches, and notes, are today among the most valuable sources of information on the tribes that inhabited the plains.

Between 1830 and 1836 Catlin made a number of journeys to the still unsettled plains, painting many tribes and collecting materials for an ethnological museum he hoped to establish. The high point was his trip up the Missouri River in 1832, during which he did the paintings and sketches seen on these pages. The artist traveled by steamboat to Fort Union, a fur-trading post on the present Montana–North Dakota line, thereby pioneering steamboat travel on the upper Missouri. At the fort he studied and painted the tribes who came to trade furs and buffalo hides: Crows, Assiniboines, and Blackfeet. Carrying his sketch pad, Catlin hunted buffaloes with the Indians, camouflaged like them with a wolfskin. This work completed, the artist and two mountain men floated down the Missouri in a dugout canoe, stopping at Indian villages that offered Catlin new subjects. At a memorable

Amazed Indians stare as Catlin paints a Mandan chief.

stopoff with the Mandans, he painted many scenes of daily life and religious ritual. On later trips he visited the Comanches, and the Cherokees and other transplanted southeastern tribes in what is now Oklahoma.

An early Indian sympathizer, Catlin pleaded in vain for the Indians' right to maintain their traditional ways of life. The hundreds of paintings and sketches he created remain as an enduring monument to a culture that has vanished from the earth. His own museum never materialized, but much of his work is in the Smithsonian Institution in Washington, D.C.

Catlin's meticulous painting of a Mandan village shows the central plaza; people lounge on the domed roofs of the earth-and-timber lodges. Grotesque figures on poles in the foreground guard the sacred medicine lodge. Beyond the stockade is the village burial ground.

the lodge." Catlin went on to marvel at the stoicism of the youths in the face of this flesh-tearing agony, which they quietly endured until pain rendered them unconscious.

Among the tribes of the plains torture played a major role in many rituals. The vision quest, common to all Indians of the region, was of particular importance, and it was through a regimen of self-denial and torture that a young man could make contact with his personal

protector from the spirit world by calling forth a vision. Normally, one's patron appeared in the form of an animal or bird: the buffalo, elk, bear, and eagle were common, but even mosquitoes or mice might appear. To the Indians such conjuring was vital to a brave's success, particularly when he hunted the buffalo, the primary staple of the Indians in both the eastern and western plains.

It had not always been so. Before the horse's arrival in the 17th century, the

Plains tribes lived on corn and the relatively few buffaloes they could kill on foot. Bands of warriors (and sometimes squaws as well) would stampede the animals and drive them over cliffs. Sometimes—covered with wolfskins—the Indians would sneak up on the herds until they were within bow-and-arrow or even lance-throwing distance; there they would strike, making only a few kills before the herds thundered off in alarm. The horse changed all this.

Mandan warriors celebrate the harvest with a corn dance, using symbolic cornstalks, ears of corn, and food bowls. The actual work of farming, however, was done by the women.

This is one of 13 paintings that accompanied Catlin's book describing the *Okipa* ritual. The sacred, torture-filled ceremony brought prestige to participants and their kin.

Knights of the High Plains

In this George Catlin painting a Crow chief, his long hair flowing in the wind, and his steed both wear eagle-feather bonnets.

"Something happens to a man when he gets on a horse, in a country where he can ride forever," wrote historian William Brandon. "It is quite easy to ascend to an impression of living in a myth. He either feels like a god or closer to God. There seems never to have been a race of plains horsemen that was not either fanatically proud or fanatically religious. The Plains Indians were both."

These were the tribes that novels, films, and television shows have made into an American legend—tribes of fearless, befeathered warriors mounted on swift ponies, raiding the sedentary Indians to the east and warring for bounty and glory among themselves and upon all trespassers; peoples who nomadically pursued the buffalo and raised their tepees on the grassy plains that stretched from today's Canada to the American Southwest and from the Missouri River to the Rockies. Few of these Indians were native to the area. The proud Cheyennes had farmed along the upper Missouri; the Ojibwas, Crees,

and Blackfeet had been hunters of the eastern woodlands; the Sioux and the Crows had been sedentary agriculturalists on the prairies; and the Shoshones and the Comanches had hunted and foraged the barren lands beyond the Rockies. By the early 1700's these and many others had arrived on the plains, either pushed from the east by advancing white settlement or actively choosing to abandon their former way of living for the new opportunities that the acquisition of the horse gave to buffalo hunting. Rapidly they evolved a hunting-raiding-warring society that had reached its height by the time the whites arrived.

Sharing the same environment, the Indians of the High Plains came to share similar values, worship similar spirits with similar rites, and obey similar codes of conduct. In a remarkably short time they even developed a common sign language by which peoples speaking different tongues could communicate with one another. Of this sign language, trapper Osborne Russell wrote: "It is impossible for a person not acquainted with the Customs of Indians to form a correct idea in which [way] a continuous conversation is held by hours between two individuals who cannot understand each other's language."

Peoples of Glory

The Indians of the High Plains took to riding as an eagle takes to flight. They soon devised all manner of equestrian tactics for surrounding buffalo herds and picking them off from horseback, one by one—a game they found both thrilling and perilous.

With the mobility and speed that the horse gave to the Indians of the High Plains, all thoughts of agricultural pursuits disappeared. The tribes became wholly nomadic and spent most of the

year in pursuit of the herds. Entire families went along on the chase, carrying their scant belongings on a travois, a frame made from wooden poles and drawn along the ground by a horse.

In times of plenty only the choicest morsels of buffalo meat were taken, but when the pickings were slim or household and hunting supplies were needed, the buffalo became a veritable supermarket-on-the-hoof for the Indians. Hides, for example, became tepee covers, clothing, robes, moccasin tops, quivers, medicine bags, shields, drums, saddles, stirrups, dolls, and in later days gun cases. Hair was used for pillows, ropes, medicine balls, and ornaments. Horns made fine cups, spoons, and ladles, while the bones were fashioned into knives, shovels, war clubs, and dice. Even the stomach had its uses: its contents became skin ointments, while its liner was used as a water container.

The Code of the Warrior

For the Indian brave only one activity rivaled the buffalo hunt in his affections, and that was war. For these Indians, warfare bore little resemblance to the white man's concept of hostilities. Although certain tribes, like the Crow and the Blackfoot, were hereditary enemies who slaughtered each other at every opportunity, the white man's primary reason for warfare—to settle disputes over ownership of territory—was rarely a reason for combat among the Plains Indians. They sometimes did battle over hunting rights in a given area, but had no real conception of land ownership. Instead, they fought over matters of personal honor or in order to acquire horses. In some High Plains tribes young men joined military societies—by coveted invitation—but these were usually more like fraternal organizations than standing armies. On festive occasions, wearing their society's distinctive regalia, they took part in processions, dancing and singing their group's special songs. They engaged in competitions with other societies, but in wartime did not necessarily fight as a group. Any young man who wished to do so could declare himself a war leader and gather a band of braves as followers for a swift raid on the pony herd of a rival tribe or to make a knifelike thrust into their camp for the purpose of counting *coup*.

Of all the Indian practices, counting *coup*—from the French word for a

Following the buffalo herds, a band of Crows move their buffalo-skin tepees on travois sledges. Even the dogs are pressed into service as draft animals for pulling light loads.

blow—was perhaps the most misunderstood by whites. Counting *coup* simply consisted of touching an enemy with one's hand or with a short rod, called a *coup* stick. It could be the most dangerous of tactics, requiring an Indian to gallop into the midst of heavily armed rivals, make his touch, and then gallop out again. Occasionally, the courage needed was more apparent than real, as when, for example, a warrior touched a fallen enemy before the man who had killed or wounded him could reach his victim, or when one cunning brave, hidden on a cliff, lowered a stone on a rope to touch an enemy and then claimed *coup* for his valor. But however a *coup* was accomplished, it brought far more glory to a brave than a fistful of enemy scalps. Indeed, in some tribes a richly plumed headdress—each feather notched according to the circumstances of the *coup* it commemorated—was a badge of courage worn even more proudly than a white soldier's chestful of campaign ribbons and medals.

This, then, was the martial society forged by the Indians of the High Plains, a world that blossomed with the Spaniards' gift of the horse, only to wither and die when confronted by the superior technology and unappeasable appetite for land of the white pioneers.

The Buffalo Hunt, Thrilling Spectacle and Hazardous Livelihood

Killing buffaloes demanded great skill in both horsemanship and marksmanship. Even when badly wounded the huge beasts could live for hours, remaining dangerous to the end unless hit in a vital spot. After the Indians acquired firearms from the whites they still preferred their short, light bows, which were easy to handle on horseback and powerful enough to send an arrow through a buffalo at close range. A hunter could send off eight arrows in the time it took to reload a gun.

This Catlin painting captures the excitement of a buffalo chase as a mounted Indian plunges into the midst of the scattering herd.

Alfred Jacob Miller depicted these Indian hunters as they give a yell of triumph over a buffalo that has just been killed. Their prayers, offered up before the assault, have been answered.

After the hunt buffaloes were butchered on the spot—they were too heavy to drag back to camp. Miller shows a woman carving out the tender hump ribs; other favored parts were the tongue and liver.

European Travelers Discover the Great Plains

In the early 1850's Sir George Gore, a British nobleman endowed with vast wealth and a taste for adventure, decided on a bit of hunting in the American Wild West. There, according to all reports, great herds of buffalo—to say nothing of quantities of deer, elk, bear, and wild birds—awaited the honor of being slaughtered by Sir George's extensive armory. Not one to yield necessary comfort to the exigencies of wilderness life, Sir George in 1854 began his rambling three-year trek of several thousand miles across the plains to the Rockies and back accompanied by 40 servants, 3 milk cows, more than 100 horses, 27 wagons, and a full stock of fine wines and other delicacies. At night he slept beneath a striped tent, his brass bed set down upon fine rugs. By the time Sir George returned to his familiar haunts in Britain, he had disposed of some $500,000. He may have considered that a small price to pay for the adventure of a lifetime and thousands of buffaloes and other game.

Although Sir George Gore may have set a new standard for "roughing it" in style, he was hardly the first or the last European to become enthralled with the American West. Some, like Sir George, came merely to hunt; others came to observe the Indians or play at being fron-tiersmen. Still others were scientists interested in collecting plains flora and fauna. Many recorded their observations in diaries, sketches, and paintings, which became valuable records of life on the plains just before the region yielded to the white man's incursions.

Maximilian and Bodmer

One of the earliest visitors to the plains was a scholarly German natural-ist, Prince Maximilian zu Wied-Neu-wied, who toured the upper Missouri region in the 1830's in the company of Swiss artist Karl Bodmer. In addition to having a great interest in the flora and fauna of the region, Maximilian, who had studied South American Indians, showed considerable understanding of the relationship between the Plains Indians and their environment. Even at that early date he could clearly predict the results of the white man's wanton slaughter of the buffalo. While visiting John Jacob Astor's Fort Union trading post, Maximilian noted in his journal: "Every year the slaughter increases and the animals are driven further afield. The [American] Fur Company in a recent year sent 42,000 [buffalo] hides down the river. . . . The Indians depend almost entirely on these creatures . . . the Company's agents recklessly shoot

Karl Bodmer sketched Mandan women bringing wood across the Missouri River in bullboats, clumsy craft of buffalo hide.

buffalo for 'sport' often with no intention of using any part of them."

It was fortunate for historians that Maximilian had chosen Karl Bodmer to record his discoveries, for the young artist (he was only 24 when he and the peripatetic prince reached the frontier) was the most meticulously accurate draftsman of all the painters of the West. His portraits of Indians have never been surpassed in authenticity. A small music box helped him gain rapport with his Mandan and Hidatsa subjects; enchanted by its tinkling tunes, they believed it contained a small but powerful

Prince Maximilian (third from the right) converses through an interpreter with a trading party of Minnetarees at Fort Clark, on the upper Missouri. (Artist Bodmer placed himself at the far right.) White influence shows in the plume-decked top hat of the Minnetaree leader.

This Bodmer painting shows Mandan men performing their buffalo dance, an important ritual in which dancers pantomimed the activities of a hunt.

Bodmer's portraits of the Mandans (at left, Chief Mato-Tope) inspired several of them to try their own skills. At right is a painting made by one of these Indian artists.

spirit. After completing his stint with Maximilian, Bodmer returned to Europe, where he became an influential member of the Barbizon school of French painters. But his greatest work had been done in the West.

Many, perhaps most, of the foreign visitors to the plains were fascinated by the Indians and viewed their lives with a mixture of sympathy and envy. Artist Rudolf Friedrich Kurz of Switzerland found them enchanting people. While living among the Hidatsas in 1851 he noted: "Life here is much more quiet and peaceful than in civilised countries; the so-called Savage does not argue about religion, the Rights of Man, and other such matters ... he has too much sense for that." Yet the Indian life that Kurz so admired was already doomed.

In 1853 a Delaware called Black Beaver made this prediction to the German traveler Baron Balduin Möllhausen: "The time is not far off when the vast herds [of buffalo] will be only a memory. Deprived of their means of subsistence, the ... Indians ... will become the scourge of the civilisation that hems them in, and they in their turn will have to be exterminated."

Prairie à la Corne de Cerf

About 800 paces from the [Two Thousand Miles] River, the hunting or war parties of the Blackfoot Indians have gradually piled up a quantity of elks' horns till they have formed a pyramid sixteen or eighteen feet high, and twelve or fifteen feet in diameter. Every Indian who passes by makes a point of contributing his part, which is not difficult, because such horns are everywhere scattered about. ... All these horns, of which there are certainly more than 1,000, are piled up, and so wedged in, that we found some trouble in extricating, from the pyramid, a large one with fourteen antlers, which we brought away with us. The horns are partly separated from the head of the animal with the skull, and partly single horns. Some buffaloes' horns were mixed with them. The purpose of this practice is said to be a charm ... [for success] in hunting.

—Prince Maximilian's Diary, 1843

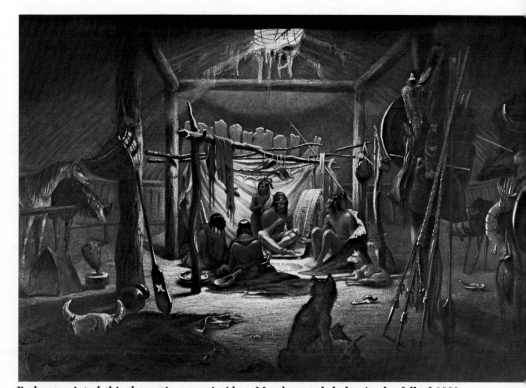

Bodmer painted this domestic scene inside a Mandan earth lodge in the fall of 1833. Sturdy and well insulated by their earthen walls, such lodges housed several families.

The Decline of the Beaver Trade

The greed of the white man for buffalo was exceeded only by his greed for beaver furs. When the 1832 rendezvous at Pierre's Hole in the Idaho country broke up after nine days, the mule train of the Rocky Mountain Fur Company began crawling eastward under a $60,000 burden of pelts. It was a good end to a good season for Fitzpatrick, Bridger, Sublette, and their partners; yet there were disquieting signs. The Rocky Mountain concern was no longer alone, for at the rendezvous several small companies had appeared, bringing their own trappers and supplies and attempting to seduce the mountain men away from their traditional loyalties. Worse yet, John Jacob Astor's American Fur Company was moving its operations into the area. Only by the most strenuous exertions had the Rocky Mountain Company's supply train beaten Astor's to the Pierre's Hole rendezvous, scooping up the cream of the year's profits before the latter could offer higher prices for pelts and lower prices for trappers' supplies.

Log-built Fort Laramie, in the heart of Sioux country (in present-day Wyoming), was the trade center for a wide area, serving trappers and Indians. In 1849 it became an army post.

The Competition

Another disturbing sign of the times was increased hostility from the Indians, for now that there were some 600 white trappers in the mountains, even traditionally friendly tribes were getting skittish. They had become alarmed by the invasion of their land and the consequent dwindling in the number of beavers and thinning of the buffalo herds. Soon after the 1832 rendezvous had ended and the trading companies' muleteers and captains had started back east, a force of white trappers and some Flathead and Nez Perce Indians clashed with some Gros Ventre Indians. The bloody battle took the lives of five whites and an unknown number of Indians.

For the Rocky Mountain Company competition from small outfits like those led by New Englander Nathaniel J. Wyeth and Capt. Benjamin Bonneville of the U.S. Army could be taken in stride. But the American Fur Company was something else entirely, and no one doubted that the next year the Astor men would be back, prepared to spend what was necessary to drive their competitors into bankruptcy. After the 1813 debacle on the Oregon coast, Astor had at first concentrated his efforts in the Great Lakes region. Then he slowly and carefully moved westward, establishing trading posts—such as Fort Union on the Yellowstone River and Fort Piegan on the Marias—and buying out or breaking up smaller firms that stood in his way. The American Fur Company's operatives even considered committing arson to discourage competitors.

In 1830 the Astor men had scored a

From major fortified trading posts trappers of competing British and American fur companies came into increasing conflict.

Attacks by Indians intent on stealing valuable cargoes were an occupational hazard of the Rocky Mountain fur trade. This party of traders is clearly getting the worst of an ambush.

In 1837 Alfred Jacob Miller painted Fort Laramie. Here the interior is thronged with Indians come to trade. All tribes were welcome except the hostile Blackfeet.

Two unkempt buckskin-clad trappers confront each other in this painting by Frederic Remington, entitled "I Took Ye fer an Injun." To survive in the harsh environment of the Rockies, mountain men had to adopt the ways of Indians they sometimes fought.

major coup by reaching an agreement with the hitherto intransigent Blackfoot Indians to open their beaver country near the mouth of the Yellowstone to the company's agents. A vast expanse of untapped wealth then fell into Astor's lap, and his increasing dominance of the U.S. fur trade placed him in a better position than ever to smash his rivals. By 1834 Fitzpatrick, Bridger, Sublette, and their partners bowed to the inevitable and agreed to sell out to Astor. But the old man did not linger to enjoy this latest triumph; before the details of the sale had been worked out, he astonished everybody by selling his own shares in the American Fur Company to his partners. Shrewd as always, Astor got out just in time. Where others expected only continued prosperity, the New York merchant foresaw disaster. By the mid-1830's the beaver trade was doomed.

A Time of Troubles

In part, this situation was due to the very success of the mountain men. They had become so efficient at tracking down and trapping beavers that they had just about denuded the more accessible rivers and streams of their wealth. Each year the mountain men were being forced to range farther afield in search of virgin territories, and even these seemed to yield fewer and fewer pelts. That their

forays into the unknown would bear rich rewards for the United States by blazing the routes of future migration was probably little considered by most trappers, who only knew that beavers were becoming scarce. And to make matters worse, the worth of each pelt was rapidly declining. A skin that had brought $6 at the rendezvous in 1832 was worth scarcely $1 a decade later, because the fact was that the day of the beaver hat, once a symbol of prosperity, was fast fading. Fashion had turned to other materials—silk from China, for example, and in Poland, Russia, and Germany a vogue for coonskin caps à la Davy Crockett swept the beaver topper into history's dustbin.

Massive presses were used to bale furs for shipment east by packhorse or river craft. A bale could weigh from 90 to 100 pounds.

A Visit to Fort Laramie

Looking back . . . upon Fort Laramie and its inmates, they seem less like a reality than like some fanciful picture of the olden time; so different was the scene from any which this tamer side of the world can present. Tall Indians, enveloped in their white buffalo-robes, were striding across the area or reclining at full length on the low roofs of the buildings which enclosed it. Numerous squaws, gayly bedizened, sat grouped in front of the rooms they occupied; their mongrel off-spring, restless and vociferous, rambled in every direction through the fort; and the trappers, traders, and *engagés* of the establishment were busy at their labor or their amusements. . . . Fort Laramie is one of the posts established by the "American Fur Company," which well-nigh monopolizes the Indian trade of this region. Here its officials rule with an absolute sway.

—Francis Parkman, *The Oregon Trail,* 1847

The Last of the Great Rendezvous

In June 1837 more than a hundred trappers, laden with furs from the last year's hunt, straggled down to the Wyoming country's Green River Valley, the site of the 13th annual rendezvous. Although the number of pelts and the profits would be less than in previous years, this rendezvous was in the grand tradition. The arrival of the American Fur Company's wagon train, with its eagerly awaited alcohol, signaled the beginning of the orgy that historian Bernard DeVoto has called "the mountain man's Christmas, county fair, harvest festival, and crowned-slave carnival of Saturn."

Between bouts of drinking, fights, games, contests, and trading for buckskins, moccasins, and squaws with the Indians who gathered to observe and cash in on the festivities, the trappers exchanged their furs for wagon-train goods to sustain themselves in the wild during the coming year. The prices they paid were about 20 times what the articles would have cost in St. Louis. When the furs were all traded and the alcohol ran out, the mountain men, nursing their hangovers and their bruises, dispersed to the wilds for another year of lonely hardship to earn the price of the next rendezvous.

There To Observe

Stewart   Miller

Two visitors at the rendezvous were an aristocratic Scot, soldier-sportsman William Drummond Stewart, and a Baltimore-born painter, Alfred Jacob Miller. Stewart, a restless veteran of Waterloo, had spent four summers hunting in the Rockies; during the winter he resided in New Orleans, where he traded in cotton. There he hired Miller to accompany him on his 1837 trip to the West and to make a permanent record of the expedition for his castle in Scotland. They traveled with the supply caravan of the American Fur Company, Miller sketching, painting, and taking notes at a furious rate for his demanding client. Once at the rendezvous, Miller painted Indians, trappers, and traders both in their riotous carryings-on and in quieter moments. Thanks to Stewart's wish to immortalize his journey, we have an on-the-spot record of this colorful episode in the history of the West.

There To Do Business

Red Elk   Meek   Carson

A motley crowd of more than 2,000 Indians, trappers, and fur-company agents flocked to the rendezvous. Shoshone Indians—some 1,500 of them—were the largest group; Red Elk, a Shoshone notable, sat for his portrait by Miller while solemnly counting his *coups*. Lords of the trappers were the free agents, far outranking those under contract to the American Fur Company. Joe Meek led a brigade of contract trappers; Kit Carson was present as an independent. Their portraits here date from much later in their careers, when Meek was a U.S. marshal in Oregon and Carson an Indian agent in Taos. But in 1837 Meek was a vigorous young man, famed among mountain men as a grizzly-bear hunter, while the slight, soft-spoken Carson was renowned as a skilled trapper and one of the toughest Indian fighters.

The Mountain Men Relaxing

Ebullient trappers work off some excess energy in an impromptu dance around the campfire to the amusement of the Indians who are looking on.

Route to Rendezvous

Stewart and Miller went by wagon train along the North Platte, then cut through South Pass.

A Suit of Armor Comes to the Plains

Stewart had many friends among the mountain men, and Jim Bridger was one of his favorites. At this rendezvous he presented Bridger with a suit of armor ordered from Scotland. Delighted with the bizarre gift, Bridger donned the casque, cuirass, and greaves and paraded in them to the wonder—and probably the derision—of the crowd. Here Bridger in his armor and other trappers look out over an Indian encampment on the Green River plains, where the tepees, whitened with clay, gleam in the sunlight. The Indians came to rendezvous not only to trade but also to enjoy the company's alcohol, feasts, and gifts. Indian squaws reaped rich rewards from the womanless mountain men, to whom the company was glad to sell trinkets at highly inflated prices.

Presenting Gifts to the Indians

Indians would not trade until their hearts were first gladdened with presents. Miller depicted a scene in which a bearded *bourgeois* (company agent) hangs a necklace around the neck of a young warrior. Other favored gifts were vermilion powder for decoration, knives, tobacco, colored beads, bright cloth, and small looking glasses.

An Eyewitness Report

At certain specified times . . . the American Fur Company appoint a "Rendezvous" . . . for . . . trading with Indians and Trappers, and here they congregate from all quarters. The first day is devoted to "High Jinks," in which feasting, drinking, and gambling form prominent parts. Sometimes an Indian becomes so excited with "Fire Water" that he commences "running a muck"—he is pursued . . . and secured. . . . "Affairs of honor" . . . are adjusted between rival Trappers—one . . . of course, receiving a complete drubbing;—all caused evidently from mixing too much Alcohol with their water. Night closes this scene of revelry and confusion. The following days exhibit the strongest contrast. . . . The Company's great tent is raised;—the Indians erect their picturesque white lodges;—The accumulated furs . . . are brought forth, and the Company's tent is a besieged and busy place. Now the women come in for their share of ornaments and finery.

—Alfred Jacob Miller
The West of Alfred Jacob Miller

Epilogue to an Era

By 1840 the beaver trade was dead—what activity there was had passed from the rendezvous site to such forts as Bent's and Laramie, where Indians could bring their pelts for trade. But even after that, here and there in the mountains a traveler might spot a weathered mountain man setting his traps and acting as if the world had not passed him by. In 1846 G. F. Ruxton, a chronicler of the Far West, reported a conversation in which a trapper, in the patois of his breed, gave voice to a dying optimism: "Howsever, beaver's 'bound to rise'; human natur can't go on selling beaver a dollar a pound; no, no, that ain't a going to shine much longer.... There was the times ... six dollars the plew [skin]—old 'un or kitten. Wagh! but it's bound to rise."

There were few, however, who shared the old man's optimism, and most of the surviving greats among the trappers had long since gone into other occupations. Some, like tale-spinning Jim Beckwourth, would even write (or dictate)

their memoirs, attempting to cash in on popular interest in the West. In his *Life and Adventures of James P. Beckwourth,* an inextricable mixture of fact and fancy, the old trapper recounted deeds of personal heroism and set down enough adventures to last even a mountain man through 20 lifetimes. "Experience has revealed to me," he wrote, "that civilized man can accustom himself to any mode of life when pelf [treasure] is the governing principle—that power which dominates through all the ramifications of social life, and gives expression to the universal instinct of self-interest." Beckwourth's colorful book caught the spirit of the mountain man's life and added new weight to the growing legend of the American West as a home of heroes.

Old Trappers in New Careers

Many trappers became hunters for trading posts and outdid the Indians in the slaughter of buffaloes—the skins of the shaggy beasts being in vogue for carriage robes, coats, rugs, and shoe lin-

Son of a Virginia planter and a slave, raconteur Jim Beckwourth gave up trapping to become a war chief of the Crow Indians.

ings. A number of others pushed on to the West Coast in search of a new life. Osborne Russell was one of the first American settlers in Oregon, and in 1848 he traveled south to California to pan for gold. There the citizens of a roaring mining camp, aptly named Hangtown, elected Russell a judge of a vigilante court, where he did his bit to keep the hangman occupied.

Bent's Fort, Key Trading Post of the Southwest

  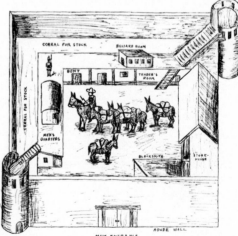

Adobe walls 14 feet high, two musketry towers, and cannon protected Bent's Fort. Trading Indians call to the lookout in the above painting by Charles Russell, a grandson of the Bent brothers' sister. The sketch at the right is by an 1844 visitor, W. M. Boggs. It shows an Indian camp outside the fort and, inside, the stock and horse corral, smithy, trader's room, and rooftop billiard room.

In all the 2,000 miles of wilderness between St. Louis and the California coast no sight was more unexpected between 1832 and the late 1840's than the turreted, flat-roofed, two-story trading post shown above. It was Bent's Fort, unsurpassed in size and importance in all the land west of the Mississippi. It could garrison 200 men and 300 animals. Its four-foot-thick walls, constructed in 1833 by Mexican laborers, were topped with blooming cacti, a belfry, and a watchtower complete with telescope. The ramparts surrounded an area 137 by 178 feet, encompassing warehouses, wagon sheds, clerks' offices, meeting halls, staff apartments, and a central square of small whitewashed guestrooms that opened onto an inner court. There stood a well and a huge press for the establishment's prime export: skins for the East.

Through the fort's iron-sheathed gate passed Cheyennes and Arapahos, Comanches and Kiowas, Utes and Gros Ventres. For the bastion was at the crosstrails of numerous tribes, and all respected the fort's owners for their honesty—a rare trait among traders. Within, the Indians could meet in a council room and also obtain weapons, trinkets, and tools in exchange for buffalo hides, which were then pressed and packed by the fort's crew of Frenchmen from St. Louis and Canadian voyageurs. Many whites found shelter there too. They feasted on game shot by Kit Carson or Tom Fitzpatrick, the post's hunters for a time, or—as one visitor wrote—on the "slap-jacks and pumpkin pies" of the cook, "a fair lady of colour, Charlotte by name, who was, as she loved to say, 'de onlee lady in de dam Injun country.'"

For several trappers the end of the beaver trade was the beginning of fame, if not fortune. Jim Bridger, Tom "Broken Hand" Fitzpatrick, and Kit Carson all went on to play major, dramatic roles in taming and settling the West. Bridger, in 1843, established a trading post on the Oregon Trail in what is now southwestern Wyoming. For a decade thereafter, hundreds of pioneers on their way west stopped at Bridger's "fort" to pick up new supplies and get information on the safest routes west.

Fitzpatrick and Carson became wilderness guides of great renown. In 1841 Fitzpatrick led for part of the way the first sizable emigrant party to the West Coast. Both men played prominent roles in John Charles Frémont's exploratory journey through the Far West in the early 1840's. Carson, in particular, caught the public's fancy for his work as Frémont's guide and became known as the pathfinder's pathfinder. But whatever excitement, adventures, and perils the post-trapping age offered, many former mountain men could not help but look back on the old freewheeling times.

The white man's trade goods and ideas had a far-reaching impact on Indian life. Venetian glass beads, such as those on the Blackfoot knife sheath (right), were prized by Plains tribes, who used them for decoration in place of dyed porcupine quills. The fiddle (below) was inspired by a European violin. To create his version of a stringed instrument, an Apache craftsman made the frame from the hollowed-out stalk of a century plant, and for the single string (not shown here) he used deer sinew. It was played with a small hunting bow.

Perhaps Washington Irving caught the spirit of the vanished age best:

No toil, no danger, no privation can turn the trapper from his pursuit. His passionate excitement at times resembles a mania. In vain may . . . cruel savages beset his path; in vain may rocks . . . precipices, and wintry torrents oppose his progress; let but a single track of beaver meet his eye and he forgets all dangers. . . . At times he may be . . . found . . . scaling . . . the most frightful precipices, searching . . . for springs and lakes unknown to his comrades, and where he may meet with his favorite game. Such is the mountaineer, the hardy trapper of the West; and such . . . is the wild, Robin Hood kind of life . . . now existing in full vigor among the Rocky Mountains.

Charlotte was kept busy, for traffic bustled. First, there were several two-man teams sent by the post to trade with the Indians. They were equipped with beads and abalone shells, brass wire, hoop iron for arrowheads, vermilion, blankets, axes, and kettles. Then, famous mountain men would come in for supplies, often gambling their peltries away while their squaws strutted about "in all the pride of beads and fanfaron, jingling with bells and bugles." Old Bill Williams, a free trapper, would order drinks for all after riding in, "his body bent over his saddle-horn . . . keen gray eyes peering from under the slouched brim of a . . . felt hat, black and shining with grease. . . . His feet were thrust into a pair of Mexican stirrups, made of wood, and as big as coal-scuttles; and iron spurs of incredible proportions, with tinkling drops attached to the rowels." Occasionally the fort was a haven for sick travelers—a government man ill with scurvy or a pioneer woman suffering a miscarriage. On their way to Santa Fe long caravans stopped there and were resupplied with flour, sugar, coffee, cloth, tobacco, weapons, and whisky.

The entrepreneurs of this astonishing oasis were two Bent brothers, Charles and William, whose father was a judge in Louisiana Territory, and their partner, Ceran St. Vrain, son of a French political émigré. The young men had abandoned the cutthroat trading of the Northwest and decided to try what is now Colorado. Grateful Cheyennes helped them choose the fort's strategic location—near the junction of the Arkansas and Purgatory Rivers—after William Bent had saved the lives of two tribesmen. Trade throve, and William became resident manager. In the late 1840's the fort also served the U.S. Army in the Mexican War. The government wanted to buy it but offered so little for it that in 1849 William abandoned it and built a smaller fort 30 miles to the east.

Charles (top right), eldest of the three Bent brothers, began trading in the 1820's by providing supplies for Northwest fur posts. Fierce competition drove him south. Later, while civil governor of New Mexico, he was killed in Taos by rebellious Indians. Both William (top left) and a younger brother, George, married kin of prominent Cheyennes, as did William's son George (below, with his wife, Magpie). William suggested the Arkansas River area for the post, as it formed the southern boundary of the fur-trade territory and lay in the heart of the buffalo country and astride the northern loop of the St. Louis–Santa Fe route. William, later an Indian agent, handled the fort's retailing; Ceran St. Vrain supervised the wholesaling.

*I have travelled near five hundred miles across Texas, and am now enabled to judge . . .
the soil, and the resources of the Country, and I have no hesitancy in pronouncing it the
finest country to its extent upon the globe. . . . There can be no doubt but the country
east of the River Grand of the north would sustain a population of ten millions of souls.*

—*Letter from Sam Houston to President Andrew Jackson, February 13, 1833*

Texas and the Great Southwest

"Dawn at the Alamo." Oil painting by Henry McArdle.

Chapter 4

White settlement of what is now the American Southwest began with the Spanish, who pushed north from Mexico in the 16th and 17th centuries. After 1821, when she won her independence from Spain, Mexico allowed Americans to trade with Santa Fe and encouraged Anglos to settle in Texas. But the vacillations of Mexican policy toward the newcomers gradually soured even the most loyal. In 1835, when the dictatorial Mexican president Santa Anna sought to clamp an iron rule on Texas, the Anglos revolted. The martyrdom of the Alamo's defenders provided Texans with a battle cry that swept them to victory at San Jacinto in 1836, giving birth to the Republic of Texas, which in 1845 became the 28th state of the United States.

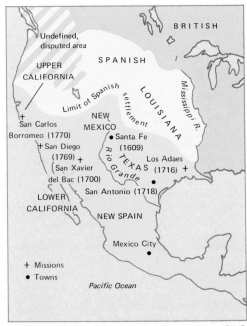

By 1770 the Spanish domain, New Spain, had spread far north from Mexico City, establishing settlements up to the frontier shown. In 1762 France had ceded to the Spaniards a vast region that resource-poor Spain could not exploit—the vaguely defined Louisiana country (which later reverted to France and was part of the Louisiana Purchase). Between 1609 and 1770 the Spaniards erected a defensive chain of missions and fortified posts that arched from Texas to California, shielding New Spain from encroachment by the French at the mouth of the Mississippi and by the Russians and British who vied for disputed sections of the Pacific Northwest.

North From Mexico

The Pueblo Indians of the upper Rio Grande Valley, here performing a corn dance, were a peaceful farming people who accepted Franciscan missionaries into their villages. But over the years resentment grew, and the Indians clung to their religion despite penances and punishments. In the 1660's a series of droughts fatal to many convinced the Indians that their gods were angered. The anti-Spanish preachings and the arrests and floggings of Popé, a medicine man, also helped to increase Indian tensions. By August of 1680 the released Popé had stirred the Pueblos to revolt. They attacked the Spanish capital of Santa Fe, setting fire to the town and temporarily driving all the Spaniards out of New Mexico.

Like the conquistadors who savaged two continents from Tierra del Fuego to Mexico, the early Spanish explorers of what is now the American Southwest roamed over a vast territory in quest of glory and gold. But finding only huddled Indian villages instead of El Dorado, they vanished from the region without a trace. It took a threat from Britain in the last quarter of the 16th century to re-awaken Spain's interest in the land to the north of Mexico.

In 1578 English seadog Francis Drake sailed his *Golden Hind* through the storm-lashed Strait of Magellan into the Pacific, where he later boldly sacked a treasure-laden Spanish galleon off Peru. The next year Drake entered a central California bay and there nailed a plaque to "a faire great post" proclaiming his queen's title to the land he dubbed New Albion. When word of Drake's forays and territorial claims reached Mexico City, a horrified Spanish viceroy made haste to plan expeditions to protect the empire's northern flank and to secure sealanes between the Americas and the Spanish-held Philippines. Apparently court officials in Madrid, preoccupied with their war with England, did not share the viceroy's alarm. Almost two decades would pass before Spanish sailors were dispatched north from Mexico to probe the California coast.

Father Kino: Missionary, Explorer, Mapmaker

San Xavier del Bac mission, in present-day Arizona, founded by Kino in 1700.

During his unmatched career in northern Sonora and southern Arizona, the indefatigable Father Eusebio Francisco Kino (c. 1644–1711) mapped this wild, farflung land in 40 expeditions and disproved the long-accepted belief that California was an island. He also pioneered in stockraising to supply the Jesuit missions. The Tyrol-born priest had taught mathematics until his request to become a missionary was granted in 1681 and he was sent to New Spain. Unlike many of his fellow missionaries, Kino tolerated the Indians' occasional backsliding into pagan ways and won their unswerving trust. Described as "merciful to others but cruel to himself," Kino shunned all personal possessions. His deathbed consisted of two calfskins, two blankets, and a packsaddle for a pillow—the same bed that he had had throughout his lifetime.

The First Spanish Settlement

In 1598 an inland expedition under mineowner Juan de Oñate was sent to establish a permanent land base that would protect New Spain's northern frontier. On April 30, 1598, in a dusty cottonwood grove near the site of what is now El Paso, Oñate proclaimed Spain's sovereignty over all the "lands, pueblos, cities, villas, of whatsoever nature now founded in the kingdom and province of New Mexico"—a vaguely defined wilderness stretching all the way from present-day Texas to California. Then, with a force of 130 soldier-settlers and their families, 8 Franciscan missionaries, and more than 100 slaves, Oñate struck northward. In his caravan he carried the necessaries of settlement: grain seed and fruit trees, a bawling herd of 7,000 lean

New Mexican Designs for Living

Living far from the mainstream of life in Old Mexico, the 18th- and early-19th-century settlers in New Mexico's isolated valleys made do with whatever materials were at hand. They evolved arts and crafts that—in the use of soft pine for most wood objects, colored clays for paints, and dyes made from native plants—took on a character uniquely their own.

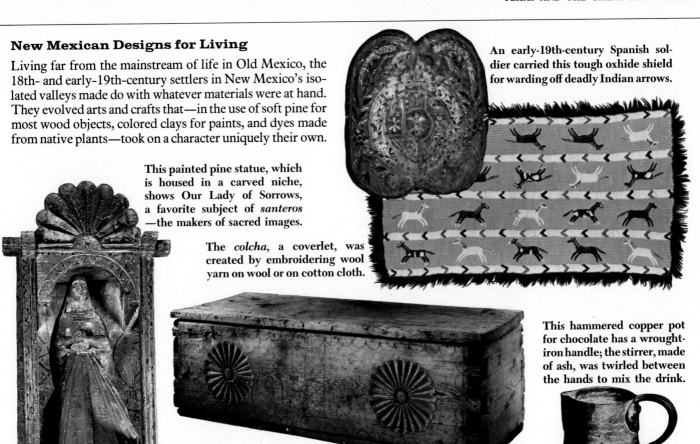

An early-19th-century Spanish soldier carried this tough oxhide shield for warding off deadly Indian arrows.

This painted pine statue, which is housed in a carved niche, shows Our Lady of Sorrows, a favorite subject of *santeros* —the makers of sacred images.

The *colcha,* a coverlet, was created by embroidering wool yarn on wool or on cotton cloth.

This hammered copper pot for chocolate has a wrought-iron handle; the stirrer, made of ash, was twirled between the hands to mix the drink.

Limited to soft pine for wood, carpenters crafted sturdy furniture by using mortise and tenon joints that were reinforced with pegs. The starkness of this chest is relieved by its carved rosettes.

Spanish cattle (ancestors of the Texas longhorns), sheep, goats, and burros, and, most significantly, a herd of horses, whose descendants would transform the entire culture of the Plains Indians. Clearly the Spaniards had come into the Southwest to stay.

At a point just south of the junction of the Rio Grande and the Rio Chama, Oñate commandeered a native pueblo (the Spanish word for a town or village and the name by which the region's settled Indians came to be known) and established the first Spanish settlement in the Southwest: San Juan. There was no trouble with the Indians except for one pitched battle in 1599, in which about 1,000 inhabitants of the tabletop pueblo of Acoma were killed.

As usual, gold fever was upon the Spaniards. Even Oñate often neglected his duties as governor to search for treasure, although he did introduce sheep to the area, which thrived there as cattle did not. Droughts and crop failures beset the colonizers, who had moved from San Juan across the Rio Grande to nearby San Gabriel, and hungry, discouraged settlers began heading back to what is now Mexico. When Oñate was accused by rivals of mismanagement, he challenged the authorities either to relieve him or to send him supplies to save the faltering colony. This ultimatum resulted in his replacement in 1609. The new governor moved the colony and capital to Santa Fe, which prospered and became an enduring outpost for Spain in the Southwest.

Missionary Efforts

The Spanish hold on the Southwest remained tenuous at best, however, for Spain—after a long war with England that had not ended until 1604—lacked the military manpower to exploit this vast realm. And with the new territory seeming to offer nothing in the way of gold and silver, there seemed little reason to press colonization. Only the missionaries were ready to continue. The first to advance were the black-robed Jesuits, who established several missions in Lower California and in the mountain valleys of the Western Sierra Madre. The Franciscans moved northward across the central plateau into present-day New Mexico and for a time into what is now Texas. In the wake of the holy men came soldiers to guard the missions and ranchers to exploit the surrounding lands.

Working ceaselessly, the friars instructed their charges not only in the Christian faith but also in such diverse skills as farming, stockraising, and carpentry. Among the most successful was Father Eusebio Francisco Kino, the great Jesuit explorer, mapmaker, and founder of missions. He arrived in what is now southern Arizona and Mexico's Sonora Province in 1687 and for 24 years labored for souls in the deserts of Arizona. After his death in 1711, however, the Arizona missions suffered 20 years of neglect as Spain turned her attention toward Texas, where a menace from the French posed a serious threat.

An Empire Gained and Lost

In 1685 Robert Cavelier, sieur de La Salle, explorer and colonizer for his sovereign, the king of France, arrived in the New World for the fourth time. He had obtained permission to establish a colony at the mouth of the Mississippi so that France's claim to the great river would be strengthened. But in the Gulf of Mexico his ships went astray, landing on the coast of present-day Texas at Matagorda Bay. The Texas outpost was soon wiped out by Indians and disease (and La Salle himself eventually murdered by his own men), but the fact that Frenchmen had landed in the region was sufficient to alarm officials in New Spain. Nor was their concern lessened when, in 1699, the French succeeded in establishing their Louisiana colony.

From Mexico City warnings of a French threat were sent to Madrid, but the languid, Francophile court paid no heed—not even when the French moved closer to Texas by planting a colony at Natchitoches on the Red River in 1714. So officials in Mexico decided to act on their own. In 1716 they dispatched an expedition into east Texas and within a year had established six missions, one of them at Los Adaes, only 15 miles from Natchitoches. It was in this region that the Spanish came upon the Indians they called Tejas (from a Caddoan Indian word for "friendly"), and from this the name "Texas" was derived. By 1718 the Spanish had founded a presidio, or garrison, and the Alamo mission at Bexar, today's San Antonio. At last Madrid's claims to Texas were backed up by a minimal Spanish presence.

Until 1761 France remained a threat to Spanish hegemony in the Southwest, but in that year France induced Spain to become its ally against Britain in the French and Indian War. As the conflict was moving toward a British victory, France, in 1762, ceded the Louisiana territory to Spain to compensate her for entering the war and to keep Louisiana out of British hands.

Comanches and Apaches

But Spain's strength was simply not equal to the opportunity. Although she managed to exert her authority in New Orleans, she did practically nothing to establish her rule in the wilderness that France had granted her, nor could she even maintain herself in the regions she had already occupied.

Long before the acquisition of Louisiana, fierce Comanche and Apache warriors were regularly raiding the Spanish missions in eastern and central Texas. In 1756, when a Lipan Apache

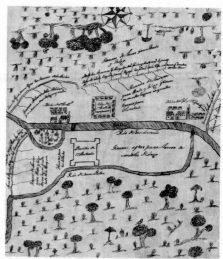

This Spanish map of 1730 shows the earliest settlements in the San Antonio area, including the Mission San Antonio de Valero (center left), later known as the Alamo.

delegation appeared at San Antonio to request a presidio and mission, Spanish soldiers and missionaries hurried north to build by the San Saba River, little realizing that the Apaches were actually more interested in protection from the Comanches than in any conversion to Christianity. Not one Apache came to the mission for religious instruction, but in 1758 the Comanches, angered by the white man's intrusion, did arrive to burn the presidio and mission and slaughter the soldiers and priests. A 300-man expedition was dispatched to punish the Indians, only to be sent scrambling back to San Antonio. Humiliated and disheartened, Spain in 1772 finally abandoned four missions and two presidios in east Texas and fell back on San Antonio to guard the approaches to Mexico.

By then a new threat had appeared. In 1768 José de Gálvez, *visitador general* of New Spain, received a dispatch telling of Russian fur traders moving south along the Pacific coast from Alaska, and officials in Madrid, recognizing imminent danger, opted to secure California with a chain of missions and presidios.

The California Missions

In the spring of 1769 a colonizing party of soldiers and settlers under the tough conquistador Don Gaspar de Portolá, together with a group of Franciscan monks led by the lame but hardy Father Junípero Serra, began the overland trek from Lower to Upper California. (The Jesuits, who had founded mis-

The labors of the Franciscan missionary Father Junípero Serra are honored in Spain, Mexico, and the state of California.

San Diego de Alcalá, founded by Father Serra in 1769, was the first of nine Franciscan missions he planted in California between what is now San Diego and San Francisco.

Adobe Sheltered Spanish Settlers in the Southwest

In an area with scant building material, the settlers of the early 1700's made homes of adobe brick, using a technique known in both the Old and New Worlds. For protection the Spanish clustered their dwellings in multifamily compounds, obtaining from the Pueblo Indians baskets and clay vessels, and teaching them how to raise both cattle and sheep.

Spanish settlers who came to New Mexico built fortified villages, each around a plaza that was large enough for residents to plant gardens and orchards. The one-story houses were attached, and all windows faced the plaza. The few doors in the outer walls, which are shown above, were only wide enough to admit a single person or animal.

A *paredcita* ("little wall") shields the fireplace from drafts.

The lower quarters of the walls in the adobe houses were painted with an ocher-color mixture of dirt and water applied with sheepskin. The tamped-clay floor was soaked with animal blood to harden the surface.

The family slept on the floor and also sat on the floor to eat their meals at a low table. The adobe fireplace served for cooking and heating the home. Corn and chili peppers were baked outdoors in a beehive-shaped earthen oven.

Blankets hang on a pole suspended from a *viga,* or roof beam.

Storage shelves are set into the wall.

A saint occupies a *nicho,* a hollow in the wall.

Comal

Strings of chilies, herbs, and a gourd for water hang from a *viga.*

Tortillas (corn cakes) are cooked on a *comal,* a sheet of copper.

All eat from a common pot of beans, using tortillas as spoons.

A woman stirs chocolate, cinnamon, vanilla, and water in a copper pitcher.

Corn for tortillas is mashed in a *metate.*

A heavy pine chest is used for storage.

Home Builders Used the Materials at Hand

To make adobe, settlers pulverized soil and added water to form a thick paste; then they molded bricks four inches thick, weighing 40 to 50 pounds each.

On a foundation of uncut stones, a worker laid dried bricks in rows mortared with thick mud. After the mortar dried, a coat of mud plaster was applied.

Pine-log roof beams, resting on bond beams, supported crisscrossed poles, which were covered with brush, a thick coat of mud plaster, and earth.

sions in Lower California, had been expelled from Spanish America by Spain's King Charles III in 1767.) After a grueling six-week march Portolá and Serra reached the site of San Diego, where they rendezvoused with other colonists who had arrived earlier by sea. Together the settlers built the mission station of San Diego de Alcalá, and then Portolá headed north to Monterey Bay. It was during this northward trek that one of his scouting parties discovered a magnificent harbor large enough to hold "not only all the navy of our most Catholic Majesty but those of all Europe"— San Francisco Bay.

Early in 1770 Serra joined Portolá at Monterey, founding the mission of San Carlos Borromeo. There, except for one year in Mexico, the great priest re-mained until his death in 1784, directing the establishment of new religious communities and the conversion of the Indians of the coastal plain from San Diego northward, most of them primitive hunters and gatherers. Responding to the promise of food and safety, thousands of them flocked to the missions, which by 1823 numbered 21. Four presidios provided military protection by assigning small detachments of soldiers to each mission. The families of the soldiers as well as traders and other settlers lived in the adobe villages that grew up around the presidios, villages that later developed into small commercial centers. With a minimum expenditure of money and manpower Spain had gained a foothold in the California country, but her power would soon prove too feeble to be maintained.

In 1820 the entire Spanish-speaking population of California and the Southwest numbered less than 50,000. Isolation, together with the venality and indolence of Spanish officials, eroded the settlers' loyalty to the mother country. Increasingly they thought of themselves not as Spaniards or even Mexicans but as "New Mexicans." When the people of Old Mexico overthrew Madrid's rule in 1821, the frontier settlements went along, though in general they neither protested nor applauded the change. Yet even as the tricolor of the fledgling Republic of Mexico was raised over San Antonio, Santa Fe, and San Diego, new forces were assembling that would undermine Mexico's New World rule from Texas to California.

A Day at Mission San José

The missions that dotted Spain's frontier in Texas had two aims: first, to convert the Indians to Christianity; second, to turn them into productive Spanish subjects whose toil would enrich and enlarge the Spanish Empire. The nomadic local Coahuiltecan Indians were eager to join the missions, which offered them a secure living and protection against raiding Apaches and Comanches. The Indian neophytes were instructed in Catholicism, the Spanish language and customs, farming, and simple handicrafts. Though treated well by Spanish standards, they pined under the regimented mission life. The shirking of work was common, and at many missions runaways were frequent. Despite these obstacles the missionaries created cohesive, self-supporting communities. One of the most successful in Texas was San José, at San Antonio, shown here on a typical day in the year 1778.

Father Antonio Margil de Jesús founded Mission San José in 1720.

Indians work on the mission farm; armed mounted guards protect them from Apache and Comanche raiders.

Women make baskets and clay pottery while tending their children.

Bread is baked in *hornos*, dome-shaped ovens of clay. Baking is a weekly event.

A woman spins wool yarn from the mission's sheep.

Young men do mission carpentry.

An old man makes arrows for the mission defense force.

A woman cooks breakfast in a copper kettle over an open fire.

San José is a sizable community; at its height it held 350 Indians.

The day begins with required prayers and hymns.

Breakfast is *atole*, gruel made of roasted corn.

The church, begun in 1768 and still uncompleted, dominates the mission. Its great bell sets the tempo of daily life. All Indian men who can be spared from other tasks help to build the church. The tower, 75 feet tall, is topped by an iron cross.

Behind the church are the missionaries' apartments, guestrooms, a kitchen and dining room, mission offices, and a storeroom for defensive arms.

SUNRISE

Mission workshops

An Indian craftsman paints with yellow, red, and blue pigments made from local stone.

A low stone wall surrounds the cemetery.

Sugarcane from the mission fields is crushed in a rotary mill; juice is boiled down in a copper-lined pan (above, left) to make brown sugar and cane syrup.

Local limestone is heated in wood-fired kilns to make quicklime, used for mortar in the church and other stone structures. The lime is ready when the stone has crumbled to powder. Water is added to the powder to make mortar; milk is added to increase its binding power and durability.

A hand-dug *acequia* ("irrigation ditch") brings water from the San Antonio River nearly two miles away. Water for drinking comes from wells.

Hides of cattle from the mission ranch are tanned in open pits.

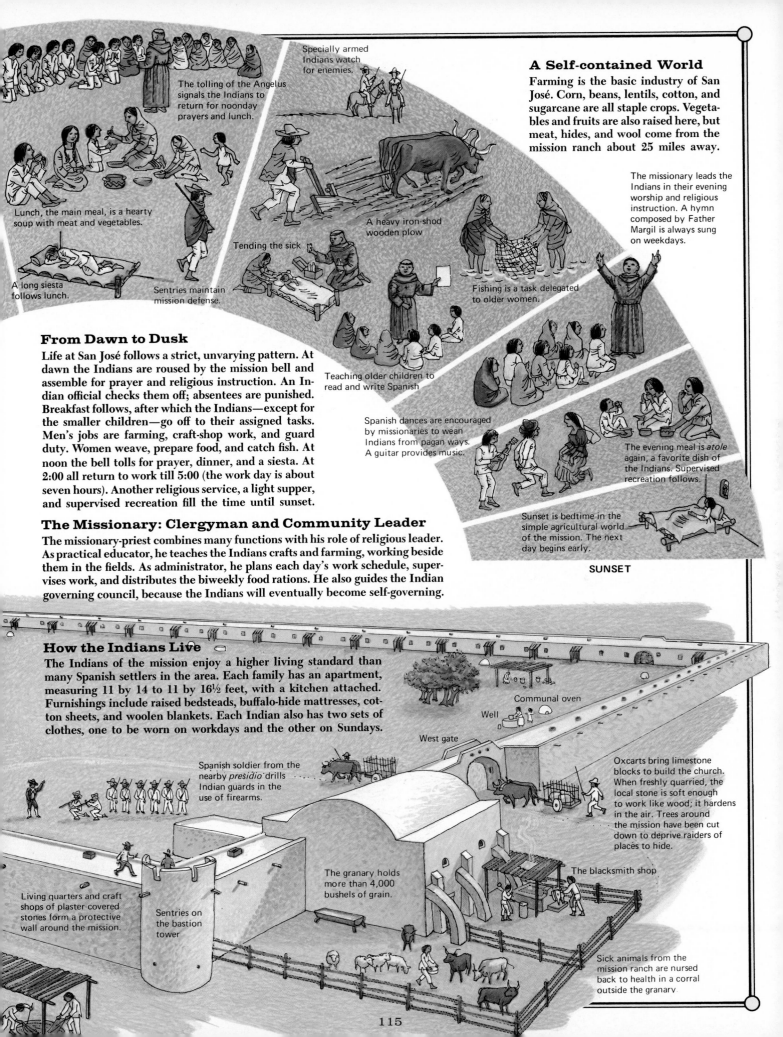

The tolling of the Angelus signals the Indians to return for noonday prayers and lunch.

Specially armed Indians watch for enemies.

Lunch, the main meal, is a hearty soup with meat and vegetables.

A long siesta follows lunch.

Sentries maintain mission defense.

A heavy iron-shod wooden plow

Tending the sick

Teaching older children to read and write Spanish

A Self-contained World

Farming is the basic industry of San José. Corn, beans, lentils, cotton, and sugarcane are all staple crops. Vegetables and fruits are also raised here, but meat, hides, and wool come from the mission ranch about 25 miles away.

The missionary leads the Indians in their evening worship and religious instruction. A hymn composed by Father Margil is always sung on weekdays.

Fishing is a task delegated to older women.

Spanish dances are encouraged by missionaries to wean Indians from pagan ways. A guitar provides music.

The evening meal is *atole* again, a favorite dish of the Indians. Supervised recreation follows.

Sunset is bedtime in the simple agricultural world of the mission. The next day begins early.

SUNSET

From Dawn to Dusk

Life at San José follows a strict, unvarying pattern. At dawn the Indians are roused by the mission bell and assemble for prayer and religious instruction. An Indian official checks them off; absentees are punished. Breakfast follows, after which the Indians—except for the smaller children—go off to their assigned tasks. Men's jobs are farming, craft-shop work, and guard duty. Women weave, prepare food, and catch fish. At noon the bell tolls for prayer, dinner, and a siesta. At 2:00 all return to work till 5:00 (the work day is about seven hours). Another religious service, a light supper, and supervised recreation fill the time until sunset.

The Missionary: Clergyman and Community Leader

The missionary-priest combines many functions with his role of religious leader. As practical educator, he teaches the Indians crafts and farming, working beside them in the fields. As administrator, he plans each day's work schedule, supervises work, and distributes the biweekly food rations. He also guides the Indian governing council, because the Indians will eventually become self-governing.

How the Indians Live

The Indians of the mission enjoy a higher living standard than many Spanish settlers in the area. Each family has an apartment, measuring 11 by 14 to 11 by 16½ feet, with a kitchen attached. Furnishings include raised bedsteads, buffalo-hide mattresses, cotton sheets, and woolen blankets. Each Indian also has two sets of clothes, one to be worn on workdays and the other on Sundays.

Communal oven

Well

West gate

Spanish soldier from the nearby *presidio* drills Indian guards in the use of firearms.

Oxcarts bring limestone blocks to build the church. When freshly quarried, the local stone is soft enough to work like wood; it hardens in the air. Trees around the mission have been cut down to deprive raiders of places to hide.

The blacksmith shop

Living quarters and craft shops of plaster-covered stones form a protective wall around the mission.

Sentries on the bastion tower

The granary holds more than 4,000 bushels of grain.

Sick animals from the mission ranch are nursed back to health in a corral outside the granary.

Southwestern Indians, Subject and Free

The Spaniards who colonized the American Southwest in the early 17th century claimed sovereignty not only over the region's lands and settlements but also over all its Indian inhabitants, whom they considered incapable of assimilating "true" civilization and hence eminently exploitable. For the most part they were scarcely aware of the cultural diversity of the three principal indigenous groups: the sedentary Pueblos, with their terraced towns and carefully tended farmlands; the raiding nomadic and seminomadic peoples, such as the Navajos, Apaches, and Comanches; and the primitive hunters of small game and gatherers of wild plants, such as the California tribes and the Coahuiltecans of southern Texas.

Of all the tribes subjugated by the Spaniards, it was this last group that most easily adapted to mission life. However, it paid dearly for its submission: by the early 19th century the Coahuiltecans and Karankawas of Texas had been virtually wiped out by white men's diseases. The so-called mission Indians of California would eventually suffer a similar fate.

The Pueblo peoples of what is now Arizona and New Mexico had an ancient, well-developed culture and ex-

The Apaches, descendants of the Athapascan-speaking hunters of Canada, probably arrived in the Southwest around 1500. They learned some farming from the Pueblo Indians, but hunting and gathering—and later raiding—were more important sources of food. Though the Apaches became expert horsemen, they preferred to do their fighting on foot and successfully resisted all Spanish attempts to subdue them.

tensive agriculture by the time Juan de Oñate encountered them along the upper Rio Grande in 1598. But generally unaggressive as they were (the tribal name "Hopi" means "peaceful ones"), they had suffered frequent raids from nomadic tribes long before the Spaniards arrived, and they could be ferocious in defense of their homes and their sacred customs. In August 1680 their long-simmering resentment of the Spanish yoke boiled over into the one

truly successful Indian rebellion against white rule in North American history. Led by an obscure Tewa medicine man known as Popé, who had twice been publicly flogged for speaking against Spanish rule, the Pueblo revolt erupted with explosive force, and within a few weeks the Spaniards had all been routed: 400 were killed and the rest driven in panic back to Mexico. Twelve years later, torn by dissension and weakened by Apache raids, the Pueblos submitted

Comanche Horsemen and Their Feats

The Comanches were unsurpassed at capturing and training wild horses (above), while as horsemen (right), they ranked among the most superb riders in the world.

In taming a wild horse, a Comanche caught it with a lasso and ran it until the animal, its breath cut off, became helpless. Then, according to artist George Catlin, "he fastens a pair of hobbles on the animal's two forefeet [and] puts a noose around its under jaw. . . . The horse makes every possible effort to escape, until its power is exhausted and it . . . yields to the power of man. He gradually advances, until able to place his hand on the animal's nose and . . . eyes; and at length to breathe into its nostrils, when it soon becomes docile. . . .

Great care is taken, however . . . not to subdue the [animal's] spirit." The training of horses and the practicing of mounted maneuvers occupied much of the young Comanche's time. In one feat a warrior would throw himself down the side of his horse and, hanging by a neck halter and steadied by a heel thrown over the horse's back, aim an arrow at an opponent or wield his 14-foot lance. Other tribes also used this stratagem, but none could match the Comanches, some of whom shot an arrow with deadly accuracy from under a horse's belly.

to reconquest by New Spain. But their revolt had led to an event of enormous significance: the dispersal of large numbers of horses to the nomadic tribes of the Southwest and the Great Plains.

Before Popé's revolt, herds of tough little Iberian horses had been kept in the pueblos for the benefit of the Spanish masters (whose word for gentleman, *caballero*, means "horseman"). After the Spaniards were routed these horses were either stolen by Navajo and Apache raiders or allowed to run wild by the Pueblos, who had little need of them. The effect was revolutionary. Those Indians who mastered the horse, as historian Walter Prescott Webb put it, "found themselves possessed of a liberty and

Mobile, mounted tribes of warriors and raiders dominated the Southwest; here and there lived farming and gathering tribes.

power which . . . made them a . . . terror to the sedentary Indians who dwelt in the periphery of their domain, to the Spaniards who came north, and later to the Americans who came west."

The Apaches and Navajos were the first Indians to become adept horsemen, using their mounts for lightning raids and equally quick escapes—though they seldom fought on horseback, never bred horses, and often used them for food, raiding for more at need. Many Apache and Navajo bands alternated raiding with agriculture as a way of life.

Ghosts and Mothers-in-law

Because they were often on the move, the southwestern raiding tribes were loosely organized, usually in relatively small kinship bands. And until they borrowed from the culture of their Pueblo prey—from whom the Navajos learned farming, herding, and weaving—they had few complex ceremonials or artifacts. The Apaches and Navajos spoke similar tongues and probably migrated to the Southwest not long before

The Lipan Apaches (above) lived in small groups that might join to form a band or break apart at will. Group affairs were directed by a chief. Driven south from the Great Plains by the Comanches, the Lipans settled in western and central Texas and northern Mexico.

the Spaniards. They possessed a rich store of mythology and a long list of taboos (one of the more curious being their belief that a man must never speak to or even look at his mother-in-law), and they shared a common horror of witches and the dead. All ghosts were thought to have malign powers, and the Apaches and Navajos buried their dead together with their possessions as quickly as possible to ward off evil.

Just as the name "Apache" was derived from a Zuni word for "enemy," the name "Comanche" came from the Ute word *Kohmahts* ("those who are always against us"). If the Apaches and Navajos were a scourge to the Spanish and their Indian subjects, the Comanches, who did not arrive in the Southwest until the early 1700's, quickly became a scourge not only to the Spaniards and the Indians associated with them but also to all the other Indians in the

region. The chief source of their power was their almost uncanny mastery of the horse. Painter George Catlin, who thought the Comanches a homely race, noted that the moment one of them "lays his hand upon his horse, his *face,* even, becomes handsome, and he gracefully flies away like a different being."

By 1750 the Comanches controlled a great swath of former Apache territory in central Texas and what is now eastern New Mexico, into which the Spaniards seldom even tried to penetrate. On this vast high plain, teeming with buffaloes, their bands grew fat and prosperous, refining their all-pervasive warrior cult and raiding Spanish and Indian settlements at will. Although the Spaniards arrogantly believed no Indians could seriously threaten European power, they never managed to subdue the Navajos, Apaches, or Comanches.

The Navajos, depicted here by Balduin Möllhausen, rivaled the Apaches in their skill with the bow and the lance. In fact, many of their customs and activities so resembled those of the Apaches that the Spanish, when first encountering them in the 1600's, called these Indians *Apaches de Navajo* after a deserted Pueblo site called Navajo, which the tribe had taken over. The Navajos lived for the most part in what is now northern New Mexico.

The Harmony of a Hopi Pueblo

True to the meaning of their name, the Hopi are a people at peace with the world. For they live their religion, and its essence is harmony. It is based on nine universes. The two highest are dwellings of the Supreme Being. Of the others, man has passed through the lower three, which are underground; he is now in the fourth, aboveground. At each emergence man is born unblemished, in harmony with all. If he can retain this purity, he will pass into a higher world. Before he entered the fourth world, man was given sacred corn, the Hopi staple. It is grown on dry plateaus, moistened only by springs—which are often dry—seepage water from the sandstone mesas, and occasional cloudbursts. The harsh environment inspires such respect for life that no game is killed without propitiation: a dead rabbit is fed cornmeal; a coyote is given a cornhusk cigarette. All villagers, as in the 1830 pueblo shown here, belong to one or more religious societies, each with a ritual chamber, or kiva, which serves as clubhouse, clinic, and shrine. Membership is matrilineal, as is family life—a daughter, for instance, gives birth at her mother's house. Birth, a Hopi Indian believes, is a byproduct of death, for after he dies and visits the underworld, his spirit may float above the earth as a rain cloud, enlivening new crops, and so bringing about rebirth.

Friendly Spirits, Sacred Rites

The dolls depict participants in holy rituals. Left: a banded, horned clown, who gives comic relief. Middle: Humis, the kachina, or spirit, who appears in July. Designs on his face and helmet, topped by eagle feathers, symbolize rain clouds and sprouting corn and squash. Right: the winter kachina named Chakwaina.

In Hopi lore evil witches, as well as man's frailty, sully life's original purity. To restore harmony, man needs the intercession of some 300 kachinas, benign messengers sent by the gods to accompany man when he emerged into the fourth world. The kachinas stay with him aboveground half the year, then descend through a hole, or *sipapu*, to the underworld. They are invoked in major rituals, such as the August rain ceremony of the societies of the Snake (symbolizing Mother Earth) and the Antelope (representing fruitful reproduction). Snake men collect serpents in the desert, sing to them, and feed them pollen. Antelope men perform foot races to "draw" the clouds so that the Snake can "suck" rain from them. On the eighth day priests conduct rites at the Antelope kiva altar (bottom, near right), prepared beforehand with gourds of purifying water and a sand depiction of rain's role in creation. On the ninth day the community convenes in the plaza of the village, where Antelope and Snake brothers stomp on the *sipapu*'s sounding board to waken the kachinas. Then the Snake men lift dozens of venomous serpents from a *kisi* pit, dance with them (below), finally carry them back to the parched plateaus—and await the blessed rain.

On the ninth day a Snake priest holds a diamondback in his mouth while his guide strokes it with an eagle feather to keep it from coiling—and striking. At left Antelope men shake gourd rattles. The performers include an albino, believed to bring good fortune.

In the village plaza (below), edged by apartments, sacred *sipapu* and *kisi* await the rain rite. Standards fly over two societies' kivas, each a subterranean room with a fire pit, an altar, and a platform, symbols of the first, second, and third worlds respectively; a ladder leads up to the fourth world. The cutaway of this Antelope kiva shows an altar painting of rain, lightning, and snakes.

Men weave a sash on a lap loom.

Hearth for firing pots

Kisi

Sipapu

Snake kiva

The *kisi* is a cottonwood bower over a snakepit. Beside it is the sounding board of a *sipapu*, a hole to the underworld. The pennant of horse hair and feathers atop the Antelope kiva ladder warns outsiders to keep away from the ritual inside.

Antelope kiva

Recess with five shelves symbolizing five worlds

The red pot below holds a sacred badge.

Ceremonial bows

Holy corn, cornmeal, water gourds

Drum

Flute, rhythm sticks

Rattles

Priest (above right) adds feathers and cornhusks to a male-female prayerstick.

A "direction man," his stylized viscera showing, guards one of the cardinal points of the compass in this 14th- or 15th-century New Mexican kiva mural.

The woman and child on the rooftop below gaze over the property. Houses belong to the women. Girls live with and are educated by their mothers. When a girl marries, the couple lives in the bride's mother's home or next door. The husband must weave two sets of wedding garments for his bride and farm the fields of his wife's family. At puberty a son leaves his family to live in a kiva until marriage. Males do all weaving.

Multistoried dwellings are made of flat stones. The topmost stones support wooden crossbeams that are covered with a waterproof layer of grass, brushwood, and mud. This forms the roof of the lower chamber, the terrace of the upper one. Stone-floored rooms are 12 feet square, their walls smoothed with mud plaster. Street-level chambers lack doors and windows but have entrance holes, with ladders, in the terrace.

An eagle, kept for its feathers, is tied to a pole on which hangs an offering for harmony. The chimneytop is a bottomless inverted pot.

From projecting roof beams food hangs to dry. Hopis adopted Spanish chilies, onions, and mutton.

A man spins cotton thread with a whorl as another weaves a blanket.

Paneless window

At right hang onions, corn, herbs, chilies, strips of mutton.

Boy peers through the doorway at his sister shaping a basket and his mother making a pot. His mother has soaked and kneaded local yellow and gray clay and molded the pot's base from a single piece of clay. She now fashions its body with spiraling clay coils. She will smooth surfaces by hand and fire the pot in ashes of cedar bark.

Entrances of lower chambers are covered with deerskin when it rains. Upper stories have paddle-shaped entrances. Water and firewood for homes are lugged up cliffside steps to the pueblo.

Wrapped in a cotton dress fastened over the right shoulder, a woman totes a sack of corn. In winter she adds a coat of rabbit fur.

To prepare *piki*, their wafer-thin cornbread, women grind corn on three stone *metates* of varying roughness. They then will mix the cornmeal with water, add ashes for leavening, and roll the dough into square, flat sheets. After baking in the hearth *piki* is rolled and stuffed with meat, nuts, beans, or chilies.

Girl of marriageable age wears her hair in two disks—"butterfly wings." A married woman parts her hair in the middle.

Girl makes a basket by coiling a rope of plaited, dyed wild grasses. Hopis also plait containers of yucca leaves. Colors are related to compass directions: yellow, north; blue, west; red, south; white, east.

Chimney hood

A greased stone on which *piki* will bake. It will be served with a cornmeal drink.

Kachina dolls, the gods' gifts to children, are made of cottonwood root and hung on walls so toddlers can learn to distinguish 300 kachinas.

Indians' clothes reflect Spanish styles.

Infant in cradleboard

Stack of *piki*

Cornmeal and gourd dipper

Throwing stick

This Hopi father and son return from an August morning's hunt in the blazing-hot plain below the mesa, atop which their pueblo perches with others. They have driven deer and rabbits into a small circle, then killed them with arrows and throwing sticks. They also have picked wild tobacco, used only ritually, and hoed fields of corn, cotton, beans, watermelons, squash, and other vegetables. The crops are planted at a time determined by a designated Sun Watcher.

Turkeys, raised for feathers, and cotton were indigenous.

Daring Adventure Becomes Big Business

Perhaps the weakest point in Spain's fragile northern perimeter—stretching from east Texas to California—was the New Mexican capital of Santa Fe, separated from Mexico City by 1,500 miles of twisting mountain trails. Though still a quiet little town of flat-roofed adobe houses in 1821, it was far from the "prairie-dog village" that one scornful contemporary visitor called it. In addition to being home to 3,000 people, Santa Fe was the commercial center for some 40,000 ranchers and estate owners in the Rio Grande Valley, and for years Missouri merchants and traders had sought access to this ready-made market for manufactured goods. As early as 1739 French fur traders Pierre and Paul Mallet had done business in Santa Fe, but Spanish officials had dealt harshly with those few Americans who had tried to follow in the Frenchmen's footsteps. Would-be traders were jailed or heavily fined and their goods confiscated.

An accidental meeting in 1821 reopened commerce with Santa Fe, but at the same time it signaled the beginning of the end for the Spanish-speaking Southwest. On September 1 of that year William Becknell left Franklin, Missouri, with a party of some 20 frontiersmen, intending to visit the Plains tribes and swap manufactured goods for the Indians' pelts and horses. Confronted by a party of Spanish-speaking soldiers in the rugged Raton Pass, the Americans assumed that jail and confiscation would follow. Instead, the soldiers were elaborately cordial, explaining that Mexico had just thrown off Spanish rule and was eager for friendly contact with the United States. Missouri traders would be more than welcome in Santa Fe. Delighted with their good fortune, Becknell and his men hastened to the New Mexi-

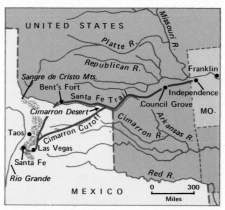

The Santa Fe Trail by way of the hazardous Cimarron Cutoff stretched some 800 miles from the Missouri border to New Mexico.

can capital, received a warm welcome from the goods-starved citizenry, and returned to Franklin in January 1822, their saddlebags heavy with Mexican silver dollars.

Two trading parties had set out from Missouri just shortly after Becknell; they returned safely to announce the happy (if misspelled) news that "the mackeson province Has de Clared Independence of the mother Cuntry and is desirous of a traid With the people of the united States." Becknell himself set forth again the following spring, this time with three heavily loaded wagons. But because wheeled vehicles could not negotiate the precipitous trail he had followed in 1821, Becknell struck south to blaze the comparatively flat Cimarron Cutoff. He very nearly did not make it. While crossing the searing 50-mile-wide Cimarron Desert, his party ran out of water. The desperate men were reduced to drinking the liquid contents of a freshly killed buffalo's stomach. Raiding Indians also plagued the party from time to time.

A Caravan of 100 Wagons

In the spring of 1824 all the Missouri traders bound for Santa Fe agreed to travel together in one well-defended caravan as protection against the "hostiles." The results of the venture were spectacular: the warring Indians kept away, and goods worth $35,000 brought a dazzling return of $190,000 in gold, silver, and furs.

The style of the Santa Fe trade had been set. From then on, except for a temporary halt during the Mexican War, ever-larger caravans made the annual trek, eventually expanding their operations to include Taos and markets in the state of Chihuahua.

By 1831 the caravan contained 100 wagons and 200 men. In an effort to aid the newly lucrative trade, Congress authorized payments to the Osage and Kansa

---

Dr. Josiah Gregg: Chronicler of Life on the Santa Fe Trail

A large caravan moved in four parallel columns, rather than in one long line, so that if hostile Indians appeared each column could quickly wheel about to create a hollow square or corral.

Ill health forced Dr. Josiah Gregg to abandon the practice of medicine in Jackson County, Missouri, and to seek relief in a trip across the High Plains to Santa Fe in 1831. For the next nine years Gregg was a trader on the Santa Fe Trail, making four round trips and living both in Santa Fe and northern Mexico. In 1844 his *Commerce of the Prairies* was published, and it remains the best account of this stirring chapter in the history of the Southwest. Little escaped Gregg's discerning eye: he wrote of the region's mountains, valleys, and plains, its rivers, animals, Indians, and natural resources—even a quietly humorous discussion of the mule's psychology (see opposite page). He was the first to note the decimation of the buffalo herds and to predict their extermination. The publication of his classic work established Dr. Gregg's literary credentials, and he served as a correspondent during the Mexican War. After the war he joined the gold rush to California, and while leading a party exploring the Trinity region of northern California in 1850, Gregg died of exposure at the young age of 43.

Indians to ensure safe passage and sent surveyors to chart the best routes. Occasional military escorts were dispatched as well, in order to help fend off the implacable Comanches who tried to rifle the wagons or run off precious livestock.

Nature presented greater dangers. Rockslides and crumbling precipices often made the mountain route nightmarish, while the shorter Cimarron Cutoff had its own horrors—withering desert heat, mirages, clouds of choking alkali dust. Overnight, spring rains turned freshets into mile-wide torrents and transformed dusty flatland into a hip-deep ocean of mud.

The New Mexican welcome, too, often wore thin. The governor in Santa Fe and his poorly paid subordinates were empowered to charge traders whatever customs duties the traffic would bear; traders never knew until they left Santa Fe how much of their profit they would be allowed to take with them. Bribery and smuggling were almost universal. The Americans, for their part, were determined to give up as little as possible for what one bitter muleskinner called "the sole use and benefit of his obesity, the Governor."

Rowdy Revels in Santa Fe

Still, traders found the risks worth running. For a time the caravans yielded an average of $130,000 each season—a handsome return of 10 to 40 percent for the men who rode the trail and for their delighted Missouri investors. And even in bad years there were other compensations. Santa Fe soon learned how best to

As a caravan nears Santa Fe, traders celebrate the end of an exhausting 10-week trip by shouting and firing rifles in the air. They will clean themselves up, don fresh clothes, and tie new crackers to their whips in anticipation of the pleasures awaiting them in town.

please the bone-weary teamsters at the end of the 800-mile trail. The La Fonda inn did a thriving business in free-flowing alcohol and all-night gambling. Willing women were also available. Their rouged cheeks, daring display of ankle, and fondness for tiny cigars symbolized thrilling depths of debauchery to frontiersmen accustomed to plainer fare back home. Drunken brawls and knife duels between Missourians and Mexican soldiers were frequent.

The result of all this bribery and carousing was that Mexicans and Americans saw each other at their worst. Local citizens came to resent the boisterous intruders, and most teamsters probably

agreed with trader Josiah Gregg, who found the New Mexicans "cunning, loquacious . . . sycophantic [and] cringing." With few exceptions, he wrote, they were untrustworthy intriguers, steeped in "bigotry and fanaticism."

The teamsters' colorful tales of the Santa Fe trade—of Indian fighting and buffalo hunting, of dark-eyed senoritas and hidden silver mines—helped fuel the land hunger of an increasingly expansionist United States. And the scornful ease with which traders eluded Mexican tariffs and ignored local laws demonstrated Mexico's powerlessness along her northern borders. New Mexico seemed ripe for the taking.

Smaller caravans marched in two lines, which formed an oval corral during halts. If Indians lurked, the animals were penned in the corral. In the background is a party of U.S. dragoons who accompanied this caravan until it arrived in Mexican territory.

"A Mule Will Be a Mule"

It is sometimes amusing to observe the athletic wagoner hurrying an animal to its post—to see him heave upon the halter of a stubborn mule, while the brute as obstinately sets back, determined not to move a peg till his own good pleasure thinks it proper to do so—his whole manner seeming to say, "Wait till your hurry's over!" I have . . . seen a driver hitch . . . a harnassed animal to the halter and . . . haul his mulishness forward, while each of his feet would leave a furrow behind; until at last the perplexed master would wrathfully exclaim, "A mule will be a mule any way you can fix it!"

—Josiah Gregg, *Commerce of the Prairies*, 1844

Santa Fe: Enticing End of the Trail

The square is vibrant with noise—the tinkle and clang of caravan bells, the hysterical braying of burros, the clatter of covered wagons; peddlers hawk, traders argue, and wagonmasters whoop their arrival. The Missouri freighters have finally rolled in; the oft-somnolent main plaza of Santa Fe is bedlam. At 10 a.m. everyone is eager to do business before the dusty midday heat drives most inside to the coolness of thick-walled whitewashed rooms or to the tree-shaded courtyards around which the one-story plastered adobe-brick dwellings are built. To the 4,000 New Mexicans in this area in 1835, the caravan's coming means an invigorating break in the isolation imposed on them by Spanish trade restrictions and by a lack of roads and navigable rivers. They have but a limited regional outlet for their pastoral trade in piñon nuts, asses, sheep, goats, and coarse wool. Lacking manufacture and craftsmen, their tools are primitive; and receiving only a trickle of overpriced goods from Mexico, they hunger for the less expensive Anglo supplies. To the Anglo-American traders Santa Fe means safety after weeks of danger; with luck, huge profits—and adventure. As one of them wrote: "Arrived at last in the strange place to which our wild love of novelty led us ... excitement tingled through our veins."

As a soldier stands guard, Albino Perez, governor of New Mexico, watches a wagon train. His palace is plain but contains offices, a guardroom, living quarters, a prison, a dirt-floor ballroom with buffalo-hide doors, and a rare luxury—glass windowpanes. In front of the flagpole runs the *acequia,* an open ditch that brings water for drinking and washing from a nearby swamp area. The town lacks a sewer system.

Grass grows on two feet of earth covering flat timber roofs.

Pitarrilla players

Acequia

Under cottonwood trees boys play *pitarrilla,* a type of checkers. Laid out on *jergas*—coarse wool carpets and blankets—is a display of round loaves of bread, sacks of cornmeal and apples, corn, apricots, melons, grapes, peaches, tomatoes, and chilies. Butchers sell mutton hung from tree limbs: the small sheep that graze the Santa Fe plateau's nutritious grasslands are very tasty. In the shade of the *portales* (arcades rimming the plaza, protecting the people from sun and rain) Pueblo Indians sell pots, bought by the townspeople for cooking and storage. Passing the vendors, a burro drags two planks; timber is found and cut far up in the mountains, so it is costly.

The sundial's inscription: "Life fleeth as a shadow."

A headband supports the shoulder bag of an Indian who, having walked from the Rio Grande Valley, comes with a month's mail—a few letters, magazines, and newspapers. He passes a boy running out with a wall poster from the palace press.

A New Mexican leads a string of burros carrying firewood for sale. Wood is piñon, a mountain scrub pine.

Oxen, with a yoke lashed to their horns, pull a *careta* laden with sacks of grain, chilies, and corn shucks to be used for mattress stuffing.

A lavishly dressed upper-class *caballero* trots in.

A wagonmaster hires a translator to help him through the vagaries of local taxes and to fill out forms for further trade far south in Chihuahua.

Its canvas top removed, a wagon is emptied of its 3,000-pound cargo. In cloth-wrapped bundles are shawls, socks, ladies' white cotton hose, hankies, shirts, pants. Two local women exclaim over calico. Beside them are bolts of cloth, felt hats, spices.

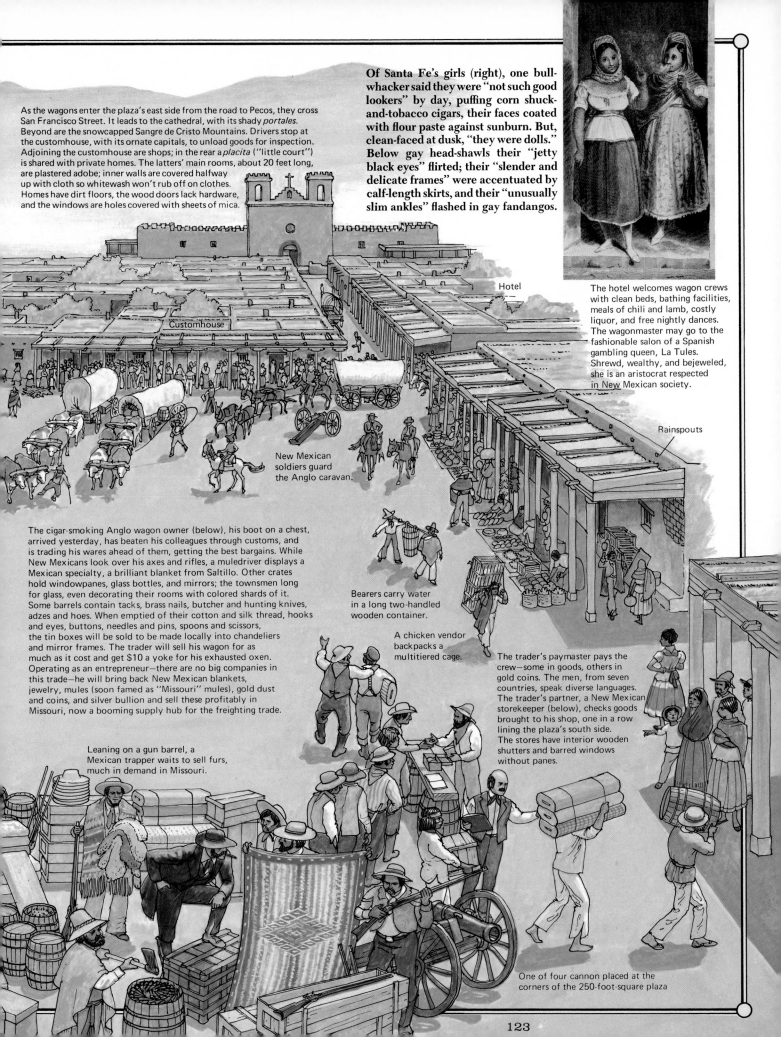

As the wagons enter the plaza's east side from the road to Pecos, they cross San Francisco Street. It leads to the cathedral, with its shady *portales*. Beyond are the snowcapped Sangre de Cristo Mountains. Drivers stop at the customhouse, with its ornate capitals, to unload goods for inspection. Adjoining the customhouse are shops; in the rear a *placita* ("little court") is shared with private homes. The latters' main rooms, about 20 feet long, are plastered adobe; inner walls are covered halfway up with cloth so whitewash won't rub off on clothes. Homes have dirt floors, the wood doors lack hardware, and the windows are holes covered with sheets of mica.

Of Santa Fe's girls (right), one bull-whacker said they were "not such good lookers" by day, puffing corn shuck-and-tobacco cigars, their faces coated with flour paste against sunburn. But, clean-faced at dusk, "they were dolls." Below gay head-shawls their "jetty black eyes" flirted; their "slender and delicate frames" were accentuated by calf-length skirts, and their "unusually slim ankles" flashed in gay fandangos.

Customhouse

Hotel

The hotel welcomes wagon crews with clean beds, bathing facilities, meals of chili and lamb, costly liquor, and free nightly dances. The wagonmaster may go to the fashionable salon of a Spanish gambling queen, La Tules. Shrewd, wealthy, and bejeweled, she is an aristocrat respected in New Mexican society.

New Mexican soldiers guard the Anglo caravan.

Rainspouts

The cigar-smoking Anglo wagon owner (below), his boot on a chest, arrived yesterday, has beaten his colleagues through customs, and is trading his wares ahead of them, getting the best bargains. While New Mexicans look over his axes and rifles, a muledriver displays a Mexican specialty, a brilliant blanket from Saltillo. Other crates hold windowpanes, glass bottles, and mirrors; the townsmen long for glass, even decorating their rooms with colored shards of it. Some barrels contain tacks, brass nails, butcher and hunting knives, adzes and hoes. When emptied of their cotton and silk thread, hooks and eyes, buttons, needles and pins, spoons and scissors, the tin boxes will be sold to be made locally into chandeliers and mirror frames. The trader will sell his wagon for as much as it cost and get $10 a yoke for his exhausted oxen. Operating as an entrepreneur—there are no big companies in this trade—he will bring back New Mexican blankets, jewelry, mules (soon famed as "Missouri" mules), gold dust and coins, and silver bullion and sell these profitably in Missouri, now a booming supply hub for the freighting trade.

Bearers carry water in a long two-handled wooden container.

A chicken vendor backpacks a multitiered cage.

The trader's paymaster pays the crew—some in goods, others in gold coins. The men, from seven countries, speak diverse languages. The trader's partner, a New Mexican storekeeper (below), checks goods brought to his shop, one in a row lining the plaza's south side. The stores have interior wooden shutters and barred windows without panes.

Leaning on a gun barrel, a Mexican trapper waits to sell furs, much in demand in Missouri.

One of four cannon placed at the corners of the 250-foot-square plaza

Americans Enter Texas

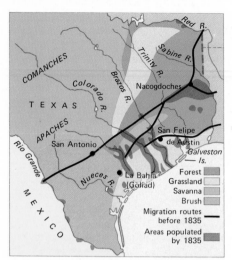

Anglo-American settlers in Texas spread through the wooded eastern area, but Mexicans preferred the dry southern grasslands.

Moses Austin's effort to obtain a land grant in Texas was aided by his proof of Spanish citizenship when he had lived in Louisiana.

From the first the rich lowlands and pine forests of east Texas had lured American adventurers. As early as 1791 Louisiana horse trader Philip Nolan, an associate of arch-plotter James Wilkinson, began traversing Spanish Texas in search of mustangs. His forays proved profitable, but Nolan may have had more than horses on his mind: he is believed by some scholars to have surveyed Spain's defenses, probably at Wilkinson's behest. In any case, his activities aroused the suspicions of Spanish officials, and when he came to Texas with 28 armed followers in 1800, ostensibly to round up more horseflesh, he was shot by Spanish soldiers.

Clearly, Texas would not fall easily, but events in central Mexico soon weakened Spain's grip. Beginning in 1810 a series of popular uprisings there absorbed Spain's attention and aroused the sympathy of the U.S. frontier. Memories of America's own revolution were still fresh in people's minds, and there were many Americans who believed an independent, republican Mexico would be more hospitable to U.S. settlers than imperial Spain had been.

In the summer of 1812 Bernardo Gutiérrez, a refugee revolutionary from Mexico, and Augustus W. Magee, an ex-U.S. Army officer, led a grandly named Republican Army of the North deep into Texas. Made up largely of river-town toughs as interested in loot as in liberty for Mexico, the 600-man force disintegrated soon after Magee died at La Bahía (now Goliad). Most of the men were later butchered by soldiers who remained loyal to Spain.

The last American expeditions into Texas were triggered by the Adams-Onís Treaty of 1819, which recognized Spain's claim to Texas in return for the cession of Florida to the United States. The treaty infuriated frontiersmen in the lower Mississippi Valley, who insisted that the Louisiana Purchase had encompassed all the lands watered by the Mississippi system—including the Red River and its tributaries. A little more pressure from U.S. diplomats, they were convinced, would have delivered Texas into American hands.

Protest meetings erupted all over the West, and one such meeting at Natchez spawned a 300-man volunteer army, eager to win for the United States what its statesmen had abandoned. Its leader was Dr. James Long, a blustery surgeon, speculator, and friend of Andrew Jackson. In June 1819 his army captured the startled border town of Nacogdoches without firing a shot. Long promptly proclaimed it the capital of the "Republic of Texas," with himself as president. He then made the mistake of leaving for Galveston Island to seek help from Gulf Coast pirate Jean Lafitte (who refused him); during Long's absence the disorderly defenders of Nacogdoches were trounced by a Spanish force.

Americans Come To Stay

Two years later Long tried again, joining the cause of Agustín de Iturbide. Although the latter did succeed in winning Mexican independence, Long was disillusioned by Iturbide's thirst for absolute power and in 1822 decided to leave Mexico City. He was killed by a nervous sentry, reportedly in an argument over his passport.

All these erratic swashbucklers provided colorful fare for American newspaper readers, but they accomplished little; U.S. settlers were still officially barred from Texas. Meanwhile, a more levelheaded American was winning Spanish sanction to found an Anglo-American colony.

In 1820 Moses Austin appeared in the Texas capital of San Antonio with an intriguing proposal for the Spanish governor: he wished to found a colony of 300 U.S. settler families in east Texas. All would be Roman Catholics of good character, he promised, and all would become loyal Spanish subjects. The governor, at first suspicious, finally approved the plan after Baron de Bastrop, an influential European living in San Antonio, interceded for Austin.

Austin returned to his Missouri home to gather a following but died before he could complete his work. At his request his son Stephen carried on; and when Spanish rule was overthrown, Stephen managed to persuade the new Mexican government to honor the contract granted to his father.

The land to which the 28-year-old Stephen Austin brought his first self-styled "Texians" in 1821, a fertile area centering on the Colorado and Brazos Valleys, was virtually empty. Other than Indians, the entire population of Texas was then no more than 4,000—most of them huddled in the towns of San Antonio, Goliad, and Nacogdoches.

San Felipe de Austin

Austin's determined pioneers cleared land, built cabins, sowed crops, repeatedly drove off the Indians, and in 1823 laid out their capital, which they called San Felipe de Austin. Their lives were rugged—"heaven for men and dogs," recalled one oldtimer, but "hell for women and oxen." Their hard work was richly rewarded, however. The alluvial soil was ideally suitable for corn and cotton. Pasturage was "inexhaustible," boasted Austin, "and green winter and summer." The forests were alive with game and the rivers with fish. One Texas pioneer wrote home that "it does not appear possible that there can be a land more lovely."

Stephen F. Austin: Founding Father of Texas

"The redemption of Texas from the wilderness, fidelity and gratitude to my adopted country, and to be inflexibly true to the interests and just rights of my settlers." Such was the code of Stephen F. Austin (1793–1836), the diminutive diplomat and statesman who colonized Texas with the plow and the rifle. During the early years of colony planting, the settlers often grew impatient with Austin's cautious handling of Mexican officials, but Austin insisted: "It was my duty to steer my precious bark [the colony] through all the shoals and quicksands regardless of the curses and ridicule of the passengers. I knew what I was about—they did not."

Born in southwestern Virginia on November 3, 1793, Stephen F. Austin was the eldest son of Moses Austin, a mineowner who moved his family of five in 1798 to what is now Missouri but was then part of Spanish Louisiana. And it was there, living among French and Spanish settlers, that Stephen learned to respect cultures other than his own—a discipline that would serve him well when he settled in Texas. At age 11 he began his formal schooling, first at Bacon Academy in Colchester, Connecticut, and later at Transylvania University in Lexington, Kentucky. Then it was back to Missouri as a mine manager, bank director, and territorial legislator; he became a circuit judge in Arkansas, a law student in New Orleans, and an editorial worker for the *Louisiana Advertiser*.

Then in 1821, when Austin was 27, came news of Moses Austin's death—and his last request regarding the Texas land grant that was Stephen Austin's inheritance. "He called me to his bedside," Maria Austin wrote her son, "and with much distress and difficulty of speech beged me to tell you to take his place and . . . go on with the business in the same way he would have done." Although Austin knew little of what his father's plans for colonization had been, he nevertheless left at once for the far frontier.

In the land to which Austin brought his 300 families (known as the Old 300) a town soon began to blossom on the lower crossing of the Brazos River—the capital of San Felipe de Austin. Yet, even as he planted roots between the Brazos and the Colorado and became the prime mover in what would become America's 28th state, Austin knew well how few his rewards would be: "A successful military chieftain is hailed with admiration and applause," he noted, "and monuments perpetuate his fame. But the bloodless pioneer of the wilder-

Stephen Austin seizes his rifle as a wounded settler reports an Indian raid. The man at the far left is Baron de Bastrop, the Mexican government's land commissioner for the Texas colony.

ness, like the corn and cotton he causes to spring where it never grew before, attracts no notice."

And after 15 years of tireless toil for Texas—years that saw him create a sturdy colony, help lead the 1835–36 revolution against Mexico, and lay the groundwork for U.S. recognition as the new republic's first secretary of state—the weary 43-year-old Austin could write: "I have no house, not a roof in all Texas that I can call my own. The only one I had was burned at San Felipe during the late invasion of the enemy. . . . I have no farm, no cotton plantation, no income, no money, no comforts. . . . All my wealth is prospective and contingent upon the events of the future. What I have been able from time to time to realize in active means has gone as fast as realized, and much faster (for I am still in debt for the expenses of my trip to Mexico in 1833, '34, and '35) where my health and strength and time have gone, which is in the service of Texas, and I am therefore not ashamed of my present poverty." Just a few weeks after he penned those words, Austin was gone—on December 27, 1836—leaving behind neither wife nor family. Yet even in his death throes he remained a man of single-minded purpose. Awakening from a dream and thinking that the United States had recognized the independence of Texas, he murmured: "Texas recognized. . . . Did you see it in the papers?"

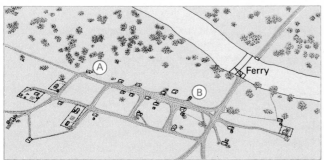

This drawing of a model of San Felipe de Austin, c. 1830, locates its straggle of cabins on the Brazos River: (A) indicates the blacksmith shop of Gail Borden, whose son later invented condensed milk; (B) shows the Cooper & Cheeves Saloon, the village's only frame building. All of the others were log cabins.

A Clash of Cultures

Pleased at Austin's progress and relieved to see the vastness of Texas being peopled at last, Mexico encouraged further immigration. A thriving Texas economy would surely benefit the whole nation, and strong settlements would provide protection against hostile Indians and discourage forays by disreputable American landgrabbers. In 1824 the Mexican Congress joined Texas with the neighboring state of Coahuila, in order to ensure a Spanish-speaking majority, and authorized the region to dispose of its lands to newcomers. The new state of Coahuila-Texas established the so-called empresario system a year later.

Fifteen promoters, Mexican and American, took advantage of its generous terms. In exchange for vast holdings, each pledged to settle 100 or more families within six years. Each family would receive one *labor* (177 acres) of farmland and a *sitio* for grazing land—a total of about 4,500 acres.

An Attractive Prospect for Settlers

New settlers received special treatment. Foreigners were exempted from taxes, tariffs, and conscription. Though the liberal Mexican constitution adopted in 1824 forbade slavery, Austin obtained a state statute permitting every Anglo-American to keep his slaves as lifetime "indentured servants." All settlers were required to be at least nominal Catholics, but only a small percentage actually was, and officials looked the other way as long as Protestants did not worship together in public.

The new immigration policy was a stunning success. There were 10,000 U.S.-born Texans in 1827 and twice that number only three years later. Their relations with Mexico City were correct and even cordial at first. Austin was honor-bound to keep his fast-growing colony loyal to the republic, and he worked hard to minimize friction. Potential troublemakers and Protestant ministers were screened out. All dealings with the central government went through the proper channels, no matter how slow or cumbersome they became. Austin was a paternalistic leader who saw his colonists as "one great family who are under my care."

But as rival empresarios arrived to settle their own land grants, it became evident that each intended to run his colony in his own way, and Austin's allegiance to Mexico sat poorly with some of them. It also annoyed another element in the turbulent Texas mix—the hundreds of squatters who for years had been drifting into the Red River region near the U.S. border. Most were hunters or hardscrabble farmers, but among them were thieves, murderers, and other fugitives from U.S. justice. Few had legal title to the lands they cleared, and fewer still heeded the dictates of far-off Mexico.

This Mexican presidial, or guard, served in the cavalry assigned to protect the Texans against Indians threatening their villages.

Though most Texans probably shared Austin's loyalty to Mexico until the Texas Revolution actually began, tensions rose steadily. Some were political in nature, but most were cultural, for Mexicans and Americans never fully trusted or understood each other.

Many Mexicans found the newcomers overbearing, ill-mannered, and—as more and more of them poured into Texas—apparently hellbent on taking over. The Anglo-Americans, for their part, usually shared the racial and cultural assumptions held by other American frontiersmen of that time: they saw themselves as a superior people, destined by Providence to subdue a wilderness that the Mexicans and their Spanish predecessors had lacked the energy or foresight to tame.

The "Fredonian Revolt"

In fact, Mexico's record of governing herself was unimpressive so far. Centuries of colonial rule had left her determined but ill-prepared to run her own affairs. Chaos below the Rio Grande meant that Texas was often left alone. This generally suited the self-reliant settlers, but isolation also had its bad side. Few troops shielded the settlements from Indians. There was no trial by jury. Local government was antiquated and inefficient.

The first clear sign of coming trouble was the comic-opera "Fredonian Re-

As the Anglo-Americans flocked to Texas, ads in *The Texas Gazette* appeared in English and in Spanish. In these Thomas Johnston seeks customers, and John Randon (right) wants to recover runaway slaves.

volt" of 1826. When an empresario named Haden Edwards, whose land grant included Nacogdoches and part of the northeast Texas squatter zone, began arbitrarily favoring his own colonists' claims at the expense of earlier settlers, Mexican officials annulled his contract and expelled him from the country. While Austin was pressing for an impartial inquiry into the controversy, Edwards' brother Benjamin rode into Nacogdoches at the head of a tiny band of men on December 16, 1826. Unfurling a red-and-white flag inscribed "Independence, Liberty and Justice," Benjamin took over the town's fort and proclaimed the "Republic of Fredonia." He had hoped for Austin's support, but the latter, after one more fruitless attempt to mediate the quarrel, prudently called out the militia from his own colony to help the Mexicans put down the insurgents. And so the Fredonian republic collapsed. The refusal of Austin's colonists—and of the Red River squatters, who had distrusted Haden Edwards' high-handedness—to support the revolt should have calmed Mexican officials, but they saw this tiny tempest as proof of American determination to wrest Texas from Mexico.

An American Offer To Buy Texas

Their fears were further aroused by continuing American agitation for the annexation of Texas, or at least part of it. Westerners remained noisily unhappy with the Adams-Onís boundary, and in 1829 President Andrew Jackson offered to buy Texas for $5 million. When the Mexicans indignantly refused, Jackson's agent repeatedly and clumsily tried to bribe them into reconsidering. Such actions, plus memories of Jackson's invasion of Spanish Florida and rumors that he had earlier advocated occupation of Texas, persuaded some Mexicans that he had been behind the Fredonian affair as well. Another ominous note was provided by U.S. newspaper advertisements that seemed to offer for sale Mexican lands to which American speculators had no title.

In 1829 the Mexican general Manuel de Mier y Terán was ordered to report on conditions in Texas. Appalled by the extent of Anglo-American influences, Terán issued a blunt warning: "Either the government occupies Texas *now*, or it is lost forever."

His warning was well timed. In Mexico the Centralists, a conservative political faction led by Mexican-born autocrats of pure Spanish descent, had seized power in 1828. Deeply distrustful of the aggressiveness and independent spirit of the Texans, they took just two years to clamp down.

General Terán's recommendations were written into the Colonization Law of 1830, which stated that citizens of "foreign countries lying adjacent to the Mexican territory" were henceforth forbidden to settle in Texas. New colonies of Mexican and European pioneers would be planted to offset the influence of the Anglo-Americans. Coastal trade between Texas and the rest of Mexico would be encouraged to solidify ties between the two; taxes and tariffs would be imposed; and troops would be garrisoned in Texas to enforce the laws.

The result was the opposite of what its authors intended. Few European settlers came, and the ban on American immigration served only to keep out the more law-abiding pioneers. Volatile squatters continued to drift across the border, and between 1830 and 1835 the U.S.-born population jumped from 20,000 to 30,000. Among these latecomers were two men destined to play key roles in the coming revolution: Sam Houston and William B. Travis. Only one aim of the 1830 act, the military occupation of Texas, was actually fulfilled—and the presence of Mexican troops had much the same effect on resentful Texans as the quartering of British Redcoats had had on an earlier generation of American revolutionaries.

Terán's Survey of Texas

When Mexican officials decided to review their past policy of encouraging Anglo-American settlement of Texas, they handed the job to Gen. Manuel de Mier y Terán, who in 1829 had become commandant general of the Eastern Interior Provinces. Terán was the right man for this task, having led an expedition that explored Texas in 1828, during which the French naturalist-artist Jean Louis Berlandier made sketches of Indians and Texas animals (see below). In reporting on this trip, Terán had noted with displeasure that Anglo-Americans outnumbered Mexicans 10 to 1 and were better fed, housed, and clothed than their Spanish-speaking neighbors. In his new report, issued in January 1830, Terán urged strong measures to curb the growing power of the newcomers and to tighten Mexico's grip on Texas by bringing in more Mexican and European colonists, strengthening the existing garrisons, and establishing new ones.

Unlike most officials in faraway Mexico City, Gen. Manuel de Mier y Terán had firsthand knowledge of life in Texas.

Acting President Anastasio Bustamante supported General Terán's proposals to dilute Anglo-American power in Texas.

Herds of combative wild swine, called javelinas, often attacked hunters. Texans disdained their meat, which was tainted by a fetid gland in the animal's back, but the Indians knew of a way to cook it in a pit to draw off all the offensive secretions.

"Let Each Man Come With a Good Rifle"

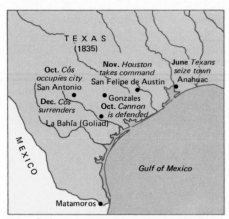

The drift into war, from the skirmish at Anahuac up to the capture of San Antonio.

On October 12, 1835, 10 days after the first shots of the Texas Revolution were fired, a force of Texans captured large stores of food and ammunition at Goliad, shown above.

The first step on the road to revolution was taken in 1832 at the port of Anahuac on Galveston Bay, where a garrison had been installed under the command of Col. John D. Bradburn, a bullying Kentuckian then in the Mexican service. He not only alienated the settlers by "borrowing" their slaves and supplies without payment but also ordered those who objected (among them firebrand attorney William B. Travis) arrested and held for military trial. In June 160 angry settlers besieged the fort, demanding Bradburn's resignation and the release of his prisoners. The officer yielded, but even so there was a skirmish between the settlers and Mexican troops—which the Texans won.

At this time all Mexico was caught up in a renewed struggle between the conservative Centralists and the Federalists, champions of the democratic constitution of 1824. Those besiegers of the Anahuac garrison hastened to point out that they did not oppose Mexican rule as such but were merely acting in support of the Federalists, who had taken power that year in a bloodless coup led by Gen. Antonio López de Santa Anna.

Two conventions of settlers held at San Felipe de Austin in 1832 and 1833 drew up a list of reforms they hoped would be sympathetically received by their "Federalist ally," Santa Anna. Among the things they requested were repeal of the clause in the 1830 Centralist law that prohibited American immigration, suspension of customs duties for three years, trial by jury, and the separation of Texas from Coahuila.

When Stephen Austin reached Mexico City in July 1833 with the Texans' proposals, he learned that President Santa Anna was away fighting rebels in the hinterlands and found the capital in turmoil because of a cholera epidemic. Austin clashed with the vice president over the slow pace of negotiations and in

October wrote a letter to officials in San Antonio urging them to begin formation of a new state without Mexican permission. When Santa Anna returned to Mexico City in November, he agreed to several of the Texans' requests, including trial by jury and repeal of the ban on American immigration, but he opposed separate statehood for Texas. Austin then left for home but was arrested when officials in Mexico City intercepted the letter he had written to San Antonio a month earlier.

Santa Anna on the March

While Austin sat helpless in a Mexico City jail, Santa Anna moved even farther from his Federalist supporters, and in the spring of 1834 he went over to the Centralists and proclaimed himself permanent president. After abolishing the federal system and installing his own puppets as state governors, he turned his attention to Texas. In January 1835 he

---

Santa Anna: Mexico's Irrepressible Leader

During a 46-year career in the army and in politics Antonio López de Santa Anna (1794-1876), unlike his idol Napoleon Bonaparte, suffered more than one Waterloo, but he regularly confounded his enemies by bouncing back into power. Born in Jalapa, Veracruz, Santa Anna began his military career as a cadet at age 15. After Mexico won its independence from Spain in 1821 he entered politics, changing sides several times. Eventually he supported the liberal Federalists against the conservative Centralists and in 1832 engineered a coup that ousted the Centralist dictator; he was elected president for the term beginning

January 1, 1833. By 1835 he had repudiated the Federalist Party and become dictator of Mexico. After his defeat by the Texans at San Jacinto in 1836, Santa Anna fell from power, but he became a hero against French invaders at Veracruz and returned to the presidency three more times: in office from 1841-44 (ousted for extravagance and incompetence); from 1846-47 (he went into exile after his defeat in the Mexican War); and from 1853-55 (overthrown and exiled after he declared himself president for life). In 1874 the blind, impoverished old man was allowed by his government to return to Mexico City where he died in 1876.

Scorning the odds against them, 300 volunteers led by Ben Milam, who died in the attack, drove General Cós' Mexican troops into San Antonio's Alamo mission in five days of house-to-house fighting. The Mexicans surrendered to the Texans on December 10, 1835.

The Mexican Soldier

This corporal of a rifleman company was typical of the soldiers in Santa Anna's army in 1835. His coat and his shako, with its brass plate and plume, were regulation from previous years. His British Baker rifle had a sword-bayonet. The switch on his cowhide pack was used, if necessary, to prod men into action.

Although courageous, many of the Mexican soldiers were Indians who did not understand Spanish and knew little about firearms. Indifferently trained by their officers, infantrymen usually fired from the hip to avoid the mulelike kick of their heavy rifles.

installed a new and extremely venal customs collector at Anahuac—stirring settlers' memories of Bradburn—and prepared to lead an army northward to cow the Texans and crush Federalist uprisings in several northern states.

Word of all this stirred the Texas radicals to action, and in June a band of 40 men under Travis forced the Anahuac garrison to evacuate once more. Texas moderates continued to press for conciliation, but when Travis and his men were ordered arrested by Mexican officials—who also made plain their intention to impose martial law throughout Texas—even the more conservative settlers were outraged. Then in September Santa Anna hardened their resolve by ordering his brother-in-law, Gen. Martín Perfecto de Cós, to reinforce San Antonio. Stephen Austin, who had been released from prison, came to the end of his patience. He signed a proclamation declaring: "There is no other remedy but to defend our rights, ourselves, and our country by force of arms."

Defiance in Gonzales

While Cós' forces slogged toward San Antonio, a cavalry detachment was sent to Gonzales to reclaim an aged brass cannon the inhabitants had once borrowed to ward off Indian attacks. The men of Gonzales not only refused to give it up but also taunted the Mexicans by placing a sign on the cannon that read, "Come and Take It!" Then, on October 2, they let fly with a load of nails, wire, and horseshoes, followed by rifle fire. The shocked Mexicans galloped toward San Antonio in disarray.

The revolution had begun. Flushed with their victory, the cocky Texans of Gonzales resolved to drive General Cós and his entire army back to Mexico. On October 12 a hastily assembled "Army of the People"—some 500 armed farmers from Gonzales and nearby settlements—set out for San Antonio with their celebrated cannon in tow. They found the city well fortified by Cós' troops and settled in for a long siege.

A Provisional Government

Meanwhile, a "consultation" of Texas leaders that had been called by Stephen Austin met in his colony's capital in November of 1835. After pointlessly reaffirming their loyalty to the now-defunct Federalist constitution, the delegates appointed a provisional governor of Texas and a 12-man ruling council. Three commissioners, Austin among them, were dispatched to the United States to solicit loans and rally volunteers, and the experienced frontiersman Sam Houston was named commander in chief of the Texas forces.

Houston knew that American aid would be crucial to success, and soon his signed pleas for help were appearing in U.S. newspapers. "Let each man come with a good rifle," he wrote, "and come soon." Once the "usurper" Santa Anna was driven from Texas, Houston vowed, those who helped defeat him would be amply rewarded with land. At Texas rallies across the United States volunteers signed up eagerly, but despite their enthusiasm Houston had few illusions about the task he faced.

Santa Anna's 6,000-man army seemed a formidable force on paper, but many of its soldiers were poorly armed and poorly trained Indian conscripts led by incompetent officers; supplies were in-

adequate and morale low. Had Houston been given his head, he might have exploited these weaknesses sooner than he did, but Texas' shaky provisional government was unwilling even to give him control of the settler-volunteers encamped outside San Antonio.

Acting on their own initiative, these men mounted a savage assault on the town, and on December 10 Cós and his 1,100-man garrison surrendered, vowing to return home and fight no more. Drunk with success, the volunteers left a skeleton force in San Antonio's adobe-walled Alamo mission and sent two foolhardy missions southward to attack the Mexicans at Matamoros. Certain that the Alamo could not long withstand a siege, Houston ordered its fortifications dismantled in January 1836—only to have his orders countermanded by the Texas provisional governor, Henry Smith. The latter dispatched the ever-ready William Travis (now a colonel in the Texas Army) to reinforce the mission, thus paving the way for one of the most celebrated tragedies in American history, the siege of the Alamo.

The Well-Remembered Alamo

At dawn on the 13th day of the siege—March 6, 1836—Gen. Antonio López de Santa Anna hurled 1,800 men against the Alamo while his band blared the savage "No Quarter" call of the "Degüello," a Spanish battle march. Twice the Mexicans charged, and twice they were sent reeling. Santa Anna then unleashed his reserves. They poured over the northern wall, where Col. William B. Travis had died, slumped near a cannon. Fighting hand-to-hand—bowie knives and clubbed rifles against bayonets—the defenders fell back to die in the convent barracks and the Alamo chapel. As the battle din subsided around 7 a.m., Santa Anna approached the Alamo, only to turn tail when a last defiant shot snapped over his head. A short time later he strolled through the smoking plaza searching for the bodies of Travis, Jim Bowie, and Davy Crockett. "It was but a small affair," Santa Anna said, but he had never been more wrong in his life. He had lost at least 600 of his men, and Texas had won a symbol and a battle cry that would crush him six weeks hence at San Jacinto.

The Texas Defenders

Travis   Bowie   Crockett

The combative, hot-tempered Colonel Travis believed the Alamo was the key to Texas and, until a few days before the final assault by Santa Anna's force of some 1,800, was confident his handful of defenders could hold out until reinforcements arrived. Near madness in grief over the deaths of his wife and two children in a plague, Jim Bowie appeared to welcome a last-ditch stand. Wrote Bowie of the Alamo: "We will rather die in these ditches than give it up to the enemy." Said Sam Houston of Bowie: "There is no man on whose ... valor I place a higher estimate." A late arrival at the Alamo was Davy Crockett—whose Tennesseans fought like tigers at the southeast wall.

The Mexican Attacker

Santa Anna, dictator of Mexico in 1836 and self-styled "Napoleon of the West."

Santa Anna directed the attack from a nearby command post, but the decisive assaults on the Alamo were led by two of his officers: Juan V. Amador and Manuel F. Castrillón. General Amador had fallen from Santa Anna's graces, but he redeemed himself when he rallied a wavering battalion and led the attack on the Alamo chapel. After leading the charge that carried the plaza, General Castrillón offered protection to six wounded men—but Santa Anna ordered the soldiers put to the sword.

This Was the Alamo in 1836

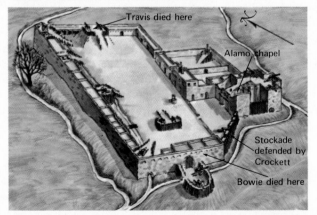

Travis died here
Alamo chapel
Stockade defended by Crockett
Bowie died here

Situated on three acres of ground about a quarter-mile east of San Antonio, the Alamo mission had been completed by Franciscan missionaries in the 1750's—so its shortcomings as a fort were considerable. Its low outer walls could be scaled by ladders, and there were no loopholes to fire through. Worse, there was a 50-yard gap in the southeast wall, which was closed only by a log stockade and earth parapet. But the walls of the Alamo chapel were 22 feet high and 4 feet thick, and as Santa Anna and his men were to discover, the Texas defenders would sell them dearly.

Bowie Died Fighting From His Bed

Armed with a brace of pistols and the knife named after him, a deathly ill Jim Bowie fought his last fight from a sickbed near the main gate of the Alamo. Bowie had come to Mexico from Louisiana about 1828 and became a Mexican citizen in 1830.

Davy Crockett's Last Stand at the Alamo

Did Davy Crockett die fighting (as in this painting) near the Alamo's southeast palisade, or was he captured with six of his men, tortured, and executed by orders of Santa Anna? New evidence has caused historians to differ as to his fate, but all agree that he died bravely.

Travis Draws the Line

Tradition has it—and the Alamo is steeped in tradition and legend—that on March 3, with the end in sight, Travis drew a line on the ground with his sword and said: "I now want every man who is determined to stay here and die with me to come across this line." All but two—desperately sick Jim Bowie and a drifter named Louis Rose, a veteran of the Napoleonic Wars a generation earlier—stepped forward. "Boys," called Bowie, "I wish some of you would . . . remove my cot over there." Four men lifted him across. Rose escaped after dark, surviving to tell his story of Travis and the line, which was not revealed until 37 years later in a thirdhand account by an illiterate woman.

The Final Message From the Defenders

Fellow citizens & compatriots—I am besieged, by a thousand or more of the Mexicans under Santa Anna—I have sustained a continual Bombardment & cannonade for 24 hours & have not lost a man—The enemy has demanded a surrender at discretion, otherwise, the garrison are to be put to the sword, if the fort is taken—I have answered the demand with a cannon shot, & our flag still waves proudly from the walls—*I shall never surrender or retreat.* Then, I call on you in the name of Liberty, of patriotism & everything dear to the American character, to come to our aid, with all dispatch—The enemy is receiving reinforcements daily & will no doubt increase to three or four thousand in four or five days. If this call is neglected, I am determined to sustain myself as long as possible & die like a soldier who never forgets what is due to his own honor & that of his country—VICTORY OR DEATH.
—W. Barret Travis
Lieutenant Colonel Comdt.

131

A War Won in 18 Minutes

On March 2, 1836, four days before the Alamo's tiny band of defenders were killed, 59 Texas leaders met in a crude frame building in the tiny village of Washington-on-the-Brazos. Shivering as the icy prairie wind whipped through the glassless windows, they declared Texas an independent republic in a document closely modeled on the American Declaration of Independence. The delegates then adopted a constitution that incorporated features from the U.S. and several state constitutions. It provided for a president who was limited to a single three-year term, an elected Congress, and a judiciary patterned after that of the United States. Slavery would be legalized, and each Texas family head would be guaranteed an ample land grant. David G. Burnet, who was a charter member of the war faction, was sworn in as interim president.

Since most Texans now favored independence, their sagging spirits lifted momentarily at the exciting news from Washington-on-the-Brazos. But hard on its heels came reports of the stunning tragedy at the Alamo. Instead of being intimidated by the defeat, however, Texans stiffened their spines. Santa Anna had unwittingly provided their cause with 182 martyrs whose fate cried out for vengeance. A Texas private named G. A. Giddings spoke for many when he wrote to his parents: "Our garrison at San Antonio was taken and massacred. If such conduct is not suffi-

cient to arouse the patriotic feelings of the sons of liberty, I know not what will. . . . Rather than be driven out of the country or submit to be a slave, I will leave my bones to blanch on the plains of Texas." (True to his word, Giddings stayed with the army and was one of the few Texans to fall at San Jacinto.)

"To the Rescue!"

Many of the Alamo's martyrs had been U.S. volunteers. American newspapers emblazoned the tragedy in their headlines and called for renewed support for the Texas struggle. "To the rescue, then, brave men of the West!" thundered the Richmond *Enquirer.* "To the rescue!" Fresh volunteers flooded across the border, while more and more Texans grabbed their rifles and saddled up.

Among the most important acts of the March convention at Washington-on-the-Brazos had been the reaffirmation of Houston's right to command. Texans had finally realized that they could no longer afford the luxury of debating whether or not orders should be obeyed, and Houston was willing to shoulder full responsibility for the struggle. "Had I consulted the wishes of all I should have been like the ass between two stacks of hay," he wrote. "I consulted none—I held no councils of war. If I err, the blame is mine."

Taking command of his small, still-unruly army at Gonzales in mid-March 1836, Houston began a zigzagging eastward retreat, always staying a step ahead of the Mexicans. He knew his force was no match for Santa Anna's oncoming army, but the weather was with him. Cold, pelting spring rains slowed Santa Anna's pace, turning cart tracks into deep bogs. Houston's only hope lay in

exhausting his pursuer, stretching the Mexican supply lines, and waiting until the Texas ranks swelled enough for his men to make a stand—or until Santa Anna made some kind of mistake.

As Houston marched, he received the disheartening news of still another Texas defeat. On March 20 a 350-man force, on its way from Goliad to join Houston's army, was caught by the Mexicans on the banks of the San Antonio River. The prisoners were marched back to Goliad where, on March 27 (Palm Sunday), they were coldbloodedly shot to death at Santa Anna's orders.

Houston on San Jacinto

It is gravely asserted by my enemies, that if the policy of certain military chieftains had prevailed the Texans would have crossed the Colorado river, annihilated the enemy and saved the people of the west from the ravages of war. If we are disposed to speculate in ifs, we may as well discuss the other hypothetical if. If the Texas army had countermarched, crossed the river and attacked the enemy, and been defeated, what then? Let the wails of the fallen of the Alamo and Goliad answer. Such speculations, seriously engaged in, are as unprofitable and vain as they are vicious. . . . The past is at least, secure and unalterable. . . . Travis, Fannin, Crockett, Bowie, were all brave and gallant spirits, they never . . . employed slander . . . their acts were open and bold; their policy of warfare was to divide, advance and conquer. My policy was to concentrate, retreat and conquer.

David G. Burnet, who toted a Bible and a pistol, was the man elected president of the provisional government of Texas.

Houston's retreat and the news of the butchery at Goliad convinced many Texans that all was lost. If even "Old Sam" avoided meeting him, Santa Anna must be truly unstoppable. Many settlers panicked, and the result was the "runaway scrape," a mass race for the U.S. border by terrified Texans from the areas abandoned by Houston's army. Many of them had burned their crops and cabins rather than see them fall into Mexican hands. The fledgling Texas government, too, was in retreat. It fell back from Washington-on-the-Brazos to tiny Harrisburg and finally took refuge in the tangled thickets of Galveston Island. Retreat was embarrassing to both the government and the army, and President Burnet bombarded Houston with letters exhorting him to stand and fight: "Sir: The enemy are laughing you to scorn. . . . You must retreat no farther. The country expects you to fight. The salvation of the country depends on you doing so."

The Battle of San Jacinto

Houston paid no attention to either the president or the homeless settlers who appeared along his line of retreat and jeered openly at the frustrated volunteers, some of whom wept for shame. Rumors spread that Houston's well-known fondness for alcohol had blurred his judgment, and at one point three of his ablest officers threatened mutiny if he did not engage the foe.

Then Santa Anna made the blunder Houston had long been waiting for. Momentarily abandoning his pursuit of Houston, he struck at Harrisburg with 900 men, hoping to seize the Texas government. The town was empty, but while Santa Anna had detoured for his attack, Houston fell in behind him. The Texas Army was now about 800 strong and eager for battle; the pursued had become the pursuer.

Santa Anna pushed on with his 900 men, still hoping to capture the Texas officials. On April 20 he camped on the banks of the San Jacinto River. Houston's army made camp a short distance away, and after a brief skirmish that afternoon the Mexicans spent the entire night preparing their defenses for an expected dawn attack.

When dawn broke on April 21, 1836, the Texans did not appear, and at midmorning 500 Mexican reinforcements arrived. The overconfident Santa Anna gave orders that his men, most of whom had been up all night, should have a hot noon meal and a rest. While the Mexican Army slept, guarded only by a skeleton force, Houston pounced.

Moving softly through the tall prairie grass, the Texans advanced to within 200 yards of Santa Anna's "Invincibles" before they were even sighted. Then as a few startled Mexicans fired a harmless volley over their heads, the Texans charged the enemy camp, yelling, "Remember the Alamo!"

The surprise was total and so was the Texas victory. Within 18 minutes the battle was won, but the pursuit of the demoralized Mexicans continued for hours. The prairie was littered with 630 enemy dead, and more than 700 Mexicans were taken prisoner—among them Santa Anna. Only 9 Texans were killed and 34 wounded.

The captured Mexican dictator's pledge of independence for Texas, which he made to secure his release, was ignored by Mexican officials who had ousted Santa Anna. But Mexico made no further serious effort to conquer Texas. A new republic had been born on the battlefield at San Jacinto.

After the massacre of the Alamo's defenders at San Antonio, Houston's army retreated eastward—pursued by Santa Anna—and the Texas government fled to Harrisburg, then to Galveston Island. When Santa Anna turned aside to attempt to seize Texas officials, Houston fell in behind him, and the fateful battle of San Jacinto followed.

The Battle of San Jacinto quickly became a rout as the Texans fired one deadly volley and lunged into the enemy camp with bowie knives and clubbed rifles, shouting, "Remember the Alamo! Remember the Alamo!" Begging for mercy, many Mexicans cried: "Me no Alamo!"

Launching the Lone Star Republic

Mexico's repudiation of the peace treaties signed by Santa Anna after the Battle of San Jacinto kept the frontier settlements of Texas in a state of alarm for 10 years. Nonetheless, the new republic bravely carried on. In its first popular election Sam Houston easily won the presidency on a platform endorsing frugality and annexation by the United States. Most Texans expected annexation to come soon, for President Jackson had long favored it personally and had been willing to wink at men and supplies pouring across the border during the revolution.

But once the war was won, Jackson stunned Texans by backing off. While Americans had thrilled to Houston's victory, they did not necessarily approve of statehood for Texas. Some feared that annexation would bring on a bloody all-out war with Mexico. Many Whigs thought the whole struggle had been engineered by Jackson and his old friend Houston simply to add a new state to the

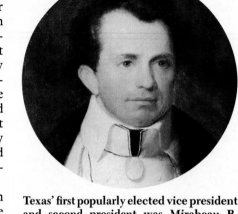

Texas' first popularly elected vice president and second president was Mirabeau B. Lamar, a strong backer of independence.

authorized funds for an official envoy.

Disappointed but determined, Houston stopped pressing for annexation, resolving to make his republic succeed on its own while waiting for a change of heart in Washington. But the Texas treasury was empty, and the war had produced a staggering debt.

From his log cabin "Executive Mansion" in Houston, the capital from 1837 to 1839, the new president fought hard to forestall financial disaster. He imposed highly unpopular taxes and issued scrip to keep the economy afloat. He slashed spending and dissuaded hot-headed volunteers from making costly forays into Mexico. He also worked

hard, if fruitlessly, to win Mexican recognition for Texas and tried to placate the frontier Indian tribes through diplomacy rather than gunfire. These peace-making efforts allowed him to cut back Texas' 3,600-man army to 600. Still, income never came close to outflow, and Houston was once forced to exhaust his personal credit just to pay his army.

Building the Texas Image

It was during the troubled early years of the republic that Texans first earned their reputation for self-reliance and swagger. Denied union with the land from which most of them had come, plagued by economic crises and foreign threats, they were still determined to make a go of it on their own. The society they built was both lusty and resilient.

One of the first acts of the new government had been the creation of a legal system broadly based on English common law. Texas towns soon attracted scores of young "cornstalk lawyers"— ill-trained but disputatious and eager to make their fortunes from the hundreds of land disputes that clogged court dockets. But despite all the attorneys, there was often little respect for law.

Texans worked hard, played hard, and displayed a fondness for settling arguments with fists, guns, bowie knives, or anything else that came to hand. Houston himself claimed that he had been challenged to 24 duels during his two presidential terms. Thievery was

Houston, Texas: "It Seems Like Magic"

This large frame building in Houston was the capitol of independent Texas from 1837 to 1839. The small building at the left housed the diplomatic staff from Texas' powerful neighbor to the north.

Texas tried to lure soldier-settlers from the United States with offers of free transportation and promises of large land grants.

Democratic Party's fold. Antislavery forces opposed annexation because it would increase slave territory, while some southerners believed Texas should remain independent so that slavery might thrive there free of opposition.

Jackson did not dare risk alienating so many voters by public calls for annexation. To do so might well have jeopardized the chances of his protege, Martin Van Buren, in the forthcoming 1836 election. Indeed, Jackson did not even extend formal recognition to the Texas republic until March 3, 1837—his last day in office—after Congress had

I arrived here on the 26th after a pleasant journey. . . . It combines more advantages and is far superior in every point of view to any situation I have yet seen in Texas for the seat of government, and commercial and mercantile operations. . . . On the 20th of January, a small log cabin and 12 persons were all that distinguished it from the adjacent forests, and now there are upwards of 100 houses going up rapidly (some of them fine frame buildings) and 1500 people. . . . The members [of government] who have arrived are well pleased, even those that opposed the location here. There are more than 100 ladies resident in town; and at a ball given on the 21st, 73 attended!! They are daily arriving! You can have no conception of the reality—it seems like magic.

—Letter from Sam Houston to Robert A. Irion, April 28, 1837

rare (except for cattle rustling and horse stealing), mainly because most Texas pioneers had so little to steal. But, observed a Texas physician, "the killing of a fellow was looked upon with greater leniency than theft."

Texans were extravagantly fond of both gambling and whisky. In 1838 a journalist reported that "the Texians, being entirely a military people, not only fought, but drank, in platoons." They were also notorious chewers of tobacco. An Austin minister once tacked up on his church the following verse admonishing his congregation:

Ye chewers of that noxious weed
Which grows on earth's most cursed sod
Be pleased to clean your filthy mouths
Outside the sacred House of God.
Throw out your "plug and cavendish,"
Your "Pig Tail," "Twist," and
    "Honeydew,"
And not presume to spit upon
The pulpit, aisles, or in the pew.

For two years Houston's economy and moderation kept the republic alive, but barely, and Texans were growing impatient for annexation. The constitution barred Houston from succeeding himself, and in 1838 the presidency was won by Mirabeau Buonaparte Lamar, a violinist, poet, and Houston foe who opposed annexation and dreamed of making Texas a powerful independent nation. Lamar opened thousands of new acres to settlers by ruthlessly driving the Cherokees of east Texas into Indian Territory and temporarily crushing the Comanches on the western border. He moved the capital to Austin in October 1839 and laid the foundations for an extensive public education system, in-

This 1840's painting shows the new capitol of Texas located in Austin. A wagon creaks past the rustic-looking building while a bored guard, at top, squats unmilitarily under a tree.

cluding a state university. By 1840 he had managed to secure recognition of the republic from Britain, France, Belgium, and the Netherlands. However, his lavish spending exceeded income by more than $4 million. The value of the Texas "red-back" dollar plunged, credit collapsed, and many fell back on the barter system.

Resolved to recoup his losses, Lamar launched his most grandiose scheme—a secret invasion of New Mexico. At one blow he hoped to corner the Santa Fe trade and extend the borders of Texas to the Pacific. An Indian-led revolt had recently disrupted New Mexico, and Lamar convinced himself that its inhabitants would not only welcome a cara-

Texas paper money came in denominations ranging from $1 to $500. However, creditors would often settle for payment in cattle.

van of Texas traders but would also rally to the Lone Star flag. In June of 1841 an expedition of 300 soldiers and civilian traders, with 24 goods wagons, set out from Austin for Santa Fe. The party almost immediately got lost. Indians picked off stragglers; prairie fires destroyed wagons. And as the Texans staggered out of the desert after 1,300 miles of confused wandering, they were seized by waiting Mexican troops, then force-marched on bleeding feet 2,000 miles to Mexico City and prison.

This fiasco exacerbated the already bad relations between Texas and Mexico and ended Lamar's career. Houston regained the presidency in the fall of 1841, swamping Lamar's candidate, David Burnet. Most Texans now agreed that, for all his private weaknesses, "[Houston] drunk in a ditch . . . is worth a thousand of Lamar and Burnet."

Austin, in south-central Texas, was a sparsely settled frontier village when Mirabeau Lamar chose it as the capital in 1839 over the opposition of former president Houston.

His right leg shattered during the Battle of San Jacinto, Houston was resting under a tree when the captured Santa Anna was brought to him. "General Santa Anna! Ah, indeed!" said Houston. The Mexican dictator expressed the hope that Houston would "be generous to the vanquished." Houston replied, "You should have remembered that at the Alamo." While the two men arranged an armistice, Erastus ("Deaf") Smith, Houston's trusty scout, sat at the left of Houston, straining to hear the discussion.

Sam Houston: First Citizen of Texas

When Sam Houston left home at the age of 20 for the War of 1812, his widowed mother enjoined him: "My son, take this musket and never disgrace it: for remember, I had rather all my sons should fill one honorable grave than that one of them should turn his back to save his life. Go," she told the strapping lad, "and remember, too, that while the door of my cabin is open to brave men, it is eternally shut against cowards." And with this call to honor for a blessing, Houston marched into the encampment of the 7th Infantry, determined to see that the homefolk would hear of him before the war ended. Hear of Houston they did, after the Battle of Horseshoe Bend in March 1814, in which he served as an ensign of the 39th Infantry. For although an arrow pierced his thigh during the first assault on this stronghold of the Creeks, he had refused an order to leave the field. And when Gen. Andrew Jackson called for officers to lead a new charge against the red men, the bleeding Houston was first to volunteer. This gesture would bring him two more wounds, but his valor won Jackson's undying respect. Later, as Old Hickory's protege, the young subaltern was to win acclaim as a congressman, senator, governor—and savior of the Lone Star Republic.

Sam Houston, one of nine children, was born on March 2, 1793, to Maj. Sam Houston—a professional soldier and veteran of the American Revolution—and his wife, Elizabeth, a gentlewoman in the tidewater fashion. But when Houston's father died on a tour of army posts, Elizabeth moved the family to Tennessee, near Maryville, a few miles from the river that separated the land of the settlers from the land of the Cherokees. Here he was enrolled in Porter Academy, and although a voracious reader fond of quoting from the *Iliad*, he failed to finish his first year of formal schooling. For from his first days in Maryville, his eyes had been fixed on the far side of the Tennessee—and his heart set on a life among the Indians. When he was 16, Houston vanished on the first of three sojourns among the Cherokees, where he was adopted by Chief Oo-loo-te-ka ("He Puts the Drum Away") and given his Indian name of Co-lon-neh ("The Raven").

Settling down at home three years later, he established a private school five miles east of Maryville, where he pros-

pered for six months, and then returned to Porter Academy as a student. This time the mysteries of geometry and the rumblings of the War of 1812 turned him from scholarly pursuits. On March 24, 1813, when a unit of U.S. Regulars passed through Maryville offering the silver dollars that were the symbols of enlistment, he stood on line to take his token.

Then came Horseshoe Bend and, two years later, promotion to second lieutenant in the 1st Infantry in New Orleans, where, for a time, he toyed with thoughts of a military career. But when a special assignment as a subagent of the Indian Bureau took him to Washington, he was rebuked by Secretary of War John Calhoun for wearing the beaded buckskins of the Cherokees, with whom he was living. Still smarting from this censure, Houston was soon outraged by charges, later disproved, that he had aided slave smugglers. When no attempt was made to punish those clearly guilty, he stomped to his quarters on March 1, 1818, and wrote his resignation.

At 25 Houston went to Nashville to read law. An apt student, he was admitted to the bar six months later and moved his practice to nearby Lebanon, where he became a

President Houston Discusses Indian Policy (1838)

Ever since the present Executive came into office, it has been his constant endeavor to establish friendly relations and secure peace with all the Indian tribes. . . . They have kept their faith, and now because we have a breathing time from war . . . are we to turn round and tell them, we only intended to deceive you . . . we are able now to do you injustice and it is the only reward we have to bestow for your friendship and confidence? . . . The Indian lands . . . their well cultivated fields and their lowing herds excite the speculators, whose cupidity, reckless of the consequences which would ensue to the country, by goading those Indians to desperation, are willing to hazard everything that is connected with the safety, prosperity or honor of our country.

Houston goes into battle at San Jacinto. "Trust in God and fear not! And remember the Alamo!" he cried.

Visiting the ramshackle three-room shanty that was President Sam Houston's executive mansion in Houston in 1837, the great naturalist and painter John James Audubon wrote in awe: "The impression made . . . by his place of abode can never be forgotten."

frequent guest at the Hermitage, Andrew Jackson's estate. And it was with Old Hickory as his patron that Houston's star soared. In 1823 he was elected to the first of his two terms in Congress. In 1827 he sat as governor of Tennessee and two years later, in a match that was the delight of Nashville's society, he married 18-year-old Eliza Allen.

But three months after the wedding, the scandalmongers had their day: Eliza had deserted Houston and taken refuge in her father's house. Now, for the first time in his career, Houston heard the hue and cry of an outraged public. Urged to "explain this sad occurrence," Houston instead resigned as governor and later declared: "This is a painful . . . affair. I do not recognize the right of the public to interfere in it." But the public would not be put off on this matter, and when Houston was burned in effigy and posted as a coward, he boarded the steamer *Red Rover* on April 23, 1829, and returned to the land of the Cherokees.

Deep in the wilderness Houston opened a trading post called Wigwam Neosho, took a girl named Tiana as his Indian bride, and "gave himself up to the fatal enchantress, alcohol." Not for long, however: shortly after his arrival, Houston became the spokesman for all the tribes that populated the land between Missouri and the Great Plains. Houston, on a mission for the Cherokee Nation, traveled to Washington, where he pleaded for justice for the Indians. Here, too, he conferred at length with his staunch friend President Andrew Jackson. And in 1832 Houston splashed across the Red River into Texas, bearing a purse and a passport provided by the president.

Triumph and Tragedy

What Texas needed was a leader "brave enough for any trial, wise enough for any emergency, and cool enough for any crisis." Or so said Sam Houston as he made his bid to be that man. At first he sided with Stephen Austin in cautioning against a break with Mexico, but when Santa Anna showed his greed for absolute power, Houston temporized no longer. On March 2, 1836, he became a signer of the Texas Declaration of Independence and on March 4 was elected commander in chief of the armies of the republic. With the Alamo doomed, Houston led his retreating army to victory at San Jacinto on April 21, 1836, and in October, at the age of 43, he

took the oath of office as president of the Republic of Texas.

In March 1837 Houston could write a friend: "You will have learned that we are independent and recognized by the United States. . . . This . . . is cause for joy. . . . My only wish is to see the country happy—at peace and retire to the Red Lands, get a fair, sweet 'wee Wifie,' as Burns says, and pass the balance of my sinful life in ease and comfort."

But when his term as president ended in 1838, Houston eschewed ease and comfort to serve in the disputatious Texas House of Representatives. He took time out in 1840 to marry Margaret Lea of Alabama, who would give him eight children, then devoted the rest of his years to his family and to Texas—serving as president for a second term (1841-44), as a U.S. senator (1846-59), and as governor (1859-61). But at this point the nation divided. When Texas seceded and Houston was called to take the Confederate oath, he refused.

Deposed from office for his defiance, the man Andrew Jackson had said would "be enrolled amongst the greatest chieftains" retired to his farm in Huntsville to become an articulate critic of Confederate policy. As his popularity returned, Houston dreamed of regaining his office. But in July 1863 a bad cold developed into pneumonia, and he died on July 26. His last words were "Texas—Texas!—Margaret—"

"Two classes of people pursued Sam Houston all his life," said a Nashville belle, "artists and women." This was no surprise to Judge Jo C. Guild, who wrote, "Houston stood six feet six inches in his socks . . . [was] of commanding and gallant bearing. . . . [He] possessed . . . courtly manners and a magnetism approaching that of General Andrew Jackson." (Houston shown here at about 60 was actually six feet two, but his personality seemed to add inches to his height.)

137

Life on a Raw Frontier

Halfway through Sam Houston's first presidential term a new immigrant tide flooded into Texas. When the Panic of 1837 threw thousands of U.S. frontiersmen off their land, Texas provided many with a second chance. Under a generous new land law, single men were granted 640 free acres and heads of families a princely 1,280 acres—plus an option to buy more at 50 cents an acre.

Soon "G.T.T." (Gone to Texas) was found scrawled across the doors of deserted cabins—and across the pages of creditors' account books—all along the U.S. frontier and in the crowded seaboard states as well. Between 1836 and 1847 the total Texas population (including slaves but not Indians) jumped from just under 40,000 to 142,000.

Many of these new settlers came in response to the republic's revival in 1841 of the old empresario system of the 1820's. Typically, a given section of the public domain was designated a colony and assigned to a proprietor, who could collect fees for surveys, moving and building costs, and other necessities from the colonists he brought in.

One of the new empresarios was a wealthy Frenchman, Henri Castro, who obtained a grant in the Medina River country between the Nueces River and the Rio Grande. It was dangerous territory, infested with hostile Indians and invaded by Mexico as recently as 1842. But in 1844 the first group of 27 French colonists, escorted by 20 Texas Rangers, boldly moved in and laid out the town of Castroville, the first permanent settlement between San Antonio and the Rio Grande. They managed to hang on through severe droughts and Indian raids, and by 1847 more than 2,000 Frenchmen had been settled in the town and surrounding area.

The Germans Go West

Germany, however, contributed by far the greatest number of European immigrants. In time they came to represent the largest foreign-born element in Texas, outnumbering even the Mexicans. The great wave of German immigration was initiated by the Mainzer Adelsverein, a society for the protection of German immigrants in Texas, organized by a group of German nobles in 1842. Two years later it published a tempting offer: each single adult who subscribed $120 would receive free passage to Texas and 40 acres; each family that subscribed $240, free passage and 80 acres. The society would provide houses, livestock, and tools, and would construct public buildings and roads for the community.

In answer to the advertisement 180 German families set out to join the society's commissioner-general, Prince Carl of Solms-Braunfels, who had preceded them to Texas. They landed on the coast at Galveston in the fall of 1844. There they learned that the land the society had bought from a pair of wily speculators was a remote wilderness, largely uninhabited save for unfriendly Indians. The following March, Prince Carl led his disheartened group to an area northeast of San Antonio and laid out the town of New Braunfels.

To the burden of building cabins, planting the first crops, and keeping the Indians at bay was added the problem of savage, unpredictable windstorms, often accompanied by driving sleet that froze unsheltered livestock—and even men—in their tracks. But the German pioneers survived, thanks more to their own hard work than to any effort of Prince Carl. Within a year of the settlement's founding the unpopular prince was replaced by the far abler Baron Hans von Meusebach, who later led a second group of German immigrants to found a settlement at Fredericksburg. Other German settlements grew up south of Fredericksburg at Sisterdale, Boerne, and Comfort and to the southeast at Seguin, Victoria, and Indianola.

The Texas Staple: Corn

While most Anglo-American farmers concentrated on growing corn and cotton and herding a few sheep, hogs, and cattle, the Germans established thriving dairy and poultry farms, grew a wide variety of vegetables and fruits, and even experimented with various strains of wheat, refusing to be satisfied with only cornmeal or with flour imported from the U.S. Midwest.

Meanwhile, the free-and-easy pioneers of eastern Texas had been abandoning their lands, some of which were exhausted by the growing of cotton, for richer regions to the west. The writer and landscape architect Frederick Law Olmsted described the sight of mile after mile of abandoned plantations in Houston County and wrote with considerable scorn of the "lazy poverty" of eastern Texas, describing encounters with settlers who left all their work to a few

Some of the most famous historical pictures of Texas life were painted by Theodore Gentilz, a young Parisian artist who came to Texas in 1844. He eventually became a merchant and art teacher in San Antonio. Gentilz recorded many aspects of the life of this colorful town so influenced by Mexico. "Invitation to the Dance" (left) shows horsemen in fancy dress serenading townsfolk at a fiesta. "Fandango" (below) depicts a ball at the "governor's palace," which Gentilz attended as a young bachelor in 1844.

Richard Petri, who emigrated with his family and settled in Fredericksburg, Texas, in the 1840's, painted this picture of his sisters milking cows and sent it to relatives in Germany.

slaves, lived in drafty, ill-made cabins, and subsisted on an unvarying diet of rancid bacon, bitter coffee, and the ubiquitous Texas cornbread. Corn was, in fact, indispensable in the conquest of the Texas wilderness. It nourished both livestock and men and grew almost untended in the virgin lands from the Red River to the Gulf.

"Picket Huts" and Plantations

The settlers' dwellings varied according to the materials at hand. In east Texas, where timber was abundant, the typical house was a one-room log cabin. In the nearly woodless south-central area dwellings were often adobe or stone. The poorest settlers sometimes made do with Mexican "picket huts," driving stakes into the ground to form walls, which were then chinked with mud and moss, and fashioning roofs of leaves or grass bound with rawhide.

As the cotton and sugar planters of eastern Texas became more affluent, many replaced their cabins with showy plantation houses of clapboard or brick, some with marble fireplaces, luxurious carpets, and furniture of mahogany and walnut, but the cutlery at the fine dining table sometimes consisted of bowie knives and forks made out of sugarcane stalks; gourds served as drinking cups.

During the almost 10 years of the Texas republic, the principal towns were Galveston, San Antonio (the most admired), Houston, and Marshall. By 1850 each had more than 1,000 inhabitants. Most town dwellings were wood-frame houses of raw, unpretentious construction, many of them on streets that filled with choking dust in summer, bottomless ooze in winter, and were studded with tree stumps no one had bothered to uproot. An editor in the town of Clarksville commented: "With a

most providential regard for their successors, the first settlers of the city left the stumps of all trees they felled just high enough to strike a man's knees."

If town streets were difficult to negotiate, getting from one settlement to another was even harder. The chief wagon roads were little more than rutted cow tracks, and water travel was a sometime thing, since most Texas streams ran to sandbars, snags, and dangerously low water in summer.

Life in those early days was rugged and often lonely, dangerous, and disappointing. The weather was violent, the economy precarious; outbreaks of such diseases as yellow fever and cholera were frequent, and relations with Mexico and the Indians uneasy. Yet to those who persevered, Texas was a special place— vast, wide open, and beautiful—that transformed immigrants from all over America and much of Europe into a proud, independent-minded new breed.

The English adventurer William Bollaert, whose journals described life in Texas in 1840-44, sketched this east Texas plantation, showing the big house and slave cabins.

The Republic's Last Days

When in 1841 Sam Houston became president of the Texas republic for the second time, he was confronted with an explosive situation. Mirabeau Buonaparte Lamar's disastrous expedition to Santa Fe had left both Mexicans and Texans in a state of simmering fury: the former outraged by Lamar's clumsy attempt to grab New Mexico, the latter equally affronted by the brutal treatment of the Santa Fe prisoners. Mexico announced her intention to reconquer all of Texas; the Texas Congress, in turn, impulsively passed an absurd resolution claiming title to six northern Mexican states plus all of California.

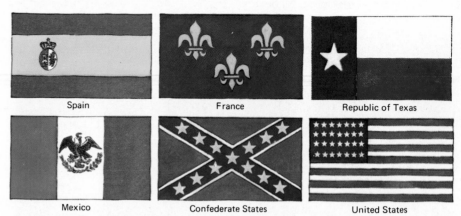

Flags of six different nations have flown over Texas soil in the last three centuries. The Lone Star remains a proud memento of Texas' brief existence as a sovereign nation.

New Clashes With Mexico

Mexico was the first to act. Beginning in February 1842 Santa Anna sent three punitive expeditions into Texas: Corpus Christi was plundered once, San Antonio twice. The result was a "runaway scrape," much like that of 1836, with panicked Texans fleeing eastward in the face of what they thought was a full-scale invasion. Declaring a public emergency, President Houston ordered the removal of the government archives from Austin—but the inhabitants of the town, fearing the permanent loss of its status as capital, refused to let them go. There followed a comic tussle (known as the Archives War) between Austin vigilantes and the Texas Rangers sent to remove the papers; the Austinites finally won the day.

Texas was ill-prepared for a full-scale confrontation with Mexico. To save money, Houston had disbanded what was left of the republic's army; three forces of volunteers had to be hastily recruited, but they were little inclined to follow anyone's commands. One group, which had been looking for a fight along the Rio Grande since November 1842, invaded the Mexican border town of Mier on Christmas Day despite orders from their commander, Gen. Alexander Somervell, to fall back to San Antonio. They were immediately surrounded by a much larger Mexican Army, forced to surrender, and marched southward in chains. The prisoners attempted a mass escape along the way, and as punishment 1 out of every 10 was executed; the rest were incarcerated in a dank prison with the survivors of Lamar's disastrous Santa Fe adventure.

The other two volunteer forces fared no better. One, under Col. Charles A. Warfield, dispatched to attack Santa Fe, included a complement of 24 mountain men who could not resist going off on their own to raid the New Mexican village of Mora; they were soon sent packing by Mexican cavalry. The second, under Maj. Jacob Snively, was authorized by President Houston to attack caravans headed for Mexico along the Santa Fe Trail. This was blatant robbery, officially sanctioned or not, and it alarmed U.S. traders, who feared for their safety. In the summer of 1843 Snively's dryland privateers were intercepted by U.S. dragoons and forced by them to give up their arms.

Retaliation against Mexico had been a dismal failure in all but one respect: it revived U.S. interest in Texas and in the annexation question. Houston realized that annexation was the best hope for Texas survival, and he proved himself a wily diplomat by creating the impression that Britain was exerting considerable influence on him. He knew the effect this would have on U.S. expansionists, who were always eager to steal a march on "Perfidious Albion."

It was true that Britain was interested in Texas and had motives of her own for wanting to keep the republic independent. British industrialists sought cheap

With death decreed by lottery in retaliation for an escape attempt, captured Texas raiders of the Mier expedition draw beans from a pot (left). Those who draw a black bean—1 man in 10—are shot (right). The "drawing of the beans" remains infamous in Texas history.

cotton and a market free of stiff U.S. tariffs for their manufactured goods. British humanitarians, who had forced the outlawing of slavery throughout the empire in 1833, hoped to persuade an independent Texas to ban the institution. By March 1843 rumors of British efforts to undermine slavery in Texas had reached Washington officials. President John Tyler, a southerner, was distinctly alarmed. So far, Houston's game was working.

In early 1843 Santa Anna, beset by a rebellion in Yucatán, sent word to Texas that he was willing to open peace negotiations. Houston had no intention of accepting his terms—to cease hostilities if Texas would acknowledge Mexican sovereignty while retaining control of its internal affairs. But he played for time, shrewdly allowing British diplomats to intercede in the negotiations. A temporary truce was signed in June, and Houston made a point of advertising his gratitude for Britain's help.

This diplomatic minuet had exactly the effect Houston hoped for. Even the aged Andrew Jackson was fooled. From his retirement he wrote that in the face of growing British influence "the safety of New Orleans, the prosperity of the great valley of the Mississippi and our whole union require the annexation of Texas." President Tyler shared Jackson's alarm and sent word to Houston that his administration would not oppose annexation if Texas would submit her request to join the Union.

The Final Round

Negotiations for a treaty of annexation proceeded smoothly till 1844. But when John C. Calhoun of South Carolina became secretary of state, he tactlessly declared that the United States had a duty to annex Texas in order to protect the South against a British plot to end slavery throughout the world. Antislavery forces seized upon Calhoun's remarks as proof that annexation was, after all, nothing more than a conspiracy of slaveholders to strengthen their position. Northern Whig support evaporated, and on June 8 the treaty was defeated in the Senate 35 to 16.

Annexation now became a burning issue in the 1844 presidential campaign. Democrat Martin Van Buren and Whig Henry Clay, vying for the presidency, were both tripped up by Texas in the end. Van Buren's opposition to annexation (he was known to fear that it would lead to war with Mexico) cost him the

The Stars and Stripes float proudly over the main plaza of San Antonio in this 1849 oil painting, for Texas was then part of the United States. But Spanish influence remained.

The Texas Navy

These schooners of the Texas Navy were drawn in 1842 by Midshipman Alfred Walke, who later took part in the battle off Campeche, where the newly equipped navy of Mexico was crippled— the last time that sailing ships defeated steamers.

The Texas Navy began as four small armed ships that disrupted Mexican seaborne supply lines in 1836. By 1840, with the backing of President Lamar, it boasted a 20-gun sloop as its flagship, plus six smaller sailing ships and a converted passenger steamer. Always short of funds, the little navy was even hired out to the rebelling Mexican state of Yucatán for $8,000 a month. For a year and a half it prevented a Mexican naval attack on Texas, and in 1843 it disabled the enemy fleet at Campeche. But that same year President Houston, desperate for money, deactivated the navy after trying—without success—to find a buyer for it.

nomination, which went to dark-horse candidate James K. Polk—like Jackson, a Tennesseean and an all-out expansionist. Clay did win his party's nomination, but his attempts to straddle the issue cost him the election. Expansionist sentiment had clearly won the day.

To get the credit for adding Texas to the Union, lameduck President Tyler hastily requested that Congress approve annexation by joint resolution, which would be easier to pass than a treaty because it did not require a two-thirds majority. Despite the opposition of antislavery forces, the resolution was passed in late February 1845, and Tyler signed it on March 1, three days before his term ended. The measure required Texas to adopt a state constitution to be approved by a convention and submitted to the president no later than January 1, 1846. These conditions were duly met, and on December 29, 1845, Texas officially became part of the United States. At ceremonies in Austin on February 19, 1846, Anson Jones, last president of the republic, formally turned over executive power to J. Pinckney Henderson, first governor of the state of Texas. "The final act in this great drama," said Jones, "is now performed; the Republic of Texas is no more."

No other race of men with the means at their command would undertake so great a journey. . . relying only on the fertility of their invention. . . .
The way lies over trackless wastes, wide and deep rivers, rugged and lofty mountains, and is beset with hostile savages. Yet . . . they are always found ready and equal to the occasion. . . . May we not call them men of destiny?

—*Jesse Applegate,* A Day with the Cow Column in 1843

"The Oregon Trail." Oil painting by Albert Bierstadt.

Chapter 5

From Sea to Sea

Even before Texas became part of the United States, venturesome Americans were pressing on toward the Pacific, to the rich, almost empty regions of the Oregon Country and California, which they believed it was their destiny to claim and settle. Trappers and traders led the advance; next came missionaries, then farmers and their families by the thousands, making the grueling continental crossing by packhorse or wagon train. By midcentury the conquest, which involved a war with Mexico, was complete.

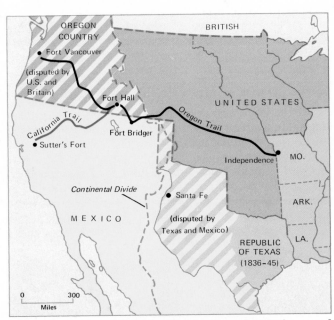

As wagon trains pushed to the West in the early 1840's, several countries contended for sovereignty over this far land. The Republic of Texas and Mexico disputed ownership of territory north of the Rio Grande; Britain and the United States jointly occupied the Oregon Country and eyed each other suspiciously, while an ever-growing number of Americans coveted Mexican California.

Utopia on the Pacific

California's vaqueros were North America's first cowboys. Above, they move a herd past the prosperous Mission San Gabriel.

In 1842 a Prussian diplomat in the United States wrote a letter to a colleague in London, extolling the virtues of a faraway land. "Upper California," Friedrich von Roenne reported, "is one of the finest countries in the world. . . . It is only necessary that it should be in the possession of an active, industrious and energetic people." If Von Roenne dreamed of seeing the Prussian banner waving over San Francisco's presidio, he was entering his nation in the struggle for the agriculturally rich Mexican province rather late in the game—well behind the Russians, British, French, and, more recently, Americans. By the time of Von Roenne's letter it was the Americans who were far ahead of all competitors in the contest to wrest California from Mexico's tenuous and often capricious rule. About 200 Americans lived in California, and many of them were prominent residents. Some had married into distinguished Mexican families, and a number had adopted both Roman Catholicism and Mexican citizenship. But their pragmatic arrangements barely concealed their ardor for annexation to the United States.

Ever since the last years of the 18th century, when California and its mother province, Mexico, were nominally ruled by Spain, Yankee sea captains had anchored along the coast and sent expeditions to trade for supplies with the ranchers and Franciscan friars in the region. They also vied with Russian and British traders in their slaughter of sea otters for the rich China market, which the great British navigator, Capt. James Cook, had opened up in 1778 after a survey of the waters off the western coast of North America.

With Mexican independence in 1821 American enterprises increased substantially. Boston's great mercantile companies sent ships around Cape Horn on a fairly regular basis. To grease the wheels of commerce, evade the high Mexican duties, and, where possible, secure trade monopolies, the Boston firms placed their agents in California to deal with the missionaries and later with the owners of the great ranchos. From their headquarters in the tiny presidio of Los Angeles or the provincial capital of Monterey, these "Bostons," as they came to be known, fanned out along the coast, contracting to buy hides for New England's shoe manufacturers (usually at $1 a-piece) and cementing relations with the leaders of California's Mexican community, which probably numbered no more than 3,300 people.

Yankee Mischiefmakers

California's sparse population, its distance from Mexico City—which never gained firm control of the province—and the jealousies rampant among the leading Mexican families made it a fertile field for Yankee mischiefmakers, who were well aware that American conquest would benefit their interests. Typical of the breed was Abel Stearns, who arrived in California in 1829 via Mexico, where he obtained a new citizenship. His dour, homely visage, which earned him the nickname Horseface, did not keep him from becoming a wealthy hide merchant in Los Angeles—nor even from marrying the 14-year-old daughter of one of the region's most powerful families. These benefits, however, did not sway Stearns from the true (and convenient) path of duty. By 1846 he was cooperating with the U.S. consul in Monterey, Thomas O. Larkin, who had been secretly instructed by President Polk to foster a "spontaneous" movement for California's separation from Mexico, a step that would lead to American annexation.

A New England-born merchant, Lar-

Indian Dwellers in a Primeval Paradise

Before the white man came in great numbers, California was home to more than 100,000 Indians. Of brownish complexion, they had broad, heavy faces and spoke a bewildering variety of dialects. Basically peace-loving peoples, most of them lived in small semipermanent villages along the coast and were gatherers and hunters who subsisted on plant foods, fish, shellfish, small game, and grubs. Thanks to a mild climate, they needed few clothes and seldom went hungry. Many had time for attending ceremonies and weaving some of the finest Indian baskets in America.

Wearing dance headdresses, these central California Indians were sketched by a German-Russian painter in 1816.

Using redbud bark, bullrushes, and strips of sedge, the Pomo Indians made superb watertight baskets.

Dome-roofed dugouts were typical homes for several California tribes. Tall baskets held acorns, a staple.

kin had reaped a fortune in California as the owner of a Monterey flour mill. As a sideline he bombarded eastern newspapers with florid descriptions of the province's beauty and wealth. Indeed, most Americans who lived in California during the 1830's and 1840's vied with one another in composing seductive letters to friends and families at home in hopes of setting off a stampede of emigration from the United States.

Ceaseless Propaganda

Of all those who heaped praise on California and scorn on its Mexican rulers, one of the most tireless was a Harvard graduate and self-proclaimed physician named John Marsh, who arrived in the province in 1836. After prospering as a doctor in Los Angeles, he bought a large parcel of land in the San Joaquin Valley. Convinced that only American immigration and American sovereignty would drive up the price of his acreage, Marsh wrote countless letters to friends in his former home, Independence, Missouri, where they were published in the local newspapers. The alluring picture he painted of life in California was especially intriguing to farm-

The lively community of Monterey had such citified entertainment as a theater. The painting is by William H. Meyers, who served as a gunner in the U.S. Navy in the 1840's.

Abel Stearns arrived in California in 1829. Less than 10 years later he had become the largest landholder in southern California.

ers burdened by low prices and high debts in the late 1830's. According to Marsh, Americans need not even stoop to manual labor; the Indians would do it all for little or no pay. "When caught young, [they] are most easily domesticated," he once wrote. "They submit to flagallation with more humility than negroes." In another letter he asserted, "The only thing we lack here is a good Government. . . . What we want most here is more people. If we had fifty families here from Missouri, we could do exactly as we please without any fear of being troubled."

Such unceasing propaganda from Americans in California was supplemented by reports from seaman and writer Richard Henry Dana, explorers Joseph Walker, Jed Smith, and James Ohio Pattie, and other travelers. All this helped to turn what had been only a tiny vanguard of traders and merchants prior to 1841 into a steady, if unspectacular, overland migration of farm families to California during the mid-1840's.

Blessed California

[This is] a country embracing four or five hundred miles of sea-coast, with several good harbours, with fine forests in the north; the waters filled with fish, and the plains covered with thousands of herds of cattle; blessed with a climate, than which there can be no better in the world . . . and with a soil in which corn yields from seventy to eighty-fold.

Monterey, as far as my observation goes, is decidedly the pleasantest and most civilised-looking place in California. . . . There are a number of English and Americans . . . who have married Californians . . . and acquired considerable property. Having more industry, frugality, and enterprise than the natives, they soon get nearly all the trade into their hands.

—Richard Henry Dana, Jr.
Two Years Before the Mast, 1840

In 1842 Monterey was a small but prosperous shipping center for American hide buyers. The key (above) shows in blue a number of its original buildings still standing today, including (A) the American consul's house; (B) the theater, California's first; (C) the customhouse; (D) the royal presidio chapel.

Bucolic Life on a California Rancho

Nowhere was frontier life as peaceful and carefree as in Mexican California in the 1820's. The population descended from the Spanish was small; the grasslands were vast. Thus estates were gigantic, grazed by huge herds of longhorns. The climate was benign; the Indians were missionary trained; poverty was nonexistent; hospitality was bountiful. The isolation meant a lack of currency, stores, and nearby towns, but this was compensated for by barter. Cattle hides and tallow were exchanged with ship captains for most supplies, from furniture and tools to silks and tortoise-shell combs. But each

rancho was self-sufficient in staple foods, the women supervising the cornfields, orchards, and gardens while the men rode the range. Each don ran his domain like a feudal lord, usually fathering over a dozen children, sheltering countless other relatives, generously lodging any passing traveler, and managing an army of Indian servants, artisans, and vaqueros, or cowhands (opposite). His days began and ended with prayers, but—without schools—he was often illiterate. His diversions were home initiated: a horserace or a cockfight or best of all a dance, the rhythms stomped in intricate steps.

Although their home is scantily furnished, the ranchero and his wife lavish color and decoration on their clothing, which glitters with spangles, embroidery, and silver buttons. The don's velveteen pants are slit up the side to reveal underdrawers, whose whiteness proves that he is a man of wealth, able to afford laundresses. The couple stands at the rear of the home, where most of the household activities take place.

A plain one-level, tile-roofed house, seen from the patio veranda, is of adobe cemented with mud. Walls five feet thick keep it cool in summer, fairly warm in winter. It lacks an interior fireplace and has an earth floor.

Wooden door

Water jug hung by rawhide

Saw

A window without glass panes

With a wooden paddle an Indian servant removes a baked loaf of bread from the *horno*, an outside oven of adobe. Next to her another woman cooks cornmeal tortillas on a sheet of metal over a stone-rimmed fire. The rancho requires many servants—one for each of the ranchero's children, two for his wife, four to grind corn, and six to prepare meals. There are also some washerwomen and a dozen spinners and seamstresses.

The don's low-heeled boots are of colored leather strips; the wife's slippers of kid.

The ranchero's father, wrapped in a serape, sits on an adobe bench. As the eldest male, he rules the family. His 50-year-old son runs the rancho and has 18 children; yet he must get the old man's approval for all major decisions and can be reprimanded with corporal punishment by the patriarch. Children, playing games, are fondly but strictly raised; when indoors, they must ask permission to sit down.

To make tallow, first the outer fat under the cowhide is removed and used for cooking or sold to traders; then the inner fat is rendered in a blubber pot (A) traded from a whaler. Partly cooled, it is poured into hide bags (B) held on stakes. When hard, 500-pound blocks are carried off (C).

Astride their finest horses, adorned with silver and embroidered trappings, vaqueros rope a grizzly. They will tie him up, pen him, bring him to the rancho, and pit him against a bull. If he kills the bull, he will be matched with another, and still another—until he dies.

At a popular rooster pull a horseman at full gallop tries to grab a bird that has been buried wattle-deep in the earth.

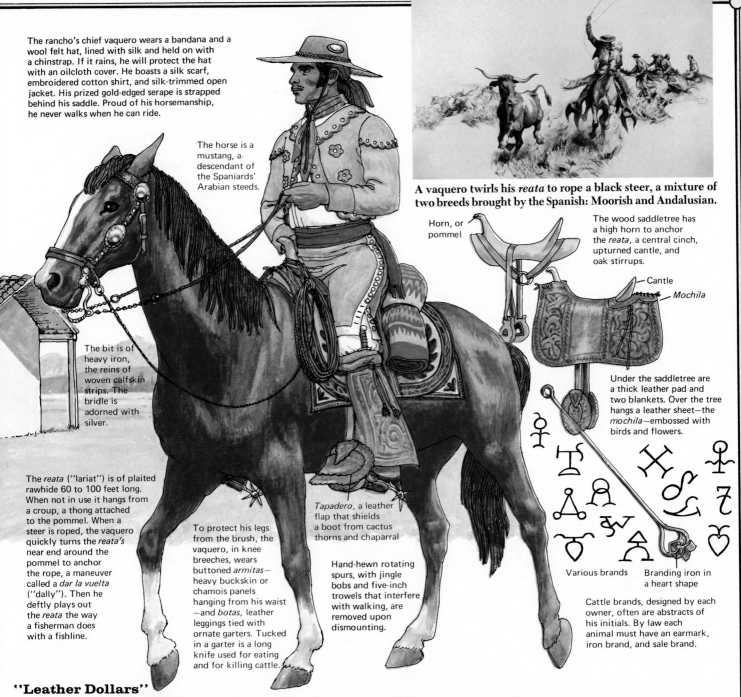

The rancho's chief vaquero wears a bandana and a wool felt hat, lined with silk and held on with a chinstrap. If it rains, he will protect the hat with an oilcloth cover. He boasts a silk scarf, embroidered cotton shirt, and silk-trimmed open jacket. His prized gold-edged serape is strapped behind his saddle. Proud of his horsemanship, he never walks when he can ride.

The horse is a mustang, a descendant of the Spaniards' Arabian steeds.

A vaquero twirls his *reata* to rope a black steer, a mixture of two breeds brought by the Spanish: Moorish and Andalusian.

Horn, or pommel

The wood saddletree has a high horn to anchor the *reata*, a central cinch, upturned cantle, and oak stirrups.

Cantle

Mochila

The bit is of heavy iron, the reins of woven calfskin strips. The bridle is adorned with silver.

Under the saddletree are a thick leather pad and two blankets. Over the tree hangs a leather sheet—the *mochila*—embossed with birds and flowers.

The *reata* ("lariat") is of plaited rawhide 60 to 100 feet long. When not in use it hangs from a croup, a thong attached to the pommel. When a steer is roped, the vaquero quickly turns the *reata*'s near end around the pommel to anchor the rope, a maneuver called a *dar la vuelta* ("dally"). Then he deftly plays out the *reata* the way a fisherman does with a fishline.

To protect his legs from the brush, the vaquero, in knee breeches, wears buttoned *armitas*— heavy buckskin or chamois panels hanging from his waist —and *botas,* leather leggings tied with ornate garters. Tucked in a garter is a long knife used for eating and for killing cattle.

Tapadero, a leather flap that shields a boot from cactus thorns and chaparral

Hand-hewn rotating spurs, with jingle bobs and five-inch trowels that interfere with walking, are removed upon dismounting.

Various brands

Branding iron in a heart shape

Cattle brands, designed by each owner, often are abstracts of his initials. By law each animal must have an earmark, iron brand, and sale brand.

"Leather Dollars"

A Yankee captain barters with the rancho's agent.

23-pound dried hide

A captain's supplies: raisins, sugar, spices, cigars, silks, calicoes, hardware, cutlery, tools

A ranchero gets his supplies by bartering with "leather dollars"—cowhides dried, scraped, beaten, and salted at the rancho, then brought to the Pacific cliffs and hurled to the beach. There sailors load them into their ships' rowboats. Captains collect hides from ranchos and some missions and sell them to boot and shoe factories back in New England.

America's First Cowboys

The mainstay of every rancho was a flamboyant, fantastically skillful horseman, the vaquero (above). Usually he was an Indian, whose forebears, under colonial law, had been forbidden to ride. Needing herdsmen, the missionaries had winked at this rule and trained Indian cowhands. When the missions became secularized, these vaqueros began working for the rancheros, who gave them huts and all necessary family supplies. The vaqueros originated most of the clothes, techniques, and terms used later by Anglo cowboys. ("Vacquero," indeed, became "buckaroo.") The vaqueros' charges—the lean, semiwild longhorns—roamed fenceless grasslands until rodeo time, when all were rounded up and, supervised by a field judge, separated according to each rancho's brand. During the late summer *matanza* ("slaughtering"), when the cattle were fattest, the vaqueros killed the animals by daringly plunging their knives into the steers' necks. The hides were stripped off, the layers of fat used for cooking and tallow. The meat was carved for steaks or fried. The best vaqueros got extra "pay" in trade goods, which they spent on fine clothes and saddles, becoming the most dazzling new sight in the West.

147

The Distant Land

In the year 1791 Yankee "sea peddler" Robert Gray, master of the merchant vessel *Columbia,* sailed into Nootka Sound in the Oregon Country, one of many eagerly pursuing the rich fur trade with China. The following spring, seeking a region not yet exploited by his competitors, Gray scoured the coast looking for a mighty river of which the Indians had spoken. On May 11, 1792, after sighting the river's broad estuary, he braved the rolling tide and whipping waves to cross its sandbar; then a party from the *Columbia* sailed some 30 miles

The Boston trader *Columbia,* commanded by Capt. Robert Gray, in winter quarters.

upstream by cutter. Naming the river after his ship, this first white man to explore Oregon's interior claimed the entire region for the United States.

British claims to the Pacific Slope dated back to 1778 and Captain Cook's voyage along the northwest coast when he too put into Nootka Sound, and Britain had not been laggard in securing her title. In the Nootka Sound treaty of 1790, Spain had recognized Britain's Oregon claim. The British representative in the Oregon Country was John McLoughlin. Officially he served from 1824 until 1846 as chief factor of the Hudson's Bay Company in the region, an immense wilderness domain stretching from the Alaska border southward to California and eastward to the slopes of the Rockies. Unofficially, however, McLoughlin served as an agent of the Crown, under orders to discourage American competition and settlement in the disputed territory. That assignment became more difficult as the years wore on because it clashed with the agent's understanding of justice and fair play.

McLoughlin well knew that Americans had as much right in the Oregon Country as the British or Canadians did. An Anglo-American agreement in 1818 had specified that the entire region was to be jointly occupied by both nations. In any case, McLoughlin was generally too hospitable to deny the shelter of his Fort Vancouver headquarters to travelers in search of help. And by 1821 Britain was ready to concede American ownership of the region between the Columbia River and the California border (the present state of Oregon), while the United States had little hope of getting territory above the 49th parallel without going to war. So the only area really in dispute lay between that parallel and the Columbia (roughly the boundaries of Washington State today).

McLoughlin's Dilemma

McLoughlin's options were not at all clear—at least not for a man who valued his personal honor above all else. Consequently, when American missionaries or settlers sought his help at his Fort Vancouver headquarters, he usually directed them to the fertile Willamette Valley south of the Columbia. But even when they opted for more northerly sites,

Two Who Opened the Way

The men shown at the right, not Americans but Quebec-born agents of the Hudson's Bay Company, left their imprint on the Oregon Country. John McLoughlin (1784-1857) was the very incarnation of the dour, righteous Scot, his formidable will backed by a powerful six-foot four-inch physique. McLoughlin entered the service of the North West Company as a 19-year-old clerk. Trained in medicine, he doubled as unpaid company physician, but his true genius lay in trading and dealing with the temperamental Indians who supplied the bulk of the company's fur catch. After the North West Company merged with its rival, the Hudson's Bay Company, McLoughlin was entrusted with the western activities of the giant enterprise. At his Fort Vancouver headquarters he set up a huge farm, a sawmill, a flour mill, and a shipyard, making his operation virtually self-sufficient. Here he ruled his vast domain as a benevolent autocrat, directing a small army of clerks, trappers, and French-Canadian voyageurs in the pursuit of beaver pelts.

Toward the Indians he was stern but fair, earning their respect and loyalty. One of his notable achievements was maintaining peace among hostile tribes and factions. He received much criticism from his associates and superiors in the company, however, for his policy of extending aid to American settlers in the Oregon Country—whether they were would-be missionaries to the Indians, farmers in search of free and fertile land, or even Americans whose plans for exploiting the region clearly conflicted with the interests of Hudson's Bay. In 1846 he resigned under a cloud. With deep

The flowing white locks of John McLoughlin earned him the Indian name White-headed Eagle. His wife was half Indian.

Peter Skene Ogden was helpful in the transfer of the rich Oregon Country from Britain to the United States after 1846.

roots in the Oregon Country, McLoughlin applied for American citizenship and claimed a huge tract of land on the Willamette River. However, an unsympathetic Congress disallowed his claim, and he died bitterly disappointed.

Peter Skene Ogden (1794-1854), the son of Tories who had fled the United States to Canada, studied law until the age of 17, then ran off to join the North West Company. Short, stocky, and powerful, with a taste for violence, he soon earned a fearsome reputation. During hostilities with the Hudson's Bay Company he captured an entire outpost of the rival he rarely denied them seed, livestock, or such protection from hostile Indians as the company could offer.

For a time American threats to British sovereignty in the Oregon Country remained more shadow than substance. Oregon was, after all, about 2,000 miles from Independence, Missouri. A few visionaries might dream of a continental dominion for the United States, but the prevailing view was probably summed up by a congressional report that stated: "Nature has fixed limits to our nation; she has kindly interposed as our Western barrier, mountains almost inaccessible. . . . This barrier our population can never pass."

One person who refused to heed such timid advice was a onetime teacher and engineer who came from Boston named Hall Jackson Kelley, a waspish, humorless man who imagined himself chosen by God to lead a great migration to the Oregon Country. In 1831 he organized an emigration society from whose headquarters flowed an incessant stream of propaganda: Oregon was paradise on earth; it was America's by right of discovery and Divine Providence; the British interloper must be expelled. Although at first few paid much attention

The majestic, perpetually snow-capped cone of Mount Hood was a landmark sought by settlers crossing the Cascades—the last obstacle on the journey to Oregon's green valleys.

to this bombast, Kelley finally managed to set off for the West with a handful of followers in November 1832.

By the time Kelley reached the Oregon Country two years later—he went by way of New Orleans, Mexico City, and California—he had dismissed all his original companions. While traveling through California, however, he had fallen in first with a trapper turned horse trader named Ewing Young and later with a band of American wanderers among whom were several reputed horse thieves. Word of the men's north-

ward trek had preceded them to Fort Vancouver. When the ailing and exhausted Kelley arrived there, he received a chilly welcome from McLoughlin, who assumed the entire group to be criminals. Because of his pitiful condition the New Englander was allowed to stay in the compound—but in a filthy hut—until a ship took him home in 1835. Once back in Massachusetts, the frustrated pioneer spent his remaining years denouncing the Hudson's Bay Company and futilely petitioning Congress to reimburse him for his expenses.

A great *canot du maître* (the name means "master's canoe"), belonging to the Hudson's Bay Company, shoots the rapids on a northern stream. Such boats served the company for transportation in the trackless wilderness of the North and West, linking trappers in remote areas with the company's Canadian headquarters in Montreal. In the 1830's the company controlled much of what is now both Canada and the northwestern United States, ruling it like an independent state. This painting is by the lady wearing the straw hat at the center of the canoe, Mrs. Edward Hopkins.

group, treating the captives with a barbarity notable even in that time and place. To escape prosecution for the alleged murder of a Hudson's Bay Company employee, he was sent to the Oregon Country, where he learned Indian diplomacy.

After the two fur companies merged, Ogden—having voyaged to London to save his job—was placed in charge of trapping operations for the Snake River country. On this assignment, which lasted several years, he explored parts of present-day Utah, California, eastern Oregon, and western Idaho, facing with his men starvation and hostile Indians.

Later he served in British Columbia and the lonely interior of the Canadian Northwest. Mellowing with age, Ogden developed tact and charm. Promoted to the rank of chief factor in 1835, he became one of two joint commanders of the Northwest area when McLoughlin resigned his post in 1846. After an Indian massacre of Americans in 1847 at the Marcus Whitman mission, in Oregon, Ogden used his influence with the Indians to rescue the survivors. Although Ogden has received little mention in history books, a city, a mountain, a valley, and a river in the present state of Utah bear his name.

Traders and Missionaries Lead the Way

Failure though it was, Hall Jackson Kelley's Oregon venture nonetheless planted a seed in the American consciousness that would eventually blossom into the great migration of which the quixotic fanatic had dreamed. This seed took root in the mind of Nathaniel Wyeth of Cambridge, a young man in the ice business who had been one of Kelley's early supporters. But unlike the older man, Wyeth was interested in Oregon for reasons neither patriotic nor spiritual. A man of energy and determination, he thought, might reap a fortune in that vast wilderness. By late 1831 Wyeth had managed to form a joint stock company with about 30 others who shared his view; a supply ship would be hired to sail round Cape Horn and meet them on the Pacific coast. The exact purpose of the venture was not specified; the participants intended to seize any opportunities that arose.

By the spring of 1832 Wyeth's party, reduced now to 24, had reached Independence, Missouri, the jumping-off

Expert fishermen, the Indians of the Oregon Country dried salmon at The Dalles, where falls and rapids forced travelers on the Columbia River to make a mile-long portage.

place for caravans headed for the annual trappers' rendezvous. Guided by the Rocky Mountain Fur Company's William Sublette, the men reached the rendezvous, but several more members abandoned the group. Wyeth and his 11 remaining followers pressed on, guided now by Sublette's brother Milton. They arrived at Fort Vancouver in October 1832—the first party of westbound Americans to negotiate what would be called the Oregon Trail.

At McLoughlin's fort they met with disastrous news. Their supply ship had foundered. Wyeth's remaining companions thereupon dissolved their firm, and most made their way back to the East and obscurity. But one man, John Ball, decided to remain in Oregon as a teacher to the Indian wives and half-breed children of the French-Canadian trappers; and two others, Solomon Smith and Calvin Tibbetts, became farmers in the Willamette Valley, where a small group of retired Hudson's Bay employees were already tilling the soil. These three men were the first Americans to take up residence in Oregon.

Men of God

Wyeth, however, still dreamed of wealth, and while heading homeward with an eastbound Hudson's Bay pack-train, he organized a second Oregon expedition. Although this, too, ended in failure, it bore important fruit. Among the men who accompanied Wyeth in the summer of 1834 were several missionaries; and unlike most of their brethren, who carried the Cross to the red men uninvited, they believed they were answering a call not only from God but from the Indians themselves.

Their conviction stemmed from an incident in 1831 when three Nez Perces and one Flathead had accompanied a fur caravan to St. Louis. The sudden appearance of these exotics from the Far West caused a considerable stir. Rumors circulated that one purpose of the Indians' journey was to recruit missionaries for the salvation of their people's souls. A letter later published in the Methodist periodical *Christian Advocate and Journal* was filled with touching if apocry-

Thomas Nuttall, Explorer for Science

Botanist and artist Nuttall collected specimens for the Harvard Botanic Garden. He painted the red thorn (right), whose berries were eaten by many travelers in the West.

Among the hardened frontiersmen and shrewd Yankee traders of Wyeth's 1834 expedition was a reclusive 48-year-old Harvard professor, Thomas Nuttall (1786-1859). One of the leading U.S. naturalists, Nuttall had joined the party at Wyeth's invitation. Eccentric and unworldly, the English-born Nuttall was no novice in wilderness exploration. In 1810 he had set out on a two-year trip that took him up the wild Missouri beyond the Mandan villages. Engrossed in his collecting, he once wandered 100 miles across the prairie without food or water—until he collapsed from exhaustion and a friendly Mandan rescued him. Puzzled by this white man who sought no wealth and seemed indifferent to danger, the Indians considered him a kind of holy madman and left him in peace.

With Nuttall in 1834 was another naturalist, John K. Townsend. The two men had a scientific orgy, ignoring discomfort in the excitement of new discoveries. Between them they collected thousands of specimens—animal, vegetable, mineral—to enrich the East's knowledge of the Rockies and the Oregon Country.

phal descriptions of the noble savages' search for God. Read from hundreds of pulpits, it generated thousands of dollars in contributions for the creation of missions in the Pacific Northwest.

Leading the men of God in Wyeth's party was 30-year-old Jason Lee. Together with his nephew and fellow clergyman, Daniel, and three laymen, he was charged by the Methodist Board of Missions with locating the supposedly brutish Flatheads, who were mistakenly believed to flatten their infants' foreheads. The board ordered Lee and his companions to "live with them, learn their language, preach Christ . . . and . . . introduce schools, agriculture, and the arts of civilized life."

After Lee's arrival in Oregon it became clear that John McLoughlin had his own plans for the minister. The factor wanted no American missionaries in the interior, where Indian resentment of their presence might well disrupt the beaver trade. He was also genuinely afraid that the whites could not be protected in the remote mountain valleys. Using the latter argument, he urged Lee to abandon the idea of the Flathead mission and instead establish himself in the Willamette Valley, where there was already one white colony—and perhaps

Jason Lee   Nathaniel Wyeth   Hall Jackson Kelley

These men, representing three forces in history, reached Oregon in 1834: the missionary Lee; the businessman Wyeth (on his second trip); the apostle of expansionism, Kelley.

Fort Nez Percés, a Hudson's Bay Company post in what is now Washington. Called Fort Walla Walla in the 1830's, it was a welcome stopover for Oregon-bound Americans.

Jason Lee's Mission

The rainy season was fast approaching, and a house was wanted to shelter us when it arrived. . . . Our house advanced but slowly, and we were caught in one violent storm of wind and rain, which was near drenching all we had, the tent which we occupied being but a poor protection. . . . Before the next storm came on we had a roof on a part of our house, and a piece of floor laid. . . . A few weeks, all the time hard at it, and the roof was completed; a good chimney made of sticks and clay, and a fire-place in one end; floors laid of plank split from the fir, and hewn on the upper side; doors procured in the same way, and hung on wooden hinges. Then a table, then stools, and finally the luxury of chairs added to our self-made comforts. Our good mansion was built of logs twenty by thirty feet . . . and lighted by four small windows, the sashes partly made by Mr. Jason Lee with his jack-knife.

—Daniel Lee and J. H. Frost
Ten Years in Oregon, 1844

some Indians in need of salvation. After prayer and thought, Lee acquiesced.

Once settled by the Willamette River, where he established a mission school near what would become the thriving town of Salem, Jason Lee underwent a conversion of his own. Along with his desire to save the heathen came a new, more earthly vision. The valley soil was superb, the climate moderate, trade routes to California and the Orient relatively easy. In short, here was a perfect spot for an American colony. Slowly the hopes of Hall Jackson Kelley were reborn in the missionary's mind.

The Great Reinforcement

At first, Lee's attempts to attract new immigrants were couched in suitably religious terms. In early 1835 he wrote to the board requesting recruits, both male and female, to aid in soul saving. Letters to the East took a long time in those days, and two years passed before Lee had his reply. It came in the form of a ship that appeared at the mouth of the Columbia bearing 13 immigrants from the East—men, women, and children dispatched by the Methodist board. One

of the women became Lee's wife in 1837, in the first Christian wedding ceremony ever to take place in Oregon.

The coming of the new recruits to Oregon merely whetted Jason Lee's appetite for additional pioneers, and the settlers themselves were becoming increasingly anxious for the protection of the American flag. Less than a year after his marriage Lee left Oregon on an overland journey to the East, to get the settlers' case before Congress and find money and new recruits for the Pacific Northwest. He was evidently a man of considerable eloquence, for though he failed to initiate any move in Congress to organize Oregon as a territory, he did find some 50 willing souls eager for adventure and anxious to establish themselves in the bountiful land beyond the mountains. On October 9, 1839, these would-be Oregonians sailed from New York, arriving at the Columbia's mouth seven months later. This Great Reinforcement, as it came to be known, firmly established the American presence in Oregon. It was only a matter of time before that presence would expand and then dominate the Oregon Country.

Indian Fishermen of the Northwest

Once they had arduously traversed the Rockies, northwest-bound settlers rolled with great relief onto a semiarid plateau. There the terrain was far easier and the Indians among the most peaceful on earth. Typified by the Colvilles, these tribes based their culture on peace and equality. They avoided wars with neighbors and, if attacked, refused to retaliate. Their chiefs mediated family or tribal quarrels so that no feuds would be kindled. And such sparks of discord as jealousy and status seeking were few because the concept of individual wealth was alien. The Colvilles considered everyone equal, even the highly respected chief. They had no social hierarchies, never took slaves, and esteemed personal autonomy.

Colville food-getting was communal, and all bounty was shared equally. After the March thaw the women gathered edible roots and lilylike camas bulbs. From moss and the bark of certain trees they made gruel. Their men collected fresh-water mollusks, hunted birds and rabbits, played games, and gambled. As soon as they spotted the silver of leaping salmon, they built summer houses of matting along riverbanks and, at a time determined by their Salmon Chief, placed weirs by the rapids and enacted a ceremony to the Fish Guardian Spirit. In autumn they climbed to higher wooded areas to pick berries and hunt. To purify themselves in honor of their prey, the men steamed themselves in ritual sweat lodges. Then they stalked bear, wolf, fox, and antelope, sometimes driving deer over cliffs. When winter came, the Colvilles retired to permanent villages of about 200 persons each. Every family had a longhouse made of grass and bullrush matting, with cubicles along the inner walls for each couple and a central aisle where they prepared meals. Lacking pottery, they used watertight baskets woven of reeds and grass, cooking by dropping hot stones into these water-filled containers.

Flatheads of the eastern plateau play a lively game of lacrosse, a sport invented by the Indians. They use a deerskin ball and racquets made of rawhide thongs.

With weirs—basket traps of willow—and spears with forked deer-bone points, Colville Indians catch salmon at the Falls of Colville. The fish will be dried on racks that are made of cedar, then packed for storage in woven-grass bags.

Three nonagricultural fishing and gathering cultures inhabited the Northwest in the 1830's and 1840's: peaceful tribes, such as the Colvilles; warlike aristocrats, such as the Nootkas and Clallams; and coastal fishermen, such as the shrewd Chinooks, who traded with both, canoeing upriver to a commerce center at The Dalles rapids.

A Chinook wife weaves a blanket of woolly hair from her dog, a now-extinct breed. Another spins thread with a spindle and whorl. A cradle headboard (left) flattens a baby's forehead—a sign of aristocracy. Indians also made rain capes of shredded cedar bark.

Having no concept of nation or tribe, the Colvilles organized their lives around the villages, each of which had a chief, a subchief, and an assembly in which all adult citizens of both sexes—including anyone marrying into the village—could have a voice. The chief kept peace, gave wise counsel, and punished with lashings the occasional thieves or rapists. During the long winter he also supervised dances and holy rites, aided by the shaman (witch doctor). The Colvilles' religion revolved around guardian spirits, usually of animal form. Before puberty each boy spent night-long vigils during which his guardian spirit would appear in a vision and become part of him for life, protecting and aiding him.

A similar respect for animal spirits permeated the religion of other fishermen across the Cascade Mountains. Along the Pacific, coastal tribes such as the Nootkas believed that if the Salmon Beings were honored, their spirits would go back to a submarine Salmon House and there acquire new bodies for next year's spawning run. The first fish taken each year was eaten ritually at an altar, and its bones were tossed back into the water so the fish would be reincarnated. Yet in many respects the Indians of the foggy, wooded coast contrasted sharply with those of the plateau, for most were warlike and status-dominated slaveowners.

Because the waters of the Pacific abounded with fish, there were food surpluses, which the Indians traded with food-short tribes for blankets and other goods. Avidly amassing possessions, they became ostentatious plutocrats. Their society was divided into commoners and nobles, with a hereditary chief who owned the village land, hunting and fishing grounds, and was served by slaves captured in raids. A noble could use his hereditary title only after performing a potlatch: inviting guests he wished to impress, he would boast about his wealth and, while delivering speeches of self-praise, give much of it away to those who were assembled. The more of his property that he gave away, the higher his status; he would even kill his slaves to show that he could afford to spare them.

Using authentic masks from various tribes, artist Paul Kane painted this scene of Northwest Coast Indians communing with the spirit world by dancing to the rhythm of a rattle and bells. The cloak in the foreground depicts stylized animals, which are the crests of one clan.

Artist John Webber, who traveled with Captain Cook, depicted the interior of a Nootka longhouse. Supported by carved posts and lighted by smoke holes, it holds several families. Behind seating platforms, baskets and wooden chests line the plank walls. Hot stones in a water-filled cooking box boil seafood. Drying fish hang from the rafters.

Clallam Indians served fish in a carved alder-wood feast dish depicting the native sea otter.

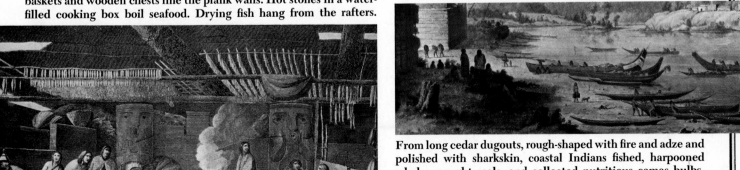

From long cedar dugouts, rough-shaped with fire and adze and polished with sharkskin, coastal Indians fished, harpooned whales, caught seals, and collected nutritious camas bulbs.

A Fever for Oregon

Even as Jason Lee was establishing his station in the Willamette Valley, other men of God were turning their eyes to the Far West. Among them was a vigorous young physician from upstate New York, Marcus Whitman, whose generally amiable manner concealed a will of steel. In December of 1834 Whitman petitioned the American Board of Commissioners for Foreign Missions to support his plan to go to Oregon under their auspices as a doctor and teacher. In reply, the board proposed that Whitman and the 55-year-old Rev. Samuel Parker, who had earlier volunteered for missionary service, reconnoiter Oregon to determine its suitability for God's work. The two men joined a packtrain bound for the annual rendezvous in the Rockies. They were hardly welcome guests among the blaspheming trappers, although Whitman gained their grudging respect by removing an arrowhead that had long been lodged in Jim Bridger's back. (When the doctor voiced his amazement at the lack of infection, the veteran mountain man remarked, "Meat don't spoil in the Rockies.")

West by Wagon

Whitman and Parker parted company after the rendezvous. Whitman hurried back east, determined, despite his ignorance of the Oregon Country, to convince his eastern superiors that new missions were desperately needed and that women and wagons could negotiate the long, perilous overland route to the Pacific Northwest.

Whitman's certainty was based only on hope, but hope became reality. Marcus Whitman was in love, and he dreamed of establishing his mission with the ebullient Narcissa Prentiss at his side. As it happened, it was easy to persuade the lady—whose religious dedication matched Whitman's own—that not

Marcus Whitman's mission at Waiilatpu included a working farm, gristmill, and blacksmith shop where Indians could learn white man's skills. The doctor's converts were few.

only she but a wagonful of household goods could make the difficult journey.

In 1836 Whitman and his bride set out into the wilderness on their godly enterprise. They were accompanied by the dour and difficult Rev. Henry Spalding (who himself had once been in love with Narcissa) and his wife. Narcissa Whitman proved an able and enthusiastic pioneer, but even her spirits sometimes flagged between the Rockies and Oregon. Though the party was accompanied on this stretch by a group of Hudson's Bay trappers headed for Fort Vancouver, the difficult terrain, the lack of fresh meat, and most of all Whitman's unyielding determination caused Narcissa no end of grief. "Husband has had a tedious time with the waggon today," she wrote in a typical diary entry. "Got set in the creek this morning while crossing, was obliged to wade considerably in getting it out. . . . It is not very greatful to my feelings to see him wear out with such excessive fatigue."

Eventually even Whitman admitted defeat, the wagon was abandoned, and they continued their journey on horseback. But he remained convinced that a large party, willing to expend the time and effort, could bring wagons over the

Oregon Trail. Already his thoughts, like those of other pious men before him, seemed to be diverging from soul saving to empire building. Though he would spend his remaining years as a missionary to the Indians, Whitman would also become one of the leading propagandists for American migration to Oregon.

Once in the Oregon Country, Whitman and Spalding set up their stations

As a visual aid for Indian proselytes, both Catholics and Protestants devised "ladders of history" slandering the rival creed. Below is a Presbyterian ladder showing the pope (at top left) tumbling down into hell.

From the Diary of Narcissa Whitman

Narcissa and Marcus Whitman

Some [of the Indians] feel almost to blame us for telling them about eternal realities. One said it was good when they knew nothing but to hunt, eat, drink and sleep; now it was bad. . . . They feel so bad, disappointed, and some of them angry, because husband tells them . . . they are all of them in the broad road to destruction. . . . Some threaten to whip him and to destroy our crops.

deep in the interior. John McLoughlin, who rightly feared for their safety, nonetheless extended his usual help.

As late as 1840 Oregon's American population amounted to fewer than 200 souls, almost all of them in the Willamette Valley. Their right to settle was implicit in the Anglo-American agreement of 1818, but no provision had been made for their governance. This suited them well enough, for in such a sparsely settled land there seemed little need for courts, legislatures, and other appurtenances of government. But the situation began to change abruptly in 1841 when Ewing Young, who had become a successful cattle rancher and probably the richest American in the Willamette Valley, died intestate, and a means had to be devised to apportion his property.

To deal with Young's estate, Jason Lee called upon American settlers to meet at Champoeg on the banks of the Willamette. The settlers created a court and formed a committee to devise a constitution and a legal code. Their work would be continued by another meeting of settlers in 1843. These Champoeg meetings laid the foundations for an organized government and gave the Ore-

In 1841, 69 pioneers took the Oregon Trail, half going north to the missions, half going south near Fort Hall to California. By 1850 over 44,000 had made the journey.

gonians a political structure with which to press for U.S. annexation.

At the same time in the East events were at last conspiring to bring the Oregon Country to the forefront of the American consciousness. The reports of missionaries received wide publicity, as did those from U.S. ships scouting the coast on official reconnaissance missions. Letters from settlers telling of rich land to be had for the taking gave hope to the farmers of the East and Midwest, who were still suffering from the economic consequences of the great panic of 1837. Above all, a new and adventurous mood

was upon the land. Gone was the belief that the Rockies were the ultimate limit of American expansion; taking its place was the popular concept that became known as Manifest Destiny, which held that the republic had a divine mission to spread from coast to coast—if not from pole to pole.

This combination of economic and ideological pressures first bore fruit in the spring of 1841, when the first wagon train of 69 pioneers set out for the Far West. Half the party made it to Oregon and the other half to California—but neither group managed to bring its wagons through. The next year a group of more than 100 traveled from Missouri to Oregon, and they too had to abandon their wagons in the mountains. Finally, in 1843 Marcus Whitman (returning to Oregon after a trip east) realized his great dream by helping to guide the first wagon train—with nearly a thousand immigrants—to the Pacific Coast. If there had been any doubt, it was now dispelled; Americans had come to Oregon to stay. Later years would bring even larger numbers, but in this year of the Great Emigration the balance tipped in favor of U.S. claims.

Jesuits Among the Indians

In the spring of 1841 six black-robed Jesuits left Westport, Missouri, with a westbound fur caravan. Their leader, burly Belgian-born Pierre Jean de Smet, had spent the previous year in the Rockies and returned with an invitation from the Flatheads to establish a mission. The first mission, in the Bitterroot Valley, was an immediate success, and the priests found the Indians eager pupils. In fact, when the Flatheads set off on their late fall buffalo hunt, they asked for a "Black Robe" to accompany them and continue their religious instruction. De Smet selected French-born Father Nicolas Point, and for five months Point stayed with the Indians on the trail and in winter camp, living their life and sharing their hardships. An untrained but enthusiastic artist, Point kept a pictorial record of his experiences. (Two of his paintings are seen at the right.) In all, Point spent six years with the Flatheads and the neighboring Coeur d'Alenes and Blackfeet, making numerous converts. (He was not impressed by the Coeur d'Alenes and Blackfeet but liked the Flatheads, among whom one usually "finds the virtues of modesty, frankness, courage, goodness and generosity.") Point's companions, notably the jovial De Smet, had equal success, and by 1847 there were three Jesuit missions in the Oregon Country. Jesuit success in gaining converts was in sharp contrast to the record of the Protestants. One cause may have been the appeal of the colorful Catholic symbolism to the Indians. But probably more important was the fact that the Jesuit missionaries were better trained and, not being colonizers, were genuinely sympathetic to the Indians.

In an imaginatively transparent tepee, Father Point welcomes a 104-year-old Spokane Indian who has snowshoed 20 miles to seek baptism.

Father Point's pupils help one another as they study the catechism.

The Prairie Schooner: America's First Mobile Home

One of the most enduring symbols of the Old West is the prairie schooner—the covered wagon—whose billowing cloth top made a wagon train look like a fleet of ships sailing over a sea of grass. The most familiar covered wagon crossing the plains and mountains in the 1840's to the promised lands of Oregon and California was a smaller, lighter relative of the big Conestoga wagon of the East. This prairie schooner was superbly designed for its job of transporting pioneer families and their goods on the five-month-long 2,000-mile journey west. The cloth top protected people and possessions from sun and rain, hail and wind, and it could be closed off entirely by drawstrings at each end. The big wheels rolled easily over humps and hollows in the trail, and wide rims helped keep them from sinking into soft ground. The wagon's 10- by 3½-foot body could take a load of a ton and a half, but experts advised keeping below this limit. The lighter the wagon, the less likely it was to bog down in muddy stream-banks or prairie sloughs—or to tire the long-suffering teams. Even so, there was not much room inside the wagon, and in decent weather most people cooked, ate, and slept outside.

A frame of hickory bows holds the wagon top, which can be rolled back for ventilation. Waterproofed with paint or linseed oil, the top is of heavy-duty canvas, often made from hemp, an important cash crop in Kentucky, Missouri, and Mississippi.

Western wagons range from plain farm wagons to five-ton freighters. The Conestoga (right), which weighs 1½ tons *empty* and carries 5-ton loads over eastern roads, was developed by Pennsylvania Germans and is too heavy for travel in the roadless West.

A "lazy board" on the side is for the driver or hitchhiker to take a rest.

Feed trough

Six mules pull a Conestoga. Its curved ends stabilize the loads on steep hills.

Because mules traditionally are mounted from the left, Conestoga drivers sit on, or walk beside, the left rear animal (above). When meeting oncoming traffic, the wagons keep to the right so the drivers afoot can see the other vehicles and can walk on the drier center of the crowned road, reinforcing the custom of right-side driving.

Perched on bundles, mother and son rest tired feet. A toolbox is on the wagon's one side, the brake lever and water bucket on the other.

The wagon box is packed to keep the center of gravity low and to avoid puncturing the cover. Heavy supplies—a plow, bed-stead, chest of drawers, stove, spinning wheel, and bags of seed—go on the bottom, carefully wrapped to avoid jostling in the springless vehicle. Then come lighter goods—kitchen utensils and clothes—wrapped and strapped down. Atop all are stored necessaries for the trip: flour and salt, a water keg, cooking pot, rifle, ax, blankets, even folding camp-stools. In bad weather the family sleeps inside, on the load. When the trail gets steeper and the oxen tire, many items will have to be abandoned.

Both oxen and mules are shod. The hooves of the stronger-legged oxen give better purchase in soft earth.

The rear wheels are about five or six feet in diameter, the front ones four feet or a bit less. The front wheels have to be smaller to permit sharp turns—a big wheel would jam against the wagon body.

Hardwood brake blocks

Massive axles support the weight of the wagon body and load. On the plains a broken axle is a calamity —and prudent wagoners usually take along a spare.

The grease bucket, filled with a mixture of animal fat and tar, hangs from the rear axle.

Iron tire (over rim)

A wagon wheel is a complex structure of many carefully fitted components. The rim is built of curved sections called felloes, pegged together at the ends or clamped by rivets and bolted to the tire. The heavy spokes fit into sockets in the felloes and in the massive hubs. The iron tire holds the wheel together and protects the rim from wear; otherwise, metal parts are kept to a minimum because of their weight and the difficulty of repairing them while on the march.

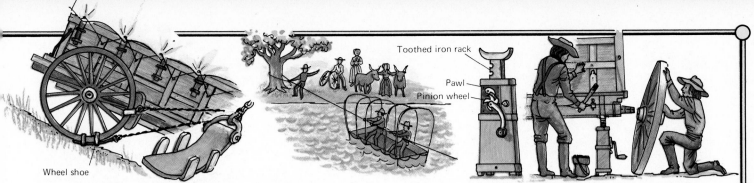

Toothed iron rack

Pawl

Pinion wheel

Wheel shoe

Jack body of heavy iron-bound wood

Tricks of Managing a Versatile Vehicle

Getting wagons up steep slopes is an exhausting task, and getting them downhill is also difficult. Brakes can slip, so the wheels are locked in place by a chain, put through the spokes and fastened to the wagon. To keep the iron tires from developing flat spots, a curved shoe is attached.

When rivers are too deep to ford, ingenious pioneers make wagon bodies watertight with a sheathing of rawhide or of tarpaulin, often coated with tallow. They remove the wheels and float the wagons across. If there is timber, they build rafts, saving time, energy, and trouble.

When a wheel needs repair, as often happens, the wagon must be jacked up so that the wheel can be removed. The heavy jack works by a rack-and-pinion system that is powered by a hand crank. A pawl locks the jack in place, keeping it from slipping and bringing down the wagon.

Sturdy Underpinnings

Oxen work in pairs, or yokes, usually three for an emigrant's team. The biggest are put next to the wagon to pull most of the load. The walking driver controls the animals with a goad, shouts, and loud cracks of his fearsome 18- to 20-foot whip, snapped above the beasts so as not to cut their flesh.

The wagon undercarriage has a rigid connecting pole that runs its length and is mortised to the rear bolster. In front it pokes through an arch in the bolster. The arch is wide enough to allow for a pivoting movement of the axle around the pole so that the front wheels can turn at bends.

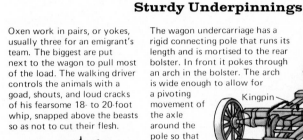

Bolster uprights to stabilize the wagon box

Brake lever

Kingpin

Hound

Singletree

Doubletree

Brake beam and brake shoes

Sand bolster

The tongue: this running gear is for horses or mules, not for oxen, which do not need "trees."

A prairie schooner's undercarriage must be strong yet maneuverable. The key to its movability is its iron or steel kingpin, which is the main front pivot, allowing the wagon to turn. The pin goes down through a wooden support, or box bolster, on which the wagon box rests (removed here to make the underpinnings visible); the two metal bolster plates on which the wagon box and the running gear swivel; the sand bolster; the connecting pole; and the axle.

The axle's outer end is tapered and conical, with its bottom surface—and the matching hub bearing below it—horizontal. As each spoke assumes the bottom position, bearing the load, it becomes perpendicular (dotted line) to the axle for maximum strength.

Axle end

Axle

Hub bearing

Cross-section profile of the axle and a wheel hub

The axle and hub are lined with iron at the points of greatest wear.

The spokes flare outward to give the wheel a dished form for greater strength.

Oxen are slow; they do up to 15 miles a day, while mules do 20 miles.

Mules Versus Oxen

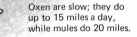

Double ox yoke of strong wood

Mule collars

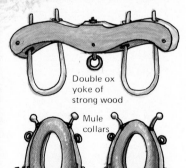

Pioneers choose mules for speed, oxen for economy. Oxen cost half the price of mules and live by eating trailside grass; mules need expensive grain. Oxen are not stolen by Indians as mules are and in an emergency can be eaten. They are also very sturdy and can withstand severe hardships.

Pioneers Take Everything They Need—And More

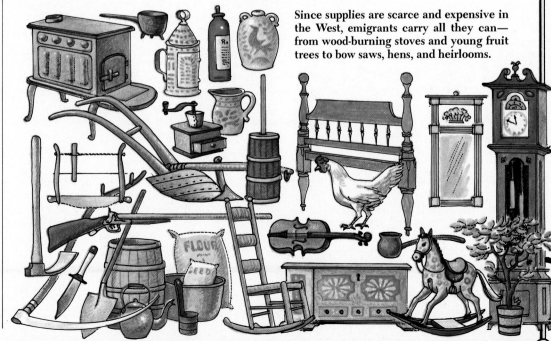

Since supplies are scarce and expensive in the West, emigrants carry all they can— from wood-burning stoves and young fruit trees to bow saws, hens, and heirlooms.

FLOUR

SEED

On the Trail From Dawn to Dusk

At Independence Rock, in what is now Wyoming, many wagon trains on the Oregon Trail camped for the night, forming corrals. Here the original Applegate train separated into smaller parties "better suited to the narrow mountain paths and small pastures in their front."

In May of 1843 some 1,000 pioneers set out from their gathering point near Independence, Missouri, for the Oregon Country. One of the leaders of the group was Jesse Applegate, who later helped to form the provisional government of what would become the state of Oregon. Here is part of his account of a day on the journey:

It is four o'clock A.M.; the sentinels on duty have discharged their rifles—the signal that the hours of sleep are over; and every wagon and tent is pouring forth its . . . tenants, and slow-kindling smokes begin largely to rise and float away on the morning air. Sixty men start from the corral, spreading as they [ride] through the vast herd of cattle and horses that form a semi-circle around the encampment, the most distant perhaps two miles away. . . . By five o'clock the herders begin to contract the great moving circle and the well-trained animals move slowly toward camp, clipping . . . grass on the way. In about an hour five thousand animals are close up to the en-

campment, and the teamsters are busy selecting their teams and driving them inside the "corral" to be yoked.

From six to seven o'clock is a busy time; breakfast is to be eaten, the tents struck, the wagons loaded, and the teams yoked and brought up in readiness to be attached to their respective wagons.

It is on the stroke of seven; the rushing to and fro, the cracking of the whips, the loud command to oxen, and what seems to be the inextricable confusion of the last ten minutes has ceased. Fortunately every one has been found and every teamster is at his post. The clear notes of the trumpet sound in the front; the pilot and his guards mount their horses, the leading division of wagons moves out of the encampment, and takes up the line of march, the rest fall into their places with the precision of clock work, until the spot so lately full of life sinks back into that solitude that seems to reign over the broad plain.

The caravan has been about two hours in motion and is now extended as widely

as a prudent regard for safety will permit. First, near the bank of the shining river [Platte] is a company of horsemen. . . . They are hunting a favorable crossing for the wagons; while we look they have succeeded . . . one of the party . . . has raised a flag, no doubt a signal to the wagons to steer their course to where he stands. . . . Some of the teamsters ride upon the front of their wagons, some walk beside their teams; scattered along the line companies of women and children are taking exercise on foot; they gather bouquets of rare and beautiful flowers that line the way.

Next comes a band of horses; two or three men or boys follow them, the docile and sagacious animals scarce needing this attention, for they have learned to follow in the rear of the wagons, and know that at noon they will be allowed to graze and rest. . . . Not so with the large herd of horned beasts that bring up the rear; lazy, selfish and unsocial. . . . They seem to move only in fear of the driver's whip.

The pilot, by measuring the ground and timing the speed of the wagons and the walk of his horses, has determined the rate of each, so as to enable him to select the nooning place, as nearly as the requisite grass and water can be had at the end of five hours' travel. . . . The wagons are drawn up in columns, four abreast, the leading wagon of each platoon on the left—the platoons being formed with that view. This brings friends together [for the noon stop] as well as at night.

At 7 a.m. the bugle sounds the daily call: "All know . . . that those not ready to take their proper places in the line of march must fall into the dusty rear for the day."

Setting Up Camp

It is now one o'clock; the bugle has sounded, and the caravan has resumed its westward journey. It is in the same order, but the evening is far less animated than the morning march; a drowsiness has fallen apparently on man and beast. . . . The sun is now getting low in the west, and at length the painstaking pilot is standing ready to conduct the train in the circle which he has previously measured and marked out, which is to form the invariable fortification for the night. The leading wagons follow him so nearly round the circle, that but a wagon length separates them. Each wagon follows in its track, the rear closing on the front, until its tongue and ox chains will perfectly reach from one to the other, and so accurate the measurement and perfect the practice, that the hindmost wagon of the train always precisely closes the gateway. As each

wagon is brought into position it is dropped from its team (the teams being inside the circle), the team unyoked, and the yokes and chains are used to connect the wagon strongly with that in its front. Within ten minutes from the time the leading wagon halted, the barricade is formed, the teams unyoked and driven out to pasture.

Everyone is busy preparing fires of buffalo chips to cook the evening meal, pitching tents and otherwise preparing for the night. . . . All able to bear arms in the party have been formed into three companies, and each of these into four watches. Every third night it is the duty of one of these companies to keep watch and ward over the camp.

It is not yet eight o'clock when the

first watch is to be set; the evening meal is just over, and the corral now free from the intrusion of the cattle or horses, groups of children are scattered over it. . . . Before a tent near the river a violin makes lively music, and some youths and maidens have improvised a dance upon the green. . . . It has been a prosperous day; more than twenty miles have been accomplished of the great journey. The encampment is a good one. . . . But time passes. . . . The violin is silent and the dancers have dispersed. Enamored youth have whispered a tender "good night" in the ears of blushing maidens, or stolen a kiss from the lips of some future bride—for Cupid here as elsewhere has been busy bringing together congenial hearts.

During the nooning a scout recounts his adventures to intent travelers. His highly embellished stories no doubt served to increase the confidence of nervous greenhorns, who depended on the scout to guide them safely through wild, unknown lands abounding in Indians.

Hardships of the Trek West

Some were prosperous New England or midwestern families with sturdy, well-provisioned wagons and ample livestock; a few were penniless frontiersmen who hitched onto wagon trains as hired hands; others were simply the young and restless, the "fiddle-footed," who could not resist the lure of a far horizon. But whoever they were, the early Oregon-bound pioneers had much in common. Many were touchy and quarrelsome; most had no knowledge of wilderness survival techniques or the hardships that lay before them, but they shared a steely determination to survive that would serve them well in meeting the brutal tests of the Oregon Trail.

The emigrants also shared a common enemy—time. They could not leave the jumping-off places along the Missouri before the prairie grass was up in early or mid-May if they expected their livestock to survive, and they had to cross the westernmost mountain barriers before the snows began to render them impassable in mid-October. That left a mere five months to cover some 2,000 miles in an era when 15 miles was a good day's travel and a rain-swollen river could delay a wagon train for two weeks.

Landmarks Along the Trail

The opening stretch of the Oregon Trail—northwestward over the blooming Kansas prairies to the Platte River in present-day Nebraska—was often a glorious lark, especially for the children. The route then followed the sinuous meanderings of the Platte, which some emigrants caustically described as a mile wide and an inch deep. The ter-

It sometimes took a man pushing each wheel and a homemade winch to work a heavy wagon up a steep mountain trail.

rain gradually became higher, more broken, and more arid. Along the river's north fork the trail went past the weird formations of Chimney Rock and Scott's Bluff to Fort Laramie in present-day Wyoming, a welcome respite where pioneers could lay in fresh supplies. Just before Independence Rock the route departed from the Platte and swung across the Rockies at the broad South Pass. The main route then dipped southwest to Fort Bridger and northwest again to Fort Hall. From there it generally followed the rim of the Snake River Canyon as far as Farewell Bend. The trail

struck northward to the beautiful valley of the Grande Ronde before crossing the Blue Mountains and reaching the mighty Columbia and a foaming gorge called The Dalles. From there on to the Willamette Valley the routes diverged. Some emigrants plunged down the river on makeshift rafts, but the cautious took one of several jolting wagon roads over the Cascade Range.

A Multitude of Mishaps

Trail discipline was difficult to enforce among the rugged individualists who traveled in the wagon trains, and quarrels over leadership, choice of route, place in line, guard duty, and other crucial matters were constant. The prairie schooners themselves—heavily laden, cumbersome, difficult to maneuver, and always in need of repair—could be a menace. Covers ripped off in windstorms, wooden wheels splintered in the alkali deserts or stuck fast in the mud, and wagons could be smashed irreparably while being windlassed down a steep grade (few early models had brakes).

The livestock, though vital, were yet another problem. Feed and water were usually ample on the Kansas grasslands except for the hindmost wagon trains in dry years. But fodder dwindled quickly on the High Plains, whose poisonous alkali springs also took a heavy toll. Cows, mules, oxen, and horses were often drowned in river crossings, run off by Indians, or terrified into stampedes by sudden thunderstorms. The loss of a good milk cow was bad enough, but the loss of a mule or ox team could leave a wagon stranded.

Crossing the Platte River, with its treacherous bed and changing current, was an adventure.

South Pass, a gentle valley through the Continental Divide, was the halfway mark for emigrants bound for Oregon. But the hardest part of the long journey still lay ahead.

Murderous Indian attacks on pioneer wagons are a staple of western lore, as this painting by George Caleb Bingham shows. In fact, although Indians often stole horses and cattle by night, they seldom attempted a direct attack on a well-disciplined wagon train.

All emigrant trains faced an endless search for potable water, firewood, and fresh meat. One traveler, Alonzo Delano, ruefully noted that after two days on the trail the bacon he had bought in St. Louis "began to exhibit more signs of life than we had bargained for, having a tendency to walk in insect form." Drinking water, too, could be very lively. Historian Francis Parkman, in his classic *The Oregon Trail*, described the emigrant's typical predicament: "When, thirsty with a long ride in the scorching sun over some boundless reach of prairie, he comes at length to a pool of water, and alights to drink, he discovers a troop of young tadpoles sporting in the bottom of his cup." Fortunately for the health of the pioneers, many women chose to boil their families' drinking water for coffee or tea so as to disguise its brackish taste—thus helping to check the spread of infectious diseases.

Water, pure or otherwise, the lack of it or a glut of it, ruled the emigrants' lives in countless ways. Crossing Kansas during particularly wet springs, the wagons could bog down, causing serious delays, and their unseasoned occupants would suffer from rheumatism and other ills. Sudden thunderstorms in open country could be downright dangerous, as pioneers and livestock were buffeted by wind and rain and frightened senseless by terrific bolts of lightning.

Water also played a part in the terrible outbreaks of cholera that in bad years plagued the emigrants at their gathering places along the Missouri and relentlessly followed them westward, striking with special force among the crowded camps and polluted wells of the Platte Valley. The many hundreds of victims usually expired with merciful speed: a pioneer might rise at dawn feeling perfectly fit and be near death by afternoon. Other diseases of the trail, less virulent but annoying enough, were scurvy, dysentery, and trachoma—the last caused by a dust-borne, eye-irritating virus.

Still another affliction, not physical but nonetheless oppressive, was engendered by the vast, empty plains themselves. Those used to domesticated landscapes felt suddenly small and insignificant. As Bernard DeVoto put it, "The little line of wagons was pygmy motion in immensity, the mind became a speck . . . always quivering with an unidentified dread."

In spite of bad weather and worse terrain, in spite of disease, dissension, and general misery, most of the exhausted emigrants made it to the banks of the Columbia. Still more hardships awaited them on the last stretch across the Cas-cade Range, but they generally managed that too. The wonder was, after all their travails, that they would ever feel the urge to pull up stakes again. But some did. Mountain man Jim Clyman, who helped guide a caravan to Oregon in 1844, wrote a letter to a Wisconsin friend describing his charges: "I never saw a more discontented community. . . . The long tiresome trip from the States, has taught them what they are capable of performing and enduring. They talk of removing to the Islands, California, Chili. . .with as much composure as you in Wisconsin talk of removing to Indiana or Michigan."

Stampedes of buffalo (this one was started by Indian hunters) were a deadly threat to wagon trains crossing the Great Plains.

New Trails West

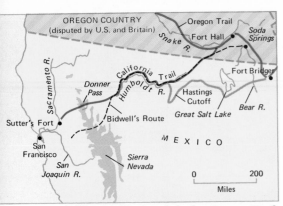

California pioneers left the Oregon Trail west of Fort Hall. The route through the Donner Pass became the California Trail.

In the winter of 1840–41 an almost palpable sense of gloom hung over the state of Missouri. Tumbling prices had put thousands of farmers deep into debt, and a raging cholera epidemic had decimated the region. In the midst of their despondency, however, many sons and daughters of earlier pioneers discerned a thin ray of hope from the Far West: the letters of John Marsh urging them to seek a bright new future in California. Hundreds of Missourians resolved to band together and blaze a trail to Marsh's verdant promised land.

By spring, however, many had backed out. In May 1841, when a recently dispossessed young schoolteacher-farmer named John Bidwell arrived at the rendezvous point at Sapling Grove, he found but one wagon waiting to accompany him on the journey. Over the next days reinforcements trickled in, but when the party at last broke camp there were only 69 men, women, and children.

Luck and Grit

By all rights the Bidwell-Bartleson party (the latter was its nominal captain) should never have made it to California. The two young men were neophytes in the wilderness. Yet they proposed to bring a wagon train to the coast through country they knew nothing about, with the sun as their only guide—even though no wagons had yet traversed the better known Oregon Trail. At first, luck was with them. A few days out of Sapling Grove they hitched up with a party of westward-bound Jesuits, including Pierre Jean De Smet, who were guided by the wilderness-wise mountain man Tom Fitzpatrick. For half the journey (as far as Soda Springs on the Bear River in what is now Idaho) the Bidwell party had the benefit of Fitzpatrick's expert direction. At the parting of the ways half the group opted for Oregon, but the rest stood firm for California, and their troubles began.

As the California-bound pioneers continued onward toward the Great Salt Lake in August, their supplies and their confidence were running low. Uncertain of the route, they dispatched two riders to Fort Hall on the Oregon Trail to engage a guide. The men returned with no guide and scant advice. They had been told simply to keep a generally westward

Elisha Stephens, who led the first wagon train across the Sierras in 1844, took what was later to become the standard route.

course, veering neither too far to the north, where they would be lost in a maze of canyons, nor too far south, where endless desert would engulf them.

Abandoning their wagons one by one, the 34 emigrants struggled on through the Great Salt Lake Desert to the Humboldt River (in present-day Nevada),

Exhausted members of the Donner party straggle through deep snow in a fruitless effort to cross the Sierra Nevada to safety.

Graves, dead animals, and smashed wagons punctuated the stretches of desert west of the Rockies that every emigrant party had to cross, whether bound for Oregon or California.

which they followed to the point where it sank underground. Game was scarce and the threat of starvation constant, but they kept going, slaughtering their oxen for food. By mid-October they had reached the foothills of the Sierras, their last major obstacle. On October 19 Bidwell noted in his diary: "Having come about 12 miles, a horrid precipice bid us stop. . . . Men went in different directions to see if there was any possibility of extricating ourselves from this place without going back but could see no prospect of a termination of the mts., mts., mountains."

Sheer grit sustained the pioneers as they trudged over the Sierras, some on bare, blistered feet. Finally, on October 29 they entered California's broad San Joaquin Valley, only a few days' hike from John Marsh's ranch. With incredible fortitude and luck, they had stumbled across most of a continent and homed in on target. Although their route across the Sierras was later superseded, their success heartened thousands.

The Donner Tragedy

A mountain man, Elisha Stephens, succeeded in bringing the first wagon train across the Sierras via the Truckee Pass in 1844. What Stephens had done, others could copy—or so thought 62-year-old George Donner, his 65-year-old brother Jacob, and the much younger James Reed as they set out in May 1846 from Independence, in Missouri. Making their way west, the already large group picked up more recruits, and when they reached the Little Sandy River in the Wyoming country in late July, they split into two trains. One proceeded to California without major mishap along the Fort Hall route, but the Donner party—by that time 89 peo-

Stunningly beautiful at other seasons, with animals drinking after dawn in mirror-clear lakes, the towering Sierras proved terrifying in winter, their lofty passes snowbound.

ple—decided to take an untested shortcut recommended by Lansford Hastings, a California land speculator who had published a western guidebook.

The decision proved fatal. Hastings Cutoff was indeed 400 miles shorter than the established California Trail from Fort Hall, but it proved far more difficult, and the party did not reach the Sierras until late October, not long before snows would be closing down the Truckee Pass (renamed Donner Pass). What followed was a season of horror and heroism, self-sacrifice, and cowardice. Strung out east of the pass, the party dug in for the winter. As supplies gave out, a scouting party of 17 young men, women, and boys was sent westward to brave the snow-clogged mountains and rally relief expeditions, but those left behind were slowly reduced to starvation. By the time survivors of the scouting party reached help, the pioneers left

behind had long since eaten their remaining livestock and most of their pets. Soon they would be subsisting on the flesh of their comrades who had already starved to death.

When the first of several rescue teams reached the forward edge of the Donner train in late February 1847, they came upon scenes of horror none would ever forget. Many survivors were half mad; others lay near death, too weak to move or be moved.

In all, 45 members of the Donner party perished in the Sierras that winter, including George Donner and his wife, Tamsen, who refused to leave her dying husband when the rescuers came. But most of the survivors recovered with remarkable speed, and some even wrote to friends back east urging them to emigrate. One letter, however, contained the prudent warning: "Never take no cut ofs and hury along as fast as you can."

Donner Survivors

James and Margaret Reed

Six of the Donner party who survived were James Frazier Reed, his semi-invalid wife, Margaret, and their four children. Paradoxically, their survival may have been due to a tragedy in the Nevada desert. While struggling up a brutal grade, Reed had quarreled with the ox driver of another family in the train when the two wagons became entangled. The man attacked Reed with his whip; Reed in self-defense drew a knife and killed him.

Banished from the train, which was low on provisions and far behind schedule, Reed rode ahead to California to bring help. (He had been sent off unarmed and

on foot, but friends secretly got food, a horse, and a rifle to him.) Narrowly missing starvation, he arrived only to be embroiled in the California phase of the Mexican War. Not for three months was he able to organize a relief expedition.

Meanwhile, Margaret, trapped in the snow, was somehow able to sustain her children's lives and morale. Reed, finally underway, led his men, burdened with heavy food packs, up the mountains. He met his wife with two of their children coming down with an earlier relief party. Reed pressed feverishly ahead, and in two days found his other children alive.

The Imperial Urge

The movement was a force long before it had a name. Indeed, by the late 1830's what historians later called the doctrine of Manifest Destiny was already an article of faith for millions of Americans. They believed that God had created upon our shores a new breed of man—predominantly English and Scottish in heritage, Protestant in faith, democratic in ideology, and white in complexion—destined to rule the continent, at least from the Atlantic to the Pacific and from the Canadian border to the Gulfs of Mexico and California. Finally, in 1845 editor John L. O'Sullivan coined the phrase that gave a title to the concept. Writing of the burning Oregon issue and U.S. claims to the entire region north to Russian Alaska's southern border, O'Sullivan asserted that the disputed territory was American, not by right of discovery or even its settlement by U.S. citizens but because of "our manifest destiny to overspread and possess the whole of the continent which

Providence has given us for the development of the great experiment of liberty and federated self-government."

Whence came this compulsion to expand, this sense of mission so selfless in theory, so self-serving in practice? Perhaps it was implicit as early as the 17th century when the colonists of Virginia and the Puritans of Massachusetts Bay began their drive to seize the Indians' lands. It was certainly present in the late 18th-century surge across the Appalachians, in the purchase of Louisiana, and in the harrying of Spain from the Floridas. But not until the late 1830's was it given an easily understood rationale, one that boldly proclaimed the moral superiority of Americans, from which their "right" of continental conquest was deduced. The premise is reflected in Richard Henry Dana's immensely popular work *Two Years Before the Mast*, memoirs of his 1834 visit to the West Coast. Dana scornfully characterized Californians as "an idle, thriftless people" who

"make nothing for themselves." He added, "In the hands of an enterprising people, what a country this might be!"

The same ideas suffused Texas' rebellion against Mexico when scores of American frontiersmen rushed to help their compatriots throw off a foreign yoke in 1836—one that was widely viewed as necessarily tyrannical and inept *because* it was foreign. By 1845 Texas would become part of the Union.

In 1844 a new president, James K. Polk, squeaked into office on a platform promising vigorous pursuit of maximum American claims in both the Southwest and Northwest. Polk's inaugural address seemed to imply that he had achieved an overwhelming mandate. "Our title to the country of the Oregon is 'clear and unquestionable,'" he asserted. His audience assumed that he meant the region all the way to the 54° 40' line, the southern border of Russian America. Privately, Polk was ready to accept a northern border at the 49th

The Whitman Massacre

A dramatic drawing shows a grim Indian assaulting Marcus Whitman while his wife tries to stop him. Actually, Narcissa rushed in after her husband had already been wounded.

Tomahas (above), a sullen Cayuse, was one of Whitman's killers; his weapon, this bronze tomahawk.

The career of medical missionary Marcus Whitman ended in terror and tragedy on a cold, wet November day in 1847. For 11 years he had preached to the Cayuse Indians but without much success. Now the Indians were growing resentful of the white men who crowded into Oregon, many of whom stopped to rest at Whitman's mission.

The last wave of settlers had brought a deadly gift: measles. To the Indians, who had never before encountered the disease, it was fatal. Whitman did what he could to treat the victims, but Indian children died while white children recovered. To the grieving Indians, it was clear that Whitman was a sorcerer. While pretending to help

them, he was thought to be secretly poisoning them with his medicines so that whites might steal their land.

November 29 brought bad news: three more Indian children had died. One belonged to Chief Tiloukaikt, who had already lost two others to the white man's sickness. After a funeral held by Whitman, Tiloukaikt and other Indians entered the mission kitchen. While the chief engaged Whitman in conversation, a warrior, Tomahas, struck the missionary from behind. Tiloukaikt hacked at Whitman's face; a third Indian shot him in the neck. After the slaughter was over, 13 whites staying at the mission were dead, one of them Whitman's wife, Narcissa.

parallel, but he knew that those who had been stirred by the "Fifty-four Forty or Fight!" slogan would have thought such a compromise akin to treason.

Meanwhile, events in Oregon had been moving swiftly. No longer was U.S. settlement restricted to the Willamette Valley. A sprinkling of Americans was living in the Puget Sound area and in missions in the interior. Britain had once hoped to keep these regions for her own, but as the fur trade declined, so did her economic interest in Oregon. In 1845 John McLoughlin himself recognized the legal authority of the settlers' provisional government on the north bank of the Columbia, and the headquarters of the Hudson's Bay Company was moved to Vancouver Island.

Famed historical painter Emanuel Leutze captured the spirit of Manifest Destiny in this massive canvas. Surmounting fearful obstacles, his pioneers express their confidence.

The Oregon Settlement

During this period the influx of settlers was making the Indians ever more restless and fearful of losing their lands. The missionaries did little to calm them or help them adjust to the inevitability of domination by America. Instead they wrangled among themselves, Catholics vying with Protestants for the salvation of souls, and both groups warning the confused Indians that eternal hellfire would be their lot if they should opt for the wrong faith. A few Indians vented their anger on mission property, and the fear of a full-scale Indian rebellion in Oregon fed renewed demands for protection by the United States.

At the same time in Washington, D.C., President Polk was acting out a complex charade, publicly supporting "Fifty-four Forty or Fight!" while quietly passing the word to the British that the 49th parallel would be acceptable. Her Majesty's envoy at first failed to take the bait, but when Polk loudly reasserted his original demand and requested that Congress repeal the joint occupation treaty, the British capitulated. With calculated hesitation Polk accepted the 49th-parallel boundary pending Senate approval, and on June 15, 1846, the pact was ratified. Whatever dismay they may have felt about this "compromise," few senators were happy about the prospect of a two-front war—for by then the United States was deeply involved in a struggle with Mexico.

Thomas Hart Benton

The self-proclaimed father of Manifest Destiny, and certainly its most vociferous expounder, was Missouri's redoubtable Senator Thomas Hart Benton. As early as 1819 Benton, then a St. Louis journalist, advocated annexing Texas, and by 1825 he was calling for an overland trail to the Pacific Coast. His expansionism was partly motivated by the desire to increase the U.S. share of the China trade, but it had deeper ideological roots as well. In the unclaimed lands of the West, Benton saw an opportunity for poor farmers and workmen from the East to become prosperous, independent farmers.

A tireless promoter of the Oregon Country, Benton realistically urged compromising with Britain on the boundary question. He was against annexing Texas in 1845 because he did not want war with Mexico. Despite his original proslavery position, he opposed the extension of slavery, even at the cost of his Senate seat.

Oregon City in 1846 was a small but steadily growing settlement located at the falls of the Willamette River. When Oregon became a territory in 1849, it was made the first capital.

165

John Charles Frémont and Kit Carson

The noted scout Kit Carson stands beside John Charles Frémont, whom he accompanied on three exploring missions.

John Charles Frémont was brilliant, unpredictable, and egotistical, a polished eastern dandy with social ambitions and powerful personal connections. Kit Carson was modest, unaggressive, steady, and of humble background. A mountain man, he was respected by his peers but little known outside that limited circle. A chance meeting on a Missouri River steamboat brought these men into a close partnership that left a permanent imprint on the history of the West.

Born in Savannah, Georgia, in 1813, Frémont and his mother, brother, and sister moved in 1818 to Charleston, South Carolina, where John Charles grew up in genteel poverty. He developed into a handsome youth with a romantic love of danger, a flair for self-dramatization, and a talent for attracting influential friends, one of whom paid for much of his education. At the age of 25 he became a second lieutenant in the elite U.S. Topographical Corps, where he soon gained a brilliant reputation as a wilderness surveyor and mapmaker.

The dashing young officer attracted the attention of Thomas Hart Benton, one of the most powerful men in American politics. At the Benton home Frémont met the senator's beautiful, talented 15-year-old daughter, Jessie. The two fell in love and despite impassioned parental opposition were secretly married in the fall of 1841. The senator soon forgave his son-in-law and became his devoted patron and protector, wangling for him a coveted appointment as chief of an expedition to map the Oregon Trail. It was on his way to begin this assignment that Frémont met Carson.

Kit Carson, born in Kentucky in 1809, grew up on a backwoods farm on the Missouri frontier. Unlike Frémont he had

no schooling. At 16 he ran away and joined a Santa Fe traders expedition. By 23 he was a free trapper, based in Taos but ranging through most of the mountain West. Though small and slight, Carson was strong and tough as a rawhide thong, a master of mountain and desert craft, and a noted Indian fighter. Despite his illiteracy he had a working command of French, Spanish, and several Indian languages and a level-headed intelligence that offset Frémont's impulsiveness.

The Bestseller That Created a Legend

Frémont had two main objectives in 1842: to make the first accurate map of the Oregon Trail and to promote westward emigration. Guided by Carson, an expedition traveled up the familiar route along the Platte, crossed South Pass, and explored the Wind River Range, where the group climbed a peak subsequently named Mount Frémont. Such exploits were not part of Frémont's instructions, but they made good promotional material. On the return trip Frémont rashly insisted on shooting the rapids of the Platte in a rubber boat he had brought for just such an occasion. The boat overturned, and some of his records were lost, along with costly scientific equipment and specimens.

This did not deter Frémont from composing an informative report, packed with accurate details, including campsites and route maps covering each average day's travel. It was also a colorful adventure story, starring Frémont and featuring Kit Carson as a semilegendary superscout. The report was an instant bestseller; much credit for its success must go to Jessie, to whom Frémont dictated the manuscript.

On a second expedition (1843–44) Frémont and Carson attempted in vain to find a passage through the Central Rockies, explored the Great Salt Lake region, and arrived at Marcus Whitman's mission in the Oregon Country in the late fall. Picking up new supplies at Fort Vancouver, Frémont then followed the eastern foothills of the Cascades down to what is now Nevada and made a foolhardy crossing of the Sierra Nevada in midwinter, barely getting his men through alive. The report on this expedition, although it contained a number of errors, corrected many mistakes in earlier maps of the region beyond the Rockies and was received enthusiastically by an expansion-minded public.

War with Mexico seemed imminent when Frémont under-

A lithograph from Frémont's report on his second expedition shows his men packing down snow so they could make camp.

Kit Carson was not easily fazed by the unexpected, but here he recoils in horror as an aged and emaciated Indian woman, abandoned by her tribe, is drawn to his campfire.

Jessie Benton Frémont

When Jessie and her new husband informed her father of their secret marriage, he stormed at Frémont, "Get out of the house and never cross my door again! Jessie shall stay here." Jessie clasped her husband's arm, saying, "Whither thou goest, I will go; and where thou lodgest, I will lodge." Jessie was a constant source of emotional support to the volatile John Charles.

took his third western reconnaissance in 1845. When war did come, he organized a volunteer battalion that aided in the conquest of California, but Frémont's glory did not last long. Accused of both mutiny and insubordination, he was court-martialed and convicted. Although pardoned from serving his sentence, Frémont resigned. Paradoxically, he gained additional public support as a martyr to military autocracy.

A disastrous fourth expedition, financed privately, followed (1848–49). The goal: to find a railroad route through the mountains. This time, without Carson's guidance, Frémont sallied forth in winter, became snowed in up in the mountains, and, leaving his men, made his way to Taos, where he recuperated in Carson's house. But once again good fortune was with him; gold was found on a huge tract of land Frémont had acquired in California, and he became rich.

Moving to California, he served a brief term as senator, and in 1856 he was nominated as the presidential candidate of the newly formed Republican Party, running on a Free Soil ticket. In the Civil War he served as a general in Missouri but was removed by President Lincoln because of military mis-

takes and an ill-timed grant of freedom to slaves, which roused much anti-Union sentiment in the critical border states. Thereafter, Frémont's star declined. He lost his lands in California, failed as a railroad promoter, and had to depend on Jessie's writings for support. He died in poverty in 1890 in New York while working on an article for a magazine.

Kit Carson, pressed into service as a scout during the Mexican War, was denied an army commission by Benton's foes in the Senate. He farmed a while in Taos and became an Indian agent from 1853 to 1861. In the Civil War he rose to the rank of general on the Union side, campaigning in the Southwest against hostile Indian tribes. He died in 1868 from complications following an accident suffered while he was on a hunting trip.

Frémont's later admirers called him the Great Pathfinder. In reality, though an enthusiastic outdoorsman, he was a poor pathfinder. For the most part he followed paths that other men had made. One prime achievement was to map these paths accurately in time for the great caravans moving west. "Path-marker" is a fitting epitaph for this man of flawed brilliance.

From Carson's Day

After serving as Frémont's guide and as a scout in the Mexican War, Carson became an Indian agent from 1853 to 1861 in Taos, his permanent home. During his years as a mountain man Carson had fought Indians and would fight them again in 1864, but his wards in Taos respected their agent and may have given him a beaded buckskin carbine sheath and gloves similar to those shown at right. Carson's seven-shot Spencer carbine, like the one here, was of the type the Union cavalry regiments had used most effectively during the final year of the Civil War.

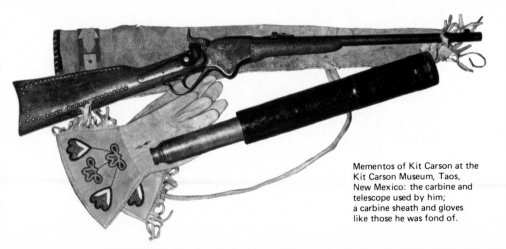

Mementos of Kit Carson at the Kit Carson Museum, Taos, New Mexico: the carbine and telescope used by him; a carbine sheath and gloves like those he was fond of.

War With Mexico Begins

President Polk may have been quite sincere when he said he wanted no war with Mexico, but he did want the fruits of war. These included Mexican recognition of the Texas annexation and the delineation of the state's southern and western border by the Rio Grande rather than the Nueces River far to the north and east. Polk was also determined to gain all Mexico's remaining possessions north of the Gila River: New Mexico (which included all of what is now Nevada and Utah, and parts of Arizona, Colorado, New Mexico, and Wyoming) and, most of all, California. To get them, he was willing to pay in cash if possible, in blood if necessary.

One of the least attractive aspects of Manifest Destiny was its racism. In a nation still overwhelmingly Protestant, Catholics were widely regarded as the Devil's disciples. In a country where only white men were truly free, where Negroes were enslaved and Indians abhorred, even antislavery men often viewed blacks and mixed bloods with scorn. (An early law drawn up by the settlers themselves barred not only slaves but free Negroes from the Oregon Country.) In a nation still proud of its English heritage the Spaniard was often viewed as crafty, immoral, and unclean. What better country for the United States to test its mettle against than Mexico—Spanish and Indian by descent, Roman Catholic in religion.

On May 8, 1846, five days before Congress declared war on Mexico, Gen. Zachary Taylor beat the Mexican Army at Palo Alto and again the next day at Resaca de la Palma. The U.S. Second Dragoons are shown here charging gallantly during one of these battles.

Given a decade of tense relations over the Texas issue and Mexico's stubborn refusal to sell lands the United States wanted, a clash between the two North American powers seemed inevitable. In fact, four years before the Texas boundary dispute led to bloodshed in 1846, a clash of sorts had already occurred.

In September 1842, while the administration of President John Tyler was trying to negotiate the purchase of California, Commodore Thomas ap Catesby Jones, an American naval commander, was aboard his ship in Peruvian waters. There he heard, and believed, a rumor that the United States and Mexico had gone to war and that Britain was stepping in to claim California for her own. Rushing northward, Jones reached Monterey Bay on October 18 and immediately landed a force, which seized the former California capital and raised the Stars and Stripes.

Two days passed before Jones learned that there was no war. Making such apologies as he could, he hauled down

James K. Polk: "I Intend To Be Myself President"

Devoid of charm, wit, or brilliance, President James K. Polk (1795-1849) left behind no fund of anecdotes or intimate friends eager to keep his memory green. But as the strongest man to hold the presidency between the terms of Andrew Jackson and Abraham Lincoln, Polk added more than 1 million square miles to the territory of the United States and reformed the federal monetary and tariff systems. Historian George Bancroft, who was Polk's secretary of the Navy, wrote that his administration, "viewed from the standpoint of results, was perhaps the greatest in our national history, certainly one of the greatest." Emphasizing his independence from pressure groups, Polk wrote shortly after his election, "I intend to be *myself* President of the U.S."

Born in North Carolina and educated at the state university, Polk studied law in Nashville, Tennessee, and was admitted to the bar in 1820. He was elected to Congress in 1825 and

spent 14 years in the House, serving as speaker from 1835 to 1839. An earnest but hardworking legislator, Polk faithfully supported the policies of President Jackson and won some notice as an ardent expansionist. But he remained merely a safe party man and was not seriously considered for the Democratic presidential nomination in 1844. Former President Martin Van Buren seemed a sure bet for the nomination until he opposed the annexation of Texas, as did the Whig Party nominee, Henry Clay. The angered Jackson then threw his influence behind Polk, and Polk became the nation's first dark-horse presidential candidate.

The Whigs dismissed the Democratic candidate with the question: "Who is James K. Polk?" But when Clay hedged on the question of the annexation of Texas and lost the votes of antislavery Whigs, Polk rode to victory on a platform that advocated the annexation of Texas and the occupation of Oregon as well.

A cartoonist depicts Polk's policies as a house of cards, but they proved durable.

Antiwar Sentiment

The United States will conquer Mexico, but it will be as the man swallows the arsenic, which brings him down in turn. Mexico will poison us.
—Ralph Waldo Emerson

the U.S. flag; after staying in Monterey 32 days to protect Americans living there from reprisals by Mexican officials, he sailed off to Los Angeles.

A point of no return was reached in U.S.-Mexican relations with the annexation of Texas on December 29, 1845. On that same day the anti-American Centralists removed the less bellicose Federalist president, José Joaquín Herrera, and began preparing for war with the United States. President Polk's emissary, John Slidell, who had been authorized to buy New Mexico and California and settle all outstanding disputes with Mexico, had been ignored.

Mexican Miscalculations

Faced by a Mexico that wanted war, Polk maneuvered to mobilize American public opinion by making Mexico strike the first blow. On January 13, 1846, he ordered Gen. Zachary Taylor with an army of some 4,000 into the disputed area between the Nueces River and the Rio Grande. Earlier, Polk had prepared for eventualities in California when he ordered the American consul in Monterey, Thomas O. Larkin, to "arouse in their [the Californians'] bosoms that love of liberty and independence so nat-

Newspaper reports of our first war on foreign soil were eagerly read and heatedly discussed throughout the nation, as portrayed in this painting by Richard Caton Woodville.

Thomas O. Larkin, U.S. consul in Monterey, played an important role in maneuvers that won California away from Mexico.

ural to the American Continent." Anticipating a rebellion in California or open war with Mexico, Polk also advised John D. Sloat, commander of the U.S. Pacific flotilla, to prepare to "possess yourself of . . . San Francisco, and blockade or occupy such other ports as your force may permit." Meanwhile, Capt. John Charles Frémont, ostensibly on a scientific survey with 60 well-armed veterans of wilderness life, had moved into California.

Aggressive Mexican officials not only felt that their army was more than a match for the American forces but that the tense Oregon situation and the divided state of public opinion in the United States would hamper that nation's war effort. These proved to be fatal miscalculations. On April 25, 1846, Mexican troops moved into the disputed Texas border region and opened fire on a detachment of Taylor's forces. The necessary incident had at last occurred, and

on May 11 President Polk, in his war message to Congress, made the questionable charge that "Mexico has . . . invaded our territory and shed American blood upon the American soil."

Although both houses of Congress voted overwhelmingly for war, few congressmen were taken in by Polk's assertions of Mexican aggression. But most rallied to the flag. Many southerners were eager for war, a fact that the growing antislavery forces construed as evidence of a plot to extend not democracy but "slavocracy" all the way to the Pacific Coast. From his study in Cambridge, poet James Russell Lowell composed his *Biglow Papers*, giving voice in Yankee dialect to northern and northwestern anger:

They jest want this Californy
So's to lug new slave-states in
To abuse ye, an' to scorn ye,
An' to plunder ye like sin.

The Conquest of California

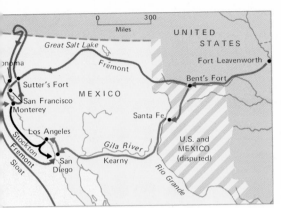

The movements of the top officers involved in the American conquest of California: Frémont, Kearny, Sloat, and Stockton.

Pío Pico, the last governor of Mexican-held California, poses for a photograph with his wife and niece. Pico was forced from his post in 1846 when troops led by Brig. Gen. Stephen W. Kearny and Commodore Robert F. Stockton (at right) occupied the province.

When John Charles Frémont appeared in California in December 1845, ostensibly to resupply his survey team, instinct and intelligence told him that, with war between the United States and Mexico near, new laurels awaited him if he could accomplish the conquest of the Mexican province. But as yet there was no war, and to calm Mexican officials he loudly proclaimed his peaceful intentions and the temporary nature of his group's stay.

By early spring, however, not only were Frémont and his men still in California, but they had ignored an order to leave, issued by Mexico's military commandant, Gen. José Castro. Moreover, they had constructed some breastworks under a defiantly waving Stars and Stripes. To dislodge them, General Castro dispatched a cavalry force, which prudently remained beyond rifle range as its leader urged Frémont to depart. To avoid initiating combat, Frémont broke camp and moved north, "slowly and growlingly," as he later recalled. He had actually crossed into Oregon when he was overtaken early in May 1846 by a young U.S. Marine lieutenant, Archibald H. Gillespie, who had come to Cal-

ifornia disguised as a merchant. Gillespie brought news of imminent war. (On May 13 war was declared, but it would be weeks before Frémont knew it.) Convinced that both duty and ambition required his presence in California, Frémont hurried south once more.

First Skirmishes in a Comic War

As Frémont reentered California, American settlers began rallying to his standard; yet without certain knowledge that war had begun he declined to commit his nation's flag to battle. His tagalong settlers, however, took the plunge on his behalf: on June 14 some 30 of them roared into the village of Sonoma, north of San Francisco. They seized its antique cannon and muskets and took as their prisoner Sonoma's commander, with whom they parleyed, over brandy, to arrange the town's surrender. This mission completed, the Americans declared California an independent republic, and over Sonoma's plaza they raised a homemade flag emblazoned with the figure of a bear.

Seldom has a sovereign nation enjoyed so short a history as the Bear Flag Republic. On July 7 John D. Sloat and the U.S. Pacific flotilla, having sailed into Monterey harbor a few days before, heralded the start of the Mexican War by occupying the California capital without a struggle. The Stars and Stripes replaced the Bear Flag in northern California, and it seemed to the Americans that they need only make a similar show of force in the southern ports and the whole province would be won.

Sloat, in ill health and anxious for retirement, soon handed over his com-

Capt. John Charles Frémont leads a band of hard-bitten explorers and American settlers from Sonoma to Monterey to join Commodore Stockton in the conquest of California.

After five days at anchor off Monterey, the capital of California, Commodore John D. Sloat, who was soon replaced by Commodore Stockton, landed men from the U.S. Pacific flotilla unopposed and raised the American flag over the customhouse on July 7, 1846.

mand to Commodore Robert F. Stockton, one of whose first acts was to dispatch Frémont and his 150-man force, known as the California Battalion, southward to make an assault on San Diego, which fell without resistance on July 29. On that same day Stockton, as much intent on glory as Frémont and far from pleased by the *Californios'* distaste for combat, concocted a proclamation. He charged that "scenes of rapine, blood, and murder" had been laid at the door of General Castro's now almost nonexistent militia. If the Mexicans refused to fight a war, Stockton would simply manufacture one. Seeking to avenge these mythical atrocities, he ventured forth from Monterey with 360 sailors and marines, and on August 6 he put into San Pedro Bay, where he declined an offer from Castro to parley. A week later Los Angeles fell to the Americans, again without a battle; as for Castro, he prudently departed for Mexico proper.

The entire coast was now in American hands, and Stockton sailed for Monterey, leaving behind Gillespie and a 50-man garrison to govern Los Angeles.

Stockton could not have made a worse choice. Gillespie, who made no effort to hide his contempt for Mexicans, succeeded in arousing the *Californios* far more than appeals to their patriotism had ever done. Within six weeks his ham-fisted rule had generated a true guerrilla movement, and on September 29, outnumbered and outgunned, Gillespie was forced to surrender to the insurgents. Their leader, with more chivalry than good sense, granted the Americans their freedom upon their promise to leave the province.

Instead of keeping his word, Gillespie joined forces with Navy Capt. William Mervine at San Pedro Bay, and together they opened a drive to retake Los Angeles. On October 8 the Americans and guerrillas clashed on the outskirts of the town. Although outnumbered four to one, the *Californios* had one advantage: an ancient cannon that had been hidden during the U.S. occupation of Los Angeles. Dragging this artillery piece from place to place, they tore gaping holes in the American lines and sent the U.S. forces reeling in retreat. The Americans, aware that in the south, at

least, they now had a rough approximation of a war on their hands, regrouped to resume the offensive. Meanwhile, from across the desert a new U.S. force under Gen. Stephen Watts Kearny was approaching California.

The Americans Prevail

Kearny, commanding the U.S. Army of the West, had earlier marched his 1,600 men from Kansas to Santa Fe and captured the town without a struggle. The general carried orders naming him commander in California and instructions to establish civil government there as soon as possible. (Stockton had similar orders from the Navy.) Believing the fight to be all but over, he proceeded westward with a 100-man detachment of his 300 dragoons, entering California in the late autumn of 1846. Early in December Kearny's men, exhausted by forced marches, were severely bloodied by *Californio* cavalry near San Diego; the general himself was wounded twice. In January 1847 the beleaguered Kearny joined forces with Commodore Stockton. Their combined 600-man army assaulted Los Angeles, routing the defenders and sending them scurrying north into the arms of Frémont, to whom they surrendered on January 13. All California was now in American hands.

A nephew of Mrs. Abraham Lincoln designed the flag of the California Bear Republic; it was raised over Sonoma in 1846.

The final battle in the conquest of California at La Mesa near Los Angeles (January 9, 1847), painted by U.S. sailor William H. Meyers.

The Mexican War

"Mr. Polk's War," the Whigs called it, scoring President James K. Polk for landgrabbing at sword point. But when Congress authorized him to call for up to 50,000 volunteers to fight in Mexico, the young men of the South and West swamped the recruitment offices. And as enthusiasm for the nation's first offensive war on foreign soil continued to spread, most people in the North and East gave it grudging support. The volunteers who filled the ranks of Gen. Zachary Taylor's army in 1846 were a disorderly lot who defied their officers and terrorized the Mexicans—robbing, murdering, and raping. Regular Army officers were disgusted by the volunteers, but these men were needed because the U.S. Army itself had numbered only around 7,000 men. Congress had neglected the Army and, as war with Mexico loomed, was debating whether to abolish the military academy at West Point. But the exploits of its graduates silenced its critics.

The Two American Generals

At the outbreak of war in April of 1846 Brig. Gen. Zachary Taylor and Maj. Gen. Winfield Scott had spent between them some 80 years in service. To his men Taylor was "Old Rough and Ready"—a feisty bantam who issued orders as he sprawled sidesaddle on a horse named Old Whitey. Scott was "Old Fuss and Feathers"—a huge, vain man, fond of showy uniforms but a serious student of war and a hell-for-leather fighting man. Democratic President Polk was not happy with either man, both of whom were in line for the Whig presidential nomination in 1848. Deciding that Taylor was the more popular, Polk picked Scott to end the war by having him march on Mexico City from the Gulf port of Veracruz. Taylor, stripped of troops given to Scott, was ordered to stand ready on the defensive in northern Mexico.

Taylor

Scott

The Shrewd Mexican Commander

Permitted by U.S. naval forces to return from exile to Mexico on his promise to end the war, Antonio López de Santa Anna ran true to form by doublecrossing the trusting President Polk. Finding peace talk unpopular among his countrymen, Santa Anna renewed the call for war and on September 17, 1846, was given command of the army.

Santa Anna

A Short, Victorious War

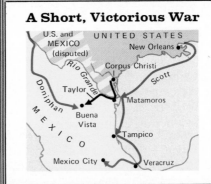

After 16 months of fighting, some 4,000 wounded and 13,000 dead—11,000 of them victims of disease and accidents—the U.S. three-pronged offensive (see map) forced Mexico to sign a peace treaty that cost her both California and the province of New Mexico in return for a payment of $15 million.

The Battle at Buena Vista

Ignoring orders to stand on the defensive, the combative General Taylor marched south with some 5,000 men and was attacked by Santa Anna's army of more than 15,000 at Buena Vista on February 22 and 23, 1847. In two days of bloody seesaw fighting Taylor's undisciplined volunteer regiments, particularly the Mississippi Rifles under the command of his former son-in-law Jefferson Davis, fought courageously against heavy odds. And when the American lines began to waver the U.S. Army's fast-moving artillery halted the Mexican forces at pointblank range (the scene at the left).

The Fall of a Seemingly Impregnable Fortress

The Chapultepec Palace, outside Mexico City, was taken by Scott's army on September 13, 1847. Among Chapultepec's defenders were teenage cadets of the Mexican Military College. These boys, called Los Niños, have become a symbol of Mexican courage.

The Halls of Montezuma

After taking Veracruz in March, breaking through towering mountains, and bypassing a trap set by Santa Anna at Cerro Gordo to reach Puebla, Scott daringly cut loose from his supply lines on August 7, 1847, and headed for Mexico City. When Britain's Duke of Wellington, conqueror of Napoleon, heard this news, he predicted: "Scott is lost—he cannot capture the city and he cannot fall back upon his base." But Scott's outnumbered army did not lose a battle in its drive toward victory. Escorted by U.S. dragoons, General Scott entered Mexico City on September 14 while the Stars and Stripes waved over the National Palace (the Halls of Montezuma). The flag had been planted there by a marine lieutenant—an act celebrated in "The Marines' Hymn." Scott then reviewed his battle-worn troops, who marched to the commands of West Point–educated officers destined for later renown: Robert E. Lee, Ulysses S. Grant, Thomas J. Jackson, and George H. Thomas.

"Doniphan's Thousand"

A Doniphan man fights a stubborn mule.

While General Taylor's army was moving into northern Mexico, the Army of the West under Gen. Stephen W. Kearny was marching from Fort Leavenworth, Kansas, to Santa Fe, New Mexico; Kearny took it on August 18, 1846, without firing a shot. In September he headed for California with 300 men after ordering Col. Alexander W. Doniphan to occupy Chihuahua, Mexico, with his 1st Regiment of Missouri Cavalry. Leading what would become one of the longest marches in U.S. military history, Doniphan crossed 90 miles of desert—called *Jornada del Muerto* ("Journey of the Dead")—routed the Mexicans at El Brazito on Christmas Day, and occupied El Paso on the 27th. Moving deeper into Mexico, "Doniphan's Thousand" defeated four times their number at the Battle of the Sacramento and took Chihuahua on March 2, 1847. Then Colonel Doniphan and his Missourians marched 600 miles through alien country to join Taylor at Monterrey, ending a campaign during which they lived off captured supplies and drew no government pay, rations, or equipment.

Peace and Its Problems

On March 17, 1848, a detachment of U.S. soldiers in Mexico City, acting on orders from President Polk, placed a distinguished-looking American under arrest. The prisoner was Nicholas P. Trist, and his crime was the negotiation of the Treaty of Guadalupe Hidalgo, which ended the Mexican War and conferred on the United States more than 500,000 square miles of land in exchange for $15 million. Only a week before, the U.S. Senate—torn by dissension among those who wished to annex all of Mexico, those who wanted just a

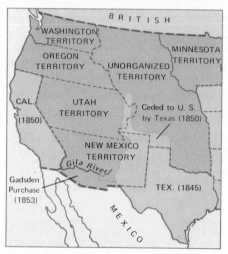

Fruits of Manifest Destiny: the Mexican War, Gadsden Purchase, and a British treaty that fixed U.S. contiguous boundaries. Year of statehood follows the state name.

few slices, and those who had damned the war from the beginning—had ratified Trist's handiwork as the best treaty possible under the circumstances.

The president's treatment of his peace commissioner was not quite as high-handed as it seemed. Although Trist had arrived in Mexico with authority to negotiate a treaty along certain specific lines, at the time he actually signed the document on February 2, 1848, he had long since been repudiated by his own government and ordered home. The vain, stiff-necked Virginian chose to ignore his recall. At the root of Trist's difficulties was his conciliatory attitude toward Mexico at a time when President Polk's demands were growing increasingly harsh because of Mexico's refusal to negotiate.

Polk also felt himself under a variety of political pressures at home: his Democratic Party had been defeated by the

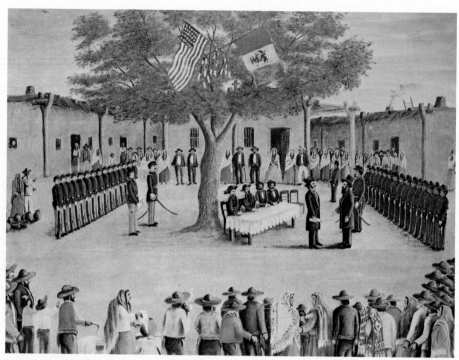

At a ceremony in the plaza of Mesilla, New Mexico Territory, on July 4, 1854, the United States took possession of land obtained from Mexico through the Gadsden Purchase.

Whigs in the 1846 congressional elections, and his program was under incessant attack from a curious coalition of extreme Manifest Destiny enthusiasts and antislavery men known as the All Mexico Movement. That the "Destinarians" desired all of Mexico was hardly surprising, but antislavery forces had previously denounced the war as a southern plot to create new slave territories. Faced with the lively possibility that large segments of the New Mexico

country might soon enter the Union as slave states, these forces sought to redress the balance by annexing Mexico proper, where slavery was outlawed.

Apprised of Trist's insubordination, Polk was furious. When he received word of the disavowed envoy's negotiations—which in fact had achieved many, but certainly not all, of the president's original objectives—he was almost beside himself. That he submitted the treaty for ratification was simply a weary

"They Mean Plunder"

The joyful news is told in every quarter with enthusiastic delight. We are such an exception to the great mass of our fellow countrymen in respect to everything else, and have been so accustomed to hear them rejoice over the most barbarous outrages committed upon an unoffending people, that we find it difficult to unite with them in their general exultation at this time; and, for this reason, we believe that by *peace* they mean *plunder*.

In our judgment, those who have all along been loudly in favor of a vigorous prosecution of the war, and heralding its bloody triumphs . . . have no sincere love of peace. . . . Had they not

succeeded in robbing Mexico of the most important and most valuable part of her territory, many of those now loudest in their professions of favor for peace would be loudest and wildest for war—war to the knife.

Our soul is sick of such hypocrisy. . . . That an end is put to the wholesale murder in Mexico is truly just cause for rejoicing; but we are not the people to rejoice; we ought rather . . . hang our heads for shame, and, in the spirit of profound humility, crave pardon for our crimes at the hands of a God whose mercy endureth forever.

—Black Abolitionist Frederick Douglass, *The North Star*, 1848

recognition of Trist's warnings that "if the present opportunity be not seized *at once,* all chance of making a treaty *at all* will be lost . . . probably forever."

Although the Mexicans had lost an empire in the American Southwest, they may have derived some comfort from watching the victors wrangle over the spoils of war. As early as 1846 Representative David Wilmot of Pennsylvania had attached to an appropriation bill an amendment to bar slavery from any new territory acquired from Mexico. The Wilmot Proviso twice failed in the Senate, but it did rouse the nation to furious debate. Until some compromise could be arranged, the new western lands would remain in a juridical limbo.

At first no compromise seemed possible. Antislavery men thundered their resolve never to permit bondage in the new territories, while in Congress southerners muttered dark threats of secession. On January 29, 1850, the aged Henry Clay of Kentucky, the Great Compromiser, rose in the Senate to give one of his last speeches. His proposal, drafted with the help of Illinois Senator Stephen A. Douglas, was to admit California immediately as a free state and to organize territorial governments in the other areas newly acquired from Mexico without any mention of slavery, leaving it to the residents to decide this question for themselves. To appease the South, Congress would pass a harsh new fugitive slave law, and the institution of slavery (but not the slave trade) would continue to be permitted in the District of Columbia. Although the plan left the slavery problem unsolved, Congress seized upon the Compromise of 1850 as a way out of an immediate sectional confrontation. Even so ardent an antislavery man as Senator Daniel Webster supported it to save the Union.

The Gadsden Purchase

The South, however, was determined to tie the Far West to its cause—if not through the institution of slavery then through mutual economic interests. For years men had dreamed of laying rails across the deserts and mountains of the trans-Mississippi country to link the West Coast with the East. No one was more eager for this venture than Jefferson Davis, who in 1853 became President Franklin Pierce's secretary of war. And no one was more determined than Davis to make sure the route of commerce would cut across the South, from New Orleans to the Pacific via Texas and

New Mexico. But there was one problem: the best route would traverse territory still in Mexican hands. To obtain these lands Davis urged the president to send James Gadsden, a South Carolina rail executive, to negotiate a treaty of cession with Mexico. On December 30, 1853, the pact was signed, and some 30,000 square miles of present-day Arizona and New Mexico were transferred to the United States for a payment of $15 million (later reduced to $10 million). With the Gadsden Purchase the U.S. borders assumed their present shape, save for Alaska and Hawaii. But before those borders could be made secure, the question of slavery would threaten the nation's very existence.

The treaty negotiated by Nicholas P. Trist (above) was, according to one politician, "negotiated by an unauthorized agent, with an unacknowledged government, submitted . . . to a dissatisfied Senate."

John R. Bartlett's Boundary Survey

The Bartlett camp at Vallecito, California. Watercolor by Seth Eastman.

The desert outside Tucson, Arizona. A pencil-and-sepia wash by Bartlett.

In 1850 bookseller and scholar John R. Bartlett was appointed U.S. commissioner to head a joint American-Mexican expedition to survey the southern boundary of the United States under the Treaty of Guadalupe Hidalgo. Bartlett had trouble sticking to the mundane job of boundary fixing; instead, he explored the Southwest extensively and later published his *Personal Narrative,* containing drawings and paintings by himself and others in the party. In 1853 Congress rejected Bartlett's proposed boundary because it left land desired for a southern rail route in Mexican hands, an oversight rectified by the Gadsden Purchase.

*As the spring and summer of 1848 advanced, the reports came faster
and faster from the gold-mines at Sutter's saw-mill. Stories reached us
of fabulous discoveries, and spread throughout the land. Everybody
was talking of "Gold! gold!" until it assumed the character of a fever.*

—William T. Sherman, Memoirs

"Sunday Morning in the Mines." Oil painting by Charles C. Nahl.

Chapter 6

The Great Rush West

The warm yellow glow of gold dust and nuggets lured thousands of eager prospectors to California in the late 1840's. Gold of a different sort—engraved tablets divinely revealed to Joseph Smith—gave birth to the Mormon religion, which led to a midcentury hegira to the Great Salt Lake and a transformation of the Utah desert into a land of plenty. To supply and transport the adventurous newcomers, daring entrepreneurs created stagecoach and freight lines and the famed Pony Express.

The nearly unsettled area between the cities of the Pacific Coast and those of the Midwest boomed when gold was discovered. Miners' camps soon peppered the hills east of Sacramento after the strike in 1848. Mining started to move eastward in the late fifties. Such gold hubs as Denver survived; others quickly became ghost towns. Finds of silver also fostered settlements. In 1859–60, 20,000 people arrived in Virginia City, then in Utah Territory, where gold and silver were mined from the rich Comstock Lode.

The Suffering of Zion

The heat of summer was already upon the land on June 24, 1844, when Joseph Smith, martyr in the making, conferred for the last time with a small group of his devoted Mormon followers on the outskirts of Carthage, Illinois. By nightfall Smith and six others had turned themselves over to the authorities to avoid the fury of a local mob bent on slaughter. Within the confines of the Carthage jail Smith could only await the possibility of a trial on trumped-up charges of treason—or the much greater probability of assassination.

Since 1830, when Smith and five followers had founded The Church of Jesus Christ of Latter-day Saints near Palmyra, New York, the life of the self-proclaimed prophet had been one compounded of triumph and tragedy, soaring pride and bleak despair. With the zeal of an Old Testament seer, he had built his church from nothing, dispatched missionaries throughout America and into Europe, and gathered thousands to his side to worship God and build Zion in the New World. At Nauvoo, Illinois, on the banks of the Mississippi, Smith and his congregation had turned a malarial swamp into one of the state's most populous and prosperous cities. There thousands of Mormons, or Saints as they sometimes called themselves, labored under his generally benevolent theocratic rule to create an ideal society, where no one went hungry

In October 1838, three days after Missouri's governor issued his "extermination order," a mob attacked the Mormon village of Haun's Mill and slew 19 unresisting men and boys.

or barefoot and no one suffered sickness unattended or was a prisoner of drink or illiteracy.

Yet Nauvoo's very success made it a target for the hatred of outsiders, all of whom the Mormons lumped together as Gentiles. For the faithful, persecution was already a familiar experience. At Kirtland, Ohio, where Joseph Smith had established his first Stake of Zion (the name given to a Mormon settlement) in the early 1830's, the Mormons had been harried and their leader tarred, feathered, and threatened with castration. Moving on to Missouri, they had suffered new persecutions. Their self-righteous assertions that God favored them over non-Mormons, their clannishness, their communal economic practices, and their antislavery sentiments had roused the bitter hatred of the highly individualistic Missourians. By

Joseph Smith, Founder of a Faith

In 1816 a 10-year-old boy named Joseph Smith (1805–44) left Vermont with his family to settle in Palmyra, New York, southeast of Rochester. The Smiths, who had lost their land after a series of crop failures, discovered that upstate New York, then a frontier, was a hotbed of religious revivalism, and the impressionable, uneducated Joseph grew up amid the conflicting claims of rival millennialist sects. At 14, according to his own account, he had the first of a series of visits by heavenly beings. When he was 17, an angel told him that he was to become a prophet. Meanwhile, he had developed a warm, winning personality and a flair for public speaking.

For a while Joseph practiced as a diviner, seeking buried treasure with the aid of a "miraculous" stone that he said allowed him to see beneath the earth.

But his career soon took a new turn. At 21, according to Mormon dogma, the angel Moroni revealed to him the location of a set of golden plates inscribed with ancient characters, which Joseph translated with the aid of a pair of magical spectacles. The task took two years; the result was the Book of Mormon. In 1830 the book was printed (the bill paid by an enthusiastic local farmer), and the new faith—with elements of doctrine similar to many found in Christian sects—was begun. From the start the church adopted the Puritan emphasis on hard work, and later it became known for its support of such reform movements as temperance, abolitionism, and communalism. Although it encountered immediate hostility, Mormonism grew rapidly. But the sect's success became the Prophet's downfall.

In a 19th-century engraving Smith receives the golden plates from the angel Moroni near Palmyra, New York.

1838 the governor of Missouri had called out the militia against them, asserting that "the Mormons must be treated as enemies and must be exterminated or driven from the State."

Faced with extermination, the Mormons had backtracked to Illinois, where Smith took advantage of a liberal law that allowed him to draft a charter establishing a virtually independent theocracy at Nauvoo. There, in the 1840's, the Mormon community prospered and expanded, but it failed to soften the hostility of its neighbors, many of whom envied the Saints' growing wealth and saw in their theocracy and communalism a threat to their own political and economic influence.

There was still another factor that set Gentile against Mormon—and even Saint against Saint. For years rumors had been spreading that Joseph Smith espoused polygamy, and by the early

Here wagon trains of Mormons driven from Missouri head for Commerce, Illinois, renamed Nauvoo by leader Joseph Smith.

1840's everyone in Nauvoo knew that Smith, as well as members of his inner circle, had cast off monogamy on the basis of a revelation from God. Within Nauvoo controversy raged over official sanction for polygamy, and the threat of schism hung in the air. Outside the town tongues clicked with disapproval, and prominent Gentiles—many of them with morals that were hardly pure—expressed outrage at this desecration of the American family. But the proud Smith, certain of the righteousness of his cause, paid little heed to dissent from within or to the growing threats from without. In 1844 he even went so far as to announce his candidacy for the office of president of the United States, thus arousing new fears of a possible Mormon dictatorship.

In June 1844 a small group of Mormon dissenters published a newspaper,

Joseph Smith tumbles out of a window of the Carthage, Illinois, jail after being shot by an anti-Mormon mob rioting below.

the Nauvoo *Expositor,* which in polite but firm language challenged the doctrine of polygamy, charged Smith with unethical financial practices, and derided his pretensions to national leadership. In response, the Nauvoo City Council ordered the opposition press destroyed as a public nuisance, and Smith, as mayor, enforced the decree with an order to the city marshal. The *Expositor*'s publishers fled to the county seat at Carthage and spread word of the confrontation. Throughout Illinois, editors and orators castigated Smith as a destroyer of freedom and cursed his followers as libertines. Mobs formed to demand that the governor disperse the Mormons and arrest their leader.

An End and a Beginning

Faced with threats on his life and vows of expulsion against his people, Smith placed Nauvoo under martial law. Donning his uniform of a lieutenant general of the Nauvoo Legion, he addressed his troops: "I have unsheathed my sword with a firm and unalterable determination that this people shall have their legal rights." As citizens of surrounding areas became fearful of their safety, the governor responded by mobilizing units of the state militia. Believing he would not receive a fair trial from his antagonists, Smith prepared to flee to the Far West. In the end, however, he was unwilling to desert his followers, and on June 24, 1844, he ordered the Nauvoo Legion to disarm. He then surrendered, with his brother Hyrum and five other Mormon leaders, to the authorities in Carthage.

A premonition of doom swept over Joseph Smith as he entered the Carthage jail. He had recently spoken many times of the possibility of mob action against him, and earlier that day he had confided to some of his closest aides: "I am going like a lamb to the slaughter; but I am calm as a summer morning." For three days he and Hyrum waited as angry

crowds gathered outside the jail. Then, late in the afternoon of June 27, the mob, the men's faces blackened to hide their identities, stormed the jail and sent bullets crashing into the bodies of Joseph and Hyrum Smith. Taking the bullets at almost pointblank range, Hyrum crumpled dead to the floor, while Joseph, with his last breath, shouted, "O Lord, my God!" and fell dead through a window to the ground below. His assailants fled the scene of their murderous act.

Yet even Smith's martyrdom, dramatic as it was, could not heal the growing disunity within his church. Hardly had his body been consigned by the faithful to a secret grave when the quarrels began to surface. Some of Nauvoo's 20,000 Mormons blamed the founder and his advisers for their predicament and, damning the yet-unacknowledged practice of polygamy as the source of the danger, looked with renewed apprehension at the rising tide of anti-Mormon feeling in surrounding communities.

For six weeks in the summer of 1844 the Saints were in doubt as to who their

Artist Henry Lewis painted Nauvoo about the time the first Mormons departed. On the skyline is their nearly finished temple.

new prophet would be. Although the senior apostle was Brigham Young, the silver-tongued Sidney Rigdon—one of the church's earliest members and a counselor to Joseph Smith—claimed the position of prophet on the basis of divine revelation. But at a mass meeting on August 8, Rigdon's bid was rejected in favor of Brigham Young's. The plainspoken Vermonter eventually decided that the survival of the faith depended on the Saints' abandonment of Nauvoo and their mass migration to some remote area where they might at last escape the malice of the Gentiles.

To the Great Salt Lake

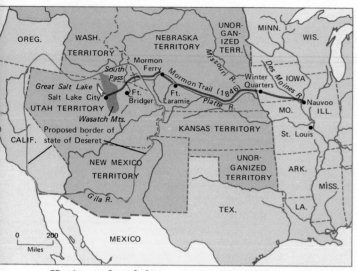

Hoping to found their own state named Deseret, the Mormons traveled 1,400 miles from Nauvoo to Salt Lake City.

Thousands of Mormons found shelter at Winter Quarters near present-day Omaha. An advance party set out for Salt Lake in April of 1847.

By mid-1845, with new anti-Mormon outrages occurring daily, Brigham Young's determination to lead his people in a modern Exodus to a "land of milk and honey" had become a necessity. He did not yet know exactly where he would take them, but that year he read the report of explorer John Charles Frémont. It referred to one place he had been considering—the valley of the Great Salt Lake, some 1,400 miles west of Nauvoo—as suitable for "civilized settlement." (Young may also have realized that the area was not sufficiently tempting to attract westering Gentiles.) Through the winter that followed, spurred by incessant Gentile demands

that the Mormons depart, he laid his plans for the mass migration, while Nauvoo familes stored supplies and got their wagons ready.

In February 1846 the first Mormon wagons left Nauvoo and crossed the icy Mississippi into Iowa. The next month Gentile attacks sent more parties scurrying across the river, and by September all but 250 families had left their Illinois Zion to the mercy of looting and burning mobs. From the first the trek was marked by superb discipline. Recognizing that survival depended upon organization, Young created a semi-military order of march. Each small group of wagons reported to a "cen-

This Mormon invention, a "roadometer," with wooden cogs geared to a wagon wheel, recorded the miles covered on a journey.

turion," who was responsible for several such detachments. Bugle calls awakened everyone in the morning, and strictly limited periods were set aside for dressing, prayers, and breakfast.

Young's intention was to move across Iowa in relatively small detachments and then establish winter quarters in Indian Territory on the west bank of the Missouri opposite what is now Council Bluffs. There the Saints would gather and wait out the winter of 1846–47 before moving on. As the first wagons set out, the families halted from time to time to mark their passage with plowed fields and sown crops. Those who followed harvested the crops and planted the fields anew. In this manner some 16,000 Mormons worked their way across the Iowa country to a camp they named Winter Quarters. Despite these carefully thought-out plans, however, the winter stopover was marked by hunger, cold, privation, and disease. The Saints' discipline and faith held firm, but by spring 700 of them were dead.

The first thin warmth of spring was hardly upon the encampment before

A Scene at Council Bluffs

This landing, and the large flat or bottom on the east side of the river, were crowded with covered carts and wagons; and each one of the Council Bluff hills opposite, was crowned with its own great camp, gay with bright white canvas, and alive with the busy stir of swarming occupants. In the clear blue morning air the smoke streamed up from more than a thousand cooking fires. Countless roads and by-paths checkered all manner of geometric figures on the hillsides. Herd boys were dozing upon the slopes; sheep and horses, cows and oxen, were feeding around them, and other herds in the luxuriant meadow of the then swollen river. From a single point I counted

four thousand head of cattle in view at one time. As I approached the camps, it seemed to me the children there were to prove still more numerous. Along a little creek I had to cross were women in greater force than *blanchisseuses* upon the Seine, washing and rinsing all manner of white muslins, red flannels and parti-colored calicoes, and hanging them to bleach upon a greater area of grass and bushes than we can display in all our Washington Square. . . . There was something joyous for me in my free rambles about this vast body of pilgrims. I could range the wild country wherever I listed.

—Thomas Leiper Kane
The Mormons, 1850

The New Leader, Brigham Young

"Prayer is good," said Brigham Young, "but when baked potatoes, and pudding, and milk are needed, prayer will not supply their place." Wearing the mantle of Joseph Smith, Brigham Young (1801–77), with his shrewd Yankee pragmatism and genius for organization, did more than any other individual to rescue the threatened Mormon Church after the death of its founder. Born in Vermont, Young was taken to western New York as a child. With only two months of schooling, he grew up to become a competent carpenter, glazier, and farmer, as well as a canny businessman, before finding a new career in the Mormon establishment. He was a master of withering sarcasm, and errant Saints were said to fear a tongue-lashing from him more than any other punishment. But in private life Young was kindly and genial, fond of dancing, music, and theater. He lived to see the self-sufficient empire he had created in the Great Basin firmly integrated into the United States as a territory.

A portrait of Brigham Young, his wife Mary Ann Angell, and their six children that was begun in Nauvoo and completed in Salt Lake City. The painter was an English Mormon convert, William W. Majors.

Brigham Young, with a pioneer band of 143 men, 3 women, 2 children, and 73 wagons, moved out across the plains to seek and settle the new Zion and prepare the way for the thousands to come. To avoid possible clashes with Gentiles, Young followed the north bank of the Platte rather than the established Oregon Trail along the river's south side. Although wet weather made travel uncomfortable in April of 1847, the Mormons still moved with the precision of a military formation on parade.

By May the Saints were happily chasing down herds of buffalo and feasting on the flesh, which they found as "sweet and tender as veal." Invigorated by the warming weather, some of them became so high-spirited that for the first time Brigham Young felt obliged to remind them of their serious purpose: "Joking, nonsense, profane language, trifling conversation and loud laughter do not belong to us. Suppose the angels were witnessing the hoe-down the other evening, and listening to the haw haws . . . would they not be ashamed of it?"

The Last Lap

Properly chastened, the Mormons returned to the trail, pushing on to Fort Laramie and beyond. Near what is now Casper, Wyoming, Young helped build two ferries to cross the river and detached a small party to remain and convey later emigrants to the other side. (Mormons could travel free; Gentiles had to pay a toll.) On Sunday, June 27—fittingly enough, the anniversary of their founder's martyrdom—the advance party crossed the South Pass.

In the Rockies they encountered trappers whom they questioned eagerly about the country that Brigham Young had by now settled on as their future home. The mountain men's reports were often most discouraging, however. Jim Bridger, for one, saw in the late spring frosts a threat to the agricultural potential of the land around the Great Salt Lake. "I'll give you a thousand dollars for the first bushel of corn you grow," he scoffed, to which Young quietly replied, "Wait and we will show you."

On July 19, 1847, a scouting party of Mormons caught their first glimpse of the Great Salt Lake. Five days later Brigham Young, who had been stricken with the mysterious mountain fever that afflicted many pioneers at high altitudes, and who was traveling behind the main party, finally looked out over the Salt Lake Valley. Mormon legend has it that the Prophet simply said, "This is the place." Later, Young recorded the event in these words: "The spirit of light rested upon me and hovered over the valley, and I felt that there the Saints would find protection and safety."

On July 22, 1847, after a trip of three months across plains and mountains, the wagons carrying the main party of Mormons rounded a hill; below lay the Great Salt Lake.

Lacking wagons and oxen, 3,000 Mormon converts from Europe loaded their possessions in two-wheeled carts and walked 1,300 miles from Iowa to Salt Lake City in the years 1856–60, making as good time as wagon trains.

Building the New Zion

The valley Brigham Young had chosen for the Saints' abode was fertile but dry, a land utterly isolated and remote from the nearest Gentile settlements. There, under the shadow of the towering Wasatch Mountains, he hoped to create a thriving Mormon community on land made productive by the careful diversion of mountain streams into irrigation canals. "No man can ever buy land here," he said, "for no one has any land to sell. But every man shall have his land measured out to him, which he must cultivate in order to keep it. Besides, there shall be no private ownership of the streams that come out of the canyons, nor the timber that grows on the hills. These belong to the people."

Young had scarcely recovered from the effects of mountain fever when he was up and about, supervising a prototype irrigation system and laying out the capital of his planned nation, Great Salt

Acting as an independent state, the Mormon Church occasionally issued its own currency, such as this $3 bill. Short of gold, the church backed its notes with livestock.

Neat irrigation ditches that bordered the streets brought a constant supply of water to the homes and gardens of Salt Lake City.

Lake City, where each adult male was to be awarded a town lot, as well as his share of farmland. "We propose to have the temple lot contain 40 acres," he declared, "that the streets will be 88 feet wide, sidewalks 20 feet, the lots to contain 1¼ acre, eight lots in a block."

Though Young's dream of escaping the sovereignty of the United States would soon end with the American victory over Mexico and the transfer of much of the Far West to U.S. control, he remained determined to shun all Gentile influences. Further, he envisaged not just an enclave around the Salt Lake but a great Mormon state to be called Deseret after the Mormon name for the honeybee, whose industry and cooperation made it a favorite symbol. Deseret

would cover all of present-day Utah and extend through much of the territory the U.S. had captured from Mexico—down to southern California, where the Saints would have a port at San Diego. Within these bounds, wrote Young, the Mormons would live in total self-sufficiency, acknowledging the ultimate sovereignty of Washington but yielding little or nothing to its direct control.

The "Starving Time"

These were heady visions indeed, but the Mormons were a resolute people. The day before Young reached the Salt Lake Valley, the Mormon scouting party had already begun the first irrigation system. In the months that followed, thousands of the faithful struggled along the Mormon Trail to join in the labors at the site of New Jerusalem. And the first crops were hardly sown when Young dispatched missionaries eastward and to Europe to seek out new converts.

Yet the first years were a bitter trial. Despite feverish activity too few crops had been harvested and too few houses built for the 3,600 Saints who arrived during the migrations of 1847 and 1848. The winter of 1848-49—the "Starving Time"—found the Mormons shivering in rude huts and tents and eating "glue soup," a concoction made of oxhide boiled in water. In the spring the faithful began anew—only to see part of their crop destroyed by insects, as had happened with previous harvests. For the swelling number of Mormons in the Salt Lake Valley the next winter, food was ample but not abundant.

Later in 1850 the Mormons suffered a setback when Congress rejected Young's plan for the state of Deseret and instead created the territory of Utah, a blow somewhat softened by the appointment of Young as territorial governor. It was also during this period that the Mormons had to give up their vision of liv-

Mormon men contributed their labor to public-works projects. In this 1874 picture volunteers stand among granite blocks for the Temple; in the rear is the Tabernacle.

USA XXXI.

ᏡᎾ ᎡᏍ ᎤᎤ ᏚᎤ ᏚᎤᎤᏓ   ᎭᏞ ᎤᏞ Ꮃ Ꮮ ᎬᏓ ᏞᎤᏓ
ᏚᎤᎤᏓ ᏅᏈ ᏔᏘ ᎤᎤ ᎰᎿ ᎤᎬᎤ ᏔᎬᏍᎵ.   ᏔᎤᏝ ᎠᏥᏈ
ᎤᎬᎤᏝᎿ ᎤᎤᎿᎢ ᏚᎤ ᏚᎤᎤᏓ ᎤᎭᎤᎤᏍ ?   ᎭᎤᏝ ᏤᎬ ᎤᎬᎤᏝᎿᎢ
ᏚᏈᏚ ᏣᎿᎤ ᏚᎤᎤᎿ ᎤᎤ ᎬᏔᎤᎤ ᎿᎢ.   ᏔᎬ ᎤᏥᎤᎤᎤ ᏚᎬ
ᏚᎤᎤᏓ ᎤᎭᎤᎤᏍ.

Young advocated spelling reform. "Let us go to school" says the first sentence of this page from a Mormon primer dated 1868.

ing totally apart from the Gentile world. After gold was discovered in California in 1848 thousands of avid prospectors tramped through Mormon territory on their way west. This was, of course, an economic boon to the Saints—who traded food and livestock to the migrants for tools, implements, manufactured goods, and sorely needed cash—and they took blatant advantage of it, charging as much as $25 a hundredweight for flour and $200 for a mule. But even as the precarious Mormon economy received a welcome boost through trade with outsiders, new reactions against the Saints' theocracy, economic practices, and tight control of the territory of Utah were building in Washington; and by 1857 pressure was mounting for a war against them.

The Desert Blooms

Desperate for a way out of the Union's sectional controversies over the slavery question, President James Buchanan responded to the growing anti-Mormon feeling in the summer of 1857 by relieving Brigham Young of the territorial governorship, appointing a Gentile in his place, and dispatching 2,500 federal troops to Utah. Young at first hurled defiance, but after a few small engagements cooler heads prevailed. In the end, the Mormon leader accepted a Gentile governor; the U.S. Army, after a symbolic march through Salt Lake City, departed and camped 44 miles southwest of the city. Both the church and Mormon-dominated society had endured, and the Civil War would soon turn the nation's attention away from the Saints' peculiar utopia.

By then the Mormon Zion was grow-

The Massacre at Mountain Meadows

This inflammatory woodcut shows Mormon "fanatics" butchering helpless emigrants.

On September 11, 1857, a wagon train of emigrants bound for California was wiped out by a group of Mormons aided by Indians. Of approximately 140 people, 120 were slain. The only survivors were children too young to bear tales. The terrible event—which took place without the sanction of the Mormon Church—was a consequence of President Buchanan's decision to send federal troops to Utah. When news that they were on the way reached the Mormons, Brigham Young forbade his people to sell supplies to Gentiles, and fanatical preachers roused the Mormons to a pitch of hysteria.

Into this situation came the Fancher wagon train. About half the party were respectable settlers from Arkansas, the rest a group of self-styled "Missouri Wildcats," some of whom boasted of having attacked Mormons and taken part in the killing of Joseph Smith. Refused supplies, they robbed and vandalized Mormon property. Worse, they threatened to round up and lead

an anti-Mormon army back to Utah from California.

Frightened and eager for vengeance, the Mormons of southwest Utah incited the local Indians to attack the wagon train as it lay encamped at the isolated oasis of Mountain Meadows. The emigrants beat off the attack and "forted up." Besieged for five days and almost out of ammunition, they accepted a Mormon promise of safe-conduct, piled their arms in a wagon, and marched off under the protection of Mormon militiamen. In a nearby brushy defile the Mormons shot the unarmed men; the Indians killed the women and many of the children.

Fearing repercussions within the church and reprisals from the U.S. government, the Mormon perpetrators blamed the massacre on the Indians and hushed up the matter. Not until 1875 was one of the participants, John D. Lee, brought to trial. In 1877 he faced a firing squad on the very site of the massacre at Mountain Meadows.

ing apace. In 1860 more than 40,000 people lived in Utah, the majority of them Mormons, and in another five years the desert was indeed blooming under a vast irrigation system that included 277 canals watering more than 150,000 acres. Salt Lake City, according to a French visitor of the time, had become a community of "order, peacefulness and industry," where "every person, from the humblest believer to Bishop or Apostle, is engaged in manual tasks. One has only to see Mormons at work to realise why their colony . . . is now so flourishing and progressive."

Enthusiastic about adobe, Brigham Young used it to build his official residence, the imposing Beehive House in Salt Lake City.

"Gold! Gold! Gold!"

It began almost as a whisper among a small party of laborers building a sawmill 40 miles from Sutter's Fort, the headquarters of John Sutter's baronial estate. Under the direction of carpenter James W. Marshall the men had been working through late 1847 beside the south fork of California's American River. On January 23, 1848, with work nearly finished, Marshall decided to make one of his periodic tests of the millrace by leaving the sluice gates open all night and allowing the river water to cascade through. When he returned the next morning, he noticed tiny yellow specks at the bottom of the millrace. After making a few simple tests, Marshall was convinced that he had found gold. A workman on the site made this laconic note: "Monday 24th this day some kind of mettle was found in the tail race that looks like goald first discovered by James Martial."

Four days later Marshall arrived at Sutter's Fort and broke the news. More tests confirmed the nature of the metal,

Two men who struck it rich outside the goldfields: Sam Brannan (left), a Mormon merchant who sold food and tools to the miners; and Levi Strauss (right), a young man from New York who manufactured durable Levi's.

New York City was plastered with clippership cards such as this one advertising passage around Cape Horn to San Francisco.

yet John Sutter was less than delighted. There, in the heart of California, he had built an almost feudal domain for himself, where his word was law. A man of few illusions, Sutter rightly sensed that if word of the find got out, his kingdom would be invaded by swarms of hard-eyed prospectors who would ravage his crops and destroy his lands. He tried to suppress news of the strike, but word inevitably got out to the tiny city of San Francisco. There, most of the 800-odd residents at first responded with skepticism. It was not until May that the stampede began in earnest.

Entrepreneur Sam Brannan

The carrier of the gold fever was one Sam Brannan, a merchant, newspaper owner, and leader of California's small community of Saints. Less saintly in practice than in preaching, Brannan had quarreled more than once with Brigham Young and would eventually be excommunicated by him for refusing to turn over tithes collected from the faithful Mormons in California.

In the rumors of gold Sam Brannan perceived his future—but not as a prospector. If there *was* gold in the diggings, he reasoned, the miners would need picks, shovels, pans, flour, coffee, and other staples. These, he guessed, could

Fame but not fortune came to James W. Marshall, who distributed this autograph card in order to publicize his great find.

be sold at incredibly high prices by the first merchant who was able to establish himself in the goldfields.

In the early spring of 1848 Brannan went to Sutter's Mill to check on the gold stories, and what he saw convinced him to lay in a supply of necessities. Then, in mid-May, he returned to San Francisco, a bottle of gold dust in his hands and a manic roar in his voice.

Pounding up and down the streets, Sam Brannan shouted, "Gold! Gold! Gold from the American River!" He grabbed pedestrians, shoved the precious bottle in their faces, and howled the news in their ears. The effect was electric, and by nightfall almost every man who could walk or ride was feverishly packing up for the American River country. Within two weeks San Francisco was a ghost town, and when the prospectors reached the goldfields, there was Sam Brannan, surrounded by tools

The Man Ruined by the Gold Rush

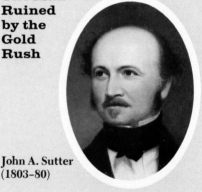

**John A. Sutter
(1803-80)**

John Augustus Sutter, an unsuccessful speculator in both Switzerland and America, reached California in 1839. Undaunted by past mishaps, this generous, charming man persuaded the Mexican governor of California to grant him some 50,000 acres east of San Francisco Bay, where he built a huge farming, ranching, and trading empire. In 1848, when gold was found in the American River, which ran through his property, Sutter tried to keep the discovery secret. But word got out. Gold seekers overran his farms and ranches, and he spent his final years vainly asking Congress to reimburse him for lands taken by prospectors.

As gold fever swept the land, San Francisco harbor became crowded with dozens of ships that had been abandoned by their crewmen who had joined the rush to the goldfields.

This caricature of a typical gold seeker, loaded with paraphernalia as he headed for California, suggests that he would shed much of it before finally reaching his goal.

and foodstuffs and ready and waiting for a bit of sharp trading.

By July all the towns and hamlets of north-central and southern California had virtually no adult males. A visitor passing through might have thought that some incredible plague had decimated the region. In the harbors of Monterey and San Francisco, ships rode empty at anchor, their crews having suddenly taken to a landsman's pursuit. Even the U.S. Army could not maintain discipline; one soldier summed up the situation with admirable succinctness: "The struggle between *right* and six dollars a month and *wrong* and seventy-five dollars a day is rather a severe one."

Hysteria Spreads

The word spread first to the Sandwich Islands (Hawaii) and from there around Cape Horn to the East Coast. On December 5, 1848, President James K. Polk gave substance to the rumors. In an address to Congress he trumpeted the news: "The accounts of the abundance of gold . . . would scarcely command belief were they not corroborated by . . .

officers in the public service." Two days later 230 ounces of glittering California gold were placed on public display in Washington, but by then such evidence was hardly necessary.

From Boston to St. Louis, from Florida to Minnesota, thousands were already laying plans, outfitting wagons, buying ship's passage, and weaving fantasies of the wealth they would glean from the new El Dorado. The day of the forty-niners was upon the nation. The greatest and most anarchic gold rush in the history of man had begun.

Where the Gold Came From

The creation of the treasure sought by the forty-niners began perhaps 150 million years ago, when gigantic plates of the earth's crust shifted, causing western North America to press against an ancient floor of the Pacific. Later, this compressed region was further crushed when upheavals thrust up a huge tilted block—part of the Sierras (right). Liquids and gases rose from deep within the earth, carrying with them minerals that penetrated cracks in the granite and formed ore veins. By 1848, at altitudes of 1,000 to 2,700 feet, the remains of these eroded veins appeared as a 120-mile-long string of gold-impregnated quartz pockets in a belt up to two miles wide. The miners called this the Mother Lode, mistakenly believing it to be one gigantic mass of gold. Lode or vein mining was too difficult to tackle with simple tools. (To finance equipment for hard-rock mining, large companies were formed.) But weathering had helped them; it had eroded small fragments of gold out of solid rock and washed into rivers quantities of the lode's golden specks. Because gold is soft and heavier than surrounding sediments, it fell in any size, from tiny grains to nuggets that settled on the streams' bedrocks and sandbars. To reach this gold, a miner simply dug in riverbanks—and dug and dug, frequently 20 feet down, washing the dirt to clear

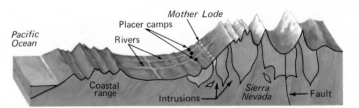

A generalized diagram (heights exaggerated) shows the site of the lode's ore pockets, partly formed by intrusions from deep down.

debris from the gold. This was called placer mining—pronounced *plah-sir* and derived from a Spanish term for gravel bank. Each miner could stake one claim (usually 50 to 100 feet long and from midstream landward to marker stakes) by leaving his tools on it, working it, and recording it for a fee at the nearest miners' camp, where disputes were settled by miners' juries. Whether he struck pay dirt (sand or gravel bearing enough gold to be profitable) was largely chance. One fellow found $26,000 in gold dust in a single summer; others in no time scooped valuable gold flakes out of crevices with horn spoons. But many found barely enough to pay for a few drinks; the expression "How much can you get up in a pinch?" comes from the custom of paying for a drink with a pinch of gold dust.

The Coming of the Argonauts

In 1848—before tens of thousands of easterners, Europeans, Latin Americans, Australians, and Chinese had swarmed to the diggings—the "Argonauts" (this name, from Greek mythology, was soon given to the gold seekers) had perhaps an even chance of making a living. The dry beds and waters of the American River and other streams were indeed rich in placer gold, and the foothills of the Sierras hid even greater, if less accessible, fortunes. Many of the early prospectors made thousands of dollars in a few months, and even the moderately lucky averaged $20 a day—hardly a king's ransom but far above contemporary wage scales for common labor.

Much of what the miners earned, however, went for necessities, whose prices soared in direct proportion to the demand. By August 1849 one miner was writing home in disgust: "Salt Pork here [San Francisco] 75 cents per lb., at the mines $200 per Barrel. Flour $2.00 per lb. . . . Potatoes about $30 a bushel. A ship load of the latter would bring *two hundred thousand dollars.*" Indeed, as Sam Brannan had foreseen, it was far easier to make a fortune by servicing the miners than by joining them. One future railroad magnate, Collis P. Huntington, for example, got a leg up on his first million by buying iron bars at $20 a ton and selling them to the forty-niners at a dollar a pound.

Once President Polk had confirmed the California strike, gold fever swept the nation with epidemic speed. A month after Polk's address, when a Pacific Mail Line ship arrived in Panama, it was greeted by a howling mob of gold seekers, ready to pay almost any price for a few feet of space. The stampede was on in earnest.

In 1849 alone, California's population rose from 20,000 to more than 100,000, and by 1852 the recently won territory had become a state with 225,000 residents. Almost all the immigrants to the West Coast were male, almost all were Argonauts, and many endured incredible hardships to reach the California goldfields, where hopes of striking it rich dwindled almost daily as the surface gold was mined out.

By Way of Cape Horn or Panama

Most migrants from the Atlantic and Gulf Coasts tried to reach California by sea. Either they could take passage aboard a clipper for the 15,000- to 17,000-mile voyage around Cape Horn and, with luck, disembark at San Francisco six months later, or they could sail to the Isthmus of Panama, travel overland to the Pacific, and when there board another vessel for the northward journey. If everything went without a hitch, the Panama route was by far the quickest; ticket agents promised arrival in the goldfields in as little as six weeks. But few who went via Panama made it in anything like that time, and many never made it at all. During the jungle trek across the isthmus and the long wait for ship's passage in Panama City, the Argonauts were often struck down by malaria, yellow fever, or cholera. Some frustrated prospectors actually tried to make it up the coast to California in small boats, only to pay with their lives for their impatience.

The route around Cape Horn was more certain, at least at first, and the earlier prospectors whiled away the voyage in relative comfort. But as the demand for space rose, so did prices, while accommodations grew ever more crowded and uncomfortable. In their haste to reach California, groups of easterners often pooled their funds to charter a ship—often an aged wreck—

All available ships (many of them leaky tubs) were pressed into service to carry eager would-be gold prospectors on the six- to eight-month trip around Cape Horn to California.

The shortcut to California via the Isthmus of Panama involved travel on fever-infested jungle rivers, then a long wait for a ship headed for San Francisco.

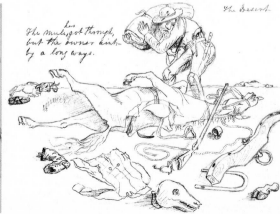

A J. G. Bruff sketch of hardships on the overland trail. His mule dead, a weary forty-niner takes up its burden.

186

A cartoonist exaggerated (only slightly) the high cost of food in California: a merchant offers to trade a pan of beans for a pan of gold and a ham for a lump of gold the same size as the ham.

One important—if recalcitrant—item needed by the forty-niner was a pack animal. Aside from digging in its hooves and refusing to move, a balky one could shed its burden by holding its breath while a pack was tightened, then letting it out.

whose unseaworthiness was concealed by a fresh coat of paint. Such vessels were no match for the brutal winds of Cape Horn, and many met their doom in the swirling waters off Tierra del Fuego.

Overland Trails

Argonauts who could not afford ship's passage or who preferred solid ground had a choice of several overland trails to the goldfields. One of these, vigorously promoted by Mississippi's Senator Jefferson Davis—who perhaps was already thinking of a railroad tying the West Coast to the South—began at Fort Smith, Arkansas, passed through Santa Fe, and then crossed the deserts of Arizona. The main trouble with this route was, of course, the intense heat and lack of water. Temperatures in the desert often reached 110°F; under the broiling sun wagon axles cracked, oxen died of thirst, and Argonauts often found themselves wandering the wastes on foot. The bones of the unlucky were left to bleach in the desert.

More popular—but, as it turned out, not much easier—were the better known Mormon and Oregon Trails over the Rockies to the California Trail, which led through the Sierras directly to the gold diggings around Sacramento. Throughout the winter of 1848-49 thousands formed wagon trains and prepared to take off from Independence, Missouri, or Kanesville (now Council Bluffs), Iowa, with the spring thaw.

They appointed captains and sergeants of the march and wrote out complex regulations for the journey. One company even elected a legislature to make laws along the trail. But none of this planning prepared the Argonauts for the misfortunes that followed. The spring of 1849 could not have been wetter. "It blew, rained, thundered & lightened tremendous heavy," as one wagon-train member recalled, and from the first the bottomless mud impeded the wagons' progress. Moreover, a raging epidemic of cholera took the lives of about 5,000

Argonauts during the early stages of their journey. Anxious to get across the Sierras before the first snows fell, the migrants abandoned enormous quantities of precious supplies and implements along the trail to lighten their wagons and gain speed. By the time the 1849 traveling season was over, the routes west had become strung-out cemeteries and junkyards. Later travelers seeking their fortunes in California had only to follow the lines of crosses and heaps of rusting cookstoves in order to find their way to the diggings.

A Prospector's Journey

[May 21, 1849.] For miles . . . an animated mass of beings broke upon our view. Long trains of wagons with their white covers were moving slowly along . . . in a few moments we took our station in the line, a component part of the motley throng of gold seekers, who were leaving home and friends far behind, to encounter the peril of mountain and plain.

[June 29.] On leaving the Missouri, nearly every train was an organized company. . . . On reaching the South Pass, we found that the great majority had either divided, or broken up entirely, making independent and helter-skelter marches towards California.

[August 10.] Reports began to reach us of hard roads ahead; that there was no grass . . . where the river disappears in the sands of the desert, and that . . . a desert of sand, with water but once in forty-five miles, had to be crossed. In our worn-out condition this looked discouraging, and it was with dread that we looked to the passage of that sandy plain.

[August 11.] There were a great many men who, having worn down their cattle and mules, had abandoned their wagons . . . their woe-begone countenances . . . excited our pity.

[September 17.] Ascending to the top of an inclined plain, the long-wished-for and welcome valley of the Sacramento, lay before me.

—Alonzo Delano, *Life on the Plains and Among the Diggings*, 1854

The Forty-niners: High Hopes and Arduous Toil

His gaunt frame is hung with a faded flannel shirt and patched trousers. A greasy slouch hat inadequately shades him from the searing summer sun. His arms are pocked with mosquito and flea bites, his hands puffy from submersion in mountain streams, his clothes alive with lice. He is the forty-niner, the Argonaut, legendary elsewhere but in California one of thousands of weary, mostly inexperienced men digging all day in temperatures over 100°F or wading for hours in icy water. Exhausted, at dusk he fixes a supper of sourdough and salt pork, occasionally varied with beans or dried apples. He probably will get scurvy and dysentery. His strained muscles ache, yet he sleeps on the damp ground. Upon the rare arrival of a family letter, he chokes up with homesickness. Is it worth it when he averages one ounce of gold dust a day, only enough to break even? Yes, of course; tomorrow he will find a $6,000 nugget—maybe. To follow the miners' activities—from the early simple panning techniques to more efficient methods developed in the 1850's—read the numbered blocks in order.

Panning Separates Heavy Gold-bearing Sand From Lighter Soil

 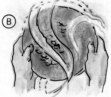  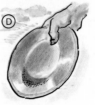  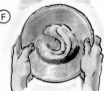

(A) Pan, three-quarters full of soil, is submerged in water and held level while the clots are broken up by stirring. (B) Pan, still submerged, is shaken quickly clockwise and counterclockwise to further loosen the gravel, then rotated ovally so the water and gravel move about, washing the lightest pebbles and sand over the edge. Held above water, the pan is again rotated sharply to resettle the heavier gold and black sand. (C) Pan is submerged again, with the near edge gradually raised to let more flotsam slip off the far edge. (D) Pan is rotated and jerked back and forth repeatedly until a crescent of black sand forms on the pan's flange, with the heaviest matter in the crease. (E) A little water is added to the pan, now held level. Pan is hit with the palm to resettle the black sand on the bottom and allow the lighter sand to rise. (F) Water is swirled slowly clockwise so the heavy sand collects on the pan's right side, the light sand on the left. The latter is washed off by dipping; only the gold-bearing black sand remains.

1. PANNING (near right) is hard, slow one-man work, even with a digging partner. At best, a miner can handle only 100 pans in a 10-hour day: most do only around 50. Yet panning is often the last step in more advanced methods employing several men to process larger quantities of earth with sluices, rockers, or long toms (below at right).

4. THE SLUICE can process 100 cubic yards of gravel daily. Made of connected riffle boxes, it retains more gold than a long tom. Carpeting at the end catches gold not trapped by riffles. Also, mercury, which has an affinity for gold, is put on the sluice bottom: it rejects sand but forms an amalgam with particles of gold. Later the gold is extracted from the amalgam with heat.

The miners' beards are caked with mud, their feet numb in soaking-wet boots. At night the men stay in tents or rough cabins.

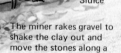

Sluice

The miner rakes gravel to shake the clay out and move the stones along a sluice, leaving gold-rich sand behind the riffles.

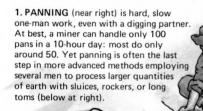

Hopper

Rocking the cradle (left), a miner pours water over gravel dumped into the hopper by digging colleagues. Rocking helps disintegrate the clay and wash the sand onto the apron, which deflects it into the foot, where gold settles behind the riffles. As many as four men team up to operate a rocker.

Riddle

Riffle box

Slats, or cleats, called riffles

Apron

Rocker

Foot

Stream

2. THE CRADLE, used in Europe, then in parts of the South, is a strainer on rockers set on an incline. Holes in its hopper bottom let sand, not stones, pass through onto a canvas apron on which some gold sticks. The sand then washes into the riffle-ridged foot.

3. THE LONG TOM, from the East is a 12-foot trough (above) tipped with an uptilted, perforated iron sheet, or riddle, and a riffle box. Water pours along it, carrying gravel shoveled into it. Large-sized stones collect atop the riddle. But fine gold-rich sediment falls through holes onto the riffle box. The device lets six to eight men work more gravel than with a pan or cradle and mine poorer gravel profitably. But it has few riffles, so some gold escapes.

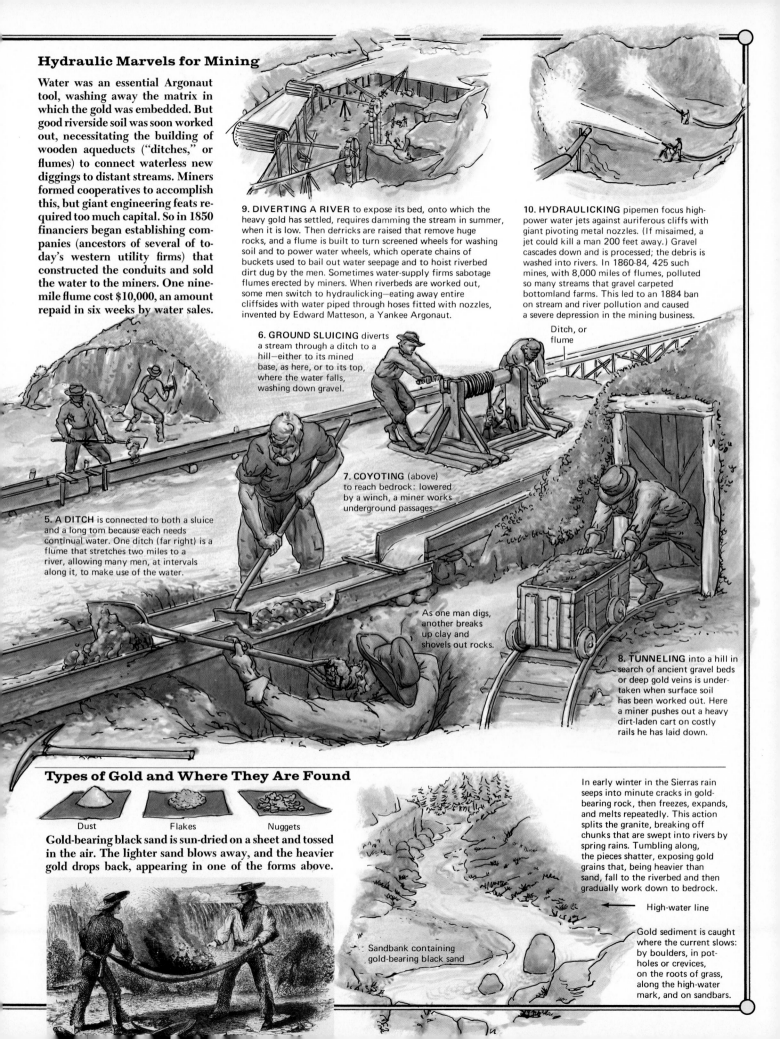

Hydraulic Marvels for Mining

Water was an essential Argonaut tool, washing away the matrix in which the gold was embedded. But good riverside soil was soon worked out, necessitating the building of wooden aqueducts ("ditches," or flumes) to connect waterless new diggings to distant streams. Miners formed cooperatives to accomplish this, but giant engineering feats required too much capital. So in 1850 financiers began establishing companies (ancestors of several of today's western utility firms) that constructed the conduits and sold the water to the miners. One nine-mile flume cost $10,000, an amount repaid in six weeks by water sales.

9. DIVERTING A RIVER to expose its bed, onto which the heavy gold has settled, requires damming the stream in summer, when it is low. Then derricks are raised that remove huge rocks, and a flume is built to turn screened wheels for washing soil and to power water wheels, which operate chains of buckets used to bail out water seepage and to hoist riverbed dirt dug by the men. Sometimes water-supply firms sabotage flumes erected by miners. When riverbeds are worked out, some men switch to hydraulicking—eating away entire cliffsides with water piped through hoses fitted with nozzles, invented by Edward Matteson, a Yankee Argonaut.

10. HYDRAULICKING pipemen focus high-power water jets against auriferous cliffs with giant pivoting metal nozzles. (If misaimed, a jet could kill a man 200 feet away.) Gravel cascades down and is processed; the debris is washed into rivers. In 1860-84, 425 such mines, with 8,000 miles of flumes, polluted so many streams that gravel carpeted bottomland farms. This led to an 1884 ban on stream and river pollution and caused a severe depression in the mining business.

6. GROUND SLUICING diverts a stream through a ditch to a hill—either to its mined base, as here, or to its top, where the water falls, washing down gravel.

Ditch, or flume

5. A DITCH is connected to both a sluice and a long tom because each needs continual water. One ditch (far right) is a flume that stretches two miles to a river, allowing many men, at intervals along it, to make use of the water.

7. COYOTING (above) to reach bedrock: lowered by a winch, a miner works underground passages.

As one man digs, another breaks up clay and shovels out rocks.

8. TUNNELING into a hill in search of ancient gravel beds or deep gold veins is undertaken when surface soil has been worked out. Here a miner pushes out a heavy dirt-laden cart on costly rails he has laid down.

Types of Gold and Where They Are Found

Dust Flakes Nuggets

Gold-bearing black sand is sun-dried on a sheet and tossed in the air. The lighter sand blows away, and the heavier gold drops back, appearing in one of the forms above.

In early winter in the Sierras rain seeps into minute cracks in gold-bearing rock, then freezes, expands, and melts repeatedly. This action splits the granite, breaking off chunks that are swept into rivers by spring rains. Tumbling along, the pieces shatter, exposing gold grains that, being heavier than sand, fall to the riverbed and then gradually work down to bedrock.

High-water line

Gold sediment is caught where the current slows: by boulders, in pot-holes or crevices, on the roots of grass, along the high-water mark, and on sandbars.

Sandbank containing gold-bearing black sand

The Riproaring Gold Camps

Looking back from the 1860's on the halcyon days of the California gold rush, Mark Twain nostalgically recalled the forty-niners as "the *only* population of the kind that the world has ever seen. . . . Two hundred thousand *young* men—not simpering, dainty . . . weaklings, but stalwart, muscular, dauntless young braves . . . the very pick and choice of the world's glorious ones."

Among the thousands who filled the gold camps that stretched for some 200 miles along the Sierras' western slopes were many who matched Twain's enthusiastic description. Determined to strike it rich, they spent hours on end in freezing rivers panning and sifting gravel—more often than not for an ounce or two of gold or nothing at all. After the relatively easy pickings had given out, they sometimes formed partnerships to build dams and divert streams so the original beds could be mined more easily. Months of arduous labor were usually required for such projects, and sometimes the rewards were only a monumental backache or a case of pneumonia.

A surprising number of the forty-niners were well-to-do young men, lured west by the promise of adventure as much as by gold. Others were driven by the hope of escaping a life of crushing poverty back east. One prospector's touching letter to his wife revealed the

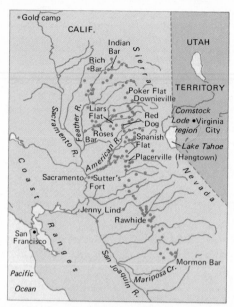

California gold mines, centered along the Sierra Nevada in the 200 miles between the Mariposa Creek and the north fork of the Feather River, yielded $81 million in 1852.

ambitions of thousands. "Jane," he wrote, "i left you and them boys for no other reason than this to come here to procure a littl property by the swet of my brow so that we could have a place of our own that i mite not be a dog for other people any longer."

Suspended between wild dreams of wealth and the more frequent reality of dry diggings, the forty-niner was often a man of mercurial temperament. A trifling argument over a card game might balloon into a gun battle; a beady-eyed stare from a passerby could set knives flashing murderously; a contested claim or a dispute over the ownership of an ounce of gold dust often ended in a bloody brawl. Yet the denizens of such camps as Poker Flat, Indian Bar, Red Dog, Rich Bar, Eureka North, and Hangtown were also capable of amazing generosity. At one camp a teenager down on his luck was given a hundred-dollar grubstake by grizzled prospectors, who then searched out a rich claim for the youngster to work.

Gamblers and "Fancy Ladies"

But in these nearly all-male, gold-obsessed societies, even the fastidious soon forgot the preachings of mothers, wives, ministers, and teachers. Former prigs became masters of profanity and vied in epic contests of verbal insult and threat. The results could be colorful, as

when one miner shouted at another, "Only let me get hold of your beggarly carcass once, and I will use you up so small that God Almighty himself cannot see your ghost!"

By the end of 1850 tens of thousands of miners—all of them forty-niners in the public's view—had poured into the California camps. Aside from white Americans, there were some 2,000 blacks, both slave and free, as well as Indians and an assortment of foreigners—from Germany, France, Ireland, England, Wales, Scotland, China, Australia, Mexico, Peru, Chile, and even Turkey. The camps also supported a floating population of professional gamblers, barkeeps, "fancy ladies," flinty-eyed merchants, and preachers. For a time, in many camps, lynch law was the only law, although more civilized systems were eventually devised. But even so, alleged lawbreakers were hanged, whipped, and occasionally mutilated on the flimsiest of evidence.

"Greasers" and "Chinks"

In some camps all foreigners were barred; in others only certain nationalities were unwelcome. California's recent masters, the Mexicans, were despised as "greasers," their claims widely ignored, and their property subject to confiscation. But of all nationalities the Chinese most often raised the hackles of their fellow prospectors. Hated for their color, scorned for their unfamiliar ways, the Chinese were even held in contempt for the diligence with which they worked diggings long since abandoned by whites as unprofitable. They were

White and black prospectors shovel what they hope will be pay dirt into a sluicebox at diggings in Spanish Flat in California.

Downieville, located in one of the richest gold-bearing areas, boasted both a bank and a church within a year of its founding.

sometimes victimized by gun-toting thugs who thought it great sport to cut off their pigtails, and on one occasion two groups of Chinese were urged into open warfare by whites. Armed with medieval lances and long swords, provided by local blacksmiths, the rival tongs whacked at one another as white onlookers cheered them on. All had a marvelous time except, of course, the eight dead and six wounded combatants—and one white who was shot by an anonymous enemy.

Less than 8 percent of California's population in 1850 was female, and women were especially scarce in the camps. But the miners made do at their wingdings by pairing off.

A drunken miner complains that toughs robbed him, then put him back on his horse after "cutting off" the poor animal's head.

A cartoonist tells of the rise and fall of a "Bully Honest Miner": he strikes it rich, blows his gold on a spree, then gets more money by salting his claim with gold dust in order to mislead a buyer. With his dishonest gains he gambles ("bucks the tiger") and is stabbed when he is caught cheating.

Occasionally, antiforeign sentiment was based on a genuine grievance; independent prospectors resented foreign operators who worked their claims with peon labor. Once, when a group of peons working for an absentee Chilean capitalist ignored orders to leave the mining camp Rose's Bar, the other prospectors strung up their foreman, mutilated one worker, and bullwhipped several others as a warning to all would-be interlopers.

Prospectors With Slaves

There was also one group of Americans who were anathema to the other miners. These were the slaveholders who relaxed while their human chattel worked the diggings on their behalf. Many years after the event, an old miner happily recalled the fate of a white Tennessean who had come to Hangtown with three slaves. After claiming what proved to be a rich digging, the Tennessean set his slaves to work. One day, when the white man arrived to collect his gold dust, the Negroes informed him that since they were on free territory, they were no longer slaves and the white man had no right to the products of their labor—unless, of course, he was willing to do a share of the work. The Tennessean appealed to the courts, only to be rebuffed; he returned to his home divested of both gold and slaves.

By the mid-1850's most of California's surface and near-surface gold was played out, and the day of the independent miner was drawing to a close. The time of the huge mining corporations, with capital and equipment to tunnel deep into the hills, had come. Gradually the old camps were abandoned, the prospectors drifting off to new diggings in Nevada or settling down to humdrum lives in the coastal towns. A wild, raucous, anarchic era had ended. A few men had grown rich; most left as poor as they had come. But all who had survived could look back on a time of high adventure and savor the moment they had left the plow, the ledger, or the textbook to seize the chance of a lifetime.

A Mining Town Is Born

Sometimes, a company of these wanderers will find itself upon a Bar, where a few pieces of the precious metal lie scattered upon the surface of the ground; of course they immediately "prospect" it. . . . If it "pays," they "claim" the spot, and build their shanties; the news spreads that wonderful "diggings" have been discovered at such a place—the monte-dealers, those worse than fiends, rush vulture-like upon the scene and erect a round tent, where, in gambling, drinking, swearing and fighting, the *many* reproduce Pandemonium . . . while a *few* honestly and industriously commence digging for gold, and lo! as if a fairy's wand had been waved . . . a full-grown mining town hath sprung into existence.
—Louise A.K.S. Clappe, *The Letters of Dame Shirley*, Indian Bar, 1852

San Francisco—Babylon on the Pacific

A patron at Madame Reiter's Bagnio takes forceful action against a woman who stole his wallet during an evening of pleasure.

To the forty-niners scouring the California diggings in the elusive search for wealth, one place increasingly became the focus of their dreams. Old ambitions and memories of home might fade, but the city of San Francisco, with its gaudy brothels, its lively gambling dens, and its elegant new mansions rising out of the hills, remained a constant goad to toil.

In 1848, when California was formally annexed by the United States, the name San Francisco was hardly even a geographical expression. Only a year earlier the tiny settlement, on its magnificent bay, had still been known as Yerba Buena—among those who knew of it at all. Fewer than a thousand people lived in San Francisco on the fateful day when that aspiring merchant-prince

Sam Brannan raised the cry of "Gold!"

If the first effect of Brannan's announcement was to depopulate the place, its long-term result was to transform San Francisco into a boomtown unlike any other. In Brannan's wake thousands of fledgling entrepreneurs eventually decided to mine the miners rather than the goldfields. Those who did not set up shop in the camps flocked to San Francisco, port of entry for the diggings.

Shantytowns and Mansions

Where there had been only barren hills sloping down to muddy flats, a confusion of shacks and substantial brick buildings sprouted to house lawyers' and physicians' offices, gambling halls, dry-goods stores, restaurants, theaters, and even an opera house. In part, the figures tell the story: by the end of 1850 San Francisco boasted a population of 30,000; and before another half decade was out some 55,000 people lived in the shantytowns, roominghouses, and mansions the gold rush had spawned.

In the race to set up shop and put down at least shallow roots, San Franciscans put a fearful strain on available supplies of labor and raw materials. Even unskilled workers were in such short supply that their wages shot up to unprecedented heights; and lumber, that most precious of commodities, zoomed from four cents a board foot to 25 times that figure. At any price it became hard to find, and many early San Francisco buildings were so-called rag houses—

squares of canvas or some other material stretched across wooden supports. Little matter that periodic fires wiped out these flimsy structures. With wealth flowing into the coffers of merchants, gamblers, and prostitutes at an extraordinary rate (at least $345 million in gold passed through the city between 1848 and the mid-1850's), rebuilding was the least of anyone's worries—a burned-out merchant could always raise cash by selling his property for at least 10 times the price of a few months earlier.

At first all the frenzy that marked San Francisco had just one purpose: to lure the prospector down from the diggings and part him from his hard-won fortune.

This view of San Francisco in 1855 shows Telegraph Hill, the city's highest point, where a semaphore reports ship arrivals.

Oddly enough, the miners often played a willing role in their own impoverishment. To the forty-niners San Francisco was a place to dine on canvasback duck and oysters, to bet hundreds on the turn of a card, to squander a fortune on a fancy lady whose rates ranged from $16 for a few minutes' conversation over a drink to more than $400 for a full night.

By the early 1850's San Francisco was swarming with ladies of the evening who came not only from New York and New Orleans but also from France, Chile, Hawaii, and China. Parisian courtesans long past their prime found instant rejuvenation in the muddy streets of San Francisco, and those who had learned the virtues of thrift in leaner times were salting away considerable fortunes for their twilight years.

At the height of the gold rush, in 1853, the city had not only 48 bawdy houses but 537 drinking establishments, 144 restaurants, and 46 gambling dens. And if the prospector survived all these without being totally fleeced, he was still in danger of being waylaid in a dark alley by gangs of toughs. But for all that, most

San Francisco's Montgomery Street, unpaved and deep in mud, offers precarious plank stepping stones for those who try to cross to the other side without wearing hip boots.

Vigilantes Dispense Quick Justice

Between 1849 and 1851 six disastrous fires raged in the city. Some of the fires were accidental, set by wood-burning stoves and kerosene or whale-oil lamps, but others were the work of criminals attracted to San Francisco because of its prosperity and high living. They used the fires as a cover to loot the city's finest homes and businesses.

On the streets of San Francisco crusading newspaper editor James King is mortally wounded by the politician James P. Casey.

Life in overcrowded, feverishly active San Francisco was dangerous as well as exhilarating in the gold-rush days. Gangs of cutthroats roamed the streets, breaking into shops and homes and murdering hapless citizens, for the agencies of law enforcement were either unable or unwilling to act.

The elite of the gangs were the "Sydney Ducks," former convicts from British penal colonies in Australia. Increasingly bold forays by the Ducks and others, plus the growing suspicion that the city's many fires were set by criminals, led to the formation of the first Committee of Vigilance on June 9, 1851.

During 10 busy weeks the committee tried, convicted, and hanged four men and forced scores of criminals to flee. The vigilantes then became inactive, and all the citizens relaxed—too soon. A new wave of violence and corruption in high places hit the city in 1854-55, bringing on another reform drive led in part by editor James King of

William (the "William" distinguished him from other James Kings in the city). One of King's chief targets was editor and politician James P. Casey, who gunned down King on May 14, 1856. To protect Casey from outraged citizens, his friends rushed him to jail where there was another prisoner, Charles Cora, who had killed a U.S. marshal. Law-abiding San Franciscans had had enough, and the second committee was organized.

The committee armed 2,500 men, seized Casey and Cora, convicted the two of murder, and hanged them on May 22. Scores of criminals were rounded up, tried, and sentenced to banishment; 500 to 800 fled to escape prosecution. Only two others—Joseph Hetherington and Philander Brace—were hanged before the committee ceased its operations in July. Although the Committee of Vigilance operated outside the law, even its critics admitted that it had acted only when the city's elected officials had failed to enforce the law.

On July 9, 1856, the local vigilantes hang convicted murderers Joseph Hetherington and Philander Brace.

visitors—at least those who were not outraged by its decadence—found San Francisco an oasis of urban delights in the western deserts. "I have seen purer liquors, better segars, finer tobacco, truer guns and pistols, larger dirks and bowie knives and prettier courtesans than in any other place," wrote one charmed visitor. "California can and does furnish the best bad things that are available in America."

Despite this unstinted praise, San Francisco's new moneyed elite soon began to itch for respectability, especially after the number of free-spending

miners began to dwindle. They exerted pressure to restrict "unseemly" activities to specially designated parts of town, far from the eyes of proper ladies and impressionable children. A great many former miners, who planned to settle permanently in the area with their families, underwent similar conversions; as one local preacher put it, they "began earnestly to manifest interest in the establishment of schools and churches."

By 1859, with the wild days of the gold rush only a memory, San Francisco was, nonetheless, established as the premier city of the Far West. In that year

writer Richard Henry Dana arrived for his first visit in more than two decades and expressed his amazement at the site's transformation. "When I awoke in the morning," he wrote of his first day there, "and looked from my windows over the city . . . with its storehouses, towers, and steeples; its court-houses, theatres, and hospitals; its daily journals; its well-filled professions . . . when I looked across the bay . . . and beheld . . . steamers . . . and capacious freighters and passenger-carriers . . . when I saw all these things . . . I could scarcely keep my hold on reality at all."

The Mining Frontier Moves Eastward

Any American prospectors of the mid-1800's who thought themselves specially favored by God might well have been forgiven that minor blasphemy. For scarcely had the easily obtained placer gold in California begun to dry up when new reports of fabulous strikes in America's far western interior made the rounds of the Sierra mining camps. Gold in the arid reaches of what is now Nevada and Arizona! Gold in the mountains of present-day Colorado, Montana, Idaho, and Wyoming! Gold in today's eastern Washington and across the border in British Columbia! The stories, magnified with endless repetition, told of nuggets as big as a man's fist, of shimmering dust just waiting to be scooped into a prospector's pan, of new bonanzas that would transform a pauper into a prince—if only a man could get there fast enough and stake a claim.

As prospectors from California, reinforced by new recruits from the East and Midwest, fanned out over the western deserts and mountain ranges, they staked not only their own claims but also those of civilization. It was they who formed the vanguard of permanent settlement in the vast interior stretching from the Missouri to the Sierras. When the new gold rushes began in the mid-1850's,

With handy ropes and a hanging tree, vigilance committees brought law and order to the Montana mining camps.

Disputes among miners were usually settled by brute force, as in this 1860 engraving of a claim-jumping brawl.

California itself was hardly played out; indeed, decades would pass before its mines ceased pouring out millions of dollars in gold annually. But the gold that remained had to be extracted from deep within the recalcitrant earth, a task requiring equipment and knowledge that only rich corporations could provide. Relatively few of the forty-niners were of the type to labor in someone else's vineyards, but many were so badly

bitten by the gold bug that they would spend the rest of their lives wandering the West in search of a new mother lode. Some actually struck rich veins of gold or silver, but most never managed to find their El Dorado.

The Gila River Country

Even while the California rush was at full tide, some prospectors were trying their luck elsewhere. In what is now

---

Gateway to the Mother Lode

Painted between 1855 and 1860, this scene shows the Sacramento waterfront from across the Sacramento River. In the center background is the well-known side-wheeler *Antelope*, queen of the Sacramento River fleet. Shuttling back and forth to San Francisco, the *Antelope* carried a huge cargo of gold from the mountain diggings down to the Pacific port every other evening.

A staid state capital, Sacramento was once a booming and roistering port. Its history began in 1839, when John Augustus Sutter founded his baronial estate of New Helvetia at the junction of the Sacramento and American Rivers. As Americans began to trickle into California, Sutter's Fort became a center for them. In 1848, after the discovery of gold near his property lured away his workers and brought hordes of trespassers who devastated his lands, Sutter was driven into near bankruptcy. He transferred his property to his son, who, the same year, founded the town of Sacramento near the fort. A lively steamboat traffic sprang up on the river, carrying

freight and passengers from San Francisco bound for the mines. Shallow-draft river steamers pushed farther up the Sacramento and its tributaries toward the Sierra Nevada. As the logical transfer point for goods and persons, Sacramento became a headquarters and supply depot for the throngs of adventurers headed for the high country. When the mining boom ended, Sacramento was already the state capital and the center of the fertile farming region of the Great Valley. It became the westernmost point of an overland mail and stage line, and in 1869 the transcontinental railroad—of which the city was one terminus—brought additional prosperity.

This photograph of a miner's cabin in Colorado suggests that its owner has tried to give it a homelike atmosphere.

Miners, like these Arizona prospectors, often arrived in clothes unsuited to the job. Most of them brought along guns as protection against thieves.

southern Arizona a strike was made in 1853 along the Gila River. Word of the bonanza filtered west; and eventually some 1,200 prospectors, suppliers, and hangers-on established the thriving community of Gila City, which "opened up," according to one account, "with a saloon to supply the necessities of life and later added a grocery store and a Chinese restaurant for the luxuries." Gila City was perhaps a model for the scores of mining towns that sprang up like toadstools throughout the Far West from the fifties through the seventies— Wickenburg and Tombstone in today's Arizona; Elk City and Oro Fino in Idaho; Diamond City, Virginia City, and Bannack in Montana; and Virginia City and Aurora in Nevada, to name just

a few. Rising out of the wilderness, they boomed for a few years, sometimes a few decades, only to lapse into somnolence and decay when the gold and silver gave out. Gila City, for example, briefly held the reputation of being the wickedest town in the West; but by 1864 its mines, which had yielded $2 million in gold, were exhausted, and the town was rapidly losing its sinful luster. A decade or so later, a traveler passing by described what remained as "three chimneys and a coyote." There were, however, other places spawned by the rush for precious metals that managed to achieve permanence and even grow into major metropolitan centers. One was Denver.

The area around Pikes Peak had long been rumored to be rich in gold. In 1850

prospectors on their way to California actually came up with traces of it, although in insufficient quantities to stay their westering course. But in 1858 pay dirt was struck by a small group of miners, and as the word spread, hopes for a California-style strike swept the nation. Particularly in the Midwest, which had been hard hit by the financial panic of 1857, there was an air of frenzied hope; and as early as March of 1859 wagon trains were forming up along the Missouri, many vehicles emblazoned with the defiant slogan "Pike's Peak or Bust!"

"Busted, by God!"

About 50,000 gold seekers flooded into the newly laid-out town of Denver, which had been created the previous winter by prospectors turned land speculators in anticipation of the rush. But few of those who came to Denver or the region's other mining camps were rewarded for their efforts, and by late spring thousands of Argonauts were broke and dispirited; by summer half of those who had reached the Rockies full of expectation were plodding homeward. Some of the "gobacks" expressed their shattered hopes by scrawling "Busted, by God!" across the tailgates of their wagons.

Still, thousands remained to try their luck just a little longer, and a few of them were rewarded—first with small gold strikes and later in the 1870's with an unexpected new bonanza in silver.

A promoter's vision in 1858: Denver within a few years was thriving as a supply base for western mining towns. By 1866, as shown here, there were even horse-drawn carriages.

The Fabulous Comstock Lode

Here the painter James Harrington depicted prospectors staking the first claim on the Comstock Lode. Henry Comstock, one of the original partners in the mine, sits at the left.

Henry T. P. Comstock was an old hand at prospecting, but he had a natural preference for loafing—and that was just what he was doing one day in June 1859 as he rode his mule along the eastern slopes of the Sierras in what is now Nevada. Enough traces of gold had been found there to keep a hard core of miners in action.

After Comstock had moseyed along for a while, he found himself beside a spring known locally as Old Man Caldwell's. Two prospectors, Peter O'Riley and Patrick McLaughlin, were hard at work, and Comstock dismounted and strolled over to their diggings. What happened next was recounted by a chronicler of the Old West known as Dan De Quille:

> Comstock . . . saw at a glance the unusual quantity of gold that was in sight. . . . He was soon . . . running his fingers through the gold, and picking into the mass of strange-looking "stuff" exposed. Conceiving at once that a wonderful discovery had been made, [he] straightened himself up . . . and coolly proceeded to inform the astonished miners that they were working on ground that belonged to him.

Actually, Comstock was claiming the land not just for himself but also for two pals, James "Old Virginny" Finney and Manny Penrod. Old Pancake, as Comstock was called, must have had a silver tongue, because a five-man partnership was formed to work the lode. (Old Virginny's share was soon bought out by Old Pancake for a bottle of booze and a blind horse.)

For a number of days the partners scratched at the earth, which yielded gold in some quantity, but they soon encountered a vein of heavy bluish quartz from which the metal was extremely difficult to extract. In late June they sent some of this perverse material to an assayer in California, who found to his astonishment that, judging by the samples, each ton of ore contained almost $1,000 in gold and $3,000 in silver. McLaughlin and O'Riley had, in fact, stumbled on one of the richest sources of precious metal ever found, and soon not only their mine but also the entire surrounding region would be famous as the Comstock Lode.

News of the Comstock Lode (so named because Comstock spent most of his time bragging about "my mine" and "my gold") set off a stampede among California miners. By June 1860 some 10,000 of them were clogging the verminous streets and alleys of a Nevada shantytown named Virginia City after

Adah Isaacs Menken and Her "Nudity" Wow the Frontier

This amusing figurine of Menken as Mazeppa is an heirloom of the Piper family. John Piper bought Maguire's Opera House, then built a fancier one.

Life in the up-and-coming metropolis of Virginia City quickened with the arrival in 1864 of the notorious Adah Isaacs Menken. The famous actress had appeared in San Francisco; but Virginia City boasted an opera house, belonging to impresario Tom Maguire, and so La Menken was persuaded to come up to the frontier town. Legends about her past preceded her, and the prospect of seeing her thrilled the townspeople.

As an accomplished schoolgirl, Adah, whose parents were Jews from New Orleans, learned French, German, Spanish, and Hebrew, translated Homer's *Iliad* from the Greek, and was also skilled in dancing, singing, and riding. Maturing into an uninhibited and temperamental beauty, she launched two successful careers. As a poetess, she was praised by Dante Gabriel Rossetti; her friends included Dickens, Swinburne, and George Sand (her son's godmother); and she was among the earliest admirers of Walt Whitman. As an actress, she was the rave of London, Paris, New York—and the American West. Her most sensational role, which Mark Twain compared more to acrobatics than to acting, was in *Mazeppa*, for which there was standing room only in Virginia City. In this drama, based on Lord Byron's poem, she was disrobed on stage—her assumed nudity was covered by flesh-colored tights—and tied to a snorting horse (which she had had carefully trained). Although the proper Victorians were shocked, enthused Virginia City miners made her an honorary fireman.

Also enjoyed were the romantic tales Adah kindled. She took her middle and last names from the first of four husbands, and in replying to gossip about love affairs, she quipped: "I never lived with Houston, it was General Jackson and Methuselah and other big men."

the hapless Old Virginny. By October the town had 154 business establishments, including a theater, a music hall, four butcher shops, and eight law offices. There were also six physicians, who kept busy attending miners poisoned by the local drinking water, which contained significant traces of arsenic as well as gold and silver.

One of the earliest Californians to arrive at the Comstock diggings was the fledgling entrepreneur George Hearst, father of the future newspaper tycoon. Among the first to hear of the fabulous find from the assayer, he arrived on the scene ahead of the good news. The $3,500 he paid for McLaughlin's share of the lode was returned to him thousands of times over. Others from the Golden State were just as quick: Comstock was gulled of his share for $10,000, while O'Riley—who was perhaps a somewhat better businessman than the others—held out for $40,000.

Speculation Fever

Most of the men who converged on Virginia City did precious little mining. They fanned out along the hillsides, staked their claims, and wove dreams of a luxurious future. But since the richest veins of ore were deeply embedded in quartz and the miners lacked the equipment needed to work them, they contented themselves with buying and selling claims at a frantic pace. "Nobody had any money," wrote one prospector, "yet everybody was a millionaire in silver claims. Nobody had any credit, yet everybody bought thousands of feet of glittering ore." Occasionally, someone made a real killing in the speculative spiral: one eastern tenderfoot parlayed a $1,000 investment into $20,000 in just a

---

Mark Twain and the Territorial Enterprise

The newspaper's handpress.

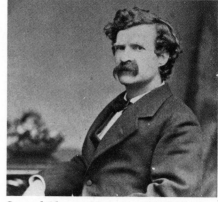

Samuel Clemens, known as Mark Twain.

The highly successful *Territorial Enterprise* set the tone for freewheeling, uninhibited frontier journalism. First published in Mormon Station (now Genoa) in present-day Nevada in 1858, it moved to Carson City and then to Virginia City in 1860. The presiding geniuses of the paper were Joseph T. Goodman and Dennis McCarthy, and one of their first reporters was young Samuel Clemens, who in 1863 began using the pen name Mark Twain. As the following brief item shows, Sam was not content to stick to bare-bones facts. To the simple news announcement "A very neat hearse arrived here yesterday, for Wilson & Keys," he added: "This is something that has long been much needed." Better yet, Sam liked to let his imagination take flight, and one sally produced "The Celebrated Jumping Frog of Calaveras County." The short story was published in New York in 1865—and Mark Twain, age 30, was on his way.

---

few months without ever once lifting a pick and shovel.

The speculative fever gradually subsided, and the smart money from San Francisco arrived on the scene. Claims were bought up and consolidated, heavy mining equipment was moved in, and by the 1870's shafts were dug thousands of feet into the mountains. Deep underground, dressed only in shoes and breechclouts, the miners labored in 120°F heat, while around their feet spurts of steamy water bubbled up from

thermal springs. One visitor to the mines reported that "there were occasional deaths, but on the whole the miners—picked men all—came through the ordeal well."

Logically enough, the cost of labor was high, but for the mineowners the profits were even higher. Gold and silver from the Nevada mines had helped finance the Union cause in the Civil War, and before the Comstock Lode gave out in the 1880's, it had poured forth more than $300 million in precious metal.

J. Ross Browne's report for *Harper's New Monthly Magazine* on Virginia City nightlife included this sketch of hurdy-gurdy girls performing their act.

Virginia City fire companies gave townsmen at least limited protection while providing volunteers with an active social life. Shown here is the Young America Engine Company on July 4, 1862.

The Stagecoach Era Opens

Mineral wealth, real and imagined, had lured thousands of Americans to the Far West; but once there, they found themselves virtually cut off from the nation's more settled regions. With railroads the principal form of long-distance travel in the East, most looked forward to the day when East and West would be linked by rail, but they knew that to build such a link was a monumental undertaking. In the meantime a more pressing need somehow had to be met: the organization of a fast, efficient overland mail service between the isolated western settlements and the East.

Even within California, organizing the simplest and most routine forms of

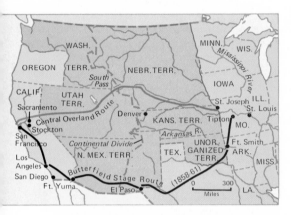

This map of the 2,800-mile Butterfield Overland Mail trail, which ran from Tipton, Missouri, to San Francisco, shows why its critics christened it the Oxbow Route.

communication seemed beyond the ability of most local officials. With the gold rush the state had grown so fast, and so many scattered mining camps had been established, that the delivery of a letter from San Francisco to the diggings at Red Dog or Hangtown was hailed as a minor miracle.

As early as 1848, the federal government began shipping mail to the West Coast via the Isthmus of Panama, a route as lengthy and uncertain for letters as it would be for the forty-niners themselves. The mail that was finally deposited at the post office in San Francisco simply piled up until some miner, coming in from the camps, could take the time to sort through it in search of letters addressed to himself and his friends. It was sheer chaos, a situation ripe for a clever entrepreneur who was eager to sell his services as a mailman.

One who saw the opportunity and

Swift-riding Plains Indians sometimes ambushed stagecoaches. In this Frederic Remington painting, "Downing the Nigh Leader," a party of Indians kills the left lead horse.

seized it was a former clerk named Alexander Todd. He had gone west with the Argonauts only to discover that his health was too delicate for hours of digging in freezing rivers. After a few inquiries had convinced Todd that prospectors would pay handsomely for mail service, he began signing up subscribers in 1849. For $2.50 Todd would carry a letter to San Francisco for posting, and for an ounce of gold dust (worth about $16) he would personally deliver such mail as he found to addressees back in the mining camps.

Day after day, Todd scoured the diggings until he had signed up hundreds of miners. Then he was off to the big city to post letters and comb through the mountains of unsorted mail for anything addressed to his clients. These activities alone brought him a handsome profit, and he was also carrying gold from the camps to places of safekeeping in San Francisco in exchange for 5 percent of its value. Without touching a pick Todd had managed to strike pay dirt.

The California Stage Company

Other entrepreneurs in California, sniffing possible windfalls, began to organize stagecoach lines, and by 1853 there were a dozen small companies running coaches between Sacramento, Stockton, and the gold diggings. A year later these competing lines were merged into a single operation, the California Stage Company, which soon became a

On rough roads passengers were usually transferred from coaches to the lighter celerity wagons with their fractious mules.

colossus, controlling most of the coach business in California and even in the Oregon Country. By 1856 it was the largest stage line in the United States, operating nearly 2,000 miles of routes.

Such developments, however, did nothing to provide reliable overland mail service between the Far West and the East. Since large federal subsidies would be needed to organize and maintain such a service, California had for years been requesting help from Congress but to no avail. Finally, in 1856 after 75,000 Californians had signed a petition, Congress agreed to act. But before anything could be accomplished, bitter sectional disputes intervened.

Northern politicians wanted a direct overland route from St. Joseph to San Francisco via the South Pass. Along this route stagecoaches would carry both passengers and the U.S. mail, the cost being partly underwritten—and a profit virtually assured—by a federal mail subsidy. But southerners, with an eye on their hoped-for rail link to the West, demanded a southern route from St. Louis—much longer, they conceded, but not subject to heavy snow in winter.

In 1857, still unable to agree on a route, Congress turned the matter over to the postmaster general, a southerner who soon awarded the coveted $600,000 annual mail subsidy to veteran express-man John Butterfield. What Butterfield proposed was a service with twice-weekly departures in each direction between San Francisco (via Los Angeles, Fort Yuma, El Paso, and Fort Smith) and Tipton, Missouri, the rail terminus from St. Louis. The North and Far West howled with anger at the use of this roundabout 2,800-mile-long trail, a huge semicircle derisively dubbed the Oxbow Route. Skeptics—and there were thousands—doubted that Butterfield could come even close to meeting the terms of his mail contract: Tipton to San Francisco delivery in 25 days.

From Missouri to San Francisco

Butterfield would not be deterred. In a year's time he spent about a million dollars preparing the route west, building nearly 200 relay and home stations—to be manned by blacksmiths, harness-makers, wheelwrights, and the like—and hiring drivers and conductors for the elegant Concord coaches and lightweight "celerity wagons" he had ordered. On September 16, 1858, he was ready to put his overland mail company to the test. On that day two coaches, one in San

To the usual discomforts of stagecoach travel were added below-zero winter storms that coated men's whiskers and horses' nostrils with ice. Deep snows could strand a stage.

Francisco and the other in Tipton, began moving in opposite directions. Aboard the westbound coach was John Butterfield himself, and at the reins was his son.

Butterfield senior rode as far as Fort Smith, Arkansas, then disembarked to await the arrival of the eastbound coach. It came in right on schedule, and Butterfield boarded it and headed back to Tipton. Once there, he rushed on to St. Louis by train and deposited the mails at the city's post office, exactly 24 days and

18 hours out of San Francisco. The westbound coach arrived at its terminus in just 23 days and 23 hours.

For the first time East and West were linked by a dependable overland mail and passenger service, a feat that President James Buchanan hailed as "a glorious triumph for civilization and the Union." Meanwhile, to the north, another ambitious venture had begun to prosper: the great freighting firm of Russell, Majors & Waddell.

A durable Concord coach passes majestic Mount Shasta in northern California. By the late 1850's stagecoaches were traveling regularly between California and the Oregon Country.

When accidents occurred, passengers had to be ready to give the driver a hand.

Jouncing West by Coach and Freighter

The travelers below are experiencing one of the greatest adventures any American has ever enjoyed, but they are too exhausted to be thrilled right now. When their 20-day trip is over, they will boast of their feat—crossing half a continent by stage (more than 2,000 bruising miles from Missouri to Sacramento), each one jammed into a space of 15 inches square, often feeling queasy from the motion, itching from sand gnats, and doing without baths or a decent night's sleep. There was suffering too from burning eyes and throats irritated by the alkali dust that also thickly coats their hair and clothes. Later they will joke about the whist and euchre played aboard; or the time the wheels sank far into the sand and everyone had to walk beside the coach for miles without water, feet crunching on the bones of prior luckless pioneers; or the day after the flash flood, when the men had to get out into hip-deep mud and push; or the terrifying descent in the Rockies, where the curves were so hairpin you could not see the lead horses, and the brakes smoked as the carriage careened down the ledgelike trail above a chasm. After they have unloaded for the last time the 25 pounds of luggage, two blankets, and water canteen allowed each of them, they will write east that the $600 fare was worth it, if only for the

The superbly crafted Concord coach was made by J. Stephens Abbott, who developed the model with wheelwright Lewis Downing in a Concord, New Hampshire, factory. He personally inspected each vehicle. The brightly varnished stages were of varied colors and sizes, had scenic views or "U.S. Mail" on their doors, and cost about $1,300. This one weighs 2,500 pounds, is 8½ feet in length and height, and 5 feet wide. It has three upholstered leather benches inside and can accommodate 9 interior and 12 rooftop passengers. The body rests on two thoroughbraces, 3½-inch oxhide strips that act as shock absorbers, keep the rig from jarring apart, and protect the horses from carriage jolts. The coach has oil lamps, basswood panels, and elm, oak, ash, and hickory running gear. Small windows and roll-up leather curtains let in air and keep out some rain and snow.

While a traveler descends, the guard-messenger, riding shotgun, and driver stay seated until all horses are unhitched. Under their "box" (seat) is a leather "boot" for tools, a water bucket, a buffalo robe, 170 pounds of mail pouches, and strongboxes.

Brake lever, operated by foot pressure, controls brakes on the rear wheels.

Express parcels, newspapers, and some luggage go into a rear boot. Extra cargo fits on the roof and under the legs of inside passengers, who may take turns trying to sleep stretched out upon it. Most will catnap sitting up. The jehu may invite a favored passenger to sit up beside him.

The best seats are behind the front boot, facing backward. Passengers on the middle bench bump knees with those on the rear bench.

A stock-tender unhooks the traces of six tired horses in four minutes. They will rest and get fodder after their 15-mile run at an average of 9 miles per hour. For the next lap a new, wilder team will take over.

Big dished wheels (the rear ones are more than five feet across) are fairly narrow—about three inches wide—for easy rolling on hard ground. (Wider farm wagon wheels are better in sand.)

The five-foot-two width between the front wheels keeps the coach from tipping. The axles are greased at each station. Few roads are graded, none are paved.

Step folds back when the stage departs.

The Reinsman's Skill

The jehu holds three pairs of reins in the fingers of his left hand, keeping his right hand free for the whip. He "talks" to the horses through the ribbons (reins). To keep his touch sensitive, the jehu seldom wears bulky gloves, thus running the risk of frostbitten fingers in the wintertime.

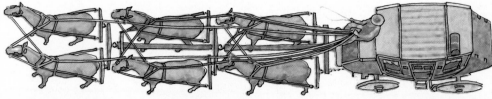

fantastic sights: vast prairie-dog towns and herds of thousands of buffalo, stupendous waterfalls and weird rock formations, and the amusing variety of fellow passengers. But on this summer evening just before the Civil War, all they can think of is that their stage has made the second of only two stops allowed them every 24 hours at a home station, and for a few hours they will be able to stretch their cramped legs, quench their thirst, and fall into a fitful sleep. Then, long before dawn, the jehu (the Biblical name given coach drivers) will holler, "All aboard! Awaaaay!" The passengers will clamber into their reliable coach and, as a fresh but half-broken team of western mustangs lurches forward at near-runaway speed, they will rattle off on a trip none will forget.

Files of Freighters Haul the Goods

Just as the stage is the conveyance for people and mail, so the freighter is the cargo carrier. Big firms do a lucrative business supplying army camps, mines, and towns. Each wagon bears up to five tons of supplies—nonperishables and canned goods on the bottom, perishables (such as sugar, flour, salt, beans) on top—and an extra tongue, yokes and axles, water keg, and tar bucket for greasing the running gear against heat and dust. Some trains, like this one, are mule-drawn, driven by mounted muleskinners; but most use oxen, prodded by bullwhackers on foot, whose whips, tipped by rawhide poppers, crack with a pop-pop heard two miles away. The dust from a freighter caravan can be seen for about 20 miles.

Leaders Swingers Wheelers Repair caboose

Pre-Civil War freighters (below right) flared outward. After the war the wagons (above) had high, straight sides and ends so they could hook in tandem. Brake levers were on the left.

The muleskinner sits on the left wheeler and holds both a brake line and the jerk line—one rein going to the left side of the left leader's bit and connected by a stick to the right leader's bit. The left leader turns left upon a long, steady pull of the jerk line, right on several short tugs.

The life of the keeper is bleak, lonely, and dangerous—some posts have escape tunnels in case of Indian attacks.

A long freight caravan clops by.

A bullwhacker snaps his whip above, not on, his 12 oxen; he says they have distinct personalities and are smarter than horses.

Some oxen will die from drinking alkali water.

The sod-roofed log home station has barns, a stable for 15 horses, and a filthy hut for the keeper, his wife, and four stockmen. In more easterly stations food is good, but western ones lack supplies; food consists of rancid bacon and corn dodgers—fried cornbread. Water is often carted from miles away. The keeper listens for the arriving jehus' bugle calls. This station is on the Central Overland Route, 600 miles shorter than the Oxbow.

Station-keeper

A passenger eats fried fat pork, mustard, stale biscuits, and sandy coffee bought in the station. A weary woman freshens up with a tin basin and towel—a grimy old shirt. Inside, she may share the bed of the keeper's wife, but male passengers must sleep on the dirt floor—drivers and guards get the few bunks. Another reinsman will drive the next 50 miles with only 10-minute stops to change horses at foodless swing stations every 15 miles.

The Formation of an Ox Train

Freighters travel with military discipline. Their general, the wagonmaster, must be resourceful, courageous, and firm with his profane, rough crew. Armed with a rifle and medicine chest, he rides up ahead. His train—rolling four abreast in open areas, single file elsewhere—stops between 10 a.m. and 2 p.m. to water and graze the oxen and again overnight when it forms a protective corral with chains linking the overlapping wagon wheels. Into this the animals, grazing outside, can be herded if an Indian attack should take place. After eating and singing by the mess wagon, each bullwhacker greases axles, gathers firewood, and crawls under his wagon to sleep until dawn on a buffalo robe.

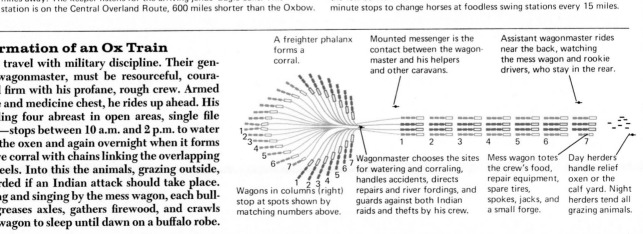

A freighter phalanx forms a corral.

Mounted messenger is the contact between the wagonmaster and his helpers and other caravans.

Assistant wagonmaster rides near the back, watching the mess wagon and rookie drivers, who stay in the rear.

Wagons in columns (right) stop at spots shown by matching numbers above.

Wagonmaster chooses the sites for watering and corraling, handles accidents, directs repairs and river fordings, and guards against both Indian raids and thefts by his crew.

Mess wagon totes the crew's food, repair equipment, spare tires, spokes, jacks, and a small forge.

Day herders handle relief oxen or the calf yard. Night herders tend all grazing animals.

The Great Freightmen

Almost immediately after Russell, Majors & Waddell was organized in 1854, the firm became the unchallenged giant of western freighting. From its bustling headquarters at Leavenworth in the new Kansas Territory, it hauled millions of pounds of supplies each year to remote U.S. Army posts scattered throughout the West. Using hundreds of wagons and thousands of oxen and men, the company devised remarkably efficient methods of moving its massive cargoes at an average rate of 15 miles per day.

There could hardly have been three more unlikely partners than William H. Russell, Alexander Majors, and William B. Waddell. Russell, a New Englander by birth and a gambler by

Before they tackle the job of yoking the oxen in a wagon corral, the bullwhackers prepare breakfast. One fries bacon while another keeps the fire going with a shovelful of bull chips.

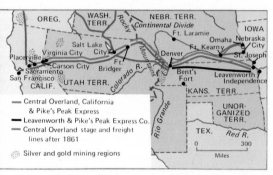

A network of wagon roads served freighters hauling supplies to booming mining towns and the Army's many forts in the West.

temperament, cut a dashing figure in New York and Washington, places he much preferred to the dusty streets of Leavenworth. But if his heart did not belong to the West, he never stopped devising new ways for himself and his partners to profit from it. He was, in short, the sort of man who could charm a fly out of a honey jar, but in the end his clever schemes backfired disastrously.

No one ever accused William Waddell of excessive charm. A plain-spoken Virginian of Scottish ancestry, he was as dedicated to squeezing a dollar as Rus-

sell was to spending it. Waddell ran the firm's day-to-day operations, bending his every effort to hold his flamboyant partner in check.

The third partner, Alexander Majors, was an outdoorsman who spent as much time as he could on the trail, pressing his teamsters onward and helping his men form up the long lines of freight wagons. Despite his expertise—it was he who organized the caravans in a highly efficient system that would be imitated throughout the West—Majors could be a trial to his subordinates. Not only did he himself refrain from drinking and cursing, he also insisted that every crewman he hired sign a solemn pledge not to swear, "nor to get drunk, nor to gamble . . . and not to do anything incompatible with the conduct of a gentleman." Needless to say, his edict was ignored when he was not present.

But drunk or sober, the crewmen proved equal to their tasks, in part because Russell, Majors & Waddell had equipped them so handsomely. After seeing the company's vast supply depot at Leavenworth, New York editor Horace Greeley wrote admiringly: "Such acres of wagons! such pyramids of extra axletrees! such herds of oxen! such regiments of drivers!"

There was good reason for Greeley's awe. In 1855 alone, the company dispatched 500 wagons, carrying 2.5 million pounds of freight, across the plains. This amounted to 20 separate wagon trains, each with its own wagonmaster, bullwhackers (teamsters), messengers, herders, and cook. The next year was another banner season, but 1857 prom-

A Charles Russell painting depicts a vigilant wagonmaster studying his freight caravan. He always rode ahead of his train to watch out for Indians and to select a likely campsite.

An angry bull and bullwhackers. Although steers, oxen were called bulls; hence the two terms "bullwhacker" and "bullwhip."

ised even greater profits: the Army had contracted with Russell, Majors & Waddell to ship about 5 million pounds of supplies westward. However, that was also the year the so-called Mormon War broke out, a conflict that was expected to increase the company's profits but instead started its long decline.

A Tottering Empire

To crush Mormon resistance, the Army dispatched 2,500 men and ordered Russell, Majors & Waddell to haul an additional 3 million pounds of supplies. Frantically, the partners sought more men, wagons, and oxen, paying top dollar for everything and everybody. The extra wagon trains were soon en route west, but three of them were attacked and burned by Mormon guerrillas, while others were the victims of heavy winter weather. The firm's losses were nearly $500,000, and to make matters worse, the Army defaulted on its promised reimbursement. The partnership never really recovered from these blows, even though 1858 brought new contracts that put 3,500 wagons and 40,000 oxen on the trails west.

To recoup the firm's fortunes, William Russell hit on a typically risky scheme. After the discovery of gold in what is today Colorado he proposed a stage line from the Mississippi Valley to Denver in order to cash in on the boom that was sure to come. But Waddell and Majors, who knew such an enterprise was doomed without a government subsidy, flatly rejected the idea. Undeterred, Russell found a new associate and began operating his Leavenworth & Pike's Peak Express Company in April 1859 and by July had added a mail route from St. Joseph, Missouri, to Salt Lake City. From the first, despite its excellent

service, the L&PP was in trouble, with costs running far ahead of revenues. Fearful that Russell's impending bankruptcy would drag them down with it, Majors and Waddell bought out the L&PP in the fall of 1859 and then extended its operations to Placerville, California. But, as might have been foreseen, the new Central Overland, California & Pike's Peak Express (usually known simply as the COC) was soon in deep trouble; discontented workers were quick to derive a name for the company from its initials: "Clean Out of Cash and Poor Pay."

Only one thing could now save the COC and its owners: a substantial mail subsidy from the government. But since the post office department was already subsidizing Butterfield's southern line, the partners had to find some dramatic way to demonstrate the superiority of their own service and of the central route west. Once more, Russell had an idea.

Just who first conceived the notion of the Pony Express—relays of riders galloping hell-for-leather across the West to deliver the mail—is unknown. But it was Russell who decided to adopt it as a means of saving his business. He gave his partners no time to protest. In January 1860 he sent a terse telegram to Leavenworth from Washington, where he had gone to seek financial assistance from the government: "Have determined to establish a Pony Express to Sacramento, California, commencing the 3rd of April. Time 10 days."

Since mules traveled faster than oxen, some merchants selling feed and luxury items were willing to pay higher rates to obtain delivery of their goods by mule-freight companies.

The Immortal Pony Express

In almost 19 months—from April 1860 through October 1861—the riders of the Pony Express galloped a total of 650,000 miles, carried 34,753 pieces of mail, and lost only one mail sack. Changing horses every 10 to 15 miles and switching riders after an average of 75 miles, the Pony Express carried the mail 1,966 miles from St. Joseph, Missouri, to Sacramento, California, in about 10 days. A record time of 7 days and 17 hours was set in March 1861 when the riders laid on the whip to bring President Lincoln's inaugural address to California. Letters, written on thin paper, cost $5 a half ounce, reduced to $1 in July 1861. The riders earned board and keep and $100 to $150 a month, depending on the length and hazards of their run. The demanding nature of their jobs was hinted at in newspaper advertisements seeking riders who were small and "daring young men, preferably orphans." Another requirement: an oath not to drink or swear on duty.

Pony Express Russell

Neither of William H. Russell's partners in the freighting firm—Alexander Majors and William B. Waddell—was in favor of starting the Pony Express. They felt that since the venture had no mail contract or guarantee of one, it could not make money. But the opportunistic Russell, always willing to take a chance and supremely self-confident, got them to go along. Russell then directed Benjamin Ficklin to oversee the building of 190 relay stations—25 home stations where riders were changed and 165 swing stations for changes of horses. Purchasing agents for the mail service were ordered to buy 500 select horses, paying some $200 for each one of them.

The Riders Were Tough and Courageous

The average age of the expressmen was 19, but one rider, William F. Cody, who later became known as Buffalo Bill, was only 15, and David Jay was 13. Records for endurance and courage were set by a number of the riders. After galloping his 76-mile relay, young Cody found that his relief had been killed. So with scant rest, he rode another 85 miles and then made the return trip—a total of 322 miles. Another rider, Bob Haslan, was set upon by Paiutes in Nevada, and during a running fight one Paiute arrow fractured his jaw and another went through his arm. But Haslan delivered the mail, traveling 120 miles in 8 hours and 10 minutes and using 13 horses. J. G. Kelley's narrowest escape came not from unfriendly Indians, dangerous mountain trails, desert heat, or blinding and bone-chilling winter blizzards but from a camp of green emigrants with itchy trigger fingers. They fired on him, thinking he was an Indian streaking in to make a hit-and-run attack.

Four Pony Express riders hold still for a photograph; several runs a week kept them on station and away from town much of the time.

The Pony Express Trail

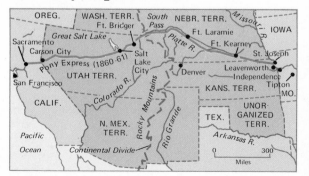

Pony Express riders braved blazing, waterless expanses, precipitous terrain, and hostile Indians as they cut mail delivery time from weeks to just days and dramatized to the nation the need for even better cross-country service.

Momentous News Is Hurried West

A letter for a Denver paper brings word of Lincoln's election.

Relay Stations Provided Fresh Mounts and Riders

Within two minutes of his arrival at a relay station, the rider was on a fresh horse and away. To save weight he carried only pistols and a knife—sometimes not even those. The leather mail sack, thrown over the saddle, was known as a *mochila*. It was a square piece of leather with pockets in each of the corners. The rider sat on it with two of the pockets in front of his legs and two behind.

The Doom of the Pony Express

An expressman rides past workers whose labor will soon send him back to a prosaic job. The completion of a transcontinental telegraph line in October 1861 ended the glory days of the Pony Express. The firm of Russell, Majors & Waddell put $700,000 in the mail venture, lost more than $200,000, and never received a penny from the government for a public service that helped unite the East and Far West at a time of disunion and civil war. Short-lived though the Pony Express proved to be, the bold undertaking left a rich heritage—a stirring example of the American pragmatic approach to the problem of conquering distance and time.

Tribute to a Pony Rider

We had a consuming desire, from the beginning, to see a pony-rider, but somehow or other all that passed us and all that met us managed to streak by in the night, and so we heard only a whiz and a hail, and the swift phantom of the desert was gone. . . . But now we were expecting one along every moment, and would see him in broad daylight. Presently the driver [of Twain's coach] exclaims: "Here he comes!" Every neck is stretched further, and every eye strained wider. Away across the endless dead level of the prairie a black speck appears against the sky, and it is plain that it moves. . . . In a second or two it becomes a horse and rider, rising and falling, rising and falling—sweeping toward us nearer and nearer . . . and the flutter of the hoofs comes faintly to the ear—another instant a whoop and a hurrah from our upper deck, a wave of the rider's hand . . . and man and horse burst past our excited faces, and go winging away like a belated fragment of a storm!
—Mark Twain, *Roughing It*, 1872

Emperors of the Trail

As glamorous as it was, the Pony Express did not persuade Congress to subsidize a central mail route, nor did it solve the financial problems of Russell, Majors & Waddell. In fact, each letter delivered via Pony Express cost the firm $16 and brought an average return of only $3. Desperate to avoid bankruptcy, William Russell appealed for help to his many Washington friends in the fall of 1860. Hope of a sort came from an Interior Department clerk who controlled millions of dollars' worth of bonds held in trust for Indian tribes.

Whether it was Russell or the clerk who conceived the plan to embezzle the Indian bonds in order to bail out the company is unclear. But the two men did enter into a conspiracy and quickly botched it. In no time at all their criminal activities were the talk of Washington; and by December 1860 Russell was in jail, and his firm was financially ruined.

Had Russell not yielded to this unfortunate temptation, the long-sought subsidy might have been obtained. By early 1861 the nation was on the brink of civil war, and the old southern mail route was clearly obsolete. But after Russell's disgrace the subsidy went to the Butterfield organization, which transferred its operations northward. Butterfield, however, was not the chief beneficiary of the

Four security guards ride shotgun on a gold shipment from Deadwood, South Dakota, in 1890. Between 1870 and 1884 bandits robbed Wells Fargo stages of almost $500,000.

demise of Russell, Majors & Waddell. That distinction went to a bluff and hard-driving businessman named Ben Holladay, whose dream was a total monopoly of all western freight and coaching operations.

By 1860 Holladay had become the chief creditor of Russell, Majors & Waddell, and in late 1861 he called in his notes, forcing the older firm into bankruptcy. The next spring he bought the partnership's assets for a total price of $500,000. Within a few years he had

nearly achieved his ambition: his Holladay Overland Mail & Express Company held a virtual monopoly on all freight and passenger service between Salt Lake City and the Missouri, and the overland mail subsidy was now his as well. He employed 15,000 people, owned 20,000 vehicles, and was grossing more than $180,000 each month from passenger, freight, and mail shipments. Holladay also had interests in steamships, distilleries, mines, and real estate.

If there was one thing Ben Holladay loathed, it was competition—however weak or insignificant. Rivals who dared contest even the smallest part of the territory this "Napoleon of the Plains" considered his own were struck down quickly. Holladay's usual procedure was to bankrupt his competitor by undercutting his rates; once the rival was demolished, he would again raise his rates and lower the standards of service.

The Behemoth of the West

There was, however, one potential rival too big and too powerful for even Holladay to swallow: Wells, Fargo & Company. It was founded by two easterners, Henry Wells and William G. Fargo, who had years of experience in the express business. Wells, Fargo & Company opened offices in San Francisco in 1852 to serve the express and banking needs of the booming mining industry. Curiously, although the partners built the most powerful private institution west of the Missouri, it seems Fargo never bothered to inspect his farflung empire, and Wells did so only once. They preferred to concern them-

Ruthless Ben Holladay

Six foot two, powerfully built, and almost insatiably ambitious, Ben Holladay (1819–87) earned this "tribute" from a rival: "Energetic, untiring, unconscionable, unscrupulous, and wholly destitute of honesty, morality or common decency."

Holladay, who by the late 1830's owned a saloon, a packing firm, and a distillery in Weston, Missouri, first achieved prominence in the freight business through his friendly contacts with the Mormons. During the Mexican War he carted supplies to the Army and made a killing by manipulating War Department contracts.

Finding his chances of becoming the number one man in the freighting business blocked by Russell, Majors & Waddell, Holladay began weaving a web to entrap the firm into selling out to him. He sold animals to RM&W on credit, letting it run up big bills, and loaned Russell money to start the ill-

fated Pony Express. As chief creditor, he took over the bankrupt firm.

By 1868 Holladay had turned to railroads, becoming the head of a line in Oregon. It was taken over by the bondholders, however, after the panic of 1873 came close to wiping him out.

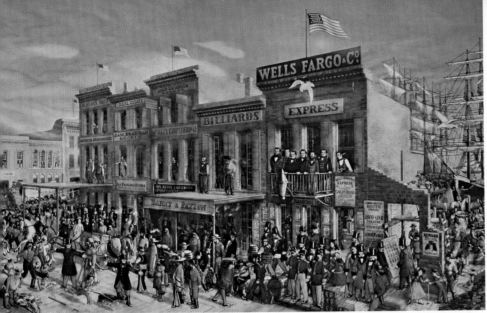

Wells, Fargo & Co. opened its first office in the center of San Francisco on Montgomery Street in 1852; business was often discussed at considerable length in the saloon next door.

Famous among Wells Fargo drivers was "Old Charley" Parkhurst. When he died in 1879, Charley was found to be a woman.

selves with long-range policy, leaving day-to-day operations in the hands of capable managers.

At first the firm concentrated on banking and shipping gold eastward by sea, but its operations soon expanded to include private mail service and the shipment of other valuables. By 1859 it had established 126 branches on the

When snowdrifts in the Sierras proved too much for horses and mules, Wells Fargo got the mail to isolated mining towns by contracting with independents such as Fenton Whiting, who operated what was called the California Dog Express (top). John A. "Snowshoe" Thompson (below) traveled across the mountains on his homemade skis.

West Coast and was expanding its operations into the Nevada mining country; Wells Fargo had become the primary link between the isolated Far West and the rest of the nation.

Oddly enough, at this time the company owned hardly any carriers. For overland transportation it contracted with local or regional stagecoach lines and for ocean shipments with steamer lines. In 1861, however, Wells Fargo took over the western portion of the central stage route from the Butterfield organization; then in 1866, after years of feuding with Ben Holladay, it bought out his vast empire for $1.8 million.

If the sale was a secret triumph for Holladay—who knew that the stagecoach would soon be doomed by the completion of a transcontinental rail link—it also suited Wells Fargo, allowing the firm to dominate every phase of the express business from the Missouri River to the Pacific.

With the coming of the railroads, Wells Fargo began to retrench on its stage operations, restricting itself to running feeder coach lines. As the railroads expanded through the Far West, the firm provided security cars on which bullion and other valuables were transported for many of the lines. But for Wells Fargo and the West as a whole, the demise of the stage was a sign that the pioneering era was coming to a close. The company would survive, but its romantic heyday had ended—the time when, according to one admirer, Wells Fargo "went everywhere, did almost anything . . . and was the nearest thing to a universal service ever invented."

This fashionably dressed gentleman is Black Bart, who robbed 28 Wells Fargo stages in less than 10 years. A company detective finally tracked him down in 1883.

Were all the teeming regions of the dawn
Unpeopled now? What devastating need
Had set so many faces pale with greed
Against the sunset? Not as men who seek
Some meed of kindness, suppliant and meek,
These hungry myriads came. They did but look,
And whatsoever pleased them, that they took.

—*John G. Neihardt,* The Song of the Indian Wars

Wars in the West

"Cavalry Charge on the Southern Plains." Oil painting by Frederic Remington.

Chapter 7

As tension mounted before the Civil War, bitter feuds erupted in the West between free-staters and proslavers. These conflicts and the sporadic border campaigns of the war itself, however, did little to stem the tide of westering miners and farmers. To make way for the whites, the government tried to confine the increasingly restive Indians on reservations run by Indian affairs agents. But the agents were often dishonest and usually ignored treaty boundaries, so Indian uprisings kept the U.S. Army busy in the West for nearly 30 years.

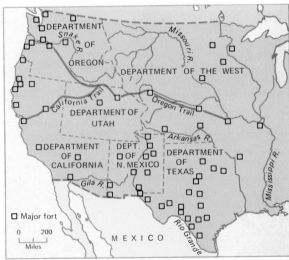

In 1860, on the eve of the Civil War, the Army's forces in the West numbered only about 10,000 men to cover 2½ million square miles. They operated from isolated army forts, with communication and coordination made even more difficult by the vast region's division into six military departments, each directed by a different commander. (After the war these departments were reorganized into two.) Usually poorly equipped and badly fed, the soldiers had to defend settlers, most of whom came by the Oregon and California Trails; protect miners and ranchers; help survey new routes; deter Indian raids; and engage in occasional battles with hostile tribesmen. During the Civil War many of the western soldiers were called back east.

The Great Powwow

The West had never seen anything like it before. On the rich grasslands some 36 miles from Fort Laramie, at a place called Horse Creek, the greatest gathering of Indian tribes in all history was taking place in this month of September in the year 1851. By the waters of the swift-flowing stream the Sioux were meeting in peace with their ancient enemies, the Crows, while chiefs of the Arikara, Cheyenne, Assiniboine, Arapaho, and Gros Ventre tribes—as well as delegates from several others—were engaged in days of council, ceremony, and feasting. In all, some 10,000 red men

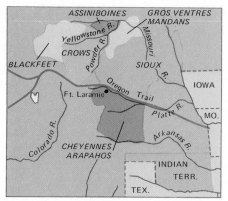

Tribes of the northern plains could travel freely over the land on both sides of the Oregon Trail until 1851, when each tribe was assigned its own area (colors above).

were gathered at the call of the Great Father and his representatives, Thomas Fitzpatrick and Col. David D. Mitchell, to make a permanent peace among the tribes and to agree formally to the free passage of the white man's wagon trains across their hunting grounds.

In the wake of the California gold strikes of 1848 the whites had left little but devastation, shooting thousands of buffalo and forcing the Plains tribes to wander farther and farther from their accustomed hunting grounds to track down the great beasts so necessary to their way of life. Despite this, the Indians had so far tolerated the white man's passage. "I have no reason to complain of the Indians," wrote government agent Fitzpatrick late in 1850, but the former mountain man expressed fears for the future if the tribes were driven to desperation by the passage of an increasing number of migrants through their territories. "What then will be the consequences should twenty thousand Indians

Agent Thomas Fitzpatrick had been a trapper with William Ashley and a co-owner later of the Rocky Mountain Fur Company.

well armed, well mounted, and the most . . . expert in war . . . turn out in hostile array against all American travellers?" wrote Fitzpatrick to his superiors. To forestall this dreadful possibility, he suggested that the government pay the Indians an annuity to compensate them for their losses.

The great powwow had been called primarily to set the amount of the compensation and to establish terms for payment. At first it seemed that the results could not have been better.

On September 8 Colonel Mitchell addressed the assembled tribesmen and expressed the position of the Great Father, who, he said, was "aware that your buffalo and game are driven off, and your grass and timber consumed by the

opening of roads and the passing of emigrants through your countries. For these losses he desires to compensate you." Then Mitchell went on to describe the government's terms for its beneficence. Each tribe must elect a primary chief to negotiate with the others and with the whites. The territory of the Great Plains would then be divided among the tribes, each one hunting only within its assigned area and each responsible for disciplining those who broke the peace. In exchange for these agreements the government would distribute $50,000 worth of supplies each year among the tribes for a period of 50 years. A crucial provision of the treaty—and one which eventually led to disaster, since it created a permanent white presence—allowed the government to build roads and forts in the Indian country.

It is unlikely that the tribal representatives understood the full consequences of the government's demands, which signified nothing less than a revolution in the Plains Indians' way of life. No longer would they be permitted to range far and freely, riding with the wind, to pursue the buffalo and one another. Instead, the tribes would be hemmed into specific areas, thus making it possible for the government to force piecemeal land cessions when it chose without arousing tribesmen in other areas. The Indians would be forced to subsist on government handouts or, at best, become farmers. For days after Mitchell's speech the tribal chiefs rose in turn to address themselves to his demands. In the end, all agreed to the government's terms, and on September 17 a primary chief from each tribe made his mark upon the treaty that the whites had drawn up.

White traders such as this one, decked out in a suit and top hat and sitting on a pile of trade goods, moved up the Missouri River as the Army built its forts in Indian country.

The Indian Agent

Lawrence Taliaferro, here over seventy, headed St. Peter's Agency, Minnesota.

An additional task for an agent was escorting Indians to Washington, D.C. Here agent Joseph R. Brown (at the far left), Sioux delegates, and officials meet to discuss an 1858 treaty.

The only important civilian official most Indians ever saw was the Indian agent, whose post was created in President Washington's day. Twelve agencies were set up in 1834 and put under the Department of the Interior in 1849. The agent provided the federal government with what little it asked to know about Indians and represented the Great White Father out in the wilds. Often, with only his wife, a subagent, and an interpreter to help him, a representative had to handle Indian relations over hundreds of square miles and also aid any whites passing through. A good agent would recruit a farmer and teacher, and his outpost would become a dot of civiliza-tion in the wilderness: log homes and an office; warehouses, a smithy, and farm buildings; a school and council houses; corn and potato fields; orchards and farm animals. He had to journey far among the tribes for powwows and entertain all Indians who came to the agency for talks. He won tribal friendships by giving the chiefs medals, flags, and supplies, feeding their people in times of need, and sending presents to their families when they died. He tried—usually in vain—to keep white poachers from encroaching on Indian lands and white traders from selling liquor to Indians. Equally unsuccessful was his attempt to vaccinate the Indians and teach them farming (they resisted both). He fined any foreigner found trading furs without a permit and tried to punish Indians who harmed whites. He also took a census, enforced the stipulations of U.S.-Indian treaties, and distributed annuities to the tribes. Unfortunately, most agents were dishonest, arranging for kickbacks from traders and pocketing annuity money, but a few were incorruptible. Lawrence Taliaferro spent more than $1,000 of his own to buy supplies for the tribes. After he retired, Sioux chiefs visited him, and Little Crow said: "My old Father, we love . . . you; we respect you. . . . Since you left us a dark cloud has hung over our nation. . . . We know your heart."

Although many looked upon the negotiations at Horse Creek as the dawning of a new age of harmony on the plains, the agreement was actually doomed from its inception. Congress immediately reduced the number of years the promised stipend would be paid, and those supplies that were delivered hardly began to compensate the Indians for all they had lost. The tribes were forced to continue far-ranging hunting expeditions that put them in sharp contention with one another for the dwindling supply of game. By 1853 Tom Fitzpatrick was deploring the Indians' plight. They were, he wrote, "in abject want of food half the year. . . . The travel upon the road drives [the buffalo] off or else confines them to a narrow path during the period of emi-gration, and the different tribes are forced to contend with hostile nations. . . . Their women are pinched with want and their children constantly crying with hunger."

A Clash on the Oregon Trail

Clearly, such a situation was bound to produce a clash between red men and white, and in 1854 a minor incident set off this tinderbox. An emigrant moving west along the Oregon Trail either abandoned or lost a lame cow that a young Sioux warrior found and butchered. Hearing of this, the owner demanded that the Sioux pay him $25 for his loss—an amount the Indians tried to shave down to $10. At this time a young lieutenant named John L. Grattan was stationed at Fort Laramie. Eager for glory and disdainful of the Indians, Grattan had once boasted that he could clear the plains of red men almost singlehandedly. The incident of the cow gave him a chance to make good his boast, and he persuaded his commanding officer to let him lead a heavily armed detachment of 30 troopers to the Sioux camp to arrest the offending Indian. When the Sioux refused to cooperate, Grattan suddenly opened fire, mortally wounding their chief. Enraged, the warriors leaped to battle; within just minutes they surrounded the entire white force and killed every man.

With this one incident the peace of the plains was broken. But before the full fury of the whites could be loosed, the U.S. Civil War intervened to give the red men a last respite.

Kansas: Prelude to Civil War

On a broiling hot day in August 1854 two parties of pioneers, wearing expressions of burning hatred, faced each other across a short stretch of prairie in Kansas. For here, on the banks of the Kaw, the two bands were enacting the prologue to a tragedy that the nation would know as Bleeding Kansas.

One party was made up of Missourians who had come west from their home state to claim the newly opened territory for the cause of slavery. They had been encamped beside the Kaw for several days when the second group arrived. These were northerners, financed by the antislavery New England Emigrant Aid Company, and they had traveled all the way from their rocky homeland to claim Kansas for free soil, free labor, and free men. Certain of their righteousness, they, like their foes, were prepared to shed their own and others' blood.

That day ended in an anticlimax: the two groups exchanged threats but not gunfire. Yet over the next six years Kansas would know little peace, as proslavery and free-state forces fought it out for control of the territory.

Only a few months earlier, most of Kansas had been part of the unorganized territory. Then Congress, after furious debate, passed the Kansas-Nebraska Act, dividing the region into two territories: Kansas in the south and Nebraska in the north. The act was based on a new compromise over the extension of slavery—one that specifically repealed the old Missouri Compromise, which had opened the state of Missouri to slavery but banned it in territories north of the 36°30′ line and east of the Rockies. Under the terms of the act residents of the two territories were to decide for themselves to admit or forbid slavery.

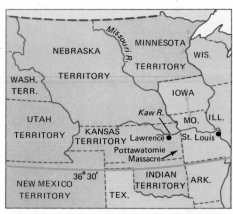

An 1854 law that allowed new territories north of the 36°30′ line to choose slavery caused great violence throughout Kansas.

In the South the Kansas-Nebraska Act was met with great rejoicing, for new territories might be opened for slavery. In the North the reaction was one of widespread revulsion and renewed determination that slavery should not extend its sway across the grasslands. Illinois Democratic Senator Stephen A. Douglas, chief sponsor of the Kansas-Nebraska Act, was heard to remark sadly that he could find his way home from Washington by the light of his burning effigies.

Out in the senator's home region, the Midwest, the act sparked the formation of a new political grouping, the Republican Party, made up mainly of so-called Conscience Whigs and Free-Soil Democrats, who were determined to reverse

Proslavery settlers and border ruffians from Missouri march on Lawrence, Kansas, the center of the free-stater forces. They took the town on May 21, 1856, destroyed the presses of two newspapers, broke into stores and houses, and wound up by burning the Free State Hotel and the home of Charles Robinson, elected governor of Kansas by the free-staters.

Proslavery forces ferry a contingent of Missouri voters across into Kansas to stuff the ballot boxes. There were more votes in the election than residents.

Missouri border ruffians stand in line at the polls; after casting their votes, they line up at the free-whisky booth.

When the ardent Lawrence free-stater Dr. John Day (seated) was seized and held in the St. Joseph, Missouri, jail in 1859, this group of heavily armed men came to rescue him.

the Kansas-Nebraska policy and bar slavery forever from the territories. (Among those who soon joined the new party was a rising Illinois lawyer and politician, Abraham Lincoln.) Meanwhile, in sternly antislavery New England, clergymen, teachers, lecturers, and writers raised money to finance right-thinking emigrants to Kansas to swell the rolls for freedom.

Thus the stage was set in the West for the first direct confrontation between North and South and their two ways of life. In Missouri the fire-eating proslavery senator David Atchison took up

the challenge and urged his constituents to "send five hundred of your young men [into Kansas] who will vote in favor of your institutions." Having issued this invitation to stuff ballot boxes, Atchison himself led a gang of Missouri rowdies into Kansas in November 1854 to vote in the first territorial election and carry the day for a proslavery delegate to Congress. But already scores of northerners, most of them from the Old Northwest, were heading west, ready to match the Missouri "border ruffians" ballot for ballot, blow for blow, and bullet for bullet.

Most of the pioneers who flocked to Kansas between 1854 and 1860, however, were more interested in securing good land than in the politics of slavery. But inevitably they too would be forced to declare their allegiance to one side or the other—if only for protection. As the split between the two groups widened, each tried to claim all of Kansas for its own—conducting separate elections for territorial legislatures and constitutions and appealing to Washington for recognition. Governors sent to Kansas by two successive Democratic administrations generally tried, without success, to hold free and fair elections, but they were rewarded by rebukes from Presidents Franklin Pierce and James Buchanan—both of them northerners with southern principles.

Increasingly, political confrontation was accompanied by bloodshed and terror, and on May 21, 1856, Kansas was catapulted toward virtual anarchy when some 800 proslavers swooped down on the antislavery center of Lawrence for an afternoon of looting and burning. Reaction was swift and awful. On May 24 fanatical John Brown led six of his followers to a proslavery settlement at Pottawatomie Creek and then watched with grim satisfaction as his men hacked five of the residents to death.

A Fanatic With a Mission

John Brown (1800-59) had long burned with a zeal to free all slaves and while living in Pennsylvania had served as an agent for the Underground Railroad, which spirited slaves out of the South. In 1849 Brown settled in a Negro community in New York; then two years later, although living in Ohio, he found time to help Negroes in Massachusetts organize a League of Gileadites to protect fugitive slaves. During those years Brown eschewed violence, but in 1855 he followed five of his sons to Kansas where proslavery and free-state settlers were poised for combat. News of the sacking of Lawrence on May 21, 1856, aroused Brown to demonic fury. The result was the massacre of five proslavery Missouri settlers at Pottawatomie Creek; and when Brown's foes marched on him, he clashed with them at Black Jack, killing 4 and capturing 25. Settlers retaliated by capturing two of Brown's sons, pillaging the settlement of Osawatomie, where Brown lived, and murdering his son Frederick.

John Brown

Wealthy supporters give arms and gold to Brown.

In 1858, as the violence in Kansas cooled, Brown made a raid into Missouri to liberate slaves. This foray may have served as a rehearsal of a plan he had earlier revealed at a meeting in Canada, a plan to start a slave insurrection in the South. On October 16, 1859, Brown and 21 men seized the federal arsenal and fire-engine house at Harpers Ferry, Virginia, but no slaves rallied to them. Within a day a company of marines led by Col. Robert E. Lee arrived and drove

Brown's men into the fire-engine house. All the men were killed (including two of Brown's sons) or captured. Brown was tried for treason, convicted, and sentenced to death. But before he was hanged on December 2, 1859, he wrote a message to the country: "I, John Brown, am now quite certain that the crimes of this guilty land will never be purged away but with blood. I had, as I now think, vainly flattered myself that without much bloodshed it might be done."

Abraham Lincoln: A Westerner in the White House

Sarah Bush Lincoln, Abe's step-mother, was a fine, strong-minded woman who insisted that he was going to be somebody. She encouraged him to read and write at home and demanded that Tom Lincoln not interfere with Abe's studying. After he was elected president, he visited Sarah; she cried and said, rightly, she was certain that she would never see him again.

maturity. Between 1847 and 1849 Lincoln served one term as a representative in Congress, where he followed the Whig line, denouncing the Mexican War as unnecessary and unconstitutional. His stand was unpopular back home, and he did not seek reelection. When his term ended, he failed to obtain an appointment he sought as commissioner of the General Land Office and then declined the post of secretary of the Oregon Territory. He returned to his law practice in Springfield, feeling that his political career was at an end.

As a lawyer, Lincoln spent much of his time bouncing over rough roads in his buggy, riding the circuit to the 14 county seats where the judge held court. Life was hard, but he enjoyed the companionship of lawyers, swapping stories spiced with rough western humor and matching wits with them in the courtroom. One veteran of numerous legal skirmishes with Lincoln said later that Lincoln was "harmless as a dove and wise as a serpent."

In 1854 the passage by Congress of the Kansas-Nebraska Act, which opened to slavery territory that previously had

Abe was a good railsplitter, but he preferred reading. "My father," he once said, "taught me to work but not to love it."

Late in 1858, when Abraham Lincoln's friends urged him to run for president, he had a short answer, "Only events can make a president." An inexorable chain of events was to propel Lincoln to the presidency; and when his election brought about secession in the South, he took his oath of office as president of a nation no longer united. In leading the country to victory in the Civil War and erasing the blot of slavery, this man of the West became a towering figure of strength and compassion, revered throughout the world.

Born on February 12, 1809, young Abe Lincoln grew up on a succession of hardscrabble farms, and his childhood was scarred in 1818 by the death of his mother. But the next year Tom Lincoln married the widowed Sarah Bush Johnston, and she gave love and understanding to the sensitive boy.

After the family moved again in 1830 to Illinois, the 22-year-old Lincoln went off on his own. Settling in New Salem (population 100), he had a succession of occupations: he managed a store and mill, served as a captain of volunteers in the Black Hawk War, ran unsuccessfully for a seat in the legislature in 1832, was joint owner of a store that soon failed, and served as postmaster and deputy surveyor. He read law books in every spare moment and in 1834 won the first of four terms in the Illinois Legislature. In March 1837 he was admitted to the bar, and the next month he moved to Springfield as the law partner of John T. Stuart.

On November 4, 1842, after a tempestuous courtship, he married Mary Todd, who was from a wealthy Kentucky family. They had four sons; only one (Robert Todd) lived to

Lincoln's Congress and the West

HOMESTEAD ACT (1862) granted a citizen the right to settle on 160 acres of unoccupied public land; he would own his grant after living on it for five continuous years.

MORRILL LAND GRANT ACT (1862) gave to the states and territories public lands, whose sale would finance the building of agricultural and mechanical arts colleges in every state—the start of the land grant colleges.

PACIFIC RAILROAD ACTS (1862 and 1864) provided land grants and loan bonds to make possible the building of the first transcontinental railroad.

This quaint hooked rug, completed in 1865, commemorates a top-hatted, bearded Abraham Lincoln, sitting at the right.

volunteers, proclaimed a blockade of the South, and suspended the writ of habeas corpus.

Despite pressure for action by Radical Republicans in Congress, Lincoln feared that an attack on slavery would cause the strategically important border slave states, particularly Kentucky and Missouri, to leave the Union. At last, he concluded that emancipation was necessary to win Negro support and influence world opinion. The final Emancipation Proclamation of January 1, 1863, freed slaves only in areas still in rebellion. But it was a promise for the future that changed the war for the Union into a war for freedom.

At Gettysburg on November 19, 1863, Lincoln delivered one of the world's great addresses, seeking to rally his countrymen to the unfinished work of the men who died there. But the bloody stalemate in Virginia in 1864 brought on a war weariness that made Lincoln doubt he would be reelected. However, the strategy of Gen. Ulysses S. Grant, supreme commander of the armies that sent Sherman smashing into Atlanta and Sheridan sweeping the Shenandoah Valley, helped give Lincoln victory over the Democratic candidate, Gen. George B. McClellan.

On Inauguration Day, March 4, 1865, the armies of the Union were poised to crush the South, and Lincoln looked ahead to a healing peace, asking the people to act "with malice toward none, with charity for all." But he did not live to work for such a peace. On April 14, five days after Gen. Robert E. Lee's army had surrendered, Lincoln was wounded by a gunshot fired at Ford's Theatre by actor John Wilkes Booth. When Lincoln died the next morning, his secretary of war, Edwin M. Stanton, who had once called him the original gorilla, said: "Now he belongs to the ages."

been free, brought Lincoln back into politics with both feet. Speaking for westerners and for those who hoped to move to new lands in the West, Lincoln said: "We want them [the territories] for homes of free white people. This they cannot be, to any considerable extent, if slavery shall be planted within them." In 1856 Lincoln finally left the Whigs and joined the new Republican Party, campaigning hard for its losing presidential candidate, John C. Frémont.

In 1858 Lincoln received the Illinois Republican nomination to oppose Senator Stephen A. Douglas, author of the Kansas-Nebraska Act, for a seat in the U.S. Senate. In accepting the nomination, Lincoln grimly declared: " 'A house divided against itself cannot stand.' I believe this government cannot endure, permanently half *slave* and half *free*." When Lincoln and Douglas hit the campaign trail to elect legislators who would support them for the Senate seat (Americans did not vote directly for senators until 1913), Douglas accepted Lincoln's challenge to debate him seven times. The debates attracted wide attention, and although Douglas won the Senate seat, Lincoln gained a national following. He became a much-sought-after speaker, and his moderate views on slavery won him the Republican presidential nomination in 1860.

Election to the Presidency

On election day Lincoln got less than 40 percent of the popular vote, but he won 17 states outright, and his total electoral vote of 180 was much greater than that of the other candidates: Douglas for the Northern Democrats, John C. Breckinridge for the Southern Democrats, and John Bell for the Constitutional Union Party.

Secessionist leaders had warned that the election of a "Black Republican" would destroy the Union, and before Lincoln's inauguration on March 4, 1861, seven states had seceded to form the Confederacy. In his inaugural address Lincoln told the South: "You have no oath registered in Heaven to destroy the government, while I shall have the most solemn one to 'preserve, protect, and defend' it." But southerners were not listening, and when Lincoln sought to send supplies to federal troops at Fort Sumter in Charleston, siege guns boomed and the Civil War began. Even before Congress met in special session on July 4, Lincoln called for

Senator Stephen A. Douglas, five feet tall and known as the Little Giant, opposed the six-foot-four Lincoln in a memorable series of debates that were conducted in Illinois in 1858.

The Civil War in the Midwest

With a whoop and a holler and innumerable torchlight processions, the Old Northwest went to the polls in November 1860 to cast its lot with the Republican Party and its presidential candidate, Abraham Lincoln. The ties of commerce and blood that had once joined the region to the South were frayed and torn. Railroads, displacing the Mississippi River trade, linked centers of the Midwest with eastern markets, and floods of immigrants from Europe—mainly Irish and German—strengthened the antislavery sentiment that New Englanders had previously brought to the West.

Even before Lincoln's inauguration, seven states (South Carolina, Mississippi, Florida, Alabama, Louisiana, Georgia, and Texas) had passed ordinances of secession and formed the Confederate States of America. Despite the conciliatory words of the new president's inaugural speech on March 4, 1861, South Carolina forces fired on Fort Sumter in Charleston on April 12, and Lincoln called for volunteers to crush the insurrection. This brought Virginia, North Carolina, Tennessee, and Arkansas into the Confederate fold, while Maryland, Kentucky, and Missouri teetered on the brink of secession.

In Missouri the threat to the Union was particularly acute. The state's prosouthern governor, Claiborne F. Jackson, was backed by rural and smalltown folk, mostly from western and southern Missouri. But in St. Louis and the surrounding areas, where German influence was strong, sentiment was overwhelmingly pro-Union. Within just months of Lincoln's election rival militias had formed, and into this explosive situation stepped Nathaniel Lyon, Union Army captain and stern abolitionist, who had been assigned to the federal arsenal in St. Louis in February 1861.

As the war approached, Lyon urged that immediate measures be taken to prevent the seizure of the arsenal by Jackson's state militia. But Lyon's prosouthern superior, Gen. William S. Harney, refused to act—even after Jackson had responded to Lincoln's request for volunteers with an outright call for insurrection. By early May the ranks of prosouthern militiamen camped out-

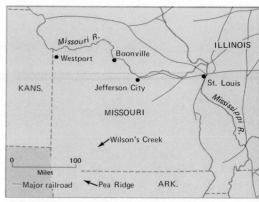

Nathaniel Lyon kept the important transport hubs of St. Louis and Jefferson City pro-Union, but most of Missouri became a no-man's-land of pro- and anti-slavers.

side St. Louis had swollen, and the threat to the city had grown acute. Luckily for the Union, however, General Harney was called away and the young captain was left in charge.

On May 10 Lyon struck. With four regiments of mostly German volunteers and one battalion of Army Regulars, he marched on the rebel encampment and easily secured its surrender. Then, in triumph, Lyon paraded his thousand prisoners through the streets of St. Louis—an act that enraged the city's secessionist minority. Rampage and riot followed the line of march, shots rang out, and before the day ended 28 citizens were dead and scores more wounded. But St. Louis, near the vital confluence of the Mississippi and Missouri Rivers, remained in Union hands.

The battle for Missouri, however, was hardly over. Governor Jackson, playing for time, now requested an interview with Lyon, who had just been promoted to brigadier general. During their meeting in St. Louis, Jackson ill-advisedly tried to play the role of potentate. If Lyon

Missourians led by Gen. Sterling Price, his arm in a sling, are beaten by Samuel Curtis' federal forces at Pea Ridge on March 8, 1862. The victory kept Missouri in the Union.

The day after suffering a setback at Big Blue (above) on October 22, 1864, federal forces were victorious at Westport, ending the South's attempts to invade Missouri.

The Cherokees and General Watie

The Cherokees were one of the Five Civilized Tribes who were forced to move to Indian Territory in the 1830's. When the Civil War began, they tried to stay clear of the whites' family quarrel. Pressured to take sides, however, they finally signed an alliance with the Confederacy in 1861, and one of their leaders, Stand Watie, became colonel of the Cherokee Mounted Rifles in the Confeder- ate Army. His command fought at Wilson's Creek, Pea Ridge, and in many skirmishes in Indian Territory. When the majority of the Cherokees rejected the Confederate treaty in 1863, Watie led the prosouthern minority and remained in the army, becoming the first Indian brigadier general. He did not surrender until June 23, 1865, more than two months after Lee's men laid down their arms.

Quantrill: The Bloodiest Guerrilla Leader

Ohio-born schoolteacher William C. Quantrill (1837–65) left the classroom in 1857 for a career as a gambler and horse thief. Getting a taste of violence in the Kansas-Missouri border warfare and liking it, Quantrill organized a pro-southern guerrilla band when the Civil War broke out. After several forays in Missouri, Quantrill was commissioned a captain by the Confederacy.

In the summer of 1863, at the peak of his power and notoriety, Quantrill led 450 men against Lawrence, in Kansas, long hated by Missourians as the hotbed of abolitionism and the center for pro-Union guerrillas known as Red Legs. Quantrill hit Lawrence early in the morning of August 21, killed at least 150 men, and destroyed property worth about $1.5 million.

Fully a match for Quantrill in sav-

William C. Quantrill

After talking to survivors, Sherman Enderton, a Kansas soldier, made this sketch of Quantrill's guerrillas pillaging Lawrence, in Kansas, on August 21, 1863.

agery were his two lieutenants: "Bloody Bill" Anderson (who fastened scalps to his horse's bridle) and George Todd. And there were three young men getting training for a life of outlawry: Frank and Jesse James and Cole Younger.

By wearing captured federal uniforms, Quantrill's men surprised their enemies, as at Baxter Springs, Kansas, where 65 out of 100 federal soldiers were killed. Early in 1865 Quantrill led a band into Kentucky, reportedly planning to go to Washington to assassinate Lincoln. On May 10, 1865, Quantrill was mortally wounded by Union guerrillas near Louisville, Kentucky.

---

would call off his troops, the governor vowed to proclaim Missouri neutral in the Civil War. At this, the outraged Lyon exploded: "Rather than concede to the State of Missouri . . . the right to dictate to my Government . . . I will see you . . . and every man, woman, and child in the State, dead and buried." As the governor prepared his departure, Lyon declared: "This means war!"

Lyon's Campaign

In early June, Nathaniel Lyon began his campaign to secure all of Missouri for the Union. With his own small garrison of Regulars reinforced by St. Louis Germans, he pushed up the Missouri River toward the state capital of Jefferson City. On the 15th the town fell without resistance, its defenders having fled to regroup and prepare themselves for battle. Lyon then moved on to Boonville, where, joined by volunteer Iowa farm boys, he routed elements of the state militia, who fled toward Arkansas and linked up with strong reinforcements moving north. With more daring than good sense, Lyon pursued the swelling southern force, and on August 10, 1861, the two armies—more than 10,000 Confederates and 5,400 Unionists—met at Wilson's Creek.

Ignoring the odds against him, Lyon attacked, and when the fighting was at its most brutal, he was killed. The bullet that stopped him also seemed to take the steam out of his successor, Maj. Samuel

Sturgis, who ordered a retreat. The victorious Confederates, however, did not follow up their advantage. Federal reinforcements arrived, and most of Missouri remained officially in Union hands. The following spring, after a victory over 16,000 Confederates at Pea Ridge on the Arkansas side of the border, Union forces fanned out into Arkansas and then smashed into the Indian Territory.

But the Union's hold on much of the region between the Mississippi and the Rockies remained tenuous. A virtual no-man's-land came into existence in southern and western Missouri, eastern Kansas, and northern Arkansas, where partisan detachments—some little more than outlaw bands—roamed free, subjecting the countryside and its residents to orgies of arson, looting, murder, and torture. It was Bleeding Kansas again but on a much larger scale. Within this zone of terror neither man nor woman, soldier nor civilian, Free Soiler nor slaveholder would be safe as long as the Civil War continued.

After Quantrill's bloody raid on Lawrence, Gen. Thomas Ewing ordered the forcible removal of civilians from the border district on the grounds that they were aiding guerrillas.

The Civil War in the Far West

While Union and Confederate forces contended for the Midwest, a new front was opening farther west in the New Mexico Territory. After the first triumphs of southern arms at Fort Sumter and Bull Run in the spring and summer of 1861, anything seemed possible to the confident Confederates—even the occupation of much of the vast territory the United States had secured in the Mexican War. Texas, since early March a part of the Confederacy, was the South's salient in the Far West, the jumping-off point for the rich mines of Colorado and the lush valleys of California. And in the thousands of southern pioneers who had surged into the West in search of gold and silver, Dixie had a potential subversive force to undermine an already weak Union authority—a force that might become a guerrilla army.

Even before the formal secession of the South, prosouthern feeling had been especially strong in the New Mexico Territory, and in March 1861 a group of settlers had met in the village of Mesilla to declare themselves and the southwestern portion of the New Mexico Territory (which they called Arizona) a part of the Confederate States of America. If these sentiments caught fire throughout the mountain region, then a bold sweep from Texas by an army of southern volunteers might well bring all the Far West to the side of the South, providing it with more than enough gold and silver to finance the war, plenty of room for slavery's extension, and an outlet on the Pacific Ocean.

The South Moves West

First, however, the secessionists had to complete their control of Texas. This task was immeasurably eased by the prosouthern sympathies of the highest Union officer in Texas, Maj. Gen. David E. Twiggs. In the weeks before Sumter, Twiggs evacuated federal outposts in response to secessionist de-

This drawing of Confederate soldiers with captured Union equipment near Camp Clark, Texas, in March 1861 was made by Carl von Iwonski, whose family came to Texas in 1845.

mands, and Texas eased into the Confederacy without a shot being fired.

The threat posed by a Texas allied with the South took on ominous proportions in the wake of two events. Throughout the spring of 1861 the federal government in Washington, fighting for its very existence, ordered the abandonment of one far western outpost after another so that the troops might be used in the war's crucial battles in the East. Only tiny Regular detachments were left behind in a scattering of forts to guard and secure the entire far western frontier. Sensing an unparalleled opportunity, Confederate Col. John R. Baylor

raised a 250-man army of Texas volunteers. In July 1861 he moved northwest from San Antonio into the New Mexico Territory to strike at Fort Fillmore, across the border from El Paso. On paper this seemed a dubious maneuver, for the fort had a 700-man garrison. But luck was with the South: at the approach of the Confederates, the Union commander panicked and ordered the evacuation of his post. His stupidity was compounded by the actions of his troops, who filled their canteens with liquor instead of water. By the time the hard-riding Texans caught up with the fleeing soldiers, the Unionists were reduced to a

A badge identified Capt. D. C. Carrington of the 2nd Regiment of Texas Mounted Rifles.

These men are members of the 8th Texas Cavalry, which fought for the Confederacy in the East, while other units, most notably the Frontier Regiment, fended off Indian raiders.

The destruction of a bridge by Confederate forces in Apache Canyon in New Mexico Territory on March 26, 1862, did not stop the headlong charge of Capt. Samuel Cook's dashing company of Colorado Volunteers, who had come to the assistance of Col. Edward Canby.

drunken rabble clamoring for surrender.

Now only Fort Union, in northeastern New Mexico, stood between the Confederates and their ambitions for far western conquest. Aware of the peril that threatened this key outpost, Col. Edward R. S. Canby, the Union commander at the fort, detached a portion of his men to reoccupy the abandoned Fort Craig, which was on the Rio Grande along the Confederate line of advance. By then, however, Baylor's volunteers had themselves been massively reinforced by some 3,000 troops under Gen. Henry Hopkins Sibley. On February 21, 1862, Sibley's force met and defeated the Fort Craig garrison at Valverde. The Union survivors under Canby fled to the shelter of the fort, five miles from the battlefield, whereupon Sibley made a mistake he would have cause to regret. The fort appeared to be bristling with cannon (many of which were actually painted logs), and he decided not to risk a siege but to continue his advance on Fort Union, the key to both Colorado and the Southwest. In March, Sibley managed to occupy both Albuquerque and Santa Fe. Meanwhile, Canby had been given precious breathing space in which to rally reinforcements to defend Fort Union.

Coloradans to the Rescue

Like most of the Far West, the newly organized Colorado Territory was split by the sectional loyalties of its recently arrived residents. In the booming mining settlement of Denver secessionist feeling was especially strong among a group of young layabouts derisively called bummers, who responded to the orders of a disreputable saloonkeeper and gambler, Charley Harrison.

At the end of May 1861 the first territorial governor of Colorado, William Gilpin—a no-nonsense man with both wilderness and military experience—arrived in Denver. Gilpin immediately began organizing a pro-Union regiment of volunteers, the so-called Pike's Peakers, which was ready for a test within a few weeks: cleaning out the bummers. Appropriately, hostilities began in a bawdy house—where an exchange of insults between bummers and Pike's Peakers led to flying fists and flashing knives—and ended in Harrison's Criterion Saloon.

With the bummers disposed of and Denver pacified, Gilpin's volunteers, now some 1,300 strong, were ready in early 1862 to help Canby, who was marching north from Fort Craig to meet the Confederate threat to Fort Union. On March 26 and 28 the two forces clashed at both Apache Canyon and Glorieta Pass, south of the fort. During the second encounter a Union major and Methodist clergyman named John M. Chivington led a daring raid on Sibley's supply train. He and his men destroyed 73 wagons and bayoneted the Confederates' entire herd of horses and mules. His supplies gone, Sibley began a retreat that continued into Texas. The Confederate threat to the mountain region and the Southwest was ended. But a new threat, this time from Indians, was about to become acute.

Col. John R. Baylor secretly recruited men to form the Texas Mounted Rifles and spearheaded the invasion of New Mexico.

Gen. Henry Hopkins Sibley, who fought with Colonel Baylor against Union Colonel Canby, was Canby's brother-in-law.

219

Indian Wars in the Southwest

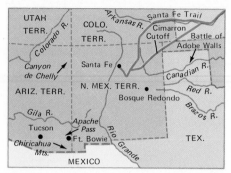

Kit Carson defeated the Navajos, forcing them into Bosque Redondo. Undefeated tribes battled Carson at Adobe Walls.

Of all the Indians in the Southwest none resisted white domination longer or more fiercely than the Navajos and the Apaches of what is now Arizona and New Mexico. The Navajos began raiding the Spaniards soon after the latter settled in the Southwest in 1598, bringing with them sheep, goats, and cattle. Spaniards and Mexicans had also had trouble for centuries attempting to tame and destroy the relatively small tribes of Apaches, made up of about three dozen autonomous bands. For their pains the whites reaped a whirlwind because the Apaches survived, acquiring a reputation for barbarity and invincibility that helped keep their enemies at bay.

At first Apache-American relations were marked by mutual respect. Those few Americans who wandered into what is now southern Arizona and New Mexico during the 1850's hardly seemed a threat, and to some Apache bands they even appeared as possible allies against such hereditary enemies as the Comanches to the east and the Mexicans south of the border. Then two separate incidents set Apaches and Americans at each other's throats.

It may have been sometime in the early 1850's—accounts differ—when an old Apache chief of the Mimbreño band was seized and unmercifully whipped by a party of American miners in the south-central part of the New Mexico Territory. Presumably, they had no idea that their victim was Mangas Coloradas, a hero of countless forays against the Mexicans and a man whose influence was exceeded only by his pride. Humiliated, Mangas Coloradas swore revenge.

The second incident came early in 1861 after a band of Pinal Apaches kidnaped a young American boy. Somehow a shavetail lieutenant became convinced that the culprits were some Chiricahua Apaches under their chief, Cochise. The lieutenant promptly arrested Cochise, his wife, son, brother, and two nephews as hostages for the safe return of the young American.

Cochise quickly escaped, but his family was left behind at the mercy of the soldiers. The furious Cochise went on a rampage, captured a stage driver and two Americans from a wagon train (whose eight Mexican drovers he then promptly killed), and offered to exchange the captives for his family. The young lieutenant stupidly refused the offer, prompting Cochise to murder his prisoners. In return, the chief's brother and two nephews were hanged.

This was hardly the moment to enrage the Apaches. The Civil War was about to begin and the western forts were to be evacuated, but the damage was done. What followed was the old story of terror and counterterror—and in 1861, with the New Mexico Territory stripped of troops, the odds lay with the Chiricahuas. In two months they slashed their way through dozens of white settlements in the Arizona country and took 150 lives.

The murders and wild rumors that followed threatened American domination of the Arizona country, as settlers hastily packed their belongings and fled to safer regions. Nor were the Apaches the only ones contending for the area. Early in the Civil War, Confederate volunteers from Texas stormed into Arizona to be welcomed by a generally prosouthern white populace. The Union responded in 1862 by sending 1,800 Californians eastward to reclaim the desert for the federal cause. By that time Cochise was allied with Mangas Coloradas, and in July the two chiefs, with 700 of their warriors, ambushed a contingent of Union soldiers in Apache Pass. The red men, however, were quickly repulsed by savage bursts from two mountain howitzers, and from this engagement Cochise learned a most valuable lesson—never to confront well-armed soldiers in open combat.

Pete Kitchen and Thomas Jeffords

Thus began a merciless guerrilla war in which every bush and rock seemed to conceal a lurking Apache. Soon the Gila River country of southern Arizona was swept clean of ranchers—all except one, the indomitable Pete Kitchen. He turned his hilltop adobe ranch house into what amounted to a fortress and dealt out such punishment to Apache raiders that they finally let him alone.

Another man in Arizona solved the Apache problem not by fighting but by talking. He was Thomas Jeffords, a six-foot New Yorker with a flaming red beard. Jeffords was superintendent of mail between Fort Bowie and Tucson. After losing 14 mail drivers in 16 months, he decided to act. Jeffords rode alone to Cochise's mountain stronghold, and the Apaches were so startled by this foolhardy stranger that they did not kill him. In the middle of their encampment Jeffords shed his rifle and six-shooter and declared his desire to speak to Cochise. When the two met, Cochise, a man of courage, recognized a kindred spirit. The men became firm friends—Jeffords remained in the camp for two days—and the Apaches never again attacked one of Jeffords' drivers.

But the war against the army and

Apache raiders head back to their hideout with a captive white girl in this painting by Harold von Schmidt. One Indian is wearing a jacket, probably stripped from a dead soldier.

A punitive expedition led by Col. Kit Carson in 1864 ran into a large force of Kiowas and Comanches at Adobe Walls in Texas. The Carson force was saved by two howitzers.

ended—or so it seemed. It would erupt again some years later, however, under another Chiricahua chief, the great Geronimo. Cochise lived out his remaining days in peace, dying on June 8, 1874, with Jeffords by his side.

For decades two of the fiercest tribes in the Southwest, the Comanches and the Kiowas, had been allies in fights against both tribal enemies and white settlers. During the Civil War hostilities between these tribes and the whites intensified. The situation reached a climax while the Army was grappling with Cochise in Arizona in 1864; Kiowa and Comanche raiders attacked a civilian wagon train on the Santa Fe Trail and took five small boys hostage. Retribution was swift: Kit Carson, then a Union Army officer, took off in pursuit of the raiders with some 350 volunteers and about 75 Ute scouts. At Adobe Walls, an abandoned trading post in the Texas Panhandle near the Canadian River, some 1,000 Comanches and Kiowas waited. But the Indians' superior numbers were offset by the Union's artillery, and the volunteers made an orderly retreat after burning down a Kiowa village as a parting gesture.

Carson, with 2 dead and 10 wounded, claimed victory, but he later admitted he was lucky to have gotten his men out of the Canadian River valley. One of the Kiowas at the Adobe Walls fight was Satanta, who would be heard from again.

other whites continued. For Mangas Coloradas there would, however, soon be peace of a sort. Weary of battle and certain of eventual defeat, he went to Gen. Joseph West in 1863 to seek peace, only to be brutally murdered at West's behest. After this atrocity Cochise's war parties redoubled their efforts; yet, even at the height of his fame, Cochise yearned for peace. Although he knew that the odds against him were too great, as long as the official policy dictated extermination, Cochise had no choice but to fight on.

A change was coming however. After a massacre in 1871 of 128 unarmed Apaches by a mob of Arizonans, eastern humanitarians applied pressure on the government to stop such slaughters. Gen. George Crook was sent to Arizona with orders to deal firmly but humanely with the Apaches. The next year Gen. Oliver O. Howard arrived with full power to make peace. The intensely religious Howard won Tom Jeffords' respect, and the two men went to see Cochise in 1872. Cochise agreed to stop fighting and go on a reservation if Jeffords was appointed Indian agent for the Chiricahua Apaches. His terms were met, and a war that had cost the United States 1,000 dead and $40 million at last

Last Stand of a Warrior Tribe

Navajo raiders menaced both white settlers and the peaceful Pueblo Indians in New Mexico. Their attacks grew bolder when U.S. troops were withdrawn during the Civil War, until finally Col. Kit Carson led about 400 men against them in 1863–64. After starving them into submission by destroying their flocks and gardens, the Americans invaded the Navajos' Canyon de Chelly stronghold. Three thousand Indians were marched 300 miles to Fort Sumner, New Mexico Territory.

Navajos under guard at the Bosque Redondo Reservation at Fort Sumner. After being held for four years, they were sent to a reservation on the present-day Arizona–New Mexico border.

These Navajos are wearing fine examples of their people's weaving and silverwork.

The Minnesota Sioux Uprising

In the Civil War summer of 1862 no place in the United States seemed more remote from the troubles of the time than the agriculturally lush state of Minnesota. True, thousands of its young men had gone off to war, and along the upper Minnesota River there lived about 6,000 eastern, or Santee, Sioux on a reservation some 150 miles long and 10 miles wide. But for the past decade these Indians, who had traded their ancestral lands and freedom of movement for a government annuity, had seemed no threat to white settlers.

In the reservation's two main centers, the Lower and Upper Agencies, church spires rose toward the sky, and the missionaries congratulated themselves on the alacrity with which their charges seemed to be taking to the hoe and the Cross. Even Little Crow, a chief of the Lower Agency region, was seen in church from time to time.

Despite their outward docility, the Sioux of Minnesota had long nursed grievances against the whites, and with most of the soldiers away at the war some Indians began to think the time had come to settle old scores. Normally, in the late summer, most of the Sioux would be away on the Dakota buffalo hunting grounds, but this year the government annuity had not yet arrived, and several local merchants had refused the necessary credit to outfit the Indians for the hunt. (The merchants' action was ill-timed, for the previous year's corn-crop failure had meant near starvation for the reservation Indians.) So the Sioux remained in Minnesota, growing increasingly restless and bitter.

This painting on a barrelhead by Anton Gág shows settlers fighting from behind a barricade during an attack on New Ulm by a small band of Sioux Indians on August 19, 1862. The only white casualty was a girl who was killed when she wandered out into the street.

After failing to capture Fort Ridgely on August 22 Little Crow led an all-out attack on New Ulm the next day. The militia repulsed daylong assaults on a stone windmill and brick post office but could not keep the Sioux from burning most of the buildings in town.

It was in this atmosphere that a small group of Sioux, returning from an unsuccessful hunt on August 17, fell to arguing and boasting among themselves. One warrior insisted that he would prove he was unafraid of whites by killing some—and dared his comrades to do the same. Four Sioux from the hunting party rode up to a farm and challenged the owner and his white guests to a shooting match. After the whites had obligingly emptied their rifles at the targets, the Indians turned on their unsuspecting hosts and killed three men and two women.

That evening the four murderers returned to the reservation and reported their crime to Little Crow. An all-night council was held, some arguing that the time was never better for war, others—including Little Crow—wavering. Finally, the chief declared himself in favor

of combat, and by the early morning of August 18 scores of braves had filtered into the Lower Agency and taken up positions. On signal they struck, firing on every white they saw except for a few they regarded as friends. A hated white merchant, Andrew Myrick—who had recently dismissed some Indians' request for credit with the imperial phrase "Let them eat grass"—was found dead, his mouth stuffed with prairie grass.

About 50 whites escaped from the Lower Agency that day to sound the alarm, but the rebellion was spreading rapidly—some 400 were slaughtered by marauding Sioux on the first day of hostilities alone. Whites hurriedly made for the protection of Fort Ridgely on the north side of the Minnesota River, but the fort, garrisoned by fewer than 80 soldiers and with no stockade, seemed a minor impediment to the Indians' of-

Although starving and defrauded of annuities, the Minnesota Sioux kept the peace until a shooting contest sparked a revolt.

Twenty-three counties in southwestern Minnesota were depopulated as settlers fled. This photograph, taken by a refugee, shows exhausted families as they rest during their flight.

fensive. Indeed, after 48 of the defenders had marched out to subdue the rebellion—only to be ambushed and all but wiped out—just 30 soldiers were left to protect the 200 refugees who had arrived on August 18.

By August 20, when Little Crow finally mounted an assault on Fort Ridgely, the fort had been reinforced. Its 180 soldiers and added civilian volunteers threw back the Sioux attackers, who then turned on the town of New Ulm, attacking it in force on August 23. All day long the red men surged toward the village, but each charge was beaten back by withering fire from its hastily organized militia. By nightfall 36 whites had died and most of New Ulm was in ashes. On August 25 the survivors evacuated the town and picked their way eastward to Mankato.

Within days of the uprising white set-tlers from western Minnesota and much of the eastern Dakota Territory were fleeing in panic toward population centers like Mankato. In all, some 30,000 whites abandoned their homes and farms, and at least 800 were killed.

Soldiers to the Rescue

Toward the end of August the Minnesota officials had calmed down sufficiently to organize a militia under Col. Henry Hastings Sibley (no relation to the Confederate general). On September 23 the colonel, with 1,600 men, caught up with Little Crow's main force near Wood Lake and subdued it. Though many of the warriors escaped—including Little Crow, who was later shot down by a young farmer—Sibley managed to round up some 2,000 Sioux prisoners and release the white captives.

In Mankato 392 of the captured Indi-ans were quickly tried and 303 sentenced to death. Most Minnesotans were eager to see the convicted Indians hanged, but Episcopal Bishop Henry B. Whipple appealed to President Lincoln for mercy: "I ask," he wrote, "that the people shall lay the blame . . . where it belongs, and . . . demand the reform of an atrocious Indian system which has always garnered for us . . . anguish and blood."

Lincoln responded by commuting the sentences of those Sioux who had only fought in battle, but on December 26, 1862, 38 braves who had been convicted of rape and murder were hanged simultaneously from a common scaffold in Mankato. Although a few raids continued into the summer of 1863, the back of the uprising had been broken, but the climactic struggle between Indians and whites had barely begun.

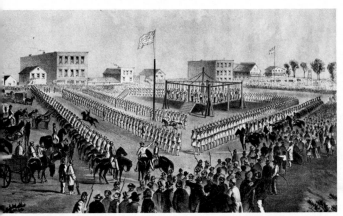

Among the 38 Sioux who were hanged in Mankato was Cut Nose, who claimed he killed whites "till his arm was tired."

After the uprising 1,700 Sioux, most of whom had not taken part, were held at Fort Snelling before being herded to a reservation in Nebraska.

Marauders and Massacre in Colorado

In the foreground Indian chiefs, headed by Black Kettle, arrive in Denver to participate in peace talks with Gov. John Evans.

Even the agony of Civil War could not halt the tide of westward expansion. Prospectors flooded into the mining country of present-day Colorado, Nevada, Arizona, Wyoming, and Montana, with would-be ranchers, townsite speculators, and numerous draft dodgers hot on their heels. In the rush of whites to secure a piece of the bonanza, Indian rights were once again trampled on, and many territories long reserved for the nomadic tribesmen were utterly denuded of buffalo. That this was often done in violation of solemn agreements between the United States and the tribes was of little concern to hunters or prospectors; most of them saw the Indians as a savage people whose disappearance would be a blessing.

The consequences of the federal government's inability or unwillingness to halt depredations against the tribes were completely predictable. The red men, pressed by hunger and fearful of losing what remained of their lands, would certainly fight to retain a hold on their heritage, and the whites were equally certain to retaliate. Even before the Civil War the moderate chiefs had begun to lose their influence as younger, more militant leaders urged resistance to the influx of whites. After the war started and hundreds of veteran troops were removed from the western forts, the High Plains and mountain regions became a tempting target for tribesmen anxious to reclaim their lands. Meanwhile, efforts of Confederate agents to rouse the Indians to rebellion may well have added fuel to the smoldering fire.

In any event, the Civil War marked the beginning of the last and bloodiest Indian resistance to white settlement and exploitation of the Far West. It was a war of episodes—of small, uncoordinated but often incredibly brutal engagements—and it would not end until the tribes were utterly broken.

The initial spread of the mining frontier into the Colorado country shortly before the Civil War met with little resistance from the region's major tribes, the Arapahos and southern Cheyennes. But as more and more prospectors swarmed onto the tribal lands (in 1859 alone more than 50,000), the Indians became suspicious and resentful. In 1861 the government induced several Cheyenne and Arapaho chiefs to sign away most of their tribes' hunting grounds in return for a small reservation in eastern Colorado—a pact that so infuriated the younger war leaders that the chiefs were forced to repudiate it.

Col. John M. Chivington was characterized by a contemporary as "a crazy preacher who thinks he is Napoleon Bonaparte."

The Isolation of Denver

Thus, tensions were already running high in 1863 when a band of Cheyenne warriors raided several small Colorado settlements. The next year, in June, an Indian war party murdered a family on an isolated Colorado ranch and then horribly mutilated their bodies. After the mangled corpses were found by whites and placed on public display in Denver, a shiver of fear passed through the town. During that same period incessant Indian raids closed down the main road to the east, leaving Denver virtually isolated.

Wild rumors of an impending attack by the Cheyennes and Arapahos swept through the city, soon to be drowned out by cries for vengeance. Already, a volunteer regiment of barroom toughs and other Denver riffraff under Col. John Chivington had been organized and was spoiling for a fight. Chivington, a former minister and the hero of the Battle of Glorieta Pass, had discovered in himself

Black Kettle (second row, second from left) in Denver for the peace parley.

Black Kettle's Letter

Sirs: We received a letter from Bent wishing us to make peace. We held a consel . . . & all came to the conclusion to make peace with you providing you make peace with the Kiowas, Commenches, Arropohoes Apaches and Siouxs. We are going to send a messenger to the Kiowas . . . about our going to make [peace] with you. We heard that you [have] some prisoners in Denver. We have seven prisoners of you which we are willing to give up providing you give up yours. . . . When we held this counsel there were few Arropohoes and Siouxs present; we want true news from you in return.

—Received at Fort Lyon
September 4, 1864

In this painting of the massacre of southern Cheyennes at Sand Creek by Chivington's men, the white flag of truce (upper right of center) hangs below the American colors.

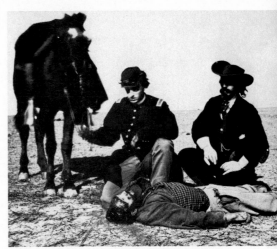

An army officer and a civilian examine the body of a hunter killed by the Cheyennes.

a great taste for battle and was now as intent on slaying heathen Indians as he had once been on saving souls. When his superior, Maj. Gen. Samuel R. Curtis, declared, "I want no peace till the Indians suffer more," the colonel was more than happy to fulfill his wishes.

Horror at Sand Creek

There appeared to be one slim chance for avoiding an all-out Indian war in Colorado. In late September of 1864 a prominent Cheyenne chief named Black Kettle appeared in Denver to negotiate for peace with the territorial governor. After conceding his inability to control many of the younger warriors, Black Kettle agreed to settle at Fort Lyon, in eastern Colorado, those of his Cheyenne and Arapaho followers who still opposed war. The new commander at the fort, saying that he was awaiting orders from General Curtis, insisted that Black Kettle camp on Sand Creek, some 40 miles from Fort Lyon. The chief agreed.

At dawn on November 29, 1864, when Black Kettle's band of about 500—including more than 300 women and children—were settled beside the stream, a detachment of about 700 of Chivington's volunteers suddenly appeared. With no warning or discussion they raked the settlement with murderous fire. In vain the Indian leader, unable to comprehend what was happening, first raised the Stars and Stripes and then a white flag of surrender. Following Chivington's order to "Kill and scalp all, big and little; nits make lice," the troopers slashed through the camp, killing every Indian who moved and then mutilating the bodies, saving some parts as grisly souvenirs of the day's action. Nei-

ther resistance nor surrender had any effect. One group of squaws and children were cut down in the midst of appealing for their lives, while a toddler lost amid the carnage was made the object of target practice by the half-crazed soldiers. Flight was the only possible hope, and indeed a few Indians did get away to spread the word through the grasslands and mountains that peace with the United States was simply not possible.

At first Denver and the nation celebrated Sand Creek as a great and noble victory of American arms. Only slowly did the truth come out, generating a wave of revulsion against Chivington and his command. "A cowardly and cold-blooded slaughter," said a shocked army judge advocate general. But by then the damage had been done, and the West was being torn by a new and bitter round of Indian wars.

The Cheyennes and Arapahos: Wandering Hunters of the Far Western Plains

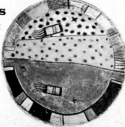

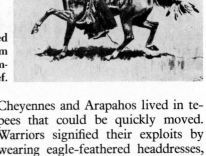

The Arapaho shield (above) is decorated with bear paws; stars, land, and sky form a background. At right, a Frederic Remington sketch of a Cheyenne war chief.

The Algonquian-speaking Cheyennes, who migrated from the upper Mississippi to the plains, had split into two groups after crossing the Missouri: the northern and the southern Cheyennes. The northern Cheyennes took up a nomadic life in the North Platte and Yellowstone River country; the southern Cheyennes roamed along the upper Arkansas River. Between the two were the Arapahos of eastern Colorado, also Algonquian-speaking Indians who had moved southwest out of Canada and northern Minnesota.

Like the other buffalo-hunting and nomadic tribes on the plains, the Cheyennes and Arapahos lived in tepees that could be quickly moved. Warriors signified their exploits by wearing eagle-feathered headdresses, which often became tall warbonnets with long tails of feathers. War shields were ornamented with feathers and, like the one above, with animal claws.

Although many of the Plains Indians had only informal tribal governments, the Cheyennes developed a strict system of rule administered by a tribal council of 44 chiefs. The tribal bands might scatter widely to hunt and find grazing grounds for their horses, but the council did give the tribe stability.

Blood on the Grasslands

Among the few Indians who had escaped the carnage at Sand Creek was Black Kettle, who fled eastward into Kansas with the remnant of his band. The old Cheyenne continued to advocate peace with the whites, but few heeded his words of restraint. A much more common feeling was expressed to a friendly white by one chief: "What do we have to live for? The white man has taken our country, killed our game, was not satisfied with that, but killed our wives and children. Now no peace. We have now raised the battle ax until death."

The year of the Sand Creek Massacre, 1864, was not even over before the pitiful tale had spread far and wide on the plains, and in December about 2,000 braves—Cheyennes, western Sioux, and Arapahos—gathered along the banks of Cherry Creek, a stream in Colorado, to plan retaliation. What followed was three years of guerrilla warfare. Summer, especially, became the season of death for the whites, as small Indian war parties thrust through the grasslands to raid settlements and wagon trains, setting houses to the torch and cutting down pioneers as they worked in the fields or tried to scramble for shelter.

The sudden explosion of warfare caught the federal government by surprise. Atrocities such as Sand Creek had led to pressure from eastern humanitarians for an immediate halt to hostilities, and in 1867 Congress authorized a peace commission to parley with tribal representatives in order to "remove the causes of war; secure the frontier settlements and railroad construction; and establish a system for civilizing the tribes." In the fall the peace commission met at Medicine Lodge Creek in Kansas with the leaders of several southern plains tribes, including the Comanches, Kiowas, Arapahos, and southern Cheyennes. One of the Cheyennes was Black Kettle.

As usual, the negotiations papered over the fundamental misunderstandings with fine words, but this time the government was determined to find a solution. The obvious one—from the white point of view—was to resettle all the Indians permanently on fixed reservations. The commission had two areas in mind: the Black Hills region for the northern tribes and the Indian Territory for the southern. The terms were not unlike those of the 1851 Horse Creek treaty: the government would provide food and supplies in exchange for which the tribesmen would promise to permit the whites free passage through their territories, allow the construction of

The 1867 Medicine Lodge Treaty gave southern tribes specific reservations in Indian Territory—what is today Oklahoma.

roads and railroads, stop their raiding, and remain on their assigned reservations except during the hunt.

But the pact was one that neither side could have lived up to, even with the best intentions. For not only did it rob the Plains Indians of their free-roaming way of life, it also imposed upon the government financial responsibilities that the Congress would fail to meet. With nothing to live on but a slim annuity and a dwindling supply of game, thousands of warriors and minor chiefs prepared to fight. By the fall of 1868 the grasslands from Kansas to Texas were crisscrossed by raiding warriors. The Army decided to punish these hit-and-run raiders with a winter campaign, knowing that the Indians of the plains usually avoided fighting in cold weather and hence would be ill-prepared to meet an attack.

Custer at the Washita River

In November soldiers of the 7th Cavalry, under the flamboyant Lt. Col. George Armstrong Custer, had the luck to pick up a fresh Indian trail in the snow. They followed it to a southern Cheyenne encampment on the Washita River, which happened to be the village of the unfortunate Black Kettle, and surrounded the camp on the night of November 26. They had not been sighted. At dawn the cavalrymen burst into the sleeping camp like avenging furies. Among the more than 100 Indian dead was Black Kettle.

This time, however, the Army paid a price for its victory. Warriors from nearby camps, roused by the firing, joined the battle and forced Custer to retreat with his Indian captives. During his withdrawal he left behind a detach-

Scouts and Indians at Beecher Island

The small island in the Arikaree River was named for an officer killed there, Lt. Frederick Beecher, nephew of Harriet Beecher Stowe, author of *Uncle Tom's Cabin*.

Among the legendary Cheyenne war leaders was the Bat, or Roman Nose. Standing six feet three, he was a commanding figure as he rode fearlessly into battle, seemingly made invincible against bullets and arrows by a magic eagle-feather warbonnet. Then in the summer of 1868, just before a small but celebrated fight at Beecher Island in eastern Colorado, Roman Nose unwittingly violated a taboo associated with his warbonnet, which meant that its power was gone: he ate food that had been touched by an iron utensil. At Beecher Island 50 volunteer scouts under Maj. George A. Forsyth withstood repeated assaults by 600 Indians. Finally, Roman Nose led a desperate charge and fell. His death so disheartened the Indians that they retreated.

Kiowa Chief Satanta, long a foe of the Army, wears part of an officer's uniform.

Soldier Hermann Stieffel painted the meeting at Medicine Lodge Creek, where the southern Cheyennes, Arapahos, Kiowas, and Comanches agreed to settle on reservations.

ment of 19 cavalrymen under Maj. Joel Elliott, who had ridden off in pursuit of some fleeing Indians. Cut off from their main force, the soldiers were surrounded by vengeance-seeking tribesmen and quickly dispatched.

Unlike Sand Creek, the Washita Massacre produced no investigation from outraged white officials. The headstrong Custer, in fact, was heartily commended by his superiors for his bold action. His victory appeared to have crushed Indian resistance on the southern plains, and in March 1869 Gen. Philip Sheridan reported that the tribes assigned to the Indian Territory were living quietly on their reservations.

Last-ditch Defiance

Soon, however, a new threat arose from the Kiowas, who had taken to marauding in the Texas Panhandle. In 1867 the Kiowas and Comanches had agreed to leave the Texas Panhandle reservation originally assigned them and had resettled on barren lands in Indian Territory. In 1871, fed up with the white man's broken promises, the Kiowas rebelled under their great chief Satanta, who had fought Carson at Adobe Walls.

After a murderous raid on a wagon train, Satanta boldly showed up at the agency near Fort Sill to draw rations, where he boasted that he had led the raid and killed seven men. The agent notified the Army, and Satanta was arrested, tried for murder in a Texas court, and sentenced to be hanged. When the Bureau of Indian Affairs and eastern humanitarians protested to the governor, he reprieved the death sentence and then paroled Satanta in 1873.

The next year Satanta joined the Comanche Quanah Parker, who set out

with 700 warriors to rid the Texas Panhandle, their traditional hunting grounds, of all the professional buffalo hunters who were wiping out the herds. Once more Adobe Walls was the scene of combat, and on June 27, 1874, the Indians besieged 28 buffalo hunters there. Thanks to the deadly accuracy of their Sharps rifles, fitted out with telescopic sights, the whites managed to hold off the red men until they wearied of their heavy losses and rode off.

Though they lost at Adobe Walls, the Kiowas and Comanches continued their raiding across the southern plains. But gradually their resolve weakened as the Army followed a scorched-earth policy, denying the warrior bands essential supplies. The once-proud red men, reduced to abject poverty, began to surrender in droves. One of those to lay down his arms was Satanta, who was led off to prison in October 1874. There, four years later, he committed suicide.

Cynthia Ann Parker: An Alien at Home

Cynthia Ann Parker and her daughter; at right is her son, the Comanche chief Quanah Parker.

In 1836 nine-year-old Cynthia Ann Parker was carried off by Comanche raiders who attacked her family home in north Texas and killed her father. Nine years later she became the wife of Chief Peta Nocona and bore him two sons, Quanah and Pecos, and a daughter, Topasannah. In 1860 Texas Rangers recaptured Cynthia Ann and her daughter, and she was joyfully welcomed by her brother and her uncle,

Isaac Parker, a prominent Texan. But Cynthia Ann mourned for her sons and several times tried to ride away and find them. When her daughter died in 1864, the grief-stricken Cynthia Ann starved herself to death. Her son Quanah ravaged the Texas frontier till 1875, when he suddenly accepted reservation life and spent the next 36 years working to improve relations between the whites and Comanches.

Logistics and Tactics in the Indian Wars

To the widely scattered ranchers, farmers, miners, and townsmen of the West, the post-Civil War Army must have seemed a frail bulwark against the ever-present threat of Indian attacks. The frontiersmen had expected that the war's end would release ample forces to subdue the unconquered tribes of the plains. Instead the people and their representatives, weary of war and of vast military expenditures, set about brutally slashing the Army's budget. A military establishment that had comprised hundreds of thousands of men was suddenly sharply reduced to 54,000 men in 1866 and to a mere 27,000 eight years later. Of these, only a fraction served in the hundred or so forts scattered from the Mississippi to the Pacific.

In some frontier forts a single company formed the entire garrison—this at a time when a company might average 30 or 40 men. Some had even fewer in service. "It is rather stupid work for an officer to go out and drill four men," said one despairing regimental officer.

Yet living on the vast stretches of the frontier were some 300,000 Indians, at least half of them potentially hostile and far superior in fighting ability to the indifferently trained soldiers of the post-Civil War Army. Their horses, too, gave them an immense advantage, for the tough little ponies could live off the plains grasslands while the larger cavalry mounts could not. Feed for army horses had to be transported along the line of

William T. Sherman, the noted general in the Civil War, commanded the Military Division of the Missouri from 1866 to 1869.

march, often slowing down the cavalry to a crawl and even forcing infantry units to retard their progress so the horse soldiers could keep pace.

Problems of logistical support complicated the Army's tasks immeasurably. On campaign most units were supplied by wagon trains, thus limiting operations to flat open country and well-established trails. Uninhibited in this way, Indian war parties often had the option of retreating through rugged country where the Army could not go.

In part, at least, Gen. George Crook corrected the Army's lack of mobility in the early 1870's. In his campaigns against the Apaches, Crook proved that pack trains of sure-footed mules could supply units in the roughest country. But efficient as the mule was, its personality did not endear it to the average enlisted man of the period. One trooper summed up the popular view of the beast by calling it "unapproached in devilment, fathomless in cunning, born old in crime, of disreputable paternity and incapable of posterity."

An Unwitting Ally

In the face of its difficulties it seems incredible that the shriveled U.S. Army was, in the end, capable of subduing the warrior societies of the frontier. But in fighting the red men, the Army had a powerful if unwitting ally: the Indian himself. With the partial exception of the Apaches, most Indians fought the Army as if it were little more than another tribe competing for temporary control of a hunting ground. Each time the Army eased its pressure in a given area, the tribesmen, not realizing that they were fighting an enemy determined on permanent control, tended to assume that they were winning.

Even if the red men had been aware of their impending doom, their highly individualistic societies of huntsmen and warriors were ill-adapted to resist a modern army. Ancient animosities among the tribes made most long-term coalitions against the whites impossible, and even within a single tribe there was little unity. Every brave was his own master, free to join an autonomous warrior band or to seek accommodation with the whites—which sometimes meant forming an active alliance with them. General Crook, for example, made effective use of friendly Apache bands in hunting down and destroying hostile elements within that nation.

As in older times, when warfare on the plains was an intertribal matter, the search for personal glory remained uppermost in the minds of the Indian warriors. If, for instance, a small band of Indian raiders rode up to an army column on the march and tapped a few of the enemy with their *coup* sticks before vanishing into the plains, the tribesmen would feel that they had won a great victory. In part, this subjugation was made inevitable by their failure to un-

The infantry spent a lot of its time, as shown here, defending supply trains. But on offensive operations the unglamorous foot soldiers often proved more dependable than the cavalry.

Although unlovely to look at and hard to handle, the pack mule kept army supplies moving in country where horses could not go.

An important post during the early fur-trading days, Fort Pierre on the Missouri was bought by the government in 1855 for the U.S. Army.

derstand that the white soldiers fought neither for glory nor for fun but to win a continent for themselves and the civilization they represented.

To achieve its aims, the Army sometimes launched massive punitive expeditions and at other times small, swift striking forces against the Indians. But in the end two combined tactics would prove most effective in subduing them: total warfare against recalcitrant Indian nations and winter campaigns. During the cold season the warrior bands, with their wives and children, were forced into temporary immobility by the fierce plains weather, the scarcity of forage and game, and the need to conserve energy and food supplies. Unable to wage war themselves, the Indians of this region found it almost inconceivable that the white soldiers could do so and hence made little provision for the defense of their encampments.

A Winter War of Terror

Taking advantage of their foe's temporary immobility, the soldiers moved across the snow-swept plains to mount surprise attacks in which the Indians were neither expected nor even allowed to surrender. Sometimes women and children were deliberately shot down; but even when they were not, their fate was often death by starvation or exposure after their men, their villages, and their horses had been destroyed. This was a war of terror, whose aim was not only to kill Indians but also to destroy the entire structure on which their nomadic lifestyle depended. If such tactics prompted men of conscience to condemn the military as a league of butchers, no one was able to devise a more effective means of accomplishing the goal that the whites would call "the winning of the West."

The U.S. Army's "Blacks in Blue"

White soldiers in the Indian fighting forces of the West called the black troopers and infantrymen brunettes, or Africans; and the Indians, apparently alluding to the blacks' curly hair, called them buffalo soldiers. The troopers of the 10th Cavalry, along with the 9th Cavalry and the black 24th and 25th Infantry, were organized in 1866 and adopted the buffalo as the central figure in their regimental crest (see emblem at right). Commanded by white officers, these "blacks in blue" won the grudging praise of Gen. William T. Sherman, who preferred white troops but said of the blacks: "They are good troops, they make first-rate sentinels, are faithful to their trust, and are as brave as the occasion calls for."

During the wars against the Apaches in the 1870's and 1880's the troopers of the 9th and 10th Cavalry matched their notably tough foes in endurance on long marches in furnacelike heat. Artist Frederic Remington, who was with the black troopers in Arizona, had this comment:

"They may be tired and they may be hungry, but they do not see fit to augment their misery by finding fault with everybody and everything. In this particular they are charming men with whom to serve. Officers have often confessed to me that when they are on long and monotonous field service and are troubled with a depression of spirits, they have only to go about the campfires of the Negro soldier in order to be amused and cheered by the clever absurdities of the men. . . . As to their bravery: 'Will they fight?' That is easily answered. They have fought many, many times. The old sergeant sitting near me, as calm of feature as a bronze

A black trooper returned from patrol and the regimental crest of the 10th Cavalry.

statue, once deliberately walked over a Cheyenne rifle pit and killed his man. One little fellow near him once took charge of stampeded cavalry horses when Apache bullets were flying."

The blacks had high reenlistment and low desertion rates and an *esprit de corps* matching that of troops in the best white regiments. While whites frequently looked upon army service as a temporary refuge, the blacks viewed it as a career. And they stuck at it despite having to bear a heavy burden of racial discrimination. Supplies given black regiments were inferior in quality and quantity, and they garrisoned the least desirable forts on the frontier. On one occasion, when the colonel of the 3rd Infantry told "nigger troops" of the 10th Cavalry not to form so close to his men while on parade, he was royally cussed out by the white Col. Benjamin Grierson of the 10th Cavalry.

In the Western Army: Boredom and Discomfort

Out west in 1875 the life of a soldier was drab and dull, completely without glamour. He usually saw little action, and this often after grueling marches in frostbite cold, parching heat, or the quagmires of flash floods. Yet he welcomed these as breaks in camp monotony. A few forts, such as Laramie (below), had more amenities than frontier farms, but most posts were crude and soldier-built, far from town, without cultural activities, and devoid of civilians except officers' wives, laundresses, and traders. The infantryman went through a rigid routine of drills, guard duty, and fatigue de-

tails—constructing buildings and roads, digging drainage ditches, cultivating gardens, fetching river water, chopping wood, and doing KP. Pay was low, but qualified men earned extra as barbers, stonemasons, or saddlers. The soldiers took turns cooking, so most meals were boiled and bad: stew, hash, baked beans, hardtack (often moldy), salt pork (sometimes maggoty), dried apples and potatoes, and coffee. At forts lacking gardens, the men came down with scurvy. Despite the efforts of post surgeons sanitation was terrible, and diseases took a far higher toll than battles with the Indians.

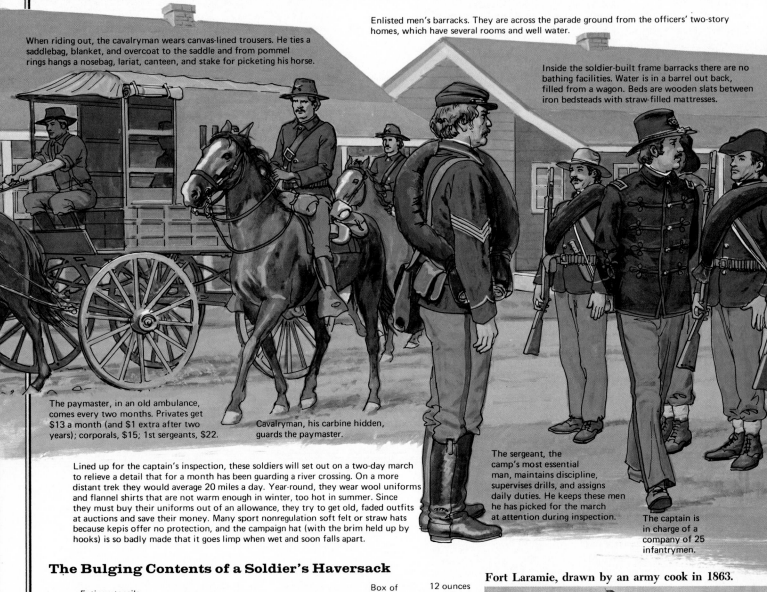

When riding out, the cavalryman wears canvas-lined trousers. He ties a saddlebag, blanket, and overcoat to the saddle and from pommel rings hangs a nosebag, lariat, canteen, and stake for picketing his horse.

Enlisted men's barracks. They are across the parade ground from the officers' two-story homes, which have several rooms and well water.

Inside the soldier-built frame barracks there are no bathing facilities. Water is in a barrel out back, filled from a wagon. Beds are wooden slats between iron bedsteads with straw-filled mattresses.

The paymaster, in an old ambulance, comes every two months. Privates get $13 a month (and $1 extra after two years); corporals, $15; 1st sergeants, $22.

Cavalryman, his carbine hidden, guards the paymaster.

The sergeant, the camp's most essential man, maintains discipline, supervises drills, and assigns daily duties. He keeps these men he has picked for the march at attention during inspection.

The captain is in charge of a company of 25 infantrymen.

Lined up for the captain's inspection, these soldiers will set out on a two-day march to relieve a detail that for a month has been guarding a river crossing. On a more distant trek they would average 20 miles a day. Year-round, they wear wool uniforms and flannel shirts that are not warm enough in winter, too hot in summer. Since they must buy their uniforms out of an allowance, they try to get old, faded outfits at auctions and save their money. Many sport nonregulation soft felt or straw hats because kepis offer no protection, and the campaign hat (with the brim held up by hooks) is so badly made that it goes limp when wet and soon falls apart.

The Bulging Contents of a Soldier's Haversack

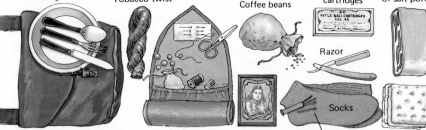

Eating utensils Tobacco twist Coffee beans Box of cartridges 12 ounces of salt pork

Razor

Socks

A haversack's items include food for one day's two meals.

"The housewife," or sewing kit

Sweetheart's picture

Matches in a cartridge case

Hardtack (12 crackers a day)

Fort Laramie, drawn by an army cook in 1863.

Lighter Moments

At all army posts pleasures depend on rank. Senior officers can have their families with them; they have houses, servants, orderlies, and lawn croquet. Noncoms are allowed to entertain company in their private rooms. Enlisted men for recreation play baseball, toss horseshoes, or drink and play cards or checkers at the traders' bars. At Laramie ordinary soldiers may attend the fort's school and use a lending library, but most do not know how to read or write.

Two noncommissioned officers enjoy music and a drink at Fort Stanton, a post in New Mexico, about 1886.

A quartermaster sergeant of the 3rd U.S. Infantry reads to a woman in his comfortable room.

Close by the barracks are a guardhouse, magazine, and surgeon's quarters.

The Indian interpreter and guide are among the few civilians allowed on the post. They dress as they please and carry their own weapons. The Army relies on them to apprehend thieves and retrieve stolen horses, to reconnoiter, and to guide the troops sent in pursuit of hostile Indians.

Above, a cavalryman in canvas stable clothes heads for the corral.

Each soldier (left) carries a haversack with a dangling tin cup, a blanket roll wrapped inside a rubber poncho, a canteen, a rifle, and ammunition in a homemade cartridge belt. Each has but one wool blanket; in winter the soldiers pool the covers and huddle together under them.

Shoes, made at the military prison, fit badly. To avoid blisters, the men soap their socks—which are tied around their pants legs—so they will not stick to their shoes.

In the foreground an orderly, in full dress uniform, arrives with a message from the post commander. The best dressed private is selected as orderly, a job coveted because he gets a pass at the end of his tour of duty, does not have to serve as a sentinel, march, or do various chores. He eats ahead of the other soldiers and spends his time sitting at headquarters.

The Principal Rifles and Pistols of the Indian Wars

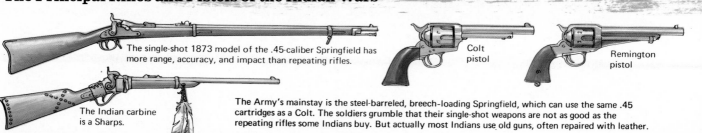

The single-shot 1873 model of the .45-caliber Springfield has more range, accuracy, and impact than repeating rifles.

Colt pistol

Remington pistol

The Indian carbine is a Sharps.

The Army's mainstay is the steel-barreled, breech-loading Springfield, which can use the same .45 cartridges as a Colt. The soldiers grumble that their single-shot weapons are not as good as the repeating rifles some Indians buy. But actually most Indians use old guns, often repaired with leather.

Red Cloud's War in the Dakota Territory

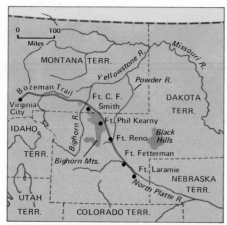

Indian wrath was aroused by the opening of the Bozeman Trail from the North Platte River to the Montana country mines and by the building of Forts Reno, Phil Kearny, and C. F. Smith to give protection to the route.

In 1866, just four years after the bloody Minnesota Sioux uprising, a council was held at Fort Laramie. In attendance were officials of the federal government and such western Sioux chiefs as Man-Afraid-of-His-Horses, Spotted Tail, and the warrior who had emerged as the most feared of all Sioux leaders—the Oglala chief Red Cloud.

For a number of years Red Cloud's bands had been attacking parties of whites who were cutting through the Powder River country's great buffalo preserve on their way to the new goldfields in present-day Montana (a route opened by John Bozeman in 1862). The Laramie council had been called to settle matters between Indians and whites.

Hardly had negotiations begun when Col. Henry B. Carrington arrived at Laramie to announce that, in keeping with War Department orders, his troops were already stationed along the so-called Bozeman Trail, constructing forts to ensure safe passage to the mines for whites. At this news Red Cloud, his face contorted with anger, exploded: "The Great Father sends us presents and wants us to sell him the road, but white chief goes with soldiers to steal the road before Indians say Yes or No." With that Red Cloud, accompanied by several other Sioux and northern Cheyenne chiefs, stormed out of the meeting.

For months after the abortive Laramie talks the soldiers could not leave their new forts along the Bozeman route without peril to their lives. In bands of 20 and 30 horsemen, or sometimes as many as 200, Red Cloud's braves waited to ambush the wood-gathering details, striking when the men were busy at their tasks. By the end of 1866, before Fort Phil Kearny, which was several miles from the nearest timber, was completed, the Indians had killed 150 soldiers and civilians and had wounded 20 more.

Even when a fort was finished, there was scant security outside its walls, and it soon became apparent that the U.S. Army force along the Bozeman was less a source of protection than a besieged host. Red Cloud's tactic of destroying Carrington's forces piecemeal reached an apogee of sorts in the Fetterman Massacre of December 21, 1866.

On that day William J. Fetterman, an impetuous young captain at Fort Phil Kearny who had boasted that he could ride through the entire Sioux Nation with 80 men, was given a chance to make good his claim. Sent out to relieve a wood detail that was under attack, Fetterman—with a force of 80 men, as it happened—let himself be lured into ambush by a wily young Sioux named Crazy Horse. The entire relief force, including its cocky officer, was wiped out.

This loss so reduced the Fort Phil

Wily strategist Chief Red Cloud (left) was content to sap the strength of the Fort Phil Kearny garrison by constant harassment. This tactic outraged Capt. William Fetterman (below), who had won battle honors in the Civil War; he denounced his superior, Col. Henry Carrington, for his caution.

Ignoring orders not to pursue Indians beyond a certain point, Captain Fetterman blundered into a Sioux ambush that cost him his life and the lives of all the men in his force.

Protected by wagon boxes lined with sheet iron and using new breech-loading rifles, U.S. soldiers repulsed a Sioux force that vastly outnumbered them.

Fort Phil Kearny, constructed in 1866, had 30 buildings that were surrounded by a high 2,800-foot-long stockade.

Kearny garrison that Carrington feared his entire command might be destroyed at any moment by the 2,000 warriors Red Cloud was said to be readying for attack. Despite a raging blizzard, the desperate commander dispatched a civilian scout, John Phillips, to ride to Laramie for reinforcements. Somehow the courier made it in four days, and within hours of his arrival men were on their way to Fort Phil Kearny.

A Momentary Peace

The dispatch of fresh troops to the Bozeman Trail forts failed to intimidate the Sioux, however. In late July 1867 Red Cloud at last felt he was strong enough—and the army garrison sufficiently weakened by his incessant attacks—to risk a direct assault on Fort Phil Kearny. With more than 1,000 warriors he rode toward the fort, but on the way he encountered a 36-man army work detail under Capt. James W. Powell. Anticipating a raid, Powell's detail had left the fort well supplied with ammunition; when Red Cloud struck, 32 of the soldiers made it to shelter behind an oval of wagon boxes. For four and a half hours they maintained a rapid, steady fire, withstanding charge after charge from the Indians until reinforcements arrived. After what came to be called the Wagon Box Fight, which took place on August 2, Red Cloud postponed his attack on Fort Phil Kearny. As it turned out, the assault would never take place, thanks to a growing sentiment in Washington to abandon the Bozeman Trail, soon to be made obsolete by a railroad.

Red Cloud, however, was willing to talk peace only if the government agreed to leave its outposts in the Sioux country: Forts Reno, Phil Kearny, and C. F.

Smith. Finally, the government took the unprecedented step of yielding to an Indian's demands, and in the spring of 1868 the forts were ordered abandoned. That summer the victorious Red Cloud burned Fort Phil Kearny to the ground.

In November 1868 Red Cloud rode into Fort Laramie to sign a treaty with the whites, a pact to which several of his fellow chiefs had already agreed. Under its terms they would settle permanently on the huge Great Sioux Reservation in the Black Hills country of the Dakota Territory, retaining their right to hunt in the Powder River region. Both the Black Hills and the Powder River would be forbidden to white exploitation.

For the moment both sides seemed satisfied: the whites had persuaded the Indians to accept a reservation, and the Indians had been able to keep whites out of their sacred Black Hills and the Pow-

der River country. But by the end of 1868 the tracks of the Union Pacific Railroad had crossed southern Wyoming, and new towns had sprung up along its right-of-way. Six years later Lt. Col. George A. Custer led his 7th Cavalry on a reconnaissance into the Black Hills—ostensibly to seek a site for a military post but actually to check out rumors of gold in the area. Custer's report, which stated that gold was indeed there, precipitated a rush into the Indian reservation. Once more a solemn treaty had proved to be worthless. And now, in a last effort to protect their dwindling lands, the Sioux and a few northern Cheyennes began to gather together a mighty army for the climactic battle of the Indian wars. The time of the Little Bighorn—popularly known as Custer's Last Stand but in reality the Indians' last stand—was drawing close.

Among the Indians who signed the Treaty of Fort Laramie in May of 1868 was the Sioux chief Man-Afraid-of-His-Horses (second from right); Red Cloud signed in November.

Custer's Legendary Last Stand

On June 22, 1876, Lt. Col. George Armstrong Custer, a nationally known hero of the Civil War, led his 7th Cavalry into Sioux territory. His object: to trap a large force of hostile Indians. Enraged over white encroachment on their hunting lands, the Sioux and northern Cheyennes had joined forces and prepared for battle. They numbered an estimated 2,500 to 3,000 warriors—probably the greatest concentration of Indian might ever assembled in the West.

Custer was eager for a fight. Earlier, he had angered President Ulysses S. Grant by giving damaging evidence against the secretary of war and involving the president's brother in trading-post corruption, and Grant had suspended Custer from his command. Restored to his regiment after the intercession of his superior, Maj. Gen. Alfred H. Terry, Custer was bent on salvaging his reputation with a smashing victory.

On the morning of June 25, after a brutal march of 40 miles, Custer's 600 or so exhausted troopers neared the huge Sioux-Cheyenne village on the Little Bighorn River in Montana Territory. Ignoring his scouts' reports of the Indians' overwhelming numbers and not waiting for the arrival of the rest of the expedition under General Terry, Custer split his command to round up what he thought was a fleeing enemy. The Indians stood their ground, and Custer rode to his death, along with more than one-third of the men in his regiment.

Leaders of the 7th Cavalry

George Armstrong Custer, lowest in his West Point class in 1861, became a brevet major general of Civil War volunteers at the age of 25 but was reduced to lieutenant colonel in the postwar Regular Army. Crusty Capt. Frederick W. Benteen, who had a solid if less spectacular war career than Custer, openly detested his flamboyant commander. Maj. Marcus A. Reno, a capable Civil War officer who lacked Indian fighting experience, proved indecisive and became a scapegoat for Custer's defeat.

Custer

Benteen

Reno

Leaders of the Indians

The deadly massing of Indian power on the Little Bighorn was directed by several outstanding warriors. Gall, a Hunkpapa chief, assailed Custer's flank and rear, while Crazy Horse of the Oglalas closed the trap on Custer. The Hunkpapa chief Rain-in-the-Face, who held a personal grudge against Colonel Custer's brother, was said to have cut out his heart. The Oglala chief Low Dog led forces that repulsed Reno and then joined in the push that finally overwhelmed Custer's command.

Gall

Rain-in-the-Face

Low Dog

Blueprint for Disaster at the Little Bighorn

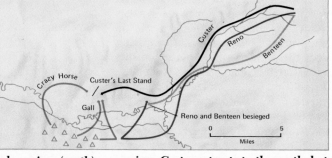

At noon on June 25 Custer divides his forces, sending Benteen and 120 men south on a scouting mission; his own men (some 225) and Reno's (112) move toward the Indian village across the river; and 129 men escort the pack train. Reno charges the village as Custer moves downriver (north), hidden by high bluffs. Heavily attacked, Reno leads a disorderly, costly retreat back across the river to a bluff, where his shaken command is joined by Benteen's men and the pack train. Surprised by Gall and his warriors, Custer retreats to the north, but Crazy Horse circles around and traps Custer's men. The Reno-Benteen force comes under heavy attack until the approach of Terry's command causes the Indians to make a retreat on the evening of June 26.

General Custer's Death Struggle—The Myth

In this highly romanticized scene painted in 1878 by H. Steinegger, a long-haired Custer, clad in his major general's Civil War uniform, defiantly wields his saber against the attacking Indians. In actuality, Lieutenant Colonel Custer was wearing buckskins and a flannel shirt during the battle; his famous long hair had been cut short for the current campaign, and he and all his men had left their sabers behind.

Low Dog's Account

They came on us like a thunderbolt. I never before nor since saw men so brave and fearless as those white warriors. We retreated until our men got all together, and then we charged upon them. I called to my men, "This is a good day to die: follow me." We massed our men, and that no man should fall back, every man whipped another man's horse and we rushed right upon them. . . . The white warriors dismounted to fire. . . . They held their horses reins on one arm while they were shooting, but their horses were so frightened that they pulled the men all around, and a great many of their shots went up in the air. . . . I did not see Gen. Custer. . . . We did not know . . . that he was the white chief.

—*Leavenworth Weekly Times*
August 18, 1881

Custer's Last Stand—A More Realistic Version

Painted in 1899 by Edgar Paxson after 20 years of research, this 6- by 10-foot picture shows the final rush of the Indians on the doomed troopers. Although many Indians had the latest repeating rifles, most used bows and arrows. Defective cartridges jammed in the troopers' single-shot carbines and had to be dug out with knives. As the ranks of the defenders thinned, the Indians finished them off with hatchets and clubs. The lone survivor was Capt. Myles Keogh's horse, Comanche; it became the regiment's mascot.

The Perils of Resistance

The defeat and death of George Custer at the Little Bighorn jolted and sobered a nation then celebrating its first hundred years of independence. To the public, if not to many of his officers, Custer had been the most dashing Indian fighter in the West, and his death had to be avenged. So the tribesmen of the northern plains were given no time to celebrate their victory. Nearly a thousand northern Cheyennes, on their way to join Sioux war leader Crazy Horse in the Powder River country, were beaten back on July 17 by Col. Wesley Merritt's 5th Cavalry at War Bonnet Creek. The defeated Cheyennes turned back to the nearby Red Cloud Agency and took no further part in the campaign.

Shortly thereafter, on September 9, 1876, the main army column under Gen. George Crook, veteran of the Apache campaigns, attacked a Sioux village near Slim Buttes, in present-day South Dakota. Driven into a blind gully near the

"Forty miles a day, on beans and hay," sang soldiers in the U.S. Army. In the winter of 1876-77 they tramped in −30°F weather.

village, the Indians dug rifle pits and fought on with grim determination for a number of hours. Finally, a mortally wounded Sioux chief, American Horse, offered to surrender if his men were not killed, and Crook accepted.

After this action, however, the summer campaign of 1876 came to a halt. The Army, by now too large and cumbersome to give effective chase to the widely scattered bands of hostiles, instead took measures against those Indians under its control. Thus, on October 23, the great Sioux Red Cloud and his followers were abruptly disarmed at their camp near Red Cloud Agency. General Crook then told the humiliated Red Cloud that the government no longer recognized him as chief of all the Sioux. Meanwhile, at several other agencies army units were ordered to seize the Indians' arms and their ponies as well—and to sell the latter and buy them cows instead.

Most disheartening of all, Congress had decided after the Custer debacle to force the Sioux to give up the Black Hills, informing them that if they refused, no more rations would be forthcoming. A few chiefs signed the new treaty, despite the fact that by its terms the Sioux gave up not only the Black Hills but also all hunting rights outside the redefined reservation.

Great numbers of Indians remained defiant, however, and Crook planned a winter campaign to bring them to heel. In late October of 1876 a column led by Col. Nelson A. Miles succeeded in tracking down Sitting Bull and his Sioux

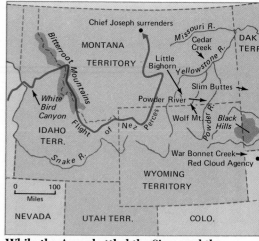

While the Army battled the Sioux and the Cheyennes, Chief Joseph led the Nez Perces on a vain escape toward Canada.

followers at Cedar Creek in Montana Territory. After a parley, during which Sitting Bull shouted that God had made him an Indian, but not an agency Indian, Miles' men attacked. Two days later some 2,000 Sioux surrendered, while Sitting Bull himself managed to escape into Canada with a few of his followers.

The End of Crazy Horse

One of the greatest warriors of the northern plains, Crazy Horse, was still to be accounted for. The ambitious Colonel Miles, with 350 hard-bitten infantrymen, decided to go after him, and on January 8, 1877, he found the Sioux war leader and some 500 Cheyenne and Sioux followers on the snowy cliffs of Wolf Mountain in Montana. Pounded by Miles' artillery and nearly blinded by a raging blizzard, the Indians were the first to withdraw from the field.

The defeat at Wolf Mountain disheartened the Indian war faction, and in the spring of 1877 more than 3,000 Sioux and Cheyennes came into the agencies to surrender. In May, Crazy Horse himself surrendered at the Red Cloud Agency, but even then he was seen as a potential threat by the Army and the Indian peace faction. He was ordered arrested and disarmed, and on September 7 he was killed in a scuffle with his captors. Thus, a little more than a year after Custer's defeat, the Indians' power on the northern plains was effectively broken.

Although this epic struggle had captured most of the public's attention, two other campaigns of the period were

Frederic Remington's painting of an army attack on Sioux Chief Crazy Horse's village does not accord with the facts. Actually, the battle took place at nearby Wolf Mountain.

equally dramatic: one was the gallant fighting retreat of the Nez Perces under their legendary chief Joseph; the other, the last-ditch stand of the Modocs in the Northwest.

Captain Jack's Rebellion

Of the once-numerous tribes of the Pacific Northwest, the Modocs had long been among the least noteworthy. The members of this small tribe, whose homeland was on the Oregon-California border, had made a few forays against white settlers in the 1850's but then agreed to share a reservation with their more numerous cousins, the Klamaths. By the late 1860's, however, friction between the two tribes became so intense that several bands of Modoc dissidents, under the leadership of a chief the whites called Captain Jack, left to settle again in their old homeland.

For a time little was done to herd the Modocs back to the reservation, but when a small army detachment arrived in 1872 to do just that, Captain Jack's warriors refused to move. When the troopers ordered the Modocs to disarm, the Indians responded with derisive laughter. A shot rang out, and a short skirmish followed in which one Indian and one soldier were killed. The Modocs then fled southward into California, wreaking vengeance on any civilians

During peace talks between the Modocs and the Army, Captain Jack murdered Gen. Edward R. S. Canby (shown above). Canby was the first U.S. general killed in an Indian war.

they chanced to see. By the time they reached the lava beds on the shore of Tule Lake, they had butchered 14 whites.

Entrenched in the meandering jumble of caves and ravines of the lava beds, the 165 men, women, and children of Captain Jack's force occupied an almost impregnable fortress—as some 325 troopers were to discover on January 17, 1873. Shrouded by fog, the 60-odd Modoc warriors easily avoided both howitzer shells and rifle fire and fought so skillfully that the troops had to withdraw. The embarrassed government then beefed up the army force to 700 men and also sent a peace commission under Gen. Edward R. S. Canby to parley with the Indians.

It was then that Captain Jack made a

fatal mistake. His medicine man had urged him to kill the general in the belief that a leaderless army would lose heart for battle. During the peace talks the Indians suddenly struck, killing Canby and another peace commissioner, a Methodist minister. Now all hope of compromise was gone. The nation was outraged, and few people quarreled with General Sherman's statement that the Modocs deserved to be exterminated. After several pitched battles the Army forced the Modocs to surrender and captured Captain Jack. He was hanged with three of his lieutenants. The surviving Modocs were shipped off to a malarial corner of the Indian Territory; the embalmed body of Captain Jack was shipped to Washington for exhibition in a museum.

The Fighting Retreat of the Nez Perces

Chief Joseph became the symbol of the heroic fight of the Nez Perces against the overwhelming forces the U.S. Army hurled against them.

Standing among the fallen, Chief Joseph reportedly told Colonel Miles: "I am tired; my heart is sick. . . . From where the sun now stands, I will fight no more forever."

The Nez Perces ("Pierced Noses") had aided the Lewis and Clark expedition in 1805 and always boasted that they had never killed a white man. When, in the 1850's, whites pushed into Nez Perce territory in the Oregon and Idaho country, the tribe agreed to cede part of its land and move onto a reservation. But over the years gold miners and settlers pressured the government, and in 1877 officials finally ordered the tribe to a new reservation in Idaho Territory. Reluctantly, Chief Joseph agreed to move. Then in June of that year a young Indian whose father had been killed by whites led a series of raids that took the lives of at least 18 settlers.

Fearing retaliation, the Nez Perces went into hiding in White Bird Canyon. After beating back an army detachment, Chief Joseph decided to lead his band of 150 warriors and 550 women, children, and older men across the Bitterroot Mountains and northward to a haven in Canada. As troops under Gen. Oliver O. Howard took the field against Chief Joseph, the public, remembering the Custer massacre, called for revenge. But the 1,700-mile retreat of the Nez Perces, in which they fought the Army to a standstill, won wide admiration. At last, however, they were trapped by Col. Nelson A. Miles' troops only 40 miles from Canada. Chief Joseph surrendered after being promised that his people would be sent back to Idaho. Instead, the government shipped them to Indian Territory, where many died. Howard and Miles protested, and the Nez Perces went to a reservation in Washington Territory.

Walking the White Man's Road

A young Navajo, Tom Torlino, poses before and after he began his education at the Carlisle Indian School in Pennsylvania.

Six years before the Little Bighorn an announcement was made that created great excitement among New Yorkers: the legendary Sioux chief Red Cloud was to lecture at Cooper Union, a free night school in the city. On a summer evening in 1870 the auditorium was jammed with people anxious to hear the famed warrior whose recent victories over the U.S. Army had forced the government to abandon the Bozeman Trail.

But if the New Yorkers had anticipated a fiery address filled with defiance, they were disappointed, for on his earlier tour through the East, Red Cloud had been shown the full power and majesty of the United States—its farms, its factories, its growing cities, and the U.S. Arsenal and Navy Yard. Where the Army in the field had failed to intimidate him, the journey had succeeded. Now there was hardly an Indian in the country more dedicated to accommodation and the peaceful adaptation of the red man to the white man's ways.

Red Cloud's Speech

Yet for all his new amiability, Red Cloud was still an ardent champion of his people. In words that were touching in their directness and their simplicity he cataloged the woes the Indians had suffered and appealed for the help of "good men" to make the tribes self-sufficient and productive. "Look at me," he cried, "I am poor and naked, but I am the Chief of the [Sioux] nation. We do not want riches, we do not ask for riches, but we want our children properly trained and brought up. We look to you for your sympathy."

As waves of applause washed over Red Cloud, he must have felt that he had

at last found powerful white allies in the struggle for justice. Yet when he returned to his homeland to counsel patience, he discovered that his words carried less and less weight. Years of warfare still lay ahead, brought on by continuing treaty violations and new white incursions into the Sioux domain.

Even so, the Sioux chief's speech marked something of a watershed in Indian-white relations, for his simple oratory helped touch off a national debate on Indian policy. The controversy continued through all the bloody encounters to come and finally ended with a complete victory for the humanitarians. But unfortunately for the Indians, the zeal of the reformers succeeded only in imposing new sorrows and degradations upon the tribes.

The reformers' basic idea was to assimilate the Indians by teaching them to become sturdy, self-sufficient farmers, distinguishable from their neighbors only by their color. But this high-minded goal was to be achieved by the most brutal kind of cultural surgery: distributing the communally held lands to individual tribesmen and wiping out the Indians' native languages, customs, religions, and tribal organizations. Even as the Army was pursuing renegade

bands in the 1870's and 1880's, men and women of sublime good will were volunteering to work among the Indians for the betterment of their lives and the salvation of their souls.

These idealists spread out among the tribes on the western reservations, determined to bring the Indian into the mainstream of American life—leading him if possible, pushing him if necessary. That few of them knew much about the Indians' multifaceted cultures or spoke any of the Indian tongues was thought of little importance, for these things were considered excess baggage that hindered the red man's transformation into an American yeoman. Sometimes, as in the case of the misguided efforts of the Indian agent Nathan Meeker to lead the Utes of Colorado into a cooperative commonwealth of farmers, the reformers' activities ended in rebellion and death. More often the consequences were less dramatic but only marginally less harmful.

Strict moralists that they were, the reformers opposed even the most innocuous of traditional activities. Until 1890, for example, the government supplied beef on the hoof as part of its annuities to the tribes. In a pitiful effort to recall the glories of the buffalo hunt, the Sioux

Valentine McGillycuddy: "Holy Medicine Man"

On September 7, 1877, U.S. Army surgeon Valentine T. McGillycuddy worked long hours in a vain attempt to save the life of wounded Chief Crazy Horse and won the respect of the Sioux and the name "Holy Medicine Man." The following year, appalled by the treatment of the Indians, he went to Washington and talked his way into the job of agent at the Pine Ridge Reservation in the Dakota Territory.

Under McGillycuddy's able, honest administration, the Sioux and Cheyennes at Pine Ridge were so prosperous that other Indians asked to join them. McGillycuddy organized an Indian police that enforced the law impartially, arresting Indians as well as whites. The whites complained loudly at the indignity of being taken into custody by Indians, while workers and freighters objected when McGillycuddy insisted that Indians build their own houses and haul their supplies from the railroad.

McGillycuddy (top center) at Pine Ridge.

McGillycuddy also outraged corrupt Indian Bureau officials who seemed to feel they had a license to steal from the red man. Soon, McGillycuddy became the most investigated man in the land as the Indian Bureau tried to oust him. Finally, in 1886, he was removed for refusing to dismiss a valued assistant.

A Panicky Agent Triggers an Uprising

Demands by land-hungry settlers and silver miners that the Utes be driven from their reservation in western Colorado had strained relations to the snapping point in the spring of 1878. Into this tense situation stepped a new agent for the reservation's White River Agency, Nathan Meeker, a visionary reformer who was bent on the instant transformation of the Ute horsemen and hunters into farmers. Roughed up by an angry chief during an argument over his program, Meeker panicked and called for troops. They arrived on September 29, 1879, and were immediately besieged. Meanwhile, warriors killed Meeker and nine employees (right) and abducted Mrs. Meeker, her daughter, and three other whites. Army reinforcements soon ended the uprising, and the hostages were released. The Utes were ousted from their reservation.

Black troopers of the 9th Cavalry gallop to aid a detachment besieged by Ute Indians on Milk Creek, near the White River Agency.

braves of the Standing Rock Agency exhibited their prowess to admiring women and children by letting the beasts run free, then lassoing them and wrestling them to the ground before dispatching them with knives. In 1888 a woman teacher at the agency, revolted by this exhibition, demanded that the government ban it. Two years later the commissioner of Indian affairs acted. "It is needless to say," he wrote, "that this bit of barbarism is a fearful hindrance to the work of civilization."

In the 1880's a similar attempt to interfere with two age-old Apache customs—the drinking of a strong native brew called tiswin and the practice of wife beating—touched off a last great rebellion under the implacable Geronimo. There were, of course, far deeper causes for resentment among the Indians—notably the arbitrary removal of many tribes from their home reserva-

tions and the widespread corruption among Indian agents and other officials—but by this time most of the red men were too broken in spirit to protest.

By the late 1870's the government began to spend considerable sums on Indian education. Both boarding and day schools were established on the reservations, and the more promising pupils were sent east to gain a smattering of "higher" learning at institutions such as Pennsylvania's Carlisle Indian School, where courses included the practical subjects of cooking, housekeeping, agriculture, and simple mechanics.

Whatever the differences between one school administration and the next, all shared a contempt for traditional Indian life. The students were forced to dress like whites, adopt white values, and, most important of all, speak the white man's tongue. "All instruction must be in the English language," read the man-

ual of regulations for Indian schools. "Pupils must be compelled to converse with each other in English, and should be properly rebuked or punished for persistent violation of this rule. Every effort should be made to encourage them to abandon their tribal language."

For some Indians this experiment in abrupt cultural transformation ended in tragedy. Of 112 Apache children sent to Carlisle beginning in 1886, for example, 30 were dead of white men's diseases within three years and another dozen were sent home seriously ill.

Of the $240 million that the federal government spent between 1868 and 1901 to support the Indians, almost one-fifth went into repressive education. Yet the government's two main goals —self-sufficiency and Indian acculturation—remained largely unrealized. This would be demonstrated in the last great Apache uprising under Geronimo.

Geronimo: Tiger of the Southwest

Geronimo (center) stands with a group of his suspicious warriors before meeting General Crook for a peace parley in March 1886.

"These tigers of the human race," Gen. George Crook wrote of the Apaches, "resented anything like an attempt to regulate their conduct, or in any way to interfere with their mode of life." And the most tigerish of all was the war leader Geronimo, who became a terror to Mexican peasants and American settlers in the Southwest—a symbol of the tenacious but doomed Indian resistance to white domination.

A Mimbreño Apache, Geronimo began life as Goyathlay ("One Who Yawns"), a name that did not seem to mark him as one most likely to succeed among a people noted for their cunning and toughness. His grandfather had been chief of an Apache band in northern Mexico, but Goyathlay's father had given up his hereditary chieftainship when he left the tribe and married into the Mimbreño Apaches.

The Murder of His Family

The Mimbreño Apaches, led by the great chief Mangas Coloradas, made a living raiding the Mexicans, and young Goyathlay did his share of riding and fighting. But his lust for blood really dated from a day in the 1850's when Mexicans killed his mother, wife, and three children. His grief at the loss of his family filled him with such hatred for the whites that he caught the attention and approval of Mangas Coloradas. Mangas Coloradas sent Goyathlay to Cochise, brilliant chief of the Chiricahuas, and to Chief Juh, of his father's people, to enlist them both against the Mexican foes.

The Mimbreños and their new allies descended upon the town of Arizpe, captured a pack train laden with ammunition and food, and fought a two-day battle with Mexican forces. The second day of battle became a hand-to-hand melee, and Goyathlay raged all over the field killing soldiers. At the height of the fighting a panicky Mexican pointed at the young man and inexplicably shouted, "Geronimo!" The cry was echoed by others, and from that day on Goyathlay was known as Geronimo (from the Spanish for Jerome).

Soon after winning his new name, Geronimo left the Mimbreños, acquired a Chiricahua wife, and accepted Cochise as his leader. When Cochise ended his long and bloody war against the whites and accepted reservation life in 1872, Geronimo continued to raid into Mexico with renegade Chiricahuas. In 1876 he began using the towering Sierra Madre of western Mexico as a stronghold to raid both sides of the

This studio picture of Geronimo was taken in 1886, the year he finally laid down his gun and went into exile in Florida.

border. But in April 1877, while he was at the Ojo Caliente Reservation in southwestern New Mexico, which he used as a supply and rest center between raids, Geronimo and 16 of his leading warriors were surrounded by Indian police led by agent John Clum and clapped into jail. Clum then marched Geronimo and his braves 400 miles to the San Carlos Reservation in eastern Arizona.

Conditions at San Carlos and other reservations seemed calculated to foment uprisings among the Apaches, as corrupt

We Must Cease

The story of one [Indian] tribe is the story of all. . . . Colorado is as greedy and unjust in 1880 as was Georgia in 1830, and Ohio in 1795; and the United States Government breaks promises now as deftly as then, and with an added ingenuity from long practice. . . . Cheating, robbing, breaking promises—these three are clearly things which must cease to be done. One more thing, also, and that is the refusal of the protection of the law to the Indians' rights of property, "of life, liberty, and the pursuit of happiness." When these four things have ceased to be done, time, statesmanship, philanthropy, and Christianity can slowly and surely do the rest. Till these four things have ceased to be done, statesmanship and philanthropy alike must work in vain, and even Christianity can reap but small harvest.

—Helen Hunt Jackson
A Century of Dishonor, 1881

homestead to farm? Nor did the Dawes Act, which finally passed in 1887, entirely overlook the Indians' inexperience in matters of finance and land titles. Under its terms no Indian would be granted full title to his holding until 25 years had passed, and in the meantime he could not sell without official permission. Further, those Indians who agreed to take up a homestead and renounce their tribal allegiance would be rewarded with U.S. citizenship.

Despite its good intentions, there was considerable mischief inherent in the Dawes Act, even though there were only a few—a very few—who clearly foresaw it. Some of these dissenters warned that most of the reservation land to be divided was far too arid for subsistence farming, much less farming for profit. They recommended that the size of the individual holdings be increased and that the Indians be encouraged to raise livestock instead of crops. But in general this advice was ignored. A handful of others predicted that loopholes in the law would permit land-hungry whites, in the words of Colorado's Senator Henry M. Teller describing a similar proposal, to "despoil the Indians of their lands and to make them vagabonds on the face of the earth."

Unfortunately, the skeptics were drowned out in the general din of approbation for the Dawes Act.

Wherever the government decided to apply its provisions, the Indians—few of whom had the inclination or the training to become farmers in any case—found themselves under pressure to lease their homesteads to white settlers for a few cents an acre or to sell off their so-called excess land for as little as 50 cents an acre. Occasionally, a strong chief would persuade his followers to hold out for a better price. In 1889 Sitting Bull, after a year of hard bargaining, forced the government to pay $1.25 for each of the 10 million acres of the Sioux reservation it wished to open for white settlement. But such small victories were rare. By that same year about 61,000 of the Indians' 215,000 square miles of reservation land had already been sold to whites, and most of the acreage allotted to individual Indians eventually came on the market despite the trusteeship provisions.

Drought, Starvation, and Epidemics

Along with reduced land holdings came shrinking allotments of food, clothing, and other supplies. The Indians, deprived of millions of acres by Congress, were now instructed to provide more of their own sustenance on their much-reduced holdings. Out in the West the years 1889 and 1890 brought drought, and in the Dakota reservations starvation and epidemics were widespread. The time was ripe for that final Indian ritual of hope and despair called the Ghost Dance and that last desperate bid for freedom that ended in the tragedy at Wounded Knee.

McGillycuddy's Lawman

Capt. George Sword

Shortly after he became the agent at Pine Ridge in 1878, Valentine McGillycuddy appointed Man-Who-Carries-the-Sword—well known for his prowess as a warrior—as captain of the first Indian police at the agency. He became Capt. George Sword. His men proved their worth when Spotted Wolf and 25 Cheyennes slipped away, presumably to join Sitting Bull in Canada. If the Cheyennes were to attack whites on the way north, troops might be summoned, and any clash would give the government an excuse to crack down on all Indians. So McGillycuddy ordered Captain Sword to bring back Spotted Wolf. Eleven days later Captain Sword and his men returned to the agency with Spotted Wolf, who was dead. He had made the mistake of resisting arrest.

A New Religion for the Indians of the Plains

The Ghost Dance religion originated in 1889. A Paiute shaman named Wovoka told a group of tribal representatives who visited him at his home in Nevada that during a seizure he believed he had visited the Great Spirit in heaven. There, he had been told that a time was coming when the buffalo would fill the plains and dead tribesmen would be restored to their families. All would live a blissful life, free of the white man and his works. Wovoka assured his followers that if they adhered to certain precepts and performed the proper ritual dance—called the Ghost Dance by whites because of its association with the resurrection of the dead—they would be given a glimpse of the marvelous world that would become theirs for eternity.

Wovoka, the Paiute messiah

The Final Clash at Wounded Knee

Sitting Bull, a great Hunkpapa war leader, was accused of using the Ghost Dance frenzy in an effort to increase his power.

The Ghost Dance cult, with its promise that all whites would disappear and all Indians would be reborn into a joyous eternal life, spread like a whirlwind across the western reservations. In 1890 it reached the lands of the Sioux in the Dakotas, but here it appeared to take on threatening overtones.

Fearful that the government would ban their new religion, the Sioux followers of the Ghost Dance took to wearing special "ghost shirts" painted with magical symbols, which they be-lieved would turn away the bullets of anyone who attacked them. As the cult spread through the Pine Ridge, Standing Rock, Cheyenne River, and Rosebud Reservations, Indian agents and army officers grew increasingly suspicious. If the ritual was so peaceful, they asked, why did its adherents need "bulletproof" garments? Aside from that, the Ghost Dance seemed to pose a direct threat to the government's program of assimilation and Christianization—although the messianic cult did have distinctly Christian aspects.

By midautumn of 1890 a kind of religious frenzy possessed many of the Sioux. They abandoned their daily tasks, emptied out the schools, and spent their days and nights dancing and chanting. White officials looked on this delirium with emotions ranging from tightlipped disapproval to growing panic. "A more pernicious system of religion could not have been offered to a people who stood on the threshold of civilization," wrote Indian agent James McLaughlin, head of the Standing Rock Agency. From Pine Ridge came another agent's panicky appeal: "Indians are dancing in the snow and are wild and crazy. . . . We need protection and we need it now." The agent's plea was quickly answered; troops were sent to the Pine Ridge and Rosebud Agencies to stand ready while the authorities debated what to do.

There was one white, however, who saw the Ghost Dance as essentially harmless. The former Indian agent Valentine McGillycuddy, dispatched by the U.S. government to assess the situa-tion, counseled patience. "I should let the dance continue," he recommended. "The coming of the troops has frightened the Indians. If the Seventh-Day Adventists prepare their ascension robes for the second coming of the Savior, the United States Army is not put in motion to prevent them. Why should not the Indians have the same privilege?" Unfortunately, few listened to McGillycuddy's warning: "If the troops remain, trouble is sure to come."

The End of Sitting Bull

Increasingly, white fear and anger focused on one Indian: Sitting Bull, the famed Hunkpapa Sioux chief and medicine man who had been one of the last to surrender to the Army and accept government authority. Actually, Sitting Bull had maintained a skeptical attitude toward the Ghost Dance, but he had also declined to interfere with it. Agent McLaughlin contended, despite evidence to the contrary, that the religious frenzy had been set off by Sitting Bull and urged that he be arrested.

In December of 1890 Maj. Gen. Nelson A. Miles, commanding the Division of the Missouri, ordered the arrest of Sitting Bull and Big Foot, a leader of the Miniconjou Sioux at the Cheyenne River Reservation. On the morning of December 15 McLaughlin's Sioux Indian police seized Sitting Bull. During a rescue attempt a fight broke out and six policemen and six Hunkpapa Sioux, including Sitting Bull, were killed.

After Sitting Bull's death some 400 of his Hunkpapas fled southward to the

Oglala Sioux at the Pine Ridge Reservation in Dakota perform the Ghost Dance, which spread east through the Great Plains from the Nevada home of the founder of the new religion. Besides prescribing the dance, shaman Wovoka warned that those who wanted to enjoy eternal bliss should avoid lying, stealing, and any form of cruelty; above all, they must do no harm to anyone, and they must never fight.

Sitting Bull, with a blanket about his waist, rebuffs officials who tried in 1889 to get the Sioux to open reservation land to whites.

Cheyenne River Reservation. With the help of Hump, a Miniconjou chief, army officers got most of the Hunkpapas to surrender at nearby Fort Bennett, but 38 of them took refuge with Big Foot, whose village was on the forks of the Cheyenne River west of Fort Bennett. Lt. Col. Edwin V. Sumner, who had been ordered to arrest Big Foot, kept his village under observation but did not try to seize the chief. Disturbed by Sumner's surveillance and worried by the approach of more troops, Big Foot decided to take his people and the Hunkpapa refugees—about 350 in all—to the Pine Ridge Reservation. They sneaked out of the village on the night of December 23 and headed south through the Dakota Badlands.

The Army pursued the fleeing Indians with elements of several cavalry units, including members of Custer's old command, the 7th Cavalry. On December 28 the soldiers caught up with Big Foot, who surrendered and accepted a military escort. That night the Indians made camp at a place called Wounded Knee Creek, about 20 miles from the Pine Ridge Agency, while some 500 troopers took up positions in the surrounding hills to prevent an escape. The next morning the commanding officer, Col. James W. Forsyth, ordered his captives to surrender their weapons.

A Wild Shot

When the Indians refused, Forsyth grew impatient and unwisely ordered his men to search the tepees and the Indians themselves for weapons. (It was dangerous to lay hands on a Sioux warrior.) A young man named Black Coyote, insulted by this rough treatment, fired a wild shot during a scuffle, and the soldiers, primed for action, retaliated with a murderous volley at close range. The warriors then fired at the soldiers, while from a low hill four Hotchkiss guns opened up, ripping into the fleeing Indians and cutting down men, women, and children until the snow was colored a bright crimson. In the confusion 25 officers and troopers died and 39 were wounded. Since the soldiers had surrounded the Indians, many of these casualties were thought to have been caused by the soldiers' own crossfire. The Indian dead numbered at least 153, by some estimates nearly 300.

So grisly was the scene that one member of the burial party recalled: "It was a thing to melt the heart of a man, if it was of stone, to see those little children, with their bodies shot to pieces, thrown naked into the pit."

The Pine Ridge Reservation Indians, whipped into a fever of fury by the carnage, gathered in a huge camp of about 4,000 at White Clay Creek, some 15 miles north of the agency. When the 7th Cavalry probed this area, it became trapped in a valley by the Sioux until rescued by several companies of the black 9th Cavalry. General Miles then had the village surrounded by 3,500 troops while he sent emissaries in to talk to the Sioux chiefs. By a show of force, plus peace overtures, Miles got the Sioux to surrender without further bloodshed on January 15, 1891. Thus the hope that had been engendered by the Ghost Dance faltered and finally vanished, and with it went the Indians' last bid for freedom.

After the carnage at Wounded Knee civilians who made up the burial party were paid $2 for each body put into a common grave in the frozen earth.

The body of Big Foot, a chief of the Miniconjou Sioux, lies frozen in the snow that covered the bloody battlefield at Wounded Knee on December 29, 1890.

I congratulate you upon the commencement of the great work [the Central Pacific Railroad] which in its results to the state of California and the Pacific Coast . . . is to be what the Erie Canal was to New York and the Eastern States. . . . We may look forward with confidence to the day . . . when the Pacific Coast will be bound to the Atlantic Coast by iron bonds.

—Leland Stanford, Governor of California, January 8, 1863

No engineering feat of 19th-century America surpassed the building of the transcontinental railroad. Neither raging blizzards nor rampaging Indians could slow the progress of the construction crews as they laid track over towering mountains and across furnace-hot prairies. The driving of the golden spike in 1869, marking the project's completion, ushered in an era of railroad building in the West that brought hundreds of thousands of settlers onto the Great Plains and beyond. And each furrow they plowed diminished what, 10 years before, had seemed a limitless frontier.

"Western Railway Station." Oil painting by Oscar Berninghaus.

Chapter 8

Rails Transform the Nation

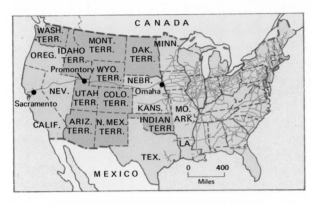

Between 1860 and 1870 the nation's rail mileage increased from 30,626 to 52,922. A cobweb of railroad lines covered the United States east of the Mississippi, particularly in the Midwest, where Chicago was the nation's great railroad center. Beyond the Mississippi, however, only one transcontinental line—the Union Pacific from Omaha, Nebraska, to Promontory, Utah Territory, and the Central Pacific from Sacramento, California, to Promontory—provided a link between the Atlantic and Pacific Coasts. In Kansas the Union Pacific's Kansas-Pacific line was laying rails westward toward Denver.

The Search for an Iron Trail

Stagecoaches jouncing along the dusty trails, lengthy trains of freight wagons crawling across the plains, graceful clipper ships battering their way around Cape Horn—these were the threads that bound the settled East to the booming Far West; but by the late 1850's nearly everyone agreed that what was needed was a transcontinental railroad to link the growing rail system of the East and Midwest with the Pacific Coast.

Undoubtedly one of the first railroad visionaries was Dr. Hartwell Carver of Rochester, New York. In 1832—just two years after America's earliest steam locomotive completed its first trial run—he began proposing a transcontinental line. Since the United States then had no more than 100 miles of track, Dr. Carver's scheme must have sounded like the ravings of a madman, particularly when he predicted such unheard-of luxuries as dining and sleeping cars.

By the mid-1840's, however, the doctor's vision had begun to seem less farfetched. Even before the United States acquired California and Oregon, the idea of a transcontinental rail line had been gaining both currency and respectability. The prime mover was a wealthy New York City merchant named Asa Whitney, who proposed that construction be subsidized by the sale of government lands in a strip 60 miles wide, stretching from Lake Michigan to the mouth of the Columbia River—a distance of about 2,000 miles. Whitney offered to buy this land (a total of almost 78 million acres) at 10 cents an acre and then sell it off piecemeal to settlers as his

Starting in 1853, routes for a transcontinental railroad were surveyed by army engineers led by Stevens and McClellan, Gunnison (his work completed by E. G. Beckwith), Whipple, and Pope and Parke.

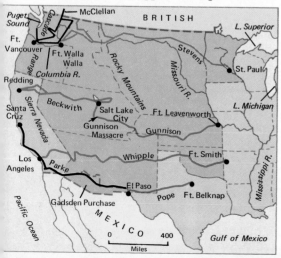

Secretary of War Jefferson Davis, a champion of the South, favored a southern route for the projected railroad to the Pacific.

line moved forward, thus keeping the railroad solvent throughout the construction period. By the time the line reached Oregon, its presence would have attracted thousands of pioneers, who would fill the vast spaces of the northern plains and provide the new railroad with both passengers and freight.

The grandeur of Whitney's scheme caught the imagination of Americans, and by the mid-1850's it had been endorsed by 16 state legislatures. But in Congress, which had to approve or deny the plan, there was no unanimity. Enthusiastic proponents suddenly turned sour at the mention of Whitney and rightly criticized him for his ignorance of the project's enormous engineering difficulties. But this was not their real objection. Unknowingly, the New York merchant had run afoul of conflicting regional ambitions. Men like Jefferson Davis from Mississippi and Senators Thomas Hart Benton of Missouri and Stephen A. Douglas of Illinois were all equally determined that their own areas should be the primary beneficiaries of a transcontinental railroad.

Senator Benton was the first to promote a route of his own choosing—the Buffalo Trail running from St. Louis along the 38th parallel to San Francisco—and in 1848 he dispatched his famous son-in-law, John C. Frémont, to survey it. Leading a party of 35, Frémont headed due west in October,

certain that he would find an easy passage through the Rockies in the vicinity of the 38th parallel. Instead, he found himself snowbound in December on a high Rocky Mountain pass. Despite the fact that 10 of his party died before help arrived, Frémont reported that the result of the survey was "entirely satisfactory."

Meanwhile, the South, increasingly disaffected from its sister states over the issue of slavery, saw its salvation in a transcontinental line that would link it with the Southwest and California. A railroad would create bonds of mutual self-interest between the new West and the Old South and give the latter increased influence in the councils of state. During the southern-influenced administration of President Franklin Pierce in the early 1850's, Secretary of War Jefferson Davis claimed a southern line would be the easiest to build and keep open during the winter months. But the fact was that neither Davis' so-called Southern Trail nor any of the other routes so far suggested had been tested against the needs of railroad builders.

In March of 1853 Congress decided

The Panama Railroad

The Panama Railroad was the first transcontinental line. Running 48 miles across the Isthmus of Panama, from Aspinwall (now Colón) on the Atlantic to Panama City on the Pacific, it delivered passengers and freight to the Pacific Mail Steamship Company for the trip to San Francisco. During the first four years of operation—from 1855 to 1859—the railroad carried close to 200,000 passengers (one-way fare, $25) and took in more than $8 million.

to seek out a practical route for a transcontinental railroad by authorizing the Army's topographical corps to conduct surveys within the next 10 months. It fell to Capt. Andrew A. Humphreys to select team leaders and designate the routes to be explored. The choice was apparently governed more by political than topographical considerations. For example, the northern route, stretching from the Great Lakes along the Missouri River to Puget Sound in the Washington Territory, was strongly supported by Illinois' powerful Senator Stephen A. Douglas, just as the Buffalo Trail was supported by Benton and the Southern Trail by Secretary Davis. A fourth route to be surveyed followed the 35th parallel from Fort Smith, Arkansas, to Los Angeles. This one had the advantage of tying in with the Mississippi Valley rail lines that linked with both northern and southern cities. Thus it could conceivably serve as a compromise that would please politicians from both the North and the South.

The Railroad Surveys

To lead the survey of the northern route, Davis chose former army officer Isaac I. Stevens, recently appointed territorial governor of Washington. The Buffalo Trail would be explored by Capt. John Williams Gunnison, the 35th parallel route by Lt. Amiel Weeks Whipple, and later the Southern Trail by Lts. John Pope and John G. Parke.

Governor Stevens' team was the first off the mark, with Stevens himself leading one party westward from St. Paul, while Capt. George B. McClellan led a second group eastward from the Washington Territory. The cautious captain

This Möllhausen painting shows the Whipple expedition, which explored New Mexico Territory, ferrying supplies across the Colorado River near a Mojave Indian village.

soon reached the conclusion that the snowy heights of the Cascades were totally impassable, and although his attitude did nothing to dampen Stevens' glowing enthusiasm for the northern route, other members of the survey team were less sanguine. One of them wrote in disgust, "The extreme northern route to the mind of all who went over it . . . seems *impracticably expensive.* A road *might* be built over the tops of the Himalayeh mountains—but no reasonable man would undertake it."

If the northern route appeared topographically unsuitable, Benton's Buffalo Trail was also discounted—but for a different reason. In late October of 1853 an advance party of Captain Gunnison's team, which had left Fort Leavenworth in June, was attacked by Paiute Indians in Utah. The captain and seven of his men were killed, and support for the Buffalo Trail quickly evaporated.

Farther to the south, along the 35th parallel route, Lieutenant Whipple's team was having much better luck. Delighted with his progress, the officer reported that the route was "not only practicable but . . . eminently advanta-

geous." Unfortunately for Whipple, however, he made an enormous error in calculating the cost of constructing a railroad along his route, overstating the amount by $75 million. Though he later corrected his mistake, the original estimate was seized upon by the route's opponents to bar construction there.

That left the Southern Trail. Davis had hoped its construction would be facilitated by the purchase of some 30,000 square miles of territory in present-day New Mexico and Arizona. But even after the Gadsden Purchase the surveying party could find no usable pass through the southern reaches of the Sierra Nevada without dipping into Mexican territory. When the secretary of war issued his preliminary report on the surveys to Congress in 1855, he still recommended the Southern Trail—as everyone had expected—but by this time he probably knew his cause was hopeless. The rising tide of sectionalism made it impossible to find a congressional majority for one route. Almost another decade would pass before work began on the rail line; and the route selected did not follow exactly any one of the four surveyed in 1853.

Members of the Whipple team are sketched on a petrified tree by Balduin Möllhausen, one of the artists who accompanied the survey.

A U.S. Army private sketched a feast given by Isaac I. Stevens, who made treaties with Indians during his railroad surveys.

Action at Last

The pamphlet entitled "A Practical Plan for Building the Pacific Railroad" was published in 1857 after many years of congressional bickering over railroad routes. Its author was a young engineer, Theodore D. Judah, who had searched out possible routes through the Sierras.

If Judah was passionate in his cause, he was also realistic, and his pamphlet scorched the Army's surveys: "When a Boston capitalist is invited to invest in a railroad project, he does not care to be informed that there are 999 different varieties . . . of plants and herbs. . . . He wishes to know the length of your road. He says, let me see your map and profile, that I may judge of its alignment and grades. . . . Have you any tunnels, and what are their circumstances?"

By the fall of 1860 Judah had solved, at least to his own satisfaction, one of the great problems of the proposed line: getting it across the Sierras. The route he chose was the old Donner Pass, even though he admitted that it would require several tunnels through the mountains. Once he had settled on this solution, he hurried to San Francisco and Sacramento to secure financial support for a scientific survey across the mountains. He approached seven leading Sacramento businessmen, including Leland Stanford, Charles Crocker, Mark Hopkins, and Collis P. Huntington, later known as the Big Four.

At first Judah avoided mention of his transcontinental plans; instead he softened up these cautious merchants by pointing out the profits they could reap from a railroad or even a wagon road via the Donner Pass to the Nevada mining camps.

In June of 1861 the Central Pacific Railroad Company of California (CP) was incorporated, with the Big Four among its directors and chief officers and Judah as chief engineer. After completing his survey Judah left for Washington, D.C., to lobby for government aid when the very integrity of the nation was being threatened by the Civil War.

There were several factors in Judah's favor, however. The Republican Party, then in power, already stood pledged to build a transcontinental line, and President Lincoln himself had expressed keen interest in the project. Then, too, a railroad would bind booming California and mineral-rich Nevada to the Union. Finally, the question of the route was no longer a burning political issue, since the South's rebellion had narrowed the choices considerably.

So successful was Judah's lobbying that on July 1, 1862, the Pacific Railroad Act was signed into law by President Lincoln. It authorized the Central Pacific to build a railroad and telegraph line from Sacramento to the Nevada line and created a new company, the Union Pacific (UP), to build westward from Nebraska. Both companies would be given land grants amounting to 10 square miles for each mile of track laid. The companies also would receive financial aid in the form of loan bonds payable in 30 years at 6 percent annual interest. Every mile of track laid on flatland would bring $16,000 worth of loan bonds; track through the high desert country of Utah and Nevada, $32,000 per mile; and track in the mountains, $48,000 per mile.

The Big Four Take Charge

Ground-breaking ceremonies for the Central Pacific were conducted with appropriate fanfare at Sacramento on January 8, 1863, but the fledgling railroad was not in good shape financially. Sales of stock had lagged and the Central Pacific had only $156,000 on hand. Chief engineer Judah had estimated that the first 50 miles of track would cost more than $3 million, and 40 miles of track had to be completed before the Central Pacific could obtain government loan bonds or land grants.

The Big Four pledged their personal

Engineer Theodore Judah: Practical Visionary

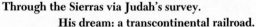

Through the Sierras via Judah's survey.
His dream: a transcontinental railroad.

Born in Bridgeport, in Connecticut, Theodore Dehone Judah (1826–63) moved with his family to Troy, New York, in 1833, when his father, the Reverend Henry R. Judah, became pastor of St. Paul's Church. A withdrawn but precocious boy, Theodore was permitted to enroll in the college preparatory course at Rensselaer Polytechnic Institute in 1837, when he was only 11 years old. There, the lectures of Professor Amos Eaton, an enthusiast of the railroad at a time when many people doubted that this wheezing, spark-spouting contraption would ever come to anything, strongly influenced young Judah.

After two years of study he left Rensselaer to take a job as a surveyor's assistant on the Schenectady & Troy Railroad and honed his engineering skills on other roads in the East. While on a job in Massachusetts, he met Anna, the daughter of the wealthy John J. Pierce of Greenfield. Theodore

and Anna were married in 1847 and moved to New York State. There he proved to be an outstanding location engineer for the Niagara Gorge and the Buffalo & New York lines.

A diligent study of the subject had made Judah a Pacific railroad enthusiast even before he went to California in 1854 to build the Sacramento Valley Railroad. He became fascinated with the challenging Sierra Nevada; and when he completed his work on the Sacramento line, he stayed in California to prowl the Sierras, seeking a route to the East. He found it and, later, the Big Four, who joined him in organizing the CP. But soon the financial manipulations of the Big Four so outraged Judah that he headed east to find investors who would help him buy control of the CP. There he died of yellow fever, which he contracted in Panama. The Big Four sent a message of sympathy to Anna and then got busy building Theodore Judah's "dream" railroad.

The CP's gateway to the East through the Sierra Nevada was the Donner Pass and nearby Donner Lake. The CP's first move was to build a wagon road linking Dutch Flat, in California, to the mines in Nevada via the Donner Pass. This painting was the work of Albert Bierstadt, an eastern artist who first came west with a government survey in 1859.

fortunes to obtain shipments of rails from the East, and Collis P. Huntington went to New York and Boston to raise money. Bankers were not interested, for there was plenty of money to be made in war contracts. Not dismayed, the Big Four managed, by a feat of geological legerdemain, to have 24 miles of flatland east of Sacramento designated mountain country. This action assured the Central Pacific an additional $768,000 in loan bonds and also helped Huntington borrow money from previously disinterested eastern bankers.

During much of 1863 Theodore Judah clashed with the Big Four because he feared they were less interested in good railroad building than in huge profits. In the fall, however, he died of yellow fever, and the Big Four had the Central Pacific firmly in their hands. But as wartime inflation pushed up costs, money again became scarce and construction lagged. So Huntington went to Washington to lobby vigorously (and buy votes) for the passage by Congress of the Pacific Railroad Act of 1864. He was joined by an expert wire-puller, the Union Pacific's Thomas C. Durant.

The 1864 act doubled the size of the railroads' land grants and offered other inducements in order to attract investors. It was particularly helpful to Durant's Union Pacific, which had yet to lay a single rail. Durant had already taken steps to assure himself a tidy profit when construction began. In 1863 he had set up the Crédit Mobilier, a construction company that would build the Union Pacific and be reimbursed by the railroad at a highly inflated rate for all

expenses incurred. (This was similar to a company the Big Four had formed for the Central Pacific in 1862 and reorganized as the Contract and Finance Company in 1867.)

The Crédit Mobilier's venture into railroad building cost Durant the services of his chief engineer, Peter A. Dey, who resigned in 1864 rather than approve a scheme to overcharge the Union Pacific for the first 100 miles of track. Even before Dey quit, Durant had tried

to hire Grenville M. Dodge, a Union general with long experience as a surveyor and railroad builder, but Dodge had refused to leave the Army. Again, Durant sought out Dodge, and in April of 1866 Dodge accepted the job of chief engineer after insisting that Durant give him complete control over the route to be followed. The next month Dodge appeared on the scene to find that the railroad had scarcely begun to inch its way across Nebraska.

Crédit Mobilier: Wrecker of Reputations

Believing that the UP would never be profitable, its vice president, Thomas Durant, decided, as he bluntly put it, "to grab a wad of money from the construction fees—and get out." In 1864 a Durant associate bought the charter of a Pennsylvania company and named it the Crédit Mobilier (French for credit on movable property). Durant then hired it to construct the UP and overcharge the railroad by millions.

Congressman Oakes Ames of Massachusetts was a stockholder in the company. In late 1867 Ames foolishly sought to win friends for the UP in Congress by selling stock—at far below its value—to members, including Schuyler Colfax, who became the vice president under Ulysses S. Grant in 1869. By 1872 rumors of the Crédit Mobilier's chicanery surfaced, and Congress investigated. Durant, whom Ames had ousted from control of the company, escaped unscathed; but Ames was censured, and he soon died.

Thomas Nast pilloried Congressmen Oakes Ames and James Brooks (above), who got stock from Ames, as "Cherubs of the Crédit Mobilier." Schuyler Colfax, shown with his family on an outing in Utah (top), was ruined by the scandal.

The Central Pacific's Big Four

Collis P. Huntington

Mark Hopkins

The Big Four of the Central Pacific Railroad were all easterners who had gone to Sacramento, California, during and after the gold-rush days. There they prospered, not as miners but as merchants, selling all manner of goods, ranging from picks, shovels, gunpowder, and fuses to groceries, cloth, and ribbon. Hardheaded, hardfisted, and alert to the main chance, these men were to turn the dreams and maps of a railroad promoter and engineer into reality.

Collis Potter Huntington, the premier wheeler-dealer of the Big Four, was a Connecticut Yankee, born in Harwinton in 1821. The son of a village tinker, he had the sharp no-nonsense look of an ax blade and a hair-trigger temper. Leaving home in 1835, he hired out as a farmhand. A year later he left the farm with $84 in his pocket and went to Oneonta, New York, to open a store with his eldest brother. Hearing of the gold rush, he bought a supply of groceries and whisky and headed for California via Panama in 1849. Stalled on the isthmus for three months by a shortage of San Francisco-bound ships, Huntington saw opportunity while others sat around and grumbled or drank too much. After selling his initial merchandise, he loaded jerked beef, potatoes, rice, and other foods in a pack and tramped back and forth across the isthmus hunting customers. He found a lot of them, and when he finally reached San Francisco he had quadrupled his original investment of $1,200.

Huntington spent one morning in the goldfields on the end of a shovel and forthwith decided to go into business, selling a variety of supplies to the miners. He opened a small store in a tent in Sacramento and in 1855 formed a partnership with Mark Hopkins. Within a year the hardware firm of Huntington & Hopkins was one of the most prosperous in California.

The oldest of the Big Four, Mark Hopkins was born in Henderson, New York, in 1813. At the age of 12 he moved with his family to St. Clair, Michigan, and at 16 he returned to New York and became a clerk in a store in Niagara County and later a partner in the firm of Hopkins & Hughes at Lockport. In 1849 he sold out his business holdings and headed for California, arriving in August. He soon opened a store in Placerville and in 1850 went into the wholesale grocery business. Soft-spoken and frugal, Hopkins possessed the ability to drive a hard bargain, which recommended him to the ruthless Huntington. Later, Huntington said of him: "I never thought anything finished until Hopkins looked at it, which is praise enough."

The Big Four Meet for the First Time

During Republican Party meetings in 1856-57 Huntington and Hopkins nodded briefly to Leland Stanford and Charles Crocker and then warmed up to them when all four men found out that they had lived in upstate New York. Huntington was later to praise Leland Stanford as "a good businessman and a clean man in all respects," but privately he was inclined to downgrade Stanford because he had gotten a comfortable start in California in 1852 with two of his brothers, who owned wholesale grocery and mining supply stores in several gold camps. The son of a tavern owner, Stanford was born in 1824 in Watervliet, New York, near Albany. Leland and his brothers cut wood to sell to the Mohawk & Hudson Railroad, and he also peddled logs and kindling in Albany. A dull student at first, he buckled down to the study of law at the age of 20 with a firm in Albany. He remained there three years and then was admitted to the bar. After his brothers went to California in 1849, Stanford married Jane Lathrop of Albany and moved to Wisconsin, where he practiced law. In 1852, when Stanford's office burned down, he sent his wife to live with her parents in Albany and headed for California, where he joined his brothers in their flourishing business. A lucky investment in a mine soon started to pay off, and in 1855 he returned to Albany, intending to settle there permanently. But his wife wanted to live in California, so Stanford went back to Sacramento in the same year and reentered the wholesale grocery business. The deliberate Stanford went into politics, winning the governorship in 1861 and ending 11 years of Democratic rule in the state.

Charles Crocker, born in Troy, New York, in 1822, was the son of a saloon owner. When his father and four brothers

The top floor of Huntington and Hopkins' store, which opened in Sacramento in 1855, was the first headquarters of the CP.

Leland Stanford sits just to the left of a large tree on his 1,700-acre farm in Palo Alto, California, surrounded by friends and family members with their children. The Stanfords' only child died at 15, and in his memory they founded Leland Stanford Junior University in Palo Alto in 1885 with an original endowment of $20 million. After Stanford's death in 1893 his widow used his great wealth to support the university and took an active part in its affairs until her death. The personal papers of both Mr. and Mrs. Stanford are now deposited in the Stanford University Libraries.

went to Indiana to get some farming land, 14-year-old Charles "Bull" Crocker was left in charge of his mother and sister at home. Muscular and pugnacious, he carved out his territory as a newspaper hawker at the Hudson River ferry and the Rensselaer & Saratoga railroad station. The family later moved to the Indiana farm, but young Charles soon left home with "a pair of socks, a cotton shirt and a linen dickey, tied up in a cotton handkerchief," and drifted on west. He joined a wagon train that reached California in 1850, tried

Leland Stanford　　　　**Charles Crocker**

mining, and in 1852 opened a dry-goods store in Sacramento. After his store burned down, Crocker shrugged off the setback and built another that soon made him well-to-do. When Theodore Judah came to Crocker, Huntington, Stanford, and Hopkins with his daring plan to pierce the Sierras with a railroad, Crocker was enthusiastic. His partners were not charmed by the manners of this hard-drinking, profane, bull-voiced man, but they came to recognize Crocker's value. When the problems of building the CP seemed insurmountable, Crocker was ready and able to take charge.

Before Crocker's Chinese coolies and white workers had

even reached the towering Sierra Nevada, the Big Four were looking for new worlds to conquer. By 1868 they had acquired the Southern Pacific Railroad Company, with an eye to gaining a rail and shipping monopoly on the West Coast. In 1869, the year that the CP and UP met at Promontory, Utah, the Big Four extended their tracks into the San Francisco Bay area and through the fertile and largely unsettled San Joaquin Valley. By building their own lines and acquiring smaller railroads, the Big Four monopolized rail traffic in California and pushed their tracks north to Portland, Oregon.

The Southern Pacific then looked to the East; and by building and buying up lines in Arizona, Texas, and Louisiana, it reached New Orleans in 1883. In 1885 the Big Three (Hopkins had died in 1878) merged the Southern Pacific and Central Pacific Railroads. During these years another railroad, the Atchison, Topeka & Santa Fe, reached the Pacific; but it had to pay dearly to run its trains on the tracks of the monopolistic Southern Pacific.

The Omnipresent Southern Pacific

The Southern Pacific did much to promote agriculture and industry in its territory. Its rails opened southern California to settlers and provided vital service to lumbermen, wheat farmers, ranchers, and later to the growers of vegetables and orchard crops. The omnipresence of the Southern Pacific was driven home by the comment of a San Joaquin Valley rancher. Asked how he had improved his scrub cattle, he said: "I crossed them with a Southern Pacific locomotive." But while many observers recognized the good works of the line, critics complained loudly about the ruthless business practices and monopolistic freight rates charged by its president, Collis P. Huntington, and his associates. San Francisco newspapers regularly lambasted Huntington, Stanford, and Crocker for their ironfisted rule over the business and political life of California. Frank Norris' searing novel *The Octopus* (1901) depicted the Southern Pacific as the despoiler of farmers and workers. Huntington, who died in 1900—the last of the Big Four—remained defiant to the end. When in 1898 Edwin Markham's poem "The Man With the Hoe" protested the exploitation of workers, Huntington anonymously offered $750 for the best rebuttal to the "socialistic" work.

Building With the Union Pacific

When he took the job as chief engineer for the Union Pacific in May of 1866, Grenville Dodge was well aware of the perils and pitfalls ahead. Hardly anything had yet been accomplished to turn the railroad from a financial skylark into a work in progress. By the end of 1865 only 40 miles of track had been laid west of Omaha. The exact route the line would follow was yet to be settled, and there were other problems that had scarcely been considered—such as recruiting labor, transporting supplies to the West, staving off Indians, and finding suitable wood for ties and trestles. Just three months before the arrival of Dodge, Thomas Durant, organizer of the Union Pacific, had secured the services of two brothers, Jack and Dan Casement, who contracted to lay the track for the railroad.

Tough and resourceful, the Casements made ideal overseers, and Dodge gave them his full support. Dan scoured the country for labor and supplies, while Jack ranged up and down the line of construction, supervising the hundreds of Irish immigrants, Union and Confederate veterans, and former slaves recruited by his brother. A man of small stature but loud voice, Jack Casement became the driving wedge of the railroad, whipping his crews into superefficient units of a giant human machine.

Clockwork Efficiency

Herculean efforts were called for because the Union Pacific stood in danger of losing its government support unless 100 miles had been completed by July of 1866. But with Dodge and the Casements now in control of operations—and with Civil War veterans clamoring for jobs—construction began to proceed with almost clockwork efficiency.

Ranging several hundred miles west of the tracklayers, surveying parties scoured the countryside, mapping out the precise route the road was to follow. Behind them came the grading crews, who carried not only picks and shovels but also rifles to ward off Indian attacks. And finally, there were the tracklayers themselves, the ironmen, inching the road forward rail by rail. As the line advanced into the open plains, hardwood for ties became virtually unobtainable. The crews had to gather the region's soft cottonwood and treat it chemically to improve its durability. For one tie in five, however, eastern hardwood was used, giving at least a degree of strength to the line. Later, when the tracks neared the mountains, plenty of hardwood ties could be obtained.

As soon as the ties were down, the ironmen followed with the rails. Five men lifted each rail, another crew placed it across the ties, and spikers finally drove it into place. The men worked in every season in all kinds of weather;

Jack Casement rode herd on all his UP construction crews, thus living up to his title: "Champion Tracklayer of the Continent."

droughts, floods, and blizzards might slow progress, but they did not halt the Union Pacific for long. In 1866, 265 miles of track were laid, so that by the end of the year the road was near Nebraska's western border. Those who had once scoffed and jeered became converts, convinced that Dodge and the Casements could accomplish miracles.

One factor almost as uncontrollable as the weather was the Indian. The High Plains tribes were growing increasingly restive at the approach of the iron horse. The Sioux and Cheyennes had reason enough for being alarmed when they saw white hunters slaughtering thousands of precious buffalo to feed the work crews, but they knew that worse was coming, since a torrent of white settlers would certainly follow in the railroad's wake. In foray after foray the red men struck at the Union Pacific, ambushing surveying and grading crews and sometimes even attacking a speeding locomotive. One group of foolhardy braves tried to capture an iron horse "on the hoof" by stretching a rawhide rope across the track. As the locomotive drew near, the Indians pulled the rope taut. Obviously, they had no concept of the impact the engine would make, and several of the braves were swept beneath the wheels.

A more serious attack from the railroad's viewpoint was carried out by the Cheyennes in August of 1867 near Plum Creek, Nebraska. There the Indians tore down telegraph wires, ripped up a section of track to form a barricade, and then waited at night in ambush. Their first victims were a telegraph repair crew of six men, traveling on a handcar, which smashed directly into the barricade. The dazed men were immediately set upon by the Cheyennes, scalping knives in hand. Incredibly, one of the crewmen—wounded and minus his scalp—managed to escape, and while lying hidden nearby, he witnessed a second inci-

UP ironmen halt their tracklaying work to pose for a photographer. Standing on the rails behind them is one of scores of supply trains.

254

As the UP's tracks invaded Indian hunting lands, the red men resisted bitterly, attacking the surveyors and, as here, ripping up rails.

dent. This time a freight train came barreling along the track and piled up on the barricade; the engineer and fireman, badly hurt, were finished off by the Indians. Four men in the caboose escaped and warned another train of the danger. Meanwhile, the Indians swarmed over the wreckage, ripping open cars loaded with supplies. During the confusion the scalpless repairman made his escape.

In general, however, the Indians proved no match for the seasoned and well-armed workmen of the Union Pacific. But there were plenty of other problems, among them the distracting presence of the inevitable armies of prostitutes, pimps, gamblers, and thugs who followed the line westward, setting up shop in the hell-on-wheels towns that rose along the right-of-way. Jack Casement was no puritan; he knew his men needed their pleasures, but he was determined not to let progress be impeded by the raffish hangers-on, and after several workers had been killed, he clamped down hard. At Julesburg, Nebraska, he armed a group of ironmen, seized several of the most offensive gamblers, and strung them up. When Dodge later asked, "Are the gamblers quiet and behaving?" Casement laconically replied, "You bet they are, General. They're out there in the graveyard."

A Threat From Within

Perhaps the most serious threat to the Union Pacific's progress came from within. Durant continued to show more interest in lining his own pockets than in building a railroad. Despite his promise not to interfere with Dodge's manage-

ment of construction, Durant was constantly trying to lengthen the route in order to get more land grants and government aid. Finally, in 1868, Dodge faced him down. "You are now going to learn," the engineer shouted, "that the men . . . will take orders from me and not from you! If you interfere there will be trouble!"

This was no idle boast. Oakes Ames, who was also feuding with Durant, soon announced to Durant that Gen. Ulysses S. Grant, the Republican candidate for president, would be in Laramie in July and wanted to hear the two sides of the Dodge-Durant disagreement. Not only was Grant Dodge's friend from Civil War days, but he was expected to win the November election, and his word would carry weight. During a meeting at Fort Sanders, near Laramie, Dodge flatly declared he would quit if Durant or anyone else again tried to change his routes. Grant then turned to Durant and laid down the law. "The government," he announced calmly, "expects the railroad company to meet its obligations. And the government expects General Dodge to remain with the road as its chief engineer until it is completed." Stung by Grant's rebuke, Durant beat a hasty retreat. "I withdraw my objections," he stated, grasping his chief engineer's hand. "We all want Dodge to stay with the road."

Durant's surrender was a triumph for Dodge. Still, there remained almost 10 months of backbreaking labor before the Union Pacific could unite with its rival from the East and span the continent with twin ribbons of iron.

Workers had to put down tools and take up guns to defend themselves against Indians.

From the Chief Engineer

At one time we were using at least 10,000 animals, and most of the time from 8,000 to 10,000 laborers. The bridge gangs always worked from five to twenty miles ahead of the track, and it was seldom that the track waited for a bridge. To supply one mile of track with material and supplies required about forty cars, as on the plains everything—rails, ties, bridging, fastenings, all railway supplies, fuel . . . and supplies for men and animals on the entire work—had to be transported from the Missouri River. Therefore, as we moved westward, every hundred miles added vastly to our transportation. Yet the work was so systematically planned and executed that I do not remember . . . the work being delayed a single week for want of material.

—Grenville M. Dodge
How We Built the Union Pacific Railway, 1910

255

The Saga of the Central Pacific

Bluff and outspoken Charlie Crocker, the president of the Big Four's construction company, liked to think of himself as a practical man. Although a businessman at least as diligent as his three partners in the pursuit of wealth, he also relished being in the thick of the action. Not for him was the usual financier's role of raising money or lobbying in Congress.

When the railroad's army of laborers began to chip away at the monstrous bulk of the Sierra Nevada, Crocker was often there to urge them on and to share at least some of the dangers—rockslides, avalanches, and below-zero temperatures—that took hundreds of them to their doom. Although the former dry-goods merchant would lean on a chief engineer and a construction boss for advice, he was the field marshal, rallying troops, plotting strategy, and supervising the battles of men against mountains.

One of Crocker's biggest problems was a shortage of labor. California was a boom country during the Civil War and early postwar years, and the large mining concerns on the Sierras' western slopes offered workers handsome wages. Across the mountains were the equally alluring gold and silver fields of Nevada. Hundreds of laborers must have asked themselves why they should endure backbreaking work on the railroad for $35 per month when such dazzling opportunities lay close at hand. Most of those who did sign up for the Central Pacific construction gangs stayed just long enough to secure a free ride to the railhead, then scattered across the mountains to the Nevada diggings.

The innumerable difficulties of railroad building scarcely fazed Crocker. To forestall any threat from the Indians—even though the tribes of the Pacific Slope were not so dangerous as those of the plains—he hit upon a simple expedient: petty bribery. Tribal chiefs and other notables were presented with free lifetime passes on the Central Pacific's coaches; lesser braves would be permitted the hospitality of freight cars.

The problem of maintaining an adequate labor supply grew even more acute as the railroad began its ascent of the Sierras. The more difficult and dangerous the terrain and the more demanding the work, the less willing were the brawny Irishmen, who made up most of the construction force, to continue at their tasks. But at length Crocker's fertile brain came up with a solution in the form of a large, untapped resource: California's Chinese. In dismal shantytowns within San Francisco and Sacramento, Chinese veterans of the gold rush had become servants, laundrymen, and peddlers, whose yellow skins, strange clothing, and mysterious ways made them anathema to white workers. Early in

Spidery trestles carried the CP's tracks across huge ravines. In 1877 Chinese coolies, using one-man and horse-pulled dumpcarts, filled in the temporary Secrettown trestle with dirt.

During the record snows in the winter of 1867 the CP used up to a dozen locomotives to hammer a "bucker" plow through 40-foot drifts, while hundreds of hand shovelers were kept busy as well.

As another means of coping with the heavy snows, the CP built 37 miles of snowsheds to protect its tracks. Work crews grumbled at "railroading in a barn," but the sheds succeeded in doing the job.

1865 Crocker urged his construction boss, James Harvey Strobridge, to hire Chinese coolies, but Strobridge at first refused. He feared a violent reaction from the white crewmen and doubted that the diminutive, frail-looking Asiatics were physically capable of breaking the granite of the mountains, grading and blasting a right-of-way through precipitous wooded trails, or laying ties and spiking rails. But Crocker would not let go. After all, he pointed out, these people's ancestors had built the Great Wall of China.

A Successful Experiment

Reluctantly, Strobridge agreed at last to try out the Chinese, 50 of whom appeared at the railhead one day in their characteristic floppy blue trousers, their long pigtails swinging rhythmically as they walked. The white workers howled with laughter at the sight of the little men, then spat racial insults and curses at them. The Chinese paid no attention. Obeying the instructions of their gang leader, they hefted their picks and shovels and went to work with a will that astonished all who watched them.

So successful was this first experiment that Crocker immediately hired another 50 Chinese workers and then another, eventually exhausting California's supply. Undaunted, he then recruited workers from China itself, eventually bringing over thousands to toil from dawn to dusk and through every conceivable extreme of weather and terrain. Disciplined, sober, and positively fearless, the Chinese actually seemed to revel in danger. They died by the scores in snow avalanches, but the survivors merely redoubled their efforts, as if the completion of the railroad might bring their fallen comrades back to life.

The Search for Supplies

Almost as desperate as the early shortage of labor was the constant scarcity of supplies. Despite boom conditions there was very little industry in California, and almost every article needed to build a railroad—from spikes to rails, from shovels to locomotives—had to be shipped from the East, either via the Isthmus of Panama or by the longer, if less expensive, route around Cape Horn. Rails that cost $91.70 a ton at an eastern mill might bring as much as $141 in San Francisco after freight charges were added. Wartime and post-war inflation piled dollar upon dollar, and some vital materials were extremely difficult to obtain at any price. During the Civil War, for example, the Big Four's Washington lobbyist feuded bitterly with Secretary of War Edwin Stanton over allocations of blasting powder, and only a direct appeal to President Lincoln himself kept operations from coming to a halt.

Through it all Crocker and his crews persevered. From September 1, 1865, to May 8, 1866, only eight miles of track were finished, but in the next six months—as more Chinese workers arrived and wartime shortages began to ease—another 28 miles of Sierra track

During the blasting of the 63-foot-deep, 800-foot-long Bloomer Cut in California, construction boss Strobridge lost an eye.

were laid, bringing the railroad into the most difficult reaches of the mountains. During the entire 12 months that followed, only 15 miles of track went down, as the crews inched and blasted their difficult way across the blizzard-ridden Sierras. But before the spring of 1868 was out, the Central Pacific was racing down the Sierras' eastern slopes to the desert flatland below. There the crews gobbled up the miles—and the government subsidies and land grants that went with them—at a frantic pace, racing against the westward-building Union Pacific. By the early spring of 1869 the Central Pacific had swept across Nevada and invaded Utah. The moment for the joining of the rails was drawing near.

Between Ogden and Promontory, Utah, the rival graders of the CP and UP began leveling parallel roadbeds not many feet apart to lay more track and thus qualify for more land grants and loan bonds. The CP's Chinese and the UP's Irishmen often mingled, with little blood being shed, but one grading gang frequently had to dodge rocks hurled by another crew's blast.

The Transcontinental: A "Handmade" Railroad

The Central Pacific, building east out of Sacramento, California, and the Union Pacific, building west out of Omaha, Nebraska, laid a total of 1,776 miles of track ahead of schedule and without the aid of bulldozers, steam shovels, or pneumatic drills. The transcontinental was a "handmade" road, using man and animal power.

The CP had the tougher supply problem. California produced plenty of food, as well as timber for ties, trestles, and tunnels, but all other equipment—rails, locomotives, cars—had to be shipped from the East around South America or freighted across Panama and carried by ship to San Francisco, where it was put on riverboats bound for Sacramento. Then the crews had to lay track through the towering and seemingly unconquerable Sierra Nevada.

West of Omaha for more than 1,000 miles there were no important settlements, no industries, and very little farm produce. Each mile of track laid by the UP required 40 carloads of supplies—rails, ties, and other equipment, plus food for the men and animals at work—that had to be transported from Omaha over the newly laid track of the road.

The Central Pacific's Chinese Excelled at Every Task Given Them

Charles Crocker solved the CP's labor problem by hiring Chinese coolies—small and undernourished-looking but as tireless and industrious as ants. Using picks, shovels, two-wheeled dumpcarts, and wheelbarrows, the Chinese quickly proved their worth as graders to doubting whites; they took over the building of many miles of stone walls in the mountains to protect the CP tracks from snow avalanches and hand-drilled and blasted 15 tunnels. The Summit Tunnel alone was 1,659 feet long.

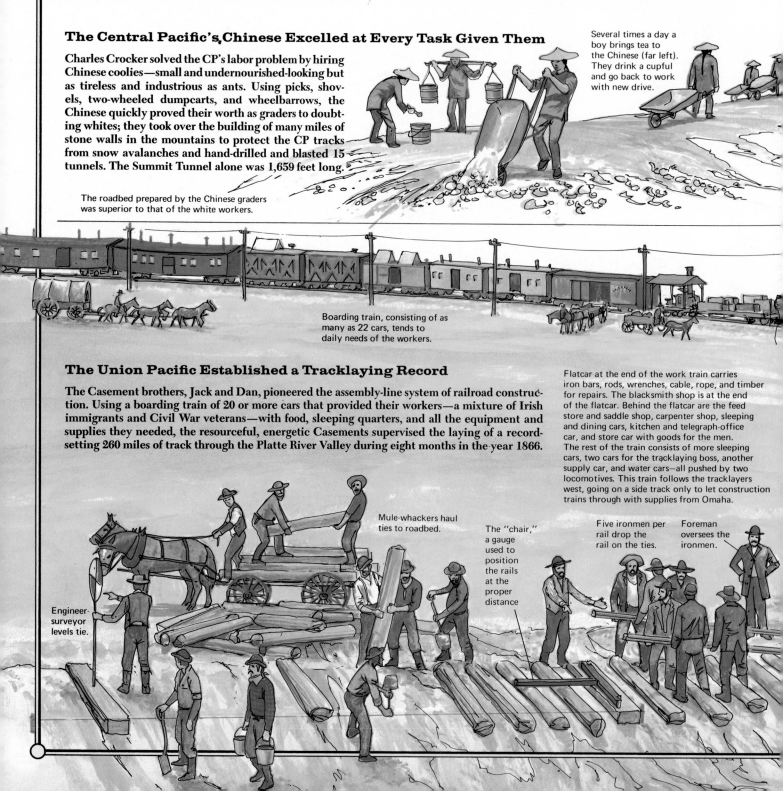

Several times a day a boy brings tea to the Chinese (far left). They drink a cupful and go back to work with new drive.

The roadbed prepared by the Chinese graders was superior to that of the white workers.

Boarding train, consisting of as many as 22 cars, tends to daily needs of the workers.

The Union Pacific Established a Tracklaying Record

The Casement brothers, Jack and Dan, pioneered the assembly-line system of railroad construction. Using a boarding train of 20 or more cars that provided their workers—a mixture of Irish immigrants and Civil War veterans—with food, sleeping quarters, and all the equipment and supplies they needed, the resourceful, energetic Casements supervised the laying of a record-setting 260 miles of track through the Platte River Valley during eight months in the year 1866.

Flatcar at the end of the work train carries iron bars, rods, wrenches, cable, rope, and timber for repairs. The blacksmith shop is at the end of the flatcar. Behind the flatcar are the feed store and saddle shop, carpenter shop, sleeping and dining cars, kitchen and telegraph-office car, and store car with goods for the men. The rest of the train consists of more sleeping cars, two cars for the tracklaying boss, another supply car, and water cars—all pushed by two locomotives. This train follows the tracklayers west, going on a side track only to let construction trains through with supplies from Omaha.

Mule-whackers haul ties to roadbed.

The "chair," a gauge used to position the rails at the proper distance

Five ironmen per rail drop the rail on the ties.

Foreman oversees the ironmen.

Engineer-surveyor levels tie.

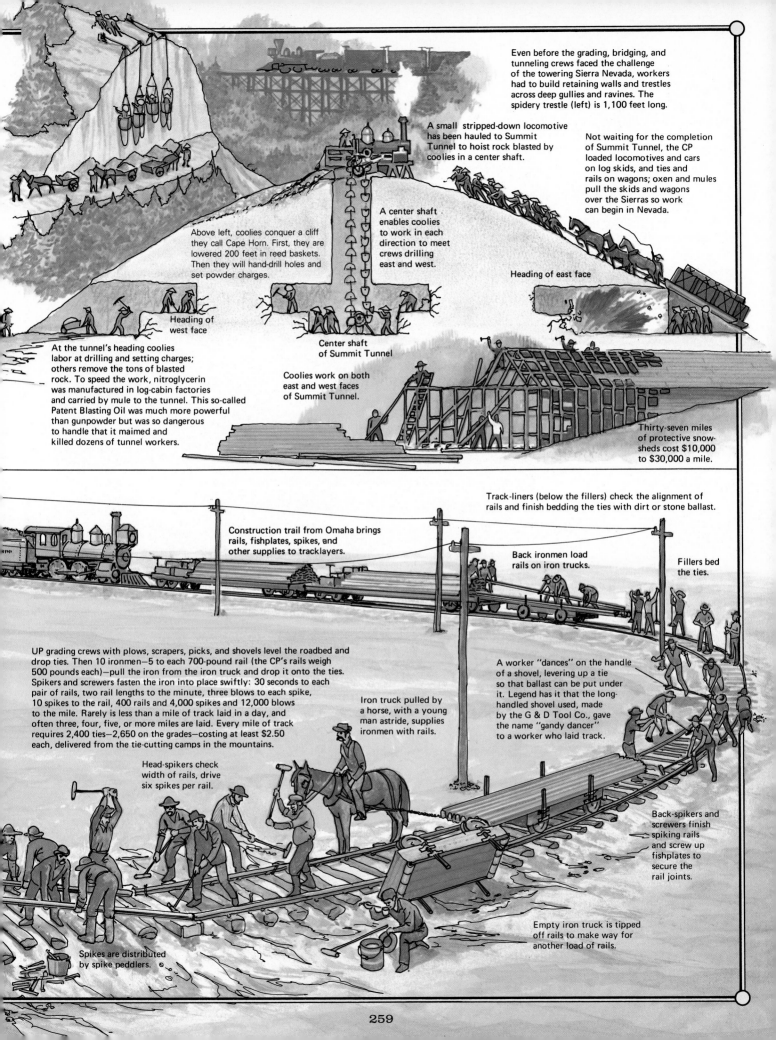

Even before the grading, bridging, and tunneling crews faced the challenge of the towering Sierra Nevada, workers had to build retaining walls and trestles across deep gullies and ravines. The spidery trestle (left) is 1,100 feet long.

A small stripped-down locomotive has been hauled to Summit Tunnel to hoist rock blasted by coolies in a center shaft.

Not waiting for the completion of Summit Tunnel, the CP loaded locomotives and cars on log skids, and ties and rails on wagons; oxen and mules pull the skids and wagons over the Sierras so work can begin in Nevada.

A center shaft enables coolies to work in each direction to meet crews drilling east and west.

Heading of east face

Above left, coolies conquer a cliff they call Cape Horn. First, they are lowered 200 feet in reed baskets. Then they will hand-drill holes and set powder charges.

Heading of west face

At the tunnel's heading coolies labor at drilling and setting charges; others remove the tons of blasted rock. To speed the work, nitroglycerin was manufactured in log-cabin factories and carried by mule to the tunnel. This so-called Patent Blasting Oil was much more powerful than gunpowder but was so dangerous to handle that it maimed and killed dozens of tunnel workers.

Center shaft of Summit Tunnel

Coolies work on both east and west faces of Summit Tunnel.

Thirty-seven miles of protective snow-sheds cost $10,000 to $30,000 a mile.

Track-liners (below the fillers) check the alignment of rails and finish bedding the ties with dirt or stone ballast.

Construction trail from Omaha brings rails, fishplates, spikes, and other supplies to tracklayers.

Back ironmen load rails on iron trucks.

Fillers bed the ties.

UP grading crews with plows, scrapers, picks, and shovels level the roadbed and drop ties. Then 10 ironmen—5 to each 700-pound rail (the CP's rails weigh 500 pounds each)—pull the iron from the iron truck and drop it onto the ties. Spikers and screwers fasten the iron into place swiftly: 30 seconds to each pair of rails, two rail lengths to the minute, three blows to each spike, 10 spikes to the rail, 400 rails and 4,000 spikes and 12,000 blows to the mile. Rarely is less than a mile of track laid in a day, and often three, four, five, or more miles are laid. Every mile of track requires 2,400 ties—2,650 on the grades—costing at least $2.50 each, delivered from the tie-cutting camps in the mountains.

A worker "dances" on the handle of a shovel, levering up a tie so that ballast can be put under it. Legend has it that the long-handled shovel used, made by the G & D Tool Co., gave the name "gandy dancer" to a worker who laid track.

Iron truck pulled by a horse, with a young man astride, supplies ironmen with rails.

Head-spikers check width of rails, drive six spikes per rail.

Back-spikers and screwers finish spiking rails and screw up fishplates to secure the rail joints.

Empty iron truck is tipped off rails to make way for another load of rails.

Spikes are distributed by spike peddlers.

The Race to the Last Spike

An amendment to the Pacific Railroad Act of 1864 had turned the building of the transcontinental line into a cross-country tracklaying race to collect government land grants and loan bonds. The Central Pacific could build as far as it might beyond the California-Nevada border, and the Union Pacific could lay track as far west as its money and materials would allow. The race appeared to favor the CP, which had conquered the Sierra Nevada and would have an easier time crossing the Nevada desert to the Great Salt Lake. The UP still had to build through the Wasatch Range, which it would reach in the winter of 1868-69. President Brigham Young of the Mormon Church had thundered against the UP after being told the only practical rail route in Utah went through Ogden, not Salt Lake City. When the CP also selected the Ogden route, Young cooled down and took a contract to grade 150 miles of UP roadbed, enabling the UP to reach Ogden ahead of the CP. But since no meetingplace had yet been selected for the two roads, the CP sent its graders eastward, past Ogden. The UP countered by pushing Irish grading crews 168 miles west of that town.

Stanford's Missed Opportunity

Under pressure from the government to stop building rail lines that met nowhere, the CP and UP agreed to a junction at Promontory in the Utah Territory. On May 10, 1869, Leland Stanford, president of the CP, swung a silver-headed maul to tap the last spike (a golden spike for the ceremony) into a hole drilled in a laurel tie, the last to be laid. Stanford missed and then handed the maul to Thomas Durant, vice president of the UP. He politely missed too, but the telegraph operator, ignoring Stanford's faulty aim, had already tapped: "Done." This message set off a series of celebrations from San Francisco to the eastern seaboard.

Thomas Hill's highly imaginative painting of Leland Stanford, president of the CP, preparing to drive the last spike, peopled the ceremony with dignitaries who were not there. Stanford (A), in the drawing at right, was present but the rest of the Big Four were not: Collis Huntington (B), Mark Hopkins (C), Charles Crocker (D). Nor was engineer Theodore D. Judah (E), who had died six years earlier.

The Site

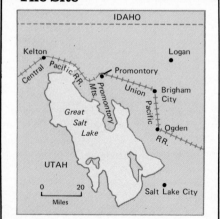

Promontory, Utah, where the rails of the UP and the CP finally met, is some 70 miles northwest of the Mormon metropolis of Salt Lake City.

The Shot

During preparations for the last-spike ceremony, construction superintendents J. H. Strobridge of the CP and Samuel Reed of the UP brought out the special laurel tie. The final two rails were then carried forward—the UP rail by an Irish squad, the CP rail by Chinese workers. As the rails arrived, a man called over to photographer Charles Savage: "Now's the time, Charlie. Take a shot!" The word "shot" jolted the nervous Chinese. Seeing the camera pointed at them, they dropped their rail and scattered. Finally, they were persuaded to come back and resume the job of putting down the rail.

Bret Harte's Tribute

What was it the Engines said,
    Pilots touching—head to head
Facing on the single track,
    Half a world behind each back?
[East:]
"I have chased the flying sun,
    Seeing all he looked upon,
Blessing all that he has blessed. . .
All his clouds about my crest;
And before my flying feet
    Every shadow must retreat."
[West:]
"You brag of your East! *You* do?
    Why, *I* bring the East to *you!*
All the Orient, all Cathay,
Find through me the shortest way;
And the sun you follow here
    Rises in my hemisphere."

Handshakes, Hilarity, and Champagne

When the last spike had been driven, two locomotives, the CP's *Jupiter* (left) and the UP's *No. 119*, chugged ahead and touched cowcatchers. Workers swarmed over them, and their engineers broke bottles of champagne in celebration of the great achievement. In the center CP's Samuel S. Montague shakes hands with Grenville M. Dodge of the UP. This photograph did not please Leland Stanford, who was a teetotaler.

Before the festivities Promontory had been just another hell-on-wheels town along the UP right-of-way, with the usual collection of stores, gambling dens, brothels, and bars.

Westward Ho!

The UP lost no time in distributing this poster throughout the country, announcing coast-to-coast travel by railroad (less than four days from Omaha to San Francisco) and promising passengers the luxury of palace sleeping cars.

"May God Continue the Unity of Our Country"

After the ceremonies at Promontory were completed, *No. 119* and *Jupiter* took turns crossing the rails that joined the UP and CP.

Once the celebrants had cleared the track, UP and CP workers rushed in with their tools, removed the last spike and the last tie, then bedded a regular tie and drove in iron spikes. This tie was quickly attacked by souvenir hunters with knives. The last tie, of laurel, was destroyed in the San Francisco fire of 1906, but the last spike is now at Stanford University. On its sides are the dates of the ground breaking and the completion of the railroad, the names of officials and directors of the CP, and a short prayer: "May God continue the unity of our Country as this Railroad unites the two great Oceans of the world."

The last spike, with a weight of 18 ounces, was valued at $350 in 1869.

The Perils and Pleasures of Railroad Travel

For a nation accustomed to thinking of transcontinental travel in terms of the snail's pace of an ox wagon or the body-bruising eternity of a stagecoach ride, the possibility of speeding from coast to coast in eight days was a heady thought. Less than a week after the joining of the rails at Promontory, Utah, on May 10, 1869, there were scheduled trains running on the new line—one westbound from Omaha and one eastbound from Sacramento—every day.

For the rich, and those with the leisure to travel and a taste for adventure, the opening of coast-to-coast service made a tour of the West something of a social necessity. And compared with a European vacation, crossing the United States by rail was not only an adventure but also a bargain. A first-class ticket from the Atlantic Coast, via connecting rail lines to Omaha and thence over the Union Pacific–Central Pacific tracks to Sacramento and on to San Francisco by steamboat, cost $173. Sleeping-car accommodations added $2 per night to the bill. An additional $4 per day entitled passengers to accommodations aboard the ultraluxurious once-a-week Pacific Hotel Express, which featured meals served on board, thus sparing the passengers the necessity of wolfing down food at trackside restaurants.

By 1885 three more major transcontinental railroads—the Southern Pacific, the Northern Pacific, and the Atchison, Topeka & Santa Fe—had been completed, linking the entire Mississippi Valley, north to south, with the states of the Pacific Coast. As the plains became settled in the 1870's and 1880's, the major traffic along these lines increasingly came not from easterners or Californians off on some long-distance jaunt but from day-coach passengers going relatively short distances. Cowhands or

Eating at a railroad station was a catch-as-catch-can affair. As passengers bit into soggy sandwiches, the conductor bawled, "All aboard," and everyone dashed for the train.

hunters, scruffy miners off to new diggings, farmers buying supplies in market towns, school teachers, or commercial travelers—they neither needed nor could afford the luxurious accommodations that first-class passengers expected.

Glimpses of the passengers in the unupholstered and often insufficiently heated day coaches provided many occupants of the luxurious palace cars with their only view of the workaday West. One fastidious first-class traveler wrote of these fellow riders: "They are not elegant . . . but bearded and mustached individuals dressed in ragged garments, carrying dirty bundles, and with revolvers stuck in their belts."

One place where the rich were forced to mingle with the day-coach riders was at the trackside eateries that dotted the right-of-way in the days before dining

cars became standard features of long-distance trains. Here all was pandemonium as dude and miner, society matron and cowhand jostled one another and screamed for attention. Those who were lucky—very lucky—managed to get a cup of lukewarm coffee and a serving of undercooked meat of doubtful ancestry.

The food problem was greatly alleviated in the late 1870's and early 1880's by an English-born restaurateur named Frederick Henry Harvey, who opened a chain of depot restaurants along the Santa Fe line. Serving good food at moderate prices, Harvey added to his popularity by staffing the well-ordered establishments with trim, presentable young waitresses whose presence in the frontier towns of the plains and mountains lent an unaccustomed aura of gentility to the surroundings. The Harvey Girls even inspired poetry of a sort, and one ardent swain wrote of his favorite: "She was winsome, she was neat, she was gloriously sweet and she certainly was very good to me."

Hotels on Wheels

While Fred Harvey was establishing modest amenities for western railroad passengers, George Pullman, inventor of the folding upper berth, worked the men of his Pullman Palace Car Company overtime to produce elegant dining cars, sumptuously appointed parlor cars, and sleepers for the growing transcontinen-

Depot dining became a pleasure when Fred Harvey established his Harvey Houses on the Santa Fe. His waitresses, "young women of good character," were paid $17.50 a month, plus room and board in a strictly chaperoned dormitory. Love blossomed across many a lunch counter, however, and about 5,000 Harvey Girls eventually settled down in the Southwest as the wives of local farmers and ranchers.

FRANK LESLIE'S
ILLUSTRATED
NEWSPAPER

No. 855—Vol. XXXIII.] NEW YORK, FEBRUARY 17, 1872. [Price, 10 Cents.

UTAH.—TRAINS OF CARS ON THE UNION PACIFIC RAILROAD SNOW-BOUND IN A DRIFT NEAR OGDEN.—From a Sketch by J. B. Schuyler.

For several months of the year the transcontinental lines had to fight howling blizzards. Here Chinese workers, laboring under the supervision of white foremen, dig out a snowbound train near Ogden, Utah Territory.

On coaches it was a case of first come, first served for the weary passengers as they improvised sleeping arrangements while the train rattled and bumped its way through the night and made bone-jolting stops and starts at each station. In contrast to the crowded, dirty, and uncomfortable accommodations (above), travelers in one of the Pullman Palace Car Company's newest sleeping cars (right) enjoyed the privacy and cushioned, curtained comfort of lower and upper berths, prepared for them by attentive porters, who converted the beds into seats again the next day.

tal carriage trade. With their fittings of burnished walnut, heavy damask draperies, and deep plush seats that could be converted into comfortable beds, Pullman's cars were often studies in Victorian excess. But most excessive of all were the menus offered by the dining cars: one 12-course Christmas dinner featured such delicacies as oysters, lobster, roast game, and plum pudding—not to mention the finest French vintages with each course.

But even for first-class passengers, wrapped in their cocoons of luxury, there were certain inconveniences. The pervasive dust of the western plains was an element to be reckoned with, and ladies were advised to wear capacious linen dusters over their dresses to protect themselves. Occasionally, cowboys out for a lark or desperadoes in search of treasure would invade the sacred precincts of the palace cars to fire off a few rounds and spread panic among the swells. Usually less dangerous to life and limb, but more so to the pocketbook, were the hordes of professional card sharps who plied their trade in the parlor cars. One was George Devol, reputed to have taken his victims for a grand total of $2 million.

Without a doubt the single greatest source of discomfort and even danger for railroad travelers was the violent weather of the plains and mountains. Spring floods regularly washed away hastily laid tracks and jerry-built trestles, and rampaging blizzards that swept across much of the West from late fall until spring caused big delays. In early 1875 a Denver-bound train out of Kansas City ran directly into the teeth of one such howler. Eleven days passed before the train limped into its destination. The passengers, half frozen by the subzero temperatures, had been reduced to a diet of canned oysters, a shipment of the delicacy having been found aboard.

And so it was on the transcontinental routes—elegance and luxury cheek by jowl with discomfort and danger. But the piercing whistle of the steam engine was a harbinger of great things to come. It was the iron horse that brought the multitudes from Europe and the settled East to fill America's last wilderness.

For the Avid Reader

One of probably hundreds of useless devices invented for travelers, the Stevens kerosene lamp was to be fastened on the coat to permit reading at night. The stench from the oil and the heat would have been unbearable.

Railroaders Met the Challenge of the West

The farflung plains, deserts, and towering mountains, and the vagaries of weather—ranging from tornadoes and floods to blizzards lasting weeks—challenged the stamina and courage of western railroad men. The work took a heavy toll in lives; several hundred engineers, firemen, brakemen, and conductors were killed or injured every year. But their ranks were quickly filled by youngsters eager to make their way up from lowly locomotive wiper to engineer or from a brakeman, risking his life on bucking boxcars, to the all-powerful conductor on a crack passenger train.

Vital to the western railroads, where single-track lines stretched for hundreds of miles, were the telegraphers. They were the eyes and ears of the tracks, transmitting the train dispatchers' orders to the conductors and thus preventing many a rear-end or head-on collision. Before the telegraphers went to work in 1851 there was no way to tell quickly if a track was clear; if a train was overdue, a crew on a handcar might have to go and look for it. The telegraph—conceived to speed communication—permitted railroads to schedule more trains over each single track and to run them in greater safety.

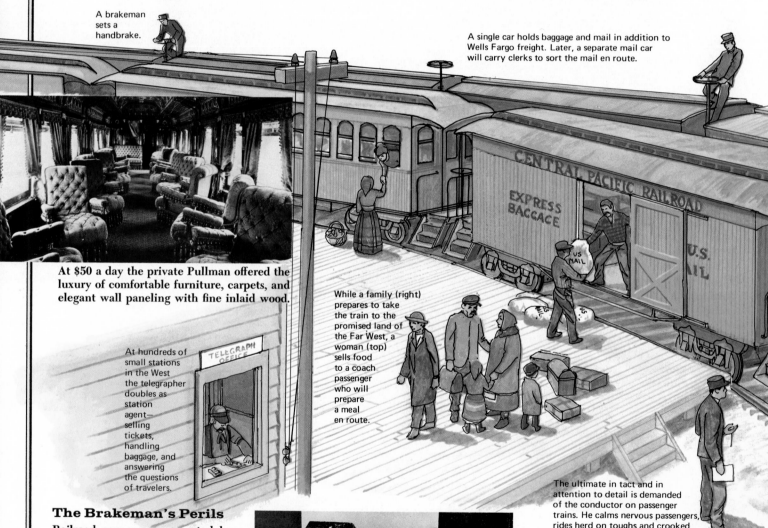

Before the days of airbrakes, which permitted the engineer to control all the cars on a train, the brakeman on a freight had to run across the tops of the cars (a dangerous business on a snowy night) to set the handbrakes. If they were not applied evenly, a disastrous break-in-two might occur, sending half a dozen cars plunging off the track. If the brakes were set too tight, a skidding wheel would be flattened. The brakeman who ruined a $45 wheel was fined a month's pay—$45.

A brakeman sets a handbrake.

A single car holds baggage and mail in addition to Wells Fargo freight. Later, a separate mail car will carry clerks to sort the mail en route.

At $50 a day the private Pullman offered the luxury of comfortable furniture, carpets, and elegant wall paneling with fine inlaid wood.

At hundreds of small stations in the West the telegrapher doubles as station agent—selling tickets, handling baggage, and answering the questions of travelers.

While a family (right) prepares to take the train to the promised land of the Far West, a woman (top) sells food to a coach passenger who will prepare a meal en route.

The ultimate in tact and in attention to detail is demanded of the conductor on passenger trains. He calms nervous passengers, rides herd on toughs and crooked gamblers, receives messages from the telegraphers, and transmits them to the engineer.

The Brakeman's Perils

Railroad cars were connected by a devil's device known as a link-and-pin coupler. It required the brakeman to guide the link of one car into the drawbar of another and insert the pin. If the drawbars of two cars were not aligned, the colliding vehicles might injure the brakeman. In 1868 an automatic "knuckle" coupler, which connected cars on contact, was invented, permitting the brakeman to direct the operation from a safe distance.

Open   Locked

Fistlike coupler locks together on contact.

The automatic coupler was not made compulsory by federal law until 1893.

The 4-4-0 (left), having speed and power, was used on the first transcontinental lines; the 4-6-0 (center) hauled both passengers and freight; and the 2-8-0 was the most popular heavy freight locomotive in the late 1800's.

To add traction, sand drops from the dome through a tube onto the track ahead of the drive wheels.

The Railroad Workhorses

Steam locomotives were identified by three digits: the first indicated the number of wheels under the front truck; the second, the number of driving wheels; the third, the number of additional trailing wheels. The front truck had a swiveling wheel assembly to help the engine round curves.

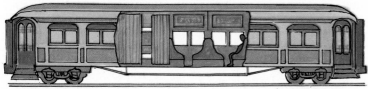

The great benefactor of passengers was George H. Pullman, whose sleeping car featured the upper berth that swung into the ceiling of the car when not in use.

In dining cars first-class passengers could sit down to elaborate meals ordered from long and varied menus.

Balloon smokestack

Screened cinder guard

Whistle

Engineer

Cab

Bell

Coal-oil head lamp

Tender

8

Drive wheels

The cupola is the lookout post from where a brakeman can observe the operation of the train and spot any signs of trouble.

Caboose

Link-and-pin coupling

Aside from shoveling as much as two tons of coal in a half hour, the fireman makes sure that the locomotive's valves are properly lubricated with tallow.

The lordly engineer can have his locomotive decorated like a Christmas tree—red wheels, gray smokestack, yellow cab, and so on. As a final touch, he usually changes the tone of the whistle with wooden plugs so that it is easily recognized.

Front truck wheels

The caboose, or "crummy," at the end of a freight train is the crew's home-away-from-home. It has from four to six bunks, supply lockers, and a stove, table, and desk for the conductor who is in command.

Pilot, or

The Search for Settlers

Red lines show federal land grants to railroads in 1871, when the grants ended. They covered over 131 million acres, an area equal to that of the 12 northeastern states (green).

In the early days the great trunk and branch lines reaching westward from the Mississippi Valley were as poor in revenue as they were rich in land. Until they could sell their vast real-estate holdings to ranchers, farmers, and merchants—whose presence would generate profitable freight traffic—the specter of bankruptcy would haunt the lines.

In 1870, the year after the first transcontinental road opened for business, prospects were still cloudy. Although the Homestead Act of 1862 had caused a rush to the West, even the most populous regions were still far from thickly settled. Minnesota, which would become the starting point for two new transcontinental rail lines—the Great Northern and the Northern Pacific—counted only 440,000 people, while Kansas and Nebraska between them had fewer than half a million, largely in their eastern portions. The Dakota country,

from which two states would be carved, had a mere 14,000 and present-day Arizona fewer than 10,000. Even the long-settled state of Oregon and Washington Territory claimed only 115,000.

Within two decades, however—after all the western trunk lines save the Great Northern had been completed—these figures had changed dramatically. By the time of the 1890 census Kansas and Nebraska had grown to more than a million residents each, Minnesota to 1.3 million, the two Dakotas to more than a half million, and the Pacific Northwest states to 675,000. The desert of Arizona Territory boasted almost 90,000 settlers. The great empty was empty no longer.

Even in a nation long accustomed to sudden spurts of population, constant westward migration, and the arrival of many thousands of foreigners each year, these figures were astonishing. To a large extent, the railroads themselves had generated this fantastic explosion. The mere presence of a line brought hordes of settlers to farm the virgin lands. Some took advantage of federal homestead legislation, but more bought land from speculators and from the railroads themselves. To speed up the influx and to dispose of their holdings, the railroads established land offices in major American cities and dispatched agents to Europe to recruit immigrants.

This task was not always easy, for much of the western interior had a long and dismal reputation for aridity and death-dealing cold. The first job of the railroad pitchmen was to scotch these

The stuff dreams are made of: hopeful emigrants visit a land office in Kansas to study maps of acreage available to them.

stories, which they did with an enthusiasm unhindered by even the shadow of truth. All over Europe they touted places like Kansas and the Dakotas as having soil so fertile that it required only the "tickling" of a plow to bring forth "the laughter of bountiful harvests." To back up these effusive claims, the railroads produced brochures complete with endorsements from supposed settlers and colorful illustrations depicting radishes as big as melons and fields of flatland choked with corn and wheat.

There were, of course, many skeptics who remained unconvinced, who spoke darkly of drought. For them the promoters merely advanced the pseudoscientific theory that, at the time, was

James J. Hill of the Great Northern Railway

When bandits robbed a Great Northern train near Ephrata in Washington, Hill took this as a personal attack on himself.

James J. Hill (1838–1916), the last of the great railroad builders, got his start as a clerk for a packet boat line in St. Paul, Minnesota, in 1856. By the mid-1860's he was operating a fuel company and a steamship line on the Red River. After wangling financial backing he and three associates took over the bankrupt St. Paul & Pacific Railroad in 1878 and by 1893 had constructed the Great Northern to Puget Sound. Meanwhile, he brought in settlers, hired experts to aid wheat farmers and cattlemen, and helped develop the orchard and timber businesses in the Pacific Northwest. By the early 1900's he controlled one-third of the rail mileage in the West. Hill was a strange man. He could grab a shovel and help

dig out a snowbound train, while sending chilled workers back for coffee in his private car; yet he fired a clerk simply because he did not like his name—which was Charles Swinburne Spittles.

endorsed by a number of prominent naturalists. According to this wishful prophecy, the mere plowing of the soil would guarantee rain: moisture from the newly turned land would ascend to the clouds and then fall back to earth to water the crops. One Colorado newspaper proclaimed that the "increase of railroads has the effect of producing more showers. The concussion of air and rapid movement produced by trains and engines affects the electrical conditions of the atmosphere."

It is doubtful that much of this optimistic talk was taken seriously; yet there was a growing body of hard evidence to support the contention that the plains region, properly irrigated and seeded with cold-resistant strains of wheat and corn, was capable of producing bumper crops to feed the burgeoning populations of Europe and America. In the minds of millions, transplanting oneself and family seemed worth the risk, with government land available for a pittance and the railroads' for $4 or $5 an acre.

The Emigrant Trails

In order to recruit foreigners—especially entire European communities that would buy up thousands of acres and travel as a unit—the railroads offered all manner of inducements. Among them might be free inspection trips for community representatives, cut-rate steamship and train tickets for the entire group, free transportation of household goods, and the right to pay for land in small installments.

Most immigrants, however, came to the United States with only their families and lacked the resources to demand any special privileges at all. After an ocean voyage in steerage they were packed into squalid, slow-moving trains, with one stove in each car serving for both cooking and heating. For an extra charge the railroads provided passengers with straw mattresses to sleep on.

In these westward-moving tenements on wheels, children were born, old people died, husbands and wives quarreled and made up, ancient feuds between different national and ethnic groups flared up anew, and a constant babel in a dozen tongues precluded all hope of rest. Yet the journey could somehow be endured, for at its end was the promise of a parcel of virgin land. There, with luck, hard work, and cunning, even the most benighted European peasant might hope to transform himself into the prosperous lord of his own domain.

"Ad astra per aspera."

Northern Kansas.

AN INVITATION

IS HEREBY EXTENDED TO EVERYBODY DESIRING A CHOICE HOME IN THE

FINEST COUNTRY

IN THE WORLD,

TO VISIT THE PLACES

DESCRIBED IN THIS FOLDER.

THE MAP IS A NEW AND ACCURATE ONE, showing the location of towns and railroads, as they were December 31, 1887.

COME

To Northern Kansas

And Locate in the State that is

ALWAYS AT THE FRONT.

BRING YOUR FAMILY

To the State that offers you FERTILE LANDS, PROSPEROUS TOWNS, plenty of CHURCHES and SCHOOLS, and

NO SALOONS.

This railroad brochure promised newcomers "fertile lands" and "prosperous towns" —in short, the good life without any saloons.

Crossing the Country on an Emigrant Train

It was a troubled uncomfortable evening in the cars. There was thunder in the air, which helped to keep us restless. A man played many airs upon the cornet, and none of them were much attended to, until he came to "Home, sweet home." It was truly strange to note how the talk ceased at that, and the faces began to lengthen. I have no idea whether musically this air is to be considered good or bad; but it belongs to that class of art which may be best described as a brutal assault upon the feelings. . . . An elderly, hardlooking man, with a goatee beard and about as much appearance of sentiment as you would expect from a retired slaver, turned with a start and bade the performer stop that "damned thing." "I've heard about enough of that," he added; "give us something about the good country we're going to." A murmur of adhesion ran round the car; the performer took the instrument from his lips, laughed and nodded, and then struck into a dancing measure; and like a new Timotheus, stilled immediately the emotion he had raised.

—Robert Louis Stevenson
Across the Plains, Written in 1879

To lure settlers to the West, railroads offered cut-rate emigrant fares (note the ticket at the right) and promised a pleasant journey. But the passengers (below) had to travel for endless days in cars that were sweltering in summer and frigid in winter.

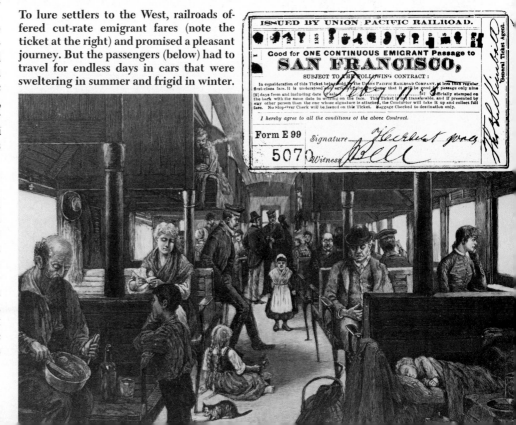

ISSUED BY UNION PACIFIC RAILROAD.

Good for ONE CONTINUOUS EMIGRANT Passage to

SAN FRANCISCO,

SUBJECT TO THE FOLLOWING CONTRACT:

Form E 99   Signature

5070   Witness

The Railroad and the Indians

Throughout the 19th century the vast majority of white Americans—including even the humanitarians most sympathetic with the Indians' plight—believed implicitly that the red man must yield before the inexorable westward advance of white civilization. There was no need for a conspiracy of ill-intentioned politicians and bloodthirsty generals to plot a grand strategy for the Indians' subjugation. In fact, some of the soldiers who bore the burden of fighting the tribes expressed a grudging admiration for their foe. Gen. George Crook, perhaps the most successful of all Indian fighters, once told a graduating class at West Point that "with all his faults . . . the American Indian is not half as black as he has been painted. He is cruel in war, treacherous at times, and not over cleanly. But so were our forefathers."

Crook's viewpoint may have been less representative than that old frontier saying sometimes attributed to Gen. Philip Sheridan: "The only good Indian I ever saw was a dead Indian." But no matter what the whites felt about these adversaries, it was believed by more and more people that two opposing ways of life simply could not coexist in one nation, no matter how broad its expanse. If white men were to farm the Great Plains, mine the mountains beyond, build towns and cities, and connect far-flung regions with a vast network of rails, there could be no room for thundering herds of buffalo or nomadic tribesmen wandering the landscape

freely in pursuit of the shaggy beasts. Further, if whites were to claim the land and divide it into privately held parcels of real estate, there could be no room for tradition-bound peoples who regarded the earth as the Creator's gift to all—peoples to whom such concepts as boundaries, private ownership, and progress were virtually meaningless.

The Vanishing Buffalo

In the end it was the railroads, stretching across the vastness of the plains, that became the final and most deadly engines of destruction for the Indians of the West. For the great transcontinental lines not only made the settlement of the interior frontier a practical possibility by linking the remotest regions with markets far to the east and west, they also doomed the tribes in much more direct ways. As rail lines grew in size and complexity, they gave the Indian-fighting army a new and deadly mobility, allowing the men in blue to stand sentinel over vast reaches of wilderness and bring overwhelming force against rebellious tribes in a far shorter time than had previously been possible.

More important still was the railroads' role in accomplishing the near extinction of the buffalo, without which the tribesmen of the High Plains knew they must give up their way of life as hunters and warriors. But before they would bend the knee and accept the cramped degradation of reservation ex-

Train of woe for the beleaguered red man: two Indians watch resignedly as a smoke-trailing iron horse crosses a nearby trestle.

istence, they would fight. For these were the years of the great Indian wars and the last generation of great Indian heroes. Yet valor alone was not enough. Forays against railroad men and settlers, even victories over the U.S. Army, could not bring back the buffalo or seriously impede the progress of the iron horse, with its cargo of woe for the red man. The situation was succinctly summed up late in 1872 by the U.S. commissioner of Indian affairs as he followed the building of the second transcontinental line. "The progress . . . on the Northern Pacific Railroad will of itself . . . leave the ninety thousand Indians ranging between the two transcontinental lines as incapable of resisting the Government as are the Indians of New York or Massachusetts."

Train ride to exile: Geronimo (front row, third from right) and his Apache band are being taken east in 1886 to a detention center in Florida.

Train ride to the promised land: farmers with their families, miners, land speculators, and footloose adventurers swap gossip and plans as they wait for a train at the UP station in Omaha, Nebraska. The sign indicates that many of these travelers are heading for the Black Hills country (in the Dakota and Wyoming Territories), which had been one of the last holdouts of the Indians until it was taken from them in 1876.

Professional Hide Hunters Slaughter the Thundering Herds

When the Union Pacific's surveyors began driving their stakes in the Platte River Valley in the mid-1860's, Sioux Chief Red Cloud warned them to turn back: "We do not want you here," he said. "You are scaring away the buffalo." However, the surveyors persisted and were followed by grading and tracklaying crews. Then came the professional hunters, hired by the railroad to provide buffalo meat for its workers. A skilled marksman, using a heavy Sharps rifle and staying downwind from a herd, could kill some 150 animals in a day. Other hunters also decimated the herds to obtain buffalo robes, but the wholesale killing and shameful waste really began in the early 1870's after eastern tanneries found that buffalo hides could be made into commercial leather. In 1872–73 alone, the railroads hauled 1,250,000 hides from the plains. When the hunters moved on, farmers often harvested the buffalo bones they left behind and took them to the railroad, where they were shipped east to be processed into carbon or fertilizer. By 1900 the buffalo population had dwindled from 75 million (before the whites arrived) to about 1,000.

Through the efforts of a Kansas frontiersman known as Buffalo Jones and Dr. William T. Hornaday, of the New York Zoological Park, new herds were started in the early 1900's. Today, there are some 10,000 buffalo in federal game preserves.

When a buffalo herd blocked the track, as frequently happened on the Union Pacific and Kansas Pacific Railroads, passengers wantonly shot the animals from the coaches, not for hides or meat but just for the sheer joy of killing.

Piles of sun-dried buffalo hides await shipment east by railroad. Below, two expert skinners wield their knives while in the background a horse, pulling on a rope, helps them rip the hide from a slain buffalo.

In this Frederic Remington painting a mourning warrior calls for supernatural help to bring back the disappearing buffalo.

"Ma" [says the eastern girl] "do cowboys eat grass?" "No, dear," says the old lady, "they're part human," an' I don't know but the old gal had 'em sized up right. If they are human, they're a separate species. I'm talkin' about the old-time ones, before the country's strung with wire . . . an' a cowpuncher's home was big. It wasn't where he took his hat off, but where he spread his blankets. . . . He don't need no iron hoss, but covers his country on one that eats grass an' wears hair.

—*Charles M. Russell*, Trails Plowed Under

"A Tight Dally and a Loose Latigo." Oil painting by Charles M. Russell.

Chapter 9

Cowboys and Cattle Kings

During the latter years of the 19th century, the times and the land combined to produce a great western epic. The manpower was furnished by the cowboy—vigorous, hard-riding, and soft-spoken. The action began after the Civil War with trail drives north from Texas and climaxed when huge cattle companies seized vast tracts of land and discouraged interlopers by a ready use of hired gunmen. When the epic ended in the 1890's, the nation fell heir to the legend of cowboy, gambler, lawman, and outlaw.

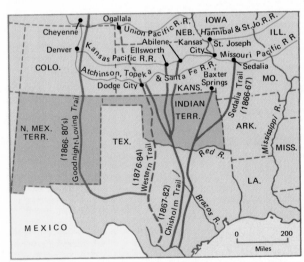

To realize a profit on their vast herds of cattle, Texas ranchers had to get them to railheads for shipment east. Here are the trails they followed to cattle towns that sprang up almost overnight as the railroads moved west. The Goodnight-Loving Trail was blazed after the northern and western ranges were found suitable for cattle.

Birth of the Beef Bonanza

There was a time, in the late 1870's and early 1880's, when a man on horseback could crisscross the Great Plains of North America—from the Mexican to the Canadian borders, from Kansas to the Rockies—and rarely be out of sight of cattle. In this region, half the size of Europe, there were only about six communities with more than 5,000 residents; yet it was a world literally teeming with life. A veritable sea of steers, jostling one another for patches of grass, were eating themselves into shape for their destiny—the slaughterhouses of Chicago and Kansas City and ultimately the dinner plates of America and Europe.

The strains of cattle that covered the vast grasslands of the West, where the buffalo had recently roamed free, combined the hardiness of the Texas longhorn with the meatiness of the Angus and Hereford. As these millions of animals fattened on their seemingly limitless range, men as faraway as New York, London, and Edinburgh also waxed fat on the profits brought in by the cattle.

As amazing as the vast extent of the American cattle range was the speed with which the beef industry grew after centuries of neglect. For almost 300 years herds of longhorns—descendants of bulls and cows brought into Mexico by Spanish conquistadors—had been multiplying almost unnoticed, gradually filling the grasslands of southeastern

A formidable beast when aroused, the longhorn was once described as being three-fifths horn and hooves and the rest hair. The most famous of the longhorns was Charles Goodnight's "Old Blue." He led Goodnight's herds north, picking the best place for the cattle to rest for the night and seeming to calm them during storms with his reassuring bawl.

This painting by Theodore Gentilz shows Mexican vaqueros examining a trail across the Texas prairie. Before the Civil War almost all the cowhands in Texas were vaqueros.

Cowboy Lingo

Airin' the lungs: cussin'
Biscuit shooter: the ranch cook
Colorado mockingbird: a burro
Dally: a half-hitch of rope around a saddle horn used when roping
Dog house: the bunkhouse
Flea trap: a cowboy's bedroll
Greasy belly: a cook
Gut hooks: spurs
Hay shaker: a farmer
Hot rock: a biscuit
Idaho brain storm: a tornado
Kack: a saddle
Kack biscuit: a saddle sore
Latigo: a leather strap used to fasten a saddle on a horse
Maniac den: a sheep wagon or camp
Maverick: an unbranded animal
Necktie social: a hanging
Tasting gravel: thrown from a horse
Walking whisky vat: a drunkard
—Ramon F. Adams, *Western Words*

Texas. But few people saw much commercial potential in them; the markets for their meat, hides, and tallow were distant and virtually unreachable.

By the early years of the 19th century tens of thousands of longhorns were running wild on the Texas prairies. Untended for the most part, they were a far cry from the manageable herds of later years. One observer of the Texas plains spoke of their "ferocious disposition" and warned: "A footman is never safe when a herd is in his vicinity." He also concluded that the longhorn was "fifty times more dangerous . . . than the fiercest buffalo."

Not until the post-Mexican War period was any real effort made to mine the potential wealth represented by Texas cattle. It was then that the first major

drives were mounted, with ranchers rounding up thousands of cantankerous animals from the open range, branding them, and then herding them northward to the markets of the Midwest or, in the 1850's, toward the gold camps of the Far West. But at that time the demand was still too small and too far away to offer adequate recompense for the discomforts and perils faced on the trail.

Early Years in Texas

For those few who made the infant Texas beef business their career, it was a hard and financially unrewarding life. Charles Goodnight, who was later to become one of the great cattle barons, recalled his early years in Texas with a tinge of bitterness. In 1857 he and his stepbrother hired out as cowhands to

272

In the 1850's the vaqueros trailed herds of cattle from the ranchos in southern California to the mining towns in the north. Although cattle raising was a major industry in Spanish California, herds were kept close to home. When settlers living in the Oregon Country wanted cattle, they had to send a delegation to purchase animals and drive them home.

watch over about 400 head in exchange for a quarter of the calves born to the herd that year. "As the end of the first year's branding resulted in only 32 calves for our share," he wrote, "we figured out that we had made between us, not counting expenses, 96 dollars."

Despite such discouraging statistics a few ranchers and would-be ranchers, including Goodnight, kept at it. As early as 1853 a longhorn herd was given temporary shelter on the Illinois prairie, fattened up, and then driven all the way east to New York City to provide its citizens with the rare sight of jostling steers jogging down the narrow city streets to the slaughterhouse. Another potential market for Texas beef in the 1850's was California, whose formerly thriving cattle industry had declined. By the time of the gold rush and its accompanying population explosion, there were thousands of beef-famished Argonauts. Inevitably, rumors reached Texas that Californians would willingly pay the astronomical sum of $200 a head. Several of the most courageous (or foolhardy) Texas stockmen rounded up their herds from the range and began the long and incredibly dangerous trek to the Sierra diggings.

During the 1850's some 50,000 Texas steers started on the journey through New Mexico and Arizona to California, but few of the stockmen were able to bring enough animals through to secure a profit. When at last the southern California ranchers woke up and began driving the remnants of their own herds to the gold diggings, beef prices fell sharply and the Texas boomlet ended.

After the Civil War, in which Texas had cast her lot with the doomed Confederacy, the Lone Star State was desperate for northern dollars. Her only immediate resource was the estimated 5 million head of cattle that roamed the grasslands, most of them untended, unbranded, and unclaimed. At home these hardy, self-reliant beasts—which had been crossbred with eastern cows to produce several strains—were virtually worthless, but they would be incredibly valuable in the North if some way could be found to get them to market.

Ranchers and Rustlers

Ranchers like Charles Goodnight returned from the war to find their herds scattered all over the range—and there was no way even honest men could tell which of the calves born in the last half decade were theirs. In this situation the distinction between rancher and rustler nearly vanished, and when Goodnight later reported that "certain scattered men . . . could not resist the temptation and went to branding those cattle for themselves," he might have been speaking of himself. Of the 8,000 head he and his brother collected in 1864-65 more than a few were mavericks, picked up on the grasslands.

There were good reasons for ranchers and drovers to ignore the niceties, for rumor had it that cattle worth, at most, $3 or $4 a head in Texas would fetch $40 a head in Missouri, where they could be shipped eastward from the newly built railheads at Sedalia or St. Joseph. Determined to share in the bonanza regardless of the perils of what came to be called the Long Drive, the Texas ranchers began rounding up their herds and hiring trail hands.

John Wesley Iliff: An Early Cattle King

After three years of college in Ohio, John Wesley Iliff refused his father's offer of $7,500 worth of land on the family farm and accepted $500 instead. In 1857 he headed for Kansas.

While Charles Goodnight was getting his start in Texas, another rugged individualist, one John Wesley Iliff (1832-78), was sinking roots in the Colorado country. The Ohio-born Iliff moved from Kansas to Denver during the 1859 gold rush and opened a store with two partners. In 1862 he bought a small herd of longhorns and established a ranch on the South Platte River in northeastern Colorado. He also became a stock dealer, buying cattle in Indian Territory and driving herds to New Mexico to supply army posts. In 1868 he trailed a herd into Wyoming to feed the men building the Union Pacific Railroad.

Iliff rode with his men, shared their hardships, and paid good wages, but he firmly opposed drinking. "Cows and whisky do not mix" was a favorite expression of his. He did not carry a gun but was always ready to use his fists to settle an argument.

When Iliff died at the age of 46, his obituary called him the cattle king of the plains and the most successful of all the cattle merchants in the West.

North from Texas

Between the Texas range, with its super-abundance of cattle, and the new rail-heads in Missouri lay hundreds of miles of rough country, all but unknown to the Texas ranchers. The way north crossed part of Texas itself, a corner of the Indian Territory, a piece of Arkansas, and some of Missouri. Most of the stockmen who vowed in that spring of 1866 to reach the Sedalia railhead before the first autumn freeze expected that the going would be tough, but none of them knew just how tough.

The Long, Hard Trail

Through the winter of 1865–66 the owners of Texas herds made their preparations for the Long Drive. Cattle by the thousands were rounded up and branded. Cowboys were signed on at $25 to $40 per month, usually six men for every 1,000 head of cattle. If the owner himself decided against making the journey, a trail boss had to be hired. The best of these were tough, canny horsemen with hair-trigger reflexes, men who could smell out danger, impose discipline, and maintain the respect of the drovers. They were well worth their princely salaries of $125 a month.

In March of 1866 dozens of ranchers, trail bosses, horse wranglers, and cooks, and hundreds of cowhands finally began moving some 260,000 jittery cattle. Each of the stockmen was determined to get his herd to Sedalia in order to cash in on the maximum price—which would mean as much as $100,000 profit on every 3,000 head. In what became a

trial-and-error trek to Missouri, the stockmen took several different routes. Some pushed directly north through the Indian Territory; others made a sharp eastward detour into Arkansas to avoid Indians. But however they went, man and nature seemed to be conspiring to bedevil them. Stampedes, which might be set off by a thunderclap, a rifle shot, or even the sudden clanking of a chuckwagon pan, were a constant menace. Many a night the cowboys rode among their nervous herds and softly sang lullabies in an effort to calm the cattle—or perhaps themselves.

Abnormally heavy rains turned the Texas prairies into a mass of oozy mud. River crossings proved deadly to man and beast as the raging waters of the Brazos and the Red pushed a tangle of struggling cattle, drovers, and horses inexorably downstream or sucked them into swirling eddies. Farther north, the surviving cattle became totally unmanageable among the hills and forests of the Ozark Plateau, bolting in terror at unfamiliar obstacles.

For those who took the Indian Territory route, there were the tribes to contend with. The Indians were often less than delighted to see vast herds, under the watchful eyes of white men, trampling their fields and devouring the grass on which their own animals depended. In retaliation, some Indian bands raided the drovers' supply wagons and stampeded their cattle—and then kept whatever strays they could capture or demanded some in tribute for rounding up

the scattered beasts. A few insisted on payment in money, perhaps 10 cents a head, before they would allow the animals to cross their lands. But even after such transactions, the Texans discovered no easy route across the Indian Territory. The tribesmen, determined to protect their holdings from damage, insisted upon the drovers keeping to narrow paths that were soon nibbled bare of grass by the advance guard of cattle, leaving little for those that came after.

Among the cattlemen on the drive north through the Indian Territory in that spring of 1866 was a young Iowan

In payment for the safe passage of a herd through Indian lands, the trail boss signals that the warrior can take one of the animals.

A river crossing could prove dangerous if the cattle became mired in quicksand or panicked in deep water and began to swim in circles.

Frederic Remington depicted a vigilant point man with his always reliable lead steer trailing a herd northward to Missouri.

named George Duffield, who had purchased a thousand head of longhorns earlier that year. Duffield's odyssey, like those of most stockmen on the drive, was one long catalog of woe, which he recorded in his daily journal. Only a few days into the drive, he suffered the first of several stampedes. "Travelled 10 miles," he wrote. "Big Stampede lost 200 head of cattle." Two weeks later there was a "Big Thunder Storm. . . . Stampede lost 100 beeves hunted all day found 50 all tired. Everything discouraging." Beyond the Red River: "Stampede last night . . . am in the Indian country . . . believe they scare the Cattle to get pay to collect them."

Eventually, Duffield and the remains of his herd made it to the Missouri border, only to find that his fellow citizens were even less hospitable than the Indians. For the Texas longhorns carried a dread disease, Texas fever, spread by ticks. Texas cattle were immune to its effects, but the Missouri stock had no immunity at all. Backed by an 1861 law that forbade the entry of diseased cattle into the state, the Missouri farmers formed armed posses and confronted the cattle drovers.

As if this were not enough, the Texans also had to contend with remaining members of the guerrilla bands that had scourged the countryside during the Civil War. Using the excuse of Texas fever as a cover for their atrocities, these border ruffians attacked the drovers and

A savage storm, with roaring thunder and blinding lightning, has frightened the cattle; and the cowboy, in this painting by Frederic Remington, is attempting to halt a stampede.

rustled their herds, sending scores of cowboys to early graves. A 19th-century account of the cattle trade summed up the situation: "The southwestern Missouri roads leading to Sedalia were the scenes of the worst of the work of these outlaws. . . . When outright murder was not resorted to as the readiest means of getting possession of a herd . . . drovers were flogged until they had promised to abandon their stock, mount their horses, and get out of the country."

Starving Cattle

Confronted with such opposition, few cattlemen made it through to the Sedalia railhead that year. Instead, herd after herd came to a dead stop at Baxter Springs, Kansas, near the border between the Indian Territory and Missouri. As the drovers waited for the blockade to end, autumn frosts killed the grass in the vicinity, causing thousands of cattle to die of starvation. Those who turned their herds east or west to avoid the pileup at Baxter Springs often found the weight of their cattle so reduced by trail's end that they were almost worthless. Thus the Long Drive of 1866, which had begun with so much hope, ended in despair. Yet the stockmen knew that the cattle business would prosper if trails leading to new and more receptive markets were opened. And in the spring of the very next year those trails were finally blazed.

The Trail to Kansas

After the failure of 1866, Texas cattlemen might have been expected to spend the next year licking their wounds before attempting to make any major new drives to the railheads. But the drive had proved that there was indeed a market, so once again many of the ranchers began moving up the Sedalia Trail. A number of them met the same reception they had had in 1866, but some were luckier. Late starters on the trail had not yet turned east into Missouri when they were intercepted by an agent of a cattle buyer named Joe McCoy, who informed them that there was an easier and safer route to market. At a tiny hamlet called Abilene in north-central Kansas, along the route of the Kansas Pacific Railroad, McCoy was in the process of establishing vast pens to receive Texas cattle. From there the stock would be shipped eastward in open cars to Kansas City and thence to the stockyards of Chicago via the Hannibal and St. Joseph Railroad, which had offered the shipper highly favorable terms for carrying the animals.

As far as the Texans were concerned, McCoy's scheme had one overwhelming advantage. McCoy himself was to put it this way: "The plan was to establish at some accessible point a depot or market to which a Texan drover could bring his stock unmolested . . . to establish a market whereat the Southern drover and Northern buyer would meet upon an equal footing, and both be undisturbed by mobs or swindling thieves."

Clara McDonald Williamson of Iredell, Texas, often saw the cattle moving north on the Chisholm Trail, and years later she recalled the Long Drive to Kansas in this painting.

Abilene, when McCoy selected it as the center of his operations, was, in his words, "a very small, dead place, consisting of about one dozen log huts." But despite its seeming lack of facilities, the West's first cattle town had obvious natural advantages that the wily McCoy was quick to see. For one thing, it could be reached from Texas via an established route—soon to be known as the Chisholm Trail. Still another advantage was the fact that in central Kansas there were no irate farmers armed against diseased Texas cattle and no outlaws forming their own kind of reception committee—at least not yet.

By 1871: 700,000 Animals

From the first, Abilene prospered as a center of the cattle trade. Even though McCoy began operations relatively late in 1867, some 35,000 animals passed through the town that year on their way to market. By 1871 the number had risen to an astounding 700,000, only to fall off precipitously later in the decade as facilities were opened at railheads farther to the south and west.

But the drives northward still took a steady toll of men and livestock through stampedes, drownings at river crossings, and occasional raids by rustlers. And periodically there were panics brought on by the the tick-borne Texas fever, which the longhorns passed on to vulnerable northern stock. Indeed, for several months in 1868 the epidemic was so bad that the receiving stockyards at Abilene and slaughterhouses farther east were forbidden to import them. Thousands of animals backed up on the grasslands around Abilene as they had near Baxter Springs. Such panic over Texas fever plagued the cattlemen for many

Longhorns take over the streets of Abilene, Kansas, as dignitaries turn out with a band, bunting, and appropriate speeches to welcome the first trail herd to arrive from Texas.

Although scientists believed that insects could not carry fever, some Texas ranchers held that the deadly disease carried by southern cows was transmitted by ticks. But, as the humorous drawing (above) that appeared in 1874 suggests, early efforts to fight tick fever proved highly ineffectual.

Cowpunchers load longhorns onto a train at Wichita, in Kansas, in 1874. Cowpunchers were so named because they used metal-tipped poles to prod cattle out of the shipping pens into railroad cars.

years—increasing in intensity as more and more farmers moved westward across Kansas—and time and again the bottom fell out of the longhorn market.

During the prosperous days, however, there were significant changes in the nature of the cattle business. Texas ranchers driving their herds northward could not help but notice that their cattle thrived on the Kansas grasses, even when forced to winter over in the region while awaiting sale and transportation east. Inevitably, the stockmen began to wonder about the utility of the drives. After all, Kansas and points north and west offered what was necessary to maintain a herd—an abundance of nutritious grass, water, and empty land. Why endure the dangers and expense of driving cattle north?

New Cattle Towns

At first, the ranchers settled in the vicinity of Abilene and then—as the extension of the railroads brought forth new cattle towns to the south and west—in places like Ellsworth, Wichita, and Dodge City, each of which enjoyed for a time a central role in the cattle-raising and cattle-droving business. But it was all too good to last, for most of Kansas was too fertile and too well watered to be left to the ranchers. By the early 1870's the agricultural frontier was moving into regions claimed by the cattlemen; and the farmers, backed by the state legislature, were determined to blanket the region with homesteads and plow the grasses under in favor of wheat and corn. As the farmers spread west-

ward, more and more of Kansas was declared off limits to trail herds. And the ever-growing number of plowmen wanted no truck with the Texas cattle, which trampled their crops and bore on their bodies the fatal tick.

By the early 1880's just about all of Kansas was closed to drovers; and as in Missouri years before, trail bosses seeking entry were faced down by armed, grimly determined farmers. By then, however, the closing of the state made little difference. For two railroads—the Southern Pacific and the Santa Fe—

crossed Texas, making shipment possible from there. Moreover, the cattle frontier itself—outrunning the advance guard of farmers and following the westward-moving railheads—had expanded far to the west and north. Railroads now cut through the most remote reaches of the High Plains, making cattle ranching practical in Colorado, Wyoming, and Montana. And the Texas longhorn was no longer king of the range, having been replaced by mixed breeds that, among other advantages, carried no deadly ticks.

Chisholm's Wagons Mark the Trail to Kansas

Trader Jesse Chisholm never drove any Texas cattle north to Kansas; nevertheless, he gave his name to the great trail.

The part of the Chisholm Trail actually used by the trader. The trail ran from the coastal plains of Texas northward through Indian Territory to the railheads located in Kansas.

The half-Cherokee Jesse Chisholm (c. 1806-68) had a trading post on the Arkansas River near present-day Wichita, Kansas, and was highly respected by the Indians. In 1865 Chisholm pointed his trade wagons southward into Indian Territory, where he planned to trade with tribes in the region of Fort Cobb on the Washita River. When a herder heading north from Texas crossed into Indian Territory, he found Chisholm's wagon ruts and followed them north into Kansas. During his trips Chisholm ransomed white captives from the Indians and also held open house for tribesmen who came to trade and seek his advice. After his death Chisholm, who the Indians said spoke "with a straight tongue," was given a grave marker by whites that stated, "No one left his home cold or hungry."

Skill and Daring at Roundup Time

The one event every cowboy anticipated eagerly was the noisy, dusty, dangerous, and utterly exhausting bedlam of the open-range roundup. On this occasion he would meet old pals and make new ones—and would prove his worth. Before barbed wire confined each rancher's cattle to their home range, everyone's stock grazed everywhere and had to be found and rounded up twice a year: in the spring to brand the new calves (the main scene below) and in the fall to select those animals that would be driven (bottom, far right) to distant stockyards and railheads. Since the roundup covered about 50 square miles, it was planned with military precision. A starting date was approved by the stockmen's association. Holding areas for each day's cattle harvest were picked by the cooperating ranchers. Then the roundup crews were dispatched. When the cattle they drove in had been handled, the tired, hungry men from many ranches would head for the chuckwagon and, over grub and scalding coffee, swap the news and stories that made the grueling roundup the high point of their rugged lives.

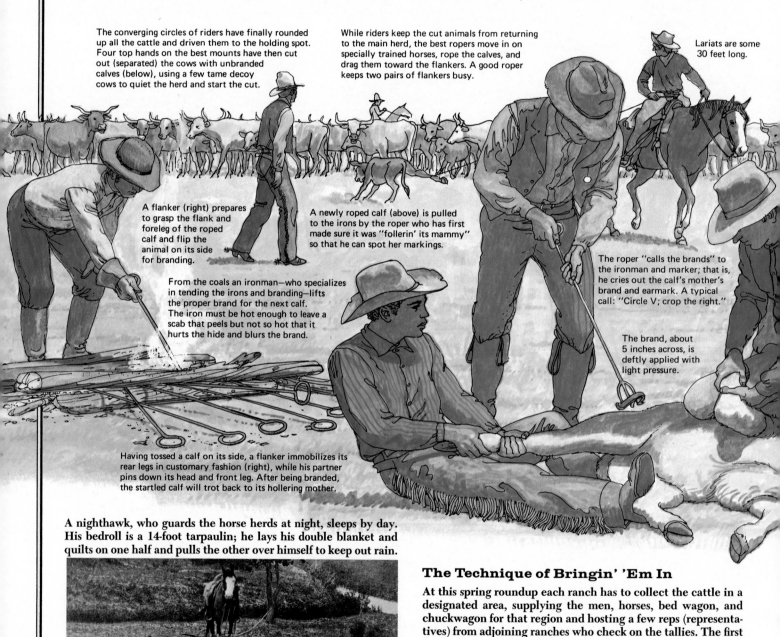

The converging circles of riders have finally rounded up all the cattle and driven them to the holding spot. Four top hands on the best mounts have then cut out (separated) the cows with unbranded calves (below), using a few tame decoy cows to quiet the herd and start the cut.

While riders keep the cut animals from returning to the main herd, the best ropers move in on specially trained horses, rope the calves, and drag them toward the flankers. A good roper keeps two pairs of flankers busy.

Lariats are some 30 feet long.

A flanker (right) prepares to grasp the flank and foreleg of the roped calf and flip the animal on its side for branding.

A newly roped calf (above) is pulled to the irons by the roper who has first made sure it was "follerin' its mammy" so that he can spot her markings.

The roper "calls the brands" to the ironman and marker; that is, he cries out the calf's mother's brand and earmark. A typical call: "Circle V; crop the right."

From the coals an ironman—who specializes in tending the irons and branding—lifts the proper brand for the next calf. The iron must be hot enough to leave a scab that peels but not so hot that it hurts the hide and blurs the brand.

The brand, about 5 inches across, is deftly applied with light pressure.

Having tossed a calf on its side, a flanker immobilizes its rear legs in customary fashion (right), while his partner pins down its head and front leg. After being branded, the startled calf will trot back to its hollering mother.

A nighthawk, who guards the horse herds at night, sleeps by day. His bedroll is a 14-foot tarpaulin; he lays his double blanket and quilts on one half and pulls the other over himself to keep out rain.

The Technique of Bringin' 'Em In

At this spring roundup each ranch has to collect the cattle in a designated area, supplying the men, horses, bed wagon, and chuckwagon for that region and hosting a few reps (representatives) from adjoining ranches who check on the tallies. The first men out—the wagon bosses—ride ahead at dawn, choosing the hubs of the zones to be scoured that day. They send their men in pairs to circle these areas and then turn back, driving all cattle before them. The lead drive men, on the most experienced, enduring horses, work the outer circle and must search ravines where the cattle might be hiding. The men, one to two miles apart, converge with their beasts upon the holding spot. While two riders keep the herd in place, the others change mounts and begin cutting out all those cows with calves that must be branded.

In his book the tallyman marks the number, sex, and owner of each calf, calling out: "Star K outfit, one calf; Circle Nine Ranch, one calf . . ." He is chosen for honesty and clerical accuracy and is often a respected older man unable to do strenuous work. His tally will show the number of animals in each herd. Animals from distant ranches will be cut out and driven to their home ranges by their reps.

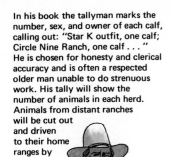

The Art of Roping

Roping is the cowboy's hardest learned skill. The experts are perfect judges of distance and speed and are assigned to rope the saddle horses and ride into the milling herd to heel out calves. Because roping can scar a steer's hide or break its leg, grown cattle are roped only if they have run away or need doctoring. This is done, as shown at right, if the man is alone; if he has a partner, he will rope the forefeet, his colleague the hind, and stretch the animal on the ground. The roper cannot let the steer be pulled from the side, for his horse will be jerked to the ground.

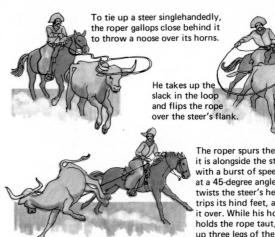

To tie up a steer singlehandedly, the roper gallops close behind it to throw a noose over its horns.

He takes up the slack in the loop and flips the rope over the steer's flank.

The roper spurs the horse until it is alongside the steer, then with a burst of speed rides off at a 45-degree angle. The rope twists the steer's head around, trips its hind feet, and flips it over. While his horse holds the rope taut, he ties up three legs of the steer. If the animal is thrown too hard, its neck may break.

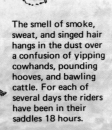

The smell of smoke, sweat, and singed hair hangs in the dust over a confusion of yipping cowhands, pounding hooves, and bawling cattle. For each of several days the riders have been in their saddles 18 hours.

The marker tosses into a pail the sliver he has cut from the calf's ear to match its mother's earmark. The bits of ear will be counted as a countercheck to the tallyman. The marker will castrate any male calf swiftly with the same sharp pocketknife. The wound usually heals quickly but sometimes gets infected with screwworms. Marking, branding, and castration take but a few seconds. By late afternoon this herd will have been processed and let loose. After supper the men will sleep in bedrolls.

Mexican John, the XIT Ranch cook, makes pies in his chuckwagon. In the drawers are food, liquor, medicine, plates, and cutlery. He cooks in large pots and Dutch ovens on an open fire, feeds up to 30 men three meals a day, then moves to a new roundup site before nightfall. Staple fare is pinto beans, bacon, biscuits, and "SOB stew" (stewed entrails). But a good cook —more than anyone else the key to a good roundup—can produce gingerbread, "spotted pup" (rice and raisins), and "shivering Liz" (jelly dessert).

Tricks of the Trail

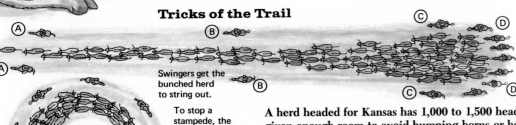

Swingers get the bunched herd to string out.

To stop a stampede, the riders race past the galloping cattle and turn them into the center of the herd.

After running in a circle the animals will stop gradually.

In the rear will come the bed wagon, the chuckwagon (which the cook will drive ahead in the afternoon to fix supper), and the remuda of 100 to 300 saddle horses cared for and corraled by the wrangler. He also fetches water and collects wood or cow chips for the cook's fire. At night the chuckwagon's tongue is pointed in the direction of tomorrow's travel.

A herd headed for Kansas has 1,000 to 1,500 head, nudged along at a slow pace and given enough room to avoid bumping horns or hooves and to allow for grazing. The trail drivers, about one man per 150 head, are made up of several types. The point riders (A), the most experienced, keep the herd on the trail and are the first to swim a river or drive native cattle away. They change the herd's course, veering in the desired direction: the lead cows swerve away from the rider approaching them and toward the rider veering away. The swing riders (B) and flank riders (C) keep cattle from wandering off and retrieve any that do. The drag riders (D), with whip and rope, contend with the weak, lazy, or footsore critters at the dusty rear. Ahead of the herd the trail boss rides to locate a high, dry, cooler spot near water for the herd to bed down in at night.

"Wicked" Cattle Towns

Their names were Abilene, Wichita, Hays City, Dodge City, Ellsworth, Ogallala, and Caldwell, to name a few. Most were born shabby and kept a scruffy look even in their days of prosperity—their dusty streets, walkways of wooden planks, sleazy saloons, gambling dens, bordellos, and false-front stores lending them a sense of impermanence. These were the cattle towns, where, according to films and television, good guys in white and bad guys in black fought it out with six-shooters on the main streets while the respectable citizenry scuttled for cover. And if some of the wilder tales were to be believed, barroom brawls regularly culminated in sudden death, with the victims being carted off to resting places like Dodge City's notorious Boot Hill.

Although popular dime novels and eastern newspapers grossly exaggerated

Dressed-up cigar-smoking cowhands buy flowers from youngsters awed by their finery. Just down the street the men will find racier attractions offered by the town.

the violence of the cattle towns, these places were in fact at least as colorful—if not nearly as bloody—as the popular imagination has always painted them. Some (notably Ellsworth, Caldwell, and Dodge) had acquired their seamy reputations well before they became cattle centers—reputations based on the presence of a raffish collection of railroad men, soldiers, buffalo hunters, and camp followers, plus the virtual absence of any system of law. Indeed, the coming of the cattle trade was often the signal for towns like Dodge or Wichita to settle down, organize local governments, and become at least moderately respectable. A good year for cattle sales meant plenty of hard money, not only for itinerant gamblers, barkeeps, and ladies of the evening but also for bootmakers, dry-goods merchants, grocers, financiers, and other citizens of substance. As historian Robert R. Dykstra phrased it in his book *Cattle Towns,* "The problem for the cattle town people was not to rid themselves of visitors prone to violence, but to suppress the violence while retaining the visitors."

The Peace Officers' Iron Rule

Andy Adams, a veteran of the cattle trade, summed up the situation from the drovers' standpoint in his *Log of a Cowboy:* "Dodge is one town where the average bad man . . . finds himself badly handicapped. The buffalo hunters and range men have protested against the iron rule of Dodge's peace officers, and nearly every protest has cost human life. Don't ever get the impression that you can ride your horses into a saloon, or shoot out the lights. . . . Most cowboys think it's an infringement on their rights to give up shooting in town, and if it is, it

These high-spirited Texans engage in a brisk game of mounted pool while a companion restrains the anguished manager.

stands, for your six-shooters are no match for Winchesters or buckshot; and Dodge's officers are as game a set of men as ever faced danger." Though Adams was probably exaggerating the human toll this law-and-order policy exacted, in other respects his picture was accurate.

In order to keep the cattle trade while attracting more permanent businesses, town officials had to walk a careful tightrope. The best way to do this seemed to be to provide the rowdier pleasures the Texas cowpokes were so fond of while at the same time controlling those pleasures and extracting considerable income from them. Newly incorporated towns were quick to pass laws establishing a lucrative system of fines for such offenses as gambling and prostitution and carrying concealed weapons. This income filled the town coffers admirably, enabling some localities to offer tax advantages to legitimate

Dodge City, spawned by the arrival of the Santa Fe in 1872, was a center of the buffalo hide and bone trade, but it really boomed after 1876 when it became a railhead for Texas cattle. As shown here in the foreground, the tracks ran along the main street of the town.

A cowboy who believes he has been cheated at cards brandishes his six-gun. Actually, cowboys were required by law to check their hardware at the sheriff's office while in town.

business and to pay for police officers.

Contrary to legend, in the Kansas cattle towns a marshal's lot was not usually a glamorous one, and certainly not a lonely one. The more sensible businessmen and politicians were not about to risk either their own safety or their city's reputation by hiring only one gun-happy officer with more enthusiasm for mayhem than commonsense. There were arrests to be made—preferably without bloodshed—fines to be levied, bibulous cowboys to be pacified, records to be kept, sidewalks to be repaired, and the occasional stray steer to be removed. All of this fell within the lawman's duties (even for such legendary marshals as "Wild Bill" Hickok of Abilene and Wyatt Earp of Wichita), and for such work a preening gunslinger was singularly unsuited. Most towns had at least five police on call in the cattle season.

Mayhem Within Reason

When a cowboy came into Abilene, Dodge, or Wichita after months on the trail, what he wanted was booze, bawds, music, and merriment. The townsmen themselves were eager to cater to these whims—within reason—but they were totally unwilling to turn the entire town over to the cowboys. Occasionally the merchants, in their eagerness to maintain control, hired the wrong people to uphold the law. Such was the case in Ellsworth during the panic of 1873, when thousands of unsold cattle and restless cowboys flooded the surrounding area. The townsfolk added to their police force a desperado known as

"Happy Jack" Morco, an illiterate loudmouth whose trigger finger worked better than his brain. Morco had soon alienated the Texans so thoroughly that the cattlemen threatened to burn the town and take their trade elsewhere. At that, the local tradesmen woke up and dismissed Morco, who refused to be disarmed and was shot dead by one of his police colleagues.

In at least one case a town marshal made an effortless transition from law enforcement to lawbreaking. Marshal Henry N. Brown of Caldwell, a former gunfighter, yielded to temptation after two relatively quiet years on the force and held up the bank at the neighboring town of Medicine Lodge, killing two people in the process. In a rare instance of a cattle town's vigilante justice, the

outraged citizens of Medicine Lodge promptly shot the marshal and lynched his three henchmen.

Despite such incidents law enforcement generally proved to be lucratively lenient and surprisingly effective. From 1870 to 1885 the documented homicide rate for the five chief cattle towns—Caldwell, Wichita, Dodge, Ellsworth, and Abilene—came to a rather ungrand total of 45. Some of these incidents, such as the shooting of a Caldwell woman by a drunken husband, had no connection with the cattle business at all, and of those that did, few were the result of the kind of blistering gunfight so dear to the hearts of western film addicts. All in all, contemporary evidence suggests that, even though the cattle towns were indeed raw and colorful, their wilder tendencies were leavened with a judicious dose of American pragmatism.

Cowboys in search of women's company after lonely months on the trail visited ladies such as these, posed in front of the house in which they entertained their customers.

The Range Expands

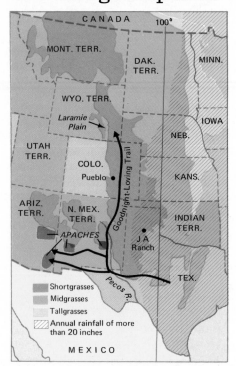

As the railroads built westward from the Missouri River, herds moved north on trails out of Texas to the rail-town shipping pens.

There is an invisible line, corresponding roughly to the 100th meridian and cutting through the Dakotas, Nebraska, Kansas, Oklahoma, and Texas, where the high grass of the eastern plains gives way to the short grass of the western. East of this line, where the rainfall averages from 20 to 25 inches per year and the soil is rich in nutrients, lies one of the world's most productive agricultural regions. West of it, all the way to the Rockies, the annual rainfall drops to as little as five inches, and the aridity plus the lime-rich soil does not encourage the growth of grains but does provide the vegetation with plentiful calcium for grazing animals. Much of this latter region, with its bitterly cold winters and hot, arid summers, had long been dismissed as the Great American Desert, unfit for any of the uses of civilization. Yet it was here that the cattle empires of the open range achieved their brief dominion and the cowboy culture flourished to make its deep impact on the American consciousness.

As early as 1850 a Capt. Richard Grant began wintering cattle successfully on the open ranges of Utah, having established a thriving trade in which he exchanged fresh cattle (at a handsome profit) for the trail-weary stock of west-bound migrants. Later in the decade winter ranges were established in what is now Wyoming and Montana as well. But it was a dramatic incident during the winter of 1864–65 that provided the most popular proof of the northern and western plains' suitability for large-scale ranching. In that year a drover named E. S. Newman found himself snowbound with a small supply train on the Laramie Plains. Hunkering down to wait out the winter, he drove off his oxen to fend for themselves, certain they would die of starvation or exposure. But when spring came, the astonished Newman found the animals alive and healthy: they had pawed through the snow with their hooves to expose as much grass as they could eat.

The Goodnight-Loving Trail

Not long after Newman made his discovery, still another area of far western grassland was opened up to cattle by Charles Goodnight and his partner, Oliver Loving. In the spring of 1866, when most Texas ranchers had their hopes pegged on Missouri railheads, the two men began looking elsewhere for a beef market. They decided to move their herds to the Colorado country by way of New Mexico, where government agents had recently established reservations for the Navajos and Apaches and were faced with the need to secure food for their charges.

Having gathered a herd of some 2,000 longhorns, the partners began the drive to New Mexico on June 6, 1866, following the old Butterfield Overland Mail route in order to make use of any waterholes still open there. However, there proved to be an 80-mile stretch with no water at all, and one drover who later took the same trail had this recollection: "Another day of sizzling heat. The cattle became feverish, unmanageable. . . . The lead cattle turned back, wandering aimlessly. . . . The cattle congregated into a mass of unmanageable animals, milling and lowing in their fever and thirst. . . . They finally turned back and the utmost efforts of every man failed to stop them. . . . We threw our ropes in their faces . . . we shot them, but in defiance of smoke and lead, they walked sullenly toward the line of horsemen. . . . In some cases they walked against our horses, and we realized that the herd was going blind."

Goodnight himself recalled a scene when, after three days of tortured thirst, the desperate animals approached the waters of the Pecos. After running the final miles to the river, "those behind pushed the ones in the lead right on across [the Pecos] before they had time to stop and drink." The crush at the river

Buffeted by a Montana blizzard, cowboys ride with the cattle, probably to cut fences so the animals, drifting with the wind, will be able to keep moving and not freeze to death.

282

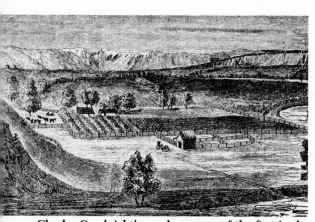

Charles Goodnight's ranch was one of the first in the Colorado country with an orchard and cornfields.

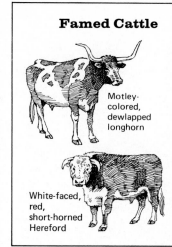

Famed Cattle

Motley-colored, dewlapped longhorn

White-faced, red, short-horned Hereford

Unlike the Old World, America had no indigenous cattle. The first cows, Spanish longhorns, were black; and their descendants throve in the wild, becoming heavier boned and taller on the southwestern prairie and brush. Able to fend off wolves and endure thirst, hunger, and cold, these long-legged, thin, and swift longhorns were the first ranch cattle in Texas, the first driven to Kansas. But their meat was lean, stringy, and tough, and they did not reach a mature weight (some 1,200 pounds) until 10 years old. So the ranchers of the West crossbred the animals with fatter and tenderer European stock, such as Herefords.

was so great that more than 100 cattle were drowned or trampled to death.

For Goodnight and Loving the terrors of the trail were compensated for by government agents at the Navajo reservation, who paid $12,000 in gold for a portion of the much-reduced herd. Then, while Goodnight returned to Texas with the treasure, Loving drove the remaining cattle northward into Colorado to provide beef for miners. He did not live to take advantage of the region's vast expanses of rich grasslands, free for the taking, for he died from an infected Indian arrow wound. Goodnight, however, was luckier. In 1868, weary of the trail, he established an immense ranch in Colorado and became one of the first cattlemen in that region.

Goodnight's experiment on the Colorado range was an immediate success. Soon the hard-bitten cattleman was dabbling in high finance and expressing an unexpected interest in the arts by building an opera house in the town of Pueblo. But his grand gestures were doomed to failure, for hard on Goodnight's heels came a host of other ranchers seeking quick fortunes, and by 1869 the overstocked Colorado range was bursting with a million cattle. Then came the panic of 1873, and in two years Goodnight was wiped out.

The Texas Panhandle

With typical grit, Goodnight surveyed the wreckage of his career and vowed to find a new, unpopulated range for his remaining 1,600 longhorns. His goal was the Texas Panhandle, a region too arid for most stockmen but one in which Goodnight was sure there was a hidden, well-watered valley—the place where, in years past, immense herds of buffalo must have grazed. With only that

Two cowboys ride through rugged land searching for a summer range with an adequate supply of water. Early ranchers had to move their herds in order to avoid overgrazing.

conviction to guide him, Goodnight headed south with a small crew and his herd. Wandering aimlessly around the Panhandle, they chanced on a Mexican sheepherder who knew of the place Goodnight sought. The Mexican led the cattleman to the fabled valley of Palo Duro, which could be reached only by a narrow buffalo trail. One look convinced Goodnight that he had found what he wanted, and he hurried back to Colorado to secure financial support from an English moneylender, John Adair.

After establishing his new JA Ranch in the Palo Duro, Goodnight began to crossbreed his stringy longhorns with Shorthorn and Hereford stock, gradually developing one of America's finest beef herds. Eventually the ranch covered

more than 200 square miles and contained some 100,000 head of cattle; and Goodnight himself became a legend in his own time—a stockman-trailblazer who had led the way into the northern plains and the Panhandle and proved their ability to support beef cattle.

Meanwhile, the cattle frontier itself had been spreading through the entire northern plains. From Wyoming and Montana to the Dakota country crossbred stock combining longhorn durability with the meaty tenderness of Angus and Hereford were fattening on the grasslands. Newly built ranch houses and corrals were scattered across the range, and more and more cowboys and financiers were filtering in. The age of the cattle baron was about to begin.

Home on the Range

In the beginning, before the days of the great cattle barons and their big-city backers, there was often little distinction between a cowhand and a rancher. Actually, many men were both. A Texan struggling to set up his own spread sometimes found it necessary to hire himself out for a season or two to earn the cash needed for a seed herd. Once he had enough to buy 20 or 30 head, he had only to find a likely piece of land on which to settle—and by the 1870's this might be in Texas itself or anywhere from Arizona and New Mexico to the Dakota country, Wyoming, or Montana. Land was cheap, much of it even free under recently enacted homestead legislation, but many cattlemen did not bother to register a homestead claim to a quarter section along a river or stream. Instead, they merely squatted on choice land and let their cattle roam over the surrounding acreage.

After a 15-hour day rounding up cattle and branding calves and stray steers, these bone-weary cowboys have eaten their evening meal and will soon crawl into their bedrolls.

Making a Go of It

The early years for a rancher were apt to be tough, as the seed stock slowly fattened and multiplied on the open range while the owner, usually working alone, rode over the vast grasslands and tried to keep his herd together. Luxuries were virtually nonexistent, and during his first years in business a rancher might live in an earth dugout, a buffalo-hide tent, a wagon, or the crudest kind of cabin. But in the normal course of events profits were high; an original investment of $100 in a herd might bring as much as $700 a year or two later, with the profits being plowed back into the business. Eventually, after four or five years, there might be something left over for building a house and hiring a few cowhands. But even then the rancher usually re-

mained "one of the boys." He would join his hired hands in riding along the edges of the unfenced ranch, and he would participate in the twice-yearly roundups, when cattle that had strayed were gathered in and all the recently born calves were branded.

In the early 1880's an Englishman named Reginald Aldridge and two companions visited a moderately prosperous Panhandle ranch that the three men were considering buying. In his memoirs of ranching life Aldridge penned a description of the place, which was fairly typical for its time. It was, he wrote, "considered the most comfortable in the Panhandle. There was a good five-room house, where the proprietor lived, together with his foreman and a woman who cooked, etc. At a little distance there was a smaller house, containing kitchen

and diningroom, and beyond that was a pickethouse where the men slept, one room of which was fitted up as a blacksmith's forge, and another used as a saddleroom. . . . There were, besides, a milkhouse, a store-room for provisions, a vegetable garden, a small horse pasture, and a field of rye. . . . The owner claimed to have about two thousand and six hundred head of cattle."

The Cowboy's Life

Next to the cattle themselves, of course, the most important element in making a ranch successful was the quality and dedication of the hired hands—the cowboys. Several decades of pulp fiction, Hollywood movies, and television serials have painted the cowboy much larger than life, making him out to be a knight of the sagebrush, a drawling individualist of old Anglo-American stock, ever ready to give up his life to defend the honor of womanhood, ever eager to risk his neck to halt a stampede or round up a gang of rustlers. In fact, there were cowboys who fitted this standard hero description, but there were many more who existed from year to year as common casual laborers, glad to have the money earned from their riding and lassoing abilities. Often their daily lives were surrounded by petty restrictions laid down by their bosses. One cattle owner even forbade the game of mumblety-peg within the limits of his spread, while on many ranches liquor, cussing, and gambling all came under

This steer is being separated, or cut out, from the main herd. When it tries to dodge back to rejoin the herd, the alert cutting horse will anticipate and skillfully block its moves.

The lonely line rider: he spends months living in a line camp (shown here), patrolling the ranch's farflung boundary and keeping the cattle from straying.

Some of the black cowboys who worked on western ranches had been born and raised in Texas, while others were young men who had originally come from the Southeast in order to avoid the racial prejudice and hard times that followed the Civil War.

The Seasonal Chores in a Cowboy's Life Are Rough and Varied

During the winter the rancher dismisses unneeded hands, keeping only the most favored to repair gear, get firewood, cut the ice on the waterholes, bring in sick cows or calves, find cattle that have drifted, and drive them to the home range and onto snow-free grass. Some cowboys live in line camps—isolated cabins from which they patrol the ranch's distant reaches.

The crucial fall job is rounding up the steers and driving them to distant stockyards and railheads. There the cowpuncher will have fun and may spend much of his earnings on a fine saddle, which costs more than a horse. Some of the cowboys quit; others may ride a train back to the ranch while a few hands drive home the horses and chuckwagon. Since cows and calves winter on the range, the latter are weaned—switched from suckling to grazing—to build the cows' strength and accustom the calves to grassland survival.

In the spring a cowhand must check the range to see where water conditions are best and move the stock there. Flash floods may trap cattle, or cows may get mired in mudholes, and the cowhand must rescue them. He has to find, gather in, and bring back to the corral the horses that have been turned out on the range for the winter. Above all, spring is the time for breaking broncs and training new horses and for rounding up the cattle in order to brand the rumps and notch the ears of new calves.

In summer chores there are regional differences. In Texas, cattle must be examined for screwworms and waterholes inspected in case some have dried up. And in Montana and Wyoming, as well as Texas, bulls must be scattered to appropriate ranges for mating and motherless calves brought back and cared for at the ranch. Work slackens, and some hands are let go; they often drift from ranch to ranch, doing odd chores (haying became one in the 1880's) in exchange for their chow.

the owner's interdict. And the work was hard: the typical cowboy lived in the saddle for weeks on end, rode line through blizzards and heat waves, risked his life in roundups and market drives but was lucky if he made as much as $30 a month.

Yet there was a romance to the cowboy's life—something about living on horseback in a vast country that was attractive to thousands, including white American farm boys, Englishmen and Scots, Germans and Frenchmen, and a large number of Mexican-Americans and blacks (the last two groups made up perhaps as much as a third of all cow-

hands). In the 1870's and 1880's running away from home to become a cowboy had much the same attraction for youths as joining the circus. One old cowpoke recalled his early infatuation in words that thousands of others might have uttered: "I always wanted to be a cowpuncher. When I was a little kid on the farm in East Texas I couldn't think of nothin' else. . . . Once in a while someone would drive a bunch of cattle by our place. I couldn't have been more'n eight years old when I followed one bunch off. . . . I had an uncle livin' down the road about four miles. He happened to see me goin' by his place.

"'Whatcha doin', kid?'

"'A-working stock,' says I.

"He finally talked me into goin' on back home with him—I stuck it out until I got to be about fifteen. Then I pulled out for good."

If it was romance that first propelled youngsters into the cowboy's life, there was something more that kept many from seeking less arduous occupations after a spell on the High Plains. Perhaps it was that in its time ranch life was the ultimate in male society, a life in which a premium was placed on personal courage in the face of many kinds of dangers: rustlers, marauding Indians, stampedes, rattlesnakes, droughts, and blizzards. From shared danger came a sturdy comradeship among those who rode the grasslands, and out of many disparate backgrounds there emerged a recognizable type, described by Theodore Roosevelt in his memoirs of ranching days in Dakota. "Cowboys," he observed, are from "every land, yet [the foreigners] soon become indistinguishable from their American companions. . . . All have a certain curious similarity . . . existence in the west seems to put the same stamp upon each. . . . Sinewy, hardy, self-reliant, their life forces them to be both daring and adventurous, and the passing over their heads of a few years leaves printed on their faces certain lines which tell of dangers quietly fronted and hardships uncomplainingly endured."

Broncbusting at the Ranch

"Cowboys is noisy fellers with bow legs and brass stomachs that rides hosses and hates any kind of work they can't do on one." Thus did an old hand describe his breed. Unlike the wild-riding fancy dressers of fiction, the lean and leathery cowboys, who from 1865 to 1885 extended the vaqueros' skills into the profession of cowpunching, dressed fairly somberly and usually rode at a trot. They were fiercely independent, yet extremely loyal to the ranches that hired them; notorious for practical jokes and tall tales, yet modest and impeccably honest; indifferent to personal suffering, yet tender with sick calves; little schooled in "book larnin'," yet able to forecast the weather from the behavior of cattle;

hard-drinking in town, yet hard-working on the job. For about $25 a month a cowhand worked at an often dangerous round of chores. He had to doctor a steer's screwworms, pull cows out of bogs, dehorn cattle, watch for overgrazing, lead any blizzard-stranded animals to wind-cleared grass, plow firebreaks, work roundups and drives, and patrol the ranch's borders in all weather. What he gloried in was his cow pony; but the job of catching and breaking one was rugged, as shown on this Montana ranch in the early spring of 1880. Professional "bronc peelers" did much of the breaking, yet all cowboys tried their luck, claiming, "There ain't no hoss that can't be rode; there ain't no man that can't be throwed."

The remuda, or cavvy—a herd of broken and partly broken horses—is fenced in by the corral. A horse is put in the remuda when it is about 4 years old; by 6 it is fairly well trained and at 10 truly experienced.

Each remuda horse is known by name. In late fall the animals are turned out on the range. In spring, weak and sometimes sick with distemper, they are fed grain.

After roping a bronc and letting it calm down, a professional rough-string rider "tops it off." Over its jaws he uses a rawhide bosal (noseband), which rubs the hide, making the bronc's head easier to control. The quirt keeps up a steady rhythm until the horse, bawling from fear, quits bucking. The cowboy will ride it for about an hour, then repeat these steps for several days if necessary. The peeler works six to eight broncs a day and gets $5 for breaking each horse. He always approaches a horse slowly, from the front, talking softly to it, quieting it. Most of the horses are a solid color; cowboys have a prejudice against paints.

Only geldings are used in remudas since mares and stallions are temperamental. Each cowboy is responsible for a string of 7 to 10 horses, keeping their tails thinned and shortened and their hooves trimmed and shod. According to their varying bents, some geldings are trained as cutting horses, adept at separating a steer from the herd. Others become night horses, calm and sure-footed; still others are used as rope horses, trained to keep the lariat taut after the cowboy has roped an animal.

Riding a rough bronc strains a man's abdomen, neck, and spine. Jarring may make him bleed from the mouth and ears and even faint. But a quirt's blow between the ears of the horse stops it from rearing over backward. A high-bucking horse is a high roller, or sun-fisher.

The bronc peeler's chaps are leather "batwings."

The breaker's single-rigged saddle has one nearly central cinch. On the fence is a double-rigged (two-cinch) saddle with a leather-covered iron horn, a leather saddle skirt that will rest on a blanket on the horse's back, and fenders (leather shields that protect the horse from the rigging's chafing).

Horn

Saddle skirt

Strings for tying objects like slickers and blankets onto the saddle

A top roper is sent to catch a remuda horse. To avoid frightening it, he flips a "hoolihan loop" up from the ground, not twirling it overhead.

Latigo

Fender

Cinch

The spade bit has a sharp plate that lies across the tongue; pulled back, it makes the horse stop. It can cut the mouth if handled roughly but in sensitive hands manipulates the horse with only the faintest touch.

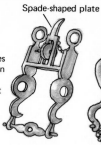

Spade-shaped plate

Curved port

The half-breed bit has a gentler plate, like a curved V. It is easier on the horse than the spade bit but needs firmer tugging.

Horsemanship differs considerably between cowboys of the northern and southern plains. The northerners, influenced by migrating California vaqueros, use a very light touch on the reins, which are fastened to spade bits, and rope in the dally style: instead of tying the lariat's near end to the saddle horn—as southern plains cowboys do for speed—they hold it until the slack of the coils is played out, then turn it twice around the saddle horn. The southern plains cowpunchers, influenced by Texas vaqueros, use the half-breed bit and a heavier touch.

Catching a wild horse for training, a cowboy ropes the stallion and takes a half-hitch, or dally, around the horn of his saddle with the lariat. He is leaning to his left to counterbalance the weight of the struggling horse.

The cowhand's hat provides shade and occasionally serves as a water pail for the horse and its rider. The boots are of fine leather and high to protect the man's calves. The heels slope inward so they will not catch in the stirrups if the rider falls and so they can dig in the ground when he stands and pulls on an animal he has roped.

Bunkhouse

Chuckhouse

Main house

Man washes with a bucket of water from a stream. The towel is a sack.

Cowhands wear collarless cotton or wool shirts, the sleeves held with garters; pants of wool or sackcloth; open vests to hold matches, cigarette paper, and tobacco; and bandanas that can be tied over the face as protection against dust or can be used to wipe away sweat.

A cowboy repairs his saddle by the sod-roofed, dirt-floored building. It is made of logs chinked with clay, papered inside with old newspapers and heated with a small stove. The crude furniture is homemade.

Rough as it is, this ranch is less primitive than many. The owner's wife and a male cook feed the men hot biscuits, beans, sourdough bread, venison and bacon, beef, boiled potatoes, dried fruit, molasses instead of sugar, and much coffee. The wife keeps hens out back and is proud of her cake recipes that need but one egg. Supplies are bought—flour in 100-pound sacks—only once or twice a year in a distant town. Any stranger passing by is given free food and shelter. The beds are boards with hay ("Montana feathers") mattresses, their legs in kerosene tins to keep out bedbugs. Because of the heat and because skunks, rattlers, and rats come indoors in summer, the cowhands usually sleep on the ground outside.

These protective chaps are cold weather angora "woolies."

Techniques of Training a Cow Pony

Snubbing post

With the horse pulled to the snubbing post the buster slips on a hackamore.

Having gently lifted the saddle onto the hobbled horse, he pulls the latigo.

Twisting its ear to distract the horse, the buster swiftly mounts it. He must still get his right foot in the stirrup.

In the early days a cowboy would bust a horse by throwing it repeatedly with a lariat, then mounting it and exhausting the animal into submission by raking it with spurs and whipping it. Later, ranchers hired professional breakers who gentled the unbroken horses, using spurs and the quirt only to stop the bucking. A dangerous step was to slip the 40-pound saddle on with one hand and, with a wire, grasp the cinch ring on the mount's far side and then fasten a latigo on it.

Touching the horse repeatedly with a slicker accustoms it to the feel of flapping objects. The cowboy will mount and dismount a dozen times, patting the horse.

The Age of the Cattle Barons

For those in the American cattle business the years of the late 1870's and early 1880's were a marvelous, heady, wildly optimistic time. The profits that could be made raising livestock on the grasslands seemed just about unlimited; if anything, the money multiplied at a faster rate than the animals themselves. Ranches in the West, some of which covered areas as big as Massachusetts and Vermont combined, were the feeding grounds for hundreds of thousands of cows. (To the cattlemen, steers, heifers, cows, and bulls were all lumped together under the designation "cows.") If most of the millions of acres on which these animals grazed were the public domain, which would eventually be carved up into homestead plots, few people at first contested the ranchers' claims to the land.

Gold on the Hoof

During these brief halcyon years, when shares in vast spreads were selling like stock in diamond mines, the ranchers benefited from a rising market. Everybody who had anything to do with American ranching expected to get rich overnight, and many did. Year in and year out, the steers brought higher and higher prices, for there seemed to be no limit to the nation's (or Europe's) appetite for American beef.

Reports of sudden riches circulated throughout the West, spread to travelers heading east, and found their way into the clubrooms of London, Edinburgh, and Paris. There was, for example, the story about a servant girl on the plains whose boss, being short of cash, paid her in cows. With an original herd of 15 cattle, permitted to graze and multiply on her master's range, she realized the sum of $25,000 in 10 years.

Even the cattlemen's trade journals, whose prose was as dry as the plains dust, did not hesitate to promise almost unimaginable riches to the investor. One issue of the *Breeder's Gazette* during this period put the case in terms that could set the most cautious Wall Street investor's heart thumping in anticipation: "A good size steer when it is fit for the butcher market will bring from $45.00 to $60.00. The same animal at its birth was worth but $5.00. He has run on the plains and cropped the grass from the public domain for four or five years, and now, with scarcely any expense to its owner, is worth forty dollars more than when he started on his pilgrimage. A thousand of these animals are kept nearly as cheaply as a single one, so with a thousand as a starter and an investment of but $5,000 in the start, in four years the stock raiser has made from $40,000 to $45,000."

It was hardly surprising that financiers from both Wall Street and Europe (particularly the British Isles) were eager to pump an unprecedented infusion of capital into the Great Plains. They formed joint stock companies to buy out

The French Marquis de Mores sat on a horse well, but his ambition far exceeded his ability to manage his many enterprises.

and combine ranches, bring in new breeds of cattle, and recruit managers and cowboys to run the whole show. Grizzled old ranchers with the smell of cow dung embedded in their skins suddenly found themselves near-celebrities, as eastern dudes and European dandies hung on their every word and marveled at their business acumen. To be sure, many of these ranchers were a lot shrewder than they looked, and one of the most daring and unusually imposing of them all was Alexander Hamilton Swan, who managed to parlay one Wyoming cattle herd into a vast beef empire. In 1883 he persuaded a group of Scottish financiers to buy out five-sixths of his holdings for $2.4 million, while he and a partner retained the remaining stock and Swan himself stayed on as general manager of the new enterprise, the Swan Land and Cattle Company, Ltd.

A Fortune in the Millions

As a breeder and promoter, Swan had no equal; by the mid-1880's the company's herds totaled 120,000 head, among them 500 prize Herefords that Swan had imported from England to improve the breed. Swan's personal fortune was estimated at $2 million to $3 million. But he was an inveterate risk taker, eventually overextending his credit and expanding the company's holdings to such a degree that in 1887 a combination of bad weather and low prices brought the whole empire crashing down. The unhappy Scottish investors were forced to sell off large portions of their holdings as the company's stock plummeted in

The first homes of many cattle barons were log cabins with sod roofs. Later, some built substantial houses, like this Wyoming home, and shipped in furnishings from the East.

These wives proved to be capable helpmates of their cattle baron husbands. Augusta Kohrs (left) fired the male cook and ran her husband Conrad's house herself. Aubony Stuart (center), Granville's Shoshone wife, bore him nine children. Mary Ann Goodnight fought loneliness on Charles' isolated ranch by making pets of three of the chickens.

value, and Swan died a bankrupt and forgotten man.

Many foreign investment syndicates sent representatives of their own to oversee their vast American properties, but some Europeans came over in person. Most spent money with incredible prodigality to establish themselves as cattle barons, while at the same time re-

A Rancher Remembers

Cattle baron Granville Stuart, an early settler in a wild land that later became the territory and state of Montana, had a key role in its great economic development.

One night on the drive . . . something startled the herd. Instantly every animal was on its feet and the tramping of flying hoofs and rattling horns sounded like artillery. . . . In an instant every man was in the saddle after them. The night was pitch dark and there was nothing to guide us but the thunder of hoofs. . . . Through the rain and mud and pitch dark, up and down banks and over broken ground, they all went in a mad rush, but the boys succeeded in holding the herd. . . . Some were in the saddle twenty-four hours.

—Granville Stuart
Forty Years on the Frontier, 1925

producing as nearly as possible the luxurious lifestyles they had left behind. Among these was a titled Frenchman, the Marquis de Mores, who settled on the Dakota Badlands with 20 servants to staff the mansion he had built in the town of Medora (founded by the marquis himself and named after his wife, New York heiress Medora von Hoffman). The ambitious Frenchman's interests included beef and sheep ranches, a stagecoach line, a refrigerator-car company, a slaughterhouse, and a firm that specialized in shipping Columbia River salmon to the dining tables of New York's wealthy. Not much of a businessman, however, he soon began losing money and in 1889 finally departed from America for the friendlier climes of his native France.

The Rich Sweet Life

Other foreigners did much better. One, a Scot named Murdo Mackenzie, managed the immense Matador Ranch, which had holdings in both Texas and Montana. Thanks to Mackenzie's almost legendary frugality, the Matador paid a steady 15 percent to investors for three decades. Most impressive of all was the English-financed XIT Ranch, which in the late 1880's added 15,000 square miles of Montana range to its already considerable Texas holdings and then went on to establish a trail between the two spreads that ran through a total of seven states.

For the cattle barons of the bonanza days life could hardly have been sweeter. The land and the grass were free, or

The Cheyenne Club

Established in 1880 by some wealthy ranchers in the frontier town of Cheyenne, Wyoming Territory, the Cheyenne Club was an oasis of gentility within the sound of a coyote's howl. Its three-story building had rooms for reading, billiards, and card playing and a fine restaurant and bar. The club's board of governors ran a tight ship, and members could be disciplined for drunkenness, profanity, and gambling, or expelled for an act "so dishonorable in social life as to unfit the guilty party for the society of gentlemen." The high-living C. M. Oelrichs, one of the club's original founders, was suspended for 30 days for hitting a bartender. His brother Harry was censured for profanity. And when the brothers refused to accept their punishment, the board of governors ousted them from the club.

nearly so, labor costs low, and beef prices rising. As a result of gentlemen's agreements, ownership of acreage along a stream gave the owner grazing rights to all the land stretching back from it; and there were rules controlling brands and roundups so that when a man's cattle strayed off "his" range, they would be returned. But with homesteaders arriving to stake out claims and increasing numbers of ranchers overstocking the land with cattle, the casual use of public-domain land could not continue. Some ranchers chose to move farther west to areas where free grass was still available. Others tried to buy or rent the land they needed. But this was expensive, and acquiring tracts vast enough for the huge herds amassed by the cattle barons proved difficult. Therefore, a number of big ranchers turned to rougher methods to enforce their claims: fencing public land and using the six-shooter and man-made prairie fires and stampedes to ward off newcomers.

The Johnson County War

Cattle barons versus small ranchers and farmers; the haves against the have-nots. That was the Johnson County War in Wyoming in 1892. Infuriated when juries refused to convict accused rustlers, the cattle barons took the law into their own hands, bringing in Texas gunmen to help them kill off suspected cattle thieves. But within 36 hours after the invaders killed two rustlers on Powder River, they were besieged by several hundred fighting-mad cowboys, small ranchers, and farmers who were convinced that the cattle barons were out to eliminate the small man and seize his land under the guise of punishing the lawless. Not forgotten was the fate of Jim Averell and Ella "Cattle Kate" Watson in 1889. Averell, who operated a store and saloon, had regularly denounced the cattle barons as landgrabbers. Cattle Kate, Averell's onetime paramour, "entertained" cowboys and accepted stolen cattle as payment. After Averell had successfully contested the land claims of Albert J. Bothwell in the Sweetwater Valley, both he and Cattle Kate were lynched by cattlemen led by Bothwell.

The Haves

Cattle baron members of the Cheyenne Club—the opposition press called them the Cheyenne ring—dominated the Wyoming Stock Growers' Association and planned the invasion to rid northern Wyoming of rustlers. Fully aware of their intentions were the state's two U.S. senators—Francis E. Warren and Joseph M. Carey—and Acting Governor Amos W. Barber, who saw to it that the state militia did not interfere. At the far left and center of the picture at the left, which was taken after the invaders were rounded up, are Maj. Frank Wolcott and W. C. Irvine, the chief organizers and leaders of the invasion.

The Have-Nots

The first and only victims of the invaders were Nick Ray and, shown here, Nate Champion, the so-called king of the cattle thieves. Jack Flagg, another target of the cattle barons, approached Champion's cabin while it was under siege and was fired on but escaped to help rouse the countryside against the invading forces. When the cattlemen and their hired gunslingers neared Buffalo, the seat of Johnson County, on April 10, 1892, a messenger warned them that the town was full of armed men. The invaders fell back to the TA Ranch, 14 miles from Buffalo, where they were besieged by some 300 small ranchers, farmers, and townsmen recruited by Sheriff Red Angus of Johnson County.

Ella "Cattle Kate" Watson

Her reputation as a hard-riding rustler was manufactured by the cattlemen after they hanged her in 1889.

The Battleground

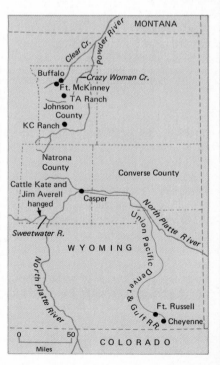

The gunmen imported from Texas arrived in Casper by train on April 6 and headed north on horseback. Their primary target was Buffalo, where they planned to kill Sheriff Red Angus, who had been elected by the anti-cattle baron element, and then fan out to kill all the rustlers in Johnson, Natrona, and Converse Counties. The invaders, slowed by heavy mud and snow, made the fatal mistake of wasting time killing Nate Champion and Nick Ray at the KC Ranch and had to hole up at the TA Ranch when their intended victims organized an attack.

Hunters and Hunted

After small ranchers and down-on-their-luck cowboys waged a stealthy war against the big cattlemen with lariat and branding iron, the latter (above) hanged suspected rustlers.

A Burr in the Cattle Baron's Hide

The cattle barons and their underlings were never tried for murder, but public opinion turned against them when a former ally deserted their side. For almost eight years Asa Shinn Mercer (above), publisher of the *Northwestern Livestock Journal* in Cheyenne, had supported the cattle barons and their dominant Republican Party machine. But a few months after the invasion of Johnson County, Mercer switched to the Democratic Party and began denouncing the barons. Advertisers boycotted his paper, and he was beaten and sued, but Mercer persisted in his course. In 1894 he published his little book with the long title, *The Banditti of the Plains, or the Cattlemen's Invasion of Wyoming in 1892*, which kept alive the memory of the Johnson County War.

The Invasion's Ignominious End

Hearing from a panicky Governor Barber that their friends were besieged at the TA Ranch, Senators Warren and Carey hurried to the White House and persuaded President Benjamin Harrison to call out federal troops, who are shown here in Buffalo. The cavalry rescued the invaders and then locked them up at Fort Russell, Wyoming.

An Ark of Safety

The besiegers of the TA ranch house lashed the running gears of two wagons together to build a movable breastworks, called an ark of safety, or a go-devil. Two thicknesses of eight-inch logs, six feet high, were then wired together and mounted on the wagon gears. The plan was to push the ark, which could shelter 40 men, close enough to the TA house to permit the attackers to throw dynamite bombs into it. On April 13 the ark was nearing effective range when three troops of the 6th Cavalry arrived. Sheriff Angus agreed to a cease-fire, and Colonel Van Horn of the cavalry arranged for the surrender. Amazingly, only one man of the 45 defenders had been wounded.

Land of Violence

From the time when the first American pioneers entered the grasslands of Texas to the day when the frontier itself was no more, the West was in many ways a magnet for mayhem. There were, of course, plenty of places west of the Mississippi where respectable folk did their best to impose law and order, where gunfights were unknown, lynchings unheard of, and even barroom brawls rare events. And chances were pretty fair that a typical week in New York City in the 19th century recorded more rampage than a month on the vast plains.

What set the West apart, however, was that there the violence was romanticized

Two dead soldiers lie outside a saloon in Hays, Kansas, following a drunken brawl.

to a remarkable degree and thus made palatable—at least to those who were never personally victimized by it. For the ethos of the West, with its stress on direct individual action rather than abstract reasoning and its suspicion of social restraints, helped make the region a haven for gunslingers (on both sides of the law), con men, and thugs—most of whom, fortunately, shot at one another, not at law-abiding citizens.

Many things conspired to make the law of the gun so important on the American frontier. First, there was the need to oust the Indians, a process that inevitably brutalized many of the victors as it destroyed their victims. There was also the Civil War, which generated passions of hatred and bitterness along the Kansas-Missouri border and unleashed gangs of looters and murderers. These lawless bands became the training grounds for many of the West's most notorious desperadoes. Then there was the nature of the West's population in the early days—overwhelmingly young, male, and footloose.

Geography, too, played its role. On the vast western landholdings, where the nearest neighbor—and courts of law—could easily be 50 miles away, men tended to think of themselves as lords of all they surveyed. Having built up huge

herds on land long considered to be worthless desert, the great cattle barons counted physical possession as more than nine-tenths of the law. When farmers, sheepmen, and new ranchers began crowding onto the plains, they regarded the cattle barons as monopolists. The cattle barons, in turn, looked upon them as interlopers and as potential thieves. The disputes that arose over land, water, and rustling became the most emotional issues on the range, often settled by a well-placed bullet.

Perhaps the most significant reason why the West was a relatively lawless place was the simple fact that it was so sparsely populated. There were just not enough ordinary citizens, let alone lawyers and judges, to establish the law as an effective force.

The Code of the West

No society, however, can exist without rules of some kind, and along the frontier there emerged a body of customs that came to be known as the Code of the West. Despite its attractive features—the code was romantic, mannerly, and idealistic—it was hardly an adequate substitute for law. According to its tenets a man's word was his bond, rustling and horse stealing were evil, and shooting an unarmed man was con-

---

The Cowboy's Weapons: All-purpose Tools of His Trade

Colt revolvers and Winchester rifles were favorite weapons of the cowboy. With them he shot rattlers and predatory animals and occasionally fended off rustlers or rene-gade Indians. He also used his Colt as a hammer to drive in fence staples and the iron-shod butt of his Winchester to crush coffee beans when he wanted to boil a pot of coffee.

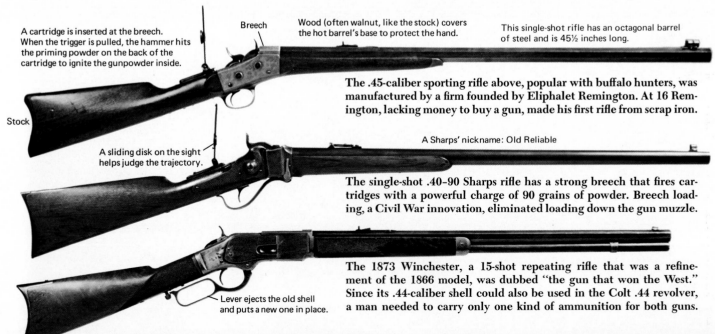

A cartridge is inserted at the breech. When the trigger is pulled, the hammer hits the priming powder on the back of the cartridge to ignite the gunpowder inside.

Breech

Wood (often walnut, like the stock) covers the hot barrel's base to protect the hand.

This single-shot rifle has an octagonal barrel of steel and is 45½ inches long.

Stock

A sliding disk on the sight helps judge the trajectory.

Lever ejects the old shell and puts a new one in place.

The .45-caliber sporting rifle above, popular with buffalo hunters, was manufactured by a firm founded by Eliphalet Remington. At 16 Remington, lacking money to buy a gun, made his first rifle from scrap iron.

A Sharps' nickname: Old Reliable

The single-shot .40–90 Sharps rifle has a strong breech that fires cartridges with a powerful charge of 90 grains of powder. Breech loading, a Civil War innovation, eliminated loading down the gun muzzle.

The 1873 Winchester, a 15-shot repeating rifle that was a refinement of the 1866 model, was dubbed "the gun that won the West." Since its .44-caliber shell could also be used in the Colt .44 revolver, a man needed to carry only one kind of ammunition for both guns.

temptible (therefore many men tended to go unarmed). Strangers were to be treated with hospitality—as long as they did not outstay their welcomes—and, finally, a bargain sealed with a handshake was as good as any agreement drawn up by lawyers.

Most often such simple constraints worked well enough, especially after the western cattlemen's associations added to them a body of strictly enforced rules concerning matters like cattle branding, land use, and water rights. Remarked one observer of this state of affairs, "I've seen many a transaction in steers, involving more than $100,000, closed and carried out to the letter with no semblance of a written contract."

But if the code had this kind of transaction to its credit, it had a dark side as well. Wherever the law was weak or men were impatient with its delays, the code was likely to be enforced by vigilante bands. A powerful ranch owner—one who insisted on strict and even prudish standards of behavior for his own hired hands—might give a tolerant wink to his equally powerful neighbor's informal rustling of a few cattle. But let his cows be stolen by professional rustlers and the stockman would become revenge personified. Sometimes, gunmen hired by cattle barons drilled suspected cattle thieves with bullets. Sometimes they got the wrong men. And sometimes they

Catering to eastern ideas of the trigger-happy West, Frederic Remington painted the blazing guns of the townspeople after a cowboy's "Argument With the Town Marshall."

used the excuse of punishing rustlers as a means to frighten off legitimate farmers and sheepmen—ranchers only learned about the turn of the century that cattle and sheep, if properly controlled, could share a range.

Sometimes the economic rivalry between cattlemen and sheepmen played a part in the spiraling vengeance of the West's celebrated blood feuds. Such was the case with the Tewksbury-Graham feud in Arizona, which took more than 25 lives in the 1880's. It began with

family quarrels but soon became linked with the bitter struggle for the use of the open range. The Grahams and their allies supported the cattle owners; the Tewksburys, the sheepmen. During one raid by the Grahams on a Tewksbury stronghold a determined Tewksbury woman marched herself out into a hail of Graham bullets to bury two of her clan's fallen. The besiegers stopped firing instantly—for, after all, the Code of the West definitely precluded the shooting of unarmed females.

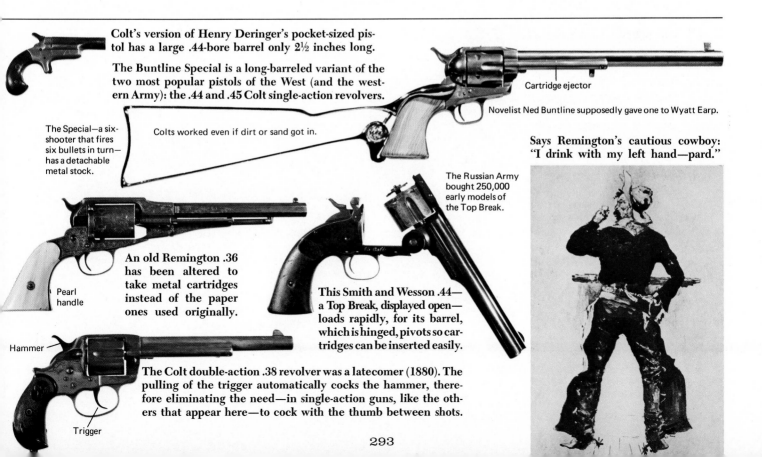

Colt's version of Henry Deringer's pocket-sized pistol has a large .44-bore barrel only 2½ inches long.

The Buntline Special is a long-barreled variant of the two most popular pistols of the West (and the western Army): the .44 and .45 Colt single-action revolvers.

Cartridge ejector

Novelist Ned Buntline supposedly gave one to Wyatt Earp.

The Special—a six-shooter that fires six bullets in turn—has a detachable metal stock.

Colts worked even if dirt or sand got in.

Says Remington's cautious cowboy: "I drink with my left hand—pard."

The Russian Army bought 250,000 early models of the Top Break.

Pearl handle

An old Remington .36 has been altered to take metal cartridges instead of the paper ones used originally.

This Smith and Wesson .44—a Top Break, displayed open—loads rapidly, for its barrel, which is hinged, pivots so cartridges can be inserted easily.

Hammer

The Colt double-action .38 revolver was a latecomer (1880). The pulling of the trigger automatically cocks the hammer, therefore eliminating the need—in single-action guns, like the others that appear here—to cock with the thumb between shots.

Trigger

293

A Gallery of the Legendary and the Notorious

Given the wide-open atmosphere of many cattle towns and mining camps, it is hardly surprising that the West spawned a bumper crop of gunslinging outlaws. More curious, perhaps, was the widespread sympathy for and fascination with the desperado. In part, the transformation in the public's mind of a bloodthirsty killer into a victim of injustice or bad breaks had its genesis in the conditions of western society. In a land where the wealthy often manipulated the law for their own advantage, the underdog outlaw came to be regarded as a symbol of defiance. Reinforcing this view was the popular press, particularly such journals as the *Police Gazette* and the dime novels, which romanticized the sordid lives of Jesse James (who claimed that wealthy enemies had hounded him into a life of crime), Billy the Kid, Belle Starr, and their ilk.

Bucktoothed Billy the Kid claimed to have killed 21.

Calamity Jane dressed as a U.S. Army scout.

Jesse and Frank James (left and center) with friend James Hart.

CLAY ALLISON. He was said to be a charming man when sober but deadly as a rattlesnake when drunk. Born in Tennessee, Allison served briefly in the Confederate Army, then went west in 1865 and became a foreman on a ranch in New Mexico. Later, after he got his own ranch and was hired by big ranchers to enforce their range rights with a gun, Allison acquired his sinister reputation as a killer. His violent, erratic behavior may have been due to brain damage. Allison's death on July 1, 1887, was embarrassing for a man who lived by the gun: probably drunk, he fell from his wagon as he was hauling supplies, and one of its wheels broke his neck.

SAM BASS. Illiterate, orphaned at 13, and forced to earn his living early, Sam Bass drifted west and wound up in Denton, Texas, where he herded cattle and worked for a freighting outfit. In 1875 Bass and Joel Collins took a herd to Kansas, collected the money due the owners, and then headed for the Black Hills. They lost their money gambling in Deadwood and tried their hand at stagecoach and train robbery. In 1877 Bass, Collins, and four other outlaws held up a Union Pacific train at Big Springs, Nebraska, and took $60,000 in gold. Lawmen caught several gang members, but Bass escaped. Betrayed by a pal, Bass was killed by lawmen at Round Rock, Texas, in 1878.

BILLY THE KID. Born in New York around 1859, he moved west in the 1860's with his widowed mother, who died in Silver City, New Mexico Territory, in 1874. In 1877 the 18-year-old Billy was working as a teamster for the Army when he shot and killed a blacksmith in a violent response to a harmless insult and was thrown into the Camp Grant guardhouse. He escaped and a few months later was hired as a cowboy by John H. Tunstall, an English merchant and rancher in Lincoln County, New Mexico. At this time rival factions were squaring off for a showdown over range rights that would soon explode in the Lincoln County War. During this conflict Tunstall was killed, and Billy murdered Sheriff William Brady. Jailed, he easily slipped his handcuffs (his wrists were large and his hands small) and, although basically a loner, he soon was riding at the head of a gang of outlaws. The newly elected sheriff, Pat Garrett, finally caught Billy in December of 1880. He was tried for the Brady murder and sentenced to hang in Lincoln. Again, Billy slipped his handcuffs, killed two guards, and escaped. Garrett trailed Billy to Fort Sumner, New Mexico, on July 13, 1881, and early the next day killed him with one shot.

CALAMITY JANE. Her name was Martha Jane Canarray, but she was known as Calamity Jane, possibly because of her threat that calamity would befall anyone who opposed her. She wore men's clothes and liked to carouse with the boys, but she stayed on the right side of the law except for drunken brawls. Born in Missouri or Illinois around 1848, she moved west in the early 1860's, served as an army teamster, and claimed to have been a scout for General George Crook. During the Deadwood smallpox epidemic in 1878 she alone helped the one doctor in town care for the sick. Until her death in 1903 she was reported seen in barrooms all over South Dakota, Wyoming, and Montana.

BUTCH CASSIDY. Christened Robert Leroy Parker, he borrowed the name of a friend who trained him as a rustler. After spending a year and a half in the Wyoming penitentiary for horse stealing, Cassidy in 1896 organized a gang of rustlers and bank robbers that soon became famous as the Wild Bunch. In the late 1890's the gang branched out and pulled off a spectacular series of train robberies. Although he was a crack shot, the affable Cassidy tried to avoid bloodshed, claiming that he had never killed a man. In 1901, when railroad detectives and lawmen began making things too hot for him, Cassidy went to South America with the Sundance Kid and the Kid's mistress, Etta Place. They kept the police in Peru, Bolivia, and Chile busy for several years, but their ultimate fate is uncertain. They may have died in a gun battle in 1909 near La Paz or, as some have said, including Cassidy's sister, lived on anonymously to a placid old age.

KID CURRY. His name was Harvey Logan, but he took the name of a man who taught him the tricks of the outlaw trade. In the 1880's Harvey and his brothers, Lonny and Johnny, fascinated by dime-novel yarns, headed west from Missouri to become cowboys. Before long they were riding with a band of rustlers. In 1897 the Logans' Hole in the Wall gang joined Butch Cassidy in Utah; the combination became one of the largest and most efficient outlaw bands ever to roam the West. During frequent clashes with posses, Kid Curry murdered five lawmen. When Butch Cassidy decided to move to South America, Kid Curry stayed behind, going on irrational killing rampages while a total of $40,000 in rewards spurred on his pursuers. Wounded in a shoot-out with police in Knoxville, Tennessee, in 1902, he was captured, tried, and sentenced to life in prison. But he lassoed the jailer with a noose made of broom wire, then eluded a massive manhunt. However, the following year he put a bullet through his brain when a posse stormed his hideout.

BOB, EMMETT, AND GRATTON DALTON.
All three brothers served briefly on the side of the law, but admiration for the James-Younger gang and the temptation of easier money led them to plot their own holdups. With Bob as their leader, they began to rob trains in 1890. Not satisfied with minor successes, they turned to an attention-getting plan—they would rob two banks simultaneously in their hometown of Coffeyville, Kansas. Wearing false whiskers, the Daltons and two henchmen rode into Coffeyville on October 5, 1892, but they were recognized; and when they emerged from the two banks, they ran into a blast of gunfire. Four citizens and four of the five gang members were killed. Emmett Dalton survived and spent 15 years in prison before he was pardoned.

BILL DOOLIN. This jovial but calculating Arkansas farmhand, a member of the Dalton gang, did not ride to Coffeyville with them, where the Daltons got shot to tatters. After that debacle Doolin organized a group in Oklahoma Territory and robbed trains and banks in the territory and several states. He was joined in these forays by Bill Dalton, who might have aided his brothers but had not ridden with them. Soon the Doolin-Dalton gang was under heavy pressure as three outstanding deputy U.S. marshals—Bill Tilghman, Heck Thomas, and Chris Madsen—got on their trail. Dalton was killed by a posse near Ardmore, Oklahoma Territory, in 1894. A year later Bill Tilghman captured Doolin, but he escaped from jail in July 1896. Within a month Heck Thomas and a posse cornered Doolin; and when he resisted, a blast from Thomas' shotgun ended his career.

JOHN WESLEY HARDIN. He began his career of crime at 15 by killing a black in 1868. When federal troops, then occupying Texas, came to arrest him, Hardin murdered three soldiers (one a Negro) and escaped. By the time he was 18 he had murdered eight men and was known as an expert gunslinger. After killing more than 40 men, often only because they were black, Mexican, or Indian, Hardin was tracked down by Texas Rangers and sent to prison. During his 15 years there he studied law, and when he was pardoned he settled in El Paso as a lawyer. But on August 19, 1895, Hardin was shot by a policeman with whom he had quarreled.

PEARL HART. Her career in crime was short, but she won fame for participating in the nation's last stagecoach holdup. At 17 Pearl Taylor married a man named Hart and moved from Canada to the Southwest. She left her husband and was working as a cook in a mining camp in 1898 when Joe Boot, a drunken miner, recruited her to help him rob the stage near Globe, Arizona. They grabbed $431 but then got lost, and a posse caught the pair three days later. Joe was sentenced to prison for 35 years and Pearl for 5. She was pardoned after serving 2½ years. Arrested in Deming, New Mexico, three years later on suspicion of involvement in a

train robbery, she was soon released—and eventually reported to be living quietly and obscurely in Kansas City.

TOM HORN. Once an army scout and a Pinkerton detective, he was hired as a professional assassin by cattle barons in Cheyenne, Wyoming, during their vendetta with sheepmen. Horn charged $500 a head. Convicted on circumstantial evidence of killing a sheep rancher's 14-year-old son, he went to the gallows in 1903.

FRANK AND JESSE JAMES. Jesse got his introduction to wholesale murder during the Civil War, when, as a teenager, he rode with one of William Quantrill's lieutenants. Meanwhile, older brother Frank was riding with Quantrill himself. To carve out a peacetime career after the war, the James boys joined forces with the Younger brothers—Bob, Cole, and Jim, who, like the

An 1887 picture of Belle Starr sporting two guns.

The bodies of Bill Powers, Bob and Gratton Dalton, and Dick Broadwell after the Coffeyville shoot-out in 1892.

Jameses, had been Missouri bushwhackers. In 1866 the thugs hit the Liberty, Missouri, bank and made off with about $60,000. During the next 10 years the James-Younger gang stole almost half a million dollars from banks and trains and killed 21 men while their fictional reputations mounted. On September 7, 1876, however, things went awry when they tackled a bank in Northfield, Minnesota. Enraged citizens turned out with shotguns and rifles, killing two gang members and wounding three as they rode out of town. The Youngers were captured two weeks later and sent to prison, but Jesse and Frank escaped and continued their careers. While living as Thomas Howard near St. Joseph, Missouri, in April 1882, Jesse James was shot in the back and killed by Bob Ford, a member of his gang. Frank James soon surrendered to authorities, was twice tried and acquitted of his crimes, and spent his declining years as a farmer.

BILL LONGLEY. Like Wes Hardin, Bill Longley hated blacks, and a Negro was his

first victim, when Longley was 15. The year was 1866, and under the Reconstruction government of Texas exslaves were getting their first taste of freedom. Longley was not prosecuted, and after killing three more blacks, he left his home near Evergreen, Texas, and wandered through the West. Working as a cowboy, gambler, teamster, and saloonkeeper, he killed some 30 men along the way, many for no other reason than their race. He then returned to his father's home in 1875, murdered Wilson Anderson, who was suspected of killing a Longley cousin, and fled to Louisiana. In 1877 Texas lawmen crossed the border, took Longley, and brought him back to stand trial for the Anderson murder. On October 11, 1878, Longley went to the gallows. Before his execution, he flippantly wrote: "Hanging is my favorite way of dying."

FLO QUICK. Dressed as a man and calling herself Tom King, she rustled cattle in the Indian Territory in the 1880's and became Bob Dalton's mistress. As Eugenia Moore or Mrs. Bryant or Mrs. Mundy, Flo charmed railroaders into giving her information about the trains the Dalton gang planned to rob. She rustled five horses used in the ill-fated Coffeyville raid in 1892 in which Bob Dalton was killed. Flo then organized a band of train robbers, but soon disappeared, and reports told of her death in a gunfight.

BELLE STARR. Desperadoes on the lam were given aid and comfort by Belle Starr, born Myra Belle Shirley. She presented Cole Younger with a daughter and later gave birth to the son of Missouri horse thief Jim Reed. Belle married a Cherokee renegade, Sam Starr, whose ranch became a hideout for outlaws. Her main job was to plan robberies, sell stolen livestock, and wangle the release of gang members on trial in Fort Smith, Arkansas. She was murdered in 1889.

THE YOUNGER BROTHERS. See **JAMES.**

Law and Order in the West

Harried town officials in the West sometimes hired gunmen as marshals to keep other gunmen in line, and not surprisingly a few of these used their badges as a shield for illegal acts. As the biographies on these pages show, there were, however, a number of superb lawmen in the West. (The judges are represented by the efficient, if controversial, Isaac C. Parker.)

Many lawmen saw no reason to make the arrest of a trigger-happy outlaw a game to be played with six-shooters on a dusty street. They found that a shotgun—or just a deadly reputation as a marksman—had a salutary effect on even the deadliest gunman. And a determined lawman could accumulate quite a nest egg: the bounty on Billy the Kid was $1,500.

IRA ATEN. This great Texas Ranger and sheriff grew up in Round Rock, Texas, where train robber Sam Bass was killed. That incident caused young Ira Aten to join the Texas Rangers in 1884, and during some five years of service he helped round up rustlers and robbers, caught smugglers operating along the Mexican border, and tracked down fence cutters during the Texas range wars. In 1889 Aten went with a platoon of rangers to Fort Bend County, near Houston, to end a feud between rival political factions. When fighting broke out, state officials put the county under martial law and later appointed Aten sheriff to keep the peace. During two years in office Aten quieted the rival factions by his impartial enforcement of the laws. He then moved to Castro County in the Texas Panhandle and took up a homestead claim. Soon his neighbors told him about trouble with rustlers and corrupt politicians who controlled the county seat of Dimmit. After Aten killed one of the politicians who pulled a gun on him, the citizens threw out the spineless sheriff in 1891 and urged Aten to take the job. The political gang cleared out, and Aten then got rid of the rustlers. In the early 1900's he moved to the Imperial Valley of California, where he died in 1953.

WYATT EARP. He was an efficient lawman when he worked at it but was not the town tamer he claimed to be. Earp served uneventfully as a policeman in Wichita in 1875-76 and as assistant marshal in Dodge City on two occasions, in 1876-77 and 1878-79. He then turned up in Tombstone, Arizona Territory, with his brothers Virgil, Morgan, and James. They were joined by

Doc Holliday, an alcoholic tubercular dentist and a vicious killer. Virgil Earp became assistant marshal and later served as acting marshal. Wyatt dealt faro at a saloon, Morgan rode shotgun on the stage to Tucson, and James became a saloonkeeper. Trouble soon began building between the Earps and the Clanton and McLaury brothers, cattlemen who augmented their herds by rustling and who raised hell in Tombstone. The feuding reached a climax in the famous fight on October 26, 1881, at the O.K. Corral, in which Virgil, Wyatt, and Morgan Earp and Doc Holliday gunned down Billy Clanton and Frank and Tom McLaury. Ike Clanton escaped by diving into a doorway just ahead of a blast from Doc Holliday's shotgun. Morgan and Virgil Earp and Doc were wounded. Witnesses claimed that the killings were coldblooded murders, that two of the men were unarmed. But the Earps testified they had heard that the Clantons and McLaurys were waiting for the right moment to hit them. The Earps and Holliday were cleared by the magistrate court judge, but Virgil was suspended from office. In December Virgil's left arm was shattered by a shotgun blast, and in March 1882 Morgan was killed in an ambush. Later, Wyatt and Doc Holliday went on a rampage, hunting down and killing two men suspected of murdering Morgan, and then had to flee to Colorado ahead of a sheriff's posse. Colorado refused to extradite the men, and they decided to go their separate ways. Wyatt Earp ended his days in California, where he died on January 13, 1929.

WILD BILL HICKOK. Even allowing for exaggerated stories of his prowess, Wild Bill

was a crack shot with a six-gun and probably killed 36 men during his career as a lawman and professional gambler. Born in Illinois in 1837, Hickok was a daring army scout in the Civil War and during the Indian wars in 1868. In 1871 he attracted attention as the two-gun marshal of Abilene, but Abilene officials, who remembered the evenhanded methods of Tom Smith, got rid of Hickok after the trigger-happy marshal gunned down a boisterous cowboy and accidentally killed one of his own policemen. His career as a lawman ended, Hickok roamed the West, gambling, boozing, and getting arrested as a vagrant. Finally, in August 1876, while playing poker in a Deadwood saloon, Wild Bill was killed by a shot in the back of the head.

CHRIS MADSEN. Before he pinned on the badge of a deputy U.S. marshal, Madsen, a redheaded Dane, had fought in Italy for Garibaldi and in Africa with the French Foreign Legion, then came to America in 1870 and served with the U.S. cavalry in the Indian wars in the West. He became one of that implacable trio—Tilghman, Thomas, and Madsen. These men, who were known as the Three Guardsmen, broke the bloody grip that outlaws held on Indian and Oklahoma Territories.

BAT MASTERSON. After trying his hand at buffalo hunting and scouting for the Army, Bat showed up in Dodge City in 1877, where brother Jim ran a saloon and older brother Ed was assistant marshal. Ed later became a highly respected marshal before he was killed trying to disarm two drunken cowboys in 1878. Jim served as marshal from 1879 to 1881. Bat kept busy gambling and also served as sheriff of Ford County but was not reelected in 1879. In 1881 he traveled to Trinidad, Colorado, where he became the town marshal and continued to gamble. In the 1890's Bat dealt faro in Denver, but around 1900 officials invited him to leave. He went to New York in 1902, was arrested for cheating at cards, but local politicians helped him beat the rap. President Theodore Roosevelt then appointed him deputy U.S. marshal, and he served for two years. Until his death in 1921 Bat worked as a sports writer.

ZEKE MILLER. A black man, he served as a deputy U.S. marshal for the central district of Indian Territory from 1894 to 1907. Although he hunted down numerous outlaws, Miller never had to shoot a man to make an arrest, nor was he ever injured on duty.

A noted buffalo hunter and a crack shot, Bill Tilghman was outstanding as a marshal in Dodge City and, from 1889, as deputy U.S. marshal in Oklahoma Territory. Later, he was voted one of Oklahoma's state senators and also served as police chief in Oklahoma City.

Handsome, dapper Bat Masterson spent many hours cultivating a reputation as a fast man with a six-shooter, which discouraged other gunslingers from challenging him and left him time to indulge in his passion for gambling. Despite his celebrity as a gunfighter, there is no evidence that he killed anyone.

Isaac C. Parker won wide fame as the hanging judge of Fort Smith, Arkansas.

Wild Bill Hickok was down and out when he was murdered in a Deadwood saloon.

HECK THOMAS. This outstanding deputy U.S. marshal was a Georgian who served as a courier in the Confederate Army when he was 12. He went to Texas after the Civil War to become a private detective and the nemesis of outlaws. Evett Nix, U.S. marshal of Oklahoma Territory, heard of Thomas and hired him in 1893. Thomas packed two pistols, but his favorite weapon was a shotgun. He joined deputy marshals Bill Tilghman and Chris Madsen to track down the Dalton gang. After one of the members, Bill Doolin, who had been captured by Tilghman, broke out of jail, Thomas got on the outlaw's trail. In August 1896 he surprised Doolin and ordered him to put up his hands. Doolin swung around, snapped off a shot with his rifle, and missed. Thomas' shotgun blast did not. Two years later Thomas and Tilghman caught up with "Little Dick" West, probably the last of the Dalton gang. West chose to swap shots with the two lawmen and was killed.

BILL TILGHMAN. During his unmatched career as a deputy U.S. marshal, William M. Tilghman proved to be a man with iron nerves and a sense of humor. While trailing the Dalton gang in 1894, Tilghman and his deputy, Steve Burke, came upon two teenagers—"Cattle Anne" McDougal and Jennie "Little Britches" Stevens—at a gang hideout. Burke sat on the scratching, clawing Cattle Anne while Tilghman chased after Little Britches, who had ridden away. Not wanting to kill a girl, though she had fired at him, Tilghman downed her horse with a shot, then collared Little Britches and spanked her. The next year Tilghman tracked the Dalton gang's deadly Bill Doolin to Eureka Springs, Arkansas. Believing he could take Doolin alone, Tilghman refused the aid of Marshal Nix and a posse. Wearing a long black coat and looking like a minister, he confronted the unsuspecting Doolin and ordered him to surrender. As Doolin's hand moved to his shoulder holster, Tilghman snapped, "Bill, don't make me kill you!" Doolin finally raised his hands.

ISAAC C. PARKER. When in 1875 this former congressman from Missouri was appointed to the federal district court at Fort Smith, Arkansas, with jurisdiction over the Indian Territory, that vast area was so infested with outlaws that it was known as Robbers' Roost. In 21 years on the bench the tireless Judge Parker tried more than 13,000 defendants and sent 74 men to the huge gallows he had built outside his court for multiple executions. Parker had final authority over judgments in all crimes in Indian Territory, and his decisions could not be appealed to a higher court. (The president could, however, commute the sentence of a condemned man.) After 1889 the U.S. Supreme Court began reviewing many of the cases and reversing the decisions, but Parker was not deterred. Contending that he was dealing with the greatest concentration of criminals in the West (65 of his deputy marshals were killed in 21 years), Parker refused to tolerate anything that he felt would weaken justice in his territory. Only 36 years old when he took his demanding job, Parker literally worked himself to death, dying in 1896 at the age of 57.

JOHN SLAUGHTER. Cochise County, Arizona Territory, was fast becoming the domain of rustlers and stagecoach robbers when John Slaughter, formerly a Texas Ranger, left his ranch and became sheriff. He was a small man who gave weight to his authority with a 10-gauge shotgun loaded with buckshot. Slaughter issued an ultimatum to the outlaws: "Get out or get shot." After several desperadoes tangled with him and were buried, the rest got out.

TOM SMITH. As marshal of Abilene, he kept order not with a six-gun but with his fists. Born in New York City about 1840, Smith went west, probably a bit before the Civil War, and by 1868 was working on the Union Pacific Railroad at Bear River, a hell-on-wheels town in Wyoming Territory. When he turned up in Abilene in 1870 to take the job of town marshal, Mayor T. C. Henry wondered how long this polite, soft-spoken man would last. The rough-and-ready Texans who brought herds to Abilene were a threat to any lawman. Smith's first act was to enforce the new firearms ordinances, which banned the carrying of guns in Abilene. Within hours the marshal was challenged by Big Hank, the town bully. Smith politely asked Big Hank to hand over his gun. When the tough cursed him roundly, Smith flattened Big Hank with one punch and ordered him out of Abilene. The next morning a burly gunman named "Wyoming" Frank defied Smith, was knocked silly, and ordered to leave town. From that day on the challenges to Smith's authority were few and far between. After six months spent taming Abilene, Smith became a deputy U.S. marshal. But in 1870 the obliging Smith rode out with a sheriff to arrest a man who had been charged with murder. There was a melee as the fugitive's pal came to his aid; the weak-kneed sheriff fled, and Smith was found some hours later, his head severed.

In a sombrero and sitting on a keg, "Judge" Roy Bean dispenses justice—enemies called it injustice. His saloon and Langtry, Texas, were named for an English actress.

End of an Era

From 1882 to 1885 the beef boom was at its height. Millions of acres of western grasslands had by then been given over to cattle raising, which attracted vast amounts of investment money from the East and abroad. Many observers saw no end to the great bonanza. But from his cattle ranch in the Dakota Badlands, Teddy Roosevelt viewed the future with foreboding and assayed the recent past with nostalgia. In a remarkably accurate bit of prognostication, the future president wrote: "The free, open-air life of the ranchman, the pleasantest and healthiest life in America, is from its very nature ephemeral. The broad and boundless prairies have already been bounded and will soon be made narrow. It is scarcely a figure of speech to say that the tide of white settlement . . . has risen . . . like a flood; and the cattlemen are but the spray from the crest of the wave, thrown far in advance, but soon to be overtaken. . . . The great fenceless ranches . . . will be . . . divided into corn land, or else into small grazing farms where a few hundred head of stock are closely watched and taken care of."

At the time Roosevelt penned these words, the cattle industry had already seen many changes. The chief modification was the gradual closing off of the open range. It all began in the 1870's when Joseph Glidden and Jacob Haish, two Illinoisans who were working independently, each developed a practical form of barbed wire. Because of the lack of wood and the vast distances involved, fencing had previously been

In their drive to control vast areas of range and vital waterholes for their herds, big cattlemen sometimes ordered their cowboys to burn small ranches and drive off the cattle.

both costly and ineffective on the plains, but now barbed wire made fencing practical for the first time.

In the beginning the big ranchers looked on barbed wire with alarm, fearing that the farmers—who were arriving on the plains in increasing numbers as new ways were developed to cultivate the grasslands—would be able to fence in their claims and fence out the cattle. But soon it dawned on the beef barons that what the farmers might do, they could do too. Literally, a frenzy of fencing began as ranchers sought to secure their own holdings by enclosing fantastically large areas in barbed wire. The mammoth XIT spread in Texas ordered so much barbed wire that the staples used to fasten it to fenceposts had to be shipped in by the freight-carload. Eventually, the XIT would have 1,500 miles of fencing. In western Kansas ranchmen enclosed entire counties, and in Nebraska one man put up barbed wire

around 132 square miles of grassland, much of it public domain.

As more and more of the open range was closed to farmers and small stockmen, they began to take countermeasures. Letters of protest were dispatched to Washington. The federal government offered only moral support, however, telling the farmers that they would be within their rights to cut the fences that barred access to the public domain but offering no protection to those who attempted it. Nonetheless, the farmers persevered. They formed night-riding groups and used wire snippers to cut gaping holes in the ranchers' fences. The stockmen retaliated in kind, sending their cowhands to destroy the fences surrounding the farmers' holdings. The mad rash of fencing and cutting often led to bloodshed; and finally, in 1885, Congress enacted a law that forbade fences on the public domain and ordered all those who erected them imprisoned. For

Charles Russell depicted wolves besetting a gaunt steer, one of thousands that died during the winter of 1886–87, among the worst ever in the West.

Finding themselves fenced off the range by cattle barons, small ranchers stealthily cut the hated barbed-wire barriers.

some time, though, the law was barely enforced.

Fencing was just one of the problems the cattle barons faced in the mid-1880's. In the fall of 1885 the impossible—but inevitable—happened. There was a glut of beef, and prices plummeted by 40 percent. Then nature took a hand in adding to the stockmen's woes.

For years the grasslands had benefited from unusually moderate weather. Spring water had been plentiful, the grass had been luxuriant, and, most important of all, the winters had been mild, allowing the cattle to roam free and eat their fill the year round. The winter of 1885-86, however, held portents of disaster. It was brutally cold, and cattle by the thousands froze to death. The next summer was miserably hot and dry on the overstocked northern plains, bringing starvation as springs dried up and the grass grew scant from overcropping. A panic began among the ranchers as they dumped their animals on the market, accepting as little as $8 a head.

Then came the winter of 1886-87. The blizzards began in November, and in January the plains region was hit by the worst snowstorm in memory. In the days of the open range, cattle had been able to move ahead of the snow line to feed or paw through the snow itself, but now they were halted by fences and frozen by temperatures of nearly 70 degrees below zero. Huddled miserably against the barbed wire, they starved by the tens of thousands. In the spring when the cattlemen were at last able to survey the damage, they saw only rotting carcasses; the efforts of a lifetime had come to nothing. At least, some ranchers thought, the value of their remaining stock would now rise; but when the cattlemen dumped them on the market, the prices tumbled still more. Ranch after ranch slid into insolvency.

Changes on the Range

The great beef bonanza had come to an end. Many ranches would revive and prosper, but never again would they blanket the West to shut out farmers and sheepherders. And never again would a stockman assume that his cattle could survive the harsh plains winters unaided. In the aftermath ranching underwent significant changes. Ranches became hay farms as well as grazing ranges, and most of the herds and holdings were cut down to more manageable proportions. The way was opened for the wave of settlement Teddy Roosevelt had predicted.

This picture of a cowboy rescuing a calf that had strayed from its mother in a snowstorm points up the problem ranchers faced in safeguarding thousands of cattle spread out over vast holdings during long, hard winters. In fact, the winter of 1886–87, which ruined many cattlemen, plus the push westward of farmers across the range in the late 1880's, forced ranchers to limit the size of their lands.

Fencing the West

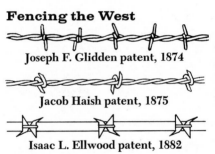

Joseph F. Glidden patent, 1874

Jacob Haish patent, 1875

Isaac L. Ellwood patent, 1882

The barbed-wire fence commended itself to the big rancher in several ways. It would keep his herds from straying, but, most important, it enabled him to control vital waterholes and streams and to keep farmers and sheepmen off the lands that he claimed as his own by right of possession if not of law. Slowly but surely, however, the Cattle Kingdom of the open range declined as the farmers' barbed wire enclosed ever-increasing expanses of grasslands. Forced to cut the size of his herds, the rancher had to breed and upgrade his cattle so that each animal would produce more beef on the hoof, and he had to grow his own feed and dig his own waterholes. As a result, ranching became a kind of stock farming, with every aspect of the herd's life brought under the cattleman's careful control.

The barbed-wire industry was entangled in litigation for a number of years as the Glidden patent owners contested the claims of their chief rival, Jacob Haish. In the above advertisement Haish stated that his wire was only "Sold on its Merits and not through the influence of threatened Lawsuits."

The Cowboy Artist

No one better captured the flavor of the Old West than Charles M. Russell (1864–1926), who at the age of 16 left his St. Louis, Missouri, home for Montana to become a cowboy. His paintings, sketches, and sculpture evoked the hunters, prospectors, cowboys, Indians, animals, and, above all, the magic of this farflung land where, as Charlie put it, "the big hills wear white robes and where the teeth of the world tear holes in the clouds." As this comment reveals, when he put down his brush and picked up a pen, he had a way with words as well.

A sensitive grassroots philosopher, Charlie wrote in a letter to his wife, Nancy: "If the hive was all drones there'd be no honey. It's the lady bee that fills the comb with sweetness. It's the same with humans. If the world was all he's, it would sour and spoil." At the time Charlie met Nancy, he was a bit of a drone, a happy-go-lucky 32-year-old cowboy turned artist who scraped by, selling a few paintings to collectors and illustrations to magazines. When work bored him or the talk in his favorite saloon paled, he would leave Great Falls, Montana, and ride out to visit the family of Ben Roberts near the town of Cascade. Ben had turned over a small building to Charlie where he could paint.

Charlie showed up in October of 1895 to find that the Roberts family had a new member. She was the motherless Nancy Cooper, who had been left in Helena by her stepfather. An attractive 16-year-old, she had an abundance of energy and intelligence, and Charlie and Nancy immediately became good friends. They were married in September of 1896 and moved into Charlie's refurbished studio-house behind the Roberts home. Gently but firmly, Nancy organized Charlie's life, putting him on a strict work schedule and later taking over the sales of his art. She felt that the easygoing Charlie placed too little value on his work and was determined to see that his genius was amply rewarded. She persuaded Charlie to move back to Great Falls, where there was a better market for

Charles Russell sketched himself and his horse, Red Bird, in a letter to Ed Botsford, who had ridden the range with him.

his art, and also got him to exhibit his works in Denver. The Denver *Times* and *Post* published some of Charlie's pictures, but he sold only enough of his work to pay for the exhibition. Charlie was disappointed, but the practical Nancy looked upon the Denver exhibit as valuable experience.

Charlie was content to let Nancy manage his life. "Any man," he said, "that can make a living doing what he likes is lucky—and I'm that." But until his death in 1926 he continued to long for the "good old days," before the plow that "turned the country grass-side down." The philosopher in Charlie made him wonder about progress: "Invention has made it easy for mankind, but it has made it no better."

There's been a shooting scrape in the local saloon, and outside the "Smoke of a .45" fogs the air as cowboys make a gun-blazing getaway.

White hunters and Indians forget past animosities as they face a crisis. A great admirer of the Indians, Russell spent a winter among the Blackfeet. "Man for man," he said, "an Injun's as good as a white man any day. When he's a good friend he's the best friend in the world." The Indians admired Russell both as a painter and as a man.

This Russell sculpture shows a bronc and rider going their separate ways.

Here the cowboys find humor in "A Bronc to Breakfast," but the hard-working, short-tempered cook is not amused as the coffee pot, skillet, and Dutch oven topple.

In his youth Charles Russell had been a working cowboy, and he probably knew from firsthand experience the deadly tangle of hooves and horns that could result from a belligerent steer and "The Broken Rope." The meticulous Russell modeled figures in clay as an aid in painting them correctly, and his wife got the idea of casting these models in bronze, as Frederic Remington was doing.

The Makings of a Myth

Fiction that left truth gasping in the dust: these magazines and dime novels by Ned Buntline (above) and others exalting western heroes and villains were highly popular.

During her 17-year career with Buffalo Bill's Wild West show, Annie Oakley was idolized in America and Europe as the "world's greatest female rifle shot." Born in 1860, she began at the age of nine or even earlier shooting game to feed her fatherless family. At 15 she outshot—and later married—a touring marksman, Frank Butler. In 1885 she went with Buffalo Bill's show and astounded audiences, shattering 943 out of 1,000 flying glass balls and splitting a playing card from 30 paces.

Born a slave in Tennessee in 1854, Nat Love made his way out west and in 1869 reached Dodge City, Kansas, where he became a cowboy working with outfits driving herds north from Texas. While in Deadwood, Dakota, he won a contest for bronc riders; as "Deadwood Dick," he gained great fame as a rodeo performer.

Even before the brief heyday of the open range—in the time of the final throes of the Indian wars and the great slaughter of the buffalo herds—a wave of fascination with the Old West had begun to sweep the nation and Europe as well. Thanks to the popular dime novels of men like E.Z.C. Judson (Ned Buntline) and later the Wild West shows of "Buffalo Bill" Cody, the West became almost as much image as reality, even while it was still being tamed.

The dime novels told cowboys how they were *supposed* to dress and act, and in their loping walks and tough-guy expressions the westerners strove to live up to their billing. These books even inspired neophyte outlaws to feats of daring. One posse is known to have tracked down three ambitious young desperadoes, only to find their saddlebags filled with dime novels celebrating the exploits of western outlaws.

The man who first fed the public's appetite for lurid dime novels had a real-life career that rivaled those of his fictional characters. While turning out some 400 pulp books and stories, and delivering temperance lectures when he was sober, Edward Z. C. Judson usually was one jump ahead of his creditors, the law, or an irate wife. Born in New York

in 1823, he joined the Navy in his teens and was appointed a midshipman in 1838 after he rescued shipmates when a boat capsized. But life at sea proved too tame for the young hero, and in 1842 he resigned and began writing blood-and-thunder thrillers. While in Tennessee in 1846, Judson killed a man in a brawl. A lynch mob promptly strung him up, but he survived when someone obligingly cut the rope. A grand jury refused to indict him, and he went to New York City. There he published a patriotic newssheet damning all things foreign and led a mob that rioted on May 10, 1849, outside the Astor Place Opera House. (The British actor William Macready was giving the farewell performance of his American tour.) For his part in this melee, which cost the lives of 22 rioters, Judson went to prison for a year. Still flaunting his superpatriotism, he became an organizer for the antiforeign Native American (Know-Nothing) Party in the early 1850's. During the Civil War he joined the Union Army, becoming a sergeant, but was dishonorably discharged in 1864.

For the next few years Judson continued to dodge creditors and "wronged" women and to churn out paperback fiction. The story goes that in 1869 he read

newspaper accounts of the exploits of Maj. Frank North and his Pawnee Scouts and headed west to see the major. The famous plainsman was not interested in becoming the hero of Judson's tall tales and pointed to 23-year-old Buffalo Bill sleeping under a wagon. "There's the man you are looking for," he said, believing he was playing a trick on his napping friend. Thus Judson discovered Buffalo Bill. Almost overnight the public idolized the young scout when Judson's story, "Buffalo Bill, the King of the Border Men," appeared in Street and Smith's *New York Weekly*. Other tales soon followed, and in 1872 they were made into a play. It drew large audiences at the Bowery Theater in New York City, where Buffalo Bill himself appeared at one performance and was roundly cheered by the audience—an experience that whetted his appetite for the kind of show business that would help perpetuate the myth of the great American West.

Buffalo Bill: Hunter, Scout, Showman, Legend

From the 1870's until the early 1900's no one better personified the West to the public than Buffalo Bill. Flamboyant and handsome, he was both a consummate showman and an authentic hero, although his boasting sometimes overshadowed his real accomplishments. In puffing up his image, however, he had plenty of accomplices—Edward Z. C. Judson (Ned Buntline) and Col. Prentiss Ingraham, who penned no fewer than 121 novels revolving around Buffalo Bill. Even European authors joined in: a Frenchman, Georges Fronval, made him the hero of 54 of his westerns.

Born William F. Cody in Iowa in 1846, he was a Pony Express rider and a scout and a soldier with the Kansas Cavalry in the Civil War before he was 20. While hunting for the food contractors of the Kansas-Pacific Railroad in 1867-68, he earned his nickname by shooting 4,280 buffalo in 18 months. As his fame spread, he took part in a buffalo-shooting contest with an army scout, Billy Comstock, an event witnessed by 100 spectators near Sheridan, Kansas. In eight hours Cody killed 69 animals; Comstock, 46. Cody was declared champion buffalo hunter of the plains, and soon after Judson published his first Buffalo Bill story.

In 1872 Buffalo Bill, his friend Texas Jack Omohundro, and Judson appeared in an overripe Judson melodrama entitled *The Scouts of the Prairie.* It opened in Chicago and all drama reviewers agreed the play was awful beyond words. The *Chicago Times* critic struggled to express his stupefaction: "It is not probable that Chicago will ever look on the like again. Such a combination of incongruous dialogue, execrable acting . . . intolerable stench, scalping, blood and thunder, is not likely to be vouchsafed to a city for a second time—even Chicago." But the audiences loved it, and the play in one form or another toured the nation for several years, drawing packed houses everywhere. Occasionally, Cody would leave the cast for a short tour of duty as an army scout in the Indian wars of the 1870's, and while serving as chief of scouts with the 5th Cavalry in the summer of 1876—shortly after Custer's defeat at the Little Bighorn—Cody killed a Cheyenne subchief, Yellow Hand, in a man-to-man shoot-out. His stock soared.

Buffalo Bill's poster tells the French, "I am coming." After giving a command performance for Queen Victoria in London in 1887, his Wild West show regularly toured the Continent.

Buffalo Bill hastened to take advantage of his fame by collaborating on stories of his adventures and producing and appearing in plays written for him. But slowly an even grander idea began to mature in his mind: he would put together a kind of frontier extravaganza to play in large outdoor arenas. Real cowboys and real Indians would take part, sharpshooters would astound the audiences with their skill, and celebrated western gunfights and stagecoach robberies would be reenacted. He got the chance to test his idea while living near North Platte, Nebraska, in 1882. The citizens wanted to celebrate the Fourth of July and asked Buffalo Bill to take charge. He came up with a rodeo and broncbusting contest and put on a ripsnorting Wild West show, which even included a herd of buffalo. The show was a huge success, and Buffalo Bill began organizing a bigger and better one.

The Wild West Show

The first official Buffalo Bill's Wild West show opened in Omaha on May 17, 1883. Aside from Buffalo Bill himself and several other marksmen, it featured among many other acts a "grand, realistic battle scene depicting the capture, torture and death of a scout by the savages." It was a smash hit, touring for nearly three decades, and wherever the show went it reinforced the growing myth of the American West.

Cody made millions—and lost them in unwise investments. According to Annie Oakley: "He was totally unable to resist any claim for assistance . . . or refuse any mortal in distress . . . and until his dying day he was the easiest mark . . . for every kind of sneak and gold-brick vendor that was mean enough to take advantage of him." In 1913 his Wild West show, burdened by debts, had to close. The final years were an anticlimax as Cody tried to make a comeback and, rebuffed by former associates, watched his health decline. But when he died in Denver in January of 1917, 18,000 people turned out to march in his funeral parade. He became, and remains, the legend of the West—a legend burnished by countless western movies, TV shows, and the several hundred rodeos held each year throughout the country.

Allowed to return from Canada, where he had fled following Custer's defeat, Sitting Bull joined Buffalo Bill's Wild West show, and the two men became great friends. During the Ghost Dance craze in 1890, when Sitting Bull was accused of fomenting an uprising, Buffalo Bill tried to see his friend and prevent trouble. But the agent, James McLaughlin, turning Cody back, ordered the arrest of Sitting Bull, who was then killed by Indian police.

Who was that early sodbuster in Kansas? He leaned at the gatepost and studied the horizon and figured what corn might do next year and tried to calculate why God ever made the grasshopper and why two days of hot winds smother the life out of a stand of wheat and why there was such a spread between what he got for grain and the price quoted in Chicago and New York.

—Carl Sandburg, The People, Yes

Settling the Plains

"Buffalo Bones Are Plowed Under." Oil painting by Harvey Thomas Dunn.

Chapter 10

A sea of grass was the West's last frontier. Onto it, between the 1860's and 1890's, rolled the greatest migration in U.S. history. Urged on by the railroads' publicity campaigns and by offers of free government land, millions of settlers penetrated the vast plains between the Mississippi and the Rockies. On treeless expanses they built sod huts and one-room schoolhouses. Aided by windmill-driven pumps, barbed wire, new farm machinery, and a special winter wheat, these staunchly individualistic farmers prospered despite incredible loneliness, drabness, grasshopper plagues, droughts, and tornadoes. Ultimately, they would transform the grasslands into the nation's breadbasket.

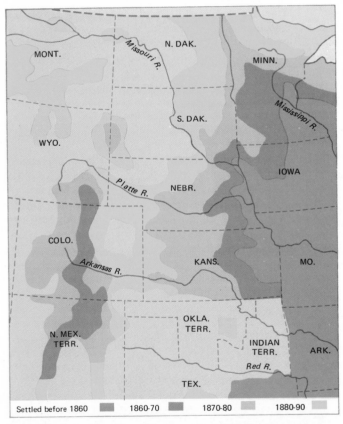

Settled before 1860 ■ 1860-70 ■ 1870-80 ■ 1880-90 ■

The plains were the last wilderness area settled in the contiguous United States. They consisted broadly of the eastern prairie plains, a flat lowland with moderate rainfall and thick grass, and the western great plains, a semiarid highland of sparse grass. Pioneers had avoided both regions because they lacked special tools to farm them. But between the 1860's and the 1880's improved farm equipment and the discovery of a way to mill hard winter wheat spurred landless farmers to swarm in, first toward tree-lined streambanks, then to the treeless plains. The Homestead Act promised them free land, but the immigrants often found that the best areas—by rivers or rails—were owned by the states, railroads, or speculators, who by 1890 controlled half a billion acres while the poor homesteaders had only 80 million. As a result, almost as many newcomers to the plains settled in small towns as on farms.

The Surge for Land

In his novel *The Emigrants,* celebrating the pioneers of the plains, the Scandinavian writer Johan Bojer had one of his characters, Kal Skaret, express his feelings as he first looked upon the land that was to be his. "Here he saw before him a whole world of splendid earth, not so much as a tree stump or a stone in it, covered with grass six feet high— enough to feed a million cows. Take your choice, Kal: a hundred and sixty acres to-day, and double as many tomorrow! Ha, ha! They'd call that an estate in the old country. He must be dreaming!"

The exaltation Kal Skaret felt would be shared by millions of immigrants to the plains in the years between 1870 and 1890, when more American soil was occupied or placed under cultivation than in the entire two and a half centuries since the landings at Jamestown. All told, 430 million acres were claimed and 225 million actually put to the plow between 1870 and 1900, and by 1890 the director of the census reported that the "unsettled area has been so broken into by isolated bodies of settlement that there can hardly be said to be a frontier line" any longer.

Like the great migrations that preceded it, the peopling of the plains drew upon both America and much of Europe for its lifeblood. Yet another element, however, was added to the mix: free black farmers. Many had to brave or evade gangs of armed whites in the employ of southern plantation owners, who were alarmed at the flight of the cheap

The forces at Fort Kearny, Nebraska, protected emigrants by scouting the area for Indians and then holding the settlers' wagons until enough assembled to form a safer train.

A family rolls into Custer County, Nebraska, probably to become one-crop corn farmers, for in this state corn yielded more per acre than wheat and needed less soil preparation.

labor. Penniless and virtually friendless in the West, a number of blacks eventually returned to the South, but many managed to achieve a share of success as plains farmers.

A second, far more numerous group of immigrants came from Europe, especially from Scandinavia and Germany, but also from Britain, Ireland, France, and even Russia. Canada also contributed to the mix (nearly 400,000 between 1880 and 1883), thanks in large measure to a favorable rate of exchange that permitted Canadian farmers to buy far more land with their dollars than they could have done at home.

Finally, there were the westering Americans, almost all work-hardened farmers from the Old Northwest and the Mississippi Valley, pushing once more for new lands, new opportunities, and new wealth. Many of them were tough

---

Where and Why Rain Falls—Or Does Not

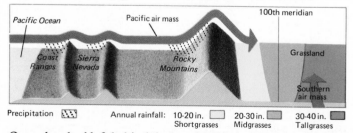

Precipitation 〰️ Annual rainfall: 10-20 in. ☐ Shortgrasses 20-30 in. ▨ Midgrasses 30-40 in. ▦ Tallgrasses

Once they had left behind the humid Mississippi River Valley, the homesteaders rolled onto the flat, drier prairie and gazed upon a sea of grass up to eight feet high. Those who continued west found that the tallgrasses (big and little bluestem and Indian grass) gradually stopped at about the 100th meridian. Beyond that, midgrasses (June and wheat grass) and then shortgrasses (gramma, needle, and buffalo grass) took over, stretching into an arid landscape. Then, and now, in the vicinity of the 100th meridian the scenery changes from green to brown. The annual rainfall, exceeding 20 inches east of the meridian, depends largely on moist southern air masses making their way northward. But yearly rainfall decreases to 10 to 20 inches west of the meridian, where east-moving air masses from the Pacific drop much of their moisture on the Rockies, which block their flow eastward. Before the Rockies were thrust upward in ancient times, all the plains had rain and forests. Afterward, the woods west of the meridian died from drought; eastward, the trees may have vanished because of prairie fires and competition from faster growing grasses. The nutrient-rich soils of the eastern plains have formed on a variety of different deposits. Among the most important are glacially eroded dust and silt picked up by the wind and deposited as a thick blanket south of the ancient glacier margin; sediment deposited in huge glacial lakes that dried up thousands of years ago; and sediment deposited by old Rocky Mountain streams. Yet the soil differs with longitude: to the east it is more acid and thick with humus, ideal for growing crops; to the west acidity is low and lime content high, creating nourishing grazing land.

veterans of the Civil War, the Indian campaigns, or the battles with the Texas cattle drovers. During the 1880's alone, Missouri, Iowa, and the states of the Old Northwest sent more than a million of their sons and daughters to the plains.

Opening the Way West

Several factors combined to open the plains to widespread agriculture in the postwar years. One was the railroads, which made the region more easily accessible. Then there were the technological innovations that rendered cultivating the treeless and relatively dry grasslands financially feasible. Barbed wire allowed the farmer to enclose his fields, keeping his own livestock in and the ranchers' trampling herds out. An improved version of the prairie plow was devised in 1868, and a modified windmill, specifically designed to harness the ever-blowing plains winds (and yet not break under their tremendous impact), made it possible to draw spring water from deep underground. New strains of wheat and improved techniques of dry farming also added to the productiveness of the plains, while laborsaving devices like the horse-drawn reaper and later the combine helped generate the extensive wheat culture that was to turn the grasslands into the breadbasket of the nation and the world.

Most important of all were the initiatives taken by the government and private interests to attract settlers to the plains. What the region had in superabundance was land, and once the Indians had been confined to reservations, most of that land was opened to settlement. The railroad companies, with their immense holdings, offered splendid inducements to immigrants. The Homestead Act of the federal government encouraged the settlement of its even vaster domains. But the promise of free land proved more important psychologically than in practice, for although the act started many a pioneer on his westward trek, once settled on his homestead, he often discovered that the act had serious flaws. The free 160 acres might have been a small empire in the well-watered East and Midwest. On the plains, however, it was barely sufficient to support a family on a subsistence-farming basis, much less provide enough space to raise a cash crop.

To secure additional acreage, farmers might buy more land from the railroads or file preemption claims on government land, which they could then purchase at

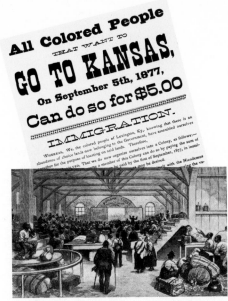

By 1880 nearly 25,000 blacks had migrated to Kansas, camping in churches and the Topeka fairgrounds (above). Penniless, few of them could afford rail fares. Most came by boat and foot, aided by black societies.

Black Exodus to the West

Although freed at last, blacks faced such harassment in the South after Reconstruction ended in 1877 that a black exodus to the West began. Benjamin "Pap" Singleton, a Tennessee carpenter known as the Black Moses, and Henry Adams, from Louisiana, recruited thousands and began leading them to Kansas. An early black western community was Nicodemus, developed by Edward McCabe, who was elected state auditor of Kansas. Nicodemus was a thriving market center until the railroad passed it by. As the number of black emigrants swelled, Kansas cities began passing laws forbidding them to settle within town limits. Many then moved on to the mountain states, Nebraska, and Oklahoma—where McCabe, one of those who pushed on, founded the city of Langston and was instrumental in establishing a university for blacks.

The Shore family, Nebraska homesteaders in 1890, used to play fiddles and the cornet at Custer County events. Blacks farmed 50,000 Nebraska acres by the early 1900's.

$1.25 per acre. An additional quarter section (160 acres) might be had free on a promise to plant trees on 40 acres of the new holding. Some settlers filed false claims under fictitious names or under the names of dependent family members in the reasonable expectation that overburdened land officials would never check up on them. Many followed the old frontier tradition of improving a claim and, once they had full title, selling it at a profit to neighboring farmers, newcomers, or land companies seeking to put together huge parcels for wheat cultivation. Thus more and more land found its way into fewer and fewer hands—which of course defeated the Homestead Act's original purpose of opening the public domain to ordinary people. In all, about 600,000 home-

steaders actually benefited from the act, while 7 million more became either tenant farmers or owners of land purchased through railroads, speculators, or the preemption law. A Kansas folksong sums up the disillusionment of many homesteaders:

How happy am I on my government claim,
Where I've nothing to lose and nothing to gain,
Nothing to eat and nothing to wear,
Nothing from nothing is honest and square.
But here I am stuck, and here I must stay,
My money's all gone and I can't get away;
There's nothing will make a man hard and profane
Like starving to death on a government claim.

A Toehold on the Plains

By the 1870's the railroads were beginning to spread their webs across the grasslands, so it was no longer necessary for settlers coming to the plains to make the entire trip by wagon. Many, of course, were farmers who already owned wagons and teams, and they often brought these chattels out west, where they could be put to good use. In fact, whatever a farmer could bring with him to the new lands constituted a leg up on the harsh environment, for on the plains a team of horses cost about $150, a wagon $75 to $125, and a sodbusting plow $15 to $30—sums that few homesteaders had readily available.

Indeed, money—cash in hand—was often the homesteader's biggest problem. Modern historians and economists have estimated that $1,000 was the minimum needed to begin profitable farming operations on a homestead. But few of the pioneers who took up residence on the public domain could claim such a handsome grubstake. Lured west by the siren song of free government land, thousands of would-be homesteaders gave scant thought to the problems of buying seed and farm implements and feeding themselves and their families before the first crop came in—or protecting themselves in the event of a disappointing first crop. The results of such lack of foresight were abandoned homesteads, a mountain of debt, and even the harrowing specter of starvation.

One reason for the suffering was that many of the plains farmers thought of themselves more as agricultural entrepreneurs than as yeomen content to earn only a modest livelihood from the soil. Throughout the post–Civil War era a get-rich-quick ethos swept the nation, and no one was immune to its effects. Wheat was the crop that promised the largest cash return, and thus it was wheat that the plains farmer favored. But, then as now, this crop depended on highly favorable weather conditions that left little margin for error. If wheat could turn the sodbuster into a capitalist, it could just as easily make him a pauper. "Don't risk your *all* on wheat," wrote a plains editorialist in 1874. "Raise corn and hogs, oats, barley, hay, flax, potatoes, sheep, cattle, poultry, bees—anything that is profitable so that if any . . . calamities befall you as they have thousands of wheat growers in the west . . . you may have some other reliance to depend on." But, seduced by dreams of riches, few farmers heeded such advice until it was too late.

Settling In

If a settler hoped to make a fortune or even a living, his first and most important task upon arriving on the plains was to choose a farm site fertile enough for profitable cultivation. Early settlers in any region of the plains had a distinct advantage, for they might be fortunate enough to find low-lying acreage fronting on a river or stream—though in some areas most of the highly desirable land was already owned by the railroads and land speculators and thus was not available for homesteading. Latecomers to a region often had to settle for less choice plots, far from surface water.

Once a pioneer had selected his land, he had to lay claim to the site, a task at first accomplished by driving in stakes at the borders of his claim or by plowing a furrow around its edges. Next came the trip to the nearest government land office to register the claim and pay a $14 filing fee. Since the land office might be more than 100 miles away, several days had to be allowed for this task or even longer if the region had just been opened and hundreds were clamoring for the land agent's attention. Thus precious time might be wasted and the sowing of the all-important first crop fatally delayed.

The crush at government land offices in newly opened areas could be mind-boggling. At Garden City, Kansas, during the 1880's officials entered and left the land office via a ladder outside a

A starving farm family, sketched in Black Jack, Kansas, in 1861, was tragic evidence that reliance on only one crop was risky.

back window to avoid the importuning crowds gathered in front. A similar scene in Gage County, Nebraska, was described in a local newspaper in 1871: "The applications poured in as fast as they could be taken care of all day, the crowd inside and out never growing smaller, for as fast as one applicant, with papers properly fixed up, would worm his way through the crowd to the door, and be cast out, panting and dripping with perspiration, another [one] would squeeze in, and become a part of the solid surging mass within."

A Letter to Norway

We have had a good year, a rich harvest both from the grain that we sowed as well as from the wild fruit and grain. We have plowed and fenced in three acres of new land. On this plot we raised ninety bushels of corn, twenty-four bushels of potatoes, and a plant called sugar cane or sorghum. This sugar cane is pressed and cooked into syrup or molasses. . . . We also got some fruit from our garden. . . . I must tell you something about a fruit called "watermelon." We have an enormous quantity of them; I can't compare them to anything I ever saw in Norway. They are as big as a child's head; some are larger. They are round, and the inside is red or yellow. The melons are sweet and juicy. . . . We sometimes sell melons to wayfarers passing by. We usually get ten cents apiece for them. However, most of the melons we shared with our friends and neighbors.

—Gro Svendsen, 1865

Taking advantage of the homestead, timber claim, and preemption laws, four sisters—Chrisman by name—each had three claims in Nebraska on which they built shacks. To comply with requirements they took turns living together in pairs in the 12 soddies.

Such scenes were common on the plains, with the confusion often compounded by rival claims for a single piece of property. In fact, claim jumping was a constant danger for the honest homesteader; a dispute over land ownership could tie up his property in litigation for many months or even years. Unscrupulous characters actually made careers of contesting claims in order to force homesteaders to buy them off, and sometimes land disputes led to violence and death—with the rightful claimant not necessarily ending up the survivor. To protect their holdings, farmers in several regions of the plains formed "claims clubs," which used vigilante methods to oust claim jumpers.

Making Do

Once a settler had completed the filing process, he was free to begin his land improvements. First of all came a shelter for himself and his family, which was sometimes an improvised tent made of bedsheets or blankets—but this proved no match for the ever-howling plains winds. Better to dig a hole in the ground or hollow out a cave in the side of a rise. In fact, a dugout was extremely cheap to build and would serve adequately until the time could be taken to build a more permanent sod hut. Oscar Babcock, a settler in Nebraska in the early 1870's, included such luxuries as a wooden door and a glass window in the dugout he built, and still his construction costs came to only $2.78—a bargain even in those days. Although such a dugout, like the more elaborate sod house that followed, was dank and dark and often overrun by bugs, it had numerous advantages besides economy. The earth was an excellent insulator, making the dwelling cool in summer and relatively easy to keep warm in winter. It required little upkeep and was practically indestructible, for it even gave protection against the fierce fires that raged across the grasslands. In the early days on the plains whole towns might be little more than assemblages of dugouts. In some, merchants sold their wares; in others, government business was carried on, while still others served as makeshift inns to serve travelers.

Relief in a Year of Hardship

Only when a pioneer had built his shelter could he take the time to plant the all-important first crop; if he put it in too late, as was often the case, he then had to face a winter, spring, and summer

A log, a plains rarity, supports a swing beside this sod house built into a bluff. The wagon is laden with newly cut sod to repair the roof. Melons (left) grow well on the grasslands.

Not all plainsmen were farmers. These Nebraskans are hunters and trappers. Pelts of fox and other animals dry on the sod wall, and the family traps hang from a projecting pole.

of hardship. Yet this could be relieved in several ways. During the 1870's and 1880's many parts of the grasslands were still wild country, abounding in game, so hunting and trapping offered a means of feeding and clothing a family. Edward Hawkes, a Nebraska settler who kept a diary, recorded his kill for January of 1876: among the creatures he bagged in a month of casual trapping were two minks, a raccoon, a beaver, and a wild cat. Another plains farmer caught so many minks one winter that he was able to make himself a fur coat. Deer and antelope, wild turkey and other game birds—especially the prairie chicken—were also present, and with luck a farmer might bag a dozen or more prairie

chickens in a single evening of hunting.

For all that, hunting alone could not maintain a farm family. Only a rich harvest could do this, and bringing it in required a combination of luck and hard work. One Kansas pioneer from England put it aptly in advising some countrymen who were considering a move to the plains: "You must make up your mind to rough it," he wrote. "You must cultivate the habit of sleeping in any kind of surroundings. . . . You must be prepared to cook your own dinner, darn your own socks if you wear them, and think yourself fortunate if you are not reduced to the position of a man I knew, who lay in a bed while his wife mended his only pair of trousers."

The Sodbuster's Innovative Home

The most inventive pioneer home was that triumph of ingenuity over adversity: the sod house. Settling in areas lacking wood, rock, and brick clay, the first soddy builders, the Mormons, may have borrowed—but then vastly improved—features from English turf shelters and Indian earth-covered lodges. Capitalizing on the tough network of grass roots firmly enmeshing plains soil, they and later plainsmen used special plows to cut turf into blocks—called Nebraska marble—which they laid like giant bricks, filling the cracks with loose soil. They left spaces for a door and windows, which were mail-ordered or bought in a distant town, along with rafters to support the weighty roof. A sodbuster could erect a 12- by 14-foot or 18- by 24-foot home (the latter shown here) in about a week, and it might survive 10 years or more. It was cheap, cool in summer, warm in winter, and virtually bulletproof, fireproof, and windproof, its walls even surviving tornadoes. But, to the despair of many a young wife, it was also dark, damp, smoky, buggy, and leaky. Sprinkling water on the dirt floor did little to allay the pervasive dust. Insects and snakes dropped from the permeable sod roof, which leaked during rainstorms—and for three days after. Mud dropped into the soup and stew, and one resourceful woman cooked flapjacks while her child held an umbrella over the stove.

The double-window soddy above has thick-based sloping walls, plank sheathing, a slat fence, and a pile of elkhorns for drying the wash. The elegant two-roomer below displays carpeting, lace curtains, an organ, framed family portraits, a stereoscope, and a bookcase that holds *The Apple Pie Alphabet.* Some soddies even had wallpaper.

Directly above the windows are short cedar poles to support the sod's weight. Cloth wadding under the poles absorbs the settling of the walls. The 12-pane windows are double-sashed but lack counterweights so are propped open with sticks. The frames, flush outside, are pegged into the walls.

Elkhorn decor

Up to the eaves the sod blocks are 4 inches thick, 1½ feet wide, and 3 feet long.

An indoor window well is a dry place to sit when the roof leaks.

Planks protect the corners of the house from the rubbing of itching cows.

Every third row the sods are laid crosswise to reduce splits at the joints.

Instead of a moldboard the plow has adjustable rods that hold up the sod strip.

The farmer brings home his grasshopper plow. Its share breaks through the grass roots, cutting the sod into long strips that are sliced into blocks.

The 16-inch-thick roof is so heavy that it is supported by a framework of cedar cut by the farmer in a distant wooded canyon. The supports: two forked interior upright poles that hold a ridgepole (which was pulled by ropes up two inclined log skids); two lower beams parallel to the ridgepole; slanting rafters; and horizontal chord rafters that direct the stress of the roof's weight onto the walls.

A muslin-sheet ceiling catches falling sod bugs and dirt—except when the roof leaks.

Roofing is of willow poles covered with layers of plum and chokecherry brush; the grass is mown from the sod bricks; and abutting slabs are of grassy sod 3 feet long, 1½ feet wide, and 6 inches thick. Eave boards keep the sod from sliding off.

Three grasses used: tall big blue stem, the sod for building and the cut grass for roof sheathing; medium-high slough grass for sheathing; short, wiry buffalo grass for sod. The house is aligned with the North Star and faces south.

Wild flowers, prairie roses, morning glories, and flower seeds from home grow on the roof.

Forked upright

Corn and onions

Kerosene lamps

The beds abut in an L shape to leave room for a sewing machine.

Behind the wife is a fuel bin.

Hay burner

The wardrobe holds the "Sunday best" clothes.

Walls are two sods thick, the blocks laid grass-down in staggered rows.

About 1½ acres of sod went into this house. Fresh sod was cut each morning, hauled by wagon or land sled, and laid while still moist and firm.

The dirt floor is hard-packed. The walls, shaved smooth with a sharp spade, are coated with a plaster of gray clay and ashes and whitewashed to deter bugs and make the room brighter.

Inside the house the mother of the children makes "white pot" (cornmeal, milk, eggs, and molasses) for a supper of venison, cornbread, turnip, parched-rye coffee, and sorghum sugar. Breakfast was fried mush and buttermilk. The plains wife keeps pigs, cows, and hens.

In his cart—his only toy except for a sled—the son pulls a watermelon. Carts were the most common toys on the plains, probably because they were so useful on a farm. Running barefoot, the boy must beware of rattlesnakes.

The baby buggy was brought from the East.

A guide that shows how deep the plow is cutting

The angle of the drawbar is adjustable.

From Plain Old Sod, a Variety of Styles

Hip-roofed soddies might have short ridgepoles, using less lumber, but extra rooms could not easily be added. An L or T shape created alcoves sheltered from the wind. A lean-to in a hillside—often a family's first shelter—was hard to ventilate, and unsuspecting cattle might crash through the roof. Fall was the best time to build, when grass roots were woody and tough. A plowed firebreak usually encircled the house.

Cost? Only Pennies

Once a sodbuster had bought land and kitchen equipment ($1, excluding the stove), his remaining expenses were minimal. The soddy above probably cost about four times these recorded outlays for a 14- by 14-foot 1872 dugout:

8- by 10-foot glass window	$1.25
18 feet of door lumber	.54
Door latch and hanging	.50
Nails (three pounds)	.19½
Stovepipe	.30

Of Water and Wind

A ready, reliable supply of water has always been the alpha and omega of successful agriculture, but its availability was far from assured on the American grasslands, especially in the regions west of the 100th meridian. Although techniques of dry farming were quickly developed on the plains to use every drop of moisture in combination with especially hardy strains of wheat, even these methods required more water than was usually available. The brutal fact was that much of the plains was at best semi-arid, despite the early spring rains that regularly drenched the region. Months might then pass before there was another drop, much less a downpour.

The first settlers on the plains usually claimed land along streams and rivers, but these often ran dry during a prolonged drought. Nevertheless, they provided at least some hope of enough water for the needs of a farm family and its stock and, if necessary, for irrigation. In addition, the presence of a stream indicated that ground water was perhaps only 15 to 40 feet beneath the surface.

Less fortunate were the pioneers who were forced to take up land far from a stream. Cisterns and barrels could be used to collect rain, but these expedients provided barely enough water to meet the personal needs of a farm family. Clearly, one of the first tasks a new settler faced was digging a well. But where to dig and how far to go before abandoning one site in favor of another were the questions.

Some, like Howard Ruede, a young pioneer who settled in Kansas in 1877, relied chiefly on their own intuition and a tolerance for backbreaking, dangerous work. He began his search for water with an auger, a sharp-pointed drill to which extra sections could be added as it was sunk deeper and deeper into the ground. Although his first exploratory bore failed to disclose any water, Ruede was certain that the precious stuff was there. Wielding a shovel, he began the arduous task of digging at the bore site, optimistically asserting that "in a hole 5 feet in diameter we will be more likely to strike a vein of water than in a hole only 2 inches in diameter." In this case, Ruede was wrong; he struck shale 25 feet down and had to begin looking elsewhere. At one point he actually struck water four feet below the surface—but the vein was on a neighbor's property. All in all, Ruede searched and dug for five months before striking a reliable water source, only eight feet below the surface.

Many High Plains farmers had to go 200 feet before striking water (occasionally wells had to be sunk as much as 500 feet into the ground). While digging and sending up buckets of dirt and rock via a winch, they were subject to awesome dangers. Cave-ins might bury them beneath tons of rubble; underground gases known as "damp" might knock them unconscious or even kill them. Abandoned wells were another danger, for they were often left uncovered—boobytraps for the unwary.

"Water Witches"

For those who needed aid in locating water, there were always the "water witches," who claimed a mystical power to divine the location of water beneath the sod. For a fee a diviner would walk up and down a homestead holding a Y-shaped stick with the joined end pointing outward. When, by some magical attraction between stick and water, the wand turned downward, the diviner pronounced that spot the proper place for digging and skedaddled with his fee. If the divining proved right, as sometimes happened, his reputation was made. If not, the plains were wide, and there were other prospective customers.

At first, buckets or hand pumps were used to draw water from a well, but by the late 1870's the characteristic multi-vaned windmill was beginning to come into widespread use. The invention of a windmill specifically adapted to the fierce, constant plains winds was, oddly enough, the work of a New Englander. According to H. N. Wade, who was long

Two famous photographers recorded the plains' taming. Solomon Butcher posed numerous families outside their soddies, displaying their choice belongings. The Nebraska couple above have a dug well, sewing machine, Christmas wreath, and birdcage—the treeless grasslands had few birds, so pet songbirds broke the silence. Laton Huffman, an army post photographer and later a Montana legislator, hated to see settlers' barbed wire scarring the wilds. He wrote resignedly of the scene shown below: "Then came the Honyocker [homesteader] with his cow in lead, his plow and his spotted sow . . . come to stay."

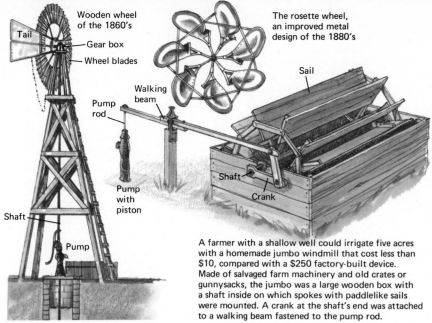

Tail

Wooden wheel of the 1860's

Gear box

Wheel blades

The rosette wheel, an improved metal design of the 1880's

Walking beam

Pump rod

Sail

Pump with piston

Shaft

Crank

Shaft

Pump

A farmer with a shallow well could irrigate five acres with a homemade jumbo windmill that cost less than $10, compared with a $250 factory-built device. Made of salvaged farm machinery and old crates or gunnysacks, the jumbo was a large wooden box with a shaft inside on which spokes with paddlelike sails were mounted. A crank at the shaft's end was attached to a walking beam fastened to the pump rod.

In river-valley areas a homemade jumbo windmill (right) worked well. But most regions required deep drilled wells. Artesian wells failed in plains soil—the water would not rise by itself—so pumping with commercial windmills (left) was needed. Gears translated the wheel's fast, erratic motion into the slow, powerful up-down thrust of a shaft fastened to the pump. A pond or tank stored the water. A dinner bell on top of the mill called the farmer from his fields.

A wooden windmill, often advertising its manufacturer, towered above those plains farms whose water tables were too deep—generally 100 to 200 feet—for hand pumping. When not in use, the tail was folded by turning a crank at the mill's base. It was the tail that kept the wheel facing into the wind.

involved in the manufacture of these devices, the plains windmill evolved in this manner: "Way back in 1854 John Burnham, who was then termed a Pump Doctor . . . suggested to Daniel Halladay, a young mechanic of Ellington, Connecticut, that it would be a good idea if a windmill could be made that would be self-governing as there was an abundance of wind all over the country that might just as well pump water and save the human energy expended.

"Mr. Halladay was a man of an inventive turn of mind, and he very quickly invented a windmill which governed itself by centrifugal force. . . . These mills were first manufactured . . . in 1854 in South Coventry, Connecticut, and a few were sold, but Mr. Burnham came to Chicago and decided that the real market . . . would be in the Western prairie states." By the 1880's thousands of these windmills were being sold. A farmer who lacked the money to buy one of Halladay's might simply build his own, since instructions for making mills were widely available. These amazingly efficient devices could pump hundreds of gallons of water from the earth each day, and by the 1890's they had become virtual symbols of plains agriculture.

The never-failing wind of the plains could be a treacherous master, however. Though it drove the mills that brought life to the plains, it could also combine with drought and heat to become a vast

destructive force. The phenomenon was noted early in the history of plains settlement by a journalist in Atchison, Kansas, who recalled the disaster of one summer's day: "At about twelve o'clock, as we were sitting in our office, we felt a gust of wind so hot and scorching that we at first supposed some building close by must be on fire, and rushed to the window to ascertain. It continued until between three and four o'clock. . . . All vegetable matter was withered . . . as though by fire, and it is feared much damage is done to the crops."

Wind and drought would continue to be the plains' greatest scourge for decades to come. The hot winds not only scorched the crops but also lifted the bone-dry topsoil, creating immense swirls of dust that were sometimes deposited hundreds of miles from their source. "Real estate moved considerably this week," reported a plains newspaper in 1880. The phenomenon was repeated periodically, reaching a climax in the great dust bowls of the 1930's. But these hot winds were just one of nature's weapons against the plains farmer.

A New Kind of Farming for the Plains

Even with improved plows for tilling and cutting sod, the homesteader found plains turf hard to manage, for the roots of the grasses extended deep down and intermeshed to form sod up to 12 feet thick. Rotting over the millennia, these roots had created fertile humus that was far thicker than in the eastern woodlands. The tallgrasses of the eastern prairies were kept moist above by rain and moist below by underground water tapped by the long roots. The midgrasses and shortgrasses of the central and western plains had shallower roots, watered by occasional rain and extending down to limy layers and dry subsoil. Once he had plowed up the moisture-holding grasslands,

the western plains farmer soon found that his topsoil blew away, and the earth baked dry. To prevent this, experimental farmer Hardy W. Campbell popularized dry farming, whereby a man let half his land (though cleared of weeds) lie fallow each year to accumulate moisture. He also tamped the soil with a subsurface packer, kept the surface blanketed with dust or mulch by cultivating after every rain, plowed deeply, and planted fewer seeds per acre than back east. Other farmers simply heeded a Sioux who, watching a pioneer turn under his grass, warned: "Wrong side up." They left the grass alone, put dairy cows to graze on it, and developed a topnotch dairy industry.

The Plagues of Nature

Dried by 100°F summers, the grasses are ignited by lightning. To stem the blaze, men plow a firebreak and, with what look like fuses, light grass ahead of the fire so it cannot feed itself.

Without mountains to interrupt the winds the plains are frequently ripped by tornadoes—such as this Garnett, Kansas, twister of 1884. These storms are formed by violently rotating air under thunderheads.

For the plainsman every season had its share of woe. Spring meant floods; summer, drought; autumn, prairie fires; and winter, arctic cold and blizzards. There were also occasional extras: swarms of grasshoppers to ravage the crops, summer hailstorms to pound them flat, and winter ice storms severe enough to topple carefully tended trees and cave in sod roofs. And no man could be fully prepared for these disasters. For a number of years running, nature might show a benign face; then, without any warning at all, she would strike savagely.

Fire and Ice

One of the worst disasters the plainsmen faced was the prairie fire. Each fall, as the grass stood limp and dry, the danger of fires rose to the flash point. Every spark from a carelessly tended campfire, every bolt of lightning threatened conflagration. Once a prairie fire had started, the walls of flame, jumping from field to field, were almost impossible to control. Yet such fires, while extremely destructive to crops, posed few dangers to human life—if a man took elementary precautions and kept his head. Caught alone on the plains, a man might use fire to fight fire, burning out a circle of grassland in order to make an island of safety for himself. But the best protection was usually a sod house; the raging infernos were unable to penetrate the damp, thick building materials. If one had warning enough, the soddy could be made even more fireproof by dousing it with water or—as one pioneer woman attempted in an emergency—with milk.

Under favorable conditions a prairie fire might last as long as six weeks, denuding tens of thousands of acres.

As distressing as the fires, and often more dangerous, were winter's subzero temperatures (as low as −40°F on the northern plains) and the accompanying blizzards. The typical plains blizzard included not only snow, which could pile up higher than the roofs of the sod houses, but also wind-driven sleet that, in minutes, could cover man and beast with a glaze of ice. Livestock caught in open pastures were sometimes so thickly coated with ice that they could not lift their heads; those that survived had to be freed from their glassy prisons by the vigorous application of clubs.

If the harvest had been poor the previous fall, or if fire had turned it to ashes,

winter posed a time of extreme peril for farm families—they might literally starve to death with no cash to buy food. In 1871 one Minnesota farmer, reduced to desperation, spoke for many others in a letter to a state official: "I have been sick for months, and my wife is not well from exposure and hunger and I thought that there was no other way than to ask you to help me—if you can let me have $25 and some close for my wife and daughter and myself as we have not close to cover our backs or heads."

In the long list of winter-borne horrors nothing quite came up to the "schoolchildren's storm" of 1888. This blizzard, which also did irreparable harm to the open-range cattle industry, derived its name from the fact that many youngsters were caught in it and died.

In summer, hot air masses sweep freely across the plains, lift up plowed topsoil, and create smothering duststorms. Before the region was farmed, the thick grasses anchored the soil.

314

A child is buried in the family's cemetery. Lacking undertakers and lumber, neighbors would bury the body as soon as possible in a sheet or in a coffin made from a wagon box.

On the way home from a wagon trip to town, this farm family was caught in a blizzard. Snowstorms blanketed the plains suddenly, with 50-mile-an-hour winds and 15-foot drifts.

The Prairie Fire

Then there is the prairie fire or, as they call it here, "Faieren." This is terrifying, and the fire rages in both the spring and the fall. Whatever it leaves behind in the fall, it consumes in the spring, so there is nothing left of the long grass on the prairies, sloughs, and marshes. It is a strange and terrible sight to see all the fields a sea of fire. Quite often the scorching flames sweep everything along in their path—people, cattle, hay, fences. In dry weather with a strong wind the fire will race faster than the speediest horse. No one dares to travel without carrying matches, so that if there is a fire he can fight it by building another and in this way save his life and prevent burns, which sometimes prove fatal. . . . I am [not] exaggerating. I assure you that all that I have told you I have experienced myself.

—Gro Svendsen, 1863

The crushed bodies of a grasshopper horde make the rails so oily the train must stop.

With typical plains capriciousness the morning of January 12, 1888, dawned bright and mild, and the children of the Dakota Territory and Nebraska trekked off to school wearing clothing more suitable to spring than winter. In the afternoon, just as they were beginning the long walk home, the sky suddenly darkened, the temperature plummeted, and a blinding storm of snow and sleet struck from the northwest. Most of the children found shelter, but a number froze to death. Among the victims discovered later were a 13-year-old girl and her younger sister. The older child had given much of her clothing to the younger in a vain effort to protect her. Near a Dakota schoolhouse nine students and their teacher were found frozen in an open field. All told, some 200 people died from exposure.

For the four years beginning in 1874 plagues of grasshoppers were the terror of the grasslands. Arriving suddenly from east of the Rocky Mountains in the summer of 1874, they came in the tens of millions like a conquering army. Hopping, flying, and marching this way and that, doubling back on their tracks, and seeking new fields to ravish, they turned millions of acres of wheat and corn into wasteland. One Kansas farmer remembered their appearance over a cornfield with bone-chilling horror. "There was not a hint of cloud in the sky," he recalled. "Then the sky suddenly became hazy and speedily darkened. . . . Then with a whizzing, whirring sound the grasshoppers came . . . in unbelievable numbers. . . . The ground was covered, in some spots to a depth of three or four inches, and trees along the creek were so loaded that large limbs were broken off. The insects fell . . . they formed a dam

and the water turned brown. . . . The hoppers landed about four o'clock. By dark there wasn't a stalk of that field of corn over a foot high left."

Efforts to stop the creatures were largely useless: they ignored farmers waving their arms in fury and fear. If millions of hoppers were consumed in the fires whose smoke it was hoped would destroy them, millions more seemed to rise unscathed. For thousands of pioneers this was the end. They had survived fire and ice, tornadoes and duststorms, economic depression and perils of every kind, but the hoppers were the final blow. Many left the plains for gentler climates; yet those who stuck it out were joined by thousands of new arrivals. The availability of free or cheap land and the hope of striking it rich on a rising wheat and corn market were still powerful attractions.

The Immigrant Tide

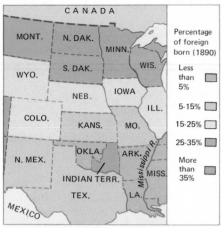

A foreigner usually came to the more northerly states. With mechanization, even in the cold climates, he could process 135 instead of 7½ acres of wheat.

It was called America fever, and during the 1870's and 1880's it swept through Europe like an epidemic. The carriers were many: agents of steamship lines and of the American railroads; publicity men hired by the western states and territories; and finally, former residents of Europe's ancient and tarnished lands, whose "America letters" to the old country spoke of a land of promise where a man could eat meat three times a day and tip his hat to no one.

In the vanguard of this unprecedented publicity campaign were the railroad companies, which were eager to sell the 181 million acres of land granted to them as bounties by the government in order to help them recover construction costs. The railroads' profits depended on the rapid settlement of the plains and the creation of a booming agricultural economy that would keep thousands of freight cars filled with the region's farm produce. The Union Pacific alone spent about $815 million to attract settlers and help them get established. The Burlington, Santa Fe, Northern Pacific, and Kansas Pacific lines were nearly as openhanded. The ornate prose in their publicity pamphlets depicted the plains as a virtual paradise. One poetically inclined huckster portrayed the Dakota Territory as a land where "mocking birds and gorgeous paroquets and cockatoos warble musical challenges to each other amid the rich foliage of the sweet-bay and mango trees."

Cutthroat Competition for Settlers

Not far behind in their avid hucksterism were the agents of the western states and territories, hired to encourage immigration from abroad. Like the railroad representatives, they tramped through Europe seeking converts and engaging in cutthroat competition with one another. C. B. Neilson, a Nebraska agent in Scandinavia, described the battle in a letter to his employers: "Dear Sir: Victory! The battle is won for our state, but it was a hard fought battle. . . . The fall

This thick-walled Nebraska sod "castle" with wooden beams was built in 1884 by a Belgian, Isadore Haumont, for only $500.

emigration to Nebraska of people with sufficient capital to commence work on our prairies will be very large. On Monday I go to Sweden and Norway, and will have easy work there. I shall try my best to beat the agent for Minnesota."

Not every American promoter wanted to lure European peasants to the plains simply to help build an agricultural empire. Some had more immediate and personal get-rich-quick schemes in mind. An English resident of Kansas, Ned Turnley by name, proposed the establishment of an English village on the Kansas plains to be known as Runnymede. A man of great ambition and few scruples, Turnley intended nothing less than the bilking of the British aristocracy. On a trip to Britain he visited many of the country's most prominent families, making them this proposal: for a fee of £500 per head he would transport the spendthrift sons of Britain's great families to his little England on the prairie and watch over them as they learned the rudiments of gracious and profitable living on the American frontier.

100 Ne'er-do-wells

Ned Turnley must have been a highly persuasive talker, for he managed to recruit about 100 ne'er-do-wells for his scheme, in the process collecting the tidy sum of £50,000. Since he was not a total charlatan, he actually built a hotel in his fledgling settlement and there sheltered his charges for several months while they hunted, drank enormous quantities of booze, and sent plaintive letters home for more money. One by one the fathers

Mennonites Brought the West's Hardiest Wheat

The religious sect's temporary longhouse village before permanent homes were built.

Communal life inside one Kansas longhouse.

Among the most valuable immigrant contributions was Turkey Red, a hard winter wheat that could survive plains weather. The seeds were brought by some 2,000 Mennonites, well-to-do German-speaking pacifist farmers from Russia's Crimea. Fearing conscription, they came in 1873–74, with Santa Fe Railroad help, and purchased nearly 100,000 acres.

By 1900, 17,000 Swedes, like these Greeley County settlers, had come to Kansas and thousands more to other plains states.

A French silk manufacturer planted 70 Kansas acres with mulberry trees and founded a silk cooperative. It failed because once they learned English, the members—here hunting rabbits for Christmas—found that they could command higher wages as farm laborers or mechanics.

The Northern Pacific Railroad carried these Russians to Bismarck, North Dakota; its winters reminded them of home.

Most inappropriate of all arrivals were these British aristocrats at Runnymede, Kansas. Staying in promoter Ned Turnley's hotel, they, their wives, and an occasional mother (in black) spurned cows and corn in favor of tennis and riding to hounds—hunting coyotes when they could not scare up a fox. They laid out a racetrack and polo field, spent their days at sports, and most of their nights drinking and frolicking.

ordered their sons home, thus dooming the Runnymede scheme.

Sometimes whole communities were transplanted from Europe to the plains. Settlements of Mennonites from Russia were among the most conspicuous and successful in Kansas and the Dakotas. In Kansas, as elsewhere, there were a number of other farming communities more redolent of the Old World than of the New—the German Catholic town of Liebenthal, for instance, and the Swedish village of Lindsborg. Even when there were no formal efforts to segregate newcomers by nationality, European immigrants usually settled where their countrymen already lived. Thus, of the 675,000 Scandinavians (including one-third of the population of Iceland) who flocked to America in the 1880's, a large

portion settled in Minnesota and the Dakotas, where the climate was similar to that of their homelands and where there were already large Scandinavian populations to welcome them and ease their way. Similarly, the Germans—of whom a quarter of a million came to the United States in 1882 alone—tended toward the central plains. Many Americans traveling through the grasslands during these years noted with amusement or dismay that European tongues seemed more prevalent than English.

Once out on the plains, most of the immigrants wasted little time wondering about the lack of tropical birds or mango trees—few had really believed the land promoters' propaganda anyway. What they found was good enough. For the vast stretches of cheap land held a

promise of independence and perhaps even prosperity. Most of the newcomers would probably have agreed with a letter written by the Reverend Olof Olsson, who had just settled in Kansas, to his Swedish countrymen in 1869: "The advantage which America offers is not to make everyone rich at once without toil and trouble, but the advantage is that the poor, who will and are able to work, secure a large piece of good land almost without cost, that they can work up little by little and become after a few years the owners of property, which rival large estates in Sweden. . . . The difficulties at the outset are so great that not every person has the courage to overcome them. The best plan is for several acquaintances to settle in a tract, where they can encourage and help each other."

The Women of the West

In the West of stories and films, women are usually secondary characters—stoic, self-sacrificing helpmates who are mere bit players in the frontier drama. In reality, however, the women of the West were much more than just wives and mothers, healers and housekeepers. They made vital contributions to the taming of a continent. Although often in the rearguard of settlement—many of them arriving in the new lands only after the men had established the first semblance of order—it was they who had to create true homes in the wilderness and organize such civilized necessities as schools, churches, and libraries.

A number of women accompanied their husbands to the plains against their better judgment, and for some their first sight of the dismal, windswept grasslands was also their last. They simply refused to settle there, forcing their husbands to retreat to more familiar and congenial surroundings.

The feeling of dread, almost of doom, experienced by these women was beautifully expressed in O. E. Rölvaag's *Giants in the Earth*, whose Scandinavian heroine Beret sensed a strange aura about the plains. "The broad expanse stretching away endlessly . . . reminded her strongly of the sea, and yet it was very different. This formless prairie had no heart that beat, no waves that sang. . . . The infinitude surrounding her on every hand might not have been

At the polls in Wyoming—the first territory to allow women the vote and, when it became a state in 1890, the first state to do so.

so oppressive . . . if it had not been for the deep silence. . . . Could no living thing exist out here, in the empty, desolate, endless wastes of green and blue? . . . How *could* existence go on, she thought desperately? If life is to thrive and endure, it must at least have something to hide behind!"

Most women pioneers set to work to prove that life was indeed possible on the plains. And hard, frustrating, agonizing work it was. The situation was particularly hard on gently bred eastern women, for whom a clean, tidy house was both a matter of deep pride and a symbol of morality. How could one keep a sod hut clean when sweeping the dirt floor merely meant spreading the grime, when bugs kept falling from the sod roof, and snakes squiggled in for shelter? How could one teach children the rudiments of cleanliness when water was so scarce and the fuel used for cooking was dried cow dung? "It was comical," wrote the editor of a plains newspaper, "to see how gingerly our wives handled these chips at first. They commenced by picking them up between two sticks. . . . Soon they used a rag, and then a corner of their apron. Finally . . . a wash after handling them was sufficient. And now? Now it is out of the bread, into the chips and back again—and not even a dust of the hands."

Far worse than the drudgery was the sheer loneliness of life on the plains. Distances were too great, and for a long

An early homesteader gathers buffalo chips for fuel. Once the herds vanished, families used twists of hay ("cats") or cornhusks. Hay, burned in special stoves, needed constant feeding and was a fire hazard. Some sod houses were nearly filled with stored cats.

Hungry for outside contact, a farm family listens to a stove salesman. Sometimes on foot, itinerants included clock repairmen, scissor grinders, and Irish and Jewish clothes peddlers.

time the population was too sparse to permit the kind of diversions that had eased the lives of the earlier woodland pioneers. At first, no community roof raisings, quilting bees, or church socials relieved the daily struggle. The cattleman and the farmer might get to town from time to time on buying and selling expeditions, but their wives usually stayed home and tended to their chores. Small wonder that the incidence of madness on the plains was much higher among women than men.

Crusaders in Petticoats

Whatever else the plainswomen were, they were not shrinking violets. Many of them took up the crusades of the Victorian Age with great gusto. Chief among these were temperance and feminism, and both achieved early success on the grasslands. In part, the women's influence stemmed from the fact that females were in short supply on the plains. If a man wanted a wife, he often had to agree to such demands as abstinence from liquor, tobacco, bad language, and gambling. "We married anything that got off the railroad" was a saying common among plainsmen, but in order to get women *on* the westbound trains, men sometimes had to abjure their most precious amusements. There was more than a hint of truth in this parody of a temperance ditty:

The man who drinks the red, red wine
Will never be a beau of mine.
The man who is a whisky sop
Will never hear my corset pop.

As the female population of the plains grew in the 1870's and 1880's, so too did the temperance movement. Even though Maine was the first state to prohibit the manufacture and sale of alcohol, the temperance crusade took root most firmly on the grasslands. The personification of the movement was Kansas' Carry Nation, who became world renowned for her hatchet-wielding forays into the saloons of Middle America.

Closely associated with temperance was the movement for women's rights. In an era when most women were legally considered not much more than men's chattel, the plains recognized women's rights, according them control over their own property and allowing them to engage in trade without their menfolk's consent. And it was in the plains region that the vote was first granted to women, with Wyoming Territory leading the way in 1869—a half century before the women's suffrage amendment was added

Sarah Sim: "I Sometimes Quite Despair"

Her hair brittle and dusty, her skin creased far beyond her age from wind, sun, and alkali water, a plains wife, who lived much like Sarah Sim, leads her milk cow.

No frontier was harder on women than the plains. And few plainswomen found it more stressful than did Sarah Sim. In 1856 she and her husband Francis, New Englanders, bought 160 Nebraska acres near Bennett's Ferry. Unlike bleaker plains areas their land had a brook, a grove, and neighbors close by. At age 32 Sarah started housekeeping with three children in a 10- by 10-foot cabin. The Sims had three cows, two oxen, a horse, pigs, and hens. They hunted prairie chickens and rabbits and gathered wild strawberries and plums. Sarah wrote her parents: "There is no school nor church. . . . There is preaching [occasionally] at private houses." The weather was very dry, the water was hard, and, she added, "it seems as if [the wind] would blow our little house away."

Then her travails began: her second child died following whooping cough and prolonged diarrhea. Her hand got badly infected, and a finger was amputated. Her husband sickened. And the first winter was bitter cold. "It almost breaks our spirits down," wrote Sarah. She became severely melancholic: "Pray for me . . . that I may overcome my present fear." But she could not. For some eight months she acted demented, tearing her clothes, biting herself and the children, breaking the windows, smashing belongings. She even attempted suicide. Finally, Francis had to tie her to their bed.

Yet, gradually, she improved and wrote, "I sometimes quite despair. . . . I would do anything to get better." Fortunately, the second winter was mild, and Francis, recovering, built additions to the home, grew potatoes and superb corn, and salted 1,560 pounds of the best pork for sale. More settlers arrived and built a school. Cheered, Sarah greeted her second spring by planting flower seeds that came from home. And although she had to face the death—from diphtheria and mumps—of four more of her nine children, she never broke down again.

to the U.S. Constitution. By 1920, when that amendment was finally adopted, all but four of the states west of the 98th meridian allowed women equal suffrage, whereas only two states east of that line had become similarly enlightened.

As gratifying as these advances may have been, they did little to alter the drudgery and monotony of frontier life. Only time and hard-won prosperity would bring the farm wife at least a degree of the comfort and security many others took for granted.

A cartoon shows hatchet-carrying Carry Nation terrorizing a Kansas saloonkeeper.

A Little Bit of Learning

Most early plains schools had a blackboard, but books—provided by parents—were usually only a Bible, hymnal, almanac, and dictionary; McGuffey's Readers; grammars and geography and arithmetic books. Boys and girls advanced by reading the next hardest book.

A rather cynical wag who took a dim view of education in rural America once observed: "The average farmer and rural teacher think of the rural school as a little house, on a little ground, with a little equipment, where a little teacher at a little salary, for a little while, teaches little children little things." There was a degree of truth in this epigram, but like many satirical summations it obscured as much as it revealed.

In many instances on the plains—as earlier in the settlement of the West—a new region was hardly opened before settlers met together to plan the schooling of their young. In 1871 an enthusiastic group in Buffalo County, Nebraska, organized a school district (and levied a tax on themselves to pay for a schoolhouse) even before they had built dwellings. Other frontiersmen, intent on more practical pursuits, were suspicious of formal education. But in the areas where the New England influence predominated, naysayers were overruled and some kind of school was established.

Frontier schools were financed by local districts, but in the early days of settlement individual subscription was more common. For each child attending school (usually for five months a year), a family might pay a fee of $1 to $1.50 a month. Teachers who earned as much as $1 per day considered themselves lucky.

Bed and Board

Parents were expected to offer bed and board for a specified period, and the more children a pioneer had, the longer he had to open his home to the teacher. Since the largest families were often least able to offer privacy, comfort, or decent fare, a schoolteacher had good reason to dread a sojourn with them. One gently bred lady wrote home of her dismay at her hosts' offerings: "Their manner of living is so different from ours that it just about used me up. For breakfast we had corn bread, salt pork and black coffee. For dinner, greens, wild ones at that, boiled pork, and cold corn bread washed down with 'beverage.' The 'beverage' . . . was vinegar and brown sugar and warm creek water."

Given the low wages, rugged living arrangements, and poor working conditions—textbooks in the earliest plains schools were scarce—the constant turnover in personnel was hardly surprising. In the course of a single school year (divided into two or three terms), a one-room schoolhouse might be presided over by as many as three different teachers. When one left, it was often impossible to secure an immediate replacement, and the school might have to close for a term.

Male teachers were especially hard to find and keep. A man well enough edu-

What Did They Read Back on the Farm?

Although incomplete, plains education succeeded surprisingly well, for by 1900 Nebraska, Kansas, and Iowa had the highest literacy rate in the nation. Farmers bought books by mail order, and larger towns often had public libraries. By 1857 Omaha boasted a library association that had a subscription to a major New York weekly.

The newspapers were the biggest goads to self-improvement. They began as publicity sheets: speculators and promoters would lay out a town, then subsidize a newspaper to advertise its advantages so as to attract residents and

investors. The paper would aim at circulation back east, for few local readers could afford a subscription, and those who were able usually paid in produce. Some papers were founded to cash in on a law requiring each homesteader to run six notices confirming that he had complied with government requirements; the cost was up to $10.

The papers' contents were primarily local gossip and announcements, editorials that blasted corruption, and advertisements. Insert pages on nonlocal news were supplied by a big-city service; and when a blizzard prevented their arrival

by mail, the local editor would dash off a few fillers, inking them by hand on wrapping paper. He generally worked in primitive quarters; one wrote that he produced the first issue of a town paper "seated upon the stump of an ancient oak . . . and [with] the top of our badly abused beaver [hat] for a table." Another editor stopped at a prairie grove, had his seven typographers cut trees, built a shed and furniture, and began printing. Poorly paid as newsmen, editors frequently held other jobs; when an issue was late, one editor explained that he had been too busy harvesting wheat.

A teacher had to instruct all ages in the one room and also build the fire and do the cleaning. States did not levy school taxes; communities financed their own schools, often putting up many one-roomers so that no child would have to walk more than three miles.

Euroi Weiner, a teacher in Custer County, Nebraska, poses on an antler chair. Many schoolmarms on the plains were teenagers.

cated to teach at all could usually find other employment at better wages. He was not apt to accept the frontier conditions, one of which was the necessity of subduing hulking 17- and 18-year-old farm boys who routinely challenged his authority. Women, however, fared better. No one expected them to engage in physical combat with their charges, and many women were sincerely dedicated to teaching, one of the few career opportunities open to them at the time. Their work also gave them a good chance to find suitable husbands on the female-starved plains.

Recruiting Women Teachers

By the time the plains were open to settlement, the schoolmarm was already an established feature of American education. Even as early as 1845 Catharine Beecher, daughter of a prominent New

England family of educators and clergymen, called for the recruitment of women into the teaching profession. Her highly influential pamphlet, "The Duty of American Women to their Country," decried the shortage of teachers on the frontier and predicted that men would never fill the gap. "It is *woman* who is to come in at this emergency and meet the demand," she wrote, adding with perhaps unconscious cynicism, "woman, whom experience and testing have shown to be the best, as well as the cheapest, guardian and teacher of childhood." By the hundreds and later by the thousands, American women—especially those of New England—answered the call of Miss Beecher.

Many of these women, dedicated as they were to both their profession and their pupils, fumed at what they saw as the low priority given education on the

plains. A school year of five months—especially in a one-room schoolhouse—seemed insufficient for even minimal instruction. "I wish I could have these children under my care for a year," one schoolmarm wrote. "How some of them would advance!" Yet the women made the best of things, fighting to overcome local prejudice and frugality, struggling to secure everything from standardized textbooks to outhouses.

For the better part of a century, the schoolmarms ruled their one-room empires on the plains like a bevy of benevolent dictators. Few were equipped to provide more than the rudiments of an education, but through their determined efforts to spread literacy and a common culture among farm boys and girls hailing from dozens of nations, they played a vital role in bringing the people of the plains into the American mainstream.

To relieve the bleak interiors, some teachers added colorful garlands of paper. The children learned to write in Spencerian script with goose quills.

The Schoolmarm

Her name was invariably Grace, Charity, or Prudence; and, if names had been always a descriptive of the personal qualities of those who bore them, she would have been entitled to all three. . . . She was somewhat angular and rather bony. Her eyes were usually blue, and, to speak with accuracy, a little cold and grayish, in their expression—like the sky on a bleak morning in Autumn. . . . In manners and bearing, she was brisk, prim, and sometimes a little "fidgety," as if she was conscious of sitting on a dusty chair. . . . She was careful of three things—her clothes, her money, and her reputation. . . . The man who courted her must do so in the most sober, staid, and regulated spirit.

—J. L. McConnel
Western Characters, 1853

Medicine on the Frontier

Of all the perils confronting the plainsman, illness was the most dreaded. Although the humid Mississippi region to the east was even more unhealthy, almost all families on the drier plains were sadly familiar with cholera, smallpox, and typhoid. As late as 1880 there were 224 deaths in what is now South Dakota from diphtheria alone. Malaria—the ague—and pneumonia were endemic. Malarial mosquitoes, unrecognized then as disease carriers, bred in moist areas by grassland rivers and were blown into drier regions. Cholera, which swept the plains in countless epidemics, was known to arrive without warning, sometimes striking—and killing—its victims in a single day.

In addition, the plains farmers of the mid-19th century still lived in a state of medical superstition. The germ theory was as yet unknown, and they thought many ailments were caused by miasmas rising from the mists or even the early morning dew. The sod huts and their privies were unhealthy—they were dark, damp, crowded, and unsanitary and had dirt floors. Contaminated food, dust-covered belongings, and bedbugs, fleas, and flies were constant aggravations. In home, school, and village, common drinking cups spread infection. Water supplies often were tainted, and the frontiersman's poor diet frequently caused scurvy and an intestinal malady dubbed bilious fever.

For most plainsmen, however, calling the doctor was a last resort. The nearest physician might live far away, and his fee could come to 50 cents a mile, plus a dollar for consultation and additional sums for medicines. This was far too

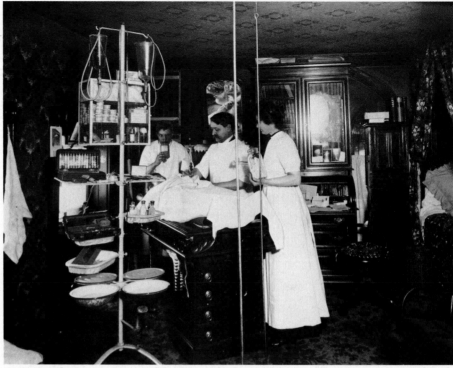

A Kansas doctor operates in his office, which in 1901 boasted a carpet, canopied bed, and—rare out west—nurse and anesthetist. The hanging bottles are for irrigating wounds.

expensive for many, well aware that the professional remedies were often no better than the folk medicines of the farmer's wife with her herbs and poultices.

Sometimes the cures the prairie wife claimed left doubt about the accuracy of the diagnosis. Typical was Mrs. Edith Wheeler of Texas, who reported: "Old Man Rufe Harper sprouted a skin cancer that the doctor swore would spread till it ate up his face. Uncle Rufe came to me . . . I remembered how my mother used to take warts off our hands with an oint-

ment made from the crushed leaves of a weed called sheep sorrel. I didn't know how it would work on cancer, but I figured it wouldn't kill Uncle Rufe. . . . To make the medicine extra strong, I mixed in gunpowder . . . and smeared that cancer with fresh applications every day. Uncle Rufe swore it burned 'worse than hell.' . . . But [after] five days that cancer slid off his face like a dried scab."

For their families' more ordinary ailments plainswomen used homemade remedies: for rheumatism, wahoo-root tea or polk root; as a physic, slippery elm; for ague, sulfur and molasses; to trigger sweating, snakeroot tea; to stanch bleeding, cobwebs. Oddly enough, for childbirth—one of the most natural of human trials—the frontier woman generally sought a doctor's help, perhaps because, due to lack of antiseptics, "childbirth fever" killed so many young women. Often, though, distances and storms prevented the physician's timely arrival, and thousands of children were born with only their fathers in attendance. Whether mother or baby survived was mostly a matter of luck. Indeed, until modern medicine got to the plains in this century, everyone's survival depended almost exclusively on good fortune.

The traveling medicine show included Indians—who shared their herbal lore—entertainment, and the sale of largely useless patent medicines, most of them not patented.

Farmers thought a healthy baby was one as fat as a pig. Most tonics were 25 percent alcohol, copiously but unsuspectingly consumed by teetotaling plainswomen and also given to infants. "Blood purifiers" were advertised as cures for everything from scrofula and epilepsy to dropsy, croup, and even cancer.

Horse liniments were hailed for humans. For internal drugs the usual dose was "one for a man, two for a horse."

A peddler of medicines in Culbertson, Nebraska. Most "remedies" sold were hokum, but in the late 1800's naive Americans made them an $80-million-a-year business.

The Plains Doctor

The paucity of medical practitioners on the frontier was particularly acute on the plains. Towns that grew around army posts had military doctors, some remarkably good. But many other communities either had no doctors at all or else mediocrities who held degrees from diploma mills, had only a year's apprenticeship with an older doctor, or were merely self-proclaimed physicians with no training. The territories initially had no medical standards, and it was not until 1880 that Nebraska passed the first law requiring that physicians register with the county clerk and be graduates of a reputable medical school—which meant a two-year course.

The most dedicated of the professionals found the career exhausting. A country doctor's office was a tent, a prairie cabin, or a room in his village home. Unable to make a living by medicine alone, he often doubled as pharmacist or dentist or supported himself through other businesses. When a patient called,

the doctor's wife would ring a bell whose special tone would summon her husband from his downstreet business office. For house calls he had to travel long distances at any hour, in all weather. He might ride by horseback or drive his buggy 30 miles to a soddy, sit up for hours with a patient, then sleep on the return trip while his horse found the way home. He acted as nurse and clergyman too, and his care was a mixture of folk remedy, medieval practice, and shrewd improvisation. He bled his patients for most ills, and for diphtheria he boiled sulfur or powdered brimstone in limewater and dripped it with a quill into the victim's nostrils. He used calomel as a cathartic, opium for diarrhea, tartar emetic to induce vomiting, Spanish fly (a drug from a beetle) to produce counterirritant blisters, and—ignorant of its true efficacy—quinine for the ague. One doctor successfully treated a severely burned man with poultices of sour milk and clay. Another reduced the irri-

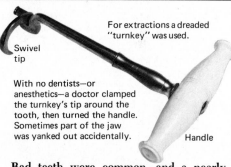

For extractions a dreaded "turnkey" was used.

Swivel tip

With no dentists—or anesthetics—a doctor clamped the turnkey's tip around the tooth, then turned the handle. Sometimes part of the jaw was yanked out accidentally.

Handle

Bad teeth were common, and a nearly toothless young girl was not unusual. A physician daubed caries with mercury or tobacco oil or else pulled out the bad tooth.

tation of bad poison ivy by immersing the child in a mudhole. The frontier doctor's forte, however, was surgery: he performed amazing amputations with a bowie knife and carpenter's saw. One did an appendectomy on a kitchen table by kerosene lamp and with no anesthetic. The long hours and rugged conditions must have driven many doctors to drink, however, for the Dakota Territory ruled it a misdemeanor if a doctor poisoned his patient while intoxicated.

The Enticements of a Prairie Town

A day in town with its sound, color, and bustle! Nothing thrilled homesteaders more. The harshness and monotony of prairie life was forgotten as the wagon, loaded with farm produce for sale or trade, rumbled toward those tantalizing sights miles away: a gleaming locomotive, fancy hats, frilled dresses, and sumptuous rarities—beer, real sugar, white bread, striped candies. Here were people to talk to. Here the storekeeper let the farmwife drape a bolt of gingham around herself longingly, although he knew she could not buy it. In reality, the typical little 1885 town below was but a couple of dozen drab, flimsy wooden buildings along a grass-centered, muddy street. But to the plainswomen, it was magical.

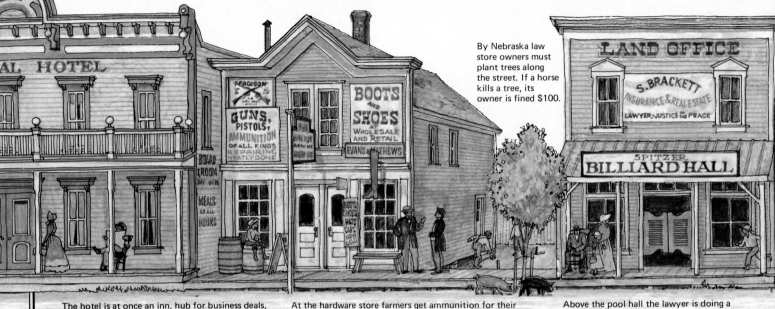

By Nebraska law store owners must plant trees along the street. If a horse kills a tree, its owner is fined $100.

The hotel is at once an inn, hub for business deals, and civic center in whose dining room politicians orate, townsmen enjoy community dances, and occasional funerals are held. Each bedroom, furnished with a washstand, bowl and pitcher, chamber pot, chair, and smoky kerosene lamp, is a cubicle partitioned with walls of brown paper —all the guests can hear one another. Beds must often be shared with one or two others. There is no bath. The main washroom has only basins, buckets, and a dirty roller towel, about which an objecting patron was admonished by the manager: "There's twenty-six men used that towel before you and you're the first one that complained."

At the hardware store farmers get ammunition for their old guns, and richer townsmen and passing ranchers buy a few new hunting rifles or pistols. Shoes and boots, bought in town, are factory-made in St. Louis and are usually purchased one or two sizes too large to allow for shrinkage when wet. Poor farm families often go barefoot, wear moccasins, or make their own shoes by tacking leather uppers onto carved wooden soles. Farmers visit town largely to sell stock and grain to buyers (who usually underpay) and to bring their grain to the mill or the grain elevator. These are located by the railroad station (not shown). There, too, are the lumberyard—which deals in train-transported boards—and a telegraph, whose telegrams are delivered from the station by messengers.

Above the pool hall the lawyer is doing a thriving business—legal work on land claims and claim jumping. He also manages farm mortgages; handles litigation over brawls, fires, and unpaid debts; and cons farmers into paying him a 10 percent commission to secure them loans. Plains lawyers are more numerous than other professionals, but many are semiliterate and poorly trained. Criminal cases are tried at the county seat. A circuit judge comes to town periodically.

Painted billboards decorate the buildings' false fronts.

False fronts suggest structures more substantial than they are.

Coal stoves are used for heating; but coal, brought by train, is very expensive.

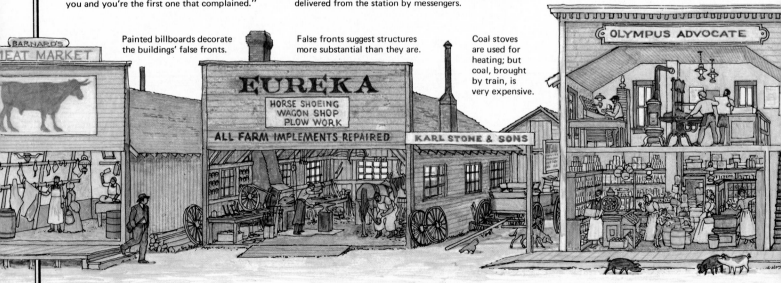

The butcher gets game (antelope, rabbit, wild turkey, prairie chicken, and duck) from homesteading hunters, beef from local ranches, and hogs from farms. Townfolk keep chickens and pigs in backyards, but they stray. The blacksmith not only shoes horses and oxen and sharpens plows but also repairs and makes farm machinery.

The general store (third from left) advertises everything from coal to coffins, needles to violin strings. Bacon, hams, luggage, and Stetsons hang from the ceiling. Dry goods line one wall, hardware another. Along a third are clothing and groceries—baking soda, salt, coffee, cheese, pickled fish, vinegar, sugar, candy, spices, and tobacco. In crannies are blankets, toys, magazines, playing cards, Bibles, and readers. By the door is the post office; mail time is announced by hoisting a flag. The store is a social center where men sit by the cracker barrel and stove, chew tobacco, talk politics, and gossip, while the women peruse fashion books and finger bolts of pretty yard goods. Purchases are usually by barter—calico for butter, a shirt for eggs.

Selecting a Town's Location

Townsites were chosen logistically, usually by business promoters. In the vast plains the hamlets had to be next to a means of transport: by a river, ferry crossing, railroad, or the crosstrails for wagon caravans (as with Junction City, Kansas). Many towns were founded by railroad companies. Others burgeoned from the rude camps of railroad-building crews (Bismarck, North Dakota, for example) or near newfound salt deposits (such as Lincoln, Nebraska) or around a gristmill (as with Enterprise, Kansas).

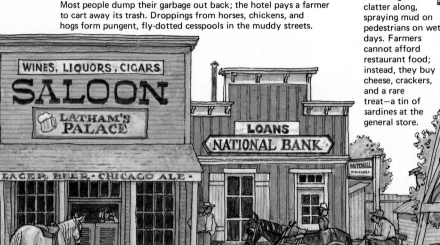

Most people dump their garbage out back; the hotel pays a farmer to cart away its trash. Droppings from horses, chickens, and hogs form pungent, fly-dotted cesspools in the muddy streets.

Buckboards and farm wagons clatter along, spraying mud on pedestrians on wet days. Farmers cannot afford restaurant food; instead, they buy cheese, crackers, and a rare treat—a tin of sardines at the general store.

Everyone fetches his water from the town's windmill-powered well, in whose tank horses and stock are watered. Here the well-keeper climbs the derrick to oil the gears. The town has no plumbing or sewers; all buildings have privies in back. There is no plentiful supply of summer ice so food must be sold and prepared quickly; and dried meat and corned beef are necessary summer fare.

Unlike saloons in cattle towns, this one has no gambling and is not roisterous. Men come for a restful beer, whisky, or bitters and conversation, or to meet clients and make deals. Some then play checkers, toss horseshoes, or visit the billiard hall. Others go to the adjoining bank, with which many have unending mortgages: the homestead mortgaged to buy farm machinery, the latter mortgaged for money until harvest time, and the first crop mortgaged for wintertime funds. The bank also lends money—at 8 to 10 percent monthly interest. In the 1850's unscrupulous banks printed their own worthless money, but this bank is federally chartered (in some towns they are state chartered). It uses national bank notes and old Civil War greenbacks as currency.

The Hotel d'Horse is the busiest place in town, a livery stable where townfolk, land hunters, loan agents, and other business transients can hire a shiny buggy—with driver if desired—for $5 a day. Drivers service the town's hotel and meet trains. Men can buy feed here and board their own horses and buggies. A part-time harness repairer and cobbler works here too. It is the first place any stranger goes to for directions—and for tips on the townsmen's foibles. Though the owner lacks police training, he doubles as town constable, a sometimes dangerous job.

Above the general store the newspaper is printed on a handpress. The editor, subsidized by a company of speculators, also dabbles in real estate and prints posters. In the loft next door a milliner sells eastern hats to a few well-to-do ladies—like the banker's wife—who will not splurge on another for several years. A farm woman enters merely to gaze wistfully at the color and frills of town fashions she cannot afford; she owns but two plain homemade sunbonnets and some calico dresses. The millinery has a discreet outside entrance so that ladies can avoid the barber shop below, where patrons enjoy the "naughty" Police Gazette. Each man has his own shaving mug, with his name and an appropriate scenic painted on it. A shave is 10 cents; a haircut (or a hot bath in back) is 25 cents.

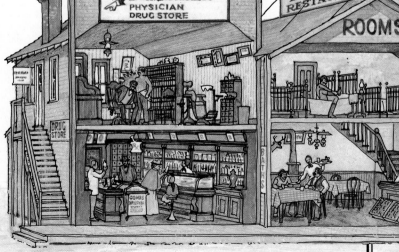

The young town still has many vacant lots between buildings. It consists only of this main street, just wide enough for a wagon to turn around in. Smart storekeepers construct boardwalks out front so customers can escape the thick dust or slushy potholes of the unpaved street, which becomes a quagmire after rain.

The doctor runs a pharmacy downstairs and practices upstairs, where he might amputate a leg, pull a tooth, or cut out a bullet. He mixes herbal nostrums, presses the pills he prescribes, and sells such patent medicines as Hoffstatter's Bitters, which is 50 percent alcohol. In glass cases he displays soaps, perfumes, even jewelry. Next door is Elaine's, where many transients stay—salesmen, horse traders, and men looking for land who find the $8-a-week hotel too expensive. For 50 cents a night they share a communal bedroom nicknamed the Potter's Field and eat Elaine's good food. She has a hired girl to set tables, serve, do dishes, make beds, empty chamber pots in the outhouse, and wash sheets once a week. By the counter is a treat: a crate of California oranges, just off the train.

Games and Gaiety Relieve the Loneliness

So nerve-shattering was the isolation on the plains that one woman, hearing that another family had settled 12 miles away, walked there, starved for conversation with another female. Although complete strangers, the two women fell into each other's arms. It is no wonder, then, that plains dwellers were great "visitin' folk." And it took so long to get to neighbors that visitors stayed all day, thoughtfully bringing a few pounds of flour or some meat. In bad times they would trek to sit up with a sick neighbor. In good times they enjoyed planting, quilting, or housewarming bees. As more settlers arrived, they created amateur theatrical groups and started lyceums, or literary societies, for readings, debates, and presentations of living tableaus. The women formed sewing circles and temperance societies that, along with church clubs and fraternal lodges, brought people together; the men, above all, loved sports, making bets on any game. They hunted, raced on foot or horse, and competed at broad jumps, marbles, and turkey shoots. They liked billiards, bowling, and croquet, playing the latter even at night with a candle on each wicket. Baseball—played without gloves or masks and with balls made of yarn from old socks, wrapped in leather from worn boots—was so popular that Wichita had a ladies' ball club.

As plains townsmen prospered, they built well-furnished Victorian homes with pleasant backyards. The family held musicales and played checkers, dominoes, euchre, seven-up, keno, mumblety-peg, drop-the-handkerchief, and "Old Mother Wobble Gobble," in which everyone copied the grimace-making antics of the leader.

As at this Englewood, Kansas, masquerade ball, the men far outnumbered the women. A rejected suitor was said to have "gotten the mitten." A boy courted by driving a special girl in a buggy or sled. A lucky one would then take his girl for a horseback ride; she rode sidesaddle, her long skirt weighted with lead.

In the late 1890's the orchestra of Clay Center, in Kansas (shown here), gave concerts and probably also played at dances. Often coming from music-loving ethnic stock, many plainsmen were amateur musicians. Wichita even boasted a home-talent minstrel troupe, and a phonograph show in Dakota schools was a big hit. Farmers came great distances for a square dance and paid 25 cents apiece for a good fiddler. To the hum of a Jew's harp, the whine of violins, and the resonance of a pitchfork triangle, plainsmen would meet at a soddy to dance. In villages a house-raising was an excuse for a calico ball: each man picked a calico kerchief from a bundle, then found the girl with the matching dress. In towns these shindigs became cotillions.

Boys enjoy watermelons on the Fourth of July, the plains' biggest celebration. Farmers and wives, bringing their own skillets, traveled miles to the nearest village. Town committees would catch thousands of catfish; supply firewood, a corn crusher, and melons; and erect a brush canopy, long table, and dance platform. There might be a band concert, militia parade, riflery competition, and various games: a ball game, a tub or sack race, or contests to catch a greased pig or climb a greased pole. After a fish fry with corn dodgers (fried cornbread), dancing began—and continued until midday on July 5th.

Little girls try a seesaw in a town backyard. They may seem overdressed—play clothes were not used—but their skirts and hats did not curtail their fun.

Youngsters also spent many happy hours sleigh riding, ice skating, going to sorghum taffy-pulls, and competing in spelling and ciphering matches, at which selected children also gave recitations, sang songs, and played musical instruments.

Toddlers on hand-carved hobbyhorses form an imaginary merry-go-round. For Christmas, plains parents whittled toys, made cornhusk dolls, and strung popcorn on whatever they found to substitute for the absent fir.

At a Sunday school picnic all ages enjoy the women's breads, cakes, pies, preserves, and other goodies. Young men assiduously attended Sunday school in order to meet girls. If a girl dated a boy frequently, she was considered "obligated" to him. Wedding feasts and dances were uproarious; and the "infair" took place the next day, when the boy and girl and her parents made a formal visit to the home of the bridegroom's family.

Hard Times on the Frontier

The first big wave of farmer-settlers had scarcely adjusted to the rigors of life on the grasslands when the dismal fact of economic depression confronted the nation. In part, the overbuilding of railroads across the plains was responsible, as huge sums were invested in projects that would not return profits for years to come. When the great brokerage house of Jay Cooke, chief underwriter for the bonds of the Northern Pacific, went bankrupt in September 1873, the shock set off ripples that plunged the nation into hard times.

Among the worst off were the plains farmers, already deep in debt either to the railroads for land purchased on time payments or to the banks from which many had borrowed to finance their agricultural operations. Indeed, even before the financial panic, thousands of pioneers had been pushed close to the edge of extinction by a series of natural disasters—prairie fires, hailstorms, and droughts. Some aid did come to the plainsmen through private charities, appropriations passed by state and territorial legislatures, and the U.S. Congress, which in 1875 overrode conservative objections to authorize the distribution of $30,000 worth of seed among destitute farmers. But all this was a drop in the bucket, as one Nebraska pioneer declared in an angry bit of doggerel:

Uncle Sam, it appears, has consented
at last
To scatter a few of his coppers
In behalf of those who, in the year that
is past,
Were cursed and cleaned out by the
hoppers.
Now I, being one of ten thousand in need,
Would willingly better my status;
So, if you can't give me my quota in seed,
Just send me a peck of potatoes.

The many afflictions besetting farmers in the early 1870's created a mood of almost unprecedented sourness. Not only were thousands destitute, but for the first time in American history farmers had begun to see themselves as a maligned minority. In the days of President Thomas Jefferson the tiller of the soil had been hailed as the backbone of the nation; now, in the post-Civil War era, America was fast becoming an industrial giant, and the urban population—even on some sections of the plains—was outstripping the rural.

Clouds of Discontent

Traditionally, America's farmers had eschewed political action, but in their distress and anger they looked to a new organization that promised them a voice in the nation's policies: the National Grange of the Patrons of Husbandry. Founded in 1867 to organize farmers and their wives into local chapters dedicated to education, culture, and socializing, the Grange grew slowly at first. But in the early 1870's, with disaster overwhelming many, there was a rush to join the organization, which was becoming increasingly reformist and less social. In 1874 nationwide Grange membership soared to 1.5 million.

Although farmers realized that there was little they could do about acts of God, they had become determined to exert their influence in any area they could: on commodity prices, grain storage charges, interest rates, and shipping costs. They accused the railroads of discriminatory practices: the Burlington line, for example, charged $1.32 per ton-mile between the Missouri River and Chicago but $4.80 west of the Missouri in 1877. When the railroads argued that the vast distances and sparse population of the plains made operations there prohibitively expensive, their critics retorted that somehow the roads managed to reduce rates during the months when barge transportation on the rivers was possible—only to raise them again when the waterways were shut down by ice.

Only a notch below the railroads in the Grangers' list of demons were the grain-elevator operators, who were accused of being in collusion with the rail companies. Typically, each town had only a single grain-elevator owner because the railroads refused to make more than one stop in each town. Thus the farmer was forced to sell to the one operator or not at all. The more venal entrepreneurs further incensed their cus-

Nebraskan Harvey Andrews and his family at his 19-month-old son's grave. Despite the tragedy of the boy's death, Andrews was fortunate in owning a stand of cedar and became wealthy selling timber to settlers.

Many new farming communities on the plains withered and died in the 1870's as the result of business failures, droughts, and plagues of grasshoppers. One artist imagined this grim scene.

Members of the Patrons of Husbandry, known as the Grangers, meet at a schoolhouse in Illinois to discuss improving the farmers' lot in the West.

One of Montgomery Ward's first price lists, offering "farmers & mechanics" goods at low wholesale prices.

This grain elevator was typical of many that received the farmers' grain for rail shipment to distribution and milling centers.

tomers by rating No. 1 grain as No. 2.

During the 1870's most of the things needed to operate a farm—plows, reapers, seed, and the cost of credit—soared in price, a direct result, the farmers charged, of monopolistic practices. As proof, they pointed to a 100 percent increase in the price of plows that had followed the merger of two major manufacturers of agricultural implements.

Too scattered to form a politically potent body on their own, the farmers found much needed allies in the small-town merchants and storekeepers of the West, who felt equally victimized by railroads and manufacturers. Together, these groups goaded the Grange into issuing the Farmers' Declaration of Independence on July 4, 1873, one which began with the familiar words "when in the course of human events" and went on to characterize tillers of the soil as people suffering from "systems of oppression and abuse." The document focused most of its ire on the railroads and

their political allies, ending with the warning that "we will give our suffrage only to such men . . . as we have good reason to believe will use their best endeavors" to reform the system.

This was no idle threat, for by the mid-1870's the Grangers held the political balance of power in several of the midwestern states. In four states Granger Laws were passed to regulate railroad rates and the activities of the owners of grain elevators. Although these laws were soon challenged in the courts as violations of private-property rights, the U.S. Supreme Court, in a series of landmark decisions, upheld the principle that government could regulate all those industries "affected with a public interest."

During this period Grangers were also forging new weapons in the economic sphere by forming consumer cooperatives. Many merchants howled in protest, but in 1872 the farsighted mail-order house of Montgomery Ward sold merchandise to the co-ops' purchasing agents and also directly to the farmers at wholesale prices.

Poorly Managed Cooperatives

Far less effective, however, were the producers' cooperatives organized by the Grangers. They had hoped that by owning their own grain elevators and farm-machinery factories they would substantially reduce their costs, but the enterprises were undercapitalized and often poorly managed, becoming easy marks for the price-slashing techniques of privately owned competitors. When the producer co-ops began to go under, many farmers who had suffered heavy

losses began to view the whole Grange movement with skepticism.

Even more destructive of the Grange as a political and economic force was the return of prosperity to the frontier in the late 1870's. With money coming into their hands once more, farmers left the Grange and shunned political action. But hard times would soon come again and with them new, more potent movements that would mobilize the farmer and make him a powerful threat to the country's status quo.

The Farmers and the Railroads

They [the railroads] have influenced legislation to suit themselves by bribing venal legislators to betray the true interests of their constituents. . . . They have by false representations and subterfuge induced the people to subscribe funds to build roads, whose rates, when built, are so exorbitant that in many instances transportation by private conveyance is less burdensome. . . . They have procured a law of Congress by which they have dispossessed hundreds of farmers of the homes that by years of toil they have built up; have induced others to mortgage their farms for roads never intended to be built, and, after squandering the money thus obtained, have left their victims to the mercy of courts over which they have held sway. They have obstructed the administration of justice.

—The Farmers' Declaration of Independence

Montgomery Ward: Storekeeper for the Plains

The famed founder of the first U.S. mail-order company.

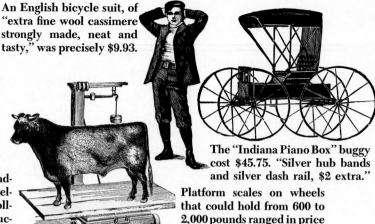

An English bicycle suit, of "extra fine wool cassimere strongly made, neat and tasty," was precisely $9.93.

This black-walnut Windsor organ, with its bevel-edged mirror, fancy scrollwork, stool, and instruction book, sold for $60.

The "Indiana Piano Box" buggy cost $45.75. "Silver hub bands and silver dash rail, $2 extra."

Platform scales on wheels that could hold from 600 to 2,000 pounds ranged in price from a mere $13.80 to $27.50.

In 1871 young Aaron Montgomery Ward was working in Chicago for C.W. & E. Pardridge, wholesalers and retailers of dry goods and notions, and spending his spare moments telling friends about his big idea: to sell direct to country people by mail at low cash prices. His friends predicted that Ward's so-called mail-order store would go broke trying to sell goods sight unseen to suspicious farmers, but he saved every cent he could, bought a small supply of likely items, and prepared to go into business. He lost his first inventory in the Great Chicago Fire of 1871, which wiped out the city's entire business district, but undaunted went back to planning and saving his money. By August of 1872, with two fellow employees of Pardridge's and a capital of only $1,600, he started Montgomery Ward & Co.

The firm's first catalogue, a one-page list of 163 articles, most of them selling for $1, was sent to the Grangers, who had a membership of nearly a million in several midwestern states. Ward's wife, Elizabeth, helped him address his first price lists and waited hopefully with him for the orders to come in. But the post-office box was often bare, and Ward's partners soon became discouraged. He bought up their shares and became sole owner of Montgomery Ward & Co. at the worst possible time. The panic of 1873 had brought ruin to many businesses and intensified the plight of the farmers.

Winning the Farmers' Confidence

Ward was convinced that hard times were an opportunity, because he had quality goods at prices even the hard-pressed farmers could afford. His job was to win their confidence. To soften their sales resistance to an unknown merchant in far-away Chicago, he began speaking at Grange meetings, explaining how he could offer quality goods at low prices. "We don't pay $40,000 a year rent," he said. "We don't employ high-priced salesmen. The goods are bought direct from manufacturers for cash, sold for cash, not sold to country retailers on six months' time, and not kept on display with salaried men to show them."

In the fall of 1873 Ward, who was running his firm on the side while working at Pardridge's, got a full-time partner, George R. Thorne, whom he had known in Michigan. Ward's family had moved from Chatham, New Jersey, to Niles,

Michigan, when he was nine. The son of a cobbler, Aaron left school at 14 to work in a barrel factory and later a brickyard. Deciding that he was not "physically or mentally suited for brick or barrel making," he went on to jobs in a shoe store and a general store, then moved to Chicago in 1866. There he clerked for the dry-goods firm of Field, Palmer & Leiter and later traveled as a salesman for other Chicago firms and a company in St. Louis. While making his rounds of country stores by train and horse and buggy, Ward hit upon the idea of a mail-order company.

Business steadily improved in 1874, and in 1875 Ward let his customers know that the then common rule of business, *caveat emptor*, or "let the buyer beware," had no place in his

"We Cheerfully Answer All Inquiries"

For a man who had dropped out of school Ward proved handy with a pen as he instructed his customers:

In writing your name and address, do not endeavor to show us a sample of spread-eagle, but rather affect the simple, plain and perfectly legible signature of John Hancock. . . . We cheerfully answer all inquiries relating to any class of merchandise, but before you ask, see that your questions are not answered in this Catalogue.

We believe in blowing our own horn. . . . From a small beginning, we are now the largest exclusively wholesale house in America devoted to supplying the consumer direct. When we introduced our system in 1872, we were looked upon with scorn by the monopolies and suspicion by the Patrons (Grangers) themselves. In the short period of three years, we have saved the consumers directly over one million dollars and, indirectly, millions by breaking up monopolies and forcing dealers to sell . . . at fair prices.

When complaints were made in 1892 about a five-cent increase in postage for the catalogue, Ward retorted:

There are about a million people in this country with more postal cards than brains who delight in sending for anything that is free. . . . Payment to cover postage is proof that you want the book.

dealings. Catalogue 13, which had grown to 72 pages, flatly stated: "We guarantee all our goods. If any of them are not satisfactory after due inspection, we will take them back, pay all expenses, and refund the money paid for them." A money-back guarantee had been used by a few big-city merchants, but Ward's was the first to adopt it as a national mail-order policy.

Ward sold to all comers but continued proudly to identify his firm as "The Original Grange Supply House." During all the years that farmers inveighed against the high prices they paid for supplies and the low prices they got for their crops, Montgomery Ward & Co. maintained cordial relations with the Grangers and later farm protest organizations. Ward's advertised in many farm publications, and it was the first advertiser in *The Farmer's Voice*, a combative weekly paper that called itself "the unofficial organ of all societies that are laboring for the well-being of the productive classes." It regularly attacked the trusts, the government, and the Republican Party. Ward's was careful to say it did not endorse the views of the *Voice*, but the firm's comments on the trusts were just as unfriendly.

The Barbed-Wire Trust

A Ward's advertisement published in 1892 declared: "There's been too great a profit in agricultural implements, that's sure. . . . Write for free Implements Catalogue that will enable you to get around the Monopoly on about 300 implements in common use." Then Ward's tackled the barbed-wire trust: "Heard the news? Barbed-wire trust broken. We are the first to give the buyers a chance at the new figures, and will guarantee our prices to be the lowest ever quoted, while the goods are the best made." When the U.S. Supreme Court blocked the government's effort to break up the sugar trust in 1895, Ward's ran an ad in the *Voice* that stated: "No trusts! The various trusts in the country say: 'Montgomery Ward & Co. cannot have our goods for the reason that they will not demand the prices we make.' The goods we purchase we pay spot cash for. The goods belong to us; we claim the right to dispose of them as we wish."

Cards like this one announced the coming of new catalogues.

The honest, outspoken Ward became one of the nation's foremost merchants, but before his death in 1913 he himself believed his greatest achievement was his successful fight to preserve Chicago's lakefront as a park for the people. In 1890 he had watched with growing outrage as the city built a scaffold near Lake Michigan to load garbage on railroad cars. He feared that this facility soon would be followed by dozens of city and private buildings. Investigating the original titles to the land, he found that they specified "public ground, forever to remain vacant of buildings." Then this pioneer environmentalist began a 20-year court fight at his own expense to protect the lakefront. "Here is a park frontage on the lake comparing favorably with the Bay of Naples," he said, "which city officials would crowd with buildings, transforming the beauty spot for the poor into the showground of the educated rich. I do not think it is right." His stubborn fight to keep the lakefront free of buildings cost him the friendship of many leading citizens, but he won. When Ward died, the *Chicago Tribune*, which had not always supported him, said: "Grant Park is Montgomery Ward's monument."

Years later, in 1946, the Grolier Club of New York included a Ward catalogue among its collection of 100 books chosen for their influence on American life. The committee that selected the books explained: "The mail order catalogue has been perhaps the greatest single influence in increasing the standard of American middle-class living. It brought the benefit of wholesale prices to city and hamlet . . . and, above all, it substituted sound quality for shoddy."

A mother and her daughters (right) study a Ward's catalogue, or "wish book," with its wondrous items. The drawing above is from the 1878 book, the first one with fashion illustrations.

The Great Dakota Boom

Harrow teams began preparation of soil on the 65,000-acre Grandin wheat farm in the Red River Valley of Dakota Territory.

In a sense the financial panic of 1873 laid the basis for a new prosperity—at least for a few. One of these few was the Northern Pacific Railroad, which had been pushed to the brink of bankruptcy by the panic and was determined to sell off its enormous land grants so that the debt-ridden line could be completed.

Part of the railroad's holdings traversed the incredibly fertile Red River Valley in western Minnesota and the northeastern portion of the Dakota Territory. In 1874, in a master stroke of enlightened self-interest, two directors of the Northern Pacific entered into a partnership with an expert Minnesota wheat grower named Oliver Dalrymple. Dalrymple was to farm 11,520 prime Red River acres in return for one-third of the profits and the acquisition of the land itself over a period of years. The idea behind this largesse was simple: if Dalrymple could harvest bumper crops of wheat on the enormous spread, word of the Red River Valley's unusual fertility would travel far and wide, precipitating a land rush to the Dakotas. This in turn would help the Northern Pacific to dispose of its vast properties and provide the line with a readymade freight business to support its extension and its future financial health.

The Bonanza Farms

From the Northern Pacific's point of view the experiment was a huge success. Not only was Dalrymple an agricultural genius, he was also an innovator. Like most of the Red River acreage, the land he farmed was dead level and virtually unobstructed. Using capital supplied by his partners, he set out to prove that Da-

kota's flat, boundless land could produce huge yields of wheat, provided the farmer adapted the methods of a factory. He bought the most up-to-date machinery—mechanical seeders, self-binding reapers, and steam-powered threshers—hired scores of laborers on a seasonal basis, and gave the world its first lesson in modern corporate farming. And what a lesson it was! At a cultivation cost of $9.50 per acre Dalrymple harvested some 25 bushels per acre. With wheat selling at 90 cents a bushel, he had a profit of more than 100 percent.

Dalrymple's triumph, as had been foreseen, touched off a rush for the fruitful Red River Valley land. Scores of eastern entrepreneurs eagerly exchanged their depreciated Northern Pacific bonds for the railroad's Dakota acreage. Publicists for Red River land toured the East to trumpet the valley's virtues; one speaker claimed (with only slight exaggeration) that if the river itself were not in the way, a man could turn one straight furrow as long as the distance between Philadelphia and Boston.

Spurred by Dalrymple's demonstration and the railroad's publicity, financiers formed syndicates that by 1878 had gobbled up nearly all the farmland in the valley. Some of the factory farms they established covered as much as 100,000 acres; many more were in the 5,000- to 10,000-acre category. Aided immeasurably in the late 1870's and early 1880's by several seasons of remarkably good weather, high wheat prices, and the availability of cheap labor, many of these farms showed record profits year after year. The Amenia and Sharon Land Company, for example, harvested 11,676 bushels of wheat on a single section of its land in 1883, making a net profit greater than the land's cost.

If the profit potential of the bonanza farms justified the huge capital outlays necessary to launch and maintain them, the financial risks were still staggering, if somewhat obscured during the boom years by favorable weather and market conditions. Just to get operations underway, the manager of the Spiritwood farm in the Red River Valley spent more

With harvesting proceeding smoothly J. L. Grandin felt free to invite friends to an elaborate hunting party in 1879. In the foreground with the two dogs are Mrs. Grandin and a Miss Hague.

To encourage sales of its land in Dakota, the Northern Pacific Railroad regularly ran excursion trains so that interested settlers and tourists could observe wheat harvests on bonanza farms along the rail route.

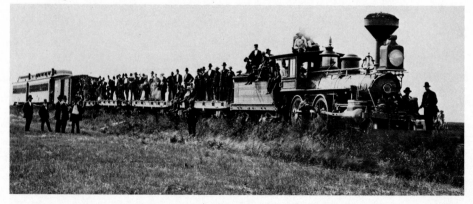

than $60,000 between 1878 and 1880—including $17,000 for plowing and $9,000 for farm machines. A modest spread of 10,000 acres required 60 gang plows, 60 mechanical seeders, 150 wagons, more than 50 self-binders, 10 steam engines, and 10 threshing machines.

Obviously, if a profit was to be turned, everything had to go off with clockwork precision. But, as the bonanza-farm entrepreneurs soon learned, not even Wall Street could control the plains weather. In the late 1880's and early 1890's a series of natural disasters, especially droughts, brought grief to investors. During those years, too, wheat prices and the yield per acre on the overplanted land began to fall.

By the late 1890's the age of the Dakota bonanza farms was over, although the Northern Pacific, which had brought them into being, was now flourishing. Most of the huge spreads were divided and sold off to small farmers.

The reign of the bonanza farms may have been brief, but their impact on plains agriculture proved considerable. First of all, they foreshadowed the corporate farms of the 20th century and the attendant decline of the family farm, developments that would be encouraged by further advances in agricultural science and technology. But of more immediate importance was the land rush into the northern and western plains precipitated by bonanza farming and by the opening of new railroad lines to the remoter corners of the plains.

The Population Boom

The Red River Valley was not the sole focus of this new land boom. A fresh wave of immigration hit Kansas, Nebraska, and the outer reaches of the Dakotas as farmers and townsite speculators swarmed west to get in on the ground floor of development. All told, the Dakotas' population increased in the 1880's from 135,177 to 539,583, while Nebraska's more than doubled to over a million. Many of the newcomers were, of course, farmers; and in the banner year of 1884 in excess of 11 million Dakota acres were claimed under the provisions of the Homestead Act, while additional millions of acres were bought from the railroads. But in the decade's last years, the hard times that had doomed the bonanza farms also slowed down the settlement of the northern plains. In fact, thousands abandoned their homesteads and retreated east to the sound of the bitter refrain:

We've reached the land of desert sweet,
Where nothing grows for man to eat,
The wind it blows with fev'rish heat
Across the plains so hard to beat.
O Dakota land, sweet Dakota land
As on thy fiery soil I stand,
I look across the plains
And wonder why it never rains.

Yet the majority of sodbusters stayed on, wrestling grimly with fierce winds, failing crops, and falling prices. During the 1890's, along with other farmers throughout the nation, they would set up such a howl of anger that the nation would be shaken to its foundations.

This work crew on the Dalrymple farm is gathering grain wired into bundles by self-binding harvesters. In 1877 Dalrymple employed 50 men who seeded 4,000 acres of wheat, which was harvested by 100 men. By 1884 Dalrymple used 1,000 workers for harvesting his wheat.

A steam-operated thresher, which replaced horse-powered equipment, separates the grain from the straw and chaff. As the mechanization of farming increased, the number of man-hours required to produce 100 bushels of grain fell to 108 in 1900, compared with 233 in 1840.

The Great Oklahoma Land Runs

Not even the feverish California gold rush of 1849 matched the explosive land run that in one day—April 22, 1889—brought more than 60,000 settlers into Indian Territory, now Oklahoma. The territory was the one remaining extensive area on the plains really suitable for successful farming. Half a century before it had been part of the great Indian reserve that stretched from the Canadian border all the way to Texas, and because this trans-Mississippi region was considered too remote to interest whites, the government had moved the Five Civilized Tribes there. The western parts of the five tribes' holdings were taken by treaties in 1866, and more than a dozen tribes from the plains were moved in. When this forced migration ended, there remained an unused area of about 2 million acres known as the Unassigned Lands, or Oklahoma District. Until the day of the great land run, U.S. troops patrolled the borders to keep whites from moving in.

Landgrabbers Eye the Unassigned Lands

In 1879 Elias C. Boudinot, a Cherokee who worked as a clerk for a House committee in Washington, came to the aid of whites who had long been urging, or "booming," the opening of the Unassigned Lands to settlement. Boudinot published an article claiming that these lands belonged to the public because they had been ceded by the Indians. Within a year Civil War veteran David L. Payne began leading forays of illegal immigrants—"Boomers"—into the Unassigned Lands, but U.S. troops drove them out. When Payne died in 1884, W. L. Couch took over leadership of the Boomers' land agitation.

Boudinot   Payne   Couch

The Road to Statehood

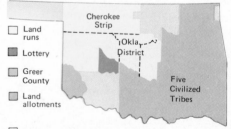

Land runs

Lottery

Greer County

Land allotments

Homestead Act and public sales

Cherokee Strip

Okla. District

Five Civilized Tribes

The Oklahoma land runs (shown in yellow) began with the opening of the Oklahoma District in 1889. In 1890 the Oklahoma Territory was organized. Runs opened other great tracts of land in the early 1890's, including 6 million acres called the Cherokee Strip. An 1896 Supreme Court decision added Greer County, Texas (orange), to the Oklahoma Territory. The Homestead Act and public sales acts opened the pink areas. In 1901 a lottery distributed the area indicated in red. The Indian Territory was thus reduced to the region occupied by the Five Civilized Tribes (green). Under the Dawes Act these lands were cut up into 160-acre plots and allotted to individual Indians. The remaining land was then opened to homesteaders. In 1907 the Oklahoma and Indian Territories joined to become the 46th state admitted to the United States. It had a population of some 1,500,000.

The Day of the Big Run

Years of Boomer agitation paid off when Congress acquired the Unassigned Lands from the Indians, and President Benjamin Harrison set April 22, 1889, as the date for the great land run. At noon a bugle call sent frenzied thousands streaming across the prairie—on fast horses, in wagons, on bicycles, on foot, and aboard six trains (passenger and freight). With farmlands and town lots enough for only a fraction of the Boomers, early arrivals were prepared to defend their claims from latecomers by rifles if necessary. Then there were the "Sooners," who sneaked in too soon (ahead of the starting time). Most of these would-be settlers lost their claims but gave Oklahoma its nickname: the "Sooner State."

The Run for the Cherokee Strip in 1893

Between 1889 and 1895 more Indian land was acquired and opened to whites by runs, the biggest being the one on September 16, 1893, which sent 100,000 people into the 6-million-acre Cherokee Strip (or Outlet). As in the 1889 run, the race was to the swift and the strong.

Guthrie: First Capital of Oklahoma

When the first Boomers leaped from trains at Guthrie on April 22, 1889, the town consisted of a water tank, the Santa Fe depot, a Wells Fargo Express shanty, and a government land office. Since President Harrison had hinted when he set the date for the land run that Guthrie would become the territorial capital, the competition for lots was intense. By nightfall more than 10,000 people had staked claims, and tents were sprouting everywhere (top right). The next day a city council and a mayor were elected, and within a few weeks the town could point to a school, a bank, and a newspaper, the *Get-up*. The deputy U.S. marshals and soldiers in Guthrie had no authority to settle land disputes; all they could do was prevent bloodshed. Fortunately, many disputes were settled by the toss of a coin or by arbitration. In 1893 Guthrie was the bustling capital of Oklahoma Territory (below right). Oklahoma became a state in 1907, and Guthrie continued as the center of government until 1910, when Oklahoma City, 30 miles to the south, was made the capital by popular vote. Guthrie's days of spectacular growth came to an end.

335

Towns Built in a Day

At first the towns resembled the hell-on-wheels settlements that sprang up along the westering tracks of the Union Pacific Railroad—jerry-built, brawling, and soon gone with the wind. But such Oklahoma land-run towns as Guthrie, Oklahoma City, Stillwater, Norman, and others looked eagerly to the future and planned for it. They immediately elected town officials, although there was no money to pay salaries. The problem was solved by fining the ever-present gamblers each morning and using the money collected for salaries and the surveying and grading of streets. One of the most pressing problems involved dealing with settlers who had put up their tents on lots that were found to be in the middle of streets when the surveyors ran their lines. One town cleared its main street by hitching mules to a heavy log and pulling it down the thoroughfare; anyone unlucky enough to be in front of the log lost his claim and had to pick up his tent and move on.

Chairs and boxes served as offices for these men who opened for business in Guthrie on the first day of the land run. There were no courts, judges, or local law enforcement, but the lawyers were kept busy making out and filing claims papers for the settlers at 25 cents to $2 apiece. They also made themselves available to help arbitrate land disputes.

Washday in Ragtown, later given the more dignified name of Anadarko when tents gave way to wooden homes and business buildings. On the Washita River southwest of Oklahoma City, Anadarko was in an area opened to settlement by lottery in August of 1901. It got a late start compared with other land-run towns in Oklahoma Territory, but in 1902 it threw a ripsnorting first anniversary celebration complete with a parade and floats.

This family on its land near Guthrie in the summer of 1889 was among 10,000 blacks who filed claims during the first run into the Unassigned Lands. Finding their opportunities limited in the South after the Civil War, thousands of blacks moved west, seeking a fresh start on land of their own. Between 1890 and 1910 the black population in Oklahoma rose 53 percent, for 27 black towns and one unincorporated community were founded during that period.

A few of the many business houses on Harrison Avenue, in Guthrie, named for President Benjamin Harrison. People showed a lot of imagination in finding ways to make a living: several men discovered red clay near Guthrie and went into the brick-making business. Another man put up a public restroom on his lot and before long made enough money to open a harness shop. Observing that a dentist in the town was swamped with patients, an enterprising blacksmith decided to take up tooth pulling as a sideline.

The first legal saloon in Oklahoma Territory was opened in Guthrie in 1890 by Moses Weinberger (center); at left is Mack O'Brien, the bartender, and at right is Ike Reed, a black porter. Tom Mix, who later became famous as a cowboy movie star, served as a bartender for a short period at the Blue Bell Saloon in Guthrie. Others who lived in the town at one time or another were humorist Will Rogers and William Wrigley, who made his first pack of chewing gum there. And Carry Nation started out from Guthrie on her saloon-smashing career.

The gambling houses in Guthrie, like most public places in this bustling town, kept busy early and late. Historian W. Eugene Hollon quotes one oldtimer: "It seems that you were always waiting your turn. You waited your turn to file on the land. You waited your turn to get a bucket of water, or waited your turn in a restaurant to get something to eat. Just about anything you wanted to do, you waited your turn."

The Hilarity Roost may have been short on space, but it offered a lively band for the entertainment of customers. Later, in 1889, the Club Theatre, the first variety hall built in the town of Guthrie, gave regular performances.

Days of Wrath

The Dakota land boom of the early 1880's had repercussions throughout the farming frontier. Year after year wheat harvests grew larger, markets expanded, and prices rose. Normally dour farmers and tightfisted bankers, traditionally wary of each other, embraced like long-lost friends, the bankers almost begging the farmers to borrow while the latter, certain of rising prices, let themselves be seduced. A new ethos swept the plains as expectations of the good life grew apace; its watchwords were "Borrow, borrow! Spend, spend! Profit, profit!—and then borrow again!" Farmers, long used to working the land with their own hands, suddenly found themselves the owners (on borrowed money) of mechanical reapers and steam-operated threshers. Down came the sod huts, up went frame houses built of expensive lumber imported from far away.

These years of easy credit and high profits—when farmland was more prized for speculative purposes than for growing crops and when the value of well-placed townsite lots rose 1,000 percent—were like a long alcoholic binge. But in 1886 and 1887 frontier farmers awoke from their dreams to a massive hangover that would last a decade.

In the wake of the short harvests of the mid-1880's tragedy began to stalk the plainsmen. A sudden and precipitous decline in commodity prices meant that they got less for the grain they did produce. The conventional wisdom—as represented by the financial community, industrialists, and many merchants—blamed the farmers' distress on worldwide overproduction of foodstuffs, despite the reduced harvests on the plains. Farmers and their representatives retorted that there were still millions of

From 1862 to the mid-1870's, when coins were scarce, the nation used paper money. There were bills for 3, 5, 10, 15, 25, and 50 cents, and the first $1 bill was also issued.

malnourished people even in the United States and that the fault lay with a distribution system presided over by interests concerned only with quick profit.

In terms of the day-to-day lives of the plainsmen, such disputes were purely theoretical. The reality was the relentless pressure from bankers and merchants for repayment of debts—and many farmers were in no position to meet their financial obligations. Foreclosure or flight became the order of the day. In Kansas alone, between 1889 and 1893, some 11,000 farmers either were dispossessed by their creditors or voluntarily left to seek new opportunities.

Not every farmer, of course, was willing to forfeit his land and equipment to the banks. A new mood of militancy swept the plains, reminiscent of the early 1870's but far more intense. A Kansas attorney and populist reformer named Mary Elizabeth Lease—known to her detractors as the Kansas Pythoness—stumped the Midwest to harangue the debt-ridden plainsmen. Addressing several thousand in the town of Paola, Kansas, she shouted: "You farmers were told . . . to raise a big crop. Well, you did, and what became of it? Six-cent corn, ten-cent oats, two-cent beef. We want the accursed foreclosure system wiped out. We will stand by our homes and use force if necessary, and we will not pay our debts to the loan sharks until the government pays its debts to us."

Another prairie radical of the late 1880's was Ignatius Donnelly, a lawyer, writer, and thunderous orator who as early as 1872 had charged: "There is an organized conspiracy in this country . . . whose sole object is to ignore and depress the agricultural interests . . . and set up, as the gods of national idolatry, a

In the early 1880's—years of agricultural prosperity in the West—farmers strove to obtain the amenities of life enjoyed by those in the East. This Nebraska family proudly poses with their new organ.

Founded in Texas around 1875, the Farmers' Alliance spread throughout the South and West in the 1880's and, as this cartoon shows, made the heads of its political opponents roll in the national and state elections of 1890.

The West's protests over high rail rates led Congress to create the Interstate Commerce Commission in 1887. W. A. Rogers shows the ICC about to lasso "Uncle Sam's Wild West (East and South) Show."

"An Unbridled Plutocracy"

We live in a commercial age—not in a military age; and the shadow that is stealing over the American landscape partakes of a commercial character. In short, the shadow is of an unbridled plutocracy . . . the names of whose members are emblazoned, not on the pages of their Nation's glory, but of its peculations; who represent no struggle for their country's liberties, but for its boodle; no contests for Magna Charta, but railroad charters . . . a plutocracy which controls the price of the bread that we eat, the price of sugar that sweetens our cup, the price of oil that lights us on our way, the price of the very coffins in which we are finally buried.

—Gen. Lloyd S. Bryce
The North American Review, March 1889

few spindles and mines. . . . If the nation is to live it must not be with one section fastened like a wolf on the vitals of the rest."

In July 1892 the varied strands of discontent within the nation were woven together in Omaha, Nebraska, when the People's Party (better known as the Populists) was formed. A coalition of farmers' organizations and the Knights of Labor (an early American labor union), the Populist Party fielded a presidential candidate that year who ran on a platform advocating a graduated income tax, the popular election of U.S. senators, restricted immigration, government ownership of the railroads, an eight-hour day for factory workers, and the free coinage of silver. These proposals hardly seem radical today, but at the time they were introduced they generated howls of anguish and derision from conservative interests.

The Silver Issue

Of all the Populist planks the silver issue was perhaps the one that most commended itself to the plains farmers. The nation's currency was based primarily on gold, which was in rather short supply. If silver, pouring out of the western mines in vast quantities, were minted at a ratio of 16 ounces to 1 ounce of gold, then the supply of money would quickly expand, its worth would drop, and farmers could pay off their debts in depreciated currency. In 1892, however, both the Republican and Democratic organizations were in the hands of hard-money men, and neither party was willing to support bimetallism. Thus the Populists hoped to gain a hammerlock on the votes of the discontented, the disaffected, and the dispossessed.

In part, at least, the Democrats managed to blunt the Populist onslaught by nominating for the vice-presidency Adlai Ewing Stevenson—a free-silver enthusiast and grandfather of the 1950's presidential candidate of the same name. A hard-money man, Grover Cleveland, headed the ticket. When the ballots were all counted, the Populist candidate, James B. Weaver, ended up a distant third behind the Republicans' Benjamin Harrison, with just over a million votes out of 12 million cast. Cleveland inched into office with just 46 percent of the popular vote.

Still, it was hardly a bad showing for a brand-new party, and some of the results seemed to portend growing strength. The Populists elected 10 congressmen, 5 senators, 3 governors, and some 1,500 members to various state legislatures. Whether these victories were a flash in the pan or a timely warning of agrarian discontent remained to be seen.

Ignatius Donnelly: Phrasemaker and Prophet

The Prince of Cranks was what his foes called him, and Ignatius Donnelly (1831–1901) replied in kind when he wrote the preamble to the Populist platform of 1892: "The fruits of the toil of millions are boldly stolen to build up colossal fortunes for a few, unprecedented in the history of mankind and the possessors of these in turn despise the Republic, and endanger liberty." Before he played an important role in organizing the Populist Party, Philadelphia-born Donnelly practiced law for a few years, then tried his hand at land speculation in Minnesota but was wiped out in 1857. Switching to politics, he served as a Republican congressman from 1862 until 1869. After he left Congress he became a reformer in search of a cause. He joined the Liberal Republican revolt against Grant in the 1872 presidential campaign, espoused the farmers' aims, and became a Greenback Democrat, advocating cheap paper money.

Donnelly's belief that the world faced destruction if reforms were de-

layed was spelled out in chilling detail in the widely read novel *Caesar's Column,* published in 1890 under a pseudonym. It described the nightmare world of 1988, ruled by a council of plutocrats who had at their command a fleet of dirigibles that were equipped with poison-gas bombs. Finally, a secret revolutionary force overthrew the plutocrats and launched an orgy of murder and looting. Fortunately, a few reformers escaped in a dirigible to Africa, where they organized a socialist state based on Populist principles.

Defeat of a Dream

At its Omaha convention in 1892 the new Populist Party had castigated the ruling establishment in these scornful words: "From the same prolific womb of governmental injustice we breed the two great classes of tramps and millionaires." Over the next few years zealous reformers did not alter that conclusion.

In 1893, shortly after President Grover Cleveland formed his second administration, another severe financial panic hit the nation, ruining thousands of businesses and driving farm prices even lower. The widespread suffering caused by the depression—some 4 million people found themselves out of work—brought a resurgence of the Populists' strength, and in the off-year

Cartoonist Homer C. Davenport pictured candidate William McKinley under the thumb of wealthy politician Mark Hanna.

elections of 1894 the party increased its vote by 42 percent and elected seven representatives and six senators. By the end of that year a growing number of farmers and small businessmen, heavily in debt, were echoing the Populist cry for free silver—depreciation of the currency through the unlimited coinage of silver. Such a step, they believed, would raise commodity prices, increase trade, and make past debts easier to pay. The Populists had hopes that the "goldbugs"—the supporters of the gold standard—would gain control of both major parties at the coming conventions. Then the forces for free silver among western Democrats and Republicans, as well as those favoring taxation, banking, and labor reform, would flock to the Populist banner and to victory in 1896.

Although the silverites had no chance to take over the Republican Party, the Democrats faced a revolt of soft-money rebels led by veteran Richard (" Silver Dick") Bland and a newcomer—the young onetime congressman from Nebraska, William Jennings Bryan. Bryan's detractors said his mouth was as wide as the Platte River and what came out was just as shallow. But Bryan brushed off the gibes and drove ahead, certain that he could lift up the downtrodden and that he was their true voice.

And quite a voice he had. In full cry—which it almost always was—it

could rattle the rafters of the most cavernous hall and galvanize an audience. At the Democratic Convention in Chicago in 1896 Bryan challenged the goldbugs—Democrats, Republicans, industrialists, and bankers—saying, "You come to us and tell us that the great cities are in favor of the gold standard. We reply that the great cities rest upon our broad and fertile prairies." He concluded with these words: "You shall not press down upon the brow of labor this crown of thorns. You shall not crucify mankind upon a cross of gold."

The convention was electrified, and Bryan won the nomination for the presidency from Bland. The Populist leaders, their thunder stolen, finally persuaded their followers to endorse Bryan.

In the campaign that followed, the most brutal in decades, Bryan traveled some 18,000 miles and made more than 600 speeches spreading the gospel of free silver. His Republican opponent, William McKinley, former Ohio governor and congressman, stood on his porch and delivered short speeches that did not upset the visiting faithful. Meanwhile, the chairman of the Republican National Committee, Mark Hanna, a millionaire Cleveland businessman, mobilized powerful financial groups to beat Bryan. The money poured in, and Hanna sent out 25 million pamphlets, mostly damning free silver, hired 1,400 speakers, and supplied buttons and ribbons to every Republican club.

On election day Bryan carried the South and the trans-Mississippi West, but it was not enough. The Populists were wrecked by his defeat, although many reforms they advocated were later adopted by the major parties.

Oddly enough, despite the defeat of the silverites, the farmers got the plentiful supply of currency they wanted. New gold discoveries greatly increased the supply of specie, which caused a rise in prices that aided farmers. As prosperity returned, the farmers made no complaint when the passage of the Currency Act of 1900 put the nation firmly on the gold standard. Yet there was something poignant about Bryan's defeat, which poet Vachel Lindsay caught:

Election night at midnight:
Boy Bryan's defeat.
Defeat of western silver.
Defeat of the Wheat. . . .
Defeat of my boyhood, defeat
of my dream.

William Jennings Bryan: Crusader from the Plains

By dramatizing the presidential campaign of 1896 as a fight between good and evil, the poor against the rich, and silver against gold, Democratic candidate William Jennings Bryan (1860–1925), the 36-year-old "Boy Orator" of Nebraska, aroused conservatives to a fever pitch of vituperation. The comment of John Hay, who had been one of Lincoln's secretaries, was among the calmer assessments of Bryan: "The Boy Orator makes only one speech. . . .

He simply reiterates the unquestionable truths that every man who has a clean shirt is a thief and should be hanged, and there is no goodness or wisdom except among the illiterates and criminal classes."

Born in Salem, Illinois, Bryan quietly practiced law in rural Illinois until 1887, when he moved to Lincoln, Nebraska, and entered politics; in 1890 he was elected to Congress. During two terms in the House, Bryan championed the farmers and free silver, and though he failed to win a U.S. Senate seat in 1894, he did not quit politics. He traveled widely and cultivated delegates to the 1896 Democratic Convention.

In 1925, shortly before his death, Bryan served as a prosecutor in the Scopes trial, in which a teacher in a Tennessee school, John T. Scopes, was convicted of teaching evolution.

Chicago, Metropolis of the Prairies

The administration building of the Columbian exposition, which featured the first extensive display of outdoor electric lighting.

This 1873 scene shows Chicago's South Water Market, where fish, lobster, eggs, meat, fruits, and vegetables could be purchased.

No city better epitomized the raw power of the growing West than Chicago. In 1850 this home of 30,000 was dismissed as the "Mudhole of the Prairies." Its buildings were slowly sinking into the mud on which they were built, and its swamplike streets were barely above the level of Lake Michigan. Then the people tackled the job of raising their city out of the mud. One of many projects involved the Tremont House. Using 5,000 jacks and 1,200 workmen, engineers raised this building eight feet. And while people were lifting Chicago by its bootstraps, so to speak, they were propelling it to a position of leadership in the West. By 1860 the population of the city had boomed to 112,000, and its streets were crowded day and night with wagons hauling cattle, hogs, wheat, corn, farm machinery, and hundreds of other native products, which were carried in and out on a total of 5,000 miles of railroad track. Increased industrial and commercial activity during the Civil War brought further spectacular growth, and by 1870 Chicago had about 300,000 residents.

The next year, however, the city that had risen from the muck faced its greatest challenge when the Great Fire of 1871 burned out three and a half square miles of buildings and gutted the business district. Rallied by Joseph Medill's editorial in the *Chicago Tribune,* which declared, "Chicago Shall Rise Again," the people went to work with a will. By 1875 hardly a trace of the fire remained, and the U.S. railroad hub went on to become the leader in meatpacking, grain trading, and the manufacture of farm machinery. In 1893, as the nation was sinking into a seemingly bottomless business depression, Chicago brushed aside the naysayers and staged the World's Columbian Exposition to demonstrate achievements in science, technology, and the arts in the 19th century and forecast new wonders. With this glittering show Chicago won attention as the "youngest of the world's great cities."

Chicago's strategic railroads in the agricultural West and its immense Union Stock Yards made it the nation's meatpacking center.

On the floor of the board of trade, known as the Pit, shouting brokers would buy and sell wheat and other grains of the West.

The paths of the pioneers have widened into broad highways. The forest clearing has expanded into affluent commonwealths. Let us see to it that the ideals of the pioneer in his log cabin shall enlarge into the spiritual life of a democracy where civic power shall dominate and utilize individual achievement for the common good.

—Frederick Jackson Turner, "Contributions of the West to American Democracy"

The West Comes

"Grand Parade of the Knights Templar." Color lithograph published by H. S. Crocker and Co.

# of Age

Between the Civil War and the turn of the century the United States had grown into an industrial behemoth—its population, agricultural yield, factory output, and steel production increasing vastly. Much of this growth was stimulated by the waxing commerce and spreading rails of the West, the bounteous area whose foodstuffs, metals, minerals, lumber, and petroleum would help to make the United States the world's richest nation. To explore still uncharted western regions, surveys were initiated, and from their discoveries—and rediscoveries—of scenic wonders arose the concept of national parks. Americans were beginning to realize that the magnificent western wilderness could vanish unless adequate preservation supplanted rampant exploitation.

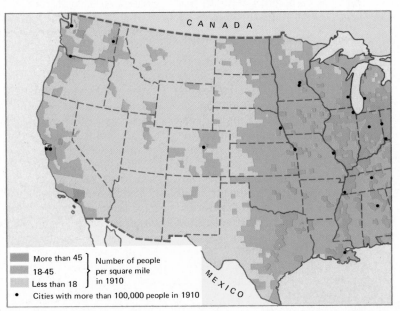

In a mere 60 years the boundless frontier vanished. Between 1850 and 1910, when the 13th census (reflected above) was taken, most good western land had been settled, largely through speculators or by homesteaders given free land. Prices for land increased 50 times from 1870 to 1910. But much soil was inhospitable, so by 1890 the Far West—California excepted—had only half as many farms as Ohio. Meanwhile, towns and cities prospered.

A Truly Scientific Survey

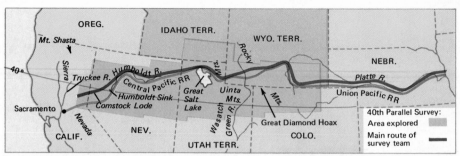

For the Army's 40th parallel survey King covered a 100-mile-wide zone flanking the railroad. Heat and malaria felled many of his men in Truckee Canyon and Humboldt Sink. On one occasion he was hit by lightning, and parts of his body temporarily turned brown.

Clarence King climbs a precipice. Inspiring leader and practical scientist, he was also a theorist on the origins of land features.

The Civil War had hardly ended when the federal government—prodded by the budding scientific community—began seeking ways to explore the unknown portions of the trans-Missouri West. From the late 1860's until the end of the next decade the government authorized a number of scientific surveys aimed at discovering the wealth of the West's barely touched domains.

Enter Clarence King

The first one to find his opportunity through America's increasing curiosity about itself was an ebullient, ambitious, and supremely self-assured young geologist named Clarence King, the offspring of a well-connected but impoverished Newport, Rhode Island, family. In the summer of 1863, a year after his graduation from Yale's Sheffield Scientific School, King crossed the continent and volunteered for a state-sponsored survey of California being conducted by another Yale man, geologist and chemist Josiah D. Whitney.

It was while exploring the California wilderness with Whitney that King hit upon the idea that would make him famous: a scientific survey of a swath a hundred miles wide, extending from the Colorado Rockies to the Sierra Nevada and centering along the 40th parallel. The object of the expedition, as summed up by King himself, was "to examine and describe the geological structure, geographical condition and natural resources of a belt of country . . . along the 40th parallel . . . with sufficient expansion north and south to include the line of the 'Central' and 'Union Pacific' railroads. . . . It should examine all rock formations, mountain ranges . . . coal deposits, soils, minerals, ores, saline and alkaline deposits . . . collect material for a topographical map of the regions traversed . . . and make collections in botany and zoology with a view to a memoir on these subjects."

By 1867 King was in Washington, assuring a charmed Secretary of War Edwin Stanton that "the deserts are not all desert; the vast plains will produce something better than buffalo, namely beef; there is water for irrigation, and land fit to receive it. All that is needed is to explore and declare the nature of the national domain." Stanton was only too happy to appoint the 25-year-old King chief of the Geological and Geographical Exploration of the Fortieth Parallel, but he warned him to get started as soon as possible because "you are too young a man to be seen about town with this appointment in your pocket—there are four major generals who want your place."

King's survey was the first major expedition to be run by a civilian, although he did have to report to the secretary of war. Moreover, it was totally staffed by scientific specialists—botanists, geologists, and mineralogists. In June of 1867 the young explorer and his handpicked crew established a base camp near Sacramento, California, and began hardening themselves for the rigors ahead. "I take a little ride every day on mule back," wrote one botanist, "and am at present afflicted with a most grievous tail."

In July the party broke camp for its first excursion into desert country. By the time the survey ended a decade later, it had ranged from California's Sierra Nevada to eastern Colorado, making in-depth studies of everything from rainfall to mineral deposits, from flora and fauna to topography.

The venture was not without its perils. In the summer of 1867, when the party was exploring the country around Nevada's Humboldt Sink, so many of its members were struck down by malaria that all retreated into the mountains to recuperate. In such conditions even scientists could grow irrational;

one botanist solemnly wrote home that "there are wells out here which are said to cause Gonorrhea." Yet the expedition also offered great compensations, as when, in 1870, King scaled Mount Shasta and discovered three active glaciers, upsetting the then-prevailing belief that no glaciers remained within the United States. And finally, there was the great diamond hoax of 1872, the unmasking of which sent King's reputation soaring to new heights.

"King of Diamonds"

That summer King heard rumors of a great "find" in gems somewhere in his region of exploration. Two drifters, it seemed, had arrived in San Francisco with a fistful of gems. Their haul was confirmed when they led a respected mineralogist, blindfolded, to their secret diggings, and the expert returned to town with more precious stones. Eager financiers promptly bought out the find for $600,000.

King was skeptical, but he also feared that if the stones proved genuine his own men would look foolish for not having discovered them, so he decided to make his own verification. With very little to go on he made some shrewd guesses about the location of the gemstone field and soon found it near the spot where the borders of Wyoming, Colorado, and Utah meet.

What King discovered astounded even him—scattered diamonds, sapphires, and rubies glittering on the ground. The stones were tucked just under the earth's surface, and one was balanced atop an anthill. Certain that the field had been salted, King hurried back to San Francisco to expose the fraud before speculators could cash in on it. For this he was hailed as a hero, the "King of Diamonds."

But exposing a swindle was a mere sideline for King, and in 1878—after a decade of surveying—he published his *Systematic Geology,* a wellspring of information on the landforms of the West. Other works that came out of the expedition vastly increased the body of knowledge concerning mineral wealth and economic potential. It was also in 1878 that King sought and was granted the directorship of the newly established U.S. Geological Survey. But of all the accolades he received, King may well have been most flattered by one from his friend Boston Brahmin Henry Adams, who called him the "best and brightest man of his generation."

Exploring the Green River area (with its Eocene period bluffs) in 1869, King discovered large coal deposits. En route there the previous year, he had ridden after and captured a soldier-escort who had deserted his expedition. This action prevented further dropouts.

At a Nevada encampment King stands in the front tent. After their first season in the field (July to November of 1867) he and his men spent the winter in Carson City and Virginia City. There the topographers from the survey worked on their maps, while others investigated the Comstock area, taking the first photographs in a U. S. mine.

The 1869 party crosses Utah's Wasatch Range. King's groups were first to spot a U.S. glacier; they also collected rocks and plants, deduced that Comstock's silver lodes were vaster than assumed, and found that the Great Basin consists of two ancient lake beds.

Confirming the Wonders of Yellowstone

Their families and friends—as well as hostile Crow Indians—tried to discourage them, warning that theirs would be "a cavalcade to hell." But the nine men meeting in Helena, Montana Territory, in August of 1870 decided to start anyway. They wanted conclusively to prove or, they skeptically thought, disprove reports of fantastic geysers, a mountain of glass, and pools of boiling paint supposedly lying in an area that Indians shunned as spirit-haunted and that early French trappers had dubbed Roche Jaune ("Yellow Rock"). The weird region had been described at length to explorers in the early 1800's by Indians, in the 1830's by trappers Joe Meek and Jim Bridger, in 1863 by a gold-seeking engineer, Walter De Lacy (who even drew a map), and in 1869 by three Montana frontiersmen who told of an inland sea and magnificent falls. Still, people would not believe. So, inadequately prepared, the nine men rode off to take a look for themselves.

They Provided Proof

The Helena nine, most of them middle-aged, were unlikely explorers. They included two merchants, a bank president, a lawyer, and an assessor; they elected the Montana surveyor general, Henry D. Washburn, their captain; and the first among them to ride off—to engage the services of the cavalry under Lt. Gustavus C. Doane—was a collector of internal revenue, Nathaniel P. Langford. Yet these unusual men proved that incredible Yellowstone Canyon really existed. Their accounts persuaded Congress to appropriate funds for an official U.S. expedition under Dr. Ferdinand V. Hayden.

Langford

Washburn

Hayden

Fantastic Journeys

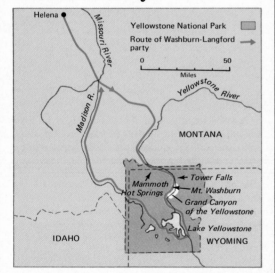

The Washburn party crossed 7,000-foot-high ridges deep in snow, then forests so dense that branches repeatedly scraped the packs off their horses. While the others explored Tower Falls, Washburn climbed a mountain—and gazed incredulously upon a tortuous yellow canyon circled by snow-capped peaks, a fabulous waterfall, a huge lake, and eerie columns of steam. Investigating the Grand Canyon, several of the men began quarreling about dividing it for personal exploitation. But one, Cornelius Hedges, proposed making it a national park. And two years later President Ulysses S. Grant did exactly that.

A Photograph of Mammoth Hot Springs

Jim Bridger told of a "petrified" rainbow, but people scoffed. Forty years later both the Washburn and Hayden expeditions found that the rainbow was an encrustation of multicolored minerals at Mammoth Hot Springs. In 1871 Hayden—a physician, geologist, naturalist, and chief of the U.S. Geological Survey of Territories—brought with him photographer-artist W. H. Jackson, who took this picture, and artist Thomas Moran, who is in it. Their dazzling pictures and paintings showed Congress the splendor of Yellowstone. Doane, who had been part of Washburn's 1870 party, also accompanied Hayden.

A Painting of Old Faithful's Show

Jackson portrays himself (right center background) photographing Old Faithful for the first time in 1871. The leading horseman is Hayden. Trying to reach the geyser in 1870, Washburn encountered many difficulties: his horses—lacking fodder and finding scant grass—were frequently mired in mud and stalked by mountain lions; one of his men was lost (later, saved); Doane suffered from an infected finger; and the exhausted explorers got food poisoning from a contaminated tin of peaches and dysentery from the water. In their sodden clothes all were severely chilled by heavy morning frosts.

Old Faithful

Those who have seen stage representations of Aladdin's Cave and the Home of the Dragon Fly, as produced in a first class theatre, can form an idea of the wonderful coloring . . . of this fairy like yet solid mound of rock growing up amid clouds of steam and showers of boiling water. . . . The period of this geyser is fifty minutes. First an increased rush of steam comes forth followed instantly by a rising jet of water which attains . . . the height of one hundred and twenty-five feet, escaping with a wild hissing sound while great volumes of steam rise up to an altitude of five hundred feet from the crater. Rainbows play around the tremendous fountains, the waters which fall about the basin in showers . . . then rush steaming to the river.

—Gustavus C. Doane's
Yellowstone Journal of 1870

Moran's "Grand Canyon of the Yellowstone" Refutes the Skeptics

Artist Thomas Moran shows the awesome beauty of the first national park. Moran, who was born in England in 1837 and came to the United States in 1844, traveled in Europe in the 1860's to continue the art studies he had begun in Philadelphia. He returned to America in 1871 in time to join Hayden's party. This painting was bought by Congress and hung in the Capitol in Washington.

The Challenge of the Colorado

The bloody battle at Shiloh in 1862 was at its height when a young Union officer raised his right arm to signal his men. Just then, a Confederate ball came hurtling toward him, smashing the upraised arm and forcing its amputation at the elbow. To some men such a wound would have meant the end of an active life but not to John Wesley Powell.

The son of a circuit-riding preacher and sometime farmer, Powell was born in New York's Genesee Valley in 1834. During his youth in Ohio and Illinois he managed to pick up enough education to qualify as a country schoolmaster. Geology was the discipline that most interested him; and although he never took a degree, during the 1850's he studied at three colleges, and by the time of his discharge from the Army he became a geology professor in Illinois. He also established and became curator of the state's natural history museum.

Geology meant fieldwork, and Powell was fascinated by the exploratory trips he made with his students in the trans-Missouri West. It was during one of these treks, in August of 1868, that the one-armed scientist clambered up a previously unscaled Rocky Mountain peak and from its summit beheld the meandering, majestic Colorado River with its deep-cut gorges. Here, atop Long's Peak, John Wesley Powell conceived his great vision. He would do what no man before him had done: he would follow the Colorado system by boat all the way from the Green River in the north and down the Colorado itself to where it joined the Virgin River (near present-day Lake Mead). That much of the system had already

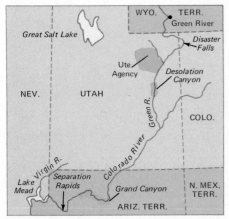

Starting at Green River, Powell's 1869 journey took him 1,037 miles to the Virgin River. He lost one boat at Disaster Falls.

Thomas Moran's painting reveals the cliffs of the Grand Canyon, at whose base Powell's boats bobbed on the Colorado River. Powell studied the area's geology, flora, and fauna.

been explored was of little concern to Powell. No one person had ever undertaken so long and arduous a journey on its inhospitable waters; and, indeed, 150 miles of the Colorado had never been conquered by boat at all.

By the early spring of 1869 Powell was in Washington, pleading for funds and equipment from federal officials. The Smithsonian Institution offered its best wishes but little practical help, and the Army authorized the would-be explorer to draw upon its surplus stores. Powell himself dipped into his own meager resources and raised enough private funds to build three sturdy oak boats and a lighter one of pine and to buy a supply of scientific instruments. He also recruited a party of nine, most of them ordinary folk with a yen for adventure but little scientific training. Among them was an army sergeant named George Young Bradley, who avowed he would "explore the river Styx" if it would get him away from the boredom of military life.

On May 24, 1869, the Powell party pushed off from the small community of Green River, in the Wyoming Territory, with Powell ranging ahead in the pine boat and the three oak vessels following, laden with supplies. The group had traveled less than two weeks before the

river struck, smashing one of the oak boats into a rock and sending its two crewmen overboard. Time and again during the journey rocks and foaming rapids would take their toll of men and supplies, and soon even the most fastidious members of the party resembled forlorn vagabonds.

Brushes with Death

Completely out of touch with civilization for 37 days, the explorers experienced almost daily perils. Once, Powell climbed a steep cliff and became trapped on a narrow ledge, where he clung desperately to a crumbling wall of sandstone with his one good arm. Just as Powell began to lose his hold, Bradley appeared on a ledge above him. Quickly divesting himself of his long-johns, he lowered them to Powell, who grabbed them and was pulled to safety.

By mid-August the party was on the edge of the Grand Canyon, where the Colorado cuts its deepest gorge and where no man had tried to pass by water before. The rocky landscape took on a brooding, almost threatening air, and the river whipped itself into an unprecedented frenzy. Most of the expedition's supplies were used up or spoiled, just when the men needed every ounce of energy for portaging and running the rapids; and for three of the party it was all too much. On August 28 they told Powell they were quitting to take their chances on an overland trek. As it turned out, all three were killed by Indians, who mistook them for another group of whites who had killed a squaw.

Ironically, the place where the ill-fated trio left the Powell party, Separation Rapids, proved to be the last great obstacle. A day's journey later, the river broadened out and the canyon walls fell away. On August 30, 1869, after more than three months on the water, the party came upon a welcome sight: a Mormon settler fishing with his sons.

Rain Does Not Follow the Plow

John Wesley Powell was heaped with fame and glory. Two years later, when he repeated his journey, he had no trouble at all raising funds or attracting scientists for the trip. Later, when Clarence King resigned as head of the U.S. Geological Survey, Powell succeeded him. In this post he used his wide knowledge of western topography to puncture the popular theory that "rain follows the plow," warning would-be settlers that the small family farm was totally out of keeping with the environment of the High Plains. Man, he held, must adapt to—or at least compromise with—the region in which he found himself or else face disaster. Powell was, of course, fundamentally correct in his assessment, but it would be some time before his words were widely heeded.

Powell with an Indian guide. A perceptive observer of the Indians, he was afraid the whites would destroy their culture.

Using his long-johns, Bradley hauls the one-armed Powell to safety. "Danger is our life now," wrote one of the party.

After each terrifying traverse of the rapids the men would reach the quiet of mirror-clear water—here, in sandy-banked Lodore Canyon.

"What a Seething and Boiling"

[August 25] We make twelve miles this morning, when we come to monuments of lava, standing in the river; low rocks, mostly, but some of them shafts more than a hundred feet high . . . then we come to an abrupt cataract. Just over the fall, on the right wall, a cinder cone, or extinct volcano, with a well-defined crater, stands on the very brink of the canyon. . . . From this volcano vast floods of lava have been poured down into the river, and a stream of the molten rock has run up the canyon three or four miles. . . . What a conflict of water and fire there must have been here! Just imagine a river of molten rock, running down into a river of melted snow. What a seething and boiling of the waters; what clouds of steam rolled into the heavens! Thirty-five miles today. Hurrah!

—John Wesley Powell, *Exploration of the Colorado River of the West and Its Tributaries*, 1875

W. H. Jackson painted topographer A. H. Thompson (far left), Powell (arm raised), and photographer John K. Hillers (far right) in Marble Canyon in 1872. Jackson based his paintings on photographs; note the similarity between Powell's pose here and at the left.

Photographers Explore the West

Some of the most spectacular explorations of the West coincided with the invention, around 1850, of a new photographic technique (opposite top) and with a Victorian Age love of landscapes. As a result, most family parlors boasted gilded baskets of scenic postcard photographs, often accompanied by stereoscopes. When photographers began taking to the wilds, they faced the logistical nightmare of toting big and bulky cameras, scores of large, heavy glass plates, chemicals, a portable darkroom, camping and mountaineering equipment,

food and firearms. In flat country W. H. Jackson carried all his equipment in a buckboard, fitted as a darkroom, and in rough terrain everything had to be backpacked up canyonsides or strapped onto mules. Once Edward Curtis' mule fell off a cliff, smashing many of the plates. For Powell's Colorado River survey John K. Hillers packed 600 large plates and several cameras into rubber sacks and put them into canvas-covered crates in the waterproof compartments of three boats; but during the expedition one boat was wrecked in the rapids.

The tent camp of Edward S. Curtis, who spent 30 years taking some 40,000 pictures that recorded the mores of Indian tribes. As a young man, he supported his widowed mother by farming their Puget Sound homestead and selling firewood. The gift of a stereoscope spurred him to build a camera. He later opened a studio in Seattle. Out photographing glaciers, he rescued a party of lost scientists, and through two of them he became the photographer on an Alaska glacier survey organized by magnate E. H. Harriman.

Perched 3,214 feet up on Overhanging Rock, W. H. Jackson focuses on Yosemite. His father taught him photography, his artist mother, painting. He sold the Union Pacific Railroad scenics of its route and became renowned for recording the Hayden survey.

Laden with camera equipment, Henry G. Peabody, whose work ranged from daguerreotypes to 35-millimeter color films, rides in the Grand Canyon. He had a studio in Boston and, with a partner, two art galleries in Chicago but moved to Pasadena after his wife's death and photographed the West for his illustrated lectures. W. H. Jackson hired Peabody to take pictures for his postcard company.

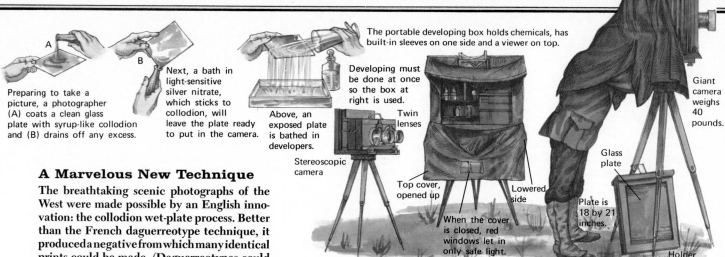

Preparing to take a picture, a photographer (A) coats a clean glass plate with syrup-like collodion and (B) drains off any excess.

Next, a bath in light-sensitive silver nitrate, which sticks to collodion, will leave the plate ready to put in the camera.

Above, an exposed plate is bathed in developers.

The portable developing box holds chemicals, has built-in sleeves on one side and a viewer on top.

Developing must be done at once so the box at right is used.

Stereoscopic camera

Twin lenses

Top cover, opened up

When the cover is closed, red windows let in only safe light.

Lowered side

Giant camera weighs 40 pounds.

Glass plate

Plate is 18 by 21 inches.

Holder

A Marvelous New Technique

The breathtaking scenic photographs of the West were made possible by an English innovation: the collodion wet-plate process. Better than the French daguerreotype technique, it produced a negative from which many identical prints could be made. (Daguerreotypes could be reproduced only as lithographs or engravings.) Plates had to be developed on the spot, however; and, with enlarging not yet practical, large plates were needed to get large pictures.

Just before taking each picture, the photographer picked out a glass plate, treated it chemically (upper left), quickly locked it into a light-tight holder, and exposed it while its coating was still wet. All the preparation and locking up of the glass plate had to be done in complete darkness.

In the 1850's the stereoscope, an English invention, became the rage in the United States. Taken with a two-lens camera, twin pictures, seen through a viewer, blended into a three-dimensional scene.

W. H. Jackson (seated) in the Tetons. A New York Union Army veteran, he went west after a romance ended and started a picture firm with his brother in Omaha.

The interplay of man and nature fascinated British-born Eadweard J. Muybridge, who emphasized the drama of Yosemite by photographing it when the sun cast deep shadows. He also recorded life in San Francisco, where he owned a bookstore, did scenics of Alaska and Central America, and pioneered in the photography of figures in motion.

The Age of Big Mining

A fever of speculation, an urge to plunge for riches against all odds, swept over America in the last decades of the 19th century. And in no endeavor did the temperatures run higher than in western mining. All across the mountainous areas of the West, from the Black Hills of Dakota through the Rockies and on to the Sierras, new reports of gold, silver, and copper deposits kept popping up—though many were literally flashes in the pan, gleaming just long enough to bring in eager prospectors by the hundreds. Other strikes, however, more than lived up to their billing, enriching investors in San Francisco and New York and sometimes even profiting the discoverers of the hidden treasures themselves. For example, the Homestake, located in the Black Hills, yielded more than $100 million in gold and $4 million in silver between the years 1877 and 1901, adding still more wealth to the already bulging coffers of California's George Hearst and his partners.

In fact, there was hardly a state or a territory of the western mountains without its share of little El Dorados. Colorado had its Leadville and Cripple Creek, where gold and silver seemed almost to flow out of the ground. Arizona Territory had Wickenburg and Tomb-stone, the latter eventually producing about $80 million in gold and silver. In 1885 the great Bunker Hill and Sullivan silver and lead reserves in Idaho were found, while gold discovered two years earlier made the Coeur d'Alene region the scene of frantic activity. In Utah, Montana, Washington, and the far frontier of Alaska there were also gold and silver rushes in the last decades of the 19th century. But of all the bonanza regions in the West none could compare in wealth or longevity to the granddaddy of them all, the great Comstock Lode.

Revival of the Comstock

From its discovery in 1859 until 1865, Nevada's fabulous Comstock Lode had been the nation's most productive source of silver and, to a lesser extent, of gold. During the Civil War the Comstock mines had produced a steady stream of specie to buttress the Union's finances, but just after the conflict came to an end the mines seemingly dried up.

By 1870 prospects looked so dim that shares in the Comstock's huge Consolidated Virginia mine were selling at a dollar apiece—and buyers were few. Yet five years later each Consolidated share stood at $700, and the mine itself was yielding $50,000 a day in precious

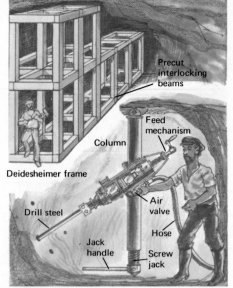

Clamped to a screw-jack column, the Burleigh drill cut holes for dynamite with the hammering action of its drill steel, which was powered by compressed air. Blasted auriferous rock went into huge crushers. The cleared tunnel was supported by a Deidesheimer frame. Burleigh drills were used in the building of the Sutro Tunnel.

metals, while other mines in and around the lode were making similar showings. Where miners had been deserting the twin towns of Virginia City and Gold Hill in droves, an influx of eager newcomers would bring the combined populations of the dusty villages to 30,000 by the year 1875.

What had happened to revive the dormant mines could be summed up in a single word: technology. Mining engineers and mineralogists, among them Clarence King, were convinced that rich veins of gold- and silver-bearing quartz lay buried in the mountains. With the backing of San Francisco financiers, engineers used a new invention—dynamite—to blast through the rock walls and make tunnels leading to the hidden veins. Drilling, which had been done by hand, became cheaper and more efficient when the Burleigh drill, powered by compressed air, was installed in 1872. Together with dynamite it made deep mining possible. The total length of the Comstock's shafts and tunnels, some of them 3,000 feet below ground, was estimated at 180 to 190 miles.

As the mines were extended deeper into the mountainsides, the danger of cave-ins became acute. To support the sagging tunnel roofs, a system of interlocking square frames made of pine and filled with waste ore was devised by a

Tabor's Rise and Fall

In April 1878 Leadville storekeeper H.A.W. Tabor (1830-99), whose luck had been mostly bad for 20 years, grubstaked two down-and-out prospectors. In a few days they hit a rich vein of silver, and Tabor's one-third share netted him $1 million. He bought other claims, including the unpromising Matchless mine, which for a time earned him $100,000 a month. Tabor made many generous gifts to Leadville civic projects and built the Tabor Grand Opera House in Denver. In 1882 he left his wife and married a young divorcée, Elizabeth Doe, and "Baby Doe" stuck with him even after he was wiped out in the panic of 1893. After his death in 1899, Baby Doe, believing the Matchless would make a comeback, went there to live in a shack and was found frozen to death in 1935.

Baby Doe wore this ermine cloak when she appeared at her husband's opera house.

Tabor worked as a slagman after going broke.

young engineer, Philip Deidesheimer. Placed atop one another to any desired height and running the length of the tunnels, these squares—which in groups resembled the walls of a honeycomb—proved equal to their task, though the pressure on the softwood was so great that the wood was often compressed to less than half its original size.

Of all the innovations employed by the Comstock mineowners the grandest in scope was the tunnel designed by German-born engineer Adolph H. J. Sutro, a four-mile-long excavation that took 10 years to build. The purpose of the tunnel was to provide easy access to the mines in the major diggings, but it also helped to solve problems concerning ventilation, water drainage, and the movement of ore. In addition, it provided an emergency escape route from fire or cave-ins for miners laboring more than 1,500 feet below the surface. Unfortunately, however, the financing of Sutro's great engineering work proved so difficult that by the time the tunnel opened in 1878, Comstock's glory days were over.

Through the 1880's and most of the 1890's mining in the lode continued on a small-scale, intermittent basis. But in 1898 the last of the major mines at the Comstock Lode closed down for good. By then the great Mother Lode had yielded up a staggering total of about $400 million in precious metals.

Sutro's Four-Mile-Long Triumph

Adolph H. J. Sutro enjoys a rare moment of relaxation during construction of his tunnel.

Sutro, who sometimes worked underground with his laborers, poses in this shaft building.

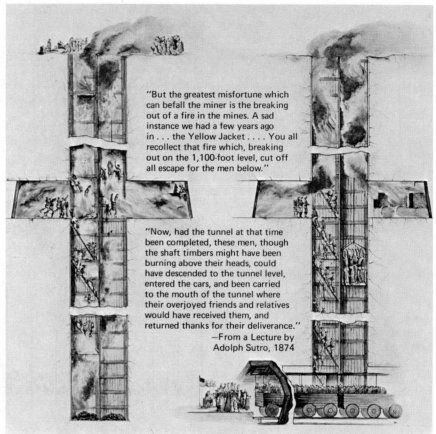

"But the greatest misfortune which can befall the miner is the breaking out of a fire in the mines. A sad instance we had a few years ago in . . . the Yellow Jacket . . . . You all recollect that fire which, breaking out on the 1,100-foot level, cut off all escape for the men below."

"Now, had the tunnel at that time been completed, these men, though the shaft timbers might have been burning above their heads, could have descended to the tunnel level, entered the cars, and been carried to the mouth of the tunnel where their overjoyed friends and relatives would have received them, and returned thanks for their deliverance."
—From a Lecture by Adolph Sutro, 1874

Sutro's diagram showing a fire in a mine with and without his tunnel. At left, the men are trapped; at right, they descend into the tunnel and make their escape.

In 1861 the 31-year-old Adolph H. J. Sutro was operating a prosperous smelter near Virginia City, which perched on the fabulous Comstock Lode. But he was nagged by the belief that the mining companies were going after the silver from the wrong direction. Instead of digging shafts straight down from the surface, he thought, why not build a tunnel beneath Mount Davidson to intersect the ore beds and enable miners to work upward into the ore as well as downward. When Sutro's smelter burned down in 1863, he did not rebuild it but took the insurance money and began promoting his tunnel.

At first all went well. Nevada and the federal government approved the tunnel, and mining companies promised to pay a royalty of $2 a ton on all ore they produced after his tunnel was in operation. But Sutro's unwise boasting that his tunnel would give him control of smelter operations aroused officials of the Bank of California. Considering Sutro a threat to their monopolistic control of the Comstock, they reneged on a promised loan and warned other financiers against investing in "Sutro's coyote hole." Next, Sutro interested the Miners Union in the tunnel's safety features, and a small loan from them permitted him to begin construction in October 1869. Wealthy San Franciscans then organized the Sutro Tunnel Company with Sutro as general superintendent. His men conquered solid rock, tons of oozing mud, and intense heat to complete his monumental project (4 miles long, 12 feet wide, and 10 feet high) in 1878. Two years later Sutro sold his tunnel stock and went to San Francisco, where he made millions in real estate and served as mayor before he died in 1898.

The Era of the Copper Kings

By the turn of the century most of the great reserves of precious metals had been fully exploited in the West. This did not mean, however, that mining was dying. Over the years western mines had been providing less glamorous metals and minerals—lead, zinc, borax, iron, coal, and copper—for the sinews of the nation's industry.

In 1844 rich iron-ore deposits had been uncovered in the Lake Superior region, but they were barely tapped until the final decades of the 19th century. Then the stupendous growth of the American steel industry brought a heavy demand for iron, and yawning pits were dug in the Mesabi Range in Minnesota and other regions to extract millions of tons of ore from the earth.

The earliest exploitation of copper deposits in the West began in the 1840's after the discovery of great reserves—in almost pure form—in Michigan's Upper Peninsula. In the next decade copper was also found in Arizona, but it was not developed extensively until the Phelps Dodge Corporation and others began operations in the 1880's. Similarly, Utah's copper deposits were not developed systematically until the 1890's.

Dawn of the Electrical Age

It was in Montana that the mining of copper really boomed with the dawning of the electrical age. In 1882 Thomas A. Edison's Pearl Street Power Station—using some 65 tons of the metal—began serving customers in New York City. By the late 1880's electric lighting had become an important business in the United States, and copper came into great demand as a conductor for transmitting electricity.

In the early years copper mining in the Butte region of Montana was incidental to the extraction of gold and silver. In 1875 a former Union soldier, Michael Hickey, staked a claim on a hill overlooking Butte and named it the Anaconda. It eventually became the world's richest copper mine, but at that time Hickey ignored the copper carbonate he found and continued his search for silver and gold.

In 1881 Marcus Daly examined the Anaconda and took an option to buy it. He then persuaded James B. Haggin, Lloyd Tevis, and George Hearst, the owners of the great Homestake mine in the Black Hills, to purchase the mine. Daly got a one-fourth interest in the

In the 1880's the poisonous smoke from this smelter at Anaconda and from others around Butte killed vegetation and animals, coated homes with soot, and turned day into night.

Anaconda and in 1882 took over development work. In May of 1883 his workers hit a vein 50 to 100 feet wide that was 55 percent copper. Daly, the first copper king, built the town of Anaconda and later engaged in a feud with another copper king, William A. Clark—a dispute that had Montana politics in an uproar for a decade.

In 1895 Daly and his partners incorporated as the Anaconda Copper Mining Company, and by 1899 Anaconda was not only the world's largest producer of copper but was in the railroad, waterpower, hotel, coal, lumber, newspaper, and electric-lighting businesses as well, with about three-fourths of Montana's workers on its payrolls. In that year Henry H. Rogers and his associates at the Standard Oil Company bought Anaconda as an important step in their drive to organize a copper trust and monopolize the industry. Standard Oil then established the Amalgamated Copper

Company as a holding company for Anaconda and other copper firms they might buy out.

Rogers and his associates had smooth sailing until they tangled with F. Augustus Heinze. Part German-Jewish and part Irish, the Brooklyn-born Heinze, who had studied at the Columbia University School of Mines, was 20 when he went to work in Butte in 1889 as a $100-a-month surveyor in the mines. He considered the riches of Butte with a calculating eye and went back to New York, where he worked for the *Engineering and Mining Journal*, then studied at a German mining university. Armed with facts on copper mining, he returned to Butte in 1892.

Heinze's first coup was to lease the rich Estella mine and rig the deal so that he got all the profits and the owner none. Seemingly having a sixth sense when it came to the geology of Butte's mines, Heinze decided to rent the abandoned

Huge shovels scoop iron ore into cars at the Mahoning mine near Hibbing on Minnesota's Mesabi Range in 1899. This open-pit mine became "the biggest hole ever made by man."

Glengarry mine and soon uncovered a rich vein of ore. Then he built his own smelter and undercut the prices charged by Clark's smelting company and Daly's smelter at Anaconda.

In the late 1890's Heinze was ready to challenge the copper king who sat on "the richest hill on earth." Heinze's weapon in his war against Amalgamated was the "law of the apex." Adopted during the California gold rush, this law gave the owner of a claim on which a vein of ore came nearest the surface the right to follow that vein no matter where it led underground. Claiming that his copper veins ran under Amalgamated's land and that he therefore had a right to them, Heinze sent as many as 37 lawyers into court to seek injunctions against Amalgamated. At one time he was involved in 133 lawsuits, and his legal maneuvers were called courthouse mining. Debonair, swashbuckling, and spellbinding as a speaker, Heinze posed as a friend of the miners and the small independents against Amalgamated and Standard Oil.

Amalgamated Strikes Back

Heinze's legal forays were ably abetted by the decisions of Judge William Clancy, a man of little education who had been put on the bench by Heinze. Finally, in October 1903, Amalgamated struck back, closing all its operations in the state and throwing some 20,000 men out of work. It did not resume operations until the governor called a special session of the legislature to pass a fair-trial law demanded by Amalgamated. This law provided for the removal of a case from a judge who was charged with prejudice by one of the parties. It was a proper statute, but Amalgamated's savage coercion of the state and its people brought widespread criticism.

After the passage of the fair-trial law Heinze's power was considerably weakened, and in 1906 he sold out to Amalgamated for $10.5 million. Heinze took his money and went to New York to try his hand at banking and stock-market speculation. But he was outmaneuvered by his old enemies at Standard Oil and all but wiped out as the panic of 1907 hit the country. Heinze went back to developing his few remaining properties in Idaho and Utah, but his old zest for combat was gone. He died suddenly in New York in 1914 at the age of 45, and Heinze's bitter foe resumed its name of Anaconda Copper Mining Company and lived on unchallenged.

Miners prepare to blast copper ore from a tunnel 1,900 feet under the Butte post office. As mining continued, the town sat on land honeycombed with miles of shafts and tunnels.

The Feud Between Daly and Clark

Both were self-made men, but no two were more dissimilar than Marcus Daly (1841–1900), generous and popular, and William A. Clark (1839–1925), tightfisted and a loner.

Daly was born in Ireland, came to America at 15, sold newspapers in New York, and then went to California to labor in the mines. In 1876 he went to Butte to investigate a silver mine.

Born in Pennsylvania, Clark was educated in Iowa and went to Colorado in 1862 to work in the mines. In 1863 he joined a gold rush to what is now Montana and made enough money to open a store in Virginia City. He later went into banking and the wholesale trade with two partners and opened the firm's bank in Butte. He soon bought the bank, developed rich mines, and built the first smelter in Butte.

At first Clark and Daly were friends, but after Daly's great copper find at the Anaconda, which the jealous Clark reportedly described as "pure luck," the friendship cooled. It vanished when the two men, both Democrats, vied for control of the party in Montana.

Marcus Daly   **William A. Clark**

In 1888 Daly's followers beat Clark when he ran for territorial delegate to Congress, and the feud was on. Daly's forces then prevented Clark's election as U.S. senator in 1893 but failed to make Anaconda the state capital. Clark had backed Helena and won. In 1899 the persistent Clark was elected to the Senate, but Daly carried charges of bribery to the Senate Committee on Elections, which refused to seat Clark. In 1901, shortly after Daly died in New York, Clark finally won a Senate seat but served only one term. He devoted the rest of his life to business affairs.

Trouble in the Mines

Light for gold miners in the Kennedy mine in California was supplied by candles. Lunch pails were hauled up after the miners ate so that they could not smuggle out ore.

To get a working mule down a mine shaft, miners lowered it in a sling to the bottom, where it remained for the rest of its life.

In the early days of the western mining boom the man who used hired labor rather than his own hands to work a claim was regarded with contempt by fellow prospectors. A forty-niner down on his luck might hire himself out for a time, but this was only a means to secure a new grubstake. Inevitably, however, as the easy diggings gave out, large corporations moved in, for they were the only ones with sufficient capital to finance the exploitation of minerals hidden deep beneath the earth. By the late 1870's the era of individual initiative had been replaced by the era of bankers, financiers, and corporate managers. Typically, a lone prospector might still be the discoverer of a lode of gold, silver, or copper, but just as typically it was a San Francisco or New York consortium that bought him out, developed the mine, and then lured hundreds of day laborers.

Conditions for these miners could often be horrible. At one of the deeper Comstock diggings the temperature hovered around 150°F, and ice was lowered by the bucketful—95 pounds per man—to give some relief. The miners carried ice in their fists to their work stations, then rubbed their bodies with it. They dipped cloths in the buckets and wrung them out on their heads to obtain momentary respites from the unbearable heat. One visitor to the Comstock recorded these impressions of its hellish pits: "Exposed to such temperatures, and breathing the stagnant air, the men spent forty-five minutes of each hour beneath the nearest air-vent, going forward to their stations for successive brief periods and returning bathed in sweat and often bent over with cramps. The pain . . . was intense."

The heat also came in liquid form. Blasting operations or air drills might expose hot underground springs, which sometimes flooded the excavations. But of all the things the miners feared, fire came first. Jammed into narrow, fetid tunnels deep in the earth, the miners believed that if a fire broke out they had no chance of escape. "Let but a splinter of pine be held in a candle," observed Dan DeQuille, the laureate of the Comstock, "and soon the smell of burning wood is detected by the miners . . . and there is a commotion, such as is seen when a hive of bees is disturbed." The men had ample reason for their dread. One blaze in 1869 trapped 45 miners, all of whom died terrible deaths.

After clashes between union men and strikebreakers at the Coeur d'Alene mines in 1892, Idaho's governor called for federal aid, and U.S. troops came in and occupied the area.

Partly because working the Comstock was so dangerous and difficult—and partly because the companies had trouble recruiting men strong enough to withstand the rigors of the Nevada diggings—workers found themselves in the unusual position for that time of being able to negotiate over wages and working conditions. At a time when respectable folk considered labor unions to be nothing better than revolutionary bands, the Comstock was already unionized, and many mines were actually closed shops. No man could be hired unless he belonged to the Miners Union, which by 1867 secured for its members the startlingly high wage of $4 per day.

Labor Struggles

If labor-management relations at the Comstock were characterized by a spirit of mutual accommodation and wary respect, such was hardly the case in the rest of the mining West. In most regions it was war to the death between the infant unions and management, each side out to destroy the other. Usually it was management that held the high cards—the courts, state militias, and major newspapers were at its command—while the unions had only the fervor of their members and their willingness to match terror with terror, murder with murder, bombing with bombing.

The battle between mine management and labor, which lasted well into the 20th century, opened at Leadville, Colorado, in 1880. The strike began when the management of one of the mines irritated the workers with regulations about smoking, talking, and loitering on the job. Meeting in protest, the miners rallied around a more basic issue—wages and hours. Joined by workers from other mines nearby, the men struck for $4 for an 8-hour day over the existing $3 to $3.50 for 10 hours. The strike closed most of the Leadville mines.

What happened then would be repeated many more times throughout the western mountains during the next decades. Management and local merchants, who depended on the mines for their income, organized into an armed alliance to frighten the miners into submission. The miners retaliated in kind, arming themselves and holding public drills. For three weeks Leadville teetered on the brink of chaos, and finally the state militia was called in to prevent violence. In the end the miners, who had no strike fund, were forced back to work at the old rate of pay.

The Making of a Radical Labor Leader

The militant career of William D. Haywood (1869-1928) was marked by trials for murder and sedition and by exile to the Soviet Union. Born in Salt Lake City, Haywood went to work in the Nevada mines at 15 and in 1896 became a charter member of the Silver City, Idaho, local of the Western Federation of Miners (WFM). Tall, powerfully built, and a forceful speaker, he was made secretary-treasurer of the WFM in 1900 and before long dominated its leadership.

After the WFM local at Cripple Creek, Colorado, was destroyed during the 1903-04 strike, Haywood became an advocate of class warfare and in 1905 helped organize the radical Industrial Workers of the World, with which the WFM was affiliated. The next year Haywood, Charles Moyer (the WFM's president), and George Pettibone were seized without a warrant in Colorado, spirited to Idaho, and indicted for the murder of Frank

William D. ("Big Bill") Haywood

Steunenberg. (As governor of Idaho, Steunenberg had dealt harshly with WFM members during a bloody strike in the Coeur d'Alene district in 1899.) Defended by Clarence Darrow, Haywood was acquitted in 1907 but broke with the WFM leaders. In 1918 he was convicted of sedition for impeding the U.S. war effort and in 1921, while awaiting a new trial, fled to the Soviet Union. Haywood died there in 1928.

During the 1899 strike against the Bunker Hill and Sullivan Company in the Coeur d'Alene area, miners drove off strikebreakers and blew up a company plant at Wardner.

The failure of the Leadville strike brought only temporary peace to the mines, however. Embittered workers all over the West now began to lend willing ears to radical labor leaders like "Big Bill" Haywood and others of the Western Federation of Miners, which had been founded in 1893.

The miners of the federation, forced to the wall by falling wages and rising prices, formed their own rifle corps to challenge the vigilante committees being established by the mining companies. With armed and desperate men on both sides, strikes often developed into bloody confrontations—as at Leadville, Cripple Creek, and Coeur d'Alene—

complete with bombings, murder, and arson on both sides. Inevitably the state militia was called in—usually as a de facto ally of the mineowners—and only rarely did a strike end with long-term gains for the miners. During the Cripple Creek, Colorado, strike of 1903-04, after one bomb killed 13 nonunion men, the militiamen rounded up hundreds of workers, imprisoned them, and then sent them out of the state. By July of 1904 the western federation local at Cripple Creek was utterly broken. The bitterness engendered by the strike and its suppression had opened a chasm between labor and management in the West that would take decades to bridge.

357

Logging in the Old Northwest

The story of western logging in America roughly parallels the story of the mining and farming frontiers. The lumber industry was, of course, born on the East Coast soon after the arrival of the first English settlers, who cut down the forests primarily to clear the land, secure materials for housing, and—in that era of wooden ships—provide timber to build the motherland's navy. When the frontier moved west, so too did lumbering activities. Water-powered sawmills were established beside the rivers of the Old Northwest and the South to produce wood for erecting towns and cities.

Only gradually did lumbering take on the aspect of a major commercial enterprise, but when it did, the devastation it wrought upon the land was awesome. For it was almost an article of faith that the land was inexhaustible; and lumbermen had no scruples about despoiling one forest after another or transforming scores of villages into towns and towns into cities, only to leave them prostrate once the timber reserves gave out.

What the lumber companies did not cut down and saw up into planks and shingles they left behind them, turning great forests into slums of nature, leaving branches, slashings, and piles of sawdust strewn all around as fodder for a bolt of

Logs were hauled from the forest to a river, and drivers moved them downstream to sawmills. Here the logs have piled into a jam, and a driver, risking his life, breaks it up.

lightning or an errant spark, causing fires that spread to timber that was still standing. By 1875 the Department of Agriculture reported that the eastern lumber companies alone were responsible for blazes that consumed 25 million acres annually.

Squatters on the Public Domain

In their gluttony the lumbermen were greatly aided by the numerous state governments that were willing to sell off public lands for as little as 10 cents an acre. In some areas, where population was sparse and the law had little force, the lumber companies merely squatted on the public domain until they had completed their work, then moved on. Loopholes in the Homestead Act and other land legislation permitted the companies to garner millions of acres intended by law for farmers.

By the post-Civil War years the lumber boom had moved into the pine forests of Michigan and Wisconsin, creating in the Old Northwest a riproaring masculine society that was easily as tough as those of the mining and ranching worlds farther west. Each winter more than 100,000 brawny lumberjacks, who were paid the standard rate of a dollar a day, moved into the Great Lakes forests to decimate the vast pine stands. Every spring the mountains of logs that

had been piled up at the riverbanks were floated downstream to the mills of Oshkosh, Hurley, Muskegon, Saginaw, and Peshtigo.

The lumberjacks themselves, after a hard, cold season of logging, followed their produce into town to live it up. The little town of Escanaba in Michigan boasted 102 bars on just one street; and there, when the jacks were in, the tanglefoot whisky flowed like water, and evenings often ended with noisy fights among rival gangs of workers. Many towns offered other diversions as well. Seney, Michigan, for example, had a brothel patrolled by fierce guard dogs trained to let customers in while preventing the girls from going out.

Sawdust Everywhere

The lumber towns, built of wood as they were, and the forests surrounding them were constantly threatened by fire. If a blaze did not start in the woodlands and spread to the towns, then it started in the towns and spread to the woodlands. Sawdust was everywhere, covering the streets and barroom floors, rising in mountainous heaps above the towns, and clogging the rivers so badly that the debris had to be burned deliberately so that the water could flow freely again. Once fires began during the hot, dry summers, they became uncontrollable. Alpena,

In 1871, the year of the Chicago Fire, a forest fire leveled Peshtigo, Wisconsin, and burned out some 1,250,000 acres of timber.

Minnesota lumberjacks relax after supper in their camp, often a 40-foot log building with no frills—just bunks, rough tables, benches, and chairs.

Each evening the choppers had to sharpen their axes, double-bitted to provide twice the cutting edge of a single bit.

Michigan, was the site of five major blazes in a decade. And in the searing fall of 1871 more than 1,000 people—four times as many as died in the Great Chicago Fire of the same year—were killed in a conflagration that devastated the area around Peshtigo, in Wisconsin.

But danger or not, employment opportunities brought hundreds of thousands to the Great Lakes forests and the sawmill towns. The high point came in 1889, when almost 10 billion board feet of lumber were cut from the woodlands of the Old Northwest. The mills in the town of Muskegon alone produced 665 million board feet and 520 million shingles in a single year. But by the turn of the century the lumber business in the Great Lakes country had gone rapidly downhill. The forests, overcut and badly ravaged by fires, no longer promised an easy profit. The Pacific Slope, with its limitless virgin forests, became the lumbermen's new lodestar. It remained only to pronounce the epitaph for the woodlands of the Old Northwest, a duty performed by one of Muskegon's dwindling population. "The finest white pine and hardwood forest," he wrote, "is now a man-made desert of fire-blasted stumps and slashings. The Muskegon River, once choked with timber as far as the eye could see, is empty. . . . There are rotting piles and moss-covered wharves where once echoed the busy refrain of forty-seven giant sawmills."

A Minnesota logging camp is depicted by painter Andrew Stenstrom. A horse-drawn water tank (foreground) ices the road to aid in sledding logs to a river.

An Evening in Camp

Thirty fine-looking, healthy, robust, well-behaved men . . . when their appetites were sated, broke up the evening in various ways. Some mended their clothes, some darned their socks, some, using the sinews of the deer, obtained of the Indians for thread, repaired their moccasins, while others employed their time in reading. The hours were relieved, too, by a little entertainment in the shape of music and dancing. . . . Of course a camp full of woodsmen could hardly be expected to pass a whole evening . . . around the big stove, without more or less indulgence in tobacco. A large number puffed away at their meerschaums, or their short, black, clay pipes. . . . No stimulants stronger than tobacco and tea were allowed in the pineries. . . . At ten o'clock the signal for retiring was given. A half hour later most of the logmen were snoring—perhaps dreaming of friends "down the river." At half past five in the morning the alarm-clock put an end to snoring and dreaming, and called the men from their beds again.

—"The Minnesota Pineries"
Harper's New Monthly Magazine, March 1868

The Pacific Coast Lumber Boom

After undercutting a huge fir with double-bitted axes, a felling crew rests before starting a cut on the back side, where a two-man saw—appropriately called the misery whip—is used.

The warning cry is "Timber-r-r!" as a towering tree falls in this forest in California.

Even as the Great Lakes forests were being denuded, lumbermen began the commercial exploitation of the majestic woodlands of the western Rockies, the Sierra Nevada, the Cascades, and the Pacific Coast. As early as 1905 a year's lumbering yields in the Far West exceeded those of the Great Lakes by 52 million board feet; by 1920 the Pacific Slope was producing four times as much as the Old Northwest. Indeed, the Far West was a lumberman's paradise, with millions of acres of inviting skyward-reaching Douglas firs, ponderosa pines, and giant redwoods and sequoias.

Actually, timber had long been a profitable West Coast industry, providing the basic building materials first for the fur traders' forts and then for the farmhouses and towns of settlers. In 1788 a Yankee merchantman had attempted to open an export market in Asia for West Coast lumber, and after the gold rushes in California and Nevada had begun, local lumber interests were hard pressed to meet the demand for their product. But large-scale exploitation of the western forests did not begin until the turn of the century, with the completion of a rail transport network into the Pacific Northwest, which made the cutting of the region's timber both feasible and profitable.

The far western lumber boom started in 1900, when railroad magnate James J. Hill, in one of history's great real-estate deals, sold off 900,000 acres of timberland to the Weyerhaeuser Company for $540 million. This purchase touched off the usual fever among speculators; one large parcel of Idaho woodland, for example, vaulted in value from $240,000 to $2.5 million in eight years.

On a skid road of half-buried logs that slopes gently downhill, some oxen haul chained trunks. So that none will tear the skids and all will slide easily, each trunk has been smoothed, bottom and front end, by ax-wielding hook tenders, and a greaser follows the oxen, daubing fish oil, old butter, or bear grease on the skids. The oxen are prodded by the nail-tipped goad of the bullwhacker, who is paid $100 per month, more than any logger. Bars sprang up beside a skid road in Seattle—hence the expression "skid row."

The Vanzer family at their Washington "stump ranch" posed for Darius Kinsey, who specialized in logging photography. Vanzer, a logger, spent his Sundays creating a farm in the middle of a forest. The outhouse (far left) is a hole formed by upraised tree roots.

For a time it seemed that the proud forests of the Far West would meet the same fate as those to the east. Hundreds of thousands of lumberjacks and millhands poured into the woodland regions, and newly erected sawmills dumped millions of pounds of sawdust along the banks of major river systems such as the Columbia and the Sacramento. Trails were slashed into the deepest forests to facilitate the movement of logs. In remote mountain areas rickety flumes were built to channel logs and semifinished planks down to fabricating plants, where the new technology of making plywood was already changing the American construction industry.

Flumes were also used to transport lumberjacks from their camps high in the mountains to the roaring towns located down at the rivers' edges. "We'd save some good timbers to ride on," recalled one lumberjack, "and Saturday night ease them into the trough and get aboard with . . . a balance pole. . . . You had to have a good sense of balance. . . . Your timber [could] take off."

As in the Great Lakes region, forest fires were a constant menace. One series of fires in the fall of 1902 swept through 700,000 acres, while eight years later some 3 million acres were blackened in a raging blaze that began in May and lasted into September. But by this time

there was a loud, persistent outcry from conservationists. The country had arrived at the limits of runaway exploitation, and even the profit-minded lumber industry had begun to acknowledge the fact that there were no longer great quantities of land to waste. New government regulations on woodland safety and forest management came into effect, and the great lumber companies began establishing tree farms to replace the timber they had cut. The nation was at last coming to the realization that the old devil-may-care attitudes of frontier days were no longer appropriate and that the land's resources must be carefully nurtured as well as exploited.

Lumber Baron

The German-born Frederick Weyerhaeuser (1834–1914) came to America in 1852 and got into the lumber business in 1860 when he and his brother-in-law bought a sawmill in Rock Island, Illinois. In 1891 Weyerhaeuser, with extensive logging operations in Wisconsin and Minnesota, moved to St. Paul and met James J. Hill, president of the Great Northern Railway. Wanting new business for his railroad, Hill sought to develop industries in the Pacific Northwest, and Weyerhaeuser

Frederick Weyerhaeuser

became his ally. By the early 1900's Weyerhaeuser's timber company and other family firms dominated the giant lumber industry in Idaho, Oregon, and Washington.

Huge logs are headed for a Seattle sawmill while ships prepare to transport Pacific Northwest lumber to ports all over the world.

Felling Trees: A Challenge to Men and Machines

Trees of New England and the Midwest were dwarfed by the giant firs, pines, and cedars of the Pacific states, where a single 24-foot log could weigh 40 tons and provide lumber for three houses. To move these monsters, loggers had to develop new tools (like extra-long axes and falling saws, the springboard and steam donkey) and use them with great skill. Everyone admired expert fallers (below right) and the donkey puncher (right), whose constant oiling and bolt-tightening kept his machine hauling log after log through the woods. Men without expertise worked as choker setters or log snipes, earning $2.50 a day for these backbreaking and dangerous jobs. In 1900 the logger's day began at 6:00 a.m. when he left his bunkhouse (a flea-infested shanty near the logging site). By 7:00 he had devoured piles of hotcakes, steak, and eggs and was tramping into the woods for a day of grueling work that could easily end in death.

Chutes and Flumes and Shay's Big Idea

A peavey, with its spike and hinged hook, to move logs

Logs come crashing down a chute to a loading platform that is higher than—and tilts down to—the railroad track so logs can be rolled onto the flatcars.

Elevated flumes, fed by reservoirs, move logs and rough boards (cut by a small portable saw in the woods) down to the sawmills. Flumes must be tended to make sure the wood does not jam up and spill out. Occasionally, a daredevil logger risks his life riding the flume boat into town.

Ephraim Shay's locomotive, using gears instead of driving rods to transmit power to its eight driving wheels, can climb grades and haul weights that would stall a conventional train. Hundreds of miles of track have been laid for these engines—introduced in 1880 by Shay, a logger in the Great Lakes area—making it possible to move large quantities of timber without dependence on rivers.

The bucker cuts a felled tree into logs (16, 24, 32, or 40 feet long) measured by his 8-foot rod. He stays alert, for the log, when cut, may shift and crush him.

Loggers remind one another to watch out for the dangerous "bite of the line" when the cable snaps taut as the donkey reels it in.

The development of the steel cable meant logs could be dragged far and jerked free of hindrances. Rope, used earlier, broke under strain.

If it is raining at 6 a.m., loggers do not work and are not paid for the day, though they still have to pay $5 a week for board. But once a day's work has begun, they keep at it even if it rains or snows.

The log snipe has beveled ("sniped") the log's front end so it will not dig into the ground.

Falling ax (left) has extra-long handle and head.

A choker setter (above) has dug a hole with his hands so he can slip the choker under the log. Now he hooks up the chain and will call for the signal to "go ahead on the main line" (reel in the cable).

Many loggers began their careers as whistle punks like the young boy above. He holds a rope that runs to the donkey engine's steam whistle and by yanking on it—one sharp yank to go ahead, two to come back, and one to stop—he can signal the donkey puncher when to start reeling in the cable. His mind may wander as he stands giving signals for five long hours between meal breaks, but one false yank would start the cable reeling in and the log lurching forward, possibly killing someone.

Donkey puncher

The steam donkey (a steam engine geared to a winchlike drum and mounted on a log sled) hisses steam, throws off cinders, and shivers and shakes when it is hauling in a huge timber. While the cable is slack the choker setter hooks it up to another log.

Patented by John Dolbeer in 1882, the steam donkey makes it possible to move timber almost anywhere. With its cable attached to a tree, it has pulled itself into place, where it is anchored by chains to other trees. Horses pull the cable out to the logs.

A nimble "river pig" maneuvers a flotilla of logs on a river drive in Washington. The logs were floated downstream to sawmills.

The cook and his helpers have a meal ready for the loggers. Plenty of food is required for men who work six days a week, 11 hours a day.

Logs nearest the steam donkey are cleared out first to make room for more distant ones.

The undercut determines the direction the tree will fall. First the fallers saw into the tree, creating the base of the undercut. Then with their axes they chop away at a 45-degree angle. An expert faller may brag that he can plant a stake in the ground and make his tree land right on it. But if wind catches the tree, it can fall anywhere.

Bottle of saw lubricant (kerosene) next to double-bitted ax

Undercut

A wooden mallet with a hardwood head pounds steel and wooden wedges.

Fallers on springboards are driving in wedges to keep the weight of the tree from binding the crosscut saw with which they make the back cut. When the back cut has almost reached the undercut, they will remove the saw's handle, pull it out of the tree, and hammer in more wedges to make the tree start to fall. If the cut end of a falling tree catches one of them, its force would probably break the faller's back; so the moment a tree starts to topple, the men will leap off their springboards and away from the tree.

Springboards permit fallers to cut above the tree's swollen bole, where pitch collects and causes the saw to stick. Also, the wood in the bole is likely to be knotty or ruined by the spread of root rot.

The crosscut saw above (invented in the 1880's) has special teeth that let it cut horizontally across the tree.

Boots with calks (pointed studs) dig into the 5-foot by 8-inch springboard. The board has a pointed metal tip that curves up and bites into the top of the notch the faller has cut in the tree.

H. Pertchik

Land of Plenty

Simon Benson, a turn-of-the-century Columbia River lumberman, did not let distance stop him when it came to marketing his timber. In the small community of San Diego, many hundreds of miles from his forest domains, Benson built a sawmill, anticipating a growing market for building materials. To transport his logs from the Columbia country to the sawmill, he designed mammoth oceangoing rafts, some of them 1,000 feet long and capable of hauling 6 million board feet of timber per trip.

In his enthusiasm for the economic potential of the West Coast, Benson was hardly alone. The three states of the Pacific tier were among the fastest growing in the nation. Between 1870 and 1900 California's population almost tripled to 1.5 million; and Washington's rose by more than 1,000 percent to 518,000, while Oregon's population more than quadrupled to 413,000.

Mining and the industries it helped spawn, including lumbering, accounted for part of the increase. Southern California's balmy climate also played a major role. By 1900 about 10 percent of those living in that region had gone there hoping that the year-round sunshine would improve their health. But, above all, it was the lure of the land that brought swarms of settlers streaming to the Far West. In 1893 the last of the five great transcontinental rail lines reached the coast. From Seattle in the north to Los Angeles in the south, a vast agricultural paradise was linked to a continental market.

At first, wheat, which flourished in

Orange pickers and growers display the bounty of a California grove. The boom began in the 1880's after the sour California orange was replaced by the sweet navel variety.

California's flat interior valleys, was the primary crop. By 1890, 2.75 million acres of the state's land were under wheat cultivation, and some 40 million bushels were produced that year. Soon fruits and garden vegetables supplemented wheat, thanks to the completion of great irrigation systems and the development of refrigerator cars in the 1880's. And in the northern part of the state, in the Sacramento, Napa, and Sonoma Valleys, the wine industry was burgeoning as vintners from Europe began experimenting with a variety of grapes. By 1900 more than 80 percent of U.S. wine was of California origin.

All this growth represented enormous profits for the railroads, which vied with one another to attract farmers to their own areas of the Pacific coast. In their eagerness to bring in settlers and the freight business that would be generated, they offered special reduced fares. In 1887, 100,000 people swarmed

into southern California after a rate war between the Southern Pacific and the Santa Fe had lowered the Kansas City–Los Angeles fare to a mere $1.

Los Angeles, the terminus of the two lines, swelled most quickly. Between 1881 and 1887 its population rose from 11,183 to more than 60,000, touching off one of the wildest bouts of speculation in U.S. history. The prices of city lots zoomed from $500 to $5,000 in less than a year, while the wealthy who sought a building lot overlooking the Pacific found that they would have to shell out about $50,000 for the privilege. A local financial panic in the late 1880's, fol-

Banking Innovator

In 1902 the death of his father-in-law brought Amadeo Peter Giannini, 32, out of early retirement from a family produce firm to take the older man's post as director of a bank in North Beach, the Italian quarter of San Francisco. When the institution refused to make more loans to workers and small businessmen, Giannini and a group of friends opened the Bank of Italy across the street in 1904. He shocked staid financiers by advertising vigorously for bank customers and encouraging small loans, some for as little as $25. After the San Francisco earthquake of 1906 the Bank of Italy won much good will by opening for business days ahead of

other banks. In 1909 Giannini went into branch banking, and his institution grew with booming California. Long before his death in 1949 the Bank of America, successor to the Bank of Italy, had about 500 branches throughout the state of California and was the largest commercial bank in the world.

Tugs tow one of Simon Benson's log rafts down the Columbia River on the first leg of its journey south to San Diego, California. The logs are secured by 175 tons of chains.

lowed by a national depression in 1893, cooled things down temporarily. But soon the discovery of oil near the city, followed by plans for a deepwater port and finally by the arrival of the nascent film industry, combined to get the city moving once again.

"The City"

If Los Angeles led the way in size and growth rate, it was its rival to the north, San Francisco, that acquired the reputation of being the most charming, vital, and sophisticated city in the West—if not in the nation. To its devotees, who were legion, San Francisco was simply "the city," and they were sure that nowhere else could one find such cosmopolitanism, so dramatic a setting, or so elegant an ambience. Here, at the turn of the century, wealthy bohemians such as writers Jack London and Frank Norris rubbed shoulders with bankers and merchants in the rococo splendor of the Palace Hotel's dining room or in the equally elegant Occidental.

With a population of 342,000 in 1900 San Francisco was the West Coast's premier city in every respect. Even the devastating earthquake of 1906 could not keep it down for long. Smug in its own self-regard, the city merely shrugged off more raucous rivals like Los Angeles in the south and Seattle in the north.

Urban contrasts: cosmopolitan San Francisco, typified by the elegant Palace Hotel, and a busy street in Los Angeles, raw and brawling but the growing rival of the Bay City.

As recently as 1880, Seattle had been a mere village of 3,500, but with the completion of a spur of the Union Pacific from Tacoma it began a great surge of growth. By 1890 the town was an important marketing and shipping center with a population of 42,000. The coming of the Northern Pacific and Great Northern Railroads, and the Yukon and Alaska gold rushes that began in the late 1890's, further enhanced Seattle's importance. Alaskan gold and the search for it generated a host of new industries and brought into the coffers of merchants, hotelkeepers, restaurateurs, and saloon owners a goodly share of the wealth pried from the north country's unyielding soil. By the beginning of the new century the Pacific Northwest had come into its own.

A Frenchman's condescending view of California's wine industry in 1878 shows Chinese workers pressing grapes with their bare feet.

The Edge Hill Vineyard produced 80,000 gallons of wine in 1877.

Wine Comes to California

California's sunshine and moderate rainfall made it a potentially superb vineyard. First to perceive this were the Spanish padres, who in 1770 introduced European cuttings to Mission San Gabriel, but the wine produced was heavy and bitter. Other southern California vintages of the early 1800's were often fortified with brandy because, being of low acidity, they tended to spoil in the warm climate. Then, in 1849, an unusual foreigner arrived, seeking not gold but a mild climate. He was Agoston Haraszthy de Mokcsa, formerly a member of the Royal Hungarian Body Guard and secretary to the viceroy of Hungary, who had immigrated to Wisconsin in 1840 and was one of the founders of what today is Sauk City. There he established a brickyard, operated a ferryboat, and planted Wisconsin's first hopyard.

But the cold was hard on his asthma; so he went to San Diego, where he fought Indians and was elected county sheriff and a member of the state legislature. Surmising that the inland Sonoma Valley would be ideal for European vines, he imported Hungarian and Persian cuttings and in 1858, near Buena Vista, planted the first large vineyard in California. A few years later a German immigrant, Charles Krug, pioneered viticulture in the Napa Valley. In the 1870's a species of plant louse devastated the industry, but resistant strains were developed, and before long California took its place as the No. 1 wine producer in the nation.

Black Gold

To the few hundred citizens of Titusville, a hamlet in the hills of western Pennsylvania, the thick, black, viscous substance that bubbled up from the earth, befouling their water and their croplands, was a monstrous curse of nature. If anyone in the mid-1850's had told them that the black stuff was potentially valuable—that in decades to come men would cheat and lie and beggar their families in a mad scramble to get it—they would have dismissed him as a madman. Nor could they have imagined that in California, Texas, Louisiana, and Oklahoma ordinary farm and grazing land would one day become enormously valuable, all because that same black liquid would be found in immense quantities beneath its soil. At best, the Pennsylvanians thought that this Seneca oil, as they called it, might have some medicinal properties; for the Seneca Indians, who had once inhabited the region, had imbibed it as a cure-all.

Outside of Titusville, however, there were a few men who thought that Seneca oil might be put to good use. As early as 1849 a Pittsburgh druggist made a fairly satisfactory lamp fuel by distilling the crude oil, and in the mid-1850's a well-known professor from Yale, chemist Benjamin Silliman, Jr., concluded that Seneca oil, properly refined, might serve as a substitute for the increasingly expensive whale oil then used for lighting. Spurred by Silliman's findings, a consortium of financiers dispatched a former railroad conductor, one Edwin L. Drake, to Titusville in May 1858 to secure mineral rights and supervise the drilling of wells. More than a year passed before Drake brought in his first well, but when he did so on August 27, 1859, his success set off a stampede into Titusville and the surrounding countryside. The little village was soon transformed into a raucous, hard-drinking boomtown—known to some wags as "Sodden Gomorrah"—in which properties that had sold for around $100 were suddenly worth a thousand times that amount. A new mineral rush was on, and the American petroleum industry, which would one day alter the very nature of the world's way of life, had been born.

Kerosene To Light the Lamps

For decades Pennsylvania oil, refined into kerosene, was America's primary means of illuminating houses and shops. For those with secure drilling rights in the oil-rich regions—and those who controlled refineries and the shipping of oil, like the young John D. Rockefeller—the new industry was a gold mine. Yet toward the end of the 19th century the demand for kerosene, tar, and lubricating oil—so far the only products made from crude oil—began to decline. Overproduction, gas lighting, and later electricity threatened the industry with ruin. No one knew that gasoline—that unwanted product of the refining process—had any potential value. It remained for a peripatetic miner from Wisconsin, Edward L. Doheny, to point the way.

Doheny was a promoter, a plunger always on the lookout for the main chance. In 1893 he hit it rich when he and a partner discovered a great pool of

The great Spindletop gusher blew out more than 80,000 barrels of oil each day for 10 whole days before the drillers could cap it.

oil below what is now downtown Los Angeles. It had long been supposed that crude oil might make an excellent fuel for driving engines, but few thought the supplies available would be sufficient. Doheny's discovery changed all that. The resulting oil boom created a surplus in California, and Doheny persuaded some railroad officials to try oil in place of coal for running their locomotives. By the late 1890's the great Santa Fe railroad had found oil so inexpensive, convenient, and efficient that it had switched over to the new fuel. Soon other railroads—and freighters and ocean liners as well—were using crude oil. America's oil boom was now on in earnest; it remained only for the general acceptance of the gasoline-driven automobile and the discovery of new oil-rich regions to turn what was already a major industry into an industrial behemoth.

The development in Europe of the gasoline-powered internal-combustion engine gave new impetus to oil exploration in the United States. By 1910 there were more than 450,000 "gas buggies" snorting along the nation's city streets and muddy rural byways. Advancing technology and the inventiveness, drive, and ambition of men like Ransom Olds, who produced his first Oldsmobile in

This is one of the first rotary rigs on Spindletop. Rotating drill bits cut through rock with greater speed and efficiency than rock-pounding drills.

To obtain financial backing for drilling at Spindletop, Austrian-born Anthony F. Lucas had to give up most of his claim in the venture, so his financial reward was small.

The lack of both real-estate and production controls allowed derricks with wood-powered rigs to proliferate on Spindletop (shown here in 1903), like too many straws in the same glass. In one year the first well's output equaled that of 37,000 wells located in the East.

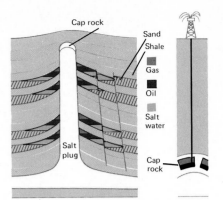

Oil From a Salt Plug

Lucas drilled atop a mile-wide 15-foot-high mound, created by an upthrusting column of salt (top left). Lighter than the overlying rock layers, the salt rose upward, making fault lines in the surrounding rock. The salt pushed through the oil shale, squeezing out petroleum and gas that collected around the plug and fault lines. Lucas hit the oil-rich cap rock (right). The salt—and oil-forming marine organisms—probably were deposited by ancient seas that once lapped over the Gulf Coast.

1899, and Henry Ford, the first to mass-produce an inexpensive car on an assembly line, helped produce millions more. But even their efforts would have been fruitless had not immense quantities of petroleum been discovered beneath the soil of Texas.

In 1901, just at the dawn of the automobile age, Texas brought in its first real gusher in a field known as Spindletop, four miles from the windswept Gulf Coast town of Beaumont. The people of Beaumont had long known that there were natural-gas deposits in the region, but only one man—he was a local real-estate dealer, Sunday-school teacher, and self-taught geologist named Patillo Higgins—was convinced that where there was natural gas there must also be oil. With every penny he could scrape up Higgins began buying land and mineral rights in the 1890's. Some $30,000 later—without having struck oil—Higgins was broke, but before he bowed out of the picture he persuaded a professional mining engineer, Anthony F. Lucas, to take over the search.

After securing backing from two Pennsylvania financiers and hiring three experienced rigmen, Lucas began drilling at Spindletop in the fall of 1900. The men built an 84-foot-high derrick and then started the long, arduous, dangerous task of boring into the earth, working around the clock through the last months of 1900. Then on January 10, 1901, as the drill pierced the earth 1,160 feet down, there was a sudden eruption of mud and rock and a hissing roar of gas. After a short silence a bubbling, heaving sound like the breath of a monster was heard below the surface. Finally, a slick of black liquid broke free, followed by a roar as a jet of oil shot out of the earth and spewed high above the derrick's top. The workers fled as the black gold spread on the ground in an ever-widening pool. By the time Lucas was fetched from Beaumont, the earth around the derrick was covered with oil to a distance of 150 feet, and still the petroleum gushed skyward at the rate of more than 3,300 barrels an hour.

Only days later were Lucas' men able to cap this first of a series of Texas gushers, and by then many thousands of gallons of oil had been wasted. But there was plenty to waste; oilmen from all over were streaming into Spindletop, and by the following year the area's production exceeded the rest of the world's.

Soon the oil bonanza would spread throughout east Texas, fueling America's technological revolution and giving

The "black gold" rush to Spindletop in 1901 swamped the quiet Texas town of Beaumont with 50,000 people—promoters, land speculators, engineers, and drillers.

birth to a generation of free-spending and wildcatting Texas oil millionaires. Whether these hard-driving speculators and prospectors were the last remaining frontiersmen or the heralds of a new age could be a matter of debate. They were, however, living links between the 19th-century bonanza West and the 20th-century West of corporate finance and development.

John Muir: Guardian of the Forests

Born in Scotland in 1838, John Muir came to America in 1849 with his father and a brother and sister to establish a farm in the Wisconsin wilderness. Shortly thereafter his mother brought over the rest of the family—four girls and two boys. John's sketchy formal education had ended when he left Scotland, but he read every book he could put his hands on. His father, a stern taskmaster, kept him busy at farm chores and would not allow him to read in the evenings. So John built a wooden clock and rigged up an "early-rising machine" that tilted his bed and got him out of the blankets and to his books. This regime enabled him to enroll at the University of Wisconsin when he was 22.

Muir left the university in 1863 and spent many months wandering through Wisconsin, Iowa, Illinois, Indiana, and Canada studying plants. After working for a time in a wagon factory in Indianapolis, where an accident that injured an eye persuaded him to "bid adieu to mechanical inventions" and take up the study of nature, he traveled on foot from Indiana to the Gulf of Mexico, keeping a daily journal of observations on plants and supporting himself by taking odd jobs. In 1868 he went to California and spent six years exploring the Yosemite Valley, then wandered on to Nevada, Utah, Oregon, Washington, and Alaska, again keeping a journal illustrated with numerous pencil sketches. In 1888 he married Louie Wanda Strentzel, the daughter of Dr. John Strentzel, who had settled in California's Alhambra Valley in 1849 and developed a prosperous fruit ranch. Muir rented and later bought part of Strentzel's ranch and set out to become an expert horticulturist. By 1891 he had made enough money to permit him to spend the rest of his life studying nature and writing. Soon he was to become a one-man indignation committee inveighing against the prodigal waste of America's forests.

In 1889 Muir had taken Robert Underwood Johnson, one of the editors of *Century Magazine,* to the Yosemite Valley and shown him the ruin brought to forested uplands by thousands of sheep ("hoofed locusts," Muir called them), which stripped the land bare of grass, causing spring floods and summer droughts in the valleys. The two men then launched a campaign that prodded Congress into establishing the Yosemite and the Sequoia National Parks in 1890. Muir's magazine articles also inspired Secretary of the Interior John W. Noble to press successfully for the passage by Congress in 1891 of the Forest Reserve Act, which empowered the president to set aside timberlands. Under this authority President Benjamin Harrison rescued some 13 million acres. Finally, in 1896, President Grover Cleveland appointed a forestry commission—as proposed 10 years before by Muir—to study wasteful lumbering practices. When the commission reported its findings in 1897, Cleveland created 13 forest reserves to protect more than 21 million acres of timber. But the ranchers, sheepmen, and lumber companies succeeded in removing most of the land from these reserves.

Muir Declares War—And Wins

The mild-mannered Muir now declared war on those who would give no thought to the needs of future generations. The battle, said Muir, was one "between landscape righteousness and the devil." His articles in *Harper's Weekly* and *Atlantic Monthly* aroused the public. In 1898, when foes of the forest reservation policy moved to end it, Muir's views prevailed.

In 1903 Muir, then the recognized leader of the drive to save America's forests and scenic wilderness areas, went on a camping trip with President Theodore Roosevelt. The president listened sympathetically to Muir and went to work. Acting under the 1891 law, Roosevelt set aside more than 100 million acres of unsold government timberland as a national

John Muir returned to his beloved Yosemite Valley in 1908 to gaze pensively at cliffs he had nimbly climbed when he was a young man.

California's stately redwoods inspired the landscape artist Albert Bierstadt to paint this splendid picture.

While Muir was campaigning hard to have the seven-square-mile valley of Yosemite declared a national park, this painting by Thomas Hill helped stir public interest in the spectacular area. Shortly before his death, Muir was saddened by the losing battle to keep Yosemite's Hetch Hetchy Valley from being converted into a reservoir. Despite the efforts of Muir and conservationists all over the nation the Raker Bill was prodded through Congress with unseemly haste, and the Hetch Hetchy was flooded.

forest reserve. And despite the opposition of acid-tongued Speaker of the House Joseph G. Cannon, who once said the government should spend "not one cent for scenery," the president established five national parks. He also designated 16 historic areas as national monuments under the Antiquities Act of 1906. The Petrified Forest and the Grand Canyon, which were designated national monuments in 1906 and 1908, respectively, later became national parks.

As president of the Sierra Club, which he helped found in 1892, Muir continued to keep an ever-watchful eye over the nation's forests. He lavished much attention on the giant redwoods, the world's largest trees, which, because they did not shrink or rot and were easy to cut and shape, were used for a wide variety of products—caskets, cigarboxes, water pipes, shingles, furniture, pencils, and organ pipes. Muir rallied conservationists who, with a few public-spirited lumbermen, were able to save some of the redwood groves. Years of effort by conservationists finally led in 1968 to the establishment of Redwood National Park in California.

In the final period of his life (he died in 1914) Muir worked on his journals, and over the years generations of nature lovers have been inspired by these words: "The forests of America, however slighted by man, must have been a great delight to God, because they were the best He ever planted."

President Theodore Roosevelt, long a champion of the great outdoors, camped with Muir in the Yosemite Valley in 1903.

Sights, Scents, and Sounds

During his walks through the woods John Muir recorded his impressions: a sketch of juniper trees at the right and, below, lines from one of his journals.

The fragrance with which one is feasted in the woods is, like the music, derived from a thousand untraceable sources. In music there are not only birds, main wind-tones, the frogs, a flutter of leaves like the clapping of small hands, squirrels, waterfalls, and the rush and trill of rivers and small brooks, but the whole air vibrates with myriad voices blended that we cannot analyze. So also we breathe fragrant violets, the rosiny pine and spicy fir, the rich, invigorating aroma of plushy bogs in which a thousand herbs are soaked . . . a combination so marvelously poised we scarce notice it on account of its excellence.

—John Muir, *John of the Mountains*, 1938

Farewell the Frontier

By all accounts March 4, 1905, in Washington, D.C., was, as President Theodore Roosevelt characteristically put it, both "dee-lightful" and "bully!" The previous November the Harvard-educated former Dakota rancher, Rough Rider, governor of New York, and vice president of the United States had been overwhelmingly elected to his first full term as president. Now, on an unusually mild and sunny March day, he stood on a Pennsylvania Avenue reviewing stand to greet the thousands of his countrymen who filed by.

In keeping with Roosevelt's reputation as an outdoorsman, rancher, and conservationist, the inauguration parade had a strong western flavor. Phalanxes of cowboys whooped and hollered their way along Pennsylvania Avenue. The 7th Cavalry regiment, George Armstrong Custer's old outfit, passed in review with horses prancing and the regimental band playing. Also in the line of march—though perhaps somewhat less enthusiastic in their tribute—was a group of Indian chiefs, among them Quanah Parker, the old Comanche, and hatchet-faced Geronimo, at one time the Apache's pride and the white man's nightmare. Now he was an aged, toothless man, trotted out of captivity from time to time for ceremonial appearances—in this case, the inauguration of a new Great White Father.

For Teddy Roosevelt, his guests, and the American people who thronged the sidewalks of the capital, it was a day of good clean fun. But it was also a reprise, a prettied-up glimpse of the American past, a nostalgic summation of the frontier experience in which all Americans had, in one way or another, taken part.

The Meaning of It All

More than a decade before March 4, 1905, the nation had already begun to sense that something had changed in America. The great open spaces of the West, where a man had once been able to take his pick of free or at least inexpensive land, were rapidly shrinking. The ever-shifting, westward-moving frontier line suddenly had nowhere left to go. The Census Bureau, after the tally of 1890, put it quite bluntly, declaring in its bulletin that "the unsettled area has been so broken into by isolated bodies of settlement that there can hardly be said to be a frontier line."

What had it all meant, this century-long national adventure of subduing and settling a continental empire? For some the answer was clear enough. For the Indians it was a tale of defeat, destruction, and despair. But what of the rest of us? Was there a meaning and a message beyond what the eye could see in the spreading checkerboard of farms, the mushrooming cities, the endless ribbons

Frederick Jackson Turner, ardent proponent of the frontier's influence on American life, hikes in western woods in 1904.

of railroad track, and all the other appurtenances of westward expansion?

In 1893 Frederick Jackson Turner, a young historian from the University of Wisconsin, read an essay, "The Significance of the Frontier in American History," to a group of fellow academics in which he attempted to answer these questions. In a brief but brilliant exposition Turner clothed the frontier experience in a new dignity. The American, he said, was unique among the peoples of the earth, and that singularity had its genesis and its flowering in the existence of the frontier. "Up to our own day," Turner stated, "American history has been in a large degree the history of the

Following the sun in pursuit of their dream, this group of pioneers appears equal to the challenge posed by the journey west.

colonization of the Great West. The existence of an area of free land, its continuous recession, and the advance of American settlement westward explain American development."

According to the intellectual orthodoxy of Turner's time America was little more than a transplanted Europe, drawing its customs and its laws from the settlers' homelands. Americans might adapt the old ways to the new environment, but their roots remained firmly implanted in European soil. Turner's thesis cast all this into doubt. With trenchant logic he asserted that Americans had cast off not only the soil of Europe but also its character. As they conquered the frontier, the frontier in turn conquered them, forcing settlers to put aside old habits in order to adapt to their harsh environment. The frontier "strips off the garments of civilization and arrays [the settler] in the hunting shirt and moccasin. It puts him in the log cabin of the Cherokee and Iroquois and runs an Indian palisade around him. Before long he has gone to planting Indian corn and plowing with a sharp stick; he shouts the war cry and takes the scalp in orthodox Indian fashion. . . . Little by little he transforms the wilderness, but the outcome is not the old Europe, not simply the development of Germanic germs. . . . The fact is, that here is a new product that is American."

Nor was it only the immigrants from abroad who were shaped by the frontier. Easterners, still half-European in outlook, who went west were also transformed by the experience. Old habits of social organization, of deference to one's supposed superiors, of yielding without protest to the tax collector's exactions and to the bureaucrat's demands were quickly shed in an environment that required and prized self-sufficiency. Thus the frontier, according to Turner, made the American the world's first truly free man. Free not just because the Constitution gave him rights, but free because the earth he farmed and the life he led impelled him toward freedom. "The wilderness ever opened the gate of escape to the poor, the discontented and the oppressed," Turner observed. "If social conditions tended to crystallize in the East, beyond the Alleghenies there was freedom."

The Living Frontier

Many modern scholars discount at least part of Turner's thesis. For example, Turner held that the United States was spared the revolutionary upheavals that afflicted much of 19th-century Europe because the frontier acted as a safety valve, drawing off surplus agricultural and factory labor in hard times and offering the poor a way out of their poverty. To a degree this may have been true in the pre–Civil War era, when thousands of New Englanders and tideland Southerners moved west. But after the Civil War it was usually farmers and the sons of farmers, already living at the outer edge of settlement, who blazed the way farther west. Relatively few from the slums of New York, Boston, or Philadelphia made their way to the hinterlands, for the cost of transportation—to say nothing of the funds needed to establish a farm—was generally far beyond their means.

Yet the mere fact that the frontier existed seems to have exerted a tremendous psychological influence on the thinking of Americans, even those for whom the West was more a dream than a reality. This still remains true today. In a thousand ways, both subtle and obvious, the shadow of the frontier continues to cast its spell over America. It lives, of course, in the rodeos, the television dramas, and the movies, but it also exists in the loping walk of the Montana ranch hand, in the drawl of the Kansas farmer, and in the dress of nearly all Americans—as their addiction to blue jeans demonstrates. More important, perhaps, the frontier is reborn every time a citizen digs in his heels and sets himself up as a minority of one against the conventional wisdom of his time. If the American character is, as many believe, a compound of optimism, orneriness, generosity, and shrewdness, if it is informal and innovative, pragmatic and democratic, then it owes much to the fact that once there was a vast wilderness where men and women could go to dream great dreams and do marvelous deeds.

The fulfillment of one family's dream: three generations of Parmenters enjoy a fine dinner at their prosperous ranch near Denver in 1889.

Bibliography

The editors wish to acknowledge their indebtedness to the authors and editors of the following books and periodicals consulted for reference.

General

BILLINGTON, RAY ALLEN. *The Far Western Frontier*. Harper & Row, 1956.
———. *Westward Expansion*. Macmillan, 1974.
BRANCH, EDWARD DOUGLAS. *Westward: The Romance of the American Frontier*. Cooper Square, 1969.
DAVIDSON, MARSHALL B. *Life in America*. Houghton Mifflin, 1974.
DICK, EVERETT. *Tales of the Frontier: From Lewis and Clark to the Last Roundup*. University of Nebraska Press, 1964.
EWERS, JOHN C. *Artists of the Old West*. Doubleday, 1973.
FERRIS, ROBERT G. (ed.). *Prospector, Cowhand, and Sodbuster*. The National Survey of Historic Sites and Buildings, Vol. XI, U.S. National Park Service, 1967.
GABRIEL, RALPH H. (ed.). *Pageant of America*. Yale University Press, 1926.
GETLEIN, FRANK. *The Lure of the Great West*. Country Beautiful, 1973.
HAWGOOD, JOHN A. *America's Western Frontiers*. Knopf, 1967.
HINE, ROBERT V. *The American West*. Little Brown, 1973.
HOFSTADTER, RICHARD, WILLIAM MILLER, and DANIEL AARON. *The American Republic*. Prentice-Hall, 1970.
HORAN, JAMES D. *The Great American West*. Bonanza, 1959.
KIRSCH, ROBERT, and WILLIAM S. MURPHY. *West of the West*. E. P. Dutton, 1967.
LAVENDER, DAVID. *The American Heritage History of the Old West*. 1965.
McCRACKEN, HAROLD. *George Catlin and the Old Frontier*. Bonanza, 1959.
MONAGHAN, JAMES (ed.). *The Book of the American West*. Bonanza, 1963.
MORISON, SAMUEL ELIOT. *The Oxford History of the American People*. Oxford University Press, 1965.
The Old West Series. Time-Life Books, 1973–76.
PAXSON, FREDERIC L. *History of the American Frontier: 1763-1893*. Houghton Mifflin, 1924.
The Pioneer Spirit. American Heritage, 1959.
RIDGE, MARTIN, and RAY ALLEN BILLINGTON. *America's Frontier Story*. Holt, Rinehart & Winston, 1969.
RIEGEL, ROBERT E., and ROBERT G. ATHEARN. *America Moves West*. Holt, Rinehart & Winston, 1971.
RUTH, KENT. *Great Day in the West*. University of Oklahoma Press, 1963.
SPENCER, ROBERT F., and JESSE D. JENNINGS. *The Native Americans*. Harper & Row, 1965.
STECKMESSER, KENT L. *The Westward Movement: A Short History*. McGraw-Hill, 1969.
STILL, BAYRD. *The West: Contemporary Records of America's Expansion Across the Continent, 1607-1890*. Capricorn Books, 1961.
———. *Urban America: A History with Documents*. Little Brown, 1974.
WOESTEMEYER, INA FAYE, and J. MONTGOMERY GAMBRILL. *The Westward Movement*. Appleton-Century, 1939.

Prologue: The Coming of the Europeans

CRAVEN, WESLEY FRANK. *The Colonies in Transition, 1660-1713*. Harper & Row, 1968.
ECCLES, WILLIAM JOHN. *The Canadian Frontier, 1543-1760*. Holt, Rinehart & Winston, 1969.
LEACH, DOUGLAS EDWARD. *The Northern Colonial Frontier, 1607-1763*. Holt, Rinehart & Winston, 1966.
POMFRET, JOHN E. *Founding the American Colonies, 1583-1660*. Harper & Row, 1970.

1. The West Beckons

ABERNETHY, THOMAS PERKINS. *The Burr Conspiracy*. Peter Smith, 1968.
BAKELESS, JOHN. *Daniel Boone*. Stackpole, 1939.
CARUSO, JOHN ANTHONY. *The Appalachian Frontier*. Bobbs-Merrill, 1959.
CHINN, GEORGE M. *Kentucky: Settlement and Statehood*. Kentucky Historical Society, 1975.
COLES, HARRY L. *The War of 1812*. University of Chicago Press, 1965.
KEATS, JOHN. *Eminent Domain: The Louisiana Purchase and the Making of America*. Charterhouse, 1973.
KINCAID, ROBERT L. *The Wilderness Road*. Bobbs-Merrill, 1947.
LECKIE, ROBERT. *The Wars of America*. Harper & Row, 1968.
MAHON, JOHN K. *The War of 1812*. University Presses of Florida, 1972.
PECKHAM, HOWARD H. *Colonial Wars: 1680 to 1762*. University of Chicago Press, 1964.
PHILBRICK, FRANCIS S. *The Rise of the West, 1754-1830*. Harper & Row, 1965.
RAWLING, GERALD. *The Pathfinders*. Macmillan, 1964.
SLOANE, ERIC. *A Museum of Early American Tools*. Funk & Wagnalls, 1964.
TUNIS, EDWIN. *Colonial Craftsmen*. World Publishing, 1965.
VAN EVERY, DALE. *A Company of Heroes*. Morrow, 1962.

2. To the Mississippi and Beyond

ANDRIST, RALPH K. *Andrew Jackson: Soldier and Statesman*. American Heritage, 1963.
ANDRIST, RALPH K., and C. BRADFORD MITCHELL. *Steamboats on the Mississippi*. American Heritage, 1962.
BALDWIN, LELAND D. *The Keelboat Age on Western Waters*. University of Pittsburgh Press, 1941.
BANTA, RICHARD ELWELL. *The Ohio*. Holt, Rinehart & Winston, 1949.
BATES, ALAN L. *The Western Rivers Steamboat Cyclopoedium*. Hustle Press, 1968.
DRAGO, HARRY SINCLAIR. *Canal Days in America*. C. N. Potter, 1972.
FOREMAN, GRANT. *Indian Removal: The Emigration of the Five Civilized Tribes of Indians*. University of Oklahoma Press, 1972.
HOLBROOK, STEWART H. *The Yankee Exodus*. Macmillan, 1950.
HUNTER, LOUIS CLARE and B. J. *Steamboats on the Western Rivers*. Octagon, 1969.
JAMES, MARQUIS. *Andrew Jackson: The Border Captain*. Bobbs-Merrill, 1933.
———. *Andrew Jackson: Portrait of a President*. Bobbs-Merrill, 1937.
KANE, HARNETT T. *Gone Are the Days*. E. P. Dutton, 1960.
PETERSEN, WILLIAM JOHN. *Steamboating on the Upper Mississippi*. Iowa State Historical Society, 1937.
RECK, FRANKLIN M. *The Romance of American Transportation*. Crowell, 1962.
SAMUEL, RAY, et al. *Tales of the Mississippi*. Hastings House, 1955.
TIBBLES, THOMAS HENRY. *Buckskin and Blanket Days*. University of Nebraska Press, 1957.
WARD, JOHN W. *Andrew Jackson: Symbol for an Age*. Oxford University Press, 1962.
WESLAGER, C. A. *The Log Cabin in America*. Rutgers University Press, 1969.
WILSON, MITCHELL. *American Science and Invention: A Pictorial History*. Bonanza, 1954.

3. Of Mountain Men and Indians

DEVOTO, BERNARD. *Across the Wide Missouri*. Houghton Mifflin, 1947.
———. *The Year of Decision: 1846*. Little Brown, 1950.
———. *The Course of Empire*. Houghton Mifflin, 1952.
———(ed.). *The Journals of Lewis and Clark*. Houghton Mifflin, 1953.
GOETZMANN, WILLIAM H. *Exploration and Empire*. Knopf, 1966.
LAVENDER, DAVID. *Bent's Fort*. Doubleday, 1954.
MORGAN, DALE L. *Jedediah Smith and the Opening of the West*. University of Nebraska Press, 1964.
OGLESBY, RICHARD. *Manuel Lisa and the Opening of the Missouri Fur Trade*. University of Oklahoma Press, 1963.
RUSSELL, CARL P. *Firearms, Traps, and Tools of the Mountain Men*. Knopf, 1967.
THWAITES, REUBEN GOLD (ed.). *The Original Journals of Lewis and Clark*. Dodd, Mead, 1904.
WEEMS, JOHN EDWARD. *Dream of Empire*. Simon & Schuster, 1971.

4. Texas and the Great Southwest

BARKER, EUGENE C. *The Life of Stephen F. Austin*. Cokesbury Press, 1926.
BOLTON, HERBERT. *The Spanish Borderlands*. Yale University Press, 1921.
DAY, DONALD, and HARRY HERBERT ULLOM (eds.). *The Autobiography of Sam Houston*. University of Oklahoma Press, 1954.
DICKEY, ROLAND. *New Mexico Village Arts*. University of New Mexico Press, 1949.
FEHRENBACH, T. R. *Comanches*. Knopf, 1974.
FEWKES, DR. J. WALTER. *Tusayan Flute and Snake Ceremonies*. Annual Report of the U.S. Bureau of American Ethnology, 1900.
GARD, WAYNE. *Rawhide Texas*. University of Oklahoma Press, 1965.
GIBSON, CHARLES. *Spain in America*. Harper & Row, 1966.
HABIG, MARION A. *San Antonio's Mission San José*. The Naylor Co., 1968.
HOGAN, WILLIAM R. *The Texas Republic*. University of Oklahoma Press, 1946.
HOLLON, W. EUGENE. *The Southwest, Old and New*. Knopf, 1961.
JAMES, MARQUIS. *The Raven: A Biography of Sam Houston*. Berg, 1968.
KOWNSLAR, ALLAN O. *The Texans: Their Land and History*. American Heritage, 1972.
LORD, WALTER. *A Time to Stand*. Harper & Row, 1961.
RICHARDSON, RUPERT NORVAL. *Texas: The Lone Star State*. Prentice-Hall, 1970.
WELLMAN, PAUL I. *Glory, God and Gold*. Doubleday, 1954.

5. From Sea to Sea

BEAN, WALTON E. *California, An Interpretive History*. McGraw-Hill, 1973.
CONNOR, SEYMOUR V., and ODIE B. FAULK. *North America Divided: The Mexican War 1846-1848*. Oxford University Press, 1971.
DRIGGS, HOWARD R. *Westward America*. Putnam's, 1942.
DUFOUR, CHARLES L. *Ten Flags in the Wind*. Harper & Row, 1967.
DUNLOP, RICHARD. *Great Trails of the West*. Abingdon Press, 1971.
HINE, ROBERT V. *Bartlett's West*. Yale University Press, 1968.
JOHNSON, PAUL C. *Pictorial History of California*. Doubleday, 1970.
LAVENDER, DAVID. *Land of Giants*. Doubleday, 1958.
———. *Westward Vision: The Story of the Oregon Trail*. McGraw-Hill, 1963.
———. *Climax at Buena Vista*. Lippincott, 1966.

———. *California: Land of New Beginnings.* Harper & Row, 1972.

———. *The Rockies.* Harper & Row, 1975.

MacKAY, DOUGLAS. *The Honourable Company.* Bobbs-Merrill, 1936.

MERK, FREDERICK. *Manifest Destiny and Mission in American History: A Reinterpretation.* Knopf, 1963.

NEVINS, ALLAN. *Frémont: Pathmarker of the West.* Longmans, Green and Co., 1955.

PADEN, IRENE D. *The Wake of the Prairie Schooner.* Macmillan, 1943.

PARKMAN, FRANCIS. *The Oregon Trail.* Signet Classics (New American Library), 1950.

POMEROY, EARL. *The Pacific Slope: A History of California, Oregon, Washington, Idaho, Utah, and Nevada.* University of Washington Press, 1973.

ROLLE, ANDREW F. *California: A History.* Crowell, 1963.

SELLERS, CHARLES. *James K. Polk.* Princeton University Press, 1957.

WAGGONER, MADELINE SADLER. *The Long Haul West.* Putnam's, 1958.

WEEMS, JOHN EDWARD. *To Conquer a Peace: The War Between the United States and Mexico.* Doubleday, 1974.

WILLIAMS, ALBERT N. *Rocky Mountain Country.* Duell, Sloan and Pearce, 1950.

6. The Great Rush West

ARRINGTON, LEONARD J. *Great Basin Kingdom: Economic History of the Latter-day Saints, 1830-1900.* University of Nebraska Press, 1958.

BIRNEY, HOFFMAN. *Zealots of Zion.* Penn Publishing Co., 1931.

BROOKS, JUANITA. *The Mountain Meadows Massacre.* University of Oklahoma Press, 1962.

CHIDSEY, DONALD BARR. *The California Gold Rush.* Crown, 1968.

DE LORENZO, LOIS. *Gold Fever and the Art of Panning and Sluicing.* ATR Enterprises, 1970.

DRAGO, HARRY SINCLAIR. *Roads to Empire.* Dodd, Mead, 1968.

EGGENHOFER, NICK. *Wagons, Mules and Men.* Hastings House, 1961.

FATOUT, PAUL. *Mark Twain in Virginia City.* Indiana University Press, 1964.

MULDER, WILLIAM, and A. RUSSELL MORTENSEN (eds.). *Among the Mormons: Historic Accounts by Contemporary Observers.* University of Nebraska Press, 1973.

PAUL, RODMAN W. *Mining Frontiers of the Far West.* University of New Mexico Press, 1963.

———. *California Gold: The Beginning of Mining in the Far West.* University of Nebraska Press, 1965.

POINT, NICHOLAS. *Wilderness Kingdom.* Holt, Rinehart & Winston, 1967.

STEGNER, WALLACE. *The Gathering of Zion: Story of the Mormon Trail.* McGraw-Hill, 1964.

WAGNER, JACK R. *Gold Mines of California.* Howell-North Books, 1970.

WALKER, HENRY PICKERING. *The Wagonmasters.* University of Oklahoma Press, 1966.

WATKINS, T. H. *Gold and Silver in the West.* American West Publishing Co., 1971.

WEBB, TODD. *The Gold Rush Trail and the Road to Oregon.* Doubleday, 1963.

WINTHER, OSCAR. *The Transportation Frontier: Trans-Mississippi West, 1865-1890.* University of New Mexico Press, 1964.

YOUNG, OTIS E., JR. *Western Mining.* University of Oklahoma Press, 1970.

7. Wars in the West

AGAR, HERBERT. *Price of Union.* Houghton Mifflin, 1950.

BRANDON, WILLIAM B. *The Last Americans.* McGraw-Hill, 1974.

DEBO, ANGIE. *A History of the Indians of the United States.* University of Oklahoma Press, 1970.

FERRIS, ROBERT G. (ed.). *Soldier and Brave.* The National Survey of Historic Sites and Buildings, Vol. XII, U.S. Department of the Interior, 1971.

GOETZMANN, WILLIAM H. *Army Exploration in the American West, 1803-1863.* Yale University Press, 1959.

GRAHAM, WILLIAM ALEXANDER. *The Custer Myth.* Stackpole, 1953.

———. *The Story of Little Big Horn.* Bonanza, 1959.

GRINNELL, GEORGE B. *Fighting Cheyennes.* University of Oklahoma Press, 1956.

JOSEPHY, ALVIN M., JR. *The Patriot Chiefs.* Viking Press, 1961.

LECKIE, WILLIAM H. *The Buffalo Soldiers.* University of Oklahoma Press, 1970.

MAILS, THOMAS E. *The Mystic Warriors of the Plains.* Doubleday, 1972.

MONAGHAN, JAMES. *Civil War on the Western Border, 1854-1865.* Little, Brown, 1955.

NADEAU, REMI A. *Fort Laramie and the Sioux Indians.* Prentice-Hall, 1967.

RICKEY, DON. *Forty Miles a Day on Beans and Hay.* University of Oklahoma Press, 1972.

SANDBURG, CARL. *Abraham Lincoln.* Harcourt Brace, 1966.

SEYMOUR, FLORA. *The Story of the Red Man.* Books for Libraries, 1970.

UTLEY, ROBERT M. *Frontiersmen in Blue.* Macmillan, 1967.

———. *Frontier Regulars.* Macmillan, 1974.

WASHBURN, WILCOMB. *The Indian in America.* Harper & Row, 1975.

ZORNOW, WILLIAM FRANK. *Kansas: A History of the Jayhawk State.* University of Oklahoma Press, 1971.

8. Rails Transform the Nation

HOLBROOK, STEWART H. *The Story of American Railroads.* Crown, 1947.

HOWARD, ROBERT WEST. *The Great Iron Trail.* Putnam's, 1962.

KRAUS, GEORGE. *High Road to Promontory.* American West, 1969.

LATHAM, FRANK. *The Transcontinental Railroad.* Watts, 1973.

9. Cowboys and Cattle Kings

ADAMS, RAMON F. *Old-Time Cow Hand.* Macmillan, 1961.

ATHERTON, LEWIS. *The Cattle Kings.* Indiana University Press, 1961.

BROWN, MARK H., and W. R. FELTON. *Before Barbed Wire.* Bramhall House, 1956.

BURKE, JOHN. *Buffalo Bill: The Noblest Whiteskin.* Putnam's, 1973.

DRAGO, HARRY SINCLAIR. *Great American Cattle Trails.* Dodd, Mead, 1965.

DYKSTRA, ROBERT. *The Cattle Towns.* Knopf, 1968.

ELMAN, ROBERT. *Badmen of the West.* Ridge Press/Pound Books, 1974.

RUSSELL, DON. *The Lives and Legends of Buffalo Bill.* University of Oklahoma Press, 1960.

Sights West. Buffalo Bill Historical Center, 1976.

SMITH, HELENA HUNTINGTON. *The War on Powder River.* McGraw-Hill, 1966.

WARD, FAY E. *The Cowboy at Work.* Hastings House, 1976.

10. Settling the Plains

ALLEN, DURWARD L. *The Life of Prairies and Plains.* McGraw-Hill, 1967.

Blacks in the Westward Movement. Smithsonian Institution Press, 1975.

BRACKE, WILLIAM. *Wheat Country.* Duell, Sloan and Pearce, 1950.

BROWN, DEE. *The Gentle Tamers.* University of Nebraska Press, 1968.

BURLEND, REBECCA and EDWARD. *A True Picture of Emigration.* The Citadel Press, 1968.

DICK, EVERETT. *Vanguards of the Frontier.* Appleton-Century, 1941.

———. *The Sod House Frontier.* Johnsen, 1954.

DRACHE, HIRAM M. *The Day of the Bonanza.* North Dakota Institute for Regional Studies, 1964.

DRURY, JOHN. *Midwest Heritage.* A. A. Wyn, 1948.

FITE, GILBERT C. *The Farmer's Frontier.* Holt, Rinehart & Winston, 1966.

GREEVER, WILLIAM S. *The Bonanza West.* University of Oklahoma Press, 1963.

KAROLEVITZ, ROBERT F. *Doctors of the Old West.* Superior Publishing Library, 1967.

PHELAN, JOHN (ed.). *Readings in Rural Sociology.* Macmillan, 1920.

PREECE, HAROLD. *Living Pioneers.* World Publishing Co., 1952.

SCHLEBECKER, JOHN T. *Whereby We Thrive: A History of American Farming, 1607-1972.* Iowa State University Press, 1975.

WEBB, WALTER PRESCOTT. *The Great Plains.* Grosset & Dunlap, 1957.

WELSCH, ROGER L. *Sod Walls.* Purcells, Inc., 1968.

11. The West Comes of Age

ANDREWS, RALPH W. *Picture Gallery Pioneers.* Bonanza, 1964.

———. *Photographers of the Frontier West.* Bonanza, 1965.

BONNEY, ORRIN H. and LORRAINE. *Battle Drums and Geysers.* Sage Books, 1970.

BURLINGAME, ROGER. *March of the Iron Men.* Scribner's, 1938.

GRISWOLD, WESLEY S. *A Work of Giants.* McGraw-Hill, 1962.

GRONER, ALEX. *The American Heritage History of American Business and Industry.* American Heritage, 1972.

HAVIGHURST, WALTER. *Wilderness for Sale.* Hastings House, 1956.

LENS, SIDNEY. *The Labor Wars.* Doubleday, 1973.

LEWIS, OSCAR. *The Big Four.* Knopf, 1938.

MARCOSSON, ISAAC F. *Anaconda.* Dodd, Mead, 1957.

McCAGUE, JAMES. *Moguls and Iron Men.* Harper & Row, 1964.

NAEF, WESTON J., and JAMES N. WOOD. *Era of Exploration: The Rise of Landscape Photography in the American West, 1860-1885.* The Metropolitan Museum of Art, Albright-Knox Art Gallery, 1975.

TERRELL, JOHN UPTON. *The Man Who Rediscovered America: A Biography of John Wesley Powell.* Weybright and Talley, 1969.

TILDEN, FREEMAN. *Following the Frontier with F. Jay Haynes, Pioneer Photographer of the Old West.* Knopf, 1964.

WILKINS, THURMAN. *Clarence King.* Macmillan, 1958.

WOLFE, LINNIE MARSH. *Son of the Wilderness: The Life of John Muir.* Knopf, 1945.

•See also works cited in quotation boxes throughout this book and the following periodicals that deal with western themes:
American Heritage. New York, New York
American History Illustrated. Gettysburg, Pennsylvania
The American West. Palo Alto, California
The Journal of American History. Bloomington, Indiana
Publications of state historical societies

Index

Page numbers in **bold** type refer to illustrations, maps, and captions.

376

Page numbers in **bold** type refer to illustrations, maps, and captions.

378

Credits and Acknowledgments

SPECIAL RESEARCH ACKNOWLEDGMENTS

Special appreciation for invaluable help in picture research is extended to the following organizations and their staffs: Bancroft Library; Buffalo Bill Historical Center; Chicago Historical Society; Denver Public Library, Western History Dept.; Museum of Fine Arts, Boston; The New-York Historical Society; New York Public Library, American History Division, Picture Collection, Prints Division, and Rare Book Division; Royal Ontario Museum; the various state historical societies of California, Colorado, Kansas, Missouri, Montana, Nebraska, Ohio, Oregon, Tennessee, and Wisconsin; Stuhr Museum, Grand Island, Nebr.; The Thomas Gilcrease Institute of American History & Art; Walters Art Gallery; Wells Fargo Bank. Special appreciation is also extended to the following individuals: Boyd Cruise, Curator Emeritus, Historic New Orleans Collection; Carl S. Dentzel, Director, Southwest Museum; Carol Forsyth, Smithsonian Institution; Diana Fox, Librarian, State Historical Society of Iowa; William Glover, The Granger Collection; Dave Helfert, Director, House Media Services, Texas House of Representatives; Roberts Jackson, Culver Pictures; Harvey L. Jones, Deputy Curator of Art, The Oakland Museum; Gerald Kearns, Library of Congress; Art McCourt, Archivist, Weyerhauser Company; Dr. Harold McCracken, Director Emeritus, Buffalo Bill Historical Center; Mrs. L. Vernon Miller; Robert D. Monroe, Chief, Special Collections Division, University of Washington Libraries; Lois Olcott Price, Director of Museum Planning, The Filson Club. Appreciation for assistance in general research is extended to: Wendell Ashton and F. Charles Graves, The Church of Jesus Christ of Latter-day Saints; Silvio Bedini, Warren Danzenbaker and Dr. Aubrey Davis, Smithsonian Institution; Barbara Blei, Stockton-San Joaquin County Public Library; Lois De Lorenzo, author *Gold Fever and the Art of Panning and Sluicing;* Miss Caroline Grimes, Curator, Harrodsburg Historical Society, Harrodsburg, Ky.; Kathy Gross, Assistant Statistician, Association of American Railroads; Leslie R. Henry, Henry Ford Museum, Dearborn, Mich.; Louis C. Hunter, author *Steamboats on the Western Rivers;* Miss Jane Hutton, Editor, *The Harrodsburg Herald;* John McLeod, Librarian, Association of American Railroads; Loring McMillen, Director, Staten Island Historical Society; Jane E. Munson, Director, Jonathan Truman Dorris Museum, Eastern Kentucky University.

ACKNOWLEDGMENTS FOR QUOTED MATERIAL

46 Alexis de Tocqueville, from *Journey to America,* translated by George Lawrence, edited by J. P. Mayer. New Haven, Yale University Press, 1960. **83** Mrs. Walter Burley, from *Chicago* by Finis Farr, © 1973 by Arlington House. **84** A. B. Guthrie, Jr., from *The Big Sky,* Copyright 1947, published by William Sloane Associates. **104** Bernard DeVoto, from *Across the Wide Missouri,* copyright 1947 by Houghton Mifflin Company. **203** William Henry Jackson, reprinted by permission of G. P. Putnam's Sons from *Time Exposure.* Copyright 1940 by William Henry Jackson. **208** John G. Neihardt, from *Song of the Indian Wars.* Copyright 1925 The Macmillan Company. Copyright renewed 1953 by the John G. Neihardt Foundation and reprinted by permission. **223** Chief Big Eagle, from *Minnesota History,* Volume 38, #3, copyright 1962 by the Minnesota Historical Society. **235** Low Dog, from *The Custer Myth* by Colonel W. A. Graham, originally published by Stackpole Books, Harrisburg, Pa. Now in a reprint edition published by Bonanza Books, a division of Crown Publishers, One Park Avenue, New York. **270** Charles M. Russell, from *Trails Plowed Under,* copyright 1927 by Doubleday, Page & Company. **272** Cowboy Lingo, from *Western Worlds: A Dictionary of The American West,* by Ramon F. Adams. Copyright 1968 by the University of Oklahoma Press. **274** James H. Cook, from *Fifty Years on the Old Frontier* (New Haven, 1923). **281 & 289** Granville Stuart, from *Forty Years on the Frontier,* edited by Paul C. Phillips. Copyright 1925 by The Arthur H. Clark Company. **304** Carl Sandburg, from *The People, Yes,* copyright 1936 by Harcourt Brace Jovanovich, Inc.; copyright, 1964, by Carl Sandburg. Reprinted by permission of the publisher. **306** "The Lane County Bachelor," from *The American Songbag* by Carl Sandburg. Harcourt Brace Jovanovich, Inc. 1927. **306** Johan Bojer, from *The Emigrants,* translated from the Norwegian by A. G. Jayne, copyright 1925 by the author, published by The Century Co., New York and London. **308 & 315,** Gro Svendsen, from *Frontier Mother: The Letters of Gro Svendsen,* edited by Pauline Farseth and Theodore C. Blegen. Northfield, Minnesota. Norwegian-American Historical Assn., 1950. **318** O. E. Rölvaag, from *Giants in the Earth.* English translation by Lincoln Concord and the author. Reprinted by permission of Harper & Row, Publishers. **319** Sarah Sim, based on "Problems in the Land of Opportunity" by Elizabeth N. Shor, *The American West* magazine, January 1976, copyright © 1976 by the American West Publishing Company, Cupertino, California. With permission by the publisher. **333** "Dakota Land," Carl Sandburg, *The American Songbag,* Harcourt Brace Jovanovich, Inc., 1927. **340** Vachel Lindsay, "Bryan, Bryan, Bryan, Bryan" from *Collected Poems.* Copyright 1920 by The Macmillan Company; renewed 1948 by Elizabeth C. Lindsay. **344** Henry Adams, from *The Education of Henry Adams,* copyright 1918 by the Massachusetts Historical Society and published by Houghton Mifflin Company. **347** Gustavus C. Doane, from *Battle Drums And Geysers,* edited by Orrin H. and Lorraine Bonney. Published by the Swallow Press, Inc., 1970. Copyright © 1970 by Orrin H. Bonney and Lorraine Bonney. **349** John Wesley Powell, from *The Exploration of the Colorado River,* © 1957 by the University of Chicago. **369** John Muir, from *John of the Mountains,* edited by Linnie Marsh Wolfe, copyright 1938 by Wanda Muir Hanna and published by Houghton Mifflin Company.

York; *middle right* Culver Pictures; *bottom right* Metropolitan Museum of Art, Rogers Fund. **70** *top* State Historical Society of Wisconsin; *bottom* The New-York Historical Society. **71** *left* Museum of Fine Arts, Boston, Bequest of Henry L. Shattuck in memory of Ralph W. Gray; *top right* The New-York Historical Society; *lower right* New York Public Library, American History Division. **72** *upper left* Chicago Historical Society; *bottom left* New York Public Library, Picture Collection; *top left* International Museum of Photography at George Eastman House; *top right* New York Public Library, Prints Division. **73** *top* Museum of the City of New York; *bottom left & right* Library of Congress. **74** *top* The Granger Collection; *bottom* The New-York Historical Society. **75** Illinois Department of Conservation. **78** *top* Deere & Company; *bottom left* University of Michigan; *bottom right* Missouri Historical Society. **79** *top left* State Historical Society of Wisconsin; *top right* J. I. Case Company. **80** *top* Culver Pictures; *bottom* Milwaukee County Historical Society. **81** *top left & right* Library of Congress; *lower left* Public Library of Cincinnati & Hamilton County. **82** *top* Courtesy of the Curators of the Bodleian Library, Oxford; *lower left & right* Oberlin College; *bottom* New York Public Library, General Research & Humanities Division. **83** *top left* Cincinnati Historical Society; *top right* The New-York Historical Society; *bottom left* Missouri Historical Society; *lower right* Private Collection. **84–85** The Walters Art Gallery. **86** *top right* Courtesy of Mrs. Peter A. Jay & the Frick Art Reference Library; *remainder* Oregon Historical Society. **87** *upper* American Museum of Natural History. **88** *bottom right* Glenbow-Alberta Institute; *remainder* Hudson's Bay Company. **89** *right* The Thomas Gilcrease Institute of American History & Art, Tulsa, Okla. **90** *left* Utah State Historical Society; *bottom right* Missouri Historical Society. **91** The Walters Art Gallery. **92** *top left* Kansas State Historical Society; *right* New York Public Library; *bottom left* National Collection of Fine Arts, Smithsonian Institution. **93** *left* The Walters Art Gallery; *bottom right* & **95** *top right* Joslyn Art Museum, Omaha, Nebr. **96** *left* National Collection of Fine Arts, Smithsonian Institution; *right* The New-York Historical Society. **97** *top* National Collection of Fine Arts, Smithsonian Institution; *bottom left* New York Public Library, Rare Book Division; *bottom right* American Museum of Natural History. **98** *top* From the Collection of Mr. & Mrs. Paul Mellon; *bottom* National Collection of Fine Arts, Smithsonian Institution. **99** *upper* New York Public Library, Rare Book Division; *bottom* The Walters Art Gallery. **100 & 101** *top left & bottom* New York Public Library, Rare Book Division; *top center* Museum of Fine Arts, Boston, Horatio Greenough Curtis Fund; *top right* & **102** *top* Northern Natural Gas Company Collection, Joslyn Art Museum, Omaha, Nebr.; *bottom right* The Granger Collection. **103** *left* The Walters Art Gallery; *top right* New York Public Library, General Research & Humanities Division; *lower right* Jefferson National Expansion Memorial, National Park Service. **104** *upper left to right:* The Thomas Gilcrease Institute of American History & Art, Tulsa, Okla.; Northern Natural Gas Company Collection, Joslyn Art Museum, Omaha, Nebr.; The Walters Art Gallery; Oregon Historical Society; Collection of Nolie Mumey; *bottom right* Courtesy of Mrs. Joseph Whyte. **105** The Walters Art Gallery. **106** *top* State Historical Society of Colorado; *left* Amon Carter Museum, Fort Worth, Tex.; *lower right* Denver Public Library, Western History Dept. **107** *top left* Collection of K. C. DenDooven; *top right* Museum of the American Indian; *middle left* State Historical Society of Colorado; *remainder* University of Oklahoma Library, Western History Collections. **108–109** Texas House of Representatives, Austin. **110** *top* Academy of Natural Sciences of Philadelphia; *lower* The John Carter Brown Library. **111** *top center* Museum of New Mexico; *remainder* Museum of Fine Arts, Boston, Collection of Dr. and Mrs. Ward Alan Minge. **112** *upper left* Title Insurance & Trust Co.; *bottom* San Diego Historical Society, Library & Manuscripts Collection; *top right* University of Texas at Austin. **114** *upper left* From the collections of the San Jacinto Museum of History Association. **116** *top right* National Collection of Fine Arts, Smithsonian Institution; *lower left* The New-York Historical Society; *lower right* American Museum of Natural History. **117** *top* Courtesy of the San Antonio Museum Association, Witte Memorial Museum, San Antonio, Tex.; *bottom* Southwest Museum. **119** *top left* Courtesy of Frank C. Hibben, University of New Mexico. **120** *bottom* **121 & 123** *top right* New York Public Library, American History Division. **124** Missouri Historical Society. **125** *top* Texas House of Representatives, Austin. **126** *top* The Thomas Gilcrease Institute of American History & Art, Tulsa, Okla.; *remainder* The Beinecke Rare Book & Manuscript Library, Yale University. **127** *bottom* Smithsonian Institution; *remainder* Museo Nacional de Historia. **128** *top right* The Beinecke Rare Book & Manuscript Library, Yale University; *bottom* Culver Pictures. **129** *left* Courtesy of the Texas State Archives; *right* New York Public Library, Picture Collection. **130** *top left to right:* University of Texas at Austin; Daughters of the Republic of Texas Library; From the collections of the San Jacinto Museum of History Association; The Granger Collection; *bottom right* Daughters of the Republic of Texas Library. **131** *top* Brass Door Galleries, Houston, Texas; *bottom* & **132** *top* Courtesy of the Texas Memorial Museum, Austin; *bottom* University of Texas at Austin. **133** *bottom* & **134** *top* Texas House of Representatives, Austin; *remainder* & **135** *top* University of Texas at Austin; *lower right* Courtesy of the Texas State Archives; *bottom* New York Public Library, Rare Book Division. **136** Texas House of Representatives, Austin. **137** *top left* From the collections of the San Jacinto Museum of History Association; *top right* University of Texas at Austin; *bottom* Library of Congress. **138** Daughters of the Republic of Texas Library. **139** *top* Collection of Russell Hamilton Fish, III; *bottom* Courtesy of the Edgar E. Ayer Collection, The Newberry Library. **140** *bottom* University of Texas at Austin. **141** *top* Courtesy of the San Antonio Museum Association, Witte Memorial Museum, San Antonio, Tex.; *lower* Courtesy of the Texas State Archives. **142–143** Butler Institute of American Art. **144** *top* California State Library, Sacramento; *bottom left* The John Carter Brown Library, Brown University; *upper right* New York Public Library, Rare Book Division; *bottom right* American Museum of Natural History. **145** *top* New York Public Library, Manuscript Division; *upper left* Security Pacific National Bank, Historical Collections; *bottom left* The Oakland Museum. **146** *bottom left* California Historical Society, San Francisco, San Marino; *bottom right* Title Insurance & Trust Co. **147** *top right* Painting by W. H. D. Koerner, reprinted by permission of Ruth Koerner Oliver. **148** *left* Massachusetts Historical Society; *remainder* Oregon Historical Society. **149** *top* Portland Art Museum, Portland, Oregon; *lower* Public Archives of Canada, Ottawa. **150** *top* Western History Collections, University of Oklahoma Library; *lower left* Reproduced from the *Dictionary of American Portraits,* published by Dover Publications, Inc., 1967; *lower right* New York Public Library, Rare Book Division. **151** *top* Oregon Historical Society; *lower* New York Public Library, American History Division. **152** *upper left* From *Wilderness Kingdom* by Nicolas Point, S. J. Translated and introduced by Joseph P. Donnelly, S. J. Copyright © 1967 by Loyola University Press, Chicago. Reproduced by permission of Holt, Rinehart and Winston, Publishers; *upper & bottom right* & **153** *top & bottom right* Royal Ontario Museum; *bottom left* Courtesy of the Glenbow-Alberta Institute; *middle right* Courtesy of the Stark Museum of Art, Orange, Tex. **154** *top* Washington State Historical Society; *bottom left* Culver Pictures; *bottom right* Oregon Historical Society. **155** *bottom* From *Wilderness Kingdom* by Nicolas Point, S. J. Translated and introduced by Joseph P. Donnelly, S. J. Copyright © 1967 by Loyola University Press, Chicago. Reproduced by permission of Holt, Rinehart and Winston, Publishers. **158** Denver Public Library, Western History Dept. **159** *top* Courtesy of the Bancroft Library; *bottom* Collection of Mr. & Mrs. J. Maxwell Moran. **160** *top* From *The West* by Bayrd Still, published by G. P. Putnam's Sons; *bottom left* The Granger Collection; *bottom right* Utah State Historical Society. **161** *top* Collection of August A. Busch, Jr.; *bottom* Utah State Historical Society. **162** *top right* Clyde Arbuckle Collection; *bottom left* California State Library, Sacramento; *bottom right* Courtesy of the Bancroft Library. **163** *top* The Thomas Gilcrease Institute of American History & Art, Tulsa, Okla.; *bottom* California State Dept. of Parks & Recreation. **164** *left* Reproduced by permission of the Caxton Printers, Ltd., Caldwell, Idaho; *upper right* Royal Ontario Museum; *bottom right* Oregon Historical Society. **165** *top* National Collection of Fine Arts, Smithsonian Institution; *lower right* Chicago Historical Society; *bottom left* American Antiquarian Society. **166** *top* Kit Carson Memorial Foundation; *bottom* New York Public Library, American History Division. **167** *top left* The Bettmann Archive; *top right* Southwest Museum; *bottom* Donna Harris. **168** *top* Courtesy of Kennedy Galleries, Inc., N.Y.; *bottom* The Bettmann Archive. **169** *top* Permanent Collection of the National Academy of Design; *bottom* California State Library, Sacramento. **170** *top center to right:* History Division, Natural History Museum of Los Angeles County; California State Library, Sacramento; Title Insurance & Trust Co.; *bottom* W. H. D. Koerner (1878–1938). **171** *top* Courtesy of the Bancroft Library; *lower right* Society of California Pioneers; *bottom* Franklin D. Roosevelt Library. **172** *top left* Library of Congress; *top right* New York Public Library, Picture Collection; *middle left* The Granger Collection; *bottom* Private Collection. **173** *top & lower right* New York Public Library, American History Division; *lower left* New York Public Library, Rare Book Division. **174** *top right* Courtesy of Mary Veitch Alexander, Curator, of the Gadsden Museum, Mesilla, New Mex. **175** *top* Library of Congress; *middle* On extended loan to the John Carter Brown Library from the Museum of Art, Rhode Island School of Design; *lower* The John Carter Brown Library, Brown University. **176–177** Courtesy of the E. B. Crocker Art Gallery, Sacramento, Calif. **178** *top* The Church of Jesus Christ of Latter-day Saints; *bottom* Culver Pictures. **179** *top* New York Public Library, American History Division; *lower left* The Church of Jesus Christ of Latter-day Saints; *lower right* New York Public Library, Prints Division. **180** *top* The Church of Jesus Christ of Latter-day Saints; *lower* Utah State Historical Society. **181** *top & bottom left* The Church of Jesus Christ of Latter-day Saints; *bottom right* The Harold Warp Pioneer Village, Minden, Nebr. **182** *top & lower left* The Church of Jesus Christ of Latter-day Saints; *bottom* Utah State Historical Society. **183** *top left* The Church of Jesus Christ of Latter-day Saints; *top right* Culver Pictures; *bottom* Utah State Historical Society. **184** *lower left* Society of California Pioneers; *top left* California Historical Society; *top center* Courtesy of Levi Strauss & Co.; *top right* Woodrow Gelman Collection; *lower right* New York Public Library, American History Division. **185** *top left* California Historical Society; *top right* Smithsonian Institution. **186** *upper left* New York Public Library, Picture Collection; *bottom left* Private Collection; *bottom right* Courtesy of the Bancroft Library. **187** *left* The New-York Historical Society; *right* The Thomas Gilcrease Institute of American History & Art, Tulsa, Okla. **189** *bottom left* New York Public Library, Picture Collection. **190** *bottom left & right* California State Library, Sacramento. **191** *upper left* Book Club of California; *bottom left* New York Public Library; *top right* Courtesy of Gene Autrey. **192** *top left* Courtesy of the Bancroft Library; *bottom left* The New-York Historical Society; *right* Yale University Art Gallery, the Mabel Brady Garvan Collection. **193** *top* Wells Fargo Bank History Room; *lower right* California State Library, Sacramento. **194** *top left* New York Public Library; *top right* Montana Historical Society; *bottom* Museum of Fine Arts, Boston, M. & M. Karolik Collection. **195** *top left* State Historical Society of Colorado; *top right* Southern Pacific; *bottom* The Huntington Library, San Marino, Calif. **196** *top* The Fine Arts Museums of San Francisco; *bottom* Collection of Mrs. Marshall F. Driggs. **197** *top left* New York Public Library, Picture Collection; *top right* Mark Twain Memorial, Hartford, Conn.; *bottom left* Courtesy of the Bancroft Library; *bottom right* Nevada Historical Society. **198** *top right* Courtesy of the Remington Art Museum, Ogdensburg, N.Y.; *lower right* The Huntington Library, San Marino, Calif. **199** *top* The Thomas Gilcrease Institute of American History & Art, Tulsa, Okla.; *bottom left* Wells Fargo Bank History Room; *bottom right* Wells Fargo Bank History Room/Ivan Essayan Photograph. **202** *top* Scotts Bluff National Monument; *bottom* The Thomas Gilcrease Institute of American History & Art, Tulsa, Okla. **203** *top left* Scotts Bluff National Monument; *top right* Great Falls Tribune; *bottom* Sy Seidman/Photo Trends. **204** *upper left* Courtesy of Sarah Russell; *upper right* St. Joseph Museum; *bottom right* State Historical Society of Colorado. **205** *top* The Thomas Gilcrease Institute of American History & Art, Tulsa, Okla.; *bottom* Scotts Bluff National Monument. **206** *top* Library of Congress; *bottom* Oregon Historical Society. **207** *top left* Wells Fargo Bank History Room/Ivan Essayan Photograph; *top right* New York Public Library, Picture Collection; *remainder* Wells Fargo Bank History Room. **208–209** Metropolitan Museum of Art, Gift of Several Gentlemen. **210** *top* Reprinted from *Broken Hand, the Life of Thomas Fitzpatrick* by LeRoy R. Hafen by permission of Old West Publishing Company; *bottom* The Thomas Gilcrease Institute of American History & Art, Tulsa, Okla. **211** Minnesota Historical Society. **212** *upper left* New York Public Library; *bottom left* The Granger Collection; *bottom right* Culver Pictures. **213** *top* Kansas State Historical Society, Topeka; *lower left* Courtesy of the State of Kansas; *lower right* New York Public Library. **214** *top & lower right* The Granger Collection; *lower left* Illinois State Historical Library. **215** *top* Greenfield Village & Henry Ford Museum; *bottom left & right* Library of Congress. **216** *upper left* State Historical Society of Missouri; *bottom left* & **217** *top* Kansas State Historical Society, Topeka; *bottom* Cincinnati Art Museum, the Edwin & Virginia Irwin Memorial. **218** *top* Library of Congress; *bottom left* The Texas Collection of Baylor University, Waco, Tex.; *bottom right* Courtesy of the San Antonio Museum Association, Witte Memorial Museum, San Antonio, Tex. **219** *top* Willard Andrews Collection; *remainder* State Historical Society of Colorado. **220** *bottom* Reprinted with permission from *The Saturday Evening Post* © 1947 The Curtis Publishing Company. **221** *top* National Park Service, U.S. Dept. of the Interior; *bottom* *left* National Archives; *bottom right* Museum of New Mexico. **222** *top* Brown County Historical Society; *lower right* & **223** Minnesota Historical Society. **224 & 225** *top left* State Historical Society of Colorado; *top right* History Division, Los Angeles County Museum of Natural History; *lower left* Museum of the American Indian, Heye Foundation; *lower right* Courtesy of the Harold McCracken Collection. **226** *left* Courtesy of the Remington Art Museum, Ogdensburg, N.Y. **227** *top & lower right* Smithsonian Institution; *lower left* The Texas Collection of Baylor University, Waco, Tex. **228** *top* Kansas State Historical Society, Topeka; *bottom* Denver Public Library, Western History Dept. **229** *top left* Courtesy of the Remington Art Museum, Ogdensburg, N.Y.; *top right* South Dakota Historical Resource Center; *remainder* National Archives. **230** *bottom right* Western History Research Center, University of Wyoming. **231** *top* Museum of New Mexico. **232** *middle left* Smithsonian Institution; *middle right* Denver Public Library, Western History Dept.; *bottom* Courtesy of the West Point Museum Collections, United States Military Academy © *The Saturday Evening Post.* **233** *top left* The Thomas Gilcrease Institute of American History & Art, Tulsa, Okla.; *top right* Denver Public Library, Western History Dept.; *bottom* Smithsonian Institution. **234** *upper left to right:* Custer Battlefield National Monument; Custer Battlefield National Monument; Smithsonian Institution; *middle left to right:* National Archives; From *The Custer Album,* courtesy of Lawrence A. Frost; Custer Battlefield National Monument. **235** *top* Library of Congress; *bottom* Buffalo Bill Historical Center, Cody, Wyo. **236** *left & bottom* New York Public Library. **237** *top* California Historical Society; *lower left* Library of Congress; *bottom* National Archives. **238** *top* Cumberland County Historical Society; *bottom* South Dakota Historical Resource Center. **239** *top* State Historical Society of Colorado; *lower* Courtesy of the Remington Art Memorial Museum, Ogdensburg, N.Y. **240** *top* Western History Collections, University of Oklahoma Library; *lower* The Bettmann Archive. **241** *top & bottom right* Arizona Historical Society Library; *bottom left* Library of Congress. **242** *middle left & right* Idaho Historical Society. **243** *top* South Dakota Historical Resource Center; *bottom* Smithsonian Institution. **244** *top* Butler Institute of American Art; *bottom* The Granger Collection. **245** *top & bottom right* Smithsonian Institution; *bottom left* Montana Historical Society. **246–247** Collection of August A. Busch, Jr. **248** *top* Library of Congress; *lower right* Courtesy of the Panama Canal. **249** *top* Courtesy of the Whipple Collection of the Oklahoma Historical Society; *bottom left* New York Public Library, American History Division; *bottom right* New York Public Library, General Research & Humanities Division. **250** *center* Southern Pacific. **251** *top* The New-York Historical Society, gift of Archer Milton Huntington; *lower right* The Oakland Museum; *bottom* The Granger Collection. **252** *top* Southern Pacific; *bottom* The Mariners Museum. **253** *top* Stanford University Museum of Art; *bottom* Southern Pacific. **254** Union Pacific Railroad Museum Collection. **255** *top* Kansas State Historical Society; *lower* Union Pacific Railroad Museum Collection. **256 & 257** *top* Southern Pacific; *bottom* The Bettmann Archive. **260** *upper* State of California, the Railroad Museum, Sacramento. **261** *top left* Culver Pictures; *top right* Sy Seidman/Photo Trends; *middle* Southern Pacific; *bottom* Union Pacific Railroad Museum Collection. **262** *top* The Bettmann Archive; *bottom* Fred Harvey Collection. **263** *left* The New-York Historical Society; *top right* New York Public Library, American History Division; *middle right* New York Public Library, Picture Collection; *bottom* The Cousley Historical Collection/Photo by Edward S. Barnard. **264** *upper left* Arthur Dubin Collection; *bottom left* Photri. **265** *middle right* & **266** *top right* The Granger Collection; *bottom left* New York Public Library, Picture Collection; *bottom right* The Bettmann Archive. **267** *top* Kansas State Historical Society, Topeka; *upper right* Union Pacific Railroad Museum Collection; *bottom* The Granger Collection. **268** *top* Chicago Architectural Photo Co., David R. Phillips Collection; *bottom left* Smithsonian Institution; *bottom right* The Granger Collection. **269** *top* The Thomas Gilcrease Institute of American History & Art, Tulsa, Okla.; *middle* New York Public Library, Picture Collection; *bottom left & right* Courtesy of the Harold McCracken Collection. **270–271** Amon Carter Museum, Fort Worth, Tex. **272** *top* Buffalo Bill Historical Center, Cody, Wyo.; *lower* Courtesy of the San Antonio Museum Association, Witte Memorial Museum, San Antonio, Tex. **273** *top* J. N. Bartfield Art Galleries, Inc., N.Y.; *lower* State Historical Society of Colorado. **274** *left* Amon Carter Museum, Fort Worth, Tex.; *right* The Granger Collection. **275** *top* New York Public Library, Art & Architecture Division; *lower* The Thomas Gilcrease Institute of American History & Art, Tulsa, Okla; **276** *top* Valley House Gallery; *bottom* W. H. D. Koerner (1878–1938). **277** *top left* New York Public Library, Rare Book Division; *top right* From *The American Cowboy,* Courtesy of the Harold McCracken Collection; *lower left* Oklahoma Historical Society. **278** *bottom left* & **279** *middle right* The Huffman Pictures, Miles City, Mont. **280** *upper left* The Bettmann Archive; *upper right* New York Public Library, Picture Collection; *bottom* Kansas State Historical Society, Topeka. **281** *top* Private Collection; *bottom* Western History Collections, University of Oklahoma Library. **282** *bottom* W. H. D. Koerner (1878–1938). **283** *top left* New York Public Library, Rare Book Division; *lower* Buffalo Bill Historical Center, Cody, Wyo. **284** *top* Mackay Collection, Montana Historical Society; *bottom* & **285** *top left* The Huffman Pictures, Miles City, Mont.; *right* From the Erwin E. Smith Collection of Range-life Photographs, Library of Congress. **286** *bottom left* The Huffman Pictures, Miles City, Mont. **287** *top left* Amon Carter Museum, Fort Worth, Tex. **288** *top* State Historical Society of North Dakota; *bottom* Wyoming State Archives & Historical Dept. **289** *far right* University of Wyoming, Western History Research Center; *middle right* Denver Public Library, Western History Dept.; *remainder* Montana Historical Society, Helena. **290** *upper & bottom left* University of Wyoming, Western History Research Center; *right* Memorial Museum Collection/Photri. **291** *top left* The Thomas Gilcrease Institute of American History & Art, Tulsa, Okla.; *top right* Anita Webb Deininger Collection/Photri; *bottom left & right* Wyoming State Archives & Historical Dept. **292** *upper left* Kansas State Historical Society, Topeka; *bottom* Buffalo Bill Historical Center, Cody, Wyo. **293** *top & bottom right* Courtesy of the Harold McCracken Collection; *remainder* Buffalo Bill Historical Center, Cody, Wyo. **294** *left* Glenn Shirley Western Collection; *center* Library of Congress; *right* Courtesy of Jack Wymore, Jesse James Museum, Liberty, Mo., by permission of Edith Lancaster McCord, granddaughter of James M. Hart, Sr. **295** *left* Western History Collections, University of Oklahoma Library; *right* & **296** *left* Kansas State Historical Society, Topeka; *right* Western History Collections, University of Oklahoma Library. **297** *top left* Glenn Shirley Western Collection; *top right* The Thomas Gilcrease Institute of American History & Art, Tulsa, Okla.; *bottom* Western History Collections, University of Oklahoma Library. **298** *top* The Thomas Gilcrease Institute of American History & Art, Tulsa, Okla.; *bottom left* Buffalo Bill Historical Center, Cody, Wyo.; *bottom right* Courtesy of Joe R. Grandee. **299** *top* Photo by Charles J. Belden, courtesy of the Buffalo Bill Historical Center, Cody, Wyo.; *bottom right* United States Steel Corp. **300** *top* The University of Texas at Austin; *bottom* & **301** *top & bottom* Amon Carter Museum, Fort Worth, Tex.; *middle left* Grand Central Art Galleries, the Eastern home of Western art; *middle right* Mackay Collection, Montana Historical Society. **302** *top right* Sy Seidman/Photo Trends; *lower right* Nebraska State Historical Society; *lower left insert* The Granger Collection; *remainder* The Cousley Historical Collection/Photo by William Sonntag. **303** *top* Buffalo Bill Historical Center, Cody, Wyo.; *bottom* Edward Vebell Collection. **304–305** South Dakota Memorial Art Center. **306** *top* The Harold Warp Pioneer Village, Minden, Nebr.; *lower right* Solomon D. Butcher Collection, Nebraska State Historical Society. **307** *top & middle* Kansas State Historical Society, Topeka; *lower* & **308** *bottom* Solomon D. Butcher Collection, Nebraska State Historical Society; *top* Kansas State Historical Society, Topeka. **309 & 310** *left* Solomon D. Butcher Collection, Nebraska State Historical Society. **312** *top* Denver Public Library, Western History Dept.; *bottom* The Huffman Pictures, Miles City, Mont. **313** *right* Solomon D. Butcher Collection, Nebraska State Historical Society. **314** *top left* Denver Public Library, Western History Dept.; *top right* Kansas State Historical Society, Topeka; *bottom* National Archives. **315** *top* South Dakota Memorial Art Center; *lower left* Denver Public Library, Western History Dept.; *lower right* The Bettmann Archive. **316** *top right* Solomon D. Butcher Collection, Nebraska State Historical Society; *bottom* The New-York Historical Society. **317** *lower left* The Haynes Foundation; *remainder* & **318** *upper left* Kansas State Historical Society, Topeka; *bottom* Chicago Architectural Photo Co., David R. Phillips Collection; *top right* & **319** *bottom* The Granger Collection; *top* South Dakota Memorial Art Center. **320** Nebraska State Historical Society. **321** *top left* National Archives; *top right* Solomon D. Butcher Collection, Nebraska State Historical Society; *bottom* Nebraska State Historical Society. **322** *top* Kansas State Historical Society, Topeka; *bottom* Minnesota Historical Society. **323** *top left* The Granger Collection; *top right* National Museum of History & Technology, Smithsonian Institution; *middle right* Nebraska State Historical Society; *lower* Smithsonian Institution. **326** *upper left* Chicago Architectural Photo Co., David R. Phillips Collection; *remainder* & **327** *top & bottom left* Kansas State Historical Society, Topeka; *middle* Chicago Architectural Photo Co., David R. Phillips Collection; *bottom right* Nebraska State Historical Society. **328** *left* Solomon D. Butcher Collection, Nebraska State Historical Society; *right* The Granger Collection. **329** *top left* The New-York Historical Society; *right* Montgomery Ward; *lower* State Historical Society of Iowa. **330 & 331** *top & bottom left* Montgomery Ward; *bottom right* Chicago Architectural Photo Co., David R. Phillips Collection. **332 & 333** *upper* The Haynes Foundation; *bottom* Chicago Architectural Photo Co., David R. Phillips Collection. **334 & 335** *top* Oklahoma Historical Society; *remainder* & **336 & 337** Western History Collections, University of Oklahoma Library. **338** *top* Chase Manhattan Bank Numismatic Collection; *middle* Solomon D. Butcher Collection, Nebraska State Historical Society; *bottom* The Bettmann Archive. **339** The New-York Historical Society. **340** *top* Yale University Press; *lower* Culver Pictures. **341** *top left & bottom right* The Bettmann Archive; *top right & bottom left* Chicago Architectural Photo Co., David R. Phillips Collection. **342–343** New York Public Library, Prints Division. **344** *left* Courtesy of the Bancroft Library. **345** *top & bottom* New York Public Library, Science & Technology Research Center; *middle* U.S. Dept. of the Interior. **346** *upper left* National Park Service; *upper center* Photri; *upper right* Reproduced from the *Dictionary of American Portraits,* published by Dover Publications, Inc., 1967; *lower right* U.S. Geological Survey. **347** *top* U.S. Dept. of the Interior; *bottom* & **348** *top* The Thomas Gilcrease Institute of American History & Art, Tulsa, Okla. **349** *top* New York Public Library, American History Division; *bottom left* Smithsonian Institution; *bottom right* U.S. Dept. of the Interior. **350** *upper left* Ralph W. Andrews Collection; *lower left* Collection of Robert Weinstein/Jack Novak; *right* Denver Public Library, Western History Dept. **351** *middle left* California State Library, Sacramento; *bottom left* National Park Service; *bottom right* Dept. of Special Collections, Research Library, University of California, Los Angeles. **352** *bottom* Denver Public Library, Western History Dept. **353** *upper left* California Historical Society; *remainder* The Huntington Library, San Marino, Calif. **354** *top* Allan G. Hooper Collection; *bottom* Minnesota Historical Society. **355** *top* Montana Historical Society; *lower left* The Granger Collection; *lower right* Reproduced from the *Dictionary of American Portraits,* published by Dover Publications, Inc., 1967. **356** *top left* California Division of Mines & Geology; *top right* Arthur B. Foote Collection; *bottom* University of Idaho. **357** *top* Library of Congress; *bottom* University of Idaho. **358** *bottom* The Granger Collection; *top* & **359** *bottom* Collection of LeRoy Stenstrom; *top* Minnesota Historical Society. **360** *top left* Culver Pictures; *top right* Harold G. Schutt Collection; *bottom* Weyerhaeuser Company Archives. **361** *top* Ralph W. Andrews Collection; *bottom left* Weyerhaeuser Company Archives; *bottom right* & **363** *top right* University of Washington Libraries; *middle right* Oregon Historical Society. **364** *top* Courtesy of Sunkist Growers, Inc. Archives; *lower left* Bank of America; *lower right* Title Insurance & Trust Co. **365** *top left* New York Public Library, American History Division; *top right* Chicago Architectural Photo Co., David R. Phillips Collection; *bottom* Wine Institute. **366** *bottom left* Spindletop Museum, Lamar University; *remainder* & **367** *top left & lower right* American Petroleum Institute Historical Photo Library. **368** *left* National Park Service, Yosemite National Park; *right* Berkshire Museum, Pittsfield, Mass. **369** *top* The Oakland Museum, Kahn Collection; *bottom left* Culver Pictures; *lower right* Reprinted from *My First Summer in the Sierra* by John Muir by permission of the Houghton Mifflin Co. **370** The Huntington Library, San Marino, Calif.; *bottom* Denver Public Library, Western History Dept. **371** Chicago Architectural Photo Co., David Phillips Collection.

Reader's Digest Fund for the Blind is publisher of the Large-Type Edition of *Reader's Digest.* For subscription information about this magazine, please contact Reader's Digest Fund for the Blind, Inc., Dept. 250, Pleasantville, N.Y. 10570.